HANDBOOK ON ORGANISATIONAL ENTREPRENEURSHIP

Handbook on Organisational Entrepreneurship

Edited by

Daniel Hjorth

Doctor of Philosophy in Business Administration and Professor of Entrepreneurship and Organisation, Copenhagen Business School, Denmark

Edward Elgar
Cheltenham, UK • Northampton, MA, USA

Published by
Edward Elgar Publishing Limited
The Lypiatts
15 Lansdown Road
Cheltenham
Glos GL50 2JA
UK

Edward Elgar Publishing, Inc.
William Pratt House
9 Dewey Court
Northampton
Massachusetts 01060
USA

A catalogue record for this book
is available from the British Library

Library of Congress Control Number: 2012939248

ISBN 978 1 84980 378 6 (cased)

Typeset by Servis Filmsetting Ltd, Stockport, Cheshire
Printed and bound by MPG Books Group, UK

Contents

List of figures   vii
List of tables   viii
List of contributors   ix
Foreword and acknowledgements   xi

Introduction: entrepreneurship in organisational contexts   1
Daniel Hjorth

PART I   APPROACHES AND PERSPECTIVES

1   Entrepreneurship as organisation creation   21
    William B. Gartner

2   Schumpeter's theories of organizational entrepreneurship   31
    Richard Swedberg

3   Entrepreneurship and the economics of the firm   49
    Nicolai J. Foss, Peter G. Klein and Per L. Bylund

4   Institutional perspectives on entrepreneurship   64
    Friederike Welter and David Smallbone

5   Evolutionary theory   79
    Martha Martinez and Howard E. Aldrich

6   Organizations, entrepreneurship and ethics   97
    Robert D. Hisrich and Claudine Kearney

7   Entrepreneurship, crisis, critique   116
    Campbell Jones and Anna-Maria Murtola

8   Gender, organizations and entrepreneurship   134
    Helene Ahl

9   Making the multiple: theorising processes of entrepreneurship
    and organisation   151
    Chris Steyaert

10 Organizational entrepreneurship: an art of the weak?   169
    Daniel Hjorth

PART II   FIELDS OF RESEARCH, PRACTICES AND
POLITICS

11   The entrepreneurial firm   193
     Saras Sarasvathy

12   Strategic entrepreneurship: an emerging approach to firm-level
     entrepreneurship   208
     Nicolai J. Foss and Jacob Lyngsie

13   Corporate entrepreneurship   226
     Donald F. Kuratko

14   Overcoming inertia: the social question in social
     entrepreneurship   242
     Ester Barinaga

15   Entrepreneurship in public organizations   257
     Anne Kovalainen and Elisabeth Sundin

16   Collective creativity: E-teams and E-teamwork   280
     Shannon O'Donnell and Lee Devin

17   Organizing reality machines: artepreneurs and the new
     aesthetic enlightenment   300
     Pierre Guillet de Monthoux

18   Organizing the entrepreneurial city   320
     Timon Beyes

19   Management as farce: entrepreneurial subjectivity in the
     creative industries   338
     Bent Meier Sørensen

20   Moving and being moved: ideas, perspectives and 59 theses on
     entrepreneurial leadership   362
     Daniel Hjorth and William B. Gartner

References   377
Index   461

Figures

2.1	A new Schumpeterian theory of innovation # 1: innovation as process	40
2.2	Elaboration on the theme of innovation as a process	42
2.3	A new Schumpeterian theory of innovation # 2: innovation as the creation of a new norm	44
2.4	Elaborations on the theme of innovation as the creation of a new norm	45
10.1	Multiplicity, series, event	181
10.2	Qualities of becoming	187
13.1	Defining corporate entrepreneurship	229
14.1	Social change matrix	252
19.1	The fold ('Foucault's diagram')	341
19.2	Unfolding #1	349
19.3	Unfolding #2	352
19.4	Unfolding #3	356

Tables

I.1   Organisational forms and modes of organising   3
6.1   Distinguishing ethics and social responsibility in
       entrepreneurial organizations from traditional management
       organizations   109
6.2   Public sector corruption perceptions index   112
8.1   Masculinity words compared to entrepreneur words   146
8.2   Femininity words compared to opposites of entrepreneur
       words   147
12.1   Key contributions to strategic entrepreneurship   215
17.1   From entrepreneur to artepreneur   317
20.1   Transition from industrial to postindustrial economy   363
20.2   Causation, effectuation and affectuation processes   373

Contributors

Helene Ahl, Jönköping University, helene.ahl@hlk.hj.se.

Howard E. Aldrich, University of North Carolina at Chapel Hill, howard_aldrich@unc.edu.

Ester Barinaga, Copenhagen Business School, eb.lpf@cbs.dk.

Timon Beyes, Leuphana University, timon.beyes@leuphana.de.

Per L. Bylund, University of Missouri, per.bylund@mizzou.edu.

Lee Devin, People's Light & Theatre, Swarthmore College, ldevin1@swarthmore.edu.

Nicolai J. Foss, Copenhagen Business School, njf.smg@cbs.dk.

William B. Gartner, Clemson University, gartner@clemson.edu.

Robert D. Hisrich, Thunderbird, School of Global Management, robert.hisrich@thunderbird.edu.

Daniel Hjorth, Copenhagen Business School, dhj.lpf@cbs.dk.

Campbell Jones, University of Auckland, campbell.jones@auckland.ac.nz.

Claudine Kearney, University of Groningen, c.kearney@rug.nl.

Peter G. Klein, University of Missouri, kleinp@missouri.edu.

Anne Kovalainen, Turku School of Economics, Anne.Kovalainen@tse.fi.

Donald F. Kuratko, Indiana University, dkuratko@indiana.edu.

Jacob Lyngsie, Copenhagen Business School, jl.smg@cbs.dk.

Martha Martinez, University of North Carolina at Chapel Hill, martinez@soc.duke.edu.

Pierre Guillet de Monthoux, Copenhagen Business School, pgm.lpf@cbs.dk.

Anna-Maria Murtola, Auckland, New Zealand, annamariamurtola@gmail.com.

Shannon O'Donnell, Copenhagen Business School, sod.lpf@cbs.dk.

Saras Sarasvathy, University of Virginia, SarasvathyS@darden.virginia.edu.

David Smallbone, Kingston University, d.smallbone@kingston.ac.uk.

Bent Meier Sørensen, Copenhagen Business School, bms.lpf@cbs.dk.

Chris Steyaert, University of St. Gallen, chris.steyaert@unisg.ch.

Elisabeth Sundin, Linköping University, elisabeth.sundin@liu.se.

Richard Swedberg, Cornell University, rs328@cornell.edu.

Friederike Welter, Jönköping International Business School, friederike.welter@jibs.hj.se.

Foreword and acknowledgements

This book has emerged from a long engagement with some of the intriguing and challenging research problems that belong to the many ways entrepreneurship and organisation are related. Many of these problems are discussed and explored within the pages of this *Handbook*, others are identified for the purpose of calling for future novel research. Still others, this is our hope, are there yet to be discovered by readers that can hopefully continue what writers contributing to this volume have initiated.

Why this *Handbook*, now? Businesses and organisations struggle with the on-going transition from an industrial into a postindustrial economy and society. This, in turn, happens in an accelerated process of globalisation, boosted in many ways by information technology. This requires that new organisation is created, opening the way for new ideas and solutions. 'Making the new happen', responding to, as well as driving, the transition, is a process in which entrepreneurship and organisation are intimately related. Indeed, some of us would argue that at the core of entrepreneurship, there has always been this organisation-creative element that differentiates it from other forms of creativity and from merely efficient handling of existing resources and without which there are neither organisations nor entrepreneurship.

This *Handbook* explores a number of approaches and perspectives through which the question of the relationship between entrepreneurship and organisation is multiplied. It also invites you into fields of research, practices and politics concerning the relationship between entrepreneurship and organisation. The point being that presently there needs to be much more focus on and much more knowledge concerning organisational entrepreneurship in order for us to understand how the world (not only business) is becoming new. Businesses achieve being *in* organisational forms that differ from what the industrial era made us expect as normal. Businesses achieve being *through* organisational forms that constantly change and that more often take forms we do not recognise as related to 'organising a start-up'. This *Handbook* is timely also in this sense; focusing on an entrepreneurship–organisation axis we believe will be crucial for how business/societies are presently changing and how such changes will affect our future societies/businesses.

The *Handbook* is not restricted to the context of business organisations for it is via various hybrid forms of organisation (and governance), including private and public organisations, that society/business further themselves into the future. We need to learn from multiple organisational contexts in order to understand what organisational entrepreneurship is and can be about. Organisational entrepreneurship, so this *Handbook* shows, is part of corporate contexts, strategic processes, firm-formation processes, societal change, public organisations, collective creativity, creative industries, art, cities and leadership.

The book opens up, i.e., increases the connective capacity of, a number of problems and discussions, by itself contextualising those processes/ practices mentioned above. This is done by applying a range of different theoretical perspectives while addressing the question of how entrepreneurship and organisation are related. We realise we will not have covered the full breadth of this topic, but hope to have moved ahead and thus potentialised the field in a way that will fuel future research debates and discussions.

Several persons' great efforts (including organisational skills) need to be recognised as absolutely indispensible for the becoming of this volume. Hallur Sigurdarson was a key force in the first wave of preparing the manuscripts. Lena Olaison, who joined the project towards its end, has done a tremendous job in finalising the manuscript and preparing it for publication. I owe both of them many thanks for their efforts. Finally, may I also extend my gratitude to the contributing authors who have generously devoted time and energy to this project, making the organisation of this creation into an entrepreneurially delightful endeavour.

Introduction: entrepreneurship in organisational contexts
Daniel Hjorth

BACKGROUND: WHY FOCUS ON ORGANISATIONAL ENTREPRENEURSHIP?

The year 2011 is significant. Not because most of this book was materialising within that time-space. Instead, there are other events that have operated as strange attractors[1] on my, and perhaps others' thinking, leading up to the suggestion and agreement to make this book. Events that have been directing its becoming to some extent. I refer to 2011 as an anniversary. One hundred years ago, some texts with significant influence on this book's becoming were published: Schumpeter's *Theorie der Wirtschaftlichen Entwicklung*, and Taylor's *Principles of Scientific Management*. I note this not as an example of megalomania or hubris, implying some kinship between this volume and those impressive oeuvres. Rather, they are emblematic of an era, and style of thinking, that have influenced our understanding of management, entrepreneurship and organisation in a most profound way. The era – industrial society and economy – is gradually coming to an end. This does not happen in an evident or easily detectable way. Indeed, many are the prophets that gesture towards various symbols or signs of such an end, gestures that certainly have sold many books. A more correct description would instead talk about the many, no doubt myriad, of small endings that gradually transform us and makes it plausible to one day refer to the present as postindustrial.

This might be a matter of genealogical sensibility, where gradual changes in the landscape, are picked up only by a travelling cartographer. The genealogist knows something through how it has and is becoming; knows by watching the movements. We're *becoming* postindustrial, but more importantly, this is a *postindustrial* becoming.

What style of thinking is then interrupted and gradually coming to an end? Various versions of answers to this question are of course found in the boardrooms of GM, in the memories of Lehman Brothers, in the visions of Google, Facebook and Twitter entrepreneurs. But also on the streets of London (riots in August 2011), Cairo, Tripoli, Damascus, Manama, Hara, Sanaa, Ammam and all the dynamic centres of the so-called Arabic

Spring of 2011 (not limited to spring, nor to 2011), for which the Facebook and Twitter entrepreneurs' products have been instrumental (Stepanova, 2011). In research, this becoming-postindustrial (popularised already by Bell, 1974) is investigated throughout multiple disciplines and fields of research, the coverage of which represents too vast a task even to be captured in a rough overview. Suffice to say that philosophy, humanities and art, as many times before, are fields from where we are provided with early signs, diagnostics, and descriptions (e.g., Benjamin, 1936[1968]). This in itself indicates that the changes are fundamental and have complex effects for systems, institutions, communities, organisations and people embodying those on a daily basis. Societies are not organised as in the industrial era (Bell, 1974; Toffler, 1980), nor are economies (Mills and Lefton, 1988). More importantly, the *becoming* of societies and economies is a different process now. More correctly – which is why it is postindustrial becoming – the multiple becomings of societies and economies bring about a new dynamic. Organisations accordingly achieve being through different processes and practices (Hedberg et al., 2002). Work–life is a different life and career (Florida, 2002); educations and dreams and desires are different too (Weinberg, 2009). Organisational Entrepreneurship stands in the middle of it all.

Entrepreneurship, as we have argued before (Steyaert and Hjorth, 2003, 2006) belongs to society and not simply to economy (Steyaert and Katz, 2004; Dey and Steyaert, 2010). Entrepreneurship is movement – a force that provides impetus to bodies' transition from passive to active – and an intensity that moves people to creative action (Hjorth and Steyaert, 2009; Hjorth and Gartner, this volume). Entrepreneurship does not add a new piece to the puzzle. That is incremental innovation (Ettlie et al., 1984). Entrepreneurship makes new orders achieve being (differentiation), orders that do not fit into the puzzle, but, by being different, require new organisation. Entrepreneurship is 'organisation-creation' (cf. Gartner, this volume) in the sense that it affirms the new – rather than what *is* – and therefore makes necessary new organisation in order for the new to work (add superior value). We can understand organisation-creation as interactions-in-the-making, i.e., relations (Massumi, 2002: 9), that prepare the world for receiving and affirming the greater value of the new:

Invention (creativity, the new idea) x entrepreneurship (organisation-creation) = innovation (of the more radical kind; new practices in which the value of the new is disclosed).

Innovation management, we know, at least since Burns and Stalker (1962), can handle *incremental* innovation for which organising (Weick, 1979)

Table I.1   Organisational forms and modes of organising

Organisational forms / Modes of organising	Mechanic	Organic	Entrepreneurial (which means *forming* as much as form)
Organisation (emphasis on hierarchy, functionalism, monologue)	Management and administration	Change management (1980s theme, see e.g. Quinn et al, 1990; Pettigrew and Longshore, 1990)	Spin-off; Management buy-outs (leaving more rigid organisational structures; e.g. Walter et al., 2006)
Organising (emphasis on holism, adaptability, dialogue)	–	Innovation management (1990–present; e.g. Drucker, 1985)	Corporate entrepreneurship (1980–1990; from 'autonomous' strategic initiatives e.g. Burgelman, 1983a; Stopford and Baden-Fuller, 1994)
Organisation creation (emphasis on intensity, potentiality, movement)	–	–	Organisational entrepreneurship (collective; affective; inventing the new and new practices for disclosing the value of the new; e.g. Spinosa et al., 1997)

mechanically or organically, are enough. For more creative responses (Schumpeter, 1947 [1962]), or 'doing things that are not generally done in the ordinary course of business routine' (Schumpeter, 1949: 259), distinct from administration and management (ibid.), organisation-creation (entrepreneurship) is needed. If we read progress into Burns and Stalker's mechanic–organic metaphorisation, in the sense that it attributes to the latter an enhanced capacity for more radical innovation, we might then add 'entrepreneurial' (see Table I.1 above).

One example could illustrate the relationship between entrepreneurship and organisation. Organisation (as the Latin *organum* and Greek *organon* suggest) is a concept describing a relational composite: parts, organs and the body in which they work, and by which the body is working. Organisation creation (entrepreneurship) would then include new parts as well as a new composition of the whole. Newness in both cases would result in a newness of the whole: new parts mean new relationships to other parts and a qualitatively different whole. For example: a mobile phone was once a new product. It changed our relationship to phoning, but also to other people, practices and to everyday life as a whole. The part (phone) meant new relationships to other parts (home, work, family . . .) which changes the whole – how to communicate, relate, work, live. Organisational entrepreneurship is thus somewhat of a tautology. Entrepreneurship is always organisational as the new order it creates (new product, service, solution) always takes place in an organisational context, which becomes different with the new order. Forming and form are thus never meaningfully separated; that would be thinking 'digitally', which will always miss the movement (cf. Massumi, 2002: 136–7). Forming, like movement, is becoming. Form is a stop, a position. This is why 'entrepreneurial' is different from 'organic'; the question is not about the dynamics of a form, but about the emergence of becoming other, differentiation, form*ing*.

This volume is both a form – handbook – and forming a field of research – organisational entrepreneurship. This means that it adds to what organisational entrepreneurship is understood to be, and, by also asking new questions, hopefully makes it become other, and makes it emerge differently. The book gathers a highly interesting collection of prominent researchers of organisational entrepreneurship. This means that they have all focused on various aspects of the relationship between entrepreneurship and organisation, not necessarily on organisation creation. Such a focus represents a specific scope, but is effective as delimitation mainly in an analytical sense. That is, our common concepts are those of entrepreneurship and organisation, but such a conceptual focus can of course house a vast number of empirical problems and objects of analysis. This means emphasis is sometimes on the organisational aspects of entrepreneurship, while at other times it is on the entrepreneurial aspects of organisation. Both are true to the analytical delimitation and underline the need to address the *relationship*. This relationship is in turn what has become more central – I will argue – in the postindustrial economy, as the primary challenge and opportunity for facilitating processes of collective creativity and innovation (cf. O'Donnell and Austin, 2008; Lindenberg and Foss, 2011). It is this shift, from the management – organisation relationship as primary, towards the entrepreneurship –organisation relationship as primary, which is characteristic for the many small changes we might refer to as signalling the dawn of the postindustrial.

From the perspective of this framing, Taylor and Schumpeter's central place is understandable. Admittedly, 1911 has too violent/rough an impact on what is included/excluded in this elaboration, positioning of the handbook. Several others should be mentioned as central for making the management–organisation relationship into the primary one in the industrial era. Not least, Elton Mayo, who in 1911 became the 'foundation lecturer' in mental and moral philosophy at the new University of Queensland, Australia (where he also held a chair in philosophy between 1919 and 1923). This was 11 years before he left for the United States, and 15 years before his labour turnover studies attracted the interest of Harvard School of Business Administration (where he was an associate professor 1926 and professor in 1929). Curiously enough, this is about the time (1927/28) Schumpeter held a visiting professorship at Harvard (where he became professor in 1932). The transition from Taylor's work – described by Mayo as pioneering the work he himself believed to be extending (Mayo, 1924: 258; O'Connor, 1999a) – to Mayo's, represents an important step in the move from a history of disciplinary oriented management thinking and practice, towards a control-oriented management thinking and practice. Mayo's psychological and philosophical studies made him focus on the workers' minds and develop theory for the proper constitution of the worker's self as auto-controlling. Studies in governmentality (governmental rationality; Burchell et al., 1991; Dean, 1999; Miller and Rose, 2008) have problematised this control-society with inspiration primarily from Michel Foucault's philosophy of power/knowledge and technologies of the self (Martin et al., 1988). From our focus on organisation (which often means contexts of formal business organisations), Taylor and Mayo accelerated the culmination of a control tied to the manager and central to organisational work (March and Simon, 1993: 57).

Thus, without this being explicitly part of a headline in any chapters included in this volume, the question of power and organisational politics is inevitable when the entrepreneurship–organisation relationship is in focus. The move from a disciplinary form of power, relying on the ideas of a Sovereign (Hobbes' work on citizenship, e.g., Leviathan, 1651 [1968]) as absolute and external authority, but also drawing on pastoral forms of power (exemplified in the Catholic Church's institutionalisation of hierarchical order), to a control form of power, is central to modernity (Foucault, 1980; Burchell, 1999; White and Hunt, 2000). What Taylor did is that he designed the manager–worker relationship from the imperatives of the production process. Control was moved from the manager to the machine (solving some of the problems of personal authority), the tempo of the machine. Time was thus economised, and normalisation of work, rather than supervision, was made into the control-mechanism that was supposed to secure productivity (Donzelot, 1988). Economic efficiency will then have to guide the kind of control needed, at the price of a passive subject to be managed. The human is reduced to the human *factor*, and optimum adaptability to the rationality of the economic system of production is then what follows from Taylor's 'principles' of management. Individual judgment and worker agency was replaced by a system of technologies of control, standards, mechanism through which management was to become 'scientific', and this way legitimise its authority over workers (legitimacy of management was thus Taylor's problem). Scientific quickly meant efficient because it is predictable and thus controllable. The Ford and Carnegie Foundations report on higher education for business and University College programmes in business administration, respectively (Gordon and Howell, 1959; Pierson, 1959) further pushed business school education towards becoming more scientific. Herbert Simon was quick to respond to this need, and what was subsequently referred to as the Carnegie School of Decision-making was richly funded accordingly (by the Rockefeller and Ford Foundations, as well from military budgets as Simon turned to problem-solving while the cold war was 'intensified'; Crowther-Heyck, 2006; Sent, 2000).

Mayo, a reader of Freud and Janet in particular, timed a major uprising in the United States (1919), where some 4 million American workers went on strike; the first US general strike was in Seattle; the Boston Police Force walked out after 3 days of looting as consequence; and inflation rose to 29 per cent in the United States (O'Connor, 1999b: 118). In this year, Mayo published *Democracy and Freedom*, and the new HBS Dean (Wallace Donham) started to build up and position the strength of the educational institution. Rockefeller, who had experienced problems with striking workers (the Ludlow disaster ended with deaths; 10 men, 2 women and 12 children), had then identified Mayo and supported his work with money that followed Mayo to the HBS (ibid.). Mayo called democracy '"a socialist theory" which "assumes that all authority derives from the State"' (Mayo, 1919, quoted in O'Connor, 1999b: 126). It is lack of successful adaption to the conditions of industrial life that is the cause of labour motivation and productivity problems, Mayo claimed (1923). The cure against the outcomes (in Mayo's world: Socialism, Syndicalism, Bolshevism) of such lack of adjustment is, according to Mayo, based on a psychological understanding. 'Following Freud, Mayo wrote that civilisation was based on the "sublimation' of primitive instincts"' (1922: 28; quoted in O'Connor, 1999b: 128). 'Heightened capacity for self-control' (ibid: 128) and reduction of psychological agitation was the cure. The counselling interview, a central technique in what was to become HRM, was at the core of this cure (O'Connor, 1999a). Mayo moves control from the machine–worker relationship, from economised time (where Taylor had placed it) to the worker him/herself and the question of normalisation (Townley, 1993). This is when subjectification is made the primary object of concern for management knowledge and practice: how to make up productive employee subjectivities, governable workers?

This elaboration of the background indicates why the shift from an industrial to a postindustrial time demands new ways of approaching, studying and analysing organisations. In particular, it makes quite evident that the manager–organisation relationship no longer can occupy our centre of attention, but will have to share this place with the entrepreneur–organisation relationship. The most important problem in postindustrial organisation is how its potential for innovation, how its capacity for collective creativity can be facilitated and nurtured (Austin and Devin, 2003; Hjorth, 2003a). This, we have gradually come to realise, is not primarily a problem of managerial control. It is a problem of organisational creativity. From the perspective of this book, this also means it is a challenge of organisational entrepreneurship.

Managers and managerial control has a place and time in such creation-processes, contributing to innovation, but it is more secondary than history suggests. We can imagine innovation processes as driven by entrepreneurial and managerial modes of organising. Various innovation-clouds, i.e., temporary assemblages of people and resources organised by attention to the different needs of the process, are driven by the entrepreneurial and managerial responses to those needs. The former operates primarily as active responses (affirming what allows for creation of the new), whereas the latter is primarily a reactive response (directed by the primacy of control and limitation). Organisational entrepreneurship is an achievement, the result of finding ways to make the active response prevail over the reactive for as long as it takes to prevent the new from collapsing under the weight of normalising procedures. In the context of business, this means responding with regards to what resources are already invested (reactive), or responding with regards to what potentialises the collective capacity for creation, and prepares the world for the new. Such preparation centres on organisation-creation, where the value of the new is inseparable from the new practices (style) needed for appreciating this value (cf. Spinosa et al., 1997). We will develop this in a later chapter when we discuss what entrepreneurial leadership could be from the perspective of this understanding of the dynamics of postindustrial organisation and its subsequent focus on the organisation–entrepreneurship relationship (see Chapter 20, Hjorth and Gartner, this volume).

ORGANISATIONAL ENTREPRENEURSHIP: OPENING A RESEARCH AGENDA

That there is a break indicating the end of the dominance of an industrial economy and the beginning of a more complex multiplicity, with the postindustrial economy at its centre, does not mean there is an exact date or decisive event. Searching for such an event is an impossible and uninteresting task. Social change is more realistically described in discursive terms. The answer to how it happens is a question of genealogy and genealogical sensitivity. One has to diagnose broadly, draw a map that includes cultural, societal, historical, technological, commercial (and so on) forces shaping the topology; the social/cultural/political/economic landscape. There are various forms of 'seismic activities' that herald the fault scarp: the centre of gravity of the global economy is moving east; higher levels of unemployment have persisted in more European economies than what historically has been the case (Eurostat 1); major financial and corporate structures in the United States have collapsed or have been saved by the government; we see a managerial class that seems to work less and less for salaries and more and more for bonuses or 'compensations' (as the language preferred by the Lehman Brothers would have it; see Richard Fuld explaining: http://www.youtube.com/watch?v=-cifEkRXc4). Virtual value and 'long tails' are becoming more and more important, and the building and maintaining thereof is an increasingly mediatised business in itself (Anderson, 2004).

The shift of ground is happening as a series of events throughout societies and, as the ICT-facilitated 'Arab Spring' of 2011 illustrated, when technology radically enhances networking communities' capacity for generation and circulation of information, this has important implications for all. When desire to become other is drastically increased by belonging, facilitated by the connectivity that ICT brings, the productive capacity of the assemblage, the multitude, is multiplied accordingly. ICT powers up the relational capacity of people, and the organisational capacity is enhanced accordingly. This provides additional arguments for the importance of organisational entrepreneurship; collective creativity as an active response to the state of things. The break (gradual, dispersed, multiple) with the dominance of the industrial style (basis for practices, meaning) of organising signals a transition, and opens towards it by questioning the continuity of habitual practices (cf. base of pyramid economics; long tail economics; social entrepreneurship; open innovation; Hart and London, 2005; Anderson, 2004; Leadbeater, 1997; Chesbrough, 2003). For students and practitioners of business, this transition marks a simultaneous change in the landscape of practicing and thinking management, leadership and entrepreneurship in organisations, and in the study of those practices and styles of thinking.

I would like to see this volume as located in this transitional zone, in the gap, looking into the landscape of the postindustrial, trying to provide new perspectives, approaches, concepts and stories both for the future of organisational–entrepreneurial practices and for the future of studying those. Of course, our primary focus is on entrepreneurship: entrepreneurship in the context of organisation. However, focusing on entrepreneurship in organisational contexts makes a non-relational understanding of entrepreneurship – related to management and leadership – impossible. Indeed, this recognition is in itself what makes practicing a contextual approach necessary and meaningful. Acknowledging that organisational entrepreneurship takes place somewhere, at some time, and is thereby part of a world where management and leadership provide most of the conditions for what can/cannot be done, makes our studies more realistic and useful. In addition, entrepreneurship is a form of organisational creativity. This makes it complex. As a process of creating new products, resources (or combinations of), logics of practice, rationales, organisations or even industries, entrepreneurship is difficult to grasp, describe, study and analyse. This book brings together examples – and I believe really exciting examples – of the scope of such study. It also manifests the multiplicity of entrepreneurship studies, when focused on organisational contexts.

The chapters in this book will all, in various ways, substantiate what the field of organisational entrepreneurship is about (as study and as practice). Before I move on to provide a short description of the book's content by relating to the various chapters, I would like to provide a framing of organisational entrepreneurship as I understand this research. Admittedly, this is offered in the spirit of what we previously have referred to as a European School of Entrepreneurship Research (Hjorth et al., 2008). Central to it is what I have emphasised already: understanding entrepreneurship contextually and a focus on creativity as the differentiating factor. Let me develop and expand on this shortly, before I turn to the chapter preambles.

The world becomes in multiple and polymorphous ways. Organisations need to respond to this. In postindustrial times, speed, flexibility and creativity are keys to building and sustaining innovation capacity as a primary competitive basis. However, for historical reasons (Taylor and Mayo as decisive 'events' in this history), the manager has acquired preferential right of interpretation when it comes to responding to those multiple and polymorphous ways. In addition, they have authorship privileges when it comes to narrating the organisation's worldview and guide to moving ahead in the landscape – the strategy. A strategy would then be a narrativisation (in the genre of management) of life-to-come that is composed and communicated for the purpose of controlling (people and resources), so as to make predictable the becoming of that life.

Organisational creation and entrepreneurship need to operate in such a strategised reality. It operates in an organisational context appropriated by an ostensive story. A story – strategy – that has delineated and appropriated a place of its own. Managerial responses to the multiple becomings of the world are attentive to the traces of previous investments. There are economic reasons for responding this way, since it means that maintaining a capacity for control is thereby supported (as traces can be used to generate statistics that help predict and forecast, i.e., financial economics is used to make management more 'scientific'). Again, this is how the reactive prevails over the active.

Organisational entrepreneurship instead operates by the logic of potentiality and intensity. Not what has been done, but what could become is the (un-)reason to act (cf. Gartner et al., 1992). Reason, in the industrial era, has been occupied by economic rationality, limiting the normal and right to what is controllable via statistics based on traces. This works well for management, primarily oriented towards control. On this theme, Drucker (1985) pointed out that there is a tendency in organisations to 'feed yesterday and starve tomorrow,' which would make decision makers deaf and blind to the broader complexity of human creativity, central to understanding and organising entrepreneurship (cf. Steyaert and Hjorth, 2003; Rindova et al., 2009). This, very much business school based, direction of attention to the economy of entrepreneurship prevents us from understanding the full organisation of entrepreneurship.

The problem is that creativity or entrepreneurship as organisation-creation cannot emerge from opposing the reactive, economically rational response to the world's multiple becomings typical of trace-oriented management. This will only generate opposition on the basis of the needs to maintain control and economic efficiency. There are no good arguments against such needs in business organisations. Indeed, since Taylor, such behaviour is easily represented as irrational, as wasting time and trying the useless – attempting to change the 'machine' and the structure it makes necessary according to the time–economy link Taylor established. Neo-institutional theory (Meyer and Rowan, 1977; DiMaggio and Powell, 1983) has shown that institutionalised and rationalised concepts are the primary sources of formal organisational structures (Townley, 2002). We should, however, also acknowledge the paradoxical nature of institutional theory (Czarniawska, 1997), i.e., that institutional processes also set rules of rationality (Scott, 1995). One cannot legitimise organisational creativity–entrepreneurship– 'against' these structures of organisations. Formal structures support control and economic efficiency understood as using resources on the basis of data provided by traces: 'costs usually depend mainly on the foregone value of the time spent on these investments' (Becker 1993: 43).

Space for creation cannot be achieved *against* management, as this will only generate stronger opposition (cf. Aldrich, 1999: 52) with reference to further trace-based 'evidence'. Instead, acknowledging a world with multiple rationalities suggests that affirming creative forces is how you make the new happen. Rationalities in Weber's sense – practical, theoretical, substantive and formal – are always tied to 'value spheres' in which certain patterns of actions and styles of living become rational; cf. Weber, 1978: 85–107; Townley, 2002). Organisational entrepreneurship has therefore a history of incubation, after dark work, skunk-work, moon-shining and creative ways to make space for the new (Hjorth, 2005). In such spaces, the 'normal' continuation of institutionalised rationalities is postponed or interrupted. The economically rational agent is driven by adjusting to the world as it is, central to rationality in human capital theory:

> [That] is any conduct which is sensitive to modifications in variables of the environment and which responds to this in a non-random way, in a systematic way, and economics can there be defined as the science of the systematic nature of responses to environmental variables. (Foucault, 2008: 269)

Entrepreneurship, as form of creativity, is rather understandable as driven by a world that could become actualised. Potentiality, desire to move beyond the limits of present capacities, rather than optimal adjustment (desire based on lack of fit with rationality dictated by traces and 'foregone value' of time spent), is the driver. Subsequently, narrative, rather than traditional scientific arguments (of the kind that uses calculation and statistics, i.e., rests on traces) are the primary ways of making space for organisational creativity. The social field is potentialised by the use of *intensive* images, convincing because they generate effects that transform people. People are moved, become-active, when a narrative of potential is produced for them (cf. Aldrich and Fiol, 1994; Lounsbury and Glynn, 2001; Hjorth, 2007). Now, there are reactive responses to the world, focused on opportunities as found or discovered, which still are described as 'entrepreneurship'. I have suggested this be called managerial entrepreneurship, since the style is reactive and dominated by the trace, and economy of 'what is', and calculative rationality. It operates by realising discovered opportunities. What I have proposed here as organisational entrepreneurship is rather active responses, an economy of 'what could become', creation of opportunities, potentialising of creative forces. This operates by actualising created opportunities. Relations, desires, bodies and stories – those are the resources of the world becoming new. Subjectivities such as 'entrepreneur' are shaped, temporarily, in relations, through storytelling: 'Imagination is the mode of thought most precisely suited to the differentiating vagueness of the virtual. [. . .] postinstrumental and preoperative' (Massumi, 2002: 134).

Narrative rationality (cf. Lyotard, 1979, on the contrast of narrative and scientific knowledge) allows for thought to participate in its own emergence. Sensation, intensity, effect, from such emerges imagination of how potential can be made to leap into the actual. We may call this entrepreneurial entrepreneurship. Managerial entrepreneurship calculates on possibilities, which is what instrumental reason is for. Nietzsche battled this tendency in human thinking to limit imagination or intuition to what experience serves us (cf. debate on Lachmann in entrepreneurship research). This only corresponds to the triumph of the negative or controlling will to power of 'higher men', as Nietzsche called them (Hjorth, 2010):

> There are things that the higher man does not know how to do: to laugh, to play and to dance. To laugh is to affirm life, even the suffering in life. To play is to affirm chance and the necessity of chance. To dance is to affirm becoming and the being of becoming. (Deleuze, 2006: 170)

The response that can differentiate and create, is the one that can affirm and thereby become active. This, again, is not so much about individuals as about relations, desires, stories, potentialities and intensities. Process philosophy and its corresponding relational approaches in research (see Steyaert, 2007, for review of process theory in entrepreneurship studies) help us shift from 'methodological individualism to a social ontology of relatedness' (Steyaert, 2007: 456). My hope is that this book's contribution to an opening of organisational entrepreneurship as a field of research will participate in making this shift.

CONTRIBUTIONS

I will not tread on the distinct voices provided by chapter authors. The concept of a *Handbook* indeed makes somewhat superfluous any editorial elaboration on chapter points and contributions. All chapters make contributions to organisational entrepreneurship as a burgeoning field of research, increasingly central to the postindustrial era. The simple structure of the *Handbook* – Part I focuses on approaches and perspectives, and Part II focuses on fields of research, practices and politics – is based on the following ideas. For this research field to develop, its antecedent ideas and relations to neighbouring fields of research need to be clarified.

Part I focuses on this while it simultaneously provides nuances to studies in organisational entrepreneurship. The different approaches and perspectives provide multiple entry points for students of organisational entrepreneurship, and contextualises problems in the traditions of other theoretical perspectives. Part II moves further into elaborating and demonstrating what organisational entrepreneurship is and how it is becoming something more. In addition, it tackles the questions of specific practice contexts, such as public organisations, art, the city, as well as the politics of organisational entrepreneurship. Part II, therefore, deals with contextualised problems and thereby, in many of the cases, invites the political challenges associated with creating the new.

Part I

William Gartner in many ways is a natural opener of this volume. His research, at least since the mid-1980s, has generated a number of ideas that have pointed towards this field of study (relating organisation and entrepreneurship). It is therefore an 'opening chapter' in several respects: written by an opener of this field; opening towards a more interdisciplinary study of entrepreneurship; and opening towards new problematisations (notably of organisation creation; and of a process view of entrepreneurship, see also Steyaert in this volume). Gartner tackles the recent focus on opportunity in entrepreneurship research, and uses a close reading of Karl Weick to argue that 'organising' subsumes both 'discovery' and 'creation' views. Organising here represents an ontological basis for entrepreneurship research; a basis that was side-tracked by the focus on opportunity.

Richard Swedberg inquires into Schumpeter's theories of organisational entrepreneurship. Swedberg thus opens towards the possibility of several theories, and he shows how those can be found in *Theory of Economic Development* (1911), in *Business Cycles* (1939), and in *Capitalism, Socialism and Democracy* (1942). Swedberg, in addition, affirms the need for new theories on organisational entrepreneurship as he goes on to show how one can theorise by the help of Schumpeter's ideas on the business firm. In this way, the chapter develops into an entrepreneurial endeavour itself – making use, in new ways, of established ideas in order to create new possibilities for future scholars of organisational entrepreneurship.

Nicolai Foss, Peter Klein and Per Bylund's chapter relate to Swedberg's in also discussing the business firm, this time related to entrepreneurs. The chapter focuses on the lack of contact between the study of entrepreneurship and the study of economic organisation, and goes on to argue that entrepreneurship theory and the theory of the firm can be usefully integrated. Focusing on entrepreneurship as judgement (providing a natural link to the theory of the firm), and as speculative, the authors ask to what extent the entrepreneur needs a firm. Understanding entrepreneurship as judgement, the case can be made that firms are needed, as judgement cannot be purchased on a market. Emphasising the importance of entrepreneurial imagination further strengthens the case that entrepreneurs need the firm as a vehicle for experimenting with imagined novel resource combinations and for realising imagined production structures.

Friederike Welter and David Smallborne focus on an institutional perspective on entrepreneurship. This chapter provides an important insight into the organisational context of entrepreneurship; the social embeddedness of entrepreneurial activity. We are introduced to institutional theory as applied in entrepreneurship research, and emphasis is placed on agency and institutional change.

Martha Martinez and Howard Aldrich relate evolutionary theory to entrepreneurship. Institutionalism is one link to the previous chapters; judgement/judging is another. Martinez and Aldrich provide a more relational and processual perspective on organisations. For entrepreneurship research, focus on organisational change is of particular interest, and this chapter centres on selection and variation to discuss the dynamics of evolutionary processes. This chapter also relates to Gartner's chapter as the authors understand entrepreneurs as people who succeed in creating organisations. Evolutionary theory – in this perspective – therefore provides a link between entrepreneurs and organisations. On the basis of their discussions, Martinez and Aldrich also assess methodological progress in research on evolutionary processes.

When Robert Hisrich and Claudine Kearney relate organisations, entrepreneurship and ethics, they base this on an overview of ethics and ethical practices of entrepreneurs and managers in the context of the current economic downturn. Particular focus is placed on codes of ethics, core values, corporate culture and corporate social responsibility of entrepreneurs and managers. The Credit Crisis provides an abundance of illustrations of the need to explore ethics and social responsibility of entrepreneurs and managers, and Hisrich and Kearney bring us into such a discussion.

Campbell Jones and Maria Murtola's chapter is related to Hisrich and Kearney's, as it also centres on crisis. This time, however, the crisis (and the concrete suffering it has brought) is the event they respond to with critique. Indeed, it is developing a critique of entrepreneurship – what it might look like and why it might matter – that forms the central challenge the authors take on. If entrepreneurship is to be sustainable, it needs to be subject to critique. Beyond a view of entrepreneurship as salvation, relating entrepreneurship to crisis means that its role is investigated anew. How is entrepreneurship connected to the crisis tendencies of capitalism? How is Schumpeter's 'creative destruction' tied to this tendency? Jones and Murtola outline a programme for a critique of entrepreneurship today.

Helene Ahl's chapter operates with a critical examination of the relationships between gender, organisations and entrepreneurship. Pursuing work on feminism, Ahl is interested in the construction of gender and resulting gender/power orders, so as to provide value for men and women in their work for gender equality. Ahl's focus in this chapter is on the consequences for women of constructions of gender, organisations and entrepreneurship: how are women positioned and how is this related to women's opportunities to be entrepreneurial in organisations? Ahl convincingly shows how the question of women's opportunities to be entrepreneurial in organisations requires critical genealogical inquiry that challenges gendered norms.

Chris Steyaert takes on the challenge of discussing the possibilities of a process perspective by inquiring into how theorising and researching themselves are part of moving, moving us and making difference possible. Steyaert's performative chapter invites us to experiment with how process perspectives can change how we do theory, research, writing and intervention. We are invited to create concepts and invent connections, to act with theory rather than to apply it. We are invited to think beyond present limits, to take part in the creation of what does not yet exist as a solid field of research, the coming together of organisation and entrepreneurship under the heading of organisational entrepreneurship.

In the chapter that ends Part I, I work with processual thinking to create concepts for organisational entrepreneurship. Meaning that I seek to move beyond the limits of our present thinking, and draw some lines to follow in future research. How is organisational entrepreneurship possible? Organisations, in the industrial era, were set up to be eminently manageable. Postindustrialism represents different demands, and collective creativity (for innovation) is now the haunted capacity of organisations. Are the organisational conditions for entrepreneurship (as organisation-creation) thereby changed? How does process thinking help us describe and analyse its contextual conditions? More specifically, I address the problematic status of the agent (and agency) in processual thinking. Does creation (as in organisation-creation) demand that we think a creator? Becoming-entrepreneur is proposed as a process characterised as an 'art of the weak', an affirmative-tactical mode of making use for the purpose of transmuting.

Part II

Saras Sarasvathy is a bridge between Part I and II. Her chapter opens up another bridge – or 'connective tissue' – between theories of micro behaviour in organisations and the macro environments we live in. Her opening question – is the entrepreneurial firm an artefact resulting from markets, or are firms and markets artefacts from entrepreneurial creation of organisations? – receives a 'both' answer that suggests we have underweighted entrepreneurial creation of organisations. The future research agenda for organisational entrepreneurship is then proposed as one that is contextual, relational and transformational. Exaptation, used to describe how the entrepreneurial form relates to its environment, forms into a concept that bridges the micro- and meso-levels of analysis and relates this chapter to the previous one (where 'tactically transmuting' describes a similar mode of relating.)

Nicolai Foss and Jacob Lyngsie bring us into the field of strategic entrepreneurship (SE), in itself an emerging area of research. This relates opportunity- and advantage-seeking under the central idea that these processes need to be considered together. Foss and Lyngsie want to explain how this field of research emerged, and their method is to investigate how it has responded to gaps in the two 'sibling' areas of research it connects. In addition, they want to describe the main tenets of SE theory, relate it to its neighbouring fields, and describe research gaps. Based on this review and description, they move on to open up SE towards a road ahead, focused on the need for micro-foundations for SE theory and linking it to organisational design theory.

Donald Kuratko's chapter brings us into the field of corporate entrepreneurship. Emphasis on creativity is clear when Kuratko writes about firms that lead customers, create markets, change their environments and even the rules of the competitive game. Kuratko relates to the question of strategy and entrepreneurship – from the previous chapter – by asking what it means, in a theoretical sense, to have corporate entrepreneurship as a firm's strategy. After describing the evolution of the field of corporate entrepreneurship, Kuratko focuses on how corporate entrepreneurship is configured as a strategy, the elements of an organisational architecture conducive to CE and the managerial roles within that architecture.

Ester Barinaga organises the emerging literature on social entrepreneurship into a conceptually oriented and a managerially oriented streams. On the basis of this, she argues for the need to develop a social approach to the study of the methods, strategies and notions used by social entrepreneurial initiatives working towards social change. Barinaga moves into this direction herself as she suggests a matrix (social change matrix) for analysing how the social change aimed at by social entrepreneurial initiatives relates to the methods used to initiate them. In doing so, she remedies the imbalance caused by research oriented primarily towards the entrepreneurial side of social entrepreneurship.

Anne Kovalainen and Elisabeth Sundin approach the topic of public sector entrepreneurship in a multidisciplinary way. They open their chapter by noting the awkward relationship between the public sector and entrepreneurship, and go on to tackle this relationship in a more 'positive' manner. New public management represents an event in the history of the public sector – entrepreneurship relationship – and Kovalainen and Sundin deal with this as they work their way towards a new presentation of entrepreneurship in public sector organisations.

Shannon O'Donnell and Lee Devin also approach the question of entrepreneurship and collective creativity from a multidisciplinary perspective. Their focus is on the creativity of teams working iteratively to create. Drawing from their experience and expertise in theatre, they use the concept of ensemble to describe how teams collaborate to collectively create innovation. They describe an intensely relational, interdependent, social, iterative and contextual process of creation. O'Donnell and Devin develop a more refined language for describing, analysing and practicing such collective creativity, crucial for the study and practice of organisational entrepreneurship.

In Pierre Guillet de Monthoux's chapter, the artistic element (introduced in the previous chapter) is even more prominent as the relationship – entrepreneur–artist – is analysed and discussed. In many ways, Guillet de Monthoux's discussion centres on the boundary between artist and entrepreneur, and as we are brought into this investigation, the distinction is often blurred. In the new approach he suggests, the blurredness is affirmed, and the concept of artepreneur is born. The key skill of the artepreneur is her capacity to create organisation as she aesthetically reclaims a lost 'sensus communis', while reshaping the public realm through Deweyian 'art as experience'.

The public realm is in focus in Timon Beyes' study of the organisation of the entrepreneurial city. Urban entrepreneurialism and the cultural-consumption-centred emphasis on an 'artistic mode of production' is either hailed or critiqued, but Beyes offers a third option in his prosaic mode of narrating the entrepreneurial city. For this option, space and organisational creativity is central. Beyes sensitises us to different imaginations of urban life and the novel forms of organising that it holds.

Bent Meier Sørensen – like Beyes – also explores the darker sides of enterprise discourse's emphasis on creative industries and (in this case) entrepreneurial employees. Sørensen practices a method of juxtaposition, a form of image analysis; something like a careful unfolding of what images say and do, revealing forces, effects and affects that may well have passed unnoticed had we not been invited to this closer scrutiny. The study, operating within an aesthetic framework, brings us into a discussion that relates the dawn of creative industries' worker subjectivity to the dusk of management (as engaged in creating worker subjectivities and entrepreneurial selves.)

Daniel Hjorth and William Gartner's elaboration on 'entrepreneurial leadership' continues the conversation with art, aesthetics and philosophy that has characterised the second half of Part II. The dynamics between leader and led, between moving people and being moved, is in focus. Entrepreneurial leadership is defined as mobilising collective creativity in organisational contexts, and this novel conceptualisation is based on process philosophy. However, our method is not too different from Sørensen's juxtaposition as we explore Odysseus' encounter with the Sirens (receptivity and spontaneity) as well as Martin Luther's 95 theses event (breaking by affirming the creative potentials) as two images from which we can learn how to conceptualise entrepreneurial leadership.

NOTE

1. Strange attractor, a metaphor from complexity science, describes what makes a system or, in this case, thinking, bifurcate (qualitatively change, differentiate). It makes sense to think about Scientific Management and Entrepreneurship as systems that cause bifurcations when they collide.

PART I

APPROACHES AND
PERSPECTIVES

1   Entrepreneurship as organisation creation
William B. Gartner

Act always so as to increase the number of choices. (Foerster, 1973 [2003]: 227)

INTRODUCTION

The purpose of this chapter is to offer some insights into why and how the phenomenon of organization creation has a strong relationship to what, I believe, is the essential nature of entrepreneurship. Indeed, I suggest that a close reading of primary historical texts in the entrepreneurship field (e.g., Cantillon, 1755 [2001]; Say, 1800 [2010]; Schumpeter, 1934 [1983]) would indicate that the phenomenon of organization creation plays a primary role in the evolution of ideas in entrepreneurship field. Also, see Herbert and Link (1988), Baumol (1993), and Bull and Willard (1993) for a history of definitions of entrepreneurship. Organization creation is about entrepreneurship, and vice versa.

As I have argued in the past (Gartner, 1985; 1988; 1990; 1993; 2008; 2007; Gartner and Brush, 2007), my view of what organization creation 'is' entails the rubric of 'organizing' (Weick, 1979), which I believe should play an encompassing ontological role (Thompson, 2011) in the entrepreneurship field. I begin with Weick's definition of organizing: 'a consensually validated grammar for reducing equivocality by means of sensible interlocked behaviors' (Weick, 1979: 3) as a starting point. I suggest that entrepreneurship must have, in some sense, some kind of 'organizing' component. What ever the entrepreneur does, or whatever the entrepreneurial activity entails, or what ever an entrepreneurial phenomenon is, must in some respects, involve the organization ('the organizing') of something: e.g., an environment, an opportunity, a market, a process, technology, group, business, a person's thoughts, etc. This, I think, is somewhat in line with a process view of entrepreneurship (Hjorth, 2003a, 2005; Steyaert and Hjorth, 2003; Steyeart, 2007;), but it should be noted that 'organizing' itself, is somewhat larger, more encompassing, and broader, than the phenomenon of entrepreneurship, itself, or as a process. Entrepreneurship, then, is a subset of what organizing is.

If this is so, then, I suggest that the core of the entrepreneurship field has 'side tracked' itself from its ontological basis in organizing by focusing on 'opportunity' (Shane and Venkataraman, 2000) as its essential nature. As Dimov (2011) recently pointed out, the focus on opportunities has not moved entrepreneurship scholarship closer to some coherent understanding of the phenomenon of either what opportunities are, or what entrepreneurship is. Be that as it may, while 'organizing' has an intuitive appeal to scholars interested in perspectives that place the process of entrepreneurship into a creation perspective (cf. Alvarez and Barney, 2007; 2010; Alvarez et al., 2012), the nature of 'organizing' is ontologically 'bigger' in such a way that it cannot be placed on one side of a dichotomy with 'creation' versus 'discovery' as separate entrepreneurial processes. This chapter is not intended to offer a correction of these interpretations or applications of the idea of organizing (Cornelissen and Clarke, 2010), rather, I hope to point out a more expansive reading of Karl Weick's ideas regarding organizing as it might be applied to entrepreneurship. I will do this by using Scott Shane's article 'Prior knowledge and the discovery of entrepreneurial opportunities' (2000) (referred to in the remainder of the paper as 'Prior knowledge') as a way to elaborate this exegesis. It is important then, to have some familiarity with this article before forging ahead. I will show that 'organizing' in entrepreneurship subsumes both ideas of 'discovery' and 'creation' into a more comprehensive and complex idea – enactment. The gist of this argument, then, is to suggest that when '(Weick, 1979)' is evoked as a citation link to any particular view of entrepreneurship, particularly that of being on the side of 'creation' versus 'discovery,' the idea of 'organizing' actually subsumes all other viewpoints. There is no contrasting viewpoint.

Organizing is all.[1]

WHAT I SEE

Scott Shane is one of the entrepreneurship field's most persuasive academic writers and thought leaders. His jointly authored article with S. Venkataraman (Shane and Venkataraman, 2000) was recently noted as the most cited article in the *Academy of Management Review* during this past decade. (And, it should be noted that I have argued that this article should serve as a foundation text (among many) for understanding the nature of entrepreneurship, see Gartner, 2001). What sets Scott Shane's work ahead of most other academic scholarship in entrepreneurship is his writing style: the way he is able to offer evidence for his views that enable him to provide a compelling story that is hard to doubt. 'Prior knowledge' is an exemplar of this. Yet, I have agonized over this article, and, have struggled with how the article marshals theory and evidence for what has become part of the basis for a 'discovery' (Alvarez and Barney,

2007; 2010) view of entrepreneurship. I believe, and will show, that the 'Prior knowledge' article provides a very narrow use of theory, methods, evidence, and interpretations for suggesting that 'discovery,' as a way of making sense about what occurred in a particular situation, actually occurs.[2] If this is the case, then, I suggest that these various perspectives on what opportunities are, as either forms of 'discovery' or 'creation,' can plausibly be subsumed under the 'organizing' umbrella. So, please follow along (make sure to have a copy of 'Prior knowledge' to look at) and see whether you see what I see in this text.

Scott Shane builds a theory of a 'discovery' view of entrepreneurship based on Kirzner's perspective that: 'opportunity, *by definition*, is unknown until it is discovered'; and one cannot search for something that one does not know exists (Kaish and Gilad, 1991: 38). As Shane goes on to quote Kirzner:

> what distinguishes *discovery* (relevant to hitherto unknown profit opportunities) from *successful search* (relevant to deliberate production of information which one knew one had lacked) is that the former (unlike the later) involves the *surprise* that accompanies the realization that one had overlooked something in fact readily available. (Kirzner, 1997a: 72; Shane, 2000: 451)

And, then Shane offers this insight:

> The above argument suggests that people do not discover entrepreneurial opportunities through search, but through recognition of the value of new information that they happen to receive through other means. (Shane, 2000: 451)

If one accepts Kirzner's ideas at face value, then one might agree with the logic of Shane's proposition:

People can and will discover entrepreneurial opportunities without actively searching for them. (Shane, 2000: 451)

But, Kirzner's idea of 'surprise' is cognitively and psychologically naïve in regards to what scientists know about how and why individuals make sense of and explain their experiences (cf. Nisbett and Wilson, 1977; Wilson and Schooler, 1991; Wilson and Dunn, 2004; Brown et al., 2008). Both eliciting and analysing introspections from individuals have significant challenges and possibilities of which Kirzner's perspective on introspections, via the idea of 'surprise,' manages to ignore or fail to appreciate. To build a theoretical foundation for 'surprise' as a way of making sense of one's situation, needs to go further than Kirzner's belief. It is necessary to place the Kirznerian worldview about 'surprise' within the context of already known scientific facts and theories from cognitive and psychological science. From this larger perspective, basing research on Kirzner's views of the nature of introspection is theoretically problematic.[3]

In addition, Kirzner's view of discovery as 'surprise' is philosophically flawed. As pointed out by Hjorth and Johannisson (2007), a view of search that requires one to look for what one knows as already existing is merely a repetition of Socrates' dialogue with Meno: Either you know what you are searching for or you do not. If you do know, you already have it, whence inquiry/learning is pointless. And if you do not know, you would not recognize it even if you stumbled on it accidentally; hence, again, inquiry/learning is impossible, pointless (cf. Hjorth and Johannisson, 2007: 46).

Various philosophers have addressed this paradox, and offer a variety of ways of considering the nature and meaning of search, particularly Kant (cf. Weatherston, 2002; Banham, 2005) and Bergson (cf. Deleuze, 1966 [1991]; Bergson, 2002), of which, it would appear, a Kirznarian theory about the phenomenon of 'surprise' simply does not hold up. So, while a theoretical underpinning for the 'surprise' of discovery might be plausible, there are a variety of other theoretical approaches that are supported by empirical evidence that put such a perspective on the nature of discovery as 'surprise' in doubt.

The empirical evidence for supporting the idea of 'surprise' also raises some significant concerns. Shane's empirical evidence about the nature of discovery is based on a series of eight cases that describe experiences of entrepreneurs involved in recognizing opportunities based on a patent for three-dimensional printing. As a way of providing evidence that entrepreneurs were surprised to recognize an opportunity until they had been made aware of the three-dimensional printing idea he offers such quotes as (Shane, 2000: 457):

> I just looked at the machine and thought about what could be done with it on a consumer level. My idea came to me immediately – Mike Padnos.

> Mike Cema showed me the 3DP process one day and my idea to make orthopedics just clicked – Stephen Campbell.

> The value it had just made sense to me when I saw the MIT machine. It was instinctive, just like if you showed someone who uses a typewriter this invention called a word processor . . . – Marina Hatsopoulos.

While it is plausible that these quotes can be interpreted as examples of 'surprise,' they could also be utilized to represent a myriad of other kinds of reasons for explaining these retrospective introspections. These quotes could be 'insights' or 'realizations' both of which do not require 'surprise.' What is more problematic about the quotes in the article used to support the idea of 'surprise,' is that they are context-less evidence: a reader has no way to fathom what questions were asked to prompt these responses, no way to see what other aspects of the interview support or disconfirm these quotes. A reader neither has access to the interview schedule or to the interviews themselves. One can believe Scott Shane's declaration: 'In all eight cases, the respondents indicated that they simply recognized the opportunity, almost by accident, as if they were surprised by the discovery' (Shane, 2000: 457).

But the evidence, per se, could be used to provide support for a variety of other beliefs. 'As if' places the perspective of 'surprise' in the realm of the possible, but these quotes and other evidence may also be subject to other interpretations and understandings which have not been offered or explored.

UNTIL I KNOW

I suggest that the quotes supporting 'surprise' and other evidence in 'Prior knowledge' that Scott Shane presents about the discovery of opportunities can be used as persuasive evidence for how and why enactment occurs in the organizing process. From a Weickian perspective, Kirznerian discovery – 'surprise' is a form of 'bracketing' (Weick, 1979: 153–7). We are always in the field of action. The nature of being alive means that: events, activities, behaviors, thoughts, 'whatever,' (i.e., stuff) are continually occurring. This is the raw data of life. This flow of stuff, the raw data of life, is material that may be paid attention to, or not. To pay attention to some of this stuff is to 'bracket' one's situation: In Weick's view – to enact it.

A discovery, then, from the perspective of organizing, is to recognize that one is, simply, paying attention to one's experience (Langer, 1997). This does not suggest that outside events are not 'real' until they are attended to, quite the opposite. Events happen all of the time. 'Bracketing' from an organizing view suggests that we will pay attention to some events and not others. And, that the experience of paying attention matters! To be 'surprised' (that is, to 'bracket') would suggest that, out of the stuff of life, individuals retrospectively notice that some events appear to be more significant than others. Opportunities, then, are not necessarily 'created' when one brackets one's ongoing 'stuff.' But, opportunities are not necessarily 'discovered,' either. For example, substitute the word 'opportunity' for 'environment' in the following quote:

> Environments are problematic, but not their substances and properties and parts. It is their existence as an entity that is problematic. How does it come to pass that an organization finds it useful to say of its flow of experience, 'we

face an environment' or 'we face the environment?' To what questions asked by organizational members is the positing of an environment or the environment an answer? Yet organizational theorists don't worry about problems such as this. They act if it is obvious what the environment is and where it is. Given these a-priori certainties, what investigators tend to dismiss is the assertion that the environment is located in the mind of the actor and is imposed by him on experience in order to make that experience more meaningful. It seldom dawns on organizational theorists to look for environments inside of heads rather than outside of them. (Weick, 2001: 185)

Inherently, from Weick's organizing perspective, the 'out there,' from which opportunities arise stems from the sense making capabilities utilized by the entrepreneur. This might be formulated, as 'prior knowledge' that the entrepreneur possesses, but a more complicated and richer perspective via organizing, would suggest something more.

ABOUT WHAT HE SAYS

What the quote above suggests, in regards to a discussion about the nature of opportunities as an aspect of entrepreneurship, is that the fundamental attribution error involves ascribing concreteness to opportunities, that is, to assume that opportunities are either external or internal to entrepreneurs, that opportunities are something to be created or discovered. Enactment in organizing, ontologically, is about *process as emergence*, so that labeling something as an opportunity is one way of bracketing the flow of experiences (the process of emergence) that individuals have.

> Thus, people invent organizations and their environments and these inventions reside in ideas that participants have superimposed on any stream of experience. This contrasts with the view that organizations and environments consist of underlying structures that are revealed to inquisitive discoverers. The one quibble I have with Popper involves the last sentence. The phrase 'should observation show that they are wrong' implies a reality underlying the appearances, an implication that I find dispensable. I don't think observation would suggest that something should be discarded because it is wrong. Instead, I think observation would simply suggest that there are alternative, arbitrary ways to make sense out of a stream of experience, and that these alternative-imposed regularities might be more useful or more esthetic, or more pleasant or more novel than the regularities currently being imposed. (Weick, 2001: 196)

As will be discussed below, Weick suggests that there are a multitude of ways that experiences are: generated, noticed, created, sensed, depicted, portrayed, identified, realized, processed, etc. He does not suggest an 'either/or' approach, rather, the necessity of variety in how we approach our situations.

Investigators who study organization-environment relations sometimes lean toward separatist imagery. Environments are separated from organizations and things happen between these distinct entities. This way of carving up the problem of organizational analysis effectively rules out certain kinds of questions. Talk about bounded environments and organizations, for example, compels the investigator to ask questions such as how does an organization discover the underlying structure in the environment? Having separated the 'two' entities and given them independent existence, investigators have to make elaborate speculations concerning the ways in which one entity becomes disclosed to and known by the other. But the firm portioning of the world into the environment and the organization excludes the possibility that people invent rather than discover what they think they see. We have tried to provide an alternative to 'discovery' formulations of organizational knowing. (Weick, 2001: 203)

It should be noted that the words 'excludes the possibility that people invent rather than discover' does not inherently imply that Weick is setting up a contrast between a discovery perspective and an inventing (creation) perspective. Rather, it would be more fruitful to consider that when we use words like 'discovery' we evoke particular ways to think about the nature of our experience, and that other words: design, invent, perceive, create, organize, formulate, conserve, enjoy, admire, etc., might also lead us towards a broader range of ways to grasp our experience.

When people talk about organizations operating on information as an environment, they often fail to specify what the raw data are or how they were created. This failure makes it difficult to understand how organizations do interpretation, how they know, or what they know. The concept of an enactment process tries to fill that gap by highlighting the difference between raw data and information and by asserting that actions generate raw data that eventually may be parsed into sensible experiences. (Weick, 2001: 193)

HOW I THINK

Discovery, then, is a way to talk about the process of 'bracketing' that occurs during enactment in the process of organizing. It is one word in a vocabulary of many possible words (Gartner et al., 2003) that might be used to describe aspects of the organizing process. And, it should be recognized that the claims that Weick (1979) makes for what organizing is, as a phenomenon, are more diversified than a 'creation' view. Rather than position Weick (1979) as a 'social constructionist' (Berger and Luckman, 1966), I suggest that he might better fit as a 'radical constructivist' (Foerster, 1973 [2003]; Harel and Papert, 1991; Glaserfeld, 1995; Avenier, 2010). From this position, the idea of 'complicate yourself' (Weick, 1979: 261–4) as well as his suggestions for requisite variety (Ashby, 1956; Weick,

1979: 188–93), suggest that, as scholars and practitioners, we have an obligation to expand our vocabulary, our tools and methods, and our theories and beliefs about what entrepreneurship may be.

The nature of variation in the organizing meta-theory begins with differences across situations, individuals, behaviors, thoughts, and actions. These differences matter. They need to be paid attention to, not only in terms of which differences are recognized, but also in terms of the differences themselves. We simply don't pay enough attention to how much 'stuff' is not attended to when we study entrepreneurship (Spinosa et al., 1997). The 'unattended to' serves as important materials for what the process of organizing might become. In considering the nature of entrepreneurship within the context of organizing, we place too much attention on 'selection' as a mechanism for what eventually becomes 'retained' as on-going organizations (Gartner, in press). We would find value in providing insights to organization studies in terms of what is made available as the process of enactment unfolds.

I believe that I have shown that the 'Prior knowledge' article can be viewed as a clear illustration of bracketing, and, that the belief of 'surprise' is one of many possible retrospective introspections that entrepreneurs could ascribe to their experiences. What should be emphasized, then, is the insight that both entrepreneurs and the scholars who study entrepreneurs are engaged in offering explanations for these entrepreneurs' experiences and that the explanations that are generated are the result of a variety of individual, cultural, language, social, etc., influences, all of which can then be interpreted through a myriad of theories, ideas, viewpoints, values, etc. While the championing of particular viewpoints is necessary as a part of the scholarly process, this makes sense, from my perspective, only when we can critically 'step back' and see a particular viewpoint within a larger context of other theories and ideas. Therefore, my earlier statement 'organizing is all' must be viewed this way as well. An 'organizing view' isn't all encompassing in so far as ideas about organizing, a theory of organizing, and, evidence generated from approaches that focus on organizing, cannot be critically evaluated and discussed. What is necessary then, are contexts for debate and discussion.

ABOUT WHAT I DO

While I seem to continue to engage in a variety of normative science activities to study the phenomenon of entrepreneurship, particularly those involving quantitative analyses of data from the Panel Study of Entrepreneurial Dynamics (Gartner et al., 2004), I am particularly drawn towards efforts that celebrate a breadth of disciplinary and methodological perspectives on specific entrepreneurial narratives (cf. Gartner, 2007, 2010). What I want to emphasize is, not that narratives are the ultimate source of data on entrepreneurial situations. Indeed, any particular narrative has significant shortcomings. Rather, I celebrate the variety of ways that scholars can demonstrate their ideas, theories, and methods using the same 'data' (the narrative). I find it significantly easier to appreciate critical thinking about the nature of entrepreneurship when I can see how others sort through similar data. I am sure that most scholars do not have to rely on such a crutch as a way to recognize and grapple with multiple views, theories, and perspectives on entrepreneurship. Yet, I sense so little irony (Rorty, 1989), particularly an irony that might reflect somewhat of a detached amusement of our scholarly efforts, which leads me to speculate that we tend to limit our making sense of the field. We tend to take too seriously the research we publish, and, thereby, fail to recognize a broader array of different ideas, theories, methods and 'results' might be available just outside the scope of the seriousness of our focus. I am not sure that the bromide is 'lighten up' (Weick, 1996), rather it might be to amass more performances in our repertoire (Campbell and Spicer, 2009).

Apropos to the idea of performance, I am intrigued with efforts to understand entrepreneurial phenomenon outside of normal genre of academic scholarship such as the journal article, book, or monograph, and to suggest other forms of knowing that would encompass the creative arts, such as novels, films, plays, paintings, performances, etc. My intrigue is not towards critical evaluations of these endeavors (which certainly would be of value, as well), but engagement in these activities (cf. Steyaert and Hjorth, 1997; 2002; Hjorth and Steyaert, 1998, 2004b). This is not an interest in starting organizations as a way to 'experience' organizing, that is, to become entrepreneurs (which, actually, is what we do, as scholars, but, this is besides the point), rather I exhort others to exercise the imagination to explore the nature of organizing. This, I believe, is the direction that Bruner (1986), Poklinghorne (1988), and others champion as ways of narrative knowing. Narrative, as I see it, is a way to explore how imagination leads to insight, rather than through analysis. For example, I believe the film *The Social Network* (Fincher, 2010) imagines aspects of the organizing process of the company *Facebook* in more insightful ways than one could surmise through scholarly analysis. Be that as it may, it is worth noting that 'Prior knowledge' can also be read as an act of the imagination: the cases, the quotes, the brief stories of the companies and the biographies of the founders are various narrative gambits (O'Connor, 2007; de Koning and Dodd, 2010) that move the reader towards imagining the process of organizing as the discovery and surprise of opportunities. But, the 'as if' in

'Prior knowledge' needs to be seen through the 'as if' of Vaihinger (1924 [1952]).

Finally, I come full-circle to Foerster's dictum 'Act always so as to increase the number of choices' (Foerster, 1973 [2003]: 227). If I was to suggest what the primary 'take-away' from this chapter might be, I would posit that our scholarship and views about the phenomenon of entrepreneurship need to focus on the 'more' rather than on the 'either/ or.' If 'variation' is a fundamental metaphor for entrepreneurship, then, our efforts must be to encompass a wider range of: theories, ideas, methods, data, genres, vocabularies, etc. that may evoke insights into what entrepreneurship is, and can be.

NOTES

1. Or as Weick (1979: 235) would suggest: 'Organizing' is a meta-theory, a theory to use as the basis to develop other theories of organization.
2. Ironically, it is the narrowness of the theory, arguments and evidence that Scott Shane provides that generates such a persuasive and compelling narrative.
3. My apologies for not offering substantially more theoretical and empirical scholarship to support my claims, in this section, and in the following sections, but the page limitations of this chapter require that such an elaboration wait for another venue.

2 Schumpeter's theories of organizational entrepreneurship
Richard Swedberg

While Schumpeter is a classic in the literature on entrepreneurship, he is less often discussed in organizational analysis. The reason for this is simple. Before the great breakthrough in organizational studies that came after World War II, practically no economist of stature focused on the organization of the firm. This is also true for Schumpeter.

Why then discuss Schumpeter in a handbook of organizational entrepreneurship? The answer is that Schumpeter did develop a very powerful theory of entrepreneurship; and one may legitimately ask if it cannot also be extended to the topic of organizations. Add to this that Schumpeter does make occasional and evocative remarks on the organization of the firm in his work; and we have two good reasons for including a chapter on Schumpeter in a handbook of organizational entrepreneurship.

In my view, it is possible to take all of Schumpeter's comments on the ways of organizing the firm, piece these together and present them as 'Schumpeter's theory of organizational entrepreneurship'. This is not what I will do in this chapter, however. As I see it, Schumpeter's view on organizations and organizational entrepreneurship shifted in emphasis as his work developed – from his classical book on entrepreneurship, *Theory of Economic Development* (1911), over *Business Cycles* (1939), to *Capitalism, Socialism and Democracy* (1942). To bring out the richness in Schumpeter's ideas, I will therefore present what he has to say in each of these works.

This is one reason why I have called this chapter 'Schumpeter's theories of organizational entrepreneurship', using 'theory' in plural rather than in singular. Another reason is that the classics are classics precisely because they have something that inspires generation after generation in different ways. Today's social scientists seek other things from Schumpeter than those who were active some time ago; and they also find other things.

After having accounted for the development of Schumpeter's ideas on new types of firms, I will also try to show how you can use Schumpeter's ideas to theorize on your own; and in this way add to Schumpeter's theories of organizational entrepreneurship. By this, I mean that you can take some ideas in Schumpeter's theory of entrepreneurship, play around with these, and in this way develop new theories of organizational entrepreneurship.

In my own view, these two ways of dealing with the great figures of the past – reading them carefully and using them to theorize on your own – belong together. You need, on the one hand, a thorough knowledge of their work in order to truly understand their core arguments. But it is also important not to let the ideas of the past take over and dominate the living present. We do not want to clone Schumpeter; one Schumpeter is enough. This is where the notion of freely theorizing or playing around with the ideas of the classics comes into the picture. This way, you can also avoid whatever is dead in their theories and add insights from what has happened after their death.

PART I: WHAT SCHUMPETER HAS TO SAY ABOUT ORGANIZATIONAL ENTREPRENEURSHIP IN HIS DIFFERENT WORKS

Schumpeter never devoted a full article or a book to the question of the firm or to the issue of organization. One reason for this may have been that economists in his generation were not very much interested in the organization of the firm. There is also the fact that in Europe – and Schumpeter spent his formative years in the Austrian–Hungarian Empire – the interest in organization was mainly directed at the organization of the state (or administration), not the organization of the firm. The one major exception to this is Max Weber, who argued that the huge capitalist firm was organized as a bureaucracy. The main gist of Weber's famous analysis of bureaucracy, however, was mainly inspired by and directed at the state, not the firm. It has also been suggested that the organization of the big German firms in Weber's days was modelled on the Prussian state (Kocka, 1980).

The Theory of Economic Development (1911)

For the student of organizations who is not familiar with Schumpeter, *The Theory of Economic Development* is the most important work to read, because this is where Schumpeter's famous theory of entrepreneurship was first presented. Since any theory of organizational entrepreneurship that draws on Schumpeter will include elements from the analysis in this work, a few words on Schumpeter's general theory of entrepreneurship are in place.

Joseph Schumpeter (1883–1950) presented his theory of entrepreneurship to a German-speaking audience in a huge and unwieldy book in 1911 (Schumpeter, 1911). It is often said that his work did not get the reception it deserved because Europe was at the time just about to enter a war. It should also be noted that when social scientists today speak of Schumpeter's theory of entrepreneurship, the work they have in mind is not the original edition from 1911, but the English translation of the second edition, which appeared in 1934 as *The Theory of Economic Development*.

The first edition from 1911 is considerably more radical in its argument than the English edition from 1934, something which has partly to do with Schumpeter's career (e.g., Swedberg, 2009a). By the 1930s, he was a full professor in the Department of Economics at Harvard University, while he was only an assistant professor at the little known University of Czernowitz when he wrote the first edition.

Schumpeter's central argument is that economic life can be conceptualized as either static and repetitive or as dynamic and ever-changing. His term for the former is 'the circular flow of economic life', and for the latter 'economic development' (Schumpeter, 1934: 3–94). While economists have worked out a satisfactory theory of the circular flow, he argues, they have not done so with economic development. To remedy this, Schumpeter suggests that economic change should be seen as central to economic analysis and as caused by entrepreneurship.

Schumpeter's famous definition of entrepreneurship is in terms of new ways of piecing together or recombining the various parts that make up the economic process. 'The carrying out of new combinations we call "enterprise"; the individuals whose function it is to carry them out we call "entrepreneurs"' (Schumpeter, 1934: 74). The key concept, in brief, is that of *combination*.

What makes entrepreneurship so difficult is that you have to overcome the resistance against novelty that exists in society. To cite *Theory*: 'all knowledge and habit once acquired becomes as firmly rooted in ourselves as a railway embankment in the earth" (Schumpeter, 1934 [1983]: 84). Or to cite another passage: 'Carrying out a new plan and acting according to a customary one are things as different as making a road and walking along it' (Schumpeter, 1934 [1983]: 85).

Schumpeter argues that the entrepreneur is driven by another set of forces than the non-entrepreneur. He is *not* primarily motivated by a desire for money. Money plays a role, but it is not the main motivating force. What gives the entrepreneur the strength to push through his ideas are instead: his 'dream . . . to found a kingdom', his 'will to conquer', and his 'joy of creating, of getting things done' (Schumpeter, 1934 [1983]: 93).

The entrepreneur does not invent, Schumpeter emphasizes, he *innovates*. The two can go together (as in the cases of, say, Edison and Nobel), but the difference is crucial. Schumpeter also famously enumerates what he means by an innovation. It is '*a new combination*', and it may take five forms (Schumpeter, 1934: 61; emphasis added). It can be (1) 'a new good', (2) 'a new method of production', (3) 'a new market', (4) 'a new source of supply of raw materials' and (5) a 'new organization' (Schumpeter, 1934 [1983]: 66).

Except for adding a few words to his description of each of these five types of innovation, Schumpeter does not elaborate or provide the reader with any concrete examples. One reason for this may have been that he wanted *The Theory of Economic Development* to be a work exclusively in economic theory; some formulations in the first edition had made the reviewers describe it as a study in economic history. There is also the fact that while posterity has fastened on Schumpeter's theory of entrepreneurship, he himself wanted to recast *all* of economic theory, and he therefore had to economize on space.

If one is interested in organizational entrepreneurship, it is obvious that one's attention is drawn to the fifth and last of Schumpeter's types of innovations: the 'new organization'. When we focus in more closely on this type, however, we immediately realize that Schumpeter had something different in mind with this type than what we do when we think of a 'new organization'. The full description of Type Five reads as follows: 'The carrying out of the new organization of any industry, like the creation of a monopoly position (for example, through trustification) or the breaking up of a monopoly position' (Schumpeter, 1934 [1983]: 66).

Schumpeter, in short, is not so much talking about the internal structure of a firm as the organization of a whole industry. As examples of entrepreneurial feats, he mentions two: the creation of a trust and the break-up of a monopoly. The reader may also recall that at the time when Schumpeter was working out his analysis in the early 1900s, economists were not very interested in the different ways that a single firm could be organized; and this may have added to his disincentive to look 'inside' the firm.

But it should also be emphasized that Schumpeter *did* go inside the individual firm at one point in *The Theory of Economic Development*. Firms, he argued, that are part of the circular flow – that is, non-entrepreneurial firms – are led by a certain type of individuals, while entrepreneurial firms are led by a very different type. Schumpeter calls the former 'mere managers' and the latter 'entrepreneurs' (Schumpeter, 1934 [1983]: 83; cf. Hjorth this volume).

What exactly does this opposition of mere managers to entrepreneurs mean for a theory of organizational entrepreneurship? One answer would be the following. While modern social scientists tend to cast the inside of a firm in terms of structures and social constructions, this is not what Schumpeter had in mind. Somewhat like Max Weber in *The Protestant Ethic and the Spirit of Capitalism*, he was instead sensitive to the idea of what we may call 'the spirit' of the firm. The head of a firm was a single individual – but this individual could either run the whole thing as a mere manager or in a totally new way. So even if the entrepreneurial firm and the ordinary firm may have looked the same to an outsider, they were very different by virtue of this fact.

Business Cycles (1939)

After *The Theory of Economic Development* (1911), Schumpeter's next major work in economics was *Business Cycles*. He worked more than 20 years on this project, and the idea was to expand on the project of constructing a new dynamic theory, by working out one of its most important components: the business cycle.

The end result was a giant work of some 1100 pages, covering the economic development of England, Germany and the United States from the mid-1700s to the mid-1900s. While Schumpeter had extremely high hopes for this work, his contemporaries ignored it. Much to his secret chagrin, they preferred Keynes' *General Theory* (1936 [1967]).

Also, posterity has bypassed *Business Cycles*, regarding it as a minor work by a major economist. Recently, however, business historian Thomas McCraw has shown that Schumpeter's study cannot only be read as a study of business cycles, but also as a useful entry into his theory of entrepreneurship, since it contains a wealth of historical examples of innovations (McCraw, 2006). Following the lead of McCraw, I will do the same, but focus on organizational entrepreneurship.

Schumpeter defines entrepreneurship somewhat differently in *Business Cycles* than in *The Theory of Economic Development*. He now emphasizes innovation more than the individual entrepreneur; and an innovation is defined in terms of the production function. 'We will simply define innovation as the setting up of a new production function' (Schumpeter, 1939: 87). The prominent reference to the production function in this definition was probably related to Schumpeter's desire to integrate his theory of entrepreneurship into the mainstream economics of the time.

One problem with doing this, however, is that the organization of the firm cannot very easily be analysed with the help of the idea of production function. This becomes clear if one looks at the way that a production function is commonly defined. Take the definition of Paul Samuelson: 'The production function is the technical relationship telling the maximum amount of output capable of being produced by each and every set of specified inputs (or factors of production); it is defined for a given set of technical knowledge' (Samuelson, 1970: 516). The firm, in other words, is reduced to a formula. Or to cite a critic of early neoclassical economics: 'in standard price theory, the firm is itself a primitive atom of the economy, an unindividuated, single-minded agent interacting with similarly unindividuated consumers and factor suppliers in the market economy' (Putterman, 1996: 5).

Just as in *The Theory of Economic Development*, Schumpeter says in *Business Cycles* that there exist five major types of innovations. 'A new form of organization' is one of these; and to exemplify what he has in mind with such a new form, he mentions 'a merger' (Schumpeter, 1939: 87). He also speaks quite a bit about what he calls 'New Firms' and how these are usually associated with some innovation. 'Most new firms are founded with an idea and for a purpose', as he puts it (Schumpeter, 1939: 94).

A new firm entails the construction of a new plant and some new technology – a 'new individual organism' (Schumpeter, 1939: 765). 'Old Firms' typically die, he says, when the idea or purpose that infused them has been exhausted. Schumpeter casts economic development in terms of evolution in *Business Cycles*; and his discussion of the birth and death of firms is reminiscent of modern population ecology. What he says about history in general is also applicable to the economy: 'history is the record of "effects" the majority of which nobody intended to produce' (Schumpeter, 1939: 1045).

Schumpeter's theoretical approach in *Business Cycles* to organizational innovations can be summarized as follows. By using the example of mergers, he has moved from exclusively speaking in terms of the whole of an industry, as in *The Theory of Economic Development*. He is still, however, mainly speaking of the outside of the firm, rather than in terms of its internal structure: a merger is two firms coming together. His interest in the spirit of the firm remains the same as before.

In the more than 1000 pages in which Schumpeter traces the economic development of England, Germany and the United States over 200 years, one can find many concrete examples of entrepreneurship and innovations that involve firms and their structures. Even if Schumpeter does not theorize these, they are nonetheless part of his universe. At one point, for example, Schumpeter mentions the 'Taylorization of work' and 'new business organizations such as department stores' (Schumpeter, 1939: 84). Both of these examples relate more to the inner structure of the firm than to its outer relations. This indicates that Schumpeter was indeed attentive to the discussion of the firm and its structure.

There also exists a section in *Business Cycles* that Schumpeter describes as '*organizational innovations*' in the table of contents (Schumpeter, 1939: xv). Since it is the only place in all of Schumpeter's work that I have been able to locate, where he addresses this issue in more than a few words, I will cite it in full. The section is to be found in a chapter called '1919–1929', so the immediate context is the 1920s and how this decade affected Germany:

> For us the interesting point is that development occurred in the course of an 'organizational rationalization' which was effected exclusively by entrepreneurial effort from within the industry and is suggestive of earlier American examples. The new Vereinigte Stahlwerke, which attained corporate existence in 1926, were a unit of control that aimed at concentration and specialization of production in optimally located plant. From 1926 to 1933 (when in the wake of the crisis another reorientation and reorganization took place) pits were reduced from 48 to 25, ironworks from 140 to 66, steel foundries from 20 to 8, rolling mills from 17 to 10. Very considerable investment was required to achieve this, and almost immediately after their foundation the Stahlwerke incurred a debt of over 500 million marks, a little more than half of which was spent on the erection of new plant and the improvement of existing plant. Their quota in the syndicate was less than 40 per cent, however. Not only such firms as Krupp, Mannesmann, and Hosch retained their independence, forming other alliances and expanding on their own, but also another group was formed under the leadership of the Rheinelbe-Union, which embarked on an extensive investment program of similar type and soon floated an issue of 800 million marks. The works – those belonging to different combinations as well as independent ones – which produced steel specialties, in 1927 formed an organization called Deutsche Edelstahlwerke. Every one of these steps was accompanied by induced innovation of the technological type, and all of them created an almost new industrial organism. That in the subsequent crisis things should have presented a picture which it was as easy as it was superficial to describe in terms of excess capacity and malinvestment will not surprise us. (Schumpeter, 1939: 765)

What we can read out of this passage is not only that firms that come together in some novel way constitute an "organizational innovation" (the reader already knows this), but also that the rationalization of industry may result in the creation of such organizational innovations. What is also of interest is Schumpeter's notion that the rationalization movement in the 1920s typically led to an "induced innovation of a technical type" in individual cases. The end result – and we are now back at the aggregate level – was "an almost completely new industrial organism" (Schumpeter, 1939: 765).

Capitalism, Socialism, and Democracy (1942)

Deeply disappointed with the reception of *Business Cycles*, which had taken Schumpeter so long to produce, he decided to write something very different and enjoyable. In 1942 this work appeared in the bookstores. It was entitled *Capitalism, Socialism, and Democracy*; and it became Schumpeter's most popular book. It was published just three years after *Business Cycles*.

In terms of organizational entrepreneurship, Schumpeter strikes a somewhat different tone in this work by concentrating exclusively on one type of firm: the giant corporation. He explicitly calls it an innovation: 'a new type of organization' (e.g., Schumpeter, 1942 [1962]: 84). He also notes that this type of firm has come to dominate important sectors of the modern economy. While it may hold a monopoly position in the market, it still has to compete. 'A monopoly is in general no cushion to sleep on' (Schumpeter, 1942 [1962]: 102).

Like Max Weber and later Alfred Chandler, Schumpeter saw the giant corporation as *the* ultimate form of the corporation in modern capitalism. Like Weber (but not like Chandler), he also feared that it would end up by stifling the vigorous type of capitalism that had made the West the undisputed leader of the world.

Schumpeter does not provide the reader of *Capitalism, Socialism, and Democracy* with the detailed kind of organizational picture of the giant firm that one can find, say, in *The Visible Hand* (Chandler, 1977). But he does discuss one aspect of this type of firm that Chandler does not broach, and this is its tendency to stifle entrepreneurship and dramatically change its nature (cf. Hjorth, 2005).

While the focus of this chapter is on Schumpeter's theories of organizational entrepreneurship or how firms can be organized in novel ways, *Capitalism, Socialism, and Democracy* discusses a related but different topic. This is how a new organization of the firm (the giant firm) can undermine and block the appearance of new innovations, including new organizational forms.

According to Schumpeter, the giant firm saps entrepreneurship of its vital force by trying to be entrepreneurial in a purely rational manner. By proceeding in this way, the nature of entrepreneurship as we know it changes; its element of 'romance' is eliminated (Schumpeter, 1942 [1962]: 132). The parts of entrepreneurship that have to do with 'personality and will power' will also become less important, he says, as much of the 'resistance' to entrepreneurship disappears. In a world where everybody is positive to what is new, those who advocate novelties will not have the same will power and independence of mind as the real entrepreneurs.

Schumpeter is not very clear in specifying how the giant firm will undermine the capacity to be entrepreneurial. The most concrete statement on this point in *Capitalism, Socialism, and Democracy* comes when he says that 'innovation itself is being reduced to routine' when 'teams of trained specialists' are employed to develop new technologies (Schumpeter, 1942 [1962]: 132). But there is no doubt that Schumpeter deeply feared that the growth of the giant firms would sap the spirit of capitalism and even undermine its capacity to survive in the long run. He does not state that this development also means that there will be less organizational innovations in the future, but that is a logical consequence of his argument

PART II: NEW SCHUMPETERIAN THEORIES OF ORGANIZATIONAL ENTREPRENEURSHIP

While Schumpeter's ideas on organizational entrepreneurship in *The Theory of Economic Development* and other works may be interesting, there is also the fact that on the whole he was not very interested in the organization of firms. As earlier mentioned, this was quite typical for Schumpeter's generation. When economists did discuss the firm, they tended to focus on combinations of firms rather than on the internal structure of the individual firm. Alfred Marshall is in this sense similar to Schumpeter. He added 'organization' to the factors of production; and introduced the idea of an 'industrial district' (Marshall, 1961 [1920]).

But going through Schumpeter's works and explicating the few passages where he does address the issue of organizational innovations, does not exhaust his contribution to today's discussion of this topic. One may also approach his theories in a different way, a way that may at first seem less objective and suitable for an exploration of the topic of Schumpeter and organizational entrepreneurship. This is to play around with Schumpeter's ideas, add to them and take away from them, all in an attempt to theorize a bit on one's own – but with the help of Schumpeter. The result of this type of exercise is what I call Schumpeterian theories of organizational entrepreneurship.

New Schumpeterian Theories # 1: Innovation as a Process and as a Separate Phenomenon

In what follows I shall present a few examples of what I call Schumpeterian theories of organizational entrepreneurship. The first of them draws on a certain ambiguity that exists in Schumpeter's concept of innovation. Sometimes Schumpeter looks at an innovation as *a distinct phenomenon in its own right* – as when he discusses a new commodity, a new form of technology and so on. But at other times Schumpeter views an innovation more as a *process*. Making an innovation is not so much about having an

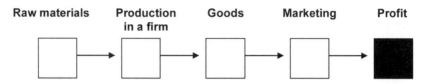

Notes: This figure shows Schumpeter's famous typology of innovations (slightly recast to make the point more clearly). Note that according to this view there will not be an innovation until the whole economic process has been carried through to its end, which in a capitalist economy means making of profit.

Figure 2.1   A new Schumpeterian theory of innovation # 1: innovation as process

idea, but pushing it through all the way: from conception to production to the market.

Schumpeter's main concept of innovation presents few surprises since it is close to the way that most people think of innovations. An innovation is 'the great new thing' as in the iPhone, Starbucks and the like (Schumpeter, 1939: 416). Or to give some examples from *Business Cycles*: 'Senfelder's lithography in 1785 and 1806; the first beet-sugar factory in 1796; Koenig and Bauer's printing press in 1814; Krupp's cast steel in 1815; first steamboat on the Weser in 1816' (Schumpeter, 1939: 282).

The second type of innovation that one can find in Schumpeter's work is much less clearly articulated; this is the innovation as a process. It is nonetheless present in his thought; and it now and then also surfaces in his formulations. An innovation is not just 'a new combination', we read at one point, but 'the carrying out of a new combination'; it is not just 'a new good' but 'the production and carrying out [of a new good]' (Schumpeter, 1934 [1983]: 65–6; 1928 [2003]: 250).

Let us stop for a moment and recall how Schumpeter speaks of innovations as new combinations in *The Theory of Economic Development*. He says that there are five types of innovation: (1) 'a new good', (2) 'a new method of production', (3) 'a new market', (4) 'a new source of supply of raw materials', and (5) a 'new organization' (Schumpeter, 1934 [1983]: 66).

Now, if we take these five innovations, rearrange them, place them next to each other and also add them up, so to speak, we notice something interesting. This is that they make up *the whole of the economic process*. There is first of all (4) *the raw material*, which is then turned into (1) *a good* with the help of (2) *a machine* in (5) *an organization*. The good is finally (3) *marketed* for a profit (see Figure. 2.1).

Looking at innovations as processes also entails a new perspective on what it means to be an entrepreneur. To innovate means more than just, say, conceive of a new good or a new market; it means to take a good all the way from conception to profit. To take the example of the iPod: you have to conceive it, produce it, market it – and make a profit.

The organization of the firm may enter into this process in one of two ways. The entrepreneur may conceive of a new type of organization; and this is what gives him the advantage (and profit). The notion of the multi-divisional firm or a franchise would be examples of such an organizational innovation.

But the firm may also be of the conventional type and just be part of, say, the production of the iPod. In this case the task of the entre-preneur is to successfully link up the activities of the firm with the new product and make a profit at the end. To paraphrase a famous saying, 'Entrepreneurship is one per cent *inspiration* and 99 per cent *perspiration.*'

Before leaving the discussion of Schumpeter's notion of the innovation as a process, it should also be noted that one can push the view of innov-ation as a process one step further. We know that Schumpeter saw the whole economic process as a combination, and we know that this was also the case with the individual innovation. The result of *combining* these two views makes us realize how many innovations are possible in theory (see Figure 2.2).

Schumpeterian Theory # 2: Innovation as the Creation of a New Norm

One may also develop Schumpeter's ideas about innovations in a different and more sociological direction. This time, let us begin with the organiza-tional innovation. When we do this we are immediately reminded of the fact that Schumpeter initially restricted the term organization very much. In *The Theory of Economic Development* he used it to refer to the collec-tive level (an industry, a cartel or a break-up of a monopoly), even if he later expanded it somewhat (to include a merger and occasionally even the internal structure of the firm, as in *Business Cycles*).

How can we remedy this narrow concept of organization and organ-izational innovation in Schumpeter's work? One answer would be that instead of viewing an organization as a cartel or a merger, we should see it as also including the internal organization of the firm. This is true – but it does not help us very much. The reason for this is that it does not make us understand what drives organizational innovations; it simply restates the obvious.

But Schumpeter also provides us with a set of excellent tools with which to theorize organizational entrepreneurship; and we may use some of these, and in this way develop a more satisfying theory. The two I have

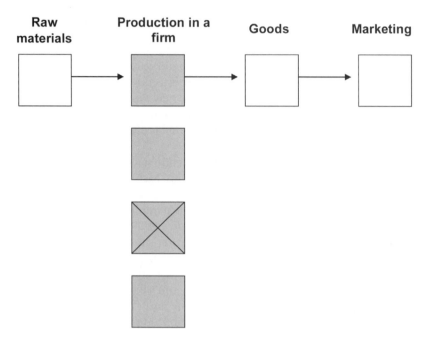

Notes: When we conceptualize the innovation as a process, we realize what huge number of innovations are possible. X indicates a change in one component of an innovation.

Figure 2.2   Elaboration on the theme of innovation as a process

in mind are *entrepreneurship as a combination* and *resistance to entrepreneurship*.[1] An innovation, as we know, consists of a novel combination of already existing elements. In theory one can imagine an enormous amount of new combinations, but one reason why so few materialize is that there exists a lot of resistance to entrepreneurship. This resistance, Schumpeter says, comes in three types. There is the resistance associated with 'the task'; the resistance associated with 'the psyche of the businessman'; and resistance from 'the social environment' (Schumpeter, 1934 [1983]: 86).

To be entrepreneurial, in other words, is to somehow be able to break down the resistance and push through a new innovation (say, in the form of a new organization) and make a profit. When this is done, Schumpeter continues, others will imitate the entrepreneur, because they want profit as well. This constitutes what Schumpeter calls the first wave of imitators.

As more and more imitate the innovation (here: the new way of organizing the firm), the level of profit goes down. By the time there is no more (entrepreneurial) profit to be had, something else has also happened: what was once an innovation has now become the generally accepted way of doing things or, in sociological terms, a norm.

Pulling together the ideas in this argument, and translating it into sociology, we get the following. There exist *norms* for how to organize the firm in the different industries, just as there exist norms for what the goods should look like, what type of machines to use, and so on. By following these norms, existing non-entrepreneurial firms can earn something like the average profit rate in the industry they are part of. This is what Schumpeter refers to as the circular flow.

But if someone can conceive of a new way of doing any of these tasks, including organizing the firm, that person may also make much more profit – entrepreneurial profit. When a new way of doing something convinces the consumers that the end product is better than the existing alternatives, this type of profit can be had. Others will then imitate – till the new way of doing things has become the accepted way of doing things or *a new norm*. Entrepreneurial profit, resistance and norms are all linked together in this Schumpeterian theory of innovations (see Figure. 2.3).

Schumpeter uses the interesting term 'competing down' for the situation where a number of imitators drive down the level of profit, in their attempt to make a profit (Schumpeter, 1939: 291). As they do this, the new model for how act is diffused. The more the competition intensifies, the more the actors accept the new way of doing things.

One may also use the term 'competing up' in the type of theory that is suggested here, because it is rarely the case that a new innovation just emerges as the result of what one single firm is doing. A more realistic scenario is that many firms start to experiment (say with a new organizational form), and that at some point a consensus begins to develop that one special version represents *the* way of doing things. Just as one speaks of multiple discoveries, one could perhaps speak of multiple innovations. How often the innovation is unique or multiple is an empirical question (see Figure 2.4).

Schumpeterian Theory # 3: A Semiotic Approach

So far I have supplied two examples of how one can create new Schumpeterian theories of organizational entrepreneurship through a bit of theorizing: you take some central ideas in Schumpeter and add to these. Another way of proceeding is to take some ideas of Schumpeter and combine them with the ideas of another thinker. As an illustration of how this can be done, I shall use the ideas of American philosopher Charles

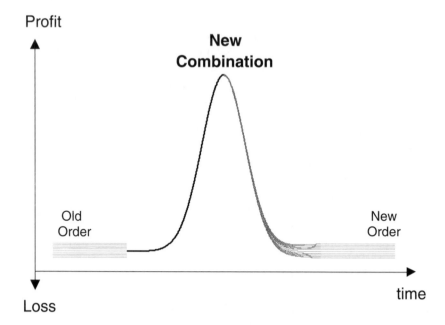

Figure 2.3   A new Schumpeterian theory of innovation # 2: innovation as the creation of a new norm

Peirce (1839–1914). Peirce is generally seen as the founder of semiotics; he was also one of the key figures in pragmatism (e.g., Brent, 1993).

Did Schumpeter ever read Peirce? There is no indication of this, either in his works or in his correspondence. Still, there exists an interesting parallelism between the ideas of Schumpeter and Peirce, and it is this parallelism that made me think that one might try to merge their thoughts or at least move them close to each other and see what happens.

Peirce's famous concept of *abduction* is very similar to that of entrepreneurship in Schumpeter. By abduction is meant the spontaneous leap that the mind makes when it discovers something new (Peirce, 1992–98). The result of the leap is a kind of *élan vital*: you suddenly just *see* something in a different light (cf. Hjorth, 2007). In modern terms, we are here dealing

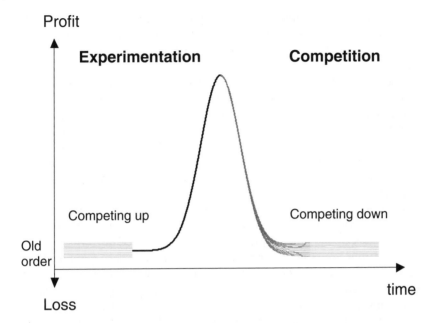

Notes: This figure expands on the basic relationship between profit and order/norm in Figure 2.3. At an early stage of the innovation process, several actors may get into the game ("*competing up*"). The number of actors decreases as the innovation takes its final shape – but goes up again as the profit of the innovator attracts an increasing number of actors. The temporary monopoly situation of the innovator is replaced by competition ("*competing down*"). One can conceive of both the curve to the left and to the right of the peak as taking other forms than what is shown here, reflecting different roads from and to the new order.

Figure 2.4   Elaborations on the theme of innovation as the creation of a new norm

with the context of discovery (how something happens), not the context of justification (how it should be presented to the community of scholars).

Peirce works out the notion of abduction within his more general theory of signs or semiotics. Reality, he argues, can be conceived in terms of signs, signs that can be relatively simple (such as a mathematical symbol) or very complex (say the notion of a firm or an organization). Human beings, according to Peirce, cast everything in terms of signs, from their most routine tasks and habits to important scientific inventions – and, we may add, innovations, including organizational innovations.

These inventions and innovations are abductions in Peirce's terminology or novel ways of viewing reality. Though Peirce never wrote on entrepreneurship, it would seem natural to say that what Schumpeter saw as a new combination or entrepreneurship is what Peirce calls abduction. And the next step would be to explore if also other parts of Peirce's theory of abduction can be used to illuminate the phenomenon of entrepreneurship.

One part of Peirce's ideas on abduction that might help to improve the theory of entrepreneurship is his notion that one can train one's skill to make abductions. You do this, he suggests, by going inside yourself and question what seems to be firm parts of reality, but which in fact are simply configurations of signs that the mind automatically arranges into some habitual configuration. We see, to use a famous example from Peirce's work, something that is green and blue; and our mind immediately puts it together: we see an azalea (Peirce, 1901).

Translated into the area of organizational entrepreneurship, a semiotic and Schumpeterian approach would look something like the following. What we see as the most natural and obvious parts of modern firms and organizations are in reality separate pieces that have been combined into very specific configurations. These configurations have become deeply ingrained habits in our minds; and we therefore take them for granted. By going inwards, however, and questioning them, we may become sensitized to this type of issue – and perhaps also succeed in challenging our habits and replace them with new and better ones.

One fact that we typically dismiss, but may want to look at much more closely, is Schumpeter's notion that having an entrepreneurial leader in a firm makes all the difference in the world. I have indicated that we may want to get a better handle on this type of statement by looking at it in terms of the concept of *spirit* – a term that in the social sciences is closely related to *The Protestant Ethic and the Spirit of Capitalism*. A firm, Weber argues, has both a 'form' as well as a 'spirit', and usually the two coincide (Weber, 1904–1905 [1958]: 64–8). The traditional firm, for example, had a traditional form and a traditional spirit. This was the case with the continental textile firm during the Middle Ages, according to Weber.

The Protestant Reformation, however, led to the introduction of a new 'spirit' in the traditional firm, while its form remained unchanged. The traditional firm became suddenly energized when it was led by entrepreneurs filled with the new 'spirit of [rational] capitalism'.

When Schumpeter conceived his ideas on entrepreneurship, economic life was much more conventional and traditional than it is today, and it was natural for him to see the entrepreneurial transformation of the spirit of a firm as the result of a single individual. Today, however, things are different and the model of the future is not so much Fordism, characterized by one great entrepreneurial idea (by Ford) that is mechanically followed by everybody else (the workers). Today the model is perhaps more along the lines of Google, where the tasks of many of the employees must be carried out in an entrepreneurial manner. Many, if not all of the employees, are supposed to challenge the way that things are done, by conceptualizing them in a novel way.

Discussion and Concluding Remarks

In this chapter I have argued that while it is possible to discern several theories of organizational entrepreneurship in Schumpeter, if one looks very closely at his work, it is also true that he never produced one major piece of analysis of the organization of the firm. Again, it was not typical for economists and social scientists to do so before World War II.

While this clearly limits Schumpeter's relevance for today's students of organizations, one may also want to consider that the classics had their own and very special way of looking at things, including organizations. And when they did so, they used their own terminology.

One can exemplify this with the scattered, but still very suggestive remarks about eighteenth century firms that one can find in Smith's *The Wealth of Nations* (1776), and about nineteenth century firms in de Tocqueville's *Democracy in America* (1830–40; for elaborations on this theme, see e.g., Jensen and Meckling, 1976 and Swedberg, 2009b). Schumpeter's remarks about the spirit of a firm belong to this category. While today's students of organizations view firms very much in terms of structures and social constructions, Schumpeter emphasized something else and much less tangible: their '*social atmosphere*', to use a term from *Business Cycles* (e.g., Schumpeter, 1939: 1038, 1046; emphasis added). When a firm is led by an entrepreneur, everything takes on a different colouring according to Schumpeter. Or in his own, much better formulation: once the entrepreneurial spirit is gone from the firm and a manager takes over, it is as if 'the air was being sucked out of it' (Schumpeter, 1939: 250).

We may ask, what is more important: the structure of a firm or its social atmosphere? Most of us would say both. A body without a skeletal structure has no form; while if there is no blood and soft tissue, there is just some bones or a skeleton. Schumpeter speaks of "organism" when he discusses industries and this metaphor should perhaps also be applied to the individual firm.

And again: one can use the classics, including Schumpeter, in a very different way, namely to theorize on one's own. One way to do so is to take some of their core ideas and add a bit to them, following T.S. Eliot's shrewd advice, "immature poets imitate; mature poets steal' (Eliot, 1921). I have supplied three examples of this way of proceeding but there are obviously many others. My hope is that the reader of this chapter will not just nod and agree that Schumpeter is a great classic – but accept the challenge and do some serious theorizing around the issue of organizational entrepreneurship.

NOTE

1. For a fuller development of the argument to come, based on the concepts of combination and resistance, see Knudsen and Swedberg (2010).

3 Entrepreneurship and the economics of the firm

Nicolai J. Foss, Peter G. Klein and Per L. Bylund

What is the relationship between entrepreneurs and business firms? Do entrepreneurs need firms to carry out their function, and do firms need entrepreneurs to survive in the competitive market process? What exactly do entrepreneurs do inside firms – establish, finance, direct, control, operate? Does the entrepreneur disappear from stage once the firm is founded, handing things off to professional managers who do not merit the label "entrepreneur"? These questions strike simultaneously at the hearts of microeconomics and management research in entrepreneurship (cf. Shane and Venkataraman, 2000). And yet the study of entrepreneurship and the study of economic organizing lack contact. In fact, the modern theory of the firm virtually ignores entrepreneurship, while the literature on entrepreneurship often sees little value in the economic theory of the firm (Foss and Klein, 2005).

This divide emerged as microeconomic analysis took important steps toward increased scientific rigor, which in effect left no room for dynamic elements such as entrepreneurs or entrepreneurship. The economic theory of the firm was subsumed into neoclassical price theory (O'Brien, 1984) and reformulated using game theory and the economics of information (Foss and Klein, 2011). As a result, modern contributions to the theory of the firm (Williamson, 1975; 1985; 1996; Milgrom and Roberts, 1992; Hart, 1995) focus on solving given optimization problems and are therefore typically static and "closed." They tend to avoid open-ended questions about where the problems come from or what is the origin of the firm. Indeed, the question of firm emergence in the market place is almost completely left out of the theoretical discourse on the firm.

In contrast, we argue in this chapter that entrepreneurship theory and the theory of the firm can be usefully integrated, and that doing so would improve both bodies of theory. Adding the entrepreneur to the theory of the firm provides a dynamic view that the overly static analysis of firm organizing cannot support. Moreover, adding the firm to the study of the entrepreneur provides important clues to how we can understand entrepreneurship.

We begin by briefly surveying the study of entrepreneurship in the economics and management literature and ask to what extent the entrepreneur, characterized in the most common ways, needs a firm. We focus on entrepreneurship as *judgment*. Judgment primarily refers to the process of businesspeople forming estimates of future events in situations in which there is no agreement or idea at all on probabilities of occurrence. It may be defined as a service that enhances the quality of decisions in novel situations that require an urgent decision, a service that is learned and has a large tacit component. Entrepreneurship represents judgment that cannot be assessed in terms of its marginal product and which cannot, accordingly, be paid a wage. It is inherently speculative. We trace this view to the economists Richard Cantillon, Frank Knight, and Ludwig von Mises. The judgment view has a direct and natural link to the theory of the firm: the entrepreneur needs a firm because judgment cannot be purchased on the market. Next, we review the main themes in the modern theory of the firm and strategic entrepreneurship, and show how entrepreneurship as judgment illuminates these issues in novel and theoretically useful ways.

In the concluding parts of the chapter, we point to the fact that resources, in contrast to the common treatment in economic theory, are fundamentally heterogeneous (Lachmann, 1956 [1978]) and therefore that resource uses are not simply data but are created as entrepreneurs envision new ways of using assets to produce goods. We make the further case that asset ownership through a firm allows the entrepreneur to experiment with novel combinations of these heterogeneous assets and thus provides a vehicle through which he or she can attempt to realize imagined production structures. From this approach a number of unconventional insights emerge, which may prove useful in further theorizing on the firm and entrepreneurship.

ENTREPRENEURSHIP: OUTCOME OR ACTION?

Entrepreneurship comes in many shapes and forms, not all of which are relevant to or can usefully be linked to the theory of the firm. We find it useful to distinguish between theories or approaches that define entrepreneurship as an *outcome* or a phenomenon (self-employment, startup companies) and those that see it as a *way of acting or thinking* (creativity, innovation, alertness, judgment, adaptation) (cf. Knight, 1942; Casson, 1982; Klein, 2008). Some "outcome" approaches deal with firms – e.g., what is the ratio of small ones to large ones in an industry or economy – but the decision to limit "entrepreneurial" behavior to small or new firms is unnecessarily restrictive, and not closely connected to the classic contributions to the economic theory of entrepreneurship associated with

Knight, Schumpeter, Kirzner, and others. "Action" approaches, what Klein (2008) calls "functional" concepts of entrepreneurship, are more useful in linking to the theory of the firm.

The economic function of the entrepreneur has been characterized in various ways: judgment, innovation, alertness, adaptation, coordination, and so on. Whereas all these functional approaches are interesting and have advantages, the notion of entrepreneurship as judgment has particularly important implications for the analysis of the business firm. Schumpeter's idea of entrepreneurship as innovation (1934) helps illuminate the process by which industries and economies expand and contract, but Schumpeter treats the entrepreneur as an uncaused cause, a pure genius who operates outside the usual constraints imposed by resource owners and other market participants and is largely independent of the firm. Kirzner's (1973; 1979; 1992; 2009) conception of entrepreneurship as "alertness" to or the discovery of profit opportunities, building on Hayek's (1978) view of competition as a "discovery procedure," attempts to elucidate the equilibrating character of the market process. Like Schumpeter's entrepreneur, however, Kirzner's discoverer does not work with firms; the Kirznerian entrepreneur does not own capital and is not subject to losses, and hence does not need a firm to exercise his function in the economy (Foss and Klein, 2012). The coordinating entrepreneur communicates "mental models" of reality (Casson, 2000) to be adopted by others, thereby creating a shared vision through which production is coordinated. This view of entrepreneurship as "cognitive leadership" (Witt, 1998, 1999) focuses almost exclusively on human resources and firm organizing relies on establishing a tacit, shared framework of goals to govern relationships among members of the entrepreneur's team. Even though charismatic leadership may be seen as a coordinating force, it is not clear why such is more entrepreneurial than other kinds of leadership or mundane managerial tasks. It is furthermore unclear in what sense the charismatic leader is primarily an economic agent and how sharing of a vision characterizes a firm.

ENTREPRENEURSHIP AS JUDGMENT

In contrast, the view of entrepreneurship as consisting of judgmental decision-making under conditions of uncertainty (Casson, 1982; Langlois and Cosgel, 1993; Foss and Klein, 2005; cf. Cantillon, 1755 [2010]) maps more naturally into theories of business strategy and organization. Judgment refers to business decision-making when the range of possible future outcomes, as well as the likelihood of individual outcomes, is unknown (what

Knight, (1921 [1985]) terms uncertainty, rather than mere probabilistic risk). Uncertainty bearing is the entrepreneur's *raison d'être*. As Mises (1949: 252) puts it, "the outcome of action is always uncertain. Action is always speculation." Consequently, "the real entrepreneur is a speculator, a man eager to utilize his opinion about the future structure of the market for business operations promising profits. This specific anticipative understanding of the conditions of the uncertain future defies any rules and systematization" (1949: 585).

Judgment is distinct from boldness, innovation, alertness, and leadership, and must be exercised in mundane circumstances, for ongoing operations as well as new ventures. While alertness tends to be passive, and perhaps even hard to distinguish from luck (Demsetz, 1983), judgment is active. Entrepreneurs "are those who seek to profit by actively promoting adjustment to change. They are not content to passively adjust their . . . activities to readily foreseeable changes or changes that have already occurred in their circumstances; rather, they regard change itself as an opportunity to meliorate their own conditions and aggressively attempt to anticipate and exploit it" (Salerno, 1993: 123). Those who specialize in judgmental decision-making may be dynamic, charismatic leaders, but they need not possess these traits. Decision-making under uncertainty is entrepreneurial, whether it involves imagination, creativity, leadership, and related factors or not.

While the view of entrepreneurship as judgment appears in many writers, it is most often associated with Knight (1921 [1985]), who introduces the concept to explain profit and the firm through the existence of uncertainty. For Knight, firm organization, profit, and the entrepreneur are closely related; they arise as an embodiment, a result, and a cause, respectively, of commercial experimentation (Demsetz, 1988a). Businesspeople use their judgment, a learned trait with a large tacit component, to form estimates of future events in situations where there is no agreement or idea at all on probabilities of occurrence. Entrepreneurship, the exercise of judgmental decision-making, therefore, cannot be assessed in terms of its marginal product and cannot be paid a wage, which means there can be no market for judgment. This is particularly because entrepreneurship is judgment about the most uncertain events, such as starting a new firm, defining a new market, and the like. The lack of basis for market pricing suggests that exercising judgment requires the person with judgment to start a firm. Consequently, judgment implies and must be exercised together with asset ownership. Judgmental decision-making is ultimately decision-making about the allocation and employment of resources; a decision-maker without capital goods cannot, to Knight, be an entrepreneur. Indeed, entrepreneurial decision-making without asset ownership constitute "mere parlor games until the money is obtained and committed to the projects" (Rothbard, 1985 [1997]: 283).

There is therefore an obvious link between entrepreneurship and the theory of the firm, particularly theories that define asset ownership as a crucial ingredient of firm organization (Hart, 1995; Williamson, 1996). The firm, in this sense, is the entrepreneur and the alienable assets he owns and ultimately controls – structured, specialized, and combined to attain the entrepreneur's imagined end. The theory of the firm is essentially a theory of how the entrepreneur exercises his judgmental decision-making – what combinations of assets he seeks to acquire, what (proximate) decisions he delegates to subordinates, how he provides incentives and employs monitoring to see that his assets are used consistently with his judgments, and so on.

DOES THE FIRM NEED AN ENTREPRENEUR?

Some concepts of entrepreneurship, and especially entrepreneurship as judgmental decision-making under uncertainty, have implications for resource ownership, and consequently for the formation and organization of firms. But this does not suggest how entrepreneurship is best incorporated into the theory of the firm, and it also does not provide sufficient clues for the role of the entrepreneur – or whether the entrepreneur is necessary for economic organization. To formulate a theoretically viable relationship between the firm and entrepreneurship, we need to look more closely to the various established theories of the firm and explore how they explain what constitutes a firm and how firm organizing fosters decision-making.

As modern, "neoclassical" economics emerged in the mid-to-late twentieth century, the firm was given "an increasingly passive role" (McNulty, 1984: 240). With the emphasis on formal, mathematical modeling, the dynamic aspects of markets that are most closely related to entrepreneurship were largely assumed away (O'Brien, 1984) and the firm became modeled simply as a production function (Williamson, 1985; Langlois and Foss, 1999). In this simplified model of the market, all firms are always on their production possibilities frontiers and always make optimal choices of their input combinations and output levels. There can be no room for entrepreneurship since the firm is but a fully transparent production possibility set and therefore any firm can do what any other firm does (Demsetz, 1988b).

The inadequacy of the traditional theory of the firm explains much of the recent interest in the many theories spawned by Coase's landmark

1937 article, "The nature of the firm." In his article, Coase introduced a fundamentally new way to think about the firm and argued that firms have no reason to exist in the world of neoclassical price theory. Because we observe firms in real life, he reasoned, there must be a "cost to using the price mechanism" (1937: 390). The entrepreneur may be able to reduce these "transaction costs" by coordinating productive activities himself, striving to "reproduce distribution of factors under atomistic competition within the business unit" (1988b: 4). However, internal organization gives rise to other kinds of transaction costs due to problems of information flow, incentives, monitoring, and performance evaluation. The boundary of the firm, then, is determined by the tradeoff, at the margin, between the relative transaction costs of external and internal exchange (Coase, 1937, 1988a). Most modern theories of the firm are Coasean in the sense that they adhere to the program established by Coase, even though their terminology, focus, and specific insights may differ.

Coase makes use of the term "entrepreneur" to denote the decision-maker in a firm, but does not share the view of entrepreneurship discussed above. Rather, the Coasean entrepreneur seems to be more engaged in the mechanical exercise of comparing the costs of organizing known transactions in given governance structures than in engaging in future-oriented speculative acts (Boudreaux and Holcombe, 1989); he exercises authority through which he "directs" labor factors to their most valued use as suggested by related prices and costs effective outside of the firm. (Here Coase (1937: 389) quotes Robbins, suggesting that the firm is dependent on the market's price system for its survival and that it must be "related to an outside network of related prices and costs.") In this sense, the Coasean entrepreneur is an authoritative imitator in a semi-static setting rather than a judgmental decision-maker as in Knight's approach.

The firm in modern organizational economics is to a large extent Coasean in that it is viewed as a contractual entity for which the economizing on transaction costs provides the best explanation to its existence, boundaries, and internal organization. Whereas the body of literature addresses all of these three issues, none of the theories in modern organizational economics provides a unified framework incorporating transaction costs of the same kind (see e.g., Foss, 1997: 175; Foss and Klein, 2008: 426; cf. Garrouste and Saussier, 2008: 23). Indeed, a possible perspective on the division of labor that exists within the modern theory of the firm is that while the principal–agent approach (Jensen and Meckling, 1976; Holmström and Milgrom, 1991, 1994) and team theory (Alchian and Demsetz, 1972; Marschak and Radner, 1972) are mainly relevant for understanding internal organization, the transaction cost (Williamson, 1975, 1985) and property rights approaches (Grossman and Hart, 1986;

Hart and Moore, 1990; Hart, 1995) are designed to explain firm boundaries. Their emphasis on different kinds of transaction costs leads to contractual imperfection, and therefore to economic outcomes inferior to the full-information, zero-transaction-cost ideal, in different ways. While principal–agent theory emphasizes costs of monitoring contractual relationships in light of potential moral hazard, the transaction cost and property rights approaches emphasize the costs of writing (complete) contracts and the costs of adjusting to unanticipated contingencies, respectively. Only transaction cost economics and the property rights approach are conventionally considered theories of the firm, strictly speaking, since the others do not explain the boundaries of the firm in terms of asset ownership (Hart, 1995).

Following the former (Williamson, 1985, 1996), organizational economics places particular emphasis on specific (or highly complementary) assets in attempting to explain the boundaries of the firm. High asset specificity means that there is a great difference in market value between an asset's present and alternative uses, which suggests investments in such exposed agents to potential hazard: once investments are made and contracts are signed, unanticipated changes in circumstances can give rise to costly renegotiation. With the value of the asset being specific to the particular transaction, one party can be "held up" by the other party attempting to extract quasi-rents through threatening to pull out of the arrangement, which would greatly reduce the value of the asset. The parties to the transaction may choose to vertically integrate the transaction to eliminate such adversarial interests and avoid costs of extensive maladaptation. Less extreme options include so-called "hybrid" arrangements: long-term contracts, partial ownership, or agreements for both parties to invest in offsetting relationship-specific investments (Ménard, 2010). Overall, parties choose a particular governance structure in order to best control the underinvestment problem, given the particulars of the relationship.

There are many ways in which entrepreneurship, and especially entrepreneurship as judgment, can be incorporated in modern organizational economics. The emphasis put on asset ownership, as well as incomplete contracting, when explaining firm organization accords well with Knight's (1921 [1985]) views, and theories of decision-making under asymmetric information illustrate the distinctiveness of entrepreneurship. Nevertheless, the modern economics of organization is still fully rooted in the neoclassical theoretical framework and has only grafted a superstructure of asymmetric information, transaction costs, and the like on top of the neoclassical theory of production (see e.g., Foss, 1996; Langlois and Foss, 1999). While notions of uncertainty, ignorance, and surprise are occasionally invoked in the literature, they serve merely as rhetorical devices to justify the assumption that contracts are incomplete (Foss, 2003) but are not themselves explained. Still, key insights from organizational economics and the concept of entrepreneurial judgment may be usefully joined into a more complete theory of economic organization.

HETEROGENEOUS ASSETS AND ENTREPRENEURIAL OWNERSHIP

The primary function of the entrepreneur is to choose among the various combinations of inputs suitable for producing particular goods according to his planned structure of production, and attempt to realize his imagined solution to perceived problems through establishing still unrealized (and unheard of) combinations of yet-to-be-created highly specialized factors and assets (Bylund, 2011). In the real world rather than the stylized neoclassical view of the market, this task consists primarily of choosing among combinations of specialized labor factors and heterogeneous capital assets whose "combinations . . . will be ever changing, will be dissolved and re-formed" (Lachmann, 1956 [1978]: 13) and guiding these factors toward wanted degrees and types of specialization. Hence, the entrepreneurial problem is extremely complicated and always subject to a high degree of uncertainty (cf. Alvarez and Barney, 2005).

Heterogeneous assets can usefully be analysed in terms of attributes (Barzel, 1997) or specificities (Lachmann, 1956 [1978]), i.e., their characteristics, functions, possible uses, etc., as perceived by the entrepreneur. Heterogeneity exists to the extent that the assets have different, and different levels of, valued attributes, and may vary over time, even for a particular asset (cf. Foss et al., 2007a). In a world of "Knightian" uncertainty, entrepreneurs are unlikely to know all relevant attributes of all assets when production decisions are made and they also cannot with certainty forecast future attributes of an asset. The latter must be discovered as assets are used in production, which means future attributes are "created" as entrepreneurs envision new ways of using assets to produce goods and, as an effect, create new capital goods. Hence Knight's approach fits well with the literature on entrepreneurial creativity, which emphasizes the open-ended nature of economic action (Alvarez and Barney, 2007a) and therefore the inherent uncertainty in (speculative) action. This is what Mises (1949: 585) calls the entrepreneur's "specific anticipative understanding of the conditions of the uncertain future," an understanding that "defies any rules and systematization," and that reaches for, while creating, the unknown future. In other words, "[w]hat distinguishes the successful entrepreneur and promoter from other people is precisely the fact that he does not let himself be guided by what was and is, but arranges his affairs on the ground of his opinion about the future. He sees the past and the present as other people do; but he judges the future in a different way" (Mises, 1949: 585).

This creation of attributes constitutes an important entrepreneurial function and suggests a distinct role for asset ownership. Since property rights are primarily held over attributes (Barzel, 1997; cf. Kim and Mahoney, 2007), the role for asset ownership results from gaining property rights to bundles of existing and future attributes. Ownership emerges as a low-cost means of allocating the rights to attributes of assets that are created or discovered by the entrepreneur–owner. Of course, asset ownership itself also provides a powerful incentive to create or discover new attributes, suggesting new opportunities for profit (cf. Alvarez and Barney, 2007a), as ownership conveys the legally recognized (and at least partly enforced) right to the income of an asset, including the right to income from new attributes.

IMPLICATIONS FOR THE THEORY OF THE FIRM

As was previously mentioned, there can be only incomplete markets for judgment due to the partial tacitness of this quality. Agents may realize rents from their human capital through three means: (1) selling labor services on market conditions, (2) entering into employment contracts, or (3) starting a firm. As Barzel (1987) argues, moral hazard implies that options (1) and (2) are often inefficient means of realizing rents (cf. Alvarez and Barney, 2004). However, there are reasons why the market may not be able to evaluate entrepreneurial services in addition to measurement difficulties and the moral hazard and adverse selection problems that follow. For instance, Kirzner (1979: 181) argues that "entrepreneurship reveals to the market what the market did not realize was available" while Casson (1982: 14) argues that "the essence of entrepreneurship is being different" especially in terms of "perception of the situation" (cf. Casson, 1997). Alvarez and Barney (2005, 2007b; cf. Hitt et al. 2001) take a different approach that builds on both Kirzner and Casson, conceiving entrepreneurs as competing for the appropriation of profit opportunities, both discovered and "created," which often involves creating firms. In these kinds of approaches, non-contractibility arises because "[t]he decisive factors . . . are so largely on the inside of the person making the decision that the 'instances' are not amenable to objective description and external control" (Knight, 1921 [1985]: 251; cf. Foss, 1993). The existence of the firm can thus be explained by a specific category of transaction costs, namely, those that close the market for entrepreneurial judgment.

Firms as Controlled Experiments

While this suggests a rationale for self-employment as compared to employment, i.e., the creation of one-person firms, we can discern reasons for the emergence of the employment contract due to capital (resource) heterogeneity. The entrepreneur acts under uncertainty in terms of the outcome of combining known attributes of heterogeneous capital assets but also regarding how to make best use of attributes discovered in the future. Under such circumstances, knowledge of the optimal sequence or execution of tasks is not likely to exist. Therefore, smaller scale entrepreneurial judgment is required on the task level as well as in the relations between tasks in order to make adjustments continuously to improve productivity and make full use of discovered attributes.

Given the limits of incomplete market contracting, the entrepreneur is better off guiding the continuously evolving system while delegating the detailed experimenting within and between specialized tasks in the established structure of production to individual members of a team of producers. Establishing market contracts in such a situation with measurement difficulties would allow any team member hold-up opportunities and the possibility to veto the guidance from the entrepreneur, thereby risking the profitability of the structure. In other words, in an ever-changing world with heterogeneous capital assets and subject to Knightian uncertainty the entrepreneur is better off creating a trusted and specialized team within the boundaries of the firm. These team members can then exercise derived judgment as proxy-entrepreneurs (Foss et al., 2007) to experiment with individual tasks in order to optimize productivity while adhering to the ends of the overall structure (for an alternative view, see e.g., Hsieh et al. 2007).

The entrepreneur remains in control of the firm through asset ownership, incomplete or open-ended contracting with team members through which they align their skills and effort to the entrepreneur's ends, and superior judgment regarding (and knowledge of) the overall structure of production and the particular ends to be achieved through the imagined and attempted production process. The firm can therefore be seen as a purposefully created structure that enables the entrepreneur to realize an imagined production process that is still non-existent in the market. In fact, as Bylund (2011) argues, the firm can be seen as an "island" of super-utilized division of labor that cannot be established in the market through contracting due to incompatibilities with the overall market structure.

Integrating the yet-to-be-realized production process in a firm is a means for the entrepreneur to artificially make real his vision for a future market structure; within the firm, the increased density of factors allows them to specialize and co-specialize to the entrepreneur's imagined process in ways and to an extent that is literally impossible outside of the firm.

Firm Emergence, Adaptation, and Evolution

Given bounded rationality and Knightian uncertainty, the ability to adapt or redeploy resources and reconfigure resource combinations – either because of unanticipated change, or because prior deployments and combinations are found to be mistakes – is critical for firm success. The ability of firms to develop new competencies in light of changing circumstances is at the heart of the dynamic capabilities approach (Teece et al., 1997) and the Penrosian understanding of the firm's subjective opportunity set (Foss et al., 2008). Such processes of emergence, adaptation, and evolution also take place across firms (Chiles et al., 2004; Burress et al., 2008). But the microfoundations of these approaches have not always been spelled out in detail.

Lachmann's (1956 [1978]) capital theory examines these readjustments from an economy-wide perspective, what he calls "reshuffling" or "regrouping." His analysis begins with the entrepreneur's production plan, or multi-period blueprint for resource acquisition and use (Lachmann, 1956 [1978]: 35). Some production plans fail, however, in the sense that they are inconsistent with the expectations and plans or consumers and other entrepreneurs, necessitating revision.

The theory of capital must therefore concern itself with the way in which entrepreneurs form combinations of heterogeneous capital resources in their plans, *and* the way in which they regroup them when they revise these plans. A theory which ignores such regrouping ignores a highly significant aspect of reality: the changing pattern of resource use which the divergence of results actually experienced from what they had been expected to be, imposes on entrepreneurs (Lachmann, 1956 [1978]: 35).

Lachmann (1956 [1978]) emphasizes that a more complex capital structure implies not only greater productivity, but also adjustment costs and path dependence. As an economy grows, its capital structure – the network of interconnected entrepreneurial production plans – becomes deeper and more complex, leading to a greater degree of capital specialization, a more advanced division of labor, and, as a result, greater economic output. But there is a danger, too: increased complexity and complementarity imply asset specificity and bilateral dependence, or "maladaptation" more generally (Williamson, 1996). Moreover, because entrepreneurial plans are continually revised, it is difficult to derive general propositions about the evolution of specific organizational structures at the firm, cluster, or industry level. "[I]ndividuals interpret the past and construct the future subjectively, [so] their knowledge differs and their expectations diverge. These differences lead them to form different plans, which interact over time to drive an ongoing process whose outcome is largely indeterminate" (Chiles et al., 2007: 474).

Applying these ideas about reshuffling and regrouping between firms and entrepreneurs to resource recombinations within firms generates important insights on organizational emergence, adaptation, and evolution. How easily are capital budgeting decisions revised? Can capital and labor be redeployed between operating units? Does increased complexity and complementarity make the firm increasingly vulnerable to "whims and vagaries" inside or outside the firm? A robust literature on the strengths and weaknesses of internal capital markets, relative to external ones, addresses this issue in part (Shin and Stulz, 1998; Rajan et al., 2000; Scharfstein and Stein, 2000; Wulf, 2002). There is much less literature on internal labor markets, however.

Research on mergers, acquisitions, and divestitures represents another attempt to get at firm-level reshuffling. Indeed, Lachmann (1956 [1978]: 97) notes that "in the modern world of large-scale enterprise the typical objects of reshuffling are as often as not whole subsidiary companies." Operating units, like resources defined at a smaller scale, are heterogeneous, have attributes (Barzel, 1997) that are discovered or created through use, have varying degrees of specificity and complementarity, and so on. Applying Lachmann's entrepreneurial capital theory to firm-level reshuffling, within or between operating units, sheds considerable light on organizational adaptation in a dynamic market setting. In this perspective, mergers, acquisitions, divestitures, and other reorganizations are best viewed as responses to valuation discrepancies that are perceived, subjectively, by entrepreneurs.

One implication is that unprofitable boundary changes should not be viewed as "mistakes," subject to tight regulatory scrutiny (Klein and Klein, 2001). A divestiture of previously acquired assets, for example, may mean simply that profit-seeking entrepreneurs have updated their forecasts of future conditions or otherwise learned from experience. Boundary changes can be viewed as a form of organizational experimentation (Mosakowski, 1997; Boot et al., 1999; Matsusaka, 2001) in which entrepreneurs seek to discover their own capabilities by trying various combinations of activities, which could include diversifying into new industries. However, while the long-term success or failure of acquisitions cannot, in general, be predicted by measures of manager control or principal–agent problems (Klein and Klein, 2001), significantly higher rates of divestiture tend to occur in clusters of mergers (see e.g., Mitchell and Mulherin, 1996; Andrade et al., 2001; Andrade and Stafford, 2004). As suggested in the literature, mergers may be driven in part by industry-specific factors, such as regulatory shocks, which means that when regulation of an industry changes, economic calculation becomes more difficult, and entrepreneurial activity is hampered.

Entrepreneurs also experiment with internal organization, notably with changing the degree of delegation and decentralization in an attempt to stimulate what may be called "derived entrepreneurship," that is, the entrepreneurial efforts that employees may engage in within the confines of the entrepreneur's overall vision. This points towards an understanding of entrepreneurship as more of a collective effort, in line with Schumpeter's notion that "the entrepreneurial function need not be embodied in a physical person and in particular in a single physical person. Every social environment has its own ways of filling the entrepreneurial function. . . . Again the entrepreneurial function may be and often is filled co-operatively" (Schumpeter, 1949). Indeed, a growing literature emphasizes the "collective" nature of many entrepreneurial activities (Cooper and Daily, 1997; Mosakowski, 1998; Aldrich, 1999; Schoonhoven and Romanelli, 2001; Ruef et al., 2003; West, 2007; Harper, 2008; Burress and Cook, 2009; Felin and Zenger, 2009).

Organizational Design

Whereas entrepreneurship activity is usually described as socially beneficial (Mises, 1949; Kirzner, 1973), some forms may be "destructive" (Baumol, 1990; Holcombe, 2002; cf. Coyne et al., 2010). Entrepreneurship may be socially harmful if it consumes resources and brings about a social loss; discovering new forms of moral hazard (Holmström, 1982), creating hold-ups (Williamson, 1996), and inventing new ways of engaging in rent-seeking activities relative to government (Baumol, 1990; Holcombe, 2002) are examples of destructive entrepreneurship. In contrast, "productive" entrepreneurship refers to the creation or discovery of new attributes leading to an increase in joint surplus. The firm and the entrepreneur may be victimized by employees engaging in destructive entrepreneurial activities. However, firms may, of course, also strongly benefit from the productive entrepreneurial activities of employees. Therefore, the internal organization of the firm should aim to control destructive and support productive entrepreneurial activities (Foss et al., 2007).

To control destructive entrepreneurship, the firm should be organized to balance the costs of destructive entrepreneurship and costs of monitoring and curbing such behavior, as employees may attempt to creatively circumvent constraints thereby imposing extra costs on the organization. Imposed constraints may have the unwanted side effect that productive entrepreneurship is stifled (see Kirzner, 1985), and, more generally, imposing (too many) constraints on employees may reduce their propensity to create or discover new attributes of productive assets. Relaxing such constraints in order to stimulate productive creation and discovery of new attributes may result in less completely specified principal–agent relationships, thereby giving agents opportunities to exercise their own, often far-reaching, judgments. This may also permit potentially destructive entrepreneurship and managing the tradeoff between productive and destructive entrepreneurship becomes a critical management task.

In this context, asset ownership is important through giving entrepreneurs the right to choose their own preferred tradeoffs. Briefly stated, ownership allows the employer–entrepreneur's preferred degree of contractual incompleteness – and therefore a certain combination of productive and destructive entrepreneurship – to be implemented at low cost. This function of ownership is particularly important in a dynamic market process, the kind stressed by Knight (in the later chapters of 1921 [1985]) and the Austrians (Hayek, 1948; Kirzner, 1973b; Littlechild, 1986). In such a context, an ongoing process of judgmental decision-making requires contractual constraints to address the changing tradeoffs between productive and destructive entrepreneurship inside the firm. The power conferred by ownership allows the employer–entrepreneur to do this at low cost (for a fuller analysis, see Foss and Foss, 2002).

CONCLUSION

As the discussion above shows, the theory of entrepreneurship and the economic theory of the firm have much to learn from each other. We have argued that the concept of entrepreneurship as judgment provides a clear link between entrepreneurship, asset ownership, and economic organization, and that their integration proves very valuable to our understanding of economic forces, market structure, and problems of organization. Similarly, the economic theory of the firm can be improved substantially by taking seriously the essential heterogeneity of capital goods and the subsequent need for entrepreneurial experimentation. Indeed, entrepreneurs without firms are stripped of an important means to pursue profits, effectuate change in the market, and attain their imagined ends. Similarly, firms without entrepreneurs are more like empty shells of automatic maximizing than the important dynamic and innovative elements that populate the real market economy.

Nonetheless, because these concepts lie fundamentally outside the standard constrained optimization framework, they are inherently difficult to model mathematically. Since modern economists have difficulty appreciating ideas that are not expressed in this familiar language, it may prove difficult to get the aforementioned insights incorporated into the economic theory of the firm. However, recent theoretical advances in strategic entrepreneurship and attempts to bridge the divide through studying entrepreneurial firms make us cautiously optimistic. We may see considerable advances in economists' understanding of the firm in a not too distant future.

ACKNOWLEDGEMENTS

This chapter draws on material in Nicolai J. Foss and Peter G. Klein (2012), *Organizing Entrepreneurial Judgment: A New Approach to the Firm,* Cambridge: Cambridge University Press.

4 Institutional perspectives on entrepreneurship
Friederike Welter and David Smallbone

INTRODUCTION

A growing number of entrepreneurship scholars have been arguing for a contextualised perspective on entrepreneurship (Johannisson et al., 2002; Davidsson, 2003; Steyaert and Katz, 2004; Baker et al., 2005; Welter, 2011), to acknowledge the heterogeneity of environment conditions, outcomes and entrepreneurial behaviours. It is important to recognise that entrepreneurship is influenced by external conditions and situations, which can impact upon personal circumstances and individual opportunity recognition. This highlights the social embeddedness of entrepreneurial activity. For example, the motives reported by entrepreneurs for starting and running businesses, which often include reference to 'independence', 'autonomy', and 'self-fulfilment', must be interpreted in the context of the environment in which they are used. Therefore, any analysis of entrepreneurship needs to be grounded in its respective context(s), if it is to accurately reflect the empirical reality because context helps us to understand when, how and why entrepreneurship happens and who becomes involved in it.

In this regard, institutional theory is a useful theoretical frame for incorporating context (Hoskisson et al., 2000), because it emphasises the different external political, economic and societal influences on individual behaviour. With regard to entrepreneurship, the institutional context has an impact on the nature, pace of development, extent of entrepreneurship and the way entrepreneurs behave. Institutions represent both constraining and enabling forces, reflecting the boundaries for individual actions. As enablers, they can assist in reducing transaction costs, uncertainty and risks of individual behaviour; whilst institutional deficiencies can add to transactions and operational costs thereby affecting the returns from entrepreneurial endeavour and constraining the pace of development of productive entrepreneurship. As a consequence, variations in institutional settings and enforcement mechanisms help to explain variations in the nature and extent of entrepreneurship across different environments. All this draws attention to the potential role of institutional theory in understanding entrepreneurial behaviour. In addition, recent developments in institutional theory, which recognise recursive influences of entrepreneurial behaviour on institutions, add another useful facet to its use in entrepreneurship research.

This chapter introduces institutional theory as applied in entrepreneurship research. The next section gives a brief theoretical overview, outlining how institutional theory can be connected to entrepreneurship research, while the following section after that presents some empirical insights. The chapter then turns to discuss future research avenues on entrepreneurship and institutions, emphasising the role of agency and institutional change as well as the need for a multilevel perspective on institutions. The chapter concludes with a brief outlook.

INSTITUTIONS AND ENTREPRENEURSHIP: A THEORETICAL OVERVIEW

Dimensions and Functions of Institutions

Institutional theory dates back to the late nineteenth and early twentieth century when American institutionalists such as Veblen, Mitchell and Commons, as well as the 'Historische Schule' (historical school) in Germany, represented by Gustav Schmoller, Werner Sombart and others, set out to describe the role of institutional legal, political and social factors in the economy. The current discussion on the embeddedness of entrepreneurship can be traced back to Schmoller, who understood human actions as embedded in and influenced by economic, political and social institutions. With this, he anticipated the main ideas of institutional theory. So called 'new' institutional theory is not a single coherent theoretical approach, but instead covers different disciplines and a variety of concepts, ranging from new institutional sociology (Scott, 1999) to new institutional economics (Williamson, 2000). Williamson (2000: 610) described new institutional economics as 'a boiling cauldron of ideas', thus emphasizing the dynamic nature of the theoretical approaches within this field. New institutional economics includes property rights theory, public choice considerations and transaction cost theory. It also incorporates North's framework of informal and formal institutions (North, 1981, 1990), which emphasises cultural and societal influences on economic phenomena and which is the framework mainly applied in entrepreneurship research.[1]

North's theoretical approach posits institutions as rules of the game in a society which regulates, both implicitly and explicitly, human behaviour. In other words, institutions represent boundaries for individual actions, which they can both enable and constrain as mentioned above. The rules of the game include 'formal' institutions, such as the constitutional, legal and organizational framework for individual actions; and 'informal' institutions, such as non-codified codes of conduct, values and norms embedded within a society. In this, institutions are 'things that constrain, enable and guide behaviour' (Nooteboom, 2002: 34).

Other authors employ *different* terms to identify and describe institutions, although the meaning only varies marginally. For example, Raiser (1997) differentiates between conventions, which he understands as societal solutions to collective choice problems; social norms, which reflect a society's (implicit) understanding of what is tolerated and acceptable behaviour and where breaches are not without consequences; and self-enforcing moral norms or values. Knight (1997) distinguishes institutions according to their enforcement mechanisms, where formal institutions are enforced by the state and informal ones by private actors. Scott (2008b) identifies three pillars of institutions, namely regulative, normative and cultural-cognitive institutions. While regulative institutions include laws and other formal rules, normative institutions reflect the norms and values of a society, or, in other words, the collective sense-making of a society. Cultural-cognitive institutions refer to the codes of conduct, which are based on individual interpretations of societal norms. Institutions also provide information on the actions of others and the way that individuals perceive and process information (Dequech, 2003).

Entrepreneurship-related formal institutions are rules governing the policies and economic structure of a country or region. Examples of formal institutions which impact on entrepreneurship include regulations for market entry and exit such as bankruptcy laws, private property regulations, laws governing commercial transactions, tax policies and the financial system. Formal institutions can create or restrict opportunity fields for entrepreneurship. The fundamental rules of a society, such as the constitution or private ownership rights, can be a major influence on the existence of entrepreneurship and the forms that it takes, whilst the legal frame exerts a major influence on the nature and extent to which productive entrepreneurship develops. Laws contribute to entrepreneurship by opening up opportunity fields, as happened in the initial stages of market reform in the post-socialist economies of Central and Eastern Europe when the introduction of private property rights allowed private enterprise to legally exist (Smallbone and Welter, 2009b). In contrast, a deficient legal infrastructure, with implementation gaps, can restrict entrepreneurship because it allows for arbitrary and discretionary actions on the part of both administrations and entrepreneurs.

Informal institutions refer to the values, norms and attitudes which are embedded as deep structures in a society (Nooteboom, 2002), guiding individual behaviour through unwritten codes of conduct. They exert an indirect influence on entrepreneurship because they can influence opportunity recognition and exploitation as well as access to resources. Examples of entrepreneurship-related informal institutions include the value society generally puts on entrepreneurship and/or the roles of women in society. Informal institutions operate at different levels: at the level of a society norms and values shape the attitudes of the population at large towards entrepreneurship; at the sector level they are reflected in codes of conduct, as set down by, for example, business associations and professions; and at the level of communities they include, for example, religious norms, kinship values or attitudes of ethnic groups.

The Interplay of Formal and Informal Institutions

Informal institutions are often equated with the 'culture' of a country or society, although this neglects the potentially interactive nature of the relationship between formal and informal institutions. Formal and informal institutions are difficult to separate in practice, due to recursive links, which draws attention to the origin of institutions. Formal institutions arise out of human actions, which mean they are socially constructed, while Williamson (2000) suggests that informal institutions mainly originate spontaneously and are self-organized. But, informal institutions might also be the outcome of purposeful human behaviour and formal institutions might result, in the long run, from uncoordinated actions of individuals (Ben-Ner and Putterman, 1998: 38). Moreover, formal and informal institutions are mutually dependent and normally co-evolve. Since informal institutions refer to the collective, tacit interpretation of individual mental perceptions (Denzau and North, 1994), they could also result from formal institutions, as a collective interpretation of these formal rules, which they can in turn modify. For example, a specific legal framework normally contains explicit regulations for implementing laws, which are complemented over time by unwritten rules providing an implicit understanding of their content. In this sense, informal institutions may fill legal gaps, which only become apparent when formal institutions such as the legal framework are applied in daily life. In the long run, this could result in revised laws and regulations, which incorporate these unwritten informal institutions.

This draws attention to the enforcement of institutions, since institutional enforcement mechanisms can impact upon the nature and extent of entrepreneurship across different environments, as well as institutional settings. Douhan and Henrekson (2010) differentiate between codified (i.e., written down) institutions and effective institutions, which reflects how they work in practice. Scott (2008b) distinguishes between three enforcement mechanisms, namely coercion, normative pressures and mimetic mechanisms. Formal institutions (or regulative elements) are enforced by coercive mechanisms, as set down in government rules and sanctions, while informal institutions are enforced by normative and mimetic mechanisms. Normative enforcement mechanisms refer to culturally sanctioned and tolerated codes of conduct, including all kinds of behavioural codes within industries and professions, families, ethnic groups and other communities.

Enforcement mechanisms legitimise individual behaviour which is of particular importance for nascent entrepreneurs and entrepreneurs in unfamiliar environments, facing a high degree of liability of newness. In environments where formal and informal institutions are in conflict, as can happen in emerging market economies, for example, where new laws and governmental regulations often contradict 'learned' behaviour, coercive mechanisms frequently force entrepreneurs to comply with regulations although they might have to draw on behaviour which is culturally accepted, but which contradicts the new legal framework (Welter and Smallbone, 2011). Williamson (1993a: 476) points out that 'transactions that are viable in an institutional environment providing strong safeguards may be non-viable in institutional environments that are weak.' Coercive enforcement is always likely to be imperfect because of the bounded rationality of human behaviour, thereby emphasising the role of trust as an important additional influence on behaviour.

Formal institutions will only work successfully if individuals are able to establish a basic level of trust in the reliability of any exchanges, but also in any sanctions and penalties that may need to be imposed. In particular, trust in institutions, or institutional trust, is essential for an efficient institutional framework, because it allows agents to enter into transactions with only limited information about the transaction partner's specific attributes (Raiser, 1999). In this regard, institutional trust allows for the use of anonymous sources in entrepreneurship, because there are legal safeguards and sanctions that may be applied in cases where the relationship fails. It is only in situations where formal and informal institutions combine to form a coherent framework that formal regulations and the rule of law will predominately shape individual behaviour, whilst in fragile settings with institutional deficiencies and conflicts, non-compliance with the formal rules becomes pervasive and normative enforcement mechanisms will typically dominate.

Institutions change over time; and institutional change can positively influence entrepreneurship where it lowers barriers to market entry and exit. However, institutional change does not have a mechanistic effect on entrepreneurship, because of the mediating influence of institutional inertia and legacies on individual behaviour as, for example, in former socialist countries (Peng, 2003; Chavance, 2008). Since informal institutions are embedded in society, they tend to change more slowly than formal institutions (North, 1990), which can result in conflicts between formal and informal institutions. This can have a major impact on entrepreneurial behaviour insofar as entrepreneurs draw on viable, but not necessarily the best courses of actions (Whyte et al., 1997), which 'may bear little resemblance to the legitimate courses of action stipulated by the formal rules' (Nee, 1998: 86).

EXPLORING THE IMPACT OF INSTITUTIONS ON ENTREPRENEURSHIP: SOME EMPIRICAL INSIGHTS

This section provides some empirical insights into studies which use institutional theory when researching entrepreneurship. Major themes which have been analysed from an institutional perspective concern the influence of formal and informal institutions on entrepreneurial behaviour (Salimath and Cullen, 2010) and the link between institutions and gender. Since institutional deficiencies can present particular challenges (and sometimes opportunities) for entrepreneurs, not surprisingly institutional approaches have been a particular feature of studies of entrepreneurship in transition and emerging market economies, where institutional deficiencies are common.

The impact of formal institutions on entrepreneurship has been well researched, with most studies relying on a macro-level design, often based on large-scale databases such as the Global Entrepreneurship Monitor, 'Doing Business' of the World Bank and similar global organizations. Studies show links between entrepreneurship and institutions (Henrekson, 2007; Douhan and Henrekson, 2010; Harbi and Anderson, 2010; Henrekson and Sanandaji, 2010), particularly in relation to economic development (Acs and Karlsson, 2002; Karlsson and Acs, 2002; Acs et al., 2008). Some show how institutions influence the nature of entrepreneurship (Davidsson and Henrekson, 2002; Henrekson and Johansson, 1999) and/or how technological developments, changes in political system and/or in laws can contribute to the creation of new opportunity fields for entrepreneurs (Davidsson et al., 2006; Smallbone and Welter 2009b, 2010b; Henrekson and Sanandaji, 2010).

The design and operation of formal institutions is directly under the influence of the state, which can also indirectly influence informal institutions, such as the values, attitudes and norms of a society through its pronouncements and actions and those of its officials. The role of the state in designing and implementing formal institutions is another recurring theme in entrepreneurship research that involves an institutional perspective. For example, Minniti (2008) asks which policies are more conducive to productive entrepreneurship while Smallbone and Welter (2010a, 2010b) analyse government policies and their contribution to creating efficient institutional frameworks in a transition country context. They point to enforcement problems associated with institutional conflicts as governments find it more difficult to change informal institutions than the formal institutional framework, especially in the short run.

Culturally embedded norms affect the extent to which a society tolerates and fosters entrepreneurial activities, as well as the number of people with previous entrepreneurial experiences and thus the number of potential role models (Shane, 2004). Cultural institutions can also influence the resources available for entrepreneurship, such as access to finance, since societies vary in the practice of saving for the future or living and spending to enjoy the moment. Cultural norms can also influence whether a society tolerates profit-making behaviour as one of the prerequisites for entrepreneurship development.

A growing body of studies have focused on the influence of informal institutions on entrepreneurship, although the results are mixed, partly because of differences in the way informal institutions are measured and other differences in research design. These studies include variations in entrepreneurial cognitions across different cultures (Busenitz and Lau, 1996; Mitchell et al., 2000); and the impact of culture and/or national environments on entrepreneurial behaviour (Basu and Altinay, 2002; George and Zahra, 2002; Hayton et al., 2002; Tan, 2002). Some studies also analyse the relation between specific informal institutions and entrepreneurship. For example, Uhlaner and Thurik (2007) examine how post-materialism influences entrepreneurship across nations; Davidsson and Wiklund (1997) show how values and beliefs impact on regional venture creation; while others have focused specifically on religion and entrepreneurship (e.g., Dodd and Seaman, 1998; Basu and Altinay, 2002; Carswell and Rolland, 2004; Audretsch et al., 2007).

Some research, again typically at the macro level, is concerned with both formal and informal institutions, for example, comparing institutional profiles across countries and measuring the degree to which a society admires and values entrepreneurial activities (Busenitz et al., 2000), or researching which types of institution influences which type of entrepreneurship. In this context, Spencer and Gómez (2004) show that normative institutions are marginally associated with self-employment, cognitive institutions explain the prevalence of small firms within a country, while regulatory institutions are associated with new listings on a country's stock exchange. In their comparative study of Vietnam, USA and Taiwan, Nguyen et al. (2009) found a significant impact of culture on the desire to set up a new venture, while results were mixed as to whether it is culture or market institutions which influence intentions and confidence during the venture creation process. Based on GEM data, Bowen and De Clercq (2008) provide empirical evidence that country-specific institutions influence the allocation of entrepreneurship into productive activities, which the authors define as high-growth entrepreneurial efforts.

Strong external environmental influences are a recurring theme in studies of entrepreneurship in emerging market economies, which has encouraged many to adopt an institutional theory framework (e.g., Peng and Heath, 1996; Yan and Manolova, 1998; Peng, 2001; Polishchuk, 2001; Smallbone and Welter, 2001; Manolova and Yan, 2002; Tan, 2002; Bruton and Ahlstrom, 2003; Peng, 2003; Welter and Smallbone, 2003; Radaev, 2004; Aidis, 2005; Aidis et al., 2008; Manolova et al., 2008; Ahlstrom and Bruton, 2010). Although in *any* context entrepreneurship is influenced by a dynamic interrelationship between individual characteristics and external conditions, in situations where the formal institutional framework is only partially installed and/or has major institutional deficiencies, the institutional context and the interplay between formal and informal institutions can become a critical factor. The specificities of the external environment in emerging economies make it a potentially more dominant influence on entrepreneurship than in a more stable business context. The role of both formal and informal institutions is often a constraining one, as the environment is characterised by a high level of uncertainty, associated with rapidly changing external conditions and major institutional deficiencies (Ahlstrom and Bruton, 2010). This might encourage illegal or semi-legal activities (Baumol, 1990) as reflected in the example of cross-border entrepreneurship in post-socialist countries, where petty traders and small-scale entrepreneurs circumvent customs and excessive border controls (Welter and Smallbone, 2009). At the same time, institutional voids can also offer opportunities for entrepreneurs as has been shown for business service firms in the Ukraine in the early 1990s (Smallbone et al., 2010). In this context, entrepreneurs frequently drew on previously learned behaviour, based on culturally embedded informal institutions, such as 'blat' or 'guanxi' (Smallbone and Welter 2009a; Puffer et al., 2010).

Puffer et al. (2010) suggest that countries such as Russia and China might develop unique balances between formal and informal institutions that better fit their (historical) contexts and situations. This is taken up by Smallbone and Welter (2012) who compare institutional change and entrepreneurship across three country settings: new EU member states from Central and Eastern Europe, the Commonwealth of Independent States (CIS) which consists of former Soviet republics and China. The authors highlight distinctive paths of institutional change and entrepreneurship development. In new member states, institutional change resulting from the accession to the European Union fostered entrepreneurship development. In CIS countries, persisting institutional deficiencies have a predominately negative effect on entrepreneurship because of the unsupportive wider political context, while in China, neither the state nor entrepreneurs show much interest in institutional change, instead they prefer to explore what they can do within the context of the (ambiguous) institutions that exist. This results in 'double entrepreneurship' (Yang, 2007) which incorporates an economic and a socio-political dimension, because entrepreneurs in China need to be able to both make a profit and to obtain socio-political security.

Few studies have researched institutional legacies and their impact on the nature and extent of entrepreneurship, as for example, Aidis and van Praag (2007) who analyse whether illegal entrepreneurial experiences during Soviet times make a difference for entrepreneurship in the contemporary period. For the Soviet Union, Rehn and Taalas (2004) showed how entrepreneurship flourished in the daily lives of individuals during the Soviet period, struggling to cope with the material shortages of the Soviet system. As a result, the authors suggested that the former USSR may be seen as a highly entrepreneurial society.

Another recurring theme in entrepreneurship studies drawing on institutional theory is the relation between institutions and gender, since both formal and informal institutions shape the role of women in a society (e.g., Baughn et al., 2006; Verheul et al., 2006; Welter and Smallbone, 2008). Examples of gender-specific formal institutions include the constitution, which may seek to ensure equal opportunities for women and men; labour market rules giving equal access to employment positions; family policies, such as specific tax regulations and the overall infrastructure for childcare; and property rights that may allow or prevent female ownership of land. Generally, institutions might restrict the nature and extent of their entrepreneurial activities if women are primarily identified with homebound roles (Welter and Smallbone 2008). For example, based on GEM data for 11 countries, Elam and Terjesen (2010) show how labour-market institutions (e.g., female business leadership, gender wage inequality and public expenditure on childcare) influence the decision to start a business indirectly through their effect on societal perceptions. Welter and Smallbone (2010) explore the impact of institutional change on women entrepreneurs in hostile and turbulent environments of Central and Eastern Europe and Central Asia. While institutional change such as the introduction of private property rights created opportunity fields for entrepreneurial men and women alike, it typically had a negative impact on women, because of the effect of a change in family policies on the subsidies for state enterprise kindergartens, which led to a lack of public childcare facilities. The authors also illustrate the diversity of behavioural responses by women to deal with the post-Soviet traditional gender role, including some who openly defied post-Soviet gender roles, while others accepted them, at least on the surface. In a post-Soviet context, business is typically considered a predominantly male territory, requiring so-called male qualities, such as strength and assertiveness. In such circumstances, women entrepreneurs break out of norms ascribing them specific roles and behaviours.

FURTHER RESEARCH DIRECTIONS ON INSTITUTIONS AND ENTREPRENEURSHIP

In reviewing the use of institutional theory in entrepreneurship studies, Bruton et al. (2010) identify three major shortcomings of its application hitherto, namely a reliance on a single perspective of institutional theory, the dominance of culture, which implies a lack of attention paid to other institutional factors, and single country studies. Salimath and Cullen (2010: 373) add to this, by pointing out a general lack of integrative theoretical frameworks that 'would contribute to an enhanced understanding of the effects of formal social institutions and national culture on entrepreneurial activity'. Our overview in the previous section shows a diversity of entrepreneurship research applying institutional theory, albeit in some cases implicitly, as well as some cross-comparative studies, but also an overreliance on culture, equating culture as a whole or single aspects with informal institutions. In addition, research which applies institutional theory implicitly treats (formal and/or informal) institutions as variables instead of using institutional theory as a conceptual lens for understanding the diversity and complexity of institutional settings, as well as the interplay between formal and informal institutions.

More fundamentally perhaps, institutional approaches have repeatedly been criticised for the lack of attention paid to human agency (Dacin et al., 2002), with underlying assumptions of 'homo economicus'. This draws attention to one of the major problems inherent in the institutional approach, which concerns the endogenous and recursive nature of both institutions and behaviour (Zafirovski, 1999). It poses the question as to how individuals can initiate change in a context, which is at the same time determining their behaviour (Koene, 2006). North (2005) emphasises the intentionality of players enacting institutional change, concluding that their grip of the respective situation influences the development of the institutional environment. Just as institutional change can influence entrepreneurial behaviour, so too in theory, at least, can entrepreneurial behaviour trigger institutional change because action develops in a 'duality between agency and structure.' (Beckert, 1999: 789). In this regard, institutional theory is complemented by structuration theory (Giddens, 1984), which allows scope for modification of institutional structures by reflexive agents. This implies that institutional change may be interpreted as an interactive learning process between entrepreneurs and those organisations designing and implementing the formal framework, such as governments.

Oliver (1991) was the first to elaborate on the role of agency within institutional theory. She suggested five types of behavioural responses to institutions, ranging from conformity or acquiescence, compromise, avoidance, deviance to manipulation. Conformity, acquiescence and compromising strategies acknowledge the existing institutional framework, with entrepreneurs adapting their behaviour accordingly. Avoidance, defiance and manipulation reflect patterns of non-conforming behaviour in relation to existing institutions. Avoidance refers to individuals or organisations concealing and buffering themselves from institutional pressures or escaping institutional rules (Oliver, 1991). In challenging environments, for example, some of the diversification strategies of entrepreneurs fall into this category (Lynn, 1998), as diversification can reduce the possibility of successful entrepreneurs attracting too much attention to themselves from the authorities, particularly in the more authoritarian states. Defiance includes entrepreneurs ignoring, circumventing or openly challenging institutional rules, which especially happens in situations where there is low potential for external enforcement. 'Manipulation' refers to active attempts to change the institutional environment, which is normally less of an option for new and young entrepreneurs because of their lack of legitimacy and power and may depend on the extent to which entrepreneurs are able to form effective business associations. The exception is where they are well connected through their personal networks, as can be frequently observed in post-Soviet states, where 'state capture' by party members turned entrepreneurs was a dominant process during the early years of the transition towards a market economy (Hellman et al., 2003).

Building implicitly on Oliver's concept, Henrekson and Sanandaji (2010) identify abiding, evading and altering as the three main mechanisms through which entrepreneurs can influence institutions. Altering includes direct actions of entrepreneurs aimed at reforming formal institutions. Abiding behaviour can trigger institutional change indirectly, for example, through disruptive actions such as the introduction of new technologies (Kalantaridis, 2007). Evasion behaviour again contributes to institutional change indirectly, because it challenges the authority of existing institutions, by weakening their effectiveness. Evasion behaviour often draws on path dependency as reflected in behavioural routines, which the authors of this chapter have previously illustrated with respect to entrepreneurial behaviour in post-socialist countries (Welter and Smallbone, 2003, 2011). Such behaviour frequently is seen as reinforcing 'inertial informality' (Chavance, 2008: 65), which has been assessed as detrimental to institutional change, particularly to change in informal institutions (Greif and Laitin, 2004). Recently, however, studies of institutional change have started to acknowledge 'positive path-dependent informality' (Chavance, 2008: 67), which draws attention to path-dependent institutional evolution through layering, conversion or recombination (Martin, 2010). Layering refers to the gradual change of informal institutions by adding new procedures or structures. Conversion includes reorientation towards new purposes; and recombination refers to changes in the combination of institutional settings. Therefore, institutional change can happen as an unintended by-product of entrepreneurial or organisational 'path-dependent' behaviour, as has been shown, for example, in various former socialist countries (e.g., Stark and Bruszt, 2001; Stark 1996; Ledeneva, 2006; Smallbone and Welter, 2009a).

The implication of this is that it is not only intentional behaviour which contributes to institutional change, but rather any entrepreneurial behaviour which implicitly or explicitly questions existing institutions. This has already been suggested by Giddens (1984) who pointed out that structures are generally quite stable, but when people ignore, replace or reproduce them differently, they can change them as an (un-)intended by-product of their actions. This could occur in situations where institutions are not legitimized in a particular economy or society (Beckert, 1999). Fligstein (1997) advocated 'institutional entrepreneurship' as one way of dealing with the role of actors in institutional theory, acknowledging that institutional entrepreneurs are not necessarily business owners, but could be politicians. Recently, the concept of institutional entrepreneurship has gained increasing attention in entrepreneurship research (e.g., Beckert, 1999, 2010; Battilana et al., 2009; Pacheco et al., 2010), although it is not without its critics.

It may be argued that the concept of institutional entrepreneurship remains blurred and its application to entrepreneurship questionable. Definitions of what constitutes institutional entrepreneurship vary across the different streams of institutional theory. For example, organizational sociologists such as DiMaggio (1988: 14) interpret institutional entrepreneurs as 'organized actors with sufficient resources' that see in new institutions 'an opportunity to realize interests that they value highly'. Based on the example of China, Daokui et al. (2006) define institutional entrepreneurs as agents who destroy prevailing market institutions during business start-up or expansion, in order for their own business to be successful. In other words, the innovation of these entrepreneurs is external to the business, having a wider impact on the whole economy. With their definition, the authors draw attention to institutional change as a result of intended individual behaviour, which might have both positive and negative effects beyond a single business. From a political economy perspective, Douhan and Henrekson (2010: 641) take this further, arguing for a distinction between business and institutional entrepreneurship with the latter reflecting actions of agents to 'exploit institutions to one's economic advantage', in contrast to business entrepreneurs who realise profits based on, for example, patents or market niches. Finally, Battilana et al. (2009) argue that for agents to qualify as institutional entrepreneurs they would need to have initiated changes that break with the existing institutional framework. In addition, they must have actively participated in implementing those changes, although it was conceded that the entrepreneurs might not be successful in implementing institutional changes. They also acknowledge that institutional entrepreneurship could be a by-product of other (entrepreneurial) actions.

The many definitions and blurred terminology raise some doubts as to whether the concept of institutional entrepreneurship, as currently defined and applied, can really add value to an institutional theory approach to entrepreneurship. So far, the concept does not appear to capture the complexities of the interplay between institutions and agents, nor does it suggest an adequate conceptual underpinning for exploring agency within institutional theory (Aldrich, 2010). A more appropriate concept to incorporate agency within institutional theory may be that of change agents, who contribute to institutional change, whether intended or a by-product of other actions, with both negative and positive outcomes. Change agents could be entrepreneurs, but they also could include officials or representatives of government or other organizational actors, as Smallbone and Welter (2012) have illustrated with reference to governments in new EU member states of Central and Eastern Europe, the CIS and China. In the former, the state actively took over as change agent, while in most CIS the state still does not fully recognise entrepreneurship and its role in fostering institutional change and economic development which leads to entrepreneurs circumventing and avoiding institutions. In China both state and entrepreneurs can be characterised as change agents, although existing entrepreneurs currently appear more interested in exploring and exploiting the existing institutional frame and institutional deficiencies than in searching for the best institutions. The case of China illustrates the interaction between institutions and organisations and/or individuals that shape institutional evolution (North, 1994), in which both organisations and entrepreneurs are players.

Institutional change, and the interplay between actors and institutions that contribute to it, is a potentially productive research avenue, as is the complexity of institutions and their impact on entrepreneurship. The various empirical studies, referred to in the previous section, show a tendency to focus on institutions at the macro level, whereas institutional theory itself acknowledges different levels of institutions. Research on ethnic entrepreneurs (Kloosterman et al., 1999; Kloosterman, 2010), for example, suggests a multi-layered analysis, based on the concept of mixed embeddedness, which recognises the diverse institutional layers at macro and micro level in which human agency is embedded, thus complementing the current institutional approach in entrepreneurship research.

This calls for multilevel research designs, which go beyond institutional profiles at country/macro level, but instead try to capture the links between institutions across the macro and micro levels. Davidsson and Wiklund (2001) report that most entrepreneurship research still focuses on the firm/business and neglects the institutional embeddedness of individual behaviour. In addition, it is suggested that the gap in multilevel institutional analysis and the focus on a single set of institutions partly result from the neglect of (more) qualitative methods, which would help to capture the richness and diversity of the institutional contexts. Gartner (2004: 212) argued that entrepreneurship research needs to understand more about the phenomenon in question by assembling what he labelled 'descriptive' evidence, demanding research which aims at understanding the phenomenon as such.

OUTLOOK

This chapter has reviewed institutional theory and its application hitherto in entrepreneurship research. One of the contributions of an institutional approach in relation to entrepreneurship is that it highlights influences on entrepreneurship that are often taken for granted, particularly in the case of research that is narrowly focused on mature market economies. An institutional approach allows for close analysis of the embeddedness of entrepreneurship within a particular context, which impacts upon the nature and extent of entrepreneurship, as well as its contribution to economic and social development. This is in line with the institutional theory approach as advocated by Powell and DiMaggio (1991) for organization studies. Both strands of institutional theory acknowledge different levels of embeddedness in which economic actions take place: political embeddedness, which emphasise the sources and means of economic action (North, 1990; Zukin and DiMaggio, 1990), cultural embeddedness, which refers to a collective understanding of society, which forms the basis for economic behaviour (North, 1990; Zukin and DiMaggio, 1990); social embeddedness, as reflected in networks of interpersonal relations (Granovetter, 1985, 2005); and cognitive embeddedness as 'ways in which the structured regularities of mental processes limit the exercise of economic reasoning' (Zukin and DiMaggio, 1990: 15–16; similarly, Denzau and North, 1994).

However, in applying institutional theory to the study of entrepreneurship, there is a need to take into account the complexity of institutions and entrepreneurship and the interrelationships between them. While institutions have an impact on the nature and extent of entrepreneurship, the interactions between institutional settings, organizations and individual actors (entrepreneurs) in turn shape the institutional evolution of economies (North, 1994). The issues arising concern the co-evolution of institutions, in particular formal and informal institutional settings; the role of actors in and for institutional change; and impediments to institutional change. These issues are of equal importance for the use of institutional theory in organisation studies. However, the question remains as to whether institutional theory can adequately analyse dynamics and processes, or whether we need to combine the insights of institutional theory with a more process-oriented approach such as evolutionary theory (cf. Martinez and Aldrich, this volume).

In seeking to move towards more in-depth investigations within an institutional frame, there is a need for longitudinal studies which could give deeper insights into historical contexts, institutional stability and change, as well as the co-evolvement of institutions and entrepreneurship over time (Scott, 2008a). There is also a need for more detailed comparative studies, with a qualitative, process-oriented perspective, in order to bring out the distinctiveness of specific institutional contexts and their links with entrepreneurship as has long been the case in organisation studies analysing different institutional contexts (Hjorth, 2008).

NOTE

1. Bruton et al. (2010), in their review, state that it is the organizational branch of institutional theory which is mainly applied in entrepreneurship studies. However, this is a result of the articles they select for review, because they rely on mainstream management and organization journals.

5 Evolutionary theory
Martha Martinez and Howard E. Aldrich

EVOLUTIONARY THEORY

The evolutionary approach may be described as a *meta-theory* because it is an overarching framework that permits the comparison and integration of other social scientific theories. Theories as diverse as population ecology (Hannan and Freeman, 1977), new institutionalism (Zucker, 1977; DiMaggio and Powell, 1983), resource dependence (Pfeffer and Salancik, 1978), and transaction cost economics (Williamson, 1985, 1991) explore evolutionary processes in organizations. In the context of organizations and organizational science, evolutionary processes arise from the interaction between strategies, structures, and environmental conditions and forces (Martinez and Aldrich, 2011). A struggle by organizations to obtain scarce resources, both social and physical, drives the process (Campbell, 1969). This struggle is characterized by competition among social actors to obtain resources ahead of their competitors or to avoid competition altogether (Barnett et al., 1994). In fact, many activities, from marketing to the development of inter-organizational alliances, stem from organizations' attempts to shield themselves from competitive pressures.

Evolutionary analyses posit that outcomes result from interactions between organizations and environments, rather than being attributable to either organizations or environments, taken separately. Every explanation is thus contingent. The effect of organizational properties depends upon environmental contexts and the effects of contexts are unknowable until organizational properties are specified. Understanding how a "fit" arises between organizations and their environments is therefore the key to comprehending trends in organizational foundings, transformation, and disbandings. Entrepreneurs and scholars usually evaluate "fit" in terms of outcomes like survival, profitability, and growth. A fit need not be perfect, but rather just the best fit, under the circumstances.

Accounts of evolutionary processes rest on identifying the selecting forces that interact with particular variations to produce organizational and population change. Compared to person-centric accounts, selection arguments can seem maddeningly indirect and impersonal. Perhaps the most difficult premise to convey is that selection derives from the *consequences* of actions, not the *intentions* of actors. Individual differences across actors are clearly still important, as some entrepreneurs and managers are more highly skilled than others at judging, envisioning, and reshaping selection environments. Nonetheless, the consequences of action are what count. Because organizational scientists often overlook this feature of evolutionary models, we think it bears repeating.

The purpose of this chapter is to provide an overview of advances in evolutionary theory and methodology, pointing out areas for future research. To accomplish this goal, we review changing views regarding the dynamics of evolutionary processes, with particular emphasis on the interrelation of selection and variation. We treat nascent entrepreneurs as people who try to start organizations and entrepreneurs as people who succeed in creating organizations. Thus, our discussion includes both entrepreneurs and the organizations they create. We explore the potential for adaptive behaviors by managers and entrepreneurs and review the role of perception and identity in evolution. A final section assesses methodological progress in research on evolutionary processes.

EVOLUTIONARY PROCESSES

Competitive struggles drive entrepreneurs and organizations to create new strategies, routines and structural elements, to select those elements that prove effective, and to extend those selected elements to other areas. Some of these new elements may require cooperation with other organizations. Therefore, the dynamics of interactions between organizations and their environments include the processes of social construction (variation), social destruction (selection), and social reproduction (retention). Variation, selection, retention, and struggle occur simultaneously rather than sequentially. Analytically, the processes may be separated into discrete phases, but in practice they are linked in continuous feedback loops and cycles. Variation generates the raw materials for selection, by environmental or internal criteria; retention processes preserve the selected variation. But retention processes also restrict the kinds of variations that may occur, and competitive struggles as well as cooperative alliances can change the character of selection criteria (Aldrich and Ruef, 2006).

When driven by competitive struggles and cooperative actions, the processes of variation, selection, and retention jointly shape the course of evolution. These processes drive change at multiple levels: between entrepreneurs and within and between organizations, organizational populations, and communities of populations. These multiple levels of social structure are nested within each other, as sources of variation and selection. From the viewpoint of *emergence*, changes in individual organizations started by entrepreneurs may affect populations, and changes in populations may affect communities. From the viewpoint of *constraint*, populations and communities are pivotal in shaping environmental forces for entrepreneurs and organizations, while communities constitute an important component of the environment for populations.

Variations across units in strategies and structures that lead to differential success in extracting resources from environments will be objects of positive selection. New types of organizations and organizational forms emerge when entrepreneurs respond to specific threats and opportunities present in their environments; entrepreneurs who are efficient at taking advantage of those opportunities and countering those threats tend to survive and be imitated by already existing organizations or new entrants. In organizational communities, populations with different characteristics enter into relationships of both competition and cooperation; those populations better able to deal with their environments are more likely to survive, whereas others are not, and characteristics of a successful population may then be diffused to other populations in the same community.

SELECTION AND ADAPTATION

Whether entrepreneurs consciously and intentionally drive variation and selection processes constitutes a central issue in evolutionary analyses. This question was formerly framed as a selection versus adaptation debate, but a paradigm shift has occurred. In the old paradigm, selection was seen as caused by forces completely exogenous to focal organizations and populations, with environmental forces treated as overwhelming and unchangeable by entrepreneurial actors. In the old view, those lucky entities that happened to have, by chance, strategies and structures that best fit the environment were the ones that survived (Aldrich, 2009). By contrast, theories currently using an evolutionary approach treat environments as subject to manipulation and transformation by entrepreneurs and organizations (Scott, 2008b). Natural limits constrain resource availability, but social forces and practices also affect access to resources and influence which entities gain legitimate access to them. Lobbying is one important way in which entrepreneurs and organizations can affect the distribution of resources. For example, early in the life of the US real estate residential industry, agents lobbied the federal government to allow tax deductions for home mortgage interest. Currently, that tax deduction plays a key role in convincing people to buy properties, thus increasing the size of the market served by agents. With this and other actions, real estate agents helped create a culture that considers owning a home superior to renting.

Adaptation was formerly seen as mostly created by entrepreneurial agency and intentionality. When studying adaptation, scholars focused on variation, distinguishing between blind variations that emerge spontaneously – as a result of mistakes, surprises, or simple unplanned deviations – from new strategies and structures aimed at solving problems and seizing opportunities. From this point of view, entrepreneurs not only generated variations but also did the selecting of which ones to retain. Adaptations through intentional variations were then treated as the direct outcome of strategic management efforts and entrepreneurial intentionality (Volberda and Lewin, 2003).

Today we would argue that entrepreneurial action can create adaptation through variation not only at the organizational level, but also through the cumulative effect of organizational actions on populations and communities. Even though particular actions might seem nearly inconsequential at the time of their enactment, their accumulated effects can be quite substantial. For example, entrepreneurs who find ways of encouraging and monitoring collective action within an industry may give an entire population an advantage over competing populations, such as through building a powerful trade association or creating economies of scope by forming industry clusters (Aldrich and Staber, 1988; Feldman et al., 2005). For example, the Research Triangle Park Area of North Carolina has attracted a cluster of biotech and pharmaceutical firms that search for new drugs, organize clinical trials, help firms deal with governmental regulations, and manufacture and package drugs. As a cluster, they benefit from complementary products and services and are a spawning ground for new firms founded by nascent entrepreneurs who have left established firms.

Even if entrepreneurs engage in intentional variations, adaptation is not a certain outcome unless it is sustained through organizational learning (Argote, 1999; Miner et al., 2001). Learning occurs when variations emerge and are affected by interactions with environments, with organizations obtaining feedback regarding the effectiveness of those strategies (Volberda and Lewin, 2003). Learning can be the result of the semi-automatic accumulation of experiences through normal organizational activities, or the final products of specialized investments in the collection, articulation, and codification of knowledge regarding specific strategies in particular environments. Entrepreneurs and managers try to understand causal mechanisms and transform them into generalized systems of rules to be applied in the future (Zollo and Winter, 2002). But the concept of "adaptation" means more than just learning something new, because the advantages of the new routines, strategies, and structures must outweigh those of the old ones by a margin large enough to compensate for the costs and disruptions normally created by any type of change (Barnett and Carroll, 1995).

In the old paradigm, selection and adaptation were completely separate processes that only intersected in the narrow of area of fit between strategies/structures and environments. The new paradigm in evolutionary theory emphasizes that selection and adaptation are not separate from each other, and in particular that adaptation strategies directly affect selection forces (Levinthal, 1991). This effect may be inherently limited, in the sense that the development of strategies and structures by a firm dedicated to shielding itself from competitive environmental forces is itself an effect on the environment. For example, many successful firms locate in particular market niches and erect barriers to entry for rivals, such as in the production of machine tools requiring a high degree of technical proficiency (Caves and Porter, 1977).

Once the required market position/structure/strategy has been achieved, there is no competitive need in the short run for further variations, learning, or adaptation (Barnett et al., 1994). Particularly in nascent industries, entrepreneurs create organizational boundaries in an attempt to claim, demarcate, and manage market segments (Santos and Eisenhardt, 2009) in ways that allow them to both control their relationships with the external environment (Pfeffer and Salancik, 1978) and to increase their efficiency in obtaining resources (Williamson, 1991). Many strategies, such as diversification of productive activities, the development of high status market positions, and monopolies created through acquisitions, have the specific purpose of protecting firms from environmental forces.

Current thinking posits that entrepreneurs' actions may not only shield organizations from selection forces but also fundamentally alter those forces. Accordingly, theorists now recognize that organizations, populations, and communities and their environments can co-evolve. For example, at the organizational level, co-evolution occurs within a population of heterogeneous firms when organizations with adaptive learning capabilities are able to interact and mutually influence each other (McKelvey, 2002; Volberda and Lewin, 2003). Particularly in the case of new organizational forms, interaction between firms shapes the structure of emerging industries (Haveman and Rao, 1997; Djelic and Ainamo, 1999; Lampel and Shamsie, 2003). For example, in the early days of the commercialization of the internet, entrepreneurs developing new ways of making online payments facilitated the growth of online merchants selling to nervous first-time customers.

Co-evolution between firms and institutions is also possible. Organized actors with sufficient resources can collectively reshape institutions by attempting to select, modify, or create them in ways that favor their interests, especially when they work purposefully together (DiMaggio, 1988; Leca and Naccache, 2006). Indeed, under certain limited circumstances, individual actors can have strong influences on institutional environments. For example, in emerging economies, dominant firms are able to affect the development of national institutions through their manipulation of social networks and in particular through using powerful political contacts (Rodrigues and Child, 2003; Child and Tsai, 2005; Dieleman and Sachs, 2008). More often, however, it is the collective actions of individuals and social entities that transform institutions (Aldrich, 2010). Particularly under conditions of institutional instability, organizational decisions about control and product strategies will affect population-level conditions like the specific control, competitive, and exchange structures in particular nations or segments of their economies (Suhomlinova, 2006). The potential for entrepreneurs to influence system-level changes is greater during crises when current institutions are incapable of resolving emerging issues (Seo and Creed, 2002; Dorado, 2005). A good example of such potential is the wave of privatizations that took place after the 1980s in Latin America. Not until hyperinflation and social instability hit the region did entrepreneurs manage to expand to new areas of the economy, transforming previously inefficient government enterprises into money-making operations.

We have previously noted the tendency in organization theory for scholars to privilege managerial and entrepreneurial intentionality as a causal force. However, for evolution to occur, it is not necessary that entrepreneurs *intend* to affect their environments. Within the daily life of organizations, in the normal processes of creating new strategies and structures, entrepreneurs affect the allocation and effective use of resources. Similarly, the actions of entrepreneurs affect environments in many ways, only some of which were intended. Indeed, environmental conditions often result from the unintended consequences of entrepreneurial action. For example, organizations in some populations move collectively from one resource space (or market segment) to another, affecting resource availability both in the original and the destination spaces, undermining the intended competitive advantage that originated the move (Dobrev, 2007).

BARRIERS TO ORGANIZATIONAL ADAPTATION

Key debates in the area of evolution center on adaptation and the extent to which it is likely or even possible for organizations. The old paradigm in evolutionary theory favored the study of selection forces because theorists considered adaptation, for good reasons, a complicated process fraught with problems. We note four salient issues: (1) the impact of increasing globalization on entrepreneurs' abilities to understand their environments; (2) the increasing complexity of technologies; (3) institutionalized rigidities inside organizations; and (4) path dependence that constrains organizational autonomy.

First, in a globalized economy, organizations face diverse and often conflicting institutional requirements. Globalization often increases uncertainty because the decentralized nature of cross-national environments means organizations and subsidiaries are affected by contradictory institutional regimes (Cantwell et al., 2010). Adaptation is difficult because individual firms have relatively limited resources, compared to the typically massive task of affecting environments. Even if resources for action were not a problem, information deficiencies would still hinder entrepreneurial control. Environmental complexity constrains entrepreneurs and managers from using their past experiences to predict the future (North, 2005).

Second, increasing complexity in technologies has made certain features of environments nearly impossible for entrepreneurs to quantify (Nelson, 2005). One example of both complexity and lack of information is the recent crisis in financial markets. Despite incredible financial and informational resources, most investors failed to predict the devastation in the housing market, caused by what was supposed to be a routine adjustment of interest rates by the Federal Reserve. The mathematical tools used to create housing derivatives were too complicated for even the most sophisticated investors to understand and apply to assessing risk.

Rational manipulation of environments may be impossible under causal ambiguity, a condition in which neither a firm nor its competitors can determine the causes of its successful performance. Because the actual causes of good performances are unknown, there is no specific strategy to be selected, reproduced inside organizations, or imitated by rivals (Powell et al., 2006). For example, did a new customer service strategy succeed because it reduced customers' waiting times, selected better trained service workers, or made competitors' services look inferior by comparison?

Third, adaptation is difficult not only because of the characteristics of environments but also because entrepreneurs face barriers to change originating in organizations themselves, particularly institutional constraints created by structure and culture. Some scholars even argue that the tasks of organizing and working within an organization are inherently in opposition to innovation and change (Weick and Westley, 1996). Institutions are collections of stable rules and roles with corresponding set of meanings that constrain suitable actions (Czarniawska, 2008b), leading humans to select activities based on their appropriateness, rather than on pragmatic or instrumental criteria (Biggart and Beamish, 2003).

Institutional theorists see organizations as self-reproducing institutionalized social structures in which myth and ceremony often take precedence over efficiency considerations (Meyer and Rowan, 1977). Government and educational institutions encourage and even mandate the use of certain procedures, and many organizations find it cheaper and more efficient to imitate others rather than to independently evaluate environmental forces and develop ad hoc strategies (DiMaggio and Powell, 1983). For example, rather than attempt to assess their own risk of discrimination lawsuits and craft firm-specific policies, many organizations simply imitate industry-standard procedures in their human resource departments.

Many researchers doubt that entrepreneurs and managers can act independently and creatively in the face of such constraints on their comprehension and behavior (Emirbayer and Mische, 1998). An ability to learn valuable behaviors so thoroughly that they become automatic gives humans a great advantage in routine situations (Aldrich, 2009), but creates a disadvantage in rapidly changing environments. Thus, the same mechanisms that facilitate the retention of successful variations, such as an emphasis on keeping and following properly documented procedures, discourage further innovation.

Fourth, from an evolutionary perspective, structure and culture are the products of prior selection processes, having co-evolved with previous environments. However, past environments may have differed greatly from current conditions. Successful adaptation to a particular environment often produces *path dependency*, a process in which a successful strategy or structure that fit past environments later becomes self-reproducing, possibly leading to a lack of fit with current environments. Path dependency has multiple causes, such as escalating commitment to favored strategies, institutional pressures, unquestioned routine, and other forms of structural inertia (Sydow et al., 2009). For example, IBM failed to recognize that profits and value added for computer products were shifting from hardware into software, and therefore failed to foresee that trying to dominate the hardware part of the industry would result in stagnation. A break from the past by diversifying into software potentially would have brought better results.

Evolutionary theorists argue that path dependency and general resistance to change typically undermine organizational survival (Miller, 1982). Although the past may offer lessons on how to deal with the current environment, "management" implies an orientation toward the future. Entrepreneurial intentionality involves not just reacting to current environmental changes, but trying to anticipate future ones. Therefore, aggressive entrepreneurs often create variations and select those they believe appropriate for an imagined but as yet unrealized future. In effect, entrepreneurs try to anticipate the effects of environmental forces and pre-empt them. From this viewpoint, environments provide stimuli and substance for internal reflections on possible improvements; entrepreneurs take this feedback and transform it into internal selection mechanisms (Zollo and Winter, 2002). But, because they lack clairvoyance, anticipating the future is a hit-or-miss endeavor.

VARIATION AND ADAPTATION IN EVOLUTIONARY THEORY

Given all the mechanisms and pressures for conformity and social repro-duction, we might question whether change and adaptation can occur at all. Environments and the selection forces they embody are extremely complex and institutional demands on organizations tend to be frag-mented, contradictory, and ambiguous. Theorists proposing that adaptive changes are possible even under these conditions note that chaotic envir-onments can provide organizations and their entrepreneurs with spaces for innovation and change (Scott, 2008). *Exogenous* changes come from shocks and jolts and from invasions of "foreign" ideas from other popula-tions and communities. *Endogenous* changes come from conflicts between elements of the environment and organizations' failures to achieve their claimed goals.

Scott (2008) argued that complex environments often not only con-strain organizations but also provide resources for creativity and innova-tion. Aldrich and Ruef (2006) identified a number of ways in which this might happen. Political turbulence can disrupt ties between established organizations and resources, rearranging organizational boundaries and freeing resources for use by new organizations. For example, every time the Chinese government enters into conflicts with Western countries, it reduces quotas or stops altogether the exporting of rare earths, which are metals used in the manufacturing of electronics such as cell phones and some green products. Such disruptions in resources have motivated mining companies to look for rare earths in other parts of the globe and have provided opportunities for Chinese manufacturers to expand their product offerings.

Government initiatives can be a strong external stimulus for many organizations, populations and communities. Regulation and deregula-tion significantly change the institutional context, affecting the type of product or services organizations can offer as well as their internal pro-cedures. Direct government support can encourage the creation of new organizations through enhanced legitimacy via the symbolic consequences of governmental action, as well as through direct subsidy (Schneiberg, 2005). The green energy industry is a clear example of such government actions. New regulations regarding fossil fuels have increased the viability of green technologies, even those that were supposedly moribund, such as the electric car. Green technologies have received direct government support from tax deductions and direct investments and have benefitted from governments giving them a prominent place in public policies. Finally, macroeconomic policies, by affecting unemployment levels and the availability of credit, can also force organizations to develop new strategies (Aldrich, 2010).

When exploring the prospects for adaptive change, we must distinguish between entrepreneurs and the managers of already established firms. Entrepreneurs are subject to environmental pressures coming from institutions in two ways. First, institutions structure the context within which entrepreneurs learn about entrepreneurship, search for resources, build their new ventures, and benefit from their efforts. Norms and values influence nascent entrepreneurs' understandings of current conditions and help shape the way in which entrepreneurial ambitions are expressed, toward traditional lines of action or toward actions that challenge the status quo.

Second, institutions provide the cultural resources with which entrepreneurs, public policy makers, investors, and others interpret the meaning of entrepreneurship. Entrepreneurs interpret opportunities while embedded in a system of cultural understandings, drawing upon and conditioned by their (learned) habitual responses to the situations they encounter (Aldrich, 2010). The roughly 7 000 000 US startup attempts per year involving around 12 million people over the past decade are a strong source of change and variation (Reynolds and Curtin, 2007).

Entrepreneurs use many "social mechanisms" as they create new ventures, encountering problem situations and drawing upon social practices from related and unrelated areas of social life to solve the problems (Gross, 2009). Changing norms and values shape and alter the construction of entrepreneurial identities, entrepreneurial intentions, and the willingness of resource providers to support new ventures. For example, in their analysis of the emergence of the wind power industry, Sine and Lee (2009) showed that at the state level, changing attitudes about the environment motivated some entrepreneurs to create new firms for ideological reasons, reflecting the new cultural schema. Their actions and resulting socio-cultural changes, in turn, opened up opportunities to entrepreneurs who were not ideologically motivated and thus not subject to the same cultural constraints. In contrast, ethnic enclaves push entrepreneurs to develop organizations that are very similar to those already existing in the community and in general discourage innovation (Waldinger et al., 1990).

Entrepreneurs are different from managers in that they lack the support of already established organizations with sizable resources; they often have to make do with whatever they have (Baker et al., 2003; Baker and Nelson, 2005). Scarcity and uncertainty force change. Because they lack resources, entrepreneurs need to come up with solutions that differ from existing practices. Most new ventures are home-based, involve little or no outside funding, and face daunting challenges getting started. While such dire circumstances may feel like disadvantages at the individual level, from an evolutionary perspective they are a potential source for change.

Entrepreneurs also differ from managers in that their activities are less organized and planned. At least in theory, managers have highly codified job descriptions and tasks they need to perform, as well as clear goals. In contrast, the activities of entrepreneurs tend to be more chaotic, ambiguous, and unplanned. Few new ventures have business plans, and even those with plans use them only to attract potential investors, rather than as blueprints for their operations (Honig and Karlsson, 2004). Because of this lack of structure, entrepreneurs have more space for spur of the moment innovations.

Can managers in already existing organizations be as adaptive as entrepreneurs? Management science at least indicates that they should try. Given the tendency of organizations toward path dependency and their need to respond to environmental demands, theorists in strategic management have emphasized that managers need to develop their firms' capacities to deal with current business demands while simultaneously being adaptive to environmental changes. This dual focus is called "ambidexterity" (Raisch and Birkinshaw, 2008).

Ambidexterity implies equal abilities to exploit current competencies by learning via refining already existing knowledge *and* exploring new business opportunities found through experimentation, play, and intentional variation (March, 1991; Baum et al., 2000; Schindehutte and Morris, 2009; Simsek, 2009). Ambidexterity can be accomplished through having a dual structure wherein some units engage in exploration and others in exploitation (Tushman and O'Reilly, 1996), or by creating an organizational culture that encourages individuals (either managers or employees in general) to divide their time between exploration and exploitation (Burgelman, 2002; Gibson and Birkinshaw, 2004). Proponents claim that ambidextrous organizations can successfully pursue both incremental changes and discontinuous or disruptive ones (Smith and Tushman, 2005). Empirical studies on the actual performance benefits of ambidexterity have been contradictory (Simsek, 2009), with some studies finding higher performance outcomes (He and Wong, 2004; Lubatkin et al., 2006), some finding that benefits are contingent (Lin et al., 2007), and others finding no effect at all (Atuahene-Gima, 2005).

COGNITION, IDENTITY AND EVOLUTIONARY CHANGE

Evolutionary theorizing, drawing upon modern cognitive psychology, posits humans who are myopic and error prone. They are embedded in organizational contexts limiting their cognitive abilities and their awareness (Small, 2009). Thus, understanding adaptation and evolution requires that entrepreneurship scholars pay special attention to humans' cognitive abilities. Researchers studying organizational strategy and cognition often start with the assumption that environments are "invented" by entrepreneurs when they select particular modes of interpretation (Starbuck, 1976; Luksha, 2008). From an evolutionary perspective, it is more precise to say that entrepreneurs do not respond to "objective" environments, but rather to their interpretations of them, which are constructed through a process of collective action or enactment (Smircich and Stubbart, 1985). If entrepreneurs are to receive full credit for adapting to changing environments, researchers must show that entrepreneurs recognize that change is necessary, are willing and committed to mobilizing resources to make change possible, and are then capable of interpreting the outcomes of such mobilization to evaluate whether the adaptation effort was successful (Huy, 1999).

A vast literature exists on managerial cognition. For the purposes of this chapter, we will only mention three issues that directly affect entrepreneurship: (1) entrepreneurs' capacities for recognizing the extent to which their environments can be analysed; (2) the link between goals and environmental risk assessments; and (3) the role of organizational identity in entrepreneurs' positioning of their organizations.

First, entrepreneurs' most important cognitive filters affect how they evaluate the degree of analysability of their environments (Daft and Weick, 1984). One could argue that causal ambiguity is not a characteristic of environments per se, but rather entrepreneurs' judgments regarding their capacities to find causes for organizational success or failure. Environments might look opaque to entrepreneurs simply because they lack cognitive abilities to recognize their diverse dimensions and how they are linked. To entrepreneurs without relevant cognitive schemata, markets based in "social media" may appear merely confusing, rather than presenting an opportunity for their firms to enter a new market niche.

Cognitive psychology tells us that once a successful action has taken place, entrepreneurs cling to the illusion of perfect control, creating explanations for successful outcomes related to the resources they control and feeling totally responsible for the outcomes that emerge. It is unlikely they will attribute their success to the favorable local, state, and national infra-structures that support their efforts, although they would no doubt nod in recognition, were these factors described to them (Aldrich, 2010). These post-facto rationalizations may affect future decision-making.

Second, goals and aspirations heavily influence the criteria entrepreneurs use to evaluate their environments. Entrepreneurs pay sequential attention to multiple goals and apply aspiration levels to each goal, with aspiration levels usually created through social comparisons (Greve, 2008). Most companies determine their aspirations by using "industry leaders" as a basis for setting performance goals. These aspirations then affect evaluations of feedback from actions taken in particular environments. Risk calculations involved in innovation decisions are heavily affected by aspirations and by the level of organizational resources. For example, studies show that managers in larger firms with ample resources perceive strategies as less risky than managers in smaller organizations (Audia and Greve, 2006). When making decisions to enter particular markets, entrepreneurs and managers do not necessarily take into consideration the state of current resources but rather their expectations concerning future ones. This principle explains why the founding of new organizations continues in mature industries, even though their markets would seem to be saturated (Lomi et al., 2010). When nascent entrepreneurs perceive higher risk, they are less likely to found firms with novel technologies (Sine et al., 2005), choosing instead to enter older industries.

Third, the concept of "identity" links entrepreneurial cognitions to the cultures and structures of organizations. Entrepreneurs' priorities and agendas depend on how an "organization" is defined. Using a "cultural codes" definition of organizational form (Aldrich and Ruef, 2006), an organizational identity consists of social codes or sets of rules specifying the features that the organization is supposed to possess (Pólos et al., 2002). Note that we did not say "how an organization defines itself." From an evolutionary perspective, identity is socially created because it arises from the interplay between organizations and their environments. Key audiences have expectations regarding the features and actions of a particular firm, and although a firm can violate those expectations, doing so can have negative consequences (Phillips and Zuckerman, 2001; Hsu and Hannan, 2005). For example, the identity of higher education institutions has been highly associated with public service and not-for-profit motives. However, a new set of for profit institutions has expanded rapidly in the

United States in the last few decades, such as the University of Phoenix. These for-profit universities have become the target of government investigations that accuse them of recruiting students by creating false expectations about the likelihood of earning degrees. Not-for-profit universities that conform to the traditional identity of a university, by contrast, have mostly escaped challenges.

The identity of individual firms stems, to some extent, from the identity of their particular populations. Historically, from the viewpoint of organizational ecology, populations were defined as collections of organizations with a common organizational form that share a geographical space at a particular point in time (Hannan and Freeman, 1977). However, the characteristics that distinguish one organizational form from another have been the subject of intense theoretical and empirical debate in recent evolutionary thinking. Earlier in population ecology research, organizational forms were practically defined as industries, industrial niches and specific types of products or markets (Carroll and Hannan, 1989). However, more recent evolutionary thinking accepts that populations are also socially defined.

Categories of organizations become organizational forms when they are recognized by social actors and achieve a taken for granted status (Hsu and Hannan, 2005). Individual firm identities are formed first by membership in specific populations and later by positions occupied within that population. Although this thinking has not been applied to organizational communities, we argue that it can be: communities are defined by a mixture of geographic proximity and audience recognition. Identities vary in their degree of flexibility and specificity, providing different "spaces" for managerial action (Zuckerman et al., 2003). Identity is not only a constraint and a motivation for action, but also a goal in itself. Meyer (2008) noted that in an expanding and globalizing world society, people and groups everywhere seem to be eager to be actors – this often takes precedence over other goals, and can produce assertions of actor identity far from any actual actor capability. In short, people inside organizations sometimes act not for the preservation of the material existence of the organization, but for the preservation of a positive and commonly accepted identity. This preservation may obstruct changes necessary for survival.

Overall, studies of cognition and identity offer a world of both structural constraint and agency. Some forces limit entrepreneurs' capacity for change, but others facilitate and even promote innovation. Entrepreneurs often inhabit a world of chaos, where intentions and results are not the same. Furthermore, even when action takes place, it may stem not from a reasoned assessment of organizational needs and capabilities but rather from a hasty response to external conditions that have been misinterpreted. Evolutionary theory teaches us that environmental signals are often filtered through socio-psychological needs.

EVOLUTIONARY RESEARCH METHODOLOGY

No description of evolutionary theory would be complete without considering the methodological advances and needs of the approach. For an empirical study to be evolutionary, it must meet certain conditions. First, to obtain unbiased conclusions about the fit between environmental forces and entrepreneurial strategies, researchers need to include not only survivors but also organizing attempts that failed to adapt to environmental demands. Second, several levels of analysis need to be included: entrepreneurs, groups, organizations, populations, and communities. Third, the logic of causality needs to be recursive. Evolutionary models posit a two-way causal street: complex entities can emerge from simpler entities, but with the range of possible emergent developments constrained by higher-order structures (Dennett, 1995). Therefore, to avoid selection bias, statistical tests of evolutionary theories require the collection and analysis of time series data (Volberda and Lewin, 2003) that includes both surviving and defunct organizations (Martinez et al., 2011). Only with time series data can researchers model the complex causal relationships created by the mutual feedback of organizational action and environmental response. Evolutionary studies need to include the historical contexts of firms and models of multilevel relationships between organizations and their nested environments (populations and communities).

We want to explore a little bit more the issue of the measurement of context. Earlier in this chapter, we explained the criteria used to evaluate the fit between environmental conditions and routines, strategies, and structures. Despite environments being theoretically central in an evolutionary theory of organizations, we believe that scholars have under-measured and under-theorized actual environmental contexts. In many studies, investigators implicitly introduce context through theories of "time" and "space." In turn, embedded in "time" and "space" are specific environmental conditions such as culture, resource constraints, political environments, and stages of economic development (Aldrich, 2009). These conditions should be systematically analysed, categorized and measured. Such systematic analysis provides accurate measurements of environmental forces and their relationship to specific organizational strategies (Martinez et al., 2011)

Within organizational science, the study of entrepreneurship has made great progress in generating the type of data that can test relationships between entrepreneurial activities and environmental conditions. Advances have been especially strong with regard to the study of firm creation and the workings of new firms. Through projects such as the Panel Study of Entrepreneurial Dynamics (PSED) carried out in the United States and the multi-national Global Entrepreneurship Monitor (GEM), a diverse team of researchers has advanced the measurement of environmental forces and made it possible for scholars to test evolutionary propositions (Reynolds et al., 2005; Reynolds, 2007). The two large-scale quantitative projects, PSED and GEM, are closely related to each other; PSED is a study of US entrepreneurs that was used as a template for the GEM surveys. We believe that the PSED data sets represent advances in the dynamic analysis of entrepreneurial processes, whereas the mostly cross-sectional GEM data sets represent advances in spatial but not dynamic analysis.

Both PSED and GEM solved the potential problem of selecting only successful entrepreneurs by using random samples of adult populations in each participant country. In terms of time-related changes in contexts, PSED offers the most advantages. PSED comprises two separate longitudinal projects, with the first enacted in 1998–2000 (PSED I) with the original screening of 64 000 adults to locate 830 nascent entrepreneurs. PSED II was begun in 2005–06 with a new sample involving the screening of 31 000 adults for a final sample of 1214 nascent entrepreneurs (Reynolds and Curtin, 2007). The PSED project provides high quality data about the early stages of entrepreneurial activities. Unlike other datasets which primarily include registered firms in their samples, PSED I and PSED II track start-ups from the very beginning. They capture the initial moments when nascent entrepreneurs began their activities, such as planning, searching for funding, making marketing, and so on. By following start-ups for more than 3 years, PSED allows researchers to use advanced statistical techniques to analyse the start-up transition process.

In terms of investigating space-related contexts, PSED includes environmental forces at both the micro and macro levels. At the micro level, PSED has information on entrepreneurs' family contexts, community characteristics, the availability of start-ups' local consumers, the development stage of their technology, the existence of other similar companies in their area, etc. At this micro level, PSED measures environmental forces using the perceptions of individuals about the cultural and competitive forces affecting them, and it also includes regional objective measures of population and urbanization levels (Reynolds, 2007).

GEM surveys started in 1999 with the participation of ten countries and that number grew to 54 participant nations by 2009, its latest data collection effort. GEM data from different countries are harmonized and put into a master database so that investigators can study different stages of entrepreneurial processes across countries. GEM merges individual level data with "objective" measures on environments obtained from standardized international data sources like the OECD, World Bank, United Nations, ILO, and others. GEM also includes National Experts Surveys designed to provide standardized scales of national cultural and societal conditions for entrepreneurship (Reynolds et al., 2005).

CONCLUSIONS

Over the past several decades, theorists and researchers have worked to refine an evolutionary paradigm capable of dealing with the complexity of entrepreneurship within modern organizations, populations, and communities. The initial evolutionary framework conceptualized environments and selection forces as all-powerful and argued that directed adaptation was a Herculean task. Since then, we have moved toward a more sophisticated approach. The new view balances the effects of agency and structure: evolutionary theory describes a world where environments create structural constraints for entrepreneurs and organizations, but also where the collective and accumulated actions of entrepreneurs within populations and communities are instrumental in creating environmental conditions.

For managers and entrepreneurs, adaptation to environmental conditions and radical transformations that challenge organizational history are improbable but not impossible. Environmental complexity, created by the dynamic interaction of economic, political, and social forces, creates opportunities for innovation and adaptation, driving evolution forward. In this world, managers and entrepreneurs have agency, but it is an agency limited by myopia and cognitive shortcomings. Humans process the feedback provided by their environments in ways that are distorted by organizational identity, goals, resources, and culture. Organizational identity, a key filter of environmental information, is both the result of intra-organizational dynamics and of the judgment of external audiences about an organization's identity, its place in its population and community and how it should behave. Cognitive distortions determine, at least partly, organizational assumptions about the analysability of the environment, risk levels, and the appropriateness of particular strategies and structures.

Despite these empirical and theoretical advances, several elements of evolutionary processes deserve further study. First, while we have made great advances in the study of cognitive filters and how they affect decision-making and adaptation processes, we need more research on how the external objective environment affects entrepreneurial evolution.

Cognition does not occur in a vacuum, but rather depends upon stimuli created by environments. Studying perception but ignoring the object that is being perceived is not sound science. The general propositions of resource dependence theory, one of the seminal theories in the evolutionary approach, have not translated into specific knowledge of how objective and social environments, in opposition to perceived environments, affect organization variation and selection. Perceptive entrepreneurs cannot ignore the reality of scarce resources.

Second, we need to continue developing a body of knowledge that can be applied to strategic management and entrepreneurial efforts. While the study of evolutionary processes is a worthwhile intellectual endeavor, if properly developed it can provide a tool for understanding the practical needs of businesses and entrepreneurs. Following its principles, we can help entrepreneurs adapt better to their environments. Although we understand general evolutionary processes, for practical applications to entrepreneurship we need to explore more specific issues and organizational areas where selection and adaptation processes may be taking place. Managers and entrepreneurs make a myriad of strategic decisions that are part of an evolutionary process, and we have just started to explore them.

Organizations are the fundamental building blocks of modern societies and studies of why and how they emerge are crucial for understanding the modern world. As we enter the second decade of the twenty-first century, entrepreneurs and organizations are remaking our world through collective action. We need encompassing schemes for understanding what is happening to us and for putting local actions and historical and global contexts. We think evolutionary theory can do that.

6 Organizations, entrepreneurship and ethics
Robert D. Hisrich and Claudine Kearney

INTRODUCTION

During the past several decades, the growing scholarly interest in entrepreneurs, entrepreneurship, corporate entrepreneurship, social entrepreneurship and new business creation has resulted in the shaping of entrepreneurship as a fundamental academic field of study. Similarly, during the past 20 years, the field of business ethics including the study of ethical behavior and societal impact of profit-seeking firms has achieved recognition and legitimacy as a rigorous and important field of study. The intersection of entrepreneurship and ethics is now receiving much needed scholarly attention. This growing body of scholarly work highlights the applicability of one field of research to another. For example, scholars point out the importance of business ethics and social responsibility among managers (Fulop et al., 2000), entrepreneurial ethics to the global economy (e.g., Bucar and Hisrich, 2001), and cross-cultural differences in ethical attitudes of entrepreneurs (e.g., Bucar et al., 2003).

There has also been a move in business activities from national to global over the last decades. Studies have shown an increase in international joint venture activity over this period. The increasing number of businesses, the opening of new markets, intense competition, and the global financial crisis are all challenging organizations today. Since the first signs of the global economic downturn, which was associated with the international credit crunch, a recession in our major trading partners, rising energy costs, adverse exchange rate movements, property crash, banking crisis, poor financial credit ratings and a severe deterioration in the construction sector, our world has been turned around. The moral and ethical corruption has been extreme and immeasurable. The recent global financial crisis has also been a crisis of trust (Duh et al., 2010). According to Garciá-Marzá (2005), trust is one of the organization's most important assets in that it enables cooperation, promotes network relationships, and facilitates effective responses to crises (Sundaramurthy, 2008). From the greedy and morally bankrupt people who have destroyed the public's trust in business to the inevitable revealing of public trading that includes unethical payoffs and vigorous back scratching. Now more than ever organizations need to take corrective action to overcome the difficulties occurring by developing an entrepreneurial spirit and ethical business practice. Understanding the factors that contribute to and influence the ethical conduct of entrepreneurs is important for the economic system of the world, particularly in the current economic climate. While businesses influence the ethical standards used in current business dealings, emerging entrepreneurial organizations set the ethical standards for the future economic system of the world (Bucar and Hisrich, 2001). Therefore, the organization's ethical behavior demands a conscious and positive attitude towards the organization's ethical codes, core values, and culture in a way that stimulates the desired achievement of business ethics and corporate social responsibility.

The purpose of this chapter is to provide an overview of ethics and the ethical practices of entrepreneurs and managers nationally and internationally in the current economic downturn, identifying opportunities for future research. We treat the entrepreneur as an individual who has founded, owns and manages the business and who created a new and different venture. Managers in corporations have authority to allocate resources but are not taking the same level of risk as entrepreneurs who founded the venture. This chapter is structured in the following manner. We review the literature on ethics and ethical business practices from a global perspective, with particular emphasis on codes of ethics, core values, corporate culture, and corporate social responsibility of entrepreneurs and managers in a dynamic and turbulent economic climate. We explore ethics and social responsibility of entrepreneurs and managers in the current economic climate.

ETHICS

Ethics refers to the *study of whatever is right and good for humans.* It can be defined as a set of principles prescribing a behavior code that explains what is right or wrong. Ethics is concerned with the study of morality: practices and activities that are considered to be a set of beliefs about right and wrong, together with the rules that govern those activities and the values to which those activities relate. Business ethics is concerned with clarifying what constitutes human welfare and the conduct necessary to promote it. It is based on moral standards: these are impartial, take precedence over self-interest and apply to everyone. Ethics is the broad field of study exploring the general nature of morals and the specific moral choices made by the individual in relationships with others. While business ethics has emerged as an important topic within academic publications in the past few decades, to date it has been treated ahistorically and with an orientation dominated by a North American perspective.

Although the English word *ethics* is generally recognized as stemming from the Greek *êthos,* meaning "custom and usage," it is more properly identified as originating from *swēdhêthos,* in which the concepts of individual morality and behavioral habits are related and identified as an essential quality of existence. Most Western authors credit the Greek philosophers Socrates (469–399 BC), Plato (427–347 BC), and Aristotle (384–322 BC) as providing the earliest writings upon which currently held ethical conceptions are based. Much earlier writings pertaining to moral codes and laws, however, can be found within both Judaism (1800 BC) and Hinduism (1500 BC). American attitudes on ethics result from three principal influences: the Judeo-Christian heritage, a belief in individualism, and opportunities based upon ability rather than social status. The United States was formed by immigrants from other countries, frequently fleeing oppression in their homelands, dedicated to creating a society where their future would be determined by their abilities and work.

Ethics guide people in dealings and taking appropriate actions with stakeholders, customers, communities and society. Cross-cultural ethical conflicts emerge when two parties differ in their ethical principles, reasoning processes or behaviors (Buller and Kohols, 1997). Literature in the field has focused increasingly on the ethical implications of transnational business operations from the perspective of the entrepreneur, the individual manager, the firm and the 'business system.' Ethics and values govern behaviors as values alone are not a sufficient basis for ethical analysis and reasoning by management. Where behaviors are guided by mutually agreed and accepted boundaries, behaviors outside the set boundaries will be deemed as "unacceptable" or "unethical." Whether behaviors are considered "unacceptable" or "unethical" is determined by the interpretation of the set boundary guidelines. However, while some behaviors are identified when the set boundary guidelines are breached, there are also behaviors that are more interpretative in nature, and cannot be clearly placed with respect to the boundary guidelines.

Ethical behavior is a precondition for an organization to achieve the status of highly credible and trustworthy, which ensures the organization's long-term success. Organizations should not just focus on profitability, but engage in actions that appear to develop some social good, beyond the interests of the organization and what is required by law (Lindgreen et al., 2008). An organization's ethical behavior demands a conscious and positive attitude from the organization's key stakeholders towards the organization's core values, culture and climate in a way that stimulates the desired achievement of business ethics (Bishop, 1991; Falkenberg and Herremans, 1995; Kaptein, 2002; Kaptein and Avelino, 2005; Mujtaba and Sims, 2006; Lindgreen et al., 2008; Belak, 2009). By operating ethically, a global venture will be in a better position to secure repeat business and make a profit, while also adding value to the customer. In doing so, the entrepreneur needs to ground the organizational culture in ethics and core values and ensure social responsibility in business practices.

CODES OF ETHICS, CORE VALUES, AND CORPORATE CULTURE

Organizations are influenced by the general environment of the society in which they operate. An organization cannot act in isolation in the marketplace. The way that an organization conducts its business activities impacts stakeholders and the wider community both internal and external to the organization. An organization's code of ethics and business value statement communicates expectations of how employees should behave in the work environment. Ethical codes refer to the standards and conduct that an organization practices in managing its internal environment and its dealings with the external environment. Such issues concern both large national and multi-national organizations such as Boston Consulting Group, Cisco, and Google, and small- and medium-sized enterprises (SMEs) such as Federal Express, Johnson and Johnson, 3M Ireland Limited, as well as public sector organizations such as civil services and universities. The importance of codes of ethics is that they: clarify the organizations' expectations of employees' behavior in various situations, and clarify what ethical codes the organization expects employees to comply with in their decisions and actions.

Most organizations accept that some form of ethical standards should govern and guide their activities. It is important to consider ethical standards in the development of the organization's core goals and objectives. Developing codes of ethics promotes ethical behavior. There are a number of advantages of implementing a code of ethics. The more employees are aware of the appropriate and expected conduct, the more likely they are to behave accordingly. They will develop a better understanding of their responsibilities and expectations and assume the appropriate level of accountability when identifying and managing business risks. A code of ethics is more than just a formal document outlining related policies. It is about integrating positive values throughout an organization. A code of ethics will not prevent every crisis, but it will ensure that employees have a clear understanding of what the organization expects. The entrepreneur or manager needs to collaborate with employees on defining the rules, regulations, policies and procedures, and make sure everyone is aware of the requirements. Following that, core business values must be instilled throughout the organization. Through frequent reinforcement, ethics will guide every decision made within the organization and become a central component in the way the organization carries out its business.

According to several authors (Morris et al., 2002; Garciá-Marzá, 2005; Belak, 2009), the ethical behavior of an organization is not possible without ethical core values, which significantly influence the development of the informal ethical structures (for example, communication on the ethical problems between entrepreneurs/managers and employees) and the development and implementation of the formal ethical structures and measures of business ethics implementation (for example, mission statement, policy manuals, training in ethics). In an organization, core values aim to convey a sense of identity to its members, enhance the stability of its social system, direct managers' attention to important issues, guide subsequent decisions by managers, and facilitate commitment to something larger than the self (Deal and Kennedy, 1982). The attitude of an organization towards the ethical core values influences the development of the ethical climate required for the organization's ethical behavior.

Entrepreneurs/managers need to ensure that the ethical standards and values that personnel exhibit in conducting business are in accordance with the organization's code of ethics and value statements. The ethical practices and values need to be fair, honest, and socially responsible. The entrepreneur and manager's reputation as well as the business reputation are influenced by ethics and organizational values. Conducting a business with integrity is just as important as bottom-line results. Ethical standards are applied anytime a decision is made or an action is taken, not just during controversial situations. In considering the ethical core values and ethical climate of an organization, the organization's culture defines the rules of ethical behavior for the development of the formal and informal measures of organization ethics implementation. The important relationship among the organization's culture, ethical climate and core values, will support the development of the informal and formal measures of implementing business ethics and will result in consistency among mission, vision, values, and culture – which is essential for the organization's long-term success (Morris et al., 2002; Garciá-Marzá, 2005; Belak, 2009).

Based on Hofstede's (1980) framework, many studies have illustrated culture has key associations between cultural values and societal outcomes. Many previous studies were conducted at the individual and country level, with few studies conducted at the group level. At country level, research issues mainly included organizational behavior, human resource management, international business studies, innovation, research and development, and societal outcomes (Bradley et al., 2006), few studies have focused on the ethical behaviors (for example, Husted, 1999, 2000, 2005). Revising a model initially proposed by Hunt and Vitell (1992), Vitell et al. (1993) provided a conceptual framework to examine how culture influences one's perceptions and ethical decision-making in business. To undertake this, they first used the cultural typology proposed by Hofstede (1980) and developed specific propositions relating Hofstede's cultural dimensions to informal and formal codes of behavior, the perception of ethical problems, the perception of the consequences of behavior, and the evaluation of the relative importance of stakeholders. The work of Vitell et al. (1993) has filled the gap in the conceptualization of business ethics relative to different influences. Furthermore, Carrol and Gannon (1997) developed a comprehensive model of the influence of culture on the ethical behaviors among managers. The origins of culture including history, resource, and geography determine the national cultures that are reflected on managerial values, beliefs, and practices. Through the primary (parenting, socialization, education, and religion) and secondary (laws, human resource management systems, and organizational culture) systems of cultural transmission, this affects the modal values and beliefs, as well as the ethical behaviors of entrepreneurs/ managers.

Organizational culture is a multifaceted construct and has been defined as encompassing the assumptions, beliefs, goals, knowledge and values shared by organizational members (Schwartz and Davis, 1981; Deal and Kennedy, 1982; Sathe, 1984; Schein, 1992). Numerous organizational cultural typologies have been identified; the most frequently cited are those of Schwartz and Davis (1981), Deal and Kennedy (1982), Sathe (1984), Cameron and Schein (1992), and Hofstede (2000). Thommen (2002) differentiates between strong and weak organizational cultures. An organization with a strong culture is one with a high level of values and high norms anchoring, a high level of agreement, as well as significant system and environment compatibility. Thommen (2002) referred to specific criteria to evaluate the strength of an organizational culture: (1) the level of anchoring, which demonstrates how much the values and norms are accepted by the co-workers; (2) the level of agreement, which defines the collective character of cultural norms and values; (3) system compatibility, which is the level of harmonization of organizational culture with all other systems of an organization; and (4) compatibility with the environment, so the organizational culture is developed in harmony with the culture of the environment in which the organization operates. Therefore, for organizations to be successful in a particular market there must be a match between the business practices to the culture of the particular market. Ohmae's

(1999) concept of "globalization" supports the view that where business practices conflict with local cultures, strategic successes are unlikely to happen.

A corporate culture that is grounded in ethical business practices is a vital ingredient for the long-term success of the organization. Failure to maintain an appropriate ethical culture and provide employees with appropriate models of ethical behavior can have a high cost for the organization (Monks and Minow, 1989). The ethical climate is most effective when members of the organization are internally motivated to behave ethically (Elango et al., 2010). The culture promoted by the entrepreneur is critical in accomplishing the appropriate ethical principles and core business values. The entrepreneur needs to assume the responsibility of determining what core competencies are needed to meet the goals and objectives of the business. Not only are the core competencies important, but the entrepreneur will need to consider the personality and character of each individual to create a viable organizational culture. Finding the most effective team and creating a positive corporate culture is a challenge for the entrepreneur but just as critical is having an innovative, marketable product.

Companies known for their ethical business practices make ethics a key element of their corporate culture. It is essential for organizations to be able to recognize and manage complex business ethics. This is the result of well-documented scandals, where the unethical behavior of leaders' had significant consequences for the organizations and their surroundings (Whitener et al., 1998; Gillespie and Dietz, 2009). The consequences of these scandals have resulted in loss of trust and credibility among employees, customers, clients, and the general public. Well-known scandals include: the questionable accounting practices at Enron and Arthur Anderson; lack of accountability at American International Group (AIG) in connection with the subprime mortgage collapse; and the Coca-Cola Company's struggles with ethical crises (Toffler and Reingold, 2004; Ferrell et al., 2008). Due to these scandals, the general public has demanded improved business ethics and greater corporate social responsibility. Avoiding the pitfalls of unethical behavior and establishing an ethical climate within the firm requires an ethical infrastructure of both formal and informal influences that control unethical behavior and promote ethical behavior (Weaver et al., 1999).

An organization's code of ethics and value statements are of significant importance and are ingrained in the organizational culture. An organization that is committed to putting its ethical principles and core business values into practice generates a work environment where personnel share common beliefs about how the business is to be conducted and how they are expected to behave in accordance with the stated ethical principles and core values. When an organization promotes behaviors that are congruent with ethical principles and core values, those ethical principles and core values nurture the corporate culture by: communicating and validating the integrity of the organization and directing personnel to do the right thing and act in a socially responsible manner. Organizations communicate their ethical principles and core value statements in annual reports to stakeholders, on their website, as part of their mission statement, and in both direct and indirect communication with employees. Organizations that are genuinely committed to ethical standards and core business values ingrain ethical behavior as a core component of their corporate culture. All personnel are expected to comply with the organization's ethical standards and value statements; failure to do so would have implications and repercussions for their role in the organization.

CORPORATE SOCIAL RESPONSIBILITY

Social responsibility is the implied, enforced, or felt obligation of entrepreneurs/managers, acting in their official capacity, to serve or protect the interests of groups other than themselves. Social responsibility requires entrepreneurs/managers to determine what is right or wrong and to make ethical decisions that nurture, protect, promote, and enhance the welfare of stakeholders and society. A socially responsible organization places a major consideration on *ethics*, focuses on the *ends*, emphasizes *obligation*, and their decision framework is *long-term* orientated. Corporate social responsibility (CSR) is concerned with the specific ethical issues facing private and public sector corporations. It means that an organization should be held accountable for any of its actions that affect stakeholders, employees, their communities, and their environment. Carroll and Buchholtz offer a four-part definition of corporate social responsibility, "the social responsibility of business encompasses the economic, legal, ethical, and discretionary (philanthropic) expectations that society has of organizations at a given point in time (2006: 35)." Their definition demonstrates current thinking on corporate social responsibility and recognizes the need to take account of changes in social environment, these may be social, legal, or political. It also reflects the degree to which an organization should move beyond the minimum obligations specified through laws, regulations and policies and how the diverse demands of stakeholders should be managed.

CSR has become one of the most distinguished topics in discussing business ethics. Particularly in Europe, political bodies such as the

European Commission have become prominent drivers for CSR. The American perspective of CSR, despite economic and legal obligations, mainly focuses on "ethical responsibility" and "corporate philanthropy" (Carroll, 1979, 1998), in most European countries with developed welfare systems, such responsibilities are primarily seen as governmental tasks (Matten and Moon, 2008). The European Commission (2001) provided a widely accepted definition of CSR that concentrates on two different aspects of corporate responsibility: as a management tool CSR should guarantee that CSR-relevant aspects become part of corporations' day-to-day business and are integrated into their governance structures. Therefore, CSR needs to ensure that corporate policies and procedures are in line with commonly accepted ethical standards and respect stake-holders' rights "in areas such as working conditions, the environment or human rights" (European Commission, 2001: 17). In a political context, CSR describes voluntary corporate engagement for an improved society and a cleaner environment. Therefore, corporations should not only contribute to economic welfare by providing appropriate products and services, paying taxes and offering secure workplaces, but they should also engage with society as good corporate citizens by undertaking additional responsibilities (Aßländer, 2011).

It is difficult to identify clear distinctions between terms such as "Corporate Responsiveness", "Corporate Citizenship", "Corporate Responsibility", "Corporate Accountability", and "Corporate Sustainability". Scholars integrate Corporate Citizenship into the concept of CSR (e.g., Leisinger, 2007, 2009). However, it has been argued that CSR should be seen as part of the broader term Corporate Citizenship, which also includes corporate social responsiveness and corporate social performance, therefore describing the broad range of social responsibility issues (Buchholtz and Carroll, 2009). For several years, many organizations have been cautiously developing policies and practices of good corporate citizenship, demonstrating to stakeholders, shareholders, politicians, and customers that it is not only socially, morally, and environmentally "right" for an organization to be a good corporate citizen, but that it also makes good business sense. Increasingly, an organization's focus in this area has been the formal development of an organization ethos of behavior, frequently expressed in the form of a code of conduct.

While codes of conduct have been in practice for many decades, more and more organizations are now including some form of commitment to corporate citizenship within them. Strong emphasis and implementation of codes of ethics and value statements alone are not sufficient in making an organization a good corporate citizen. Strong ethical practices and CSR need to be part of decisions that affect employees, stakeholders, the communities in which they operate, and society. Business thinking must be ethical because no amount of codes of conduct or legislation will generate greater integrity or more ethical behavior. Thinking ethically is fundamental to the development of good corporate citizenship. The successful code of ethical practices and corporate social responsibility of national and international business activities can mean the difference between profits versus losses in business transactions.

Entrepreneurs/managers who want their organizations to be recognized for their outstanding behavior are not only focused on the codes of ethics and core business values but are socially responsible in their decision-making strategies that affect all stakeholders. Social responsibility is demonstrated by complying with the appropriate laws and regulations in all business practices; having a safe work environment; protecting the environment; actively engaging in community affairs; support charities and projects that benefit society. For example, Toys 'R' Us supports initiatives addressing the issues of child labor and fair labor practices worldwide. Proactive entrepreneurs/managers actively embrace the need to behave in socially responsible ways, act appropriately to learn about the needs, wants, and expectations of different stakeholder groups, and willingly utilize organizational resources to promote and protect the interests of stakeholders, employees, communities and society in general. Hewlett-Packard, Johnson & Johnson, McDonalds, The Body Shop, and WalMart are multinational corporations that are at the forefront of campaigns for causes such as, recycling and resource preservation, avoiding the use of animals in drug or cosmetic testing, pollution-free environment, and reducing crime and poverty. Organizations with socially conscious entrepreneurs/managers and core values of ethical practices and business value statements are more likely to undertake business transactions in an ethical and socially responsible manner that benefits stakeholders and society.

ETHICS AND CORPORATE SOCIAL RESPONSIBILITY OF ENTREPRENEURS AND MANAGERS

It is inevitable that there cannot be ethically and socially responsible organizations without ethical and socially responsible entrepreneurs/ managers who are at times willing to sacrifice organizational objectives, interests, profit and the needs of the organization as well as their personal needs in favor of ethically and socially responsible actions. It is the entrepreneurs/managers who are responsible for developing interest in ethics and social responsibility throughout the organization and determine the most effective way to integrate these as part of the organizational strategy.

Understanding the key factors that contribute to and influence the ethical conduct and social responsibility of entrepreneurs and managers is important for the future of both the national and international economic system. Existing businesses influence the ethical standards adopted in current business transactions. Entrepreneurs live within different contexts and environments, and think differently, from managers. In examining the differences in ethical and social responsibility attitudes and behaviors between entrepreneurs and managers, it is important to understand the characteristics of the two groups. Chandler (1962) distinguished entrepreneurial and managerial roles. The entrepreneur has the ability to work out long-term general strategies and the power to allocate the necessary resources to achieve the desired goals and objectives. The power stems from the equity owned by the entrepreneur. Managerial roles are exercised through control of finance, personnel, organization, research, and information in an organization.

In a review of ten previous studies of personality characteristics of entrepreneurs and business managers, Ginsberg and Buchholtz (1989) found that these studies characterize an entrepreneur as someone who is a founder, owner and manager of a business and who creates a new and different venture. While entrepreneurs assume financial, psychic, and social risks and receive the resulting rewards of monetary and personal satisfaction and independence (Hisrich et al., 2010), managers have the authority to allocate the resources but are not taking the same risks. Specifically, financial risks assumed by managers are not of the same type and degree as the ones assumed by entrepreneurs. Entrepreneurs, more often than managers, obtain loans that are secured by their personal property and risk losing a large part of their personal wealth. Managers, on the other hand, only assume limited liability for the operations of the organization.

An entrepreneur takes risks with his or her own capital in order to sell and deliver products and services while expending significant effort to innovate. In the face of daily stressful situations and other difficulties, the possibility exists that the entrepreneur will establish a balance between ethical exigencies, economic expediency and social responsibility, a balance that differs from where the general business manager takes his or her moral stance. As distinct from corporate managers, researching entrepreneurs provide an opportunity for understanding ethics on an individual rather than collective basis. Entrepreneurs have been found to be more sensitive to the expectations of society and more critical of their performance (Humphreys et al., 1993). Entrepreneurs with a relatively new company who have few role models usually develop an internal ethical code. Entrepreneurs tend to depend on their own personal value systems more than managers when determining ethically appropriate courses of action. Drawing more on their own value system, entrepreneurs have been shown to be particularly sensitive to peer pressure and general social norms in the community, as well as pressures from their competitors. Entrepreneurs usually do not face the issue of the separation of ownership and control. Often, entrepreneurs are the founders and have a significant ownership position in their company. Unethical behavior in their organization would present an internal contradiction. As owner–managers, entrepreneurs could employ their personal values to a much greater extent than managers within large businesses (Humphreys et al., 1993), since they are not constrained by the structure of corporate organizations.

The ethical views of managers within large corporations are affected by a complex interaction between the manager's personal value system and that of senior management, frequently resulting in a manager's ethical decisions being influenced by considerations other than their personal value systems (Jackall, 1988). A manager's attitudes concerning corporate responsibility are related to the organizational climate perceived to be supportive of laws and professional codes of ethics. The differences between entrepreneurs in different types of communities and in different countries reflect, to some extent, the general norms and values of the communities and countries involved. This is the case for metropolitan as opposed to nonmetropolitan locations within a country. Internationally, there is evidence to this concerning managers in general. US managers seem to have more individualistic values than their German and Austrian counterparts.

In assessing the causes of the current economic crisis there is an indication that they include not only techno-economic aspects, but also behavioral, moral, and cultural aspects, all of which are closely interrelated. While large-scale failure of regulation and government policy can be found in the origin of the crisis, there is also negligence and greed among the different actors empowered in the process. For the entrepreneur, access to finance is one of the most significant challenges for the creation, survival, and growth of their business. The problem is exacerbated further by the current financial crisis as entrepreneurs have suffered as a result of a drastic drop in demand for goods and services and a tightening in credit terms, which are severely affecting their cash flows. While managers are not owners they are strongly affected by the crisis, large corporations do not have access to the same funds, or the number of clients prior to 2008. The economic crisis not only presents an immediate challenge that has to be managed but also provides an opportunity to address long-term problems. Entrepreneurs/managers need to rethink their strategies and behaviors when dealing with customers and clients. Both entrepreneurs

Table 6.1   Distinguishing ethics and social responsibility in entrepreneurial organizations from traditional management organizations

Entrepreneurial Organizations	Traditional Management Organizations
Founder, owner, and manager, assumes responsibility for the business operations	Assumes limited liability for the business operations
Establishes a balance between ethical exigencies, economic expediency, and social responsibility	More compliant with the organizational ethical codes of conduct
More sensitive to the expectations of society particularly peer pressure and general social norms in the community, as well as pressures from their competitors	More focused on the expectations of the organization
Ethical views are dependent on their own personal value systems. Entrepreneurs are more prone to hold ethical attitudes	Managers need to sacrifice their personal values to those of the organization. Ethical views are affected by complex interaction between the manager's personal value system and senior management
Entrepreneurs' ethical decisions are influenced by their personal value systems and assume greater personal responsibility for the outcomes	Manager's ethical decisions are influenced by considerations other than their personal value systems
Entrepreneurs with a relatively new organization who have few role models generally develop an internal ethical code	Manager's attitudes concerning corporate social responsibility are related to the organizational climate perceived to be supportive of laws and professional codes of ethics

and managers are professionals, with skills and a strong sense of accountability and responsibility. In facing the crisis both entrepreneurs/managers need to reflect on the lessons they can learn from such a situation and ensure ethical and socially responsible business practices that are transparent.

BUSINESS ETHICS: A GLOBAL PERSPECTIVE

"Business ethics is concerned with good and bad or right and wrong behavior and practices that take place within a business context" (Carroll and Buchholtz, 2006: 242). The significant increase in the number of internationally oriented businesses has impacted the increased interest in the similarities and differences in business attitudes and practices in different countries. An important aspect of business ethics in the context of globalization is represented by expectations toward "responsible" or "ethical" behavior, despite the existence of different cultural and societal standards. Cross-cultural studies are critical to understand the diversity in the perceptions of business ethics in different countries. This area has been explored to some extent within the context of culture and is now beginning to be explored within the more individualized concept of ethics.[1]

An entrepreneur/manager must consider how to conduct business in an ethical manner throughout all parts of the organization's operations. By operating ethically, the venture will be better able to secure repeat business and make a profit, while also adding value to the consumer. Consumers want to have a clear conscience about the type of company that their purchases support and knowing that a company has high ethical standards and core business values guarantees this peace of mind.

Ethics are the principles that guide an entrepreneur's/manager's decision-making and should be based on three basic values: *integrity*, *transparency*, and *accountability*. Integrity requires the entrepreneur/manager to conduct all operations and transactions with honesty and respect for the law, including refraining from bribery and other forms of corruption. Transparency demands that the entrepreneur/manager undertakes internal and external functions in an open manner and does not try to hide or disguise their actions. Finally, accountability requires the organization to record accurately all transactions and also be able to take responsibility for its decisions and actions. Conducting business in foreign markets should not change or alter the ethical principles that the entrepreneur/manager follow. While the entrepreneur/manager must continue to grow the organization's bottom line, they must make sure that these decisions are made with integrity, transparency and accountability.

Countries often establish laws and regulations to ensure that the business activities of foreign organizations are within moral and ethical boundaries that are considered appropriate. What is considered morally and ethically appropriate ranges considerably from one country to the next resulting in a wide range of laws and regulations as well as enforcement activities. A global entrepreneur/manager must take into consideration a country's laws and regulations while it carries out its business activities in an ethical manner. Sometimes this causes the global entrepreneur/manager to choose between paying substantial fines or business loss.

One set of regulatory activities that affects global entrepreneurship/management is antitrust law. These laws empower country government agencies to closely oversee and regulate joint ventures with a foreign organization, acquisition of a domestic organization by a foreign entity, or any other foreign business activity that can restrain competition or negatively affect domestic companies and their business activities. Some countries use these laws to protect their "infant industries" as they attempt to become established and grow.

Global entrepreneurs/managers are also strongly impacted by laws against bribery and corruption. In many countries, payments or favors are expected in return to do business or gain a foreign contract. To establish a foreign operation, obtain a license, or even access electricity and water, global entrepreneurs are often asked to pay bribes to government officials at all levels. Due to the increased incidences of this, the United States passed the Foreign Corrupt Practices Act in 1977, making it a crime for US executives of publicly traded companies to bribe a foreign official in order to obtain business. While this act has been very controversial and its enforcement varies, the global entrepreneur/manager must distinguish between a reasonable way of doing business in a particular country and illegal bribery and corruption. The work of the non-profit Transparency International provides a good resource for judging the level of corruption, real and perceived, in a foreign country. Table 6.2 provides the rankings for the level of public sector corruption for a selection of countries based on Transparency International's yearly survey.

The rankings listed above come from the *2011 Transparency International Corruption Perceptions Index*. This index measures the perceived levels of public-sector corruption in a given country from the opinions of both businesspeople from that country as well as country analysts from various international and local institutions. The scores are on a scale of 0–10 for each country with 10 implying highly clean public sector and zero implying highly corrupt public sectors. This data is useful for global entrepreneurs as they choose new markets to enter and assess the costs, risks, and ethical issues that they might face in doing business in a foreign market. Transparency International produces this index annually and publishes the results on its Web site www.transparency.org.

The global entrepreneur/manager is confronted with the general standards of behavior and ethics. Is it all right to cut down a rain forest and pay employees above national wages? Can you manufacture a product under different working conditions than occur in the home country yet pay wage levels far higher than average in the country? These are just some of the issues confronting the global entrepreneur as he/she does business in some foreign countries. Hopefully global entrepreneurs/managers will assert leadership in establishing standards that help promote a quality of life throughout the world.

Table 6.2   Public sector corruption perceptions index

Economy/ Country	Ranking	Score
New Zealand	1	9.5
Denmark	2	9.4
Finland	2	9.4
Sweden	4	9.3
Singapore	5	9.2
Netherlands	7	8.9
Australia	8	8.8
Switzerland	8	8.8
Canada	10	8.7
Hong Kong	12	8.4
Iceland	13	8.3
Japan	14	8.0
United Kingdom	16	7.8
Ireland	19	7.5
United States	24	7.1
France	25	7.0
United Arab Emirates	28	6.8
Portugal	32	6.1
Brunei	44	5.2
Hungary	54	4.6
South Africa	64	4.1
Italy	69	3.9
China	75	3.6
Thailand	80	3.4
India	95	3.1
Indonesia	100	3.0
Egypt	112	2.9
Vietnam	112	2.9
Bangladesh	120	2.7
Iran	120	2.7
Pakistan	134	2.5
Laos	154	2.2
Venezuela	172	1.9
Iraq	175	1.8

Notes: The rankings listed above come from the *2011 Transparency International Corruption Perceptions Index.*

Source: 2011 Transparency International Corruption Perceptions Index.

Ethics and expectations of ethics vary by country depending in part whether the country is based on the philosophies of Aristotle and Plato or Confucius, for example. In developing countries without a codified system of business laws that have been in place and enforced for a while, there is a great temptation to use bribes (facilitation payments) to expedite the business deal. Warner Osborne, Chairman and CEO of Seastone LC, in working with thousands of companies during his 20+ years' experience in China and other countries advises, "We make sure all partners we work with know we won't tolerate that [facilitation payments – bribes]." He says when dealing with foreign organizations, "We begin by establishing the ground rules – including the ethical rules that are critical to us – one-on-one verbally" (Dutton, 2008). These rules must be fully understood by each employee.

Ethical practices have been questioned in several large global companies such as Nike using overseas sweatshop labor to manufacture clothing and tennis shoes or Prudential using deceptive sales techniques to persuade policyholders to make questionable insurance choices and decisions. Recently, because of the global financial crisis, there are many questions about the financial regulator and the lending behavior of major banks and financial institutions. In determining the main cause of the global financial crisis that began in 2008 many have pointed to ethical negligence in many core areas as contributing factors for example, government flexibility on stringent standards, lending institutions that failed to scrutinize the creditworthiness of customers, customers who were less than honest on loan applications, mortgage brokers who knowingly provided loans to unqualified customers to improve their performance ratings and collect fees, and credit rating agencies that assigned inappropriate bond ratings because of conflicts of interest. From this there is clear evidence of a lack of vigilance in ethically managing stakeholder relationships.

Entrepreneurs/managers are responsible for obeying laws, and must be held accountable for any illegal and unethical actions. In order to create an ethical business climate appropriate internal codes of conduct that include expected behaviors directed toward a broad range of stakeholders must be established. There is an extensive legal and regulatory framework that governs the proper functioning of many stakeholder relationships in the business system. However, the global financial crisis of 2008 to a degree can be attributed to negligence and deficiencies in this regulatory framework. The legal and regulatory system cannot have the level and depth of detail that would be capable of anticipating every possible scenario within which unethical behavior may take place. It is also unreasonable to expect all behavior to be regulated as this would be extremely costly for individual businesses to monitor and comply with regulations that may not be specifically relevant to their business. However, entrepreneurs/managers can proactively establish appropriate ethical expectations for relating to the organization's stakeholders that contribute to ethical behavior beyond the requirements of the law.

A list of countries ranked according to their degree of transparency is indicated in Table 6.2. While New Zealand is ranked number one, Vietnam is ranked 112, Bangladesh 120, Laos 154 and Iraq 175. While the United States is ranked 24, China is ranked 75.

CONCLUSIONS

An understanding of the organization, entrepreneurship and ethics is vital to the venture's success. Entrepreneurs and managers in different ways have a strong influence on organizational ethics, core business values, corporate culture, and social responsibility. This chapter outlines the important ethical practices and business values that entrepreneurs/managers must take into account and ingrain in their corporate culture. Ethics generally refers to what is right or wrong. These beliefs guide people in their dealings with other individuals and groups, and provide the basis for determining if behavior is right or wrong. Many organizations have a formal code of ethics and core business value statements derived from societal ethics, professional ethics, and individual ethics of the entrepreneur and to a lesser degree the management team. Every entrepreneur/manager should foster a culture grounded in ethics and core values. Because being economically successful is not sufficient to create a better world. To generate more social good, profit-oriented entrepreneurs/managers should promote and engage in more ethically, socially and environmentally responsible activities, as part of their corporate strategies.

Entrepreneurs/managers need to respect the culture of other nations and aim to manage their overseas business activities in a way that will promote and contribute to the development of local communities. They must assume responsibility for implementing ethical business practices, ethical codes and standards, and for taking appropriate course of action to promote awareness of it among all those concerned. Entrepreneurs/managers must also take the voice of their organization's stakeholders, both internally and externally into consideration, and promote the development and implementation of systems that will contribute to the achievement of ethical corporate behavior.

This chapter also provides a comparison of the ethical attitudes of entrepreneurs and managers. Ethical organizational cultures are those in which ethical principles and core values are emphasized. Doing the right thing managing an ethical business that is socially responsible is not always easy. However, entrepreneurs/managers must act in an ethical and socially responsible manner. In light of the current economic climate now more than ever governments need to put great priority on the development of high quality institutions that restore trust among members of society and increase the quality of economic interactions among them. It is in the best interest of society to eliminate unethical behaviors and attitudes through education, legal and economic efforts, which is a long-term commitment. In future research, a number of countries within the United States, Asia, and Europe should be examined and their cultural differences in understanding and implementing ethical concepts should be studied in more detail to fully understand ethics in a variety of country cultures. Comparative research could usefully examine the perceptions of business ethics and corporate social responsibility of CEOs of larger corporations compared to owners of larger organizations.

NOTE

1. The material in this section was adapted from: Robert D. Hisrich (2010). *International Entrepreneurship*. Thousand Oaks, CA: Sage Publications.

7 Entrepreneurship, crisis, critique
Campbell Jones and Anna-Maria Murtola

Critique starts out from a puzzlement, a bemusement. When it comes to critique of entrepreneurship, here is our puzzle: how is it that our masters think? What, indeed, were they thinking? And what will they think of next? We know how they act – we see it every day. And we hear how they talk, as if in control of vast abilities, while at the same time hapless victims of the dictates of necessities that we could not possibly have the minds to grasp.

This situation was understood many years ago by Max Horkheimer, who identified exactly this oscillation. 'At the heart of the freedom and seeming originality of the entrepreneur' he wrote, we find equally 'an acceptance of the blind power of chance' (1972: 82). He continues:

> This dependence of the entrepreneur, arising out of the irrational character of the economic process, is manifested in a helplessness before deepening crises and a universal perplexity even among the leaders of the economy. Bankers, manufacturers, and merchants, as the characteristic literature of recent centuries shows, have completely divested themselves of humility. But simultaneously they have come to experience social reality as a superordinate but blind power. (Horkheimer, 1972: 82)

Today we seem again to be at the will of blind necessity in a time of crisis. First and foremost, the financial crisis of 2008 and the subsequent recession, global economic and national debt crises that followed. For us, critique starts not in the abstract but in response to the immediate situation before us, so in this chapter we seek to respond to this situation of crisis and to articulate some of our bemusement at the way that our masters – those who determine our collective life chances, in spite of those elected to govern them – are working through the current crisis. In doing so we will try to articulate what we consider a critique of entrepreneurship might look like and why it might matter.

In recent years we have seen contestation of entrepreneurship in a number of efforts to elaborate an academic critique of entrepreneurship (see for example Kets de Vries, 1985; Ogbor, 2000; Hjorth, 2003b; du Gay, 2004; Rehn and Taalas, 2004a, b; Armstrong, 2005; Görling and Rehn, 2008; Sørensen, 2008, 2009a; Calàs et al., 2009; Hjorth and Steyaert, 2009; Jones and Spicer, 2009). These provide important foundations for what we say here, even if they tend to remain within the polite confines of academic discourse and generally do not take seriously enough the gross inequities of what is done under cover of 'entrepreneurship'.

Critique of entrepreneurship, for us, is motivated by the concrete realities of suffering today, and the unequal and arbitrary distribution of this suffering. Alongside this it responds to the symbolic violence, the insult that accompanies injury, in the arrogance of our masters' one-sided representations of entrepreneurship as a force of salvation. If anything we want to suggest that critique of entrepreneurship should not be an optional matter, nor should critique be conceived of as a 'perspective' that one might or might not take on entrepreneurship.

Critique sets itself against dogmatism and arbitrary suffering. It is hard to imagine anything as being of durable value if it is unable or unwilling to subject itself to criticism. In this sense, entrepreneurship as such is rarely put to the test. Critique of entrepreneurship proposes such a test, a test of the kind that Immanuel Kant proposed more than two centuries ago, for the reason that without critique, it is hard to see why any particular thing should be worthy of respect or admiration. Doubt and strict criticism are, for Kant, 'proofs of a well-grounded way of thinking'.

> Our age is the genuine age of criticism, to which everything must submit. Religion through its holiness and legislation through its majesty commonly seek to exempt themselves from it. But in this way they excite a just suspicion against themselves, and cannot lay claim to that unfeigned respect that reason grants only to that which has been able to withstand its free and public examination. (Kant, 1998: 100–101)

Entrepreneurship likewise is typically exempted from free and public examination, and this is one of the reasons it raises our suspicion. Given that our goal in this chapter is to explain why critique of entrepreneurship is needed and what it might look like, this suspicion, along with the realities of crisis, bring together our considerations here.

The chapter is divided into three sections. The first section considers the relationship between entrepreneurship and crisis, and considers three aspects of this relationship: the potential of entrepreneurship as a solution to crises, the entrepreneurial opportunities said to arise from crises and the role of entrepreneurship in creating crises in the first place. Section two revisits Schumpeter's foundational concept of 'creative destruction' and shows the way that this notion, and entrepreneurship along with it, are fundamentally connected with the crisis tendencies of capitalism. Having brought together our present condition with central concepts in entrepreneurship, the third section then outlines a programme for the critique of entrepreneurship today.

ENTREPRENEURSHIP AND CRISIS

One of our central arguments in this chapter is that entrepreneurship and crisis are far less distant from each other than is often imagined. There are at least three ways in which entrepreneurship relates to crisis. First, as is most commonly acknowledged, entrepreneurship has been proposed as a solution to crises. Second, crisis has been taken as the grounds for entrepreneurial opportunities. Third, and most overlooked, is the role of entrepreneurship in the creation of crises. In this section we will discuss each of these interconnections in turn.

Entrepreneurship as a Solution to Crisis

In early 2011 the World Bank published a report with the title *Entrepreneurship Snapshots 2010: Measuring the Impact of the Financial Crisis on New Business Registration*. This report noted what will hardly be surprising news, that is, that in 2008 and 2009 there was a fall in the registration of new businesses across the world.

> Business owners and would-be entrepreneurs are often at the mercy of macro-economic conditions. This was never more true than in 2008 and 2009, when the financial crisis reverberated throughout the global economic system following the failure of several US and Western European banking institutions. (World Bank, 2011: 1)

The World Bank survey of new business registration claims to offer for the first time the ability to understand entrepreneurship within the context of the global economy and with this to be able to identify the effects on entrepreneurship of events such as the global financial crisis. By collating data from 112 countries the report also promises to be able to evaluate the way that firm creation varies between countries, and the factors that affect it. It offers insight into the impact of the financial crisis on new firm creation and the factors mediating this relationship. At the most general level, the report asks, 'What is the relationship between entrepreneurship and the business environment?' (World Bank, 2011: 3).

The way that the World Bank report conceives this relationship between entrepreneurship and crisis is revealing. First, it is never even imagined that entrepreneurship might have had any part to play in the creation of the financial crisis. In this respect entrepreneurs are treated as if they are 'at the mercy of macroeconomic conditions' (World Bank, 2011: 1), in precisely the way that Horkheimer spoke of entrepreneurs being taken as victims of a 'helplessness before deepening crises' (Horkheimer, 1972: 82).

The World Bank report nevertheless sees hope for recovery out of the crisis, and this comes in the form of new and dynamic business creation. According to the report this is exactly what entrepreneurship is about, that is, 'initiating economic enterprise' (World Bank, 2011: 7). The authors note the classic conundrum that it is almost impossible to know what entrepreneurship is: 'The concept of entrepreneurship lacks a common language' (World Bank, 2011: 6). Nevertheless, this problem is quickly swept to one side on the premise that practitioners of entrepreneurship might have a clearer idea of what entrepreneurship entails, something contradicted by decades of empirical research (Jones and Spicer, 2005).

> For practitioners, entrepreneurship has generally been viewed as the process of creating new wealth. The entrepreneurial process centres on the discovery, creation, and profitable exploitation of markets for goods and services. (World Bank, 2011: 7)

We return then to entrepreneurship as 'creating new wealth' and 'profitable exploitation of markets'. The chain of reasoning is that entrepreneurs bring about growth, which equals wealth, which in turn equals general wellbeing. Still remaining to be specified is to whom these benefits actually flow, from where they arise and with what additional consequences.

The assumptions embedded in this World Bank report are significant in their own right. Note the repeated oscillation between the entrepreneur as dependent and independent variable. Note also the way that entrepreneurship has been exempted from being conceived as having any causal role in the creation of crises. As we will seek to show, in the traditional literature on entrepreneurship there is admission of the connection between entrepreneurship and crisis. And we will furthermore speak of the dangers of an abstracted idea of entrepreneurship in which entrepreneurship is seen simply in terms of 'the discovery, creation, and profitable exploitation of markets for goods and services' (World Bank, 2011: 7).

Crisis and Entrepreneurial Opportunity

We have seen the hope that entrepreneurship will provide a solution to the crisis, by creating jobs and dragging the economy out of recession. But beyond this, many in business have directly sought to present the most recent financial crisis as a source of opportunity. By shaking up existing norms and structures, we have heard that crises enable creation of the possibility to introduce changes that might have otherwise seemed difficult if not impossible. Turbulence, change and even disaster, can then be rendered as having benefits in opening new windows of opportunity.

In late 2008, Rahm Emanuel, the former White House Chief of Staff said: 'You never want a serious crisis to go to waste. And what I mean by that is that it's an opportunity to do things that you think that you could not do before' (*Wall Street Journal*, 2008). We see in this exactly the logic of what Donald Rumsfeld described as 'shock and awe' and what Naomi Klein described as the 'shock doctrine'. Disaster capitalism involves 'the treatment of disasters as exciting market opportunities' (Klein, 2007: 6). In this we see the conscious use of crises in order to introduce radical structural changes.

In this 'crisis entrepreneurship' there is an incredible effort to see opportunities for oneself at the expense of others. To do so means to ignore or to underplay the real suffering of others and to see only the benefits that one might gain at the loss of others. Thus we see advice that those in business need to see the 'upside of the downturn'. As it has been put: 'The downturn is severe and painful, answering the prayers of every business leader who wants to make big changes in his or her organization' (Colvin, 2009: 5). Or, as Richard Branson put it, 'There are enormous opportunities when there is a crisis' (Branson, 2008), and more specifically, 'Fortunes are made out of recessions. A lot of entrepreneurs get going in the economic depths because the barriers to entry are lower' (Branson, cited in Robertson, 2009).

Such assertions of the opportunities for individual gain in a time of widespread suffering have circulated widely in popular business circles recently, in ways that have been both colourful and rich in imagination. One example of this has been in the way it has been claimed that the Chinese character for 'crisis' is constructed out of the Chinese characters for 'danger' and 'opportunity'. It is said that 'There is an ancient wisdom etched into the vocabulary of the Chinese. The written characters for the terms "threat" and "opportunity" are identical' (Nathan, 2000: 12). As the sinologist Victor Mair notes, 'A whole industry of pundits and therapists has grown up around this one grossly inaccurate statement' (Mair, 2009). Nevertheless, the factual inaccuracy of this 'curious specimen of alleged oriental wisdom' (Mair, 2009) has not discouraged widespread circulation of it as a form of evidence for the idea that crisis creates entrepreneurial opportunities.

Of course, 'opportunity' is a central concept in the theory of entrepreneurship (see Kirzner, 1973b; Shane, 2004; Short, Ketchen et al., 2010), but what is important in this way of treating opportunity in times of crisis is the almost complete moral vacuum of this discourse. Fortunes are to be made, and opportunities seized, with little or no regard for those who might be suffering at the same time or as a result of such seizing of opportunities. If entrepreneurship is simply conceived as seizing opportunities, then any seizing is as good as any other, as long as it creates a profit.

The Role of Entrepreneurship in Creating Crisis

In the World Bank report, entrepreneurs are portrayed on the one hand as hapless victims of macroeconomic forces, and on the other as agents expected to resolve the current crisis. We have also shown how crises can function as a space within which entrepreneurial opportunities can be seized. What this does not show, however, is how entrepreneurial activity is not only implicated in, but is at the very heart of, the emergence of the crisis itself.

As is well known, entrepreneurship is above all about making things change. It is about creating a break from the past, and introducing a new element into the mix. To what extent, then, and in what ways, can we implicate entrepreneurship in the creation of crises? If we look at, for instance, the innovative ideas that produced massive earnings in the financial services sector in the opening years of this century, then can we call these entrepreneurial?

One of the things that has become very clear in the fallout of the crisis is the place that financial innovation played in the lead up to the crisis of late 2008. This included the creation of a range of new financial instruments, building on and radicalising credit default swaps, derivatives, asset-backed securities, collateralised debt obligations (CDOs) and increasingly complex methods for tranching debts, increasing leveraging and pricing derivatives. Many of these financial instruments had been in operation for years, although financial innovation became *de rigueur* in the financial services sector in the first decade of the twenty-first century.

Financial innovations have been central to the development of capitalism from its very beginning, although the complexity and scope of these instruments expanded rapidly during the last third of the twentieth century. Writing in 1995, with an optimism that seems in hindsight somewhat premature, Robert C. Merton, an important figure in the expansion of financial innovations in the years to follow, wrote:

> Looking at financial innovations – from the perspective of physiology rather than pathology – one sees them as the force driving the global financial system towards its goal of greater economic efficiency. In particular, innovations involving derivatives can improve efficiency by expanding opportunities for risk sharing, by lowering transaction costs and by reducing asymmetric information and agency costs. (Merton, 1995, p. 463)

It is rather hard to decipher the basis on which Merton cleanly distinguishes the physiological from the pathological, and moreover the way that pathology is rendered marginal. Nevertheless, the view that financial innovations would create both efficiency and stability gained remarkably widespread credence up to the crisis of 2008. At investment banks such as J. P. Morgan, for example, 'in the 1990s the team had all believed, with near-evangelical fervour, that innovation would create a more robust and efficient financial world. Credit derivatives and CDOs, they assumed, would disperse risk' (Tett, 2009: 249). In 1999 Alan Greenspan, Chairman of the US Federal Reserve, said: 'these new financial instruments are an increasingly important vehicle for unbundling risks. These instruments enhance the ability to differentiate risk and allocate it to those investors most able and willing to take it' (Greenspan, 1999).

Of course, in the end, things worked out quite differently. We have seen a global financial crisis, and learned of the way that the financial innovations unleashed over the past twenty or more years have been directly implicated in that crisis. Today, 'financial innovation is widely believed to be at least partly responsible for the recent financial crisis' (Den Haan and Sterk, 2010: 707).

This causes, we will argue, significant difficulties for the promotion of innovation that we generally see in the literature on entrepreneurship. To put it simply, many of these financial innovations had serious negative consequences for a great number of people. Lack of attention to the destructive side of innovations, and above all the way that innovations create crises in the lives of others, is a peculiar blindness in entrepreneurship research. Almost as if in an effort to be value free, in this literature innovations are not judged as such. If they come to market, indeed, if they are innovations, then they are deemed to be good. Put differently, regardless of the consequences, the entrepreneurial process of innovation is deemed to be inherently virtuous in its own right. When it comes to entrepreneurship it would seem that destruction is always creative.

THE MEANING OF CREATIVE DESTRUCTION

It almost goes without saying that entrepreneurship involves creating the new. In the World Bank report the definitional difficulties of the meaning of the word 'entrepreneurship' are swept under the carpet by defining entrepreneurship as registering new businesses. For Joseph Schumpeter, the creation of the new is essential to the entrepreneurial function, and equally to the development of capitalism. 'The fundamental impulse that sets and keeps the capitalist engine in motion comes from the new consumers' goods, the new methods of production or transportation, the new markets, the new forms of industrial organization that capitalist enterprise creates' (Schumpeter, 1950: 83; see also 1934 [1983]: 66).

Schumpeter clearly recognises that the creation of the new involves overcoming obstacles and sweeping away things that are in the way. This is why he speaks of entrepreneurship as involving a process of change and creation that necessarily involves destruction. Creation in such a context is not merely an addition to how things are but a transformation that destroys previously existing relations and sets new relations and possibilities in their place. Thus Schumpeter famously evokes the image of the 'perennial gale of creative destruction' (1950: 84).

In this section we would like to specify three things. First, as Schumpeter presents it, creative destruction is an integral part of capitalism. Second, creative destruction is intimately connected with crisis. Third, the idea of creative destruction goes back much further in history than is usually acknowledged.

Creative Destruction and Capitalism

Schumpeter is clear that creative destruction is an unmistakable characteristic of capitalism. He is clear that capitalism inherently involves change. 'Capitalism, then, is by nature a form or method of economic change and not only never is but never can be stationary' (Schumpeter, 1950: 82). We must not forget that when Schumpeter introduces the idea of creative destruction, this is an account of an economic process, capitalism, and it is in this process that entrepreneurship takes place. Entrepreneurship is not the simple or immediate active force of creative destruction, but springs to life within that context. 'This process of Creative Destruction is the essential fact about capitalism. It is what capitalism consists in and what every capitalist concern has got to live in' (Schumpeter, 1950: 83). Thus when he introduces the idea of creative destruction, he writes: 'Every piece of business strategy acquires its true significance only against the background of that process and within the situation created by it . . . it cannot be understood irrespective of it' (Schumpeter, 1950: 83–84).

This place of capitalism in Schumpeter's analysis is unmistakable, even if entrepreneurship in contemporary discussions is often conceived of entirely separately. In part this is due to the widespread contemporary phenomenon of the 'fetishisation' of the entrepreneur, that is, the lifting of entrepreneurial activity from its social and above all economic situation. To this end we might recall the way that Schumpeter stressed that 'the entrepreneurial function need not be embodied in a physical person and in particular in a single physical person. Every social environment has its own ways of filling the entrepreneurial function' (Schumpeter, 1951: 255). This entrepreneurial function takes place within a broader system. It is a function or operator that makes sense only within one particular economic system, that is, capitalism.

When we speak of the entrepreneur we do not mean so much a physical person as we do a function. . . . However, all the men who actually do fulfill entrepreneurial functions have certain interests in common and, very much more important than this, they acquire capitalist positions in case of success. (Schumpeter, 1951, p. 263)

Creative Destruction and Crisis

Creative destruction also directly and inherently involves crisis. As Crandall puts it, 'a crisis is part of the process we call "creative destruction"'(2007: 432). Of course, Schumpeter had stressed in *Business Cycles* that 'capitalist evolution spells disturbance' (1939: 331). Writing in 1939 on the world crisis that followed the crisis of 1929, he wrote that the world crisis:

> was a proof of the vigor of capitalist evolution to which it was – substantially – the temporary reaction. And in any case it was – again, substantially – no novel occurrence, no unprecedented catastrophe expressive of the emergence of new factors, but only a recurrence of what at similar junctures had occurred before. (Schumpeter, 1939: 332)

We find similar ideas in a range of other economists who stress the process of motion and crisis in capitalism. Ludwig von Mises (1996) rails against the 'imaginary constructions' of those who see capitalism as stationary or circular rather than being constantly changing. Kirzner speaks of the 'incessant process of the creation and the destruction of opportunities for pure profit that makes up the discovery procedure of the market' (1982: 4). Equally, economists such as Hyman Minsky recognise the intrinsic instability of capitalism, and stress that 'business cycles and financial crises are unchanging attributes of capitalism' (2008: 194).

Earlier, Marx had mocked the 'vulgar economist, who imagines, like an inverted Archimedes, that in the determination of the market price of labour by supply and demand he has found the fulcrum by means of which he cannot so much move the world, as bring it to a standstill' (Marx, 1976: 419). Since then others have noted that disequilibrium is 'a condition internal to capitalism, not one introduced from outside the system. Indeed, equilibrium capitalism is an oxymoron, characteristic not of calm but of a state of crisis' (Storper and Walker, 1989: 48–9). For David Harvey, 'Crises are, as it were, the irrational rationalisers of an always unstable capitalism' (2010: 71). Put differently: 'Even to say "the market" is, in a way, to say crisis' (Negri, 2003: 54).

> [C]apital works by breaking down or, rather, through creative destruction achieved by crises. In contemporary neoliberal economic regimes, in fact, crisis and disaster have become ever more important as levers to privatize public

goods and put in place new mechanisms for capitalist accumulation. (Hardt and Negri, 2009: 143)

Schumpeter objects to those for whom 'the problem that is usually being visualized is how capitalism administers existing structures, whereas the relevant problem is how it creates and destroys them' (1950: 84). If the problem is to see how capitalism destroys and recreates existing structures, we will need to pay attention to which structures of life are being destroyed and what is being created in their stead.

Baumol argues that there is a clear message in the idea of creative destruction, which 'is the fact that innovation and growth force obsolete technology to be swept away without hesitation or remorse' (Baumol, 2010: 129). And clearly this 'sweeping away without hesitation or remorse' sweeps away not merely technologies, but forms of life, modes of common existence. As Baumol puts it,

> To the extent that it avoids informing us about the desirability of this process of replacement of the old by the new, the concept of creative destruction remains ambiguous. Indeed, by itself, it offers no basis on which to judge how far the process should go in order to serve the public interest most effectively. (Baumol, 2010: 129)

Baumol's argument is important in so far as he emphasises the way that creative destruction 'can generate socially damaging externalities' (2010: 136). What he fails to acknowledge, however, is the unequal and uneven distribution of these negative externalities, and along with this, the unequal distribution of the benefits of creative destruction. In this way, his claim that on balance the forces of creative destruction 'provide valuable benefits to the community' (Baumol, 2010: 136) is not only unrealistic but is excessively abstract and politically naïve.

Still, Baumol alerts us to the moral vacuum at the heart of the idea of creative destruction. We saw this also in the World Bank report, in which it was imagined that if something is created which makes a profit then it is good. This is the blind irrationalism of the idea that if something is brought to market then it is good. In this, no moral distinction is made between guns and butter. Ontologically, this means that what is brought to market is good. What we see here is a prejudice in favour of what is created over what is destroyed.

Creative Destruction is an Idea

It is important to stress that the idea of creative destruction has a long genealogy, and this is relevant for how we are going to conceive of the meaning and consequences of creative destruction. Both the term and the concept of creative destruction go much further back in history than Schumpeter's popularisation of the expression. The first clear use of this combination of words is often attributed to Werner Sombart, who wrote of the way that 'from destruction a new spirit of creation arises' (1913: 207). Sombart, who was an important source for Schumpeter although this was not always made explicit (see Michaelides and Milios, 2009), wrote that capitalism 'has a mania for innovations . . . either through elimination of competitors by the establishment of new enterprises based upon them, or – primarily – through introducing new, more profitable processes, capitalism soothes its innermost desire: to make an extra profit!' (Sombart, 1927: 87).

The concept of creative destruction has a clear lineage to Marx, for whom capitalism involved a constant process of the destruction of earlier ways of life, in which capital 'is destructive towards all of this, and constantly revolutionizes it, tearing down all the barriers which hem in the development of the forces of production, the expansion of needs, the all-sided development of production, and the exploitation and exchange of natural and mental forces' (Marx, 1973: 410; see also Elliott, 1978–79). Likewise, we hear of the 'constant revolutionizing of production, uninterrupted disturbance of all social conditions, everlasting uncertainty and agitation' (Marx and Engels, 1998: 38).

It is possible, however, to trace the idea of a process of creative destruction much further and wider. We see it in ancient images such as the idea of the reincarnation of the Phoenix, the resurrection of Christ and in Hindu ideas of constant processes of creation out of destruction. The idea of creative destruction is much more deeply embedded, and indeed more commonsensical, than might at first be thought. Reinert and Reinert (2006) argue that one of the crucial ways that the idea comes to Schumpeter is through Sombart, and in particular through the influence of Nietzsche on Sombart. We see this in the figure in Sombart of the entrepreneur as overcomer and as *Übermensch*, a figure taken from Nietzsche, who writes: 'He who has to be a creator, always has to destroy' (1969: 85).

CRITIQUE

We have sought to outline the basic interconnections between entrepreneurship and crisis. We have identified the role that financial innovations played in creating the financial crisis of 2008, and moreover, despite this, the single-minded optimism that casts entrepreneurship as a solution to that very same crisis. We have shown the way that entrepreneurship, capitalism and crisis are linked through the concept of creative destruction, which takes the entrepreneur as the linchpin in the transformations of capitalism.

Our goal in this has been to set the scene for articulating why it is that one might take a critical position regarding the very idea of entrepreneurship. What remains then is for us to spell out what we take to be central maxims for any meaningful critique of entrepreneurship. In this we more than recognise that we are not the first to propose a critique of entrepreneurship. We propose these maxims in seeking to extend the critique of entrepreneurship in a way that goes beyond previous critical work on entrepreneurship – including our own – and also because of the realities that have become increasingly clear since 2008. To this end we will here advance three maxims that we take to be foundations for the understanding and critique of entrepreneurship.

Maxim 1. Entrepreneurship cannot be separated from capitalism.

For Schumpeter, entrepreneurship and the entrepreneur are categories that make sense only by reference to their place in explaining the operation of capitalism. In Schumpeter, entrepreneurship is by definition a function within capitalism.

This reality has subsequently been eroded in discussions of entrepreneurship. Of course, in the most directly celebratory discussions of entrepreneurship we do find that entrepreneurship is praised exactly because it is taken to be part of capitalism, something that is itself considered so praiseworthy that it is hardly worth discussing. But often, the fact that entrepreneurship is an element within capitalism drops entirely out of the picture. One way of doing this is through a strategy that makes capitalism invisible by representing the capitalist economy as 'the economy' as such. A second way in which entrepreneurship is divorced from capitalism is in discussions of social entrepreneurship, of 'entrepreneurship as social change', or of general processes of 'entrepreneuring', which have nothing distinctively to do with capitalism (Rindova et al., 2009; Steyaert and Hjorth, 2006).

These strategies of naturalising capitalism by treating it as the neutral and universal backdrop of entrepreneurship and of treating entrepreneurship as something so universal that it extends beyond any particular economic set of relations both naturalise by universalisation, the former by universalising capitalism and the latter by universalising the idea of entrepreneurship.

These two positions, which seek to separate entrepreneurship from capitalism, are not merely based on a spurious historical universalisation of particular understandings of economic action. They also bring with them a radical depoliticisation of entrepreneurship. They actively disable serious contextual and structural understandings of entrepreneurship by taking the context in which entrepreneurship takes place, and indeed entrepreneurship itself, for granted. This is a problem because it is not true that capitalism is the neutral universal backdrop of all economic action, nor is entrepreneurship as currently conceived the universal basis of human interaction.

Of the two, taking entrepreneurship as the generic form of human creativity, a view that is often presented as progressive, is potentially the most pernicious. When we speak of things like social entrepreneurship, we are understanding the social in terms of economic categories, and above all the categories of capitalist economics. We have seen this extension on a constantly expanding scale with the rise of neoliberalism since the late 1970s. In the extreme, we find the redescription of all of social life in economic terms. In the university, for instance, what used to be called a charlatan is talked of as an 'academic entrepreneur'. The local community volunteer and the militant activist struggling for social justice are redescribed as 'social entrepreneurs'. In doing so, we are using economic, and specifically capitalist categories to organise social life. This has significant repercussions for how we live and how we think about life today.

This is why developments such as 'moral entrepreneurship' and 'social entrepreneurship', far from taking place on the outside of capitalism, are taking place within the most profound interior of capitalism. They involve the extension or expansion of previously limited explanations of social life to social life as such. They bring spheres of life not hitherto part of capitalism into the sphere of capitalist accumulation through their redescription. In this increasingly preposterous literature we find, for instance, claims that 'seeking autonomy, authoring and making declarations', indeed, the very idea of emancipation, is a matter of 'entrepreneuring' (Rindova et al., 2009: 477).

It is not possible to meaningfully comprehend entrepreneurship outside of capitalism and indeed as a function of capitalism. The idea of entrepreneurship has been used to extend and expand the spread of capitalism both within nations and internationally. Although entrepreneurship research is often taken to have developed out of the work of Schumpeter, perhaps the most egregious mistake of this literature has been to omit the reality of the relationship between entrepreneurship and capitalism. This has been done so as to universalise and naturalise both entrepreneurship and capitalism, and in doing so to depoliticise both. The critical position we are proposing here does not seek to politicise entrepreneurship, but rather

to undo the depoliticisation that is involved in dominant ideas of entrepreneurship. Entrepreneurship is a profoundly political category, and to
admit this means to no longer ignore or hide the realities of the operation
of capitalism.

Maxim 2. Entrepreneurship causes suffering.

Entrepreneurship is nothing if not optimistic. We saw this in the examples
above of the way that the global financial crisis has been taken as a source
of lucrative opportunities and equally in the lack of willingness to recognise the place of financial innovation in creating the crisis in the first place.
In the World Bank report we discussed, entrepreneurship is cast as a solution to the downturn. Indeed, we have seen entrepreneurship presented as
the cure for more or less all that ails the world today. It has been presented
as the cure for the economic downturn, as the resolution for desperate
poverty, and is visible in the idea that entrepreneurial ingenuity will save
us from persistent and expanding ecological crises.

What is lost in this glorification of entrepreneurship is the perpetuation
of suffering and indeed misery with which it is implicated. To see only the
'upside of the downturn' or the opportunities in times of crisis is one-sided.
It is structurally one-sided when it fails to acknowledge the realities of
suffering, and the way that suffering is not separated from entrepreneurial
activity or the operation of the capitalist economy. It is an incredibly naïve
optimism to imagine that entrepreneurial capitalism only brings good.
This represents at best only half of the truth of the matter. And as Adorno
once stressed, 'The need to lend a voice to suffering is a condition of all
truth' (1973: 17–18).

We have seen the realities of suffering that have followed the crisis of
2008, most immediately in those who have lost their homes and their jobs.
But beyond this, that suffering has not been evenly distributed. Those who
have been coded as 'subprime' and not worthy of their homes have not
been coded as such randomly, and not without reference to skin colour
(Dymski, 2009). The fact that evictions have taken place at the same time
that the luxury goods sector has shown remarkable resilience and top-end
housing and luxury yachts continue to trade strongly should focus our
attention even more sharply on the injustice of that suffering.

The critique of entrepreneurship cannot look away when jobs are lost
and communities are destroyed as a result of entrepreneurial activity.
Equally it cannot see only economic growth and fail to account for environmental consequences. It cannot see only the virtues of freedom and
not the trauma of precarious employment. It is not enough to suggest,
then, that entrepreneurship can in some particular contexts be violent

(Volkov, 2002). It is not enough to acknowledge the existence of 'violent entrepreneurs'. Beyond that we must account for the structural violence implicated in entrepreneurship. Entrepreneurship is about breaking boundaries, breaking down walls, breaking with the past. And with this, entrepreneurship involves violating what was previously valued.

Against the image in Schumpeter of the 'perennial gale of creative destruction', we might pit the alternative image that we find in Walter Benjamin of the Angel of History. In his remarkable text 'On the Concept of History', Benjamin comments on Paul Klee's painting *Angelus Novus*, which Benjamin had owned for some years. Benjamin used this image to challenge the naïve progressivist understanding of history, the implicit understanding of history that, we maintain, characterises almost all discourse on entrepreneurship. In this image, the Angel of History has its back turned to the future, and looks back at the past. 'Where a chain of events appears before *us, he* sees one single catastrophe, which keeps piling wreckage upon wreckage and hurls it at his feet' (Benjamin, 2003: 392). The Angel of History records destruction and suffering, and does so not out of negativity, but so that the storm of progress might propel us forward, not blindly to a future in which we can profit at any expense, but away from collective suffering.

We must not be dazzled by the innovations that entrepreneurial capitalism brings to market. We must also account for the rubble that is left in their path. These are not mere 'externalities', but are also part of the process. Any understanding of entrepreneurship which is not to be accused of one-sidedness must acknowledge the wreckage, the real suffering that is caused by the perennial gale of creative destruction.

Maxim 3. Entrepreneurship is an idea.

The third maxim for a critique of entrepreneurship is the recognition that entrepreneurship is not a mere blunt 'reality', but is just as much an idea. This is to say that it is a human conception, one that is also significantly invested with desires and fantasies. To say that entrepreneurship is an idea is not in any way to diminish its practical importance, but rather to recognise that entrepreneurship is a powerful idea with serious material consequences. How entrepreneurship is thought of and spoken of by the World Bank, by governments, by business leaders and by those designated as entrepreneurs has a concrete impact on our lives.

Some years ago Keynes wrote:

> the ideas of economists and political philosophers, both when they are right and when they are wrong, are more powerful than is commonly understood. Indeed the world is ruled by little else. Practical men, who believe themselves to

be quite exempt from any intellectual influences, are usually the slaves of some defunct economist (1967: 383)

Although we cannot accept that ideas alone rule the world, or that conflict over ideas takes place in a domain distinct from the terrain of vested interests, as Keynes does, we must admit the importance of ideas. To this we must add that ideas must be connected, in their complexity and very internal structure, with interests and political consequences. The critique of entrepreneurship is not a critique of particular individual entrepreneurs, but of the idea of entrepreneurship as such.

There are a number of ways in which the idea of entrepreneurship can be challenged. One strategy has been to seek to show the slipperiness of the concept, its emptiness and the way that it operates as a 'sublime object' into which almost any positive content can be filled (Jones and Spicer, 2005). Others have sought to show the way that the idea of entrepreneurship can take over the terrain of governmental policy and imagination (Armstrong, 2005). Others again have shown the gendered nature of talk of entrepreneurship (Calàs, Smircich and Bourne, 2009).

Here we have stressed the one-sided nature of the idea of entrepreneurship. We see this in the relentless optimism of entrepreneurship discourse, which fails to acknowledge the role of entrepreneurship in crisis and suffering, or sees this as the necessary eggs that must be broken if we are to make an entrepreneurial omelette. We see it also in the vacuous and uncritical repetition of platitudes and the constant efforts to remoralise entrepreneurship. Indeed, the function of the idea of entrepreneurship, we argue, is exactly to focus attention on one side of situations. The idea of entrepreneurship operates in order to sift or to filter attention. In the almost universally positive valuation of entrepreneurship, we see the way that entrepreneurship is used to decide the positive from the negative, the good from the bad. We see this at the heart of categories such as creative destruction, in which the destruction unleashed by entrepreneurial capitalism is underplayed and creation hailed. Even in efforts to balance the two, the fundamentally affirmative nature of entrepreneurship discourse ends up placing entrepreneurship on the side of the good.

Entrepreneurship is not a neutral or descriptive idea, but a fundamentally evaluative one. To speak of entrepreneurship or of an entrepreneur is already to perform a series of judgements and moral claims. In the extreme, the idea of the entrepreneur is a religious idea, as has been shown by Bent Meier Sørensen (2008). Not only in the messianic character that is attributed to entrepreneurs, but in foundational ideas, such as the creating something out of nothing, of creating the world anew from the very practice of thought.

To call these things into question is to suspect the direct mistruths of for instance the idea that the Chinese character for crisis is built on danger and opportunity. But it also means to account for how it is that there is so little suspicion in certain circles of such ideas. When we see that entrepreneurship is an idea then we can begin to see the way in which this idea operates. We can also see that it is not inevitable, that it might be right and might be wrong. It might be powerful or dangerous, and entrepreneurship is indeed a functional fiction within a broader power structure. Like all ideologies, it might not necessarily convince the masses, but it can help to reassure the dominant of the righteousness and resilience of their reign.

To seize an idea, however, is not something reassuring. Consciousness and cognition offer us remarkable freedom, the freedom to go beyond the one-sided way that the world presents itself at a particular moment. The task of criticism, as Benjamin once put it, is 'to liberate the future from its deformations in the present by an act of cognition' (Benjamin, 1996: 38). To enable us to think about something like entrepreneurship, we need to see that it is an idea, a figure of our collective imagination. To become conscious of this is not to repeat or reproduce the idea of the status quo that it produces. To think an idea is to put our minds against it in a way that releases it from the sphere of necessity and instead places it in its social, historical and political context. As Adorno writes, 'The power of the status quo puts up the facades into which our consciousness crashes. It must seek to crash through them' (1973: 17).

CONCLUSION

In a situation of crisis, we have sought here to document some of the relentless optimism that resides in the idea of entrepreneurship. We saw this in the rendering of destruction as inherently creative, in the treatment of crisis as entrepreneurial opportunity and in the idea that, despite the place of financial innovation in creating the global financial crisis, entrepreneurship is what will bring us out of crisis. This optimism, we have sought to show, is based on a perversely distorted view of the world.

It is, we have argued, grounded in at least three fundamental omissions. First, capitalism is either taken as universally beneficent, in spite of all of the evidence to the contrary, or is removed from the picture of entrepreneurship altogether. Second, suffering is directly or indirectly ignored, either by callously seeing only the opportunities that one can wrench out of the suffering of others or by the coldness of the dream that the good brought about by any change that brings a product to market will always outweigh any regrettable suffering that it may cause. Third, by tendentiously treating entrepreneurship as a purely practical matter, or by academic critics who recoil from 'theory', the fact that entrepreneurship is an idea has too often been lost.

These omissions are not politically neutral. To deny the connection of entrepreneurship and capitalism and the suffering caused by entrepreneurship, might appear to be pleasingly neutral, but it betrays the moral vacuum that lies at the heart of the thinking of entrepreneurship. In recent years some have sought to fill this vacuum by showing the socially beneficial results of entrepreneurship. We have criticised elsewhere such attempts to 'redeem' entrepreneurship (Murtola, 2008). Here we are seeking to stress the politics of these omissions, and the way that they produce particular forms of inequality and domination.

To draw attention to these things is to expose the cracks in the fantasy structure of the entrepreneurial utopia. It is to show that these cracks are not incidental or secondary. They refer to what we call, following Lacan, the 'Real' of entrepreneurship. To not see the cracks is to be deluded. Such can be a quite satisfying delusion, the idea that everyone benefits from entrepreneurial innovations, or that entrepreneurship is the answer to social ills. The important thing about the Real is that it rubs up against what is called 'reality', it knocks holes in it, it bubbles up and can overflow.

To take a critical position with respect to entrepreneurship is not merely an option. It is due to the very spread of capitalist mentality that many think that everything is a matter of perspective and that like a consumer one can pick and choose whichever perspective one likes. Critique is not a matter of 'taking a critical perspective'. Critique is human consciousness applied to the object and social world, starting from the world that we are living in right now. To *not* take a critical perspective is a defective limitation, a failure to exercise the human capacity for reason and judgement.

To not take a critical position on entrepreneurship also means contributing to the perpetuation of unnecessary suffering, to environmental degradation, to the blind laws of an irrational economic system. To not criticise entrepreneurship is to contribute to making our world more risky, unsafe and crisis-prone. It is to create ever more destruction and to hide that destruction in the loftiest and most fantastic dreams. It is to see only one side of the fantasies that have ordered our world for too long. To testify to the Real is to recognise that there are always at least two sides to things, and to pick only the shiny and charming is to seduce oneself. As that great critic Desiderius Erasmus famously said many years ago, 'In the kingdom of the blind the one-eyed man is king' (Erasmus, 2005: 57). To take a critical position and to acknowledge both sides of the dialectic of history involves opening both eyes. It also involves expressing our outrage at those one-eyed kings under whose command we presently toil.

8 Gender, organizations and entrepreneurship
Helene Ahl

An academic essay on this topic invites definitions. What is gender, what is an organization and what is entrepreneurship, and how do these relate? As space is restricted, the approach must necessarily be selective. For this reason I begin by declaring my starting point right away: I consider this feminist work, which means that the primary research interest concerns constructions of gender, that is, constructions of masculinity and femininity, and resulting gender/power orders. There is also an emancipatory interest – results from feminist research may be of value for men and women in their work for greater gender equality.

A second demarcation would be the declaration of an epistemological point of view. As most contemporary feminist scholarship, this is social constructionist work in the tradition of Berger and Luckmann (1966) and Foucault (1972). Berger and Luckman tell us that things are what we make them to be, within the limits of what can be accepted by others – it takes a group of people to agree on a certain version of social reality to make it stick. Masculinity and femininity are prime targets for social construction. Competing versions exist, making any claim to truth contestable, but they are nevertheless amazingly enduring, and so are their effects. Foucault reminds us that social constructions, or discourses in his terminology, are not innocent, but entail power arrangements with tangible consequences for men and women. The most common result by far is male superiority and female subordination.

This said, the focus of the essay is thus consequences for women of constructions of gender, organizations and entrepreneurship. How do discourses of gender, organization and entrepreneurship position women? To what extent does this provide opportunities for women to be entrepreneurial in an organization? In order to answer these questions, I will take the reader through a swift tour of past research. In the following, I first discuss gender, then organization, and third entrepreneurship, and conclude with a discussion of consequences for women's entrepreneurship in the context of organizations.

DOING GENDER

The trajectory of feminist thinking follows the trajectory of the women's movement and feminist activism (see e.g., Calás and Smircich, 1996; Weedon, 1999). Early activists fought for suffrage, for access to education and jobs, and for equality before the law. *Liberal feminist* thinking, with roots in liberal political philosophy inspired the first wave of feminist movement. This philosophy says that all human beings are equal – they are rational, self-interest seeking agents. What makes them human is their capacity for rational thinking, of which men and women are equally endowed. The only reason women have achieved less than men is that they have been deprived of resources, such as education, work opportunities and so on. Women were victims of *structural discrimination*. Without this, men and women would actualize their potential to the same degree. There is of course an unstated male norm in this philosophy – it is the self-actualizing man who is the norm, and who takes care of the children or the elderly is not an issue.

Seeing that liberal feminism took the issue only so far, the second wave of feminist activism chose a different direction. *Radical feminism* grew out of the women's movement in the 1960s. This philosophy sees sexuality, or reproduction, as the basis for women's subordination. Rape, incest, abuse, prostitution and pornography are but expressions of this. Some even count marriage as organized oppression of women. Radical feminism says that feminine traits such as caring, empathy, emotional expressiveness, endurance and commonsense are found to be lacking in men and that these traits have been devalued to the detriment of society. A separatist strategy with exclusively female groups and alternative, consensus oriented political organization is advocated, with the aim of changing the basic structure of society. Second wave feminism contained many more directions than radical feminism, some psychological, some political, some philosophical, but what unites them all is that they problematized womanhood (Harding, 1986, 1987).

What unites these philosophies is that men and women are seen as two distinct categories. The first one thinks that they are basically similar, whereas the second says that they are basically different – due to birth, or due to unavoidable gender socialization. Both have an *essentialist* view of gender – it is something tangible, measurable and tied to a physical body, and it comes in two possible versions. This meant somewhat of a dead end to feminists who observed that physical differences between men and women were too often used to legitimate social differences, even when there was no obvious reason for this. There are few, if any, systematic sex differences that have any necessary social implications. Studies of sex differences consistently show that the overlap between the sexes is much larger than the mean difference, if any, between the groups. This means that people differ, but the differences are not systematically related to a person's physiological sex (Doyle and Paludi, 1998). So there was a need for a new approach.

Consequently, third wave feminism first invented a useful distinction between sex and gender, only to later dissolve it again, but the new sex/ gender turned out to be something entirely different from the essentialist view of first and second wave feminism. The distinction between sex and gender is a distinction between physical sex and socially constructed sex, i.e., what is considered to be masculine or feminine. It was a necessary and strategic move, which made it possible to speak about oppression and injustice as results of social arrangements (which might be changed), instead of as necessary consequences of physical sex (which was seen as natural and given). The term gender opened for studies not only of masculinity and femininity as study objects in themselves, but it also opened for conceptualization of gendered phenomena at large – jobs could for example be gendered, or laws, or customs, or spaces and so on, all with consequences for men and women. Such studies also found gender orders to vary considerably in space and time, creating a useful opening for discussions of change.

But useful as it was, the sex/gender distinction quickly ran into three sorts of trouble. The first problem was that the term gender was co-opted. Forms ask you to fill out your gender today, not your sex, and they give you only the usual two options. The problem is particularly pertinent in the English language, as the word sex also refers to sexual intercourse. The word gender has come to replace one of the original connotations of the word sex. The result is that so called gender research in mainstream research journals is today mostly research on men and women, most often comparative, and most often with the predictable result – women are declared to be insufficient in one way or another (Ahl, 2004, 2006b). So the original idea with making a distinction between sex and gender was all but lost.

The second problem was philosophical. Making a distinction between sex and gender requires that one can draw a line between that which is natural and that which is constructed, a line between nature and culture. But who can do that, and on which grounds? Defining physical sex once and for all turned out to be problematic – remember South African runner Caster Semenya whose gold medal in the 2009 World Championships was questioned because her sex was questioned? However you choose to define sex – by sexual organs, hormone levels or chromosomes – there are more versions available than two. Kaplan and Rogers (1990) count at

least 17. Talking about men and women seems like a heuristic simplifica-
tion in this light. With the linguistic turn of science it was further claimed
that the language of the body determines how we understand the body.
Judith Butler (1990) claimed that the body should properly be regarded
as socially constructed, just as much as all the meanings people attach to
it. This does not mean that the body does not exist, but that it is not possible to understand the body without the confines of language and culture.
According to Butler, gender/sex (same thing) is performed. Or rather, it is
co-performed, as any successful performance requires an accepting audience (Ahl, 2007a). West and Zimmerman (1987) labelled this *doing gender*,
which is a concept that has been used widely in gender research. Men and
women sometimes go to great lengths in clothing, adornments, physical
exercise, diets and even surgery to produce socially accepted and distinctly
different male and female bodies. This *performative* or *constructionist* view
of gender is radically different from the essentialist view discussed earlier.
Masculinity or femininity (or whatever gender performance one undertakes) is not just clothing to wear on a given body, but it is all there is.

This brings me to the third problem, which is political. With such a
fluid view of gender, how is it possible to advocate women's rights? How
can one speak for a group that is not identifiable? 'Have you ever seen a
gender?' asked Mary Daly, a prominent figure in the American women's
movement (quoted in Eduards, 1995: 64), pointing to the distance between
actual men and women and their scientific representations. Iris Young
(1995) has a useful solution. Borrowing from Sartre, she introduces the
concept *gender as seriality*. She says that even if nothing essential unites
all women – or all men – they are still united in that they are *perceived*
as women or men. They must relate to gendered clothing, spaces, labour
markets, language and, foremost, to the fact that people around them
label them as women or men. People relate to this in infinitely many ways,
but relate they must. Anyone who does something outside the expected
is likely to notice it by the reactions from other people. Being seen as a
woman will therefore have repercussions on a woman's life, irrespective of
how she chooses to define herself. Thinking of gender as seriality allows
the conceptualization of women and men as categories, without assuming
that people in the same category have a common identity.

I find a constructionist view of gender productive, and as Iris Young just
saved it for emancipatory interests, this is the view of gender I will use. In
the name of consistency, this is also the view of *anything* I use, in theory,
but not in practice. It is namely impossible to question all categories at the
same time, and knowledge is always situated (Haraway, 1991). Haraway
says to declare one's standpoint (as I did in the opening paragraph) so
the reader is able to evaluate the knowledge claims made, based on his or

her own standpoint. Consequently, in the following I focus on the gendered constructions of organization and entrepreneurship, and discuss its consequences for women.

ORGANIZATIONS AND WOMEN

As most sciences, organization theory used to be a gender blind science until only a few decades ago. Organization, management and entrepreneurship theory, was written by men, for men and about men (Sundin and Holmquist, 1991). This might have been an adequate description of the management cadres of the first and middle part of last century, but whereas women's participation in organizations has increased dramatically since then, their presence in textbooks has not. Even when women were the explicit objects of organization research, such as in the famous Hawthorne experiments, they were written about as 'workers'. The Hawthorn study – one of the largest and perhaps best funded social science research projects ever – was launched when management at the Western Electric company in Hawthorn, USA, discovered in the early 1920s that operatives worked slower in order to maintain their piecework rate, even if this meant lower wages. After some 20 000 interviews and years of experiments, Elton Mayo of Harvard Business School proclaimed that social norms affected productivity, in the case of the aforementioned workers negatively. They also proclaimed that workers who have their social needs satisfied will increase productivity (Mayo, 1933, 1945). The research led to the Human Relations School, which inspired research and practice for many years to come. However, in a re-reading of the material from the study, Acker and Van Houten (1974) found that the workers who slowed down were men, for which no particular measure was taken to make them change their behaviour, while the workers who increased their productivity were a group of young women who were subject to close paternalistic surveillance and who risked losing their jobs if they did not comply. They had little choice but to increase their productivity. So, not only were the presented results gender blind, they were also misrepresentative of actual research findings. Instead of concluding that a socially satisfied worker is a productive worker one might conclude that a closely supervised and controlled worker is a productive worker (Ahl, 2006a). This shows the insufficiency of social science that disregards gender and takes gender/power relationships for granted.

When women finally entered organization theory they did it in the same way as in many other social sciences – they were made visible; their presence was noted and counted. Feminist research labels this *feminist empiricism*. It adds sex to the research agenda just as any other variable, and is referred to as the 'add women and stir' approach. Such research has found that organizations are characterized by horizontal, internal and vertical sex segregation. Horizontal gender segregation means that men and women typically have different sorts of jobs, even if they are on the same hierarchical level. A constructionist scholar would say that jobs are gendered – a teacher's job has a feminine gender connotation, whereas a flight mechanic is masculine gendered. Gender segregation is present even within professions. Internal gender segregation means that a female lawyer or doctor, for example, is likely to specialize in a different area from a male lawyer or doctor. Even if women and men are present in all sectors, women tend to be overrepresented in services, care and education, and they tend to have jobs that typically are paid less than men's jobs. Even in countries with a high proportion of female labor market partici-pation such as the United States or Sweden, there is still an average salary difference between men and women of about 20 per cent.

The term vertical sex segregation describes the fact that women are underrepresented in management positions – the likelihood of finding a woman manager diminishes the higher up you come the corporate ladder. The current figure for women CEOs in listed companies in Sweden, which according to international equality indices is one of the most gender equal in the world, is only 3 per cent (Statistics Sweden, 2010). Remunerations follow suit. Scholars talk about a *glass ceiling*, a sort of invisible roadblock which is very difficult for women to bypass.

Now, why is this? Early theorists talked about a pipeline problem. As women entered management and engineering schools later than men, they were in short supply and it would take time before they reached manage-ment levels. This argument does not hold any longer. Women have earned their MBA-degrees for decades now.

The so called women-in-management literature concentrated in giving women advice on how to make it in business. There were dress-for-success courses, courses in how to present yourself, how to learn the unspoken rules of board meetings, how to be a leader and so on. The problem with this is that it has not achieved its purpose, the reason being that it basically teaches women how to imitate an idealized masculine way of being and presenting yourself, which can never be fully achieved if you are a woman. No matter how a woman modifies her behaviour and looks, she will still be perceived as a woman by others. Programmes that teach women to be 'honorary men' (Marlow and Patton, 2005) therefore risk reinforcing gendered norms instead of challenging them.

Women in token positions, in particular, will be perceived not as indi-viduals but as representatives of their sex, and therefore often become victims of sex role stereotyping (Kanter, 1977). The presence of a token makes the majority more acutely aware of their own sex, and they may overstate differences and try to keep the token out. A related explanation is *homosocial reproduction* (Ibarra, 1992; Lindgren, 1996) which means that social groups tend to reproduce themselves – a company board consisting of white middle-class men are likely to look for new board members that are very much like themselves.

Feminists further coined the phrase 'the private is public', which means that work and family are communicating vessels – one cannot hope for change in one sector without a corresponding change in the other. As women still take the main responsibility for child and elder care and for household work, they are more likely to have interrupted careers and to work part time. Employers' and colleagues' expectations of women, be they male or female, will be affected by this. In the United States there is a 'mummy-track' and in Sweden there is resistance towards hiring women in the child-bearing years, or hiring women with small children. Women are simply seen as a less reliable labour force than men. The Swedish parental leave and child-care system which is unique in the world has not helped much. Yes, there is a paid parental leave of a year-and-a-half which may be split equally between the parents if they so wish, but mothers still take 78 per cent of it. And yes, there is low cost, public child-care of good quality available for any child aged one, but there is also a policy that parents may take paid time off for a sick child – of which mothers take 65 per cent. And in spite of being present in the work force to almost the same extent as men, women still do the majority of the unpaid household work (Statistics Sweden, 2010). In many southern European countries without the generous policies of the Scandinavian countries, women simply opt out of the work force altogether when they become mothers – or they refuse to have children. There is a problem of low nativity and a shrinking population in many European countries.

All in all, this creates a very complicated gendered landscape in organizations. Organizations are full of gendered spaces, language, symbols and practices, which men and women are left to navigate in as best they can (Acker, 1992). As women are the intruders in management, it is more difficult for them than for men. Several scholars have written about management and leadership as masculine gendered. A leader is described with words such as forceful, firm, decisive, strong, brave, charismatic and so on. When a woman is promoted to a leadership position, she is instead expected to be democratic, participative and listening. But someone still has to take the tough decisions . . . This means that it is easier for a man than for a woman to assume a leadership position. A woman who does this breaks an unwritten rule, which may be unsettling for others (Calás and Smircich, 1992). She may be resisted not only by men, but also by other women, as she challenges received understandings of gender. The same applies to people of colour or of a sexual orientation which departs from the norm. The counterpart to the glass ceiling is the glass escalator, which applies to men in women-dominated professions, such as nursing. The experience is that they are unusually quickly promoted to leadership positions, encouraged not only by superiors by also by their female colleagues (Hultin, 2003).

And last, but not least, there is the issue of sex. Gherardi (1994) explains that the first thing we do when we meet somebody is to ascribe a gender identity. And the second thing we do, says Brewis (1994), is ascribing a sexual identity. People place themselves and others in the *heterosexual matrix* (Butler, 1990) in which heterosexuality, as well as subordination of the feminine is the norm. It cannot be avoided – it is a basic part of people's way of making sense of the world. But it creates a tension in the work place. Work is a place where masculine gendered values are celebrated – work and management is supposed to be efficient, rational, neutral and impassive. Leaders are expected to display courage, strength and analytical sharpness. Stereotypical feminine values such as caring, emotion, beauty, softness, submissiveness belong to women and to the private sphere, to family, children and home. And so do love and attraction. But life does not agree to be thus partitioned. People do not leave their passions and desires at the doorstep as they enter the workplace, even if they know that they are expected to. The result is an incredibly complicated maze of norms and standards centred around ascribed gender and sexual identities that people must navigate around every day. They pertain to how we address each other, how we address a male boss, a female boss, colleagues at the same level and subordinates of either sex. They pertain to how we are allowed to talk about each other, and with whom we talk about what, and in which manner. They pertain to how we dress, depending on local and industry culture, gender and hierarchical position. And so on. It is all too easy to make a mistake; to do gender incorrectly, which will be swiftly rectified. Any break with accepted norms creates unease. Colleagues will therefore be soon to engage in 'ratification work' to restore the gender order (Brewis, 1994). Breaking a norm may thus, paradoxically, contribute to strengthening the norm.

Norms may be different at different workplaces and in different industries, regions, countries and so on, but gendered norms in one form or another are always present. As social reality must be reproduced every day in order to be maintained, this means that the easiest way of handling the challenges of everyday work is to reproduce received understandings of gender. Anything else risks becoming existentially challenging and anxiety provoking – what am I if not a 'man' or a 'woman' as I have understood it to be? Resistance toward female leaders, or homosexual men or anything else that challenges the taken for granted may be easily understood in this light. Consequently, the challenges for women who need to break the norms to get ahead in an organization are formidable. Would such a break perhaps entail an entrepreneurial act? Could entrepreneurship within an organization be thus defined? The next section looks for an answer in the entrepreneurship literature.

ENTREPRENEURSHIP AS GENDERED[1]

Part and parcel of any discussion about entrepreneurship is a discussion about the entrepreneur. Entrepreneurship scholars oscillate between defining the entrepreneur and defining entrepreneurship. Some make a distinction, some not and some claim that one or the other should be the primary research object. Economists were first in discussing entrepreneurship, and even if economic theory clearly sees entrepreneurship as a function in the economy, most theorists discuss this by defining what the entrepreneur does and by what such a person is like. The entrepreneur is, according to Czarniawska-Joerges and Wolff (1991), an archetypal figure, and whether those who govern work organizations are labelled leaders, managers or entrepreneurs is contingent upon the fashion of today. They suggest that these three roles serve three different symbolic purposes: the leader acts as a symbol embodying people's hope of control over destiny, the manager introduces order into a chaotic word, and the entrepreneur creates entire new worlds. In reality, these functions cannot be neatly separated – any one of them needs part of the other ones to function.

The entrepreneur was the central figure in early capitalism, which is also the time when classical entrepreneurship theory was formulated. In the middle of the last century this person was replaced by the manager and management theory flourished, only to be again replaced by leaders, and leadership theory during the 1970s. Today the entrepreneur is back in vogue. With the welfare state in decline all over the Western world, great hopes are put on entrepreneurship to create new businesses and new jobs to revitalize the economy. The entrepreneurship discourse therefore appears appealing to policy makers and has lately expanded not only into organizations – as this book is about – but also into the school system, into higher education and into the civil sector. More and more countries are incorporating entrepreneurship into the school curriculum, and universities have business incubators and offer entrepreneurship classes not only to business students but to students in any discipline. The most recent addition is a discourse about social entrepreneurship. These are voluntary, non-profit or business organizations founded to serve social needs that in many instances used to be the responsibilities of governments.

What is this entrepreneur who is supposed to revitalize not only the economy but also other sectors all about then? Hébert and Link (1988) explain how economists have theorized it, beginning with Cantillon who in the early 1700s defined the entrepreneur as someone who engages in exchanges for profit and exercises business judgment in the face of uncertainty. His followers added the role of the innovator. Some economists saw the capitalist as different from the entrepreneur, but for Adam Smith (1723–1790) it was one and the same. For Saint-Simon (1760–1825) the entrepreneur was the astute business leader, the skilled manager and the visionary who piloted society into the era of industrialism. Walras (1834–1910), the French economist who developed the theory of general static equilibrium saw the entrepreneur as an intermediary between production and consumption, drawn to situations of disequilibrium where opportunities for profits reside. An economy in a state of equilibrium would, however, make him superfluous. Beginning with US economist Knight (1885–1972), risk and risk taking has been perceived as an integral part of entrepreneurship. The most influential definition on entrepreneurship is attributed to Schumpeter (1883–1950). His main contribution to economics was the theory of 'economic development', which is different from general equilibrium theory. Economic development comes from within the capitalist system, and it comes in bursts rather than gradually. It is accompanied by economic growth, but in addition, it brings qualitative changes or 'revolutions', which radically transform old equilibriums. 'Add successively as many mail coaches as you please, you will never get a railroad thereby,' said Schumpeter (1934 [1983]: 64). Adding a railroad, however, would displace other means of traffic, which made him label this process 'creative destruction'.

Even if the economists aimed at theorizing entrepreneurship as a function in the economy, (as 'the market' or 'interest rates'), few resisted the temptation to describe the entrepreneur. Schumpeter devotes a whole chapter to a portrayal of this special and unusual person. Many men can sing, he says, but the Carusos are rare. First, his intuition and daring makes an entrepreneur make the right decision even though he does not have complete information. Second, he has the ability to go beyond fixed habits of thinking. 'This mental freedom presupposes a great surplus force over the everyday demand and is something peculiar and rare in nature,' writes Schumpeter (1934 [1983]: 86). Third, he is able to withstand social opposition.

What motivates this remarkable person? Schumpeter sees three motives. The first is, 'the dream and the will to found a private kingdom, usually, but not necessarily, also a dynasty' (p. 93). He says that this is closest to a medieval lordship possible to modern man, in that it offers a sense of power and independence. The second motive is the will to conquer: 'the impulse to fight, to prove oneself superior to others, to succeed for the sake, not of the fruits of success, but of success itself. From this aspect, economic action becomes akin to sport – there are financial races, or rather boxing-matches.' (p. 93). 'Finally,' writes Schumpeter, 'there is the joy of creating, of getting things done, or simply of exercising one's energy and ingenuity. This is akin to a ubiquitous motive, but nowhere else does it stand out as an independent factor of behavior with anything like the clearness with which it obtrudes itself in our case. Our type seeks out difficulties, changes in order to change, delights in ventures.' (pp. 93–94).

This fascination with the person carries through to contemporary entrepreneurship research, which inherited the definitions of entrepreneurship from economics, with Schumpeter as the most important source of inspiration. With an understanding of entrepreneurship as 'creative destruction' (Schumpeter, 1934 [1983]); 'pure alertness to as yet unexploited – because unnoticed – opportunities' (Kirzner, 1983); or 'the pursuit of opportunity without regard to resources currently controlled' (Stevenson, 1984), many envisioned entrepreneurship as an act of creativity, innovation, and ingenuity. Entrepreneurs were seen as risk takers and sometimes as daredevils. Earning a good personal profit is implicit, as is the contribution to economic growth in society. The definitions clearly centre on process: 'creative destruction, pursuit of opportunities, alertness to opportunities, breaking equilibrium'. The person who accomplishes this is seen as unique and important for society.

Consequently, most of the early research on entrepreneurs focused on who this person was, rather than on what this person did. The idea was that by identifying such a person it would be possible to select would-be entrepreneurs and thus stimulate entrepreneurship for the benefit of the economy. This is commonly referred to as the trait approach, and it dominated entrepreneurship research for several decades. It has been very productive in outlining the characteristics of entrepreneurs, but disappointingly unproductive in finding out how they differ from others, wrote Gartner (1988: 22), who when reviewing the psychological research found out that 'when certain psychological traits are carefully evaluated, it is not possible to differentiate entrepreneurs from managers or from the general population based on the entrepreneur's supposed possession of such traits.'

Attempts were then made to shift the focus solely to the function of entrepreneurial behavior, i.e., action, and away from the characteristics of the person (Gartner, 1988; Low and MacMillan, 1988), but the person kept coming back again and again. It was argued that businesses are not started by themselves. The entrepreneur is and must be an indispensable ingredient in a theory of entrepreneurship (Carland et al., 1988; Shane and Venkataraman, 2000). Consequently, even contemporary research is preoccupied with the characteristics of the entrepreneur.

Whether focusing on the entrepreneur or on entrepreneurship, the cited texts clearly envision both as having to do with economic activity of some sort. It is, as Daniel Hjorth argues, a concept firmly embedded in an enterprise discourse, which both limits the understanding of entrepreneurship and puts restrictions on what can be done in its name (Hjorth, 2005). It positions the organizational entrepreneur solely as someone who engages in economic, for-profit activity, and organizational entrepreneurship in this rendering is 'too quickly reduced to an efficiency-enhancing tool' (p. 391). It is a new version of managerialism, says Hjorth, conducting conduct by making the employee self-governed and self-regulated according to a discourse of enterprise. It is thus restrictive rather than creative. Instead, Hjorth argues for envisioning organizational entrepreneurship as 'a tactical art of creating spaces for play' (p. 388), or as 'creating disruptions and breaks with normalizing and regulating forces' (p. 396).

A similar discursive struggle as Hjorth is engaged in can be seen in the discussion of entrepreneurship in schools. Politicians want to add it to the curriculum for the same reasons as they want to stimulate entrepreneurship at large – for new businesses, new jobs and economic growth. But teachers do not embrace such a discourse (yet) and therefore translate it into stimulating independent thinking and creativity – of any sort – to the great disappointment of politicians who simply wanted them to teach the pupils how to start a business (Ahl and Berglund, 2008). The enterprise discourse seems to have the upper hand. Attempts to redefine entrepreneurship as social change exist (Steyaert and Hjorth, 2006; Calás et al., 2009), but they are so far rare.

But the enterprise discourse is not the only restriction. Another one is the gendering of the entrepreneur. In Table 8.1 below I made a list of the words used to describe the entrepreneur in economics and management research, and then juxtaposed and compared them with the words describing masculinity from Bem's (1981, 1993) widely used masculinity and femininity index (see Ahl, 2004; 2006b). Sandra Bem is a psychologist who, following thorough research in the United States, developed an index of which characteristics are generally held to describe masculinity versus femininity. In today's language one might say that she captured social constructions of gender.

Table 8.1   Masculinity words compared to entrepreneur words

Bem's Masculinity Words	Entrepreneur
Self-reliant	Self-centered, internal locus of control, self-efficacious, mentally free, able
Defends own beliefs	Strong willed
Assertive	Able to withstand opposition
Strong personality	Resolute, firm in temper
Forceful, Athletic	Unusually energetic, capacity for sustained effort, active
Has leadership abilities	Skilled at organizing, visionary
Willing to take risks	Seeks difficulty, optimistic, daring, courageous
Makes decisions easily	Decisive in spite of uncertainty
Self-sufficient	Independent, detached
Dominant, Aggressive*	Influential, seeks power, wants a private kingdom and a dynasty
Willing to take a stand	Stick to a course
Act as a leader	Leading economic and moral progress, pilot of industrialism, manager
Individualistic	Detached
Competitive	Wants to fight and conquer, wants to prove superiority
Ambitious	Achievement oriented
Independent	Independent, mentally free
Analytical	Exercising sound judgment, superior business talent, Foresighted, astute, perceptive, intelligent

Source: Ahl, 2006b: 600.

Table 8.1 shows a good match between entrepreneur words and masculinity words. Bem's femininity words do not match the list of entrepreneur words above. Is femininity then constructed as the opposite of entrepreneurship? In order to determine this, I made a list of the opposites to the entrepreneur words, using an antonym dictionary, and tried to match it with Bem's femininity words (see Table 8.2).

Besides demonstrating that entrepreneur is constructed as something positive (as the opposite words are largely negative), Table 8.2 also shows its gendering. Some of Bem's femininity words, such as loyal, sensitive to the needs of others, gentle, shy, yielding and gullible are the direct opposites of the entrepreneur words. But most of the femininity words; affectionate, sympathetic, understanding, etc., are neither on the list of words describing the entrepreneur, nor are they the opposites

Table 8.2 Femininity words compared to opposites of entrepreneur words

Bem's Femininity Scale	Opposites of Entrepreneur Words
Gentle	Cautious
Loyal	Follower, dependent
Sensitive to the needs of others	Selfless, connected
Shy	Cowardly
Yielding	Yielding, no need to put a mark on the world, subordinate, passenger, irresolute, following, weak, wavering, external locus of control, fatalist, wishy-washy, uncommitted, avoids power, avoids struggle and competition, self-doubting, no need to prove oneself
Gullible	Gullible, blind, shortsighted, impressionable, making bad judgments, unable, mentally constrained, stupid, disorganized, chaotic, lack of business talent, moody
Sympathetic, affectionate, understanding, warm, compassionate, eager to soothe hurt feelings, soft spoken, tender, loves children, does not use harsh language, cheerful, childlike, flatterable	(No match)

Source: Ahl, 2006b: 601.

of such words. The conclusion drawn is that entrepreneur is a masculine concept. I used research literature to make this point, but other authors have come to same conclusion when analysing media texts (Achtenhagen and Welter, 2005), family business (Mulholland, 1996), fiction (Smith, 2003; Smith and Anderson, 2004), education (Ahl, 2007b) or entrepreneurial regions (Wigren, 2003). The masculine gendering of entrepreneurship is all-embracing. So in addition to all the difficulties for women in organizations described in the earlier section, this presents yet another challenge. The space for a woman to engage in entrepreneurship in an organization is indeed circumscribed. A woman is firmly positioned as not-entrepreneur. And should she choose to engage in acts of creativity outside of the enterprise discourse this is positioned as not-entrepreneurship.

Is there a way to escape? May gendered norms be broken? Of course. The picture painted may seem bleak, but compared to a hundred years ago, great strides have been taken by women in joining organizations and in challenging received notions of what a woman can do. This is an act of entrepreneurship (in the expanded sense) in itself. Much has been aided by traditional liberal feminist activism aimed at removing structural barriers. Removing the last ones by structural change or by legislation would be helpful. I am here thinking of opening up all kinds of education and training, and all professions to women. Most Western countries have almost completed this transition, but some all-male pockets remain. Another much debated suggestion are quotas, designed to get more men into women-dominated organizations, more women into male-dominated organizations, and more women into top-level management. A third move would be a family policy which truly makes it possible to combine work and care for children and the elderly, *and* which splits this work equally between men and women. The Scandinavian countries are world champions in this respect, but even these countries have not taken it far enough to achieve equal opportunities for men and women, and most other places on this planet have yet a long way to go (Kantola and Outshoorn, 2007; Esping-Andersen, 2009).

Besides structural changes, what else can be done? Unfortunately, no final escape from gendered stereotypes is in sight (Ahl, 2007a). People make sense of something by picturing what it is not. Dichotomous thinking is a basic way of understanding the world, and male and female is 'the mother of all dichotomies' (McCloskey, 1985). We understand light by comparing it to dark, tall by comparing it to short and so on. Hierarchical ordering comes along. Light is better than dark, tall is better than short – or the reverse, depending on context (Needham, 1973). But if stereotypes cannot be avoided, perhaps one can fill them with a different content? Can they be ridiculed and made fun of, thus making other versions thinkable? Male and female have arguably been differently constructed in different places and at different times, so variations are possible. Renegotiations of the gender contract take place all the time, and they are also always resisted.

An old-fashioned second-wave feminist move of consciousness raising may be an appropriate strategy in this respect. As Susan Faludi (1991) demonstrated, there was a backlash in the 1980s. Feminist victories of the women's movement were lost. Gender equality is not a 'natural state' which we slowly and surely evolve towards – it is rather an ongoing project which needs continual renewal. New generations come along who have no idea of the kinds of battles their grandmothers had to fight. Young women today who encounter resistance in organizations therefore risk blaming themselves and think that they are personally inadequate, when the reason is a structural pattern beyond their control. So it is a matter of education, and a matter of continuous questioning (Ahl, 2007b).

But what can a woman in an organization who is not in the position to change national politics, organise collective action at the company, start classes in gender theory or organise consciousness raising groups do? She will need to overcome preconceived notions of both womanhood and entrepreneurship in her own mind as well as in the minds of others. If the former has been achieved, how deal with the latter, if at all possible? Direct persuasion might of course work. Or she could play around with categories by constantly evading the labels others place on her, making it difficult for others to firmly and once and for all position her. Fournier (2002) reports a case study of Italian entrepreneurs who did just that, to the great bewilderment of the researcher. Or she could move to another country, which might achieve a similar result. The first women to become full professors at European universities were also foreigners. The two types of strangeness cancelled out each other according to Czarniawska and Sevón (2008). A foreign woman was allowed things a native was not, because she was perceived foremost as a foreigner, and not as a woman. As a stranger she neglected the proper social codes of her new environment simply because she did not understand them. Czarniawska and Sevón (2008: 266) suggest that 'a native woman who transgresses the limits defined for her by her community must be mad: a foreign woman does not know better'. Not knowing better may be the best way to break gendered norms, as one can then act as if they did not exist. But this is a risky game, without any promise of success.

Clearly, whether entrepreneurship is defined as enterprise, as social change or as the creation of entire new worlds, it is not a one-woman show. No such deed can be done without associating with other people. A woman will need to get customers, colleagues, bosses and subordinates along on her endeavour, and in this process she will encounter gendered norms that must be dealt with in one way or another. Openly questioning and challenging existing gendered norms seems to be the most necessary element in making it possible for women to engage in entrepreneurship within the context of an organization. But this cannot be left to individual women alone – the chances for success are far too slim. Leaving the responsibility to individual women in organizations buys into the common sense conception of entrepreneurship as heroic deeds done by single, enterprising (and male) individuals. If a woman fails at questioning gendered norms, she will then be doubly blamed. Consequently, the common sense understanding of entrepreneurship needs to be questioned at the same time. It favours neither women, men, or new endeavours. Reconceptualizing both gender and entrepreneurship is indeed a formidable challenge, which is best undertaken collectively.

NOTE

1.   The summary of classical theories of entrepreneurship was originally published in Ahl, H.
     (2006c). Women and humanities: allies or enemies? In B. Czarniawska and P. Gagliardi
     (eds.), Management Education and Humanities. Cheltenham: Edward Elgar Publishing,
     pp. 45–66. So were Tables 8.1 and 8.2, which however first appeared in Ahl, H. (2002).
     The making of the female entrepreneur: a discourse analysis of research texts on women's
     entrepreneurship. Doctoral Dissertation. Jönköping, Jönköping International Business
     School.

Making the multiple:[1] theorising processes of entrepreneurship and organisation
Chris Steyaert

INTRODUCTION

Organizational and entrepreneurship scholars are increasingly engaging with process theory in their theoretical and analytical work. In the last 30 years or more, entire academic careers have been built around the pursuit of a process perspective of organization, and around efforts to flesh out the by now enigmatic term 'organizing'. To name a few, Karl Weick, Robert Cooper, Robert Chia, and Barbara Czarniawska have made crucial contributions, while institutional support comes from Haridimos Tsoukas, who has since 2005 re-invented the Greek Isles as places for intense philosophical exploration of process theory and for the emergence of so-called process organization studies. Such intensive encounters enable academic communities not only to support or even to institutionalize their unusual perspectives but also to notice and deal with the sometimes contradictory positions that are part of the quickly expanding range of various so-called process perspectives (Wood, 2002; De Cock and Sharp, 2007; Steyaert, 2007; Weik, 2011). Such tensions become visible when philosophical assumptions are closely scrutinized (Hernes, 2008; Weik, 2011) or when new conceptual language does not give rise to new research practices and classical ways of treating method are continued instead (De Cock and Sharp, 2007). Currently many of the contributions on process theory are oriented towards sensemaking, even when it is called a relative newcomer to process thinking (Hernes and Maitlis, 2010: 27).

What makes sensemaking central to understanding organization from a process perspective is that the making of meaning is an ongoing activity, not derived from stable concepts but instead developing within the process itself (Hernes and Maitlis, 2010). Even if sensemaking is a crucial overarching concept that can bring together various understandings of organizing, it often remains within a representational logic of research. Therefore, I will suggest moving to other approaches that take a more explicit recourse to material, embodied, and affective conditions of organizing. In particular, some of the more radical applications of process theory which take issue with a Deleuzian process ontology (Fuglsang and

Sørensen, 2006) remain scattered in the field and could become connected within a so-called non-representational or performative theory of organizing (Beyes and Steyaert, 2012). If a next generation of process theory scholars is to become visible, it will be crucial to tackle these tensions and contradictions head on by experimenting more actively with research practices and thus nudging the field of organizational entrepreneurship to become more entrepreneurial.

A process perspective, quite tautologically, is said to be focused on processes, on movements and flows, such as flux, change, transformation, alteration, metamorphosis, translation, passage, voyage. . . There is an overwhelming interest in movements (Hjorth and Steyaert, 2004b, 2009; Steyaert and Hjorth, 2003, 2006), even if we have realized for quite a while now that we are not good at thinking movements (Cooper, 1998; Chia, 1999) and that this may well continue to be so, especially if we do not intensify experimentation – which I believe can be most fruitfully undertaken through a performative mode of theorizing. Therefore, in this chapter I consider the conditions and implications that are integral parts of taking a process perspective on entrepreneurship and organization, and I examine the question of how process theory requires that we first reconsider the process of theorizing.

My main argument is that the development of process perspectives requires us to re-consider the concept of theory (in its broadest sense) and to contemplate and experiment with the process of theorizing itself. As an example, I refer to the work of Karl Weick who matched his development of a processual perspective of organizing with an equally considerable reflexivity about theorizing (Steyaert and Dey, 2007) and who can be said to represent the interpretive adoption of theorizing process (Hernes and Maitlis, 2010). I then expand on a performative understanding of theorizing, one that draws on a non-representational form of knowledge conception and that considers the material and affective situatedness of process. To support a performative approach to process theory, I suggest that theorizing (process theory) as a process implies the creation of multiplicity: *le multiple, if faut le faire,* or the multiple must be made, as Deleuze and Guattari (1988: 6) put it. To underline this creation of multiplicity, I refer to the radical process theory of Michel Serres and his practice of stepping aside, and then discuss a few examples that perform (academic) writing as the creation of multiplicity. Based on these examples, I call for more experimentation, as Deleuze and Guattari teach us, and Michel Serres urges us, if we want to prepare for a next generation of process theorists who move into a non-representational mode of research. I conclude with some prospects for future developments of process theory.

WHAT THEORY IS NOT, THEORIZING IS[2]

Scholars interested in process theory have one experience in common: they all have thought hard about how to theorize and to destabilize an essentialist understanding of theory itself. They offer a range of ways to develop non-essentialist theories, even if they do not aim for equally radical consequences (Nayak, 2008; Weik, 2011). Within this range, I distinguish between two kinds of theorizing, one that follows an interpretive logic and one that adopts a performative format. The first type can be best illustrated by the work of Karl Weick, who, as said, enriched his development of a processual perspective of organizing with a considerable reflexivity about theorizing (Weick, 1979, 1989, 1992, 1999a, 2004). Weick (1979) urged organizational scholars to stamp out nouns in favor of verbs and to think of organization as organizing; similarly, he urges us to focus less on theories as outcomes, but to pay attention to the process of theorizing. Weick's (1995) adagio, as suggested in the title of his article, is "what theory is not, theorizing is." His interest in improving theory drives him to look at and improve the theorizing process, which "we cannot improve . . . until we describe it more explicitly, operate it more self-consciously, and decouple it from validation more deliberately" (Weick, 1989: 516).

What Weick does is undercut many of the holy cows of methodology, including the whole idea of validity, and engage in more playful and imaginative theorizing, a form of theorizing that widens what can be considered the tools of thinking, representing, and selecting. In essence, Weick approaches theorizing as a form of sensemaking following his evolutionary model of organizing; he sees organizing as "an allegory for writing" and equally points out that "writing is organizing" (Czarniawska, 2003: 245). He captures the paradoxical character of theorizing in the by now renowned idea of disciplined imagination, giving form to a view that conceives theory construction as involving imagination, yet disciplined by the processes of artificial selection. Theorizing, according to Weick, requires a deliberate diversion into how we state problems, how we carry out thought trials, and what selection criteria we include in that thinking. His plea for imagination brings him to counter 'obvious', mostly analytical, principles of classical theory building and to underline the emotional side of theorizing. For instance, he says, a theorist should be "pleased" when assumptions are disconfirmed, as "a disconfirmed assumption is an opportunity for a theorist to learn something new, to discover something unexpected, to generate renewed interest in an old question, to mystify something that had previously seemed settled, to heighten intellectual stimulation, to get recognition, and to alleviate boredom" (p. 525).

Probably more than any other organizational scholar of his time, Weick is prepared to counter established views on what is scientific and what determines that science is 'proper'. In a reply to a text by Sutton and Staw, who tried to neatly define theory by stating what theory is not and by arguing in favor of what is called 'strong' theories, Weick takes a second look at what they have expelled and gives it another chance, as he believes that all these 'negatives' might be crucial in the process of theorizing. As a consequence, Weick (1995) reconsiders references, data, lists, diagrams, and hypotheses with respect to their role in the process of theory construction and in what he calls the interim struggles that bring about theoretical approximations.

While focusing on the process of theorizing, Weick comes to highlight imagination as crucial for what he calls "theory construction," as he broadens the tools and tactics of theoretical practice using a metaphor of "building." Ultimately, Weick opens up the cause of theorizing beyond the usual focus on validity and values in order to stress the significance of such causes of theorizing as plausibility and beauty. In a follow-up essay, entitled "That's moving," Weick plays with the double meaning of moving, not only to point at his continued interest in processual theories, but to emphasize and further elaborate on the role of emotions in theorizing as these can guide us in conceiving theories that matter: "the theories that matter most are those theories that have emotional resonance" (Weick, 1999b: 134). What matters for Weick are theorists who relate understanding and living, and more roughly stated, theory and practice. Drawing on Kierkegaard and Heidegger, Weick (1999b) points out that theorists should aim at narrowing "the gap between understanding and living, or between the present-to-hand stance of the spectator and the ready-to-hand stance of the agent [since they] are more likely to generate work that is judged to be moving" (p. 135).

While Weick translates his understanding of sensemaking processes onto theorizing, he is aware of how theorizing, as a process of making things explicit, might distract from the experiences of a ready-to-hand engagement and might alienate us from the world of involved actors. Therefore, he prefers implicit theories which are not "stripped of context, situation, configuration, relational meaning, and particulars" (p. 136). Yet, while theorizing is always closer to understanding in retrospect, his attempt is to close the gap by considering how we live moving forward. For a theorist or researcher, this also requires listening to how those who participate in the experiences (under study) might counter our initial ideas so that "[w]hen theorists have second thoughts that affirm our original intuitions, we are moved" (p. 138). As a consequence, tactics of theorizing follow the living format of a narrative mode; they focus on interruptions, projects, and unfolding events, and give attention to people "who keep showing up every day" (p. 140). Thus, what Weick suggests here is a "classical" interpretive and phenomenological move to relate to the everyday life-worlds of those (humans) one studies, people who should be given a voice in scholarly representations. I now turn to a performative mode, where such a move to connect is expanded to relationships with nonhuman others and with pre-personal affect. Turning to an ontological politics (Law, 2004), it is no longer enough to sketch out and interpret the life worlds of humans; instead theorizing is a practice that adds to the world through relating to forces of desire and affect.

NON-REPRESENTATIONAL THEORY

In order to "theorize" process beyond the hermeneutic worldview that Weick shares with many others (Hernes and Maithlis, 2011), I would like to point out the possibilities opened up by several scholars who pursue a radical process view of (organizational) becoming. Adopting a "weak thinking style" or ontology of movement (Chia, 1996; Viteritti, 2004), we can point out a neo-materialist (Braidotti, 2002) or a relational materialist (Thrift, 1999) version of a becoming ontology; both Braidotti and Thrift anchor this ontology within Deleuze's notion of becoming for which he draws upon the work of such process theorists and philosophers as Bergson, Nietzsche and, above all, Spinoza. According to Thrift (1999: 317), a relational materialism depends upon a conception of the world as associational, as an imbroglio of heterogeneous and more or less expansive hybrids, as a performance of many worlds. More precisely, a relational materialism is produced through "a non-representational theory" that enacts a relational, materialist, and embodied conception of processes of becoming. The main tenet of a non-representational theory (Beyes and Steyaert, 2012; Cadman, 2009) is a focus on mobile practices and on everyday life which is studied using questions about process. For example, how are everyday practices performed? How are practices and performance embodied? Which forces and capacities to act have bodies? How is performance actualized through the coexistence of a multiplicity of time–space connections?

Thinking from such a radical becoming perspective, researching and theorizing cannot extract a representation of the world (or an organization for that matter) from the world "because we are slap bang in the middle of it, co-constructing it with numerous human and non-human others" (Thrift, 1999: 297). Thrift suggests a non-representational theory which tries to alter the current primacy of representation and its allegiance to an interpretive or textualist model of the world, that seems to prioritize that which can be written down and cancels out that which is not written down. Thrift rejects the metaphor of 'building' and questions "the view that human beings are engaged in *building* discursive worlds by actively constructing webs of significance which are laid out over a physical substrate" (p. 300). This view can be traced back to the founding statements of Clifford Geertz (1964) concerning the "imposition of an arbitrary framework of symbolic meaning upon reality" (p. 39) and has been central to voicing the interpretive turn in organization studies (Hatch and Yanow, 2003). Now it gives form to a so-called building perspective where worlds are made before they are lived in: "there is an imagined separation between the perceiver and the world, such that the perceiver has to reconstruct the world, in the mind, prior to any meaningful engagement with it" (Ingold, 1995: 66; Thrift, 1999).

Referring to such various authors as Bergson, Merleau-Ponty, and Latour, Thrift argues that space and time are not neutral grids or containers of meaning but that "space and time are what we labour to produce as we go along" (p. 301). Instead of a textualist model of the world, which over-emphasizes the cognitive, the contemplative, and the representative, time and space become conceived as embodied and involved activity (Beyes and Steyaert, 2012). The world is made up of billions of happy or unhappy encounters forming a space–time complexity that reminds us of an actor network (Latour, 1997), a mediating network (Cooper and Law, 1995), or a rhizome (Deleuze and Guattari, 1998): "there are no stable and complete orders, only tentative and fractional orderings" (p. 302). The problem is rather "to explain the wonder that there can be stasis given the primacy of process" (Massumi, 2002: 7). The issue at hand is to focus upon "the linkages between the human and other humans, objects, forces, procedures, the connections and flows made possible, the becomings and capacities engendered, the possibilities thus foreclosed, the machinic connections formed that produce and channel the relations humans establish with themselves, the assemblages of which they form elements, relays, resources or forces" (Rose, 1998: 182).

Theories cannot represent these rhizomatic becomings; nor do they exist so we can see the world (or organizations) better. Rather, they form practices themselves (Bourdieu, 1977; Foucault, 1977). They are practical means of going on (Thrift, 1999) and adding to the world (Massumi, 2002). The transition from representational to relational theorizing is formulated well by Shotter (1995: 11) as "a new way of 'looking over' the play of appearances unfolding before us, such that, instead of seeing the events concerned, in terms of theories of what they supposedly represent, we see them 'relationally' – that is, we see them practically, as being embedded in a network of possible connections and relations with their surroundings."

Theories try to reformulate, change, or open up our relations with others and other things and to increase the connections that assemble 'our' lives. Theory is not about knowing what we are (as beings); instead, it focuses on what we want to or can become, on our becomings and how to alternatively 'represent' mutations, changes and transformations. Instead of representations, Braidotti (2002) speaks of figurations, seen as materialistic mappings of situated, or embedded and embodied, positions. A theory as figuration is a living map, a transformative account of the world, the self or an organization. It is upon the ruin of representation – where new ontological and epistemological questions are asked from an aesthetic vantage point – that the appeal and application of organizational research of process might become nomadic. That is, research – and the theories it performs – is no longer metaphoric (Morgan, 2006) but metamorphic; it forms a becoming for the sake of change itself. Theorizing is expansive, as it focuses upon how any being might be possible (Colebrook, 2002). Theorizing aims for the infinite potential instead of generalizing the neopositivist views on theory or contextualizing interpretive approaches. In what follows, I expand the idea that theorizing no longer serves an interest in controlling practice (as in generalization) or in understanding it through empathic relations (as in interpretation); instead, theorizing enables us to experimentally examine what it can have us become.

MULTIPLYING: STEPPING ASIDE

Theorizing in a performative mode thus enacts a becoming-entrepreneurial of research practices, an experimentation with new practices of living and thinking. This emphasis on theorizing as creation is a Serresian idea which urges us to leave home or well-known territories, concepts, and habits, to engage with other sounds and intensities and to go for the deep waters (Dey and Steyaert, 2007). Such experimentation with theorizing can most easily be explained by referring to the idea of stepping aside, a practice of experimentation, which tries to create the multiple. Stepping aside is a practice suggested by Michel Serres, who is certainly not the best-known philosopher of the 'becoming' perspective as his work is not easily co-opted (Brown, 2005), even if he actually should figure next to Whitehead in formulating a non-foundational conception of process (Brown and Stenner, 2009). Serres detests the thinking in schools that limits opportunities for creation and invention. He feels at home with the idea of Deleuze and Guattari that philosophy consists of creating concepts; like them, he sees himself as a geographer of philosophy. Also like them, he sets out to create philosophy as a logic of multiplicities; Deleuze (2000: 147) has affirmed he feels close to Serres on this point. To create multiplicity, Serres begins by literally playing along with Descartes' "cogito ergo sum" or "I think therefore I am." He enacts this in a poetic style, illustrating the pure creativity connected to the singularity of a rhizomatic subjectivity (Braidotti, 2005):

> Who am I, beyond the joy coming from this shudder of awakening, the growth of this green ivy, this dancing flame, this living fire? I think in general, I am a capacity to think something, and I am virtual. I think in general, I can think anything. I think, therefore I am indeterminate. I think, therefore I am anyone. A tree, a river, a number, an ivy, a fire, a reason or you, whatever. Proteus. I think, therefore I am Nobody. The I is nobody in particular, it is not a singularity, it has no contours, it is the blankness of all colours and all nuances, an open and translucent welcome of a multiplicity of thoughts, it is therefore I do not exist. Who am I? A blank domino, a joker, that can take any value. A pure capacity. There is nothing more abstract. I am just the plain whore of the thoughts that accost me, I wait for them, morning and evening, at the crossroads, under the statue of the angel Hermes, all wind and all weather. And, maybe, I am, maybe, if the verb to be is a joker or a blank domino, as well. (Serres, 1995b: 31)

This extensive quote comes from *Genèse* (Genesis), Serres' book on creation or, rather, the book where he unfolds his concept of creation through a performative poetics. Noise, chance, and disorder are evoked as the heralds of the doing of creation. In particular, Serres conceives of noise as the background to all existence; noise is the multiple, multiplicity, the chaos that is always there, invisible but inevitably present in things that are forming and becoming. Serres originally wanted to call the book 'Noise', but was overruled by his French publisher (Critchley, 1996).

It is as if Serres was offering a response in advance to Deleuze and Guattari's notable observation from their final book, *What Is Philosophy?*, that "we only need a little organisation to protect us against chaos" (Deleuze and Guattari, 1994: 201). With great zeal and much poetry, his *Genèse* plunges into the stream of multiplicity, and suggests throughout the whole book how multiplicity turns up again and again, how it has earned itself a place of priority. Organisation is an effect, a stabilization, which often blinds us to the multiple, the chaotic, in short to the process of becoming. In Serres' work, multiplicity is set to music. Indeed, he says, it is easier to listen to multiplicity than to conceive of it visually. Images are sound-images. Perhaps we have been able to imagine multiplicity, but have not always allowed it to sound. Hearing always continues long after seeing has stopped. Multiplicities – think of the sea – are not seen but heard. We are immersed in sound just as we are in light and air. 'Noise' is always there; it is our unbroken background, the material for our forms.

What Serres really envisions is a nomadology, a philosophy of move-ment which does not attempt to conceal multiplicity under unitary concepts, like sweeping dust under a carpet. The same holds for how we theorize relations, often prioritizing just one causal relationship. However, as Serres asks, who can claim that a relation cannot be further elucidated in more subtle relations? There is never simply one causal relation but a web of connections and relationships a researcher needs to attend to. Also it would be mistaken to consider multiplicity as a sum total, an aggregate: it is rather "a lake under the mist, the sea, a white plain, background noise, the murmur of a crowd, time" (1995b: 5). For Serres, multiplicity is not something abstract, but it belongs to the everyday: "Sea, forest, rumour, noise, society, life, works and days, all common multiples." And in all of this, time is the absolute multiplicity, a magnitude without unity. Here is where history can appear, full of sound (noise) and fury. Serres (1995b, p. 20) calls sound-noise – the Old French word *noise* – the only positive word for describing the condition for which we normally reserve only negative terms, such as dis-order.

The question is what we can do to make the multiple possible and enable the potential of the multiple. Above all, Serres (1995b: 5) believes that the usual academic habitus of arrogant truth-making needs to be altered radi-cally: "May the aforesaid scientific knowledge strip off its arrogance, its magisterial, ecclesial drapery, may it leave off its martial agressivity, the hateful claim of always being right; let it tell the truth; let it come down, pacified, toward common knowledge" (1995b: 6). Instead of holding on to interests and positions, Serres holds, creative living is dependent on those who, in their everyday life, dare to step aside and create space for what-ever (new and different) is to come, and thus initiate a process. That is the crucial question Serres describes in the following quote:

To take a place or to give up a place, that is the whole question. There are those who take places, there are those who give them up. [. . .] Those who give up their places move and flow. Their blankness is pure processuality. To yield means to take a step. To step aside, we say. Those who step aside, those who cede their place, begin, by their cession, a process. Those who take the places stabilize them and drown them in noise. Those who give up their place have already taken a step. [. . .] The only steps are steps aside. There is no step that is not a cession. Those who give up their place yield it up to all those who take places, they yield it to everyone, they always yield it. They never have a place to put their foot down, they have no rest. *They are always moving. There is no movement except by stepping aside, giving up one's place. Thus, the series of cessions makes process.* As soon as they find, discover, invent a blank space, the clamorous noisemakers who take the places race in, invade it, pin it down with noise, fury, hatred and illusion, they bury it beneath their tumult, and the original ones give up the place. The blank space is the place of the continuous cession. There is no blank white space, there are only the blank white ones who step aside. There is no blank space, there is only a blank step, the step of giving up a place, there is only a trace of a step, that white foot, exquisite, alive, in the midst of the noise. (Serres, 1995b: 76–78; my italics)

Thus, Serres sees a permanent movement through the act of stepping aside again and again. To give way is to give someone a way. Pay attention, says Serres, to those who give (a)way, for it is they who are 'on the way'. They are moving. They occupy no space, they don't silt up, they are neither immobile nor unmoved. They don't get carried away. Driven out, they float away. Away they must. Like Ulysses, they are always creating new space. They are on the move, like those in a dance, which is based on steps that open a space. Dancing is the continual creation of space, a trace of trace-making. For Serres, the dancer becomes the prototype of the person becoming. For dancing, like writing, is pure movement.

MULTIPLYING: PERFORMING SERIES

Through the practices of stepping side, theorizing can thus be attended to as an active and affective form of creating multiplicity. It requires that we deterritorialize our existing knowledge, create concepts, and orient ourselves to the affects and desires of what is possible or what is to come. In that sense, a performative mode of theorizing is a creative act of multiplication. Summarized in a slogan: to theorize (multiplicity), perform a series. To illustrate how multiplication can be performed, I now turn to a few examples of an analysis that creates a series and thus enables a process of adding to the world. Organizational entrepreneurship requires the initiation of a process of multiplying, that is unfolding new images, languages, and affects to think and enact organizational worlds differently.

A first illustration comes from Hjorth and Steyaert (2006); aiming to carve out a minor language of management education, they developed an image-based performance in which they confront a series of over a hundred images of managerial elites with a broader selection of images of elites. The images and stills of movies interact with a written dialogue in what is called "a mixage, a performative fabulation where images, music, pauses and voices intermingle" (p. 70). The agenda of this performance is to question the dominant account of managerial elites, which is increasingly inscribed in the educational programmes of American and European business schools, and to imagine other versions of what it means to educate and to form managers. As the performance is played out, we are not so much reminded of a form of theatre, but captured by a faceless expressivity that connects with the light and shadows of a room, the laughter and silence of an audience, their whispers and gasps. Through performing, the fragments of words and the images form an assemblage with its own intensities, its own speeding up and slowing down: it "forms a murmuring of understatements and a shouting of exaggerations, a cutting in with slogans and a zooming out with pauses" (p. 70). The performance is driven by an ongoing stepping aside: the usual images of management, the dominant vision on education are entered into and immersed in a series of other images, in a multiplication that lets other images become imaginable: can management education be guided by a series of alternative images – such as people without qualities, harlequins, masked clowns, angels, and troubadours?

In a similar vein, moving from the context of education to publication, Steyaert and Hjorth (2002) created a performance based on the kind of speech scholars produce in relation to specific audiences. Through creating a series of speeches, the performance again forms a mixage, one that intermingles famous speech fragments with dialogic sketches on the struggles of an academic trying to prepare a paper and a presentation for an upcoming conference. The play is not just about questioning the usual ways of publishing and giving lectures; rather, the creation of a series and the ongoing stepping aside explore alternative forms, styles, and genres of (academic) speech. They form an experimentation that affirms the myriad of other ways that academics could perform their work, and address their work to everyday men and women, as one would meet them in the square in any possible city.

A further example of creating a series to form a processual analysis comes from a study on organizational change in which the concept of change is re-invented along a Deleuzian becoming ontology and the concept of desire in specific (Lohmann and Steyaert, 2006). Aiming to enact the process of change-becoming-change, Lohmann and Steyaert (2006) present a processual analysis through what they call a cartography of affects. The change process was initiated by the wave of privatization, specifically the policy of deregulating the European electricity industry. This process created several years of change initiatives in the company being studied, a Danish utilities provider called ELEC. Following how the change develops over a 3-year period, the analysis zooms in on affective details as the employees experience these changes; it narrates their frustrations and struggles, and their comments and hesitations – along with their hopes and ideas.

Here, change is reconceptualized as a series of affective movements, a triptych of affects: waiting, confronting, and exhausting. At first, employees waited and felt insecure; then they were uncertain and confronted their uncertainty and felt irritated; later they were despondent, exhausted, and anxious. The analysis breaks with the usual format of a change study that represents a discursive change accompanied by resistance. Following the new change discourse that centers on competition and the free market, the study steps aside from this overwhelming rhetoric of change; by following the everyday lives of the employees, it gives space to an echo, an affective silence that contained the collective enunciation of living (through) change. Instead of a defeatist image of employees who resist, the analysis also creates images of employees who have the ideas, hopes, and energy to continue with the change process beyond its predefined goals.

Thus, the study by Lohmann and Steyaert is guided by the idea of re-conceptualizing the overcoded concept of change, and through a series of affects, it performs the multiplicity and intensity of change, what has also been called organizational becoming (Tsoukas and Chia, 2002). Massumi (2002: 36) summarizes affect as "the perception of one's own vitality, one's sense of aliveness, of changeability"; this might bring us to the core of processual analysis (of change). How, in our encounters with other actants, do we (learn to) sense and practice how we can change ourselves? And how can we re-invent the assemblages that already produce us? In taking a processual perspective, we encounter no a prioris, only becomings; in this case, change itself has to become (changed). As Linstead (2004) puts it, change "must be judged and evaluated according to the extent to which desire, multiplicity and creativity are emancipated," and the extent "to which the outcome is social relations which exist for the betterment of us all, rather than just for the favoured few" (pp. 9–10).

In the change study, as well as in the performances by Hjorth and Steyaert, writing participates in the invention of new possibilities of organizational life; these might come closest to what the open yet contradictory term organizational entrepreneurship aims to express. Through aesthetic forms, a series is created, a series that in its performativity produces a people to come: new realities become possible for the organizational life spheres in which we are involved. A process of organizational entrepreneurship is enacted through a form of fabulation that, through minor stories and performances, shapes imaginative alternatives and possibilities and creates counterpoints to dominant, majoritarian discourses (Biehl and Locke, 2010).

MULTIPLYING THROUGH EXPERIMENTATION

This is then my plea: Experiment! Radicalize the so-called radical process theory. By trying to distinguish between interpretive and performative approaches to theorizing process I may seem to be creating too strong a contrast, but my aim is not to do away with one form to promote another. Rather, with my plea, I try to emphasize differences in the quality of experimentation that both approaches enable. In the future, experimentation will be necessary to further develop the potential of processual perspectives through conceptual creation. Whether one opts for theorizing through sensemaking or through performing (or through other overarching concepts I do not address here), in both cases, experimentation can enable us to move beyond current habitual practices. Also Karl Weick, as we saw, has deployed tactics of experimentation, even if he continued to relate them to concepts from mainstream literature, a move that led Hernes (2008: 114) to call Weick a "radical mainstream organization theorist."

As explained earlier, a core problem has been that theorists interested in conceptualizing processes keep adhering to a representational logic of inquiry; they stall their own processual thinking by falling back on non-processual methods that freeze the movements they try to study, describe, and explain. But theorizing cannot move forward while scholars hold on to former scientific concepts of theory. Even if they claim to cling to the assumptions, concepts, and principles of process philosophy, they fail to adopt (even partially) their practices and methods of inquiry and "end up reverting to conventional non-process methods" (De Cock and Sharp, 2007: 233). For instance, in discussing the work of Langley (1999, 2007) and Van de Ven and Poole (2005), Hernes (2008: 23) makes a similar remark, noticing that these authors "tend to treat analysis as a rather classic approach to making sense of data, where the 'what' of the flow is implicitly already determined and defined by the analyst at the outset". In this respect, De Cock and Sharp (2007) point out that the very idea of process data (Langley, 1999) is virtually contradictory; they illustrate that all parts of the research process and such taken-for-granted notions as data need to be re-invented. An intention to describe pure movement remains sterile if approached with accounts "that conceive the goings on of the social world through a fixed viewpoint" (Cadman, 2009: 5).

Thus we see the challenge: to connect the wealth of understandings based on process philosophy with the ways of undertaking research into social processes such as organizational entrepreneurship, especially to overcome the problem that "process thinking is struggling to achieve an anti-interpretive movement" (De Cock and Sharp, 2007: 241). Whether an anti-interpretive movement would be enough is doubtful; what I believe is needed is a practice of theorizing differently, one that does not fall back on the usual ways of setting up (interpretive) research. I believe we must engage with experimentation, and be a bit bold, not only questioning what we have learned about theory, data, methods, and so on in our introductory course on *Wissenschaftstheorie,* but also thinking affirmatively (Weiskopf and Steyaert, 2009) and inventing new practices of research. Through stepping aside one can initiate a process of multiplication. Multiplying, as I illustrated, consists of creating a series. This is a Deleuzian tactic of conceptualizing the creation of a series – and, and, and – based on increasing the (number of) connections. The aim is to discourage a "unified plan of organization or development" and to seek "an unlimited plane in which one is always passing from one singular point to another, then connecting it to yet something else" (Rajchman, 2000: 4). This is illustrated in the style Deleuze practiced as he was writing in series or plateaus, and the ways thinking gets shaped in connections and associations, a constant multiplication. "For," as Rajchman (2000: 5) remarks, "to think is to experiment". So one cannot stay on the outside; one has to make a move, try something out, to get somewhere (Deleuze, 1990). In this, Deleuze (1990: 125) emphasizes,

> Mediators are fundamental. Creation's all about mediators. Without them nothing happens. [. . .] Whether they're real or imaginary, animate or inanimate, you have to form your mediators. It's a series. If you're not in some series, even a completely imaginary one, you're lost. I need my mediators to express myself, and they'd never express themselves without me: you're always working in a group, even when you seem to be on your own.

For Deleuze, the prime mediator to form a series was his collaboration with Félix Guattari; through it they became a multiple, a collective.

To experiment, to create such a multiplicity thus becomes in my view the leitmotiv to radicalize processual thinking. Just as one cannot commit a priori to stasis, one should not adhere a priori to an idea of flow; instead, multiplicities have to be made through experimentation "to shake up an overly rigid system," an actualized, stabilized system that Deleuze has called a stratum (Bonta and Protevi, 2004: 83). Taking a practical tack, Deleuze and Guattari (1988: 161) indicate how to proceed: "This is how it should be done: lodge yourself on a stratum, experiment with the opportunities it offers, find an advantageous place on it, find potential movements of deterritorialization, possible lines of flight, experience them, produce flow conjunctions here and there, try out continuums of intensities segment by segment, have a small plot of new land at all times." Whether you follow the more detailed instructions as illustrated by Bonta and Protevi (2004: 83) or by Fuglsang and Sørensen (2006: 16), experimentation engages with intensities to foster patterns of becoming and affirms the positive structure of difference (Braidotti, 2005). It requires changing, exploring and repeating the practices involved in researching, such as writing.

With regard to writing, Bonta and Protevi (2004: 83) suggest that we all "learn how to 'stutter in your own language', pick up some slang, or simply read, new, 'minor' authors." Writing is not based on repeating usual styles and rehearsing well-known truths, but on breaking open and cutting through majoritarian or dominant forms of expression that re-install the fiction of the author (Hjorth and Steyaert, 2006). Therefore, Deleuze and Guattari (1986: 41) argue that "[l]iving and writing, art and life, are opposed only from the point of view of a major literature." Minor literature opens up to intensities, sensations and affects, "to the sounds, marks and affects from which meanings emerge" (Colebrook, 2002: 116). Writing presupposes that we empty ourselves, so that we can open up "to possible encounters with a number of affective outsiders" (Braidotti, 2005: 306), and then hold on to that affectivity in order to mobilize our "capacities to feel, sense, process and sustain the impact in conjunction with the complex materiality of the outside; a sort of fluid but self-sustaining sensibility, or stream-of-consciousness that is porous to the outside" (Braidotti, 2005: 306–7). Writing is thus a material-affective practice of creation, a pure creativity, "an aesthetic mode of absolute immersion along with the unfolding and enfolding of one's sensibility in the field of forces one inhabits – music, colour, light, speed, temperature and intensity" (Braidotti, 2005: 307).

CONCLUSION

In this chapter, I discussed the possibilities of a process perspective by addressing one of its trickiest questions: how practices of theorizing and researching themselves become moving and how they can move us, that is increase our perception of changeability and add to our belief in making different things possible in the world. Even if process perspectives have been around for a while, they have many implications for how we 'do' theory, research, writing, and intervention, all of which need to be further clarified and experimented with. In conclusion, I offer a few summative contributions, prospects if you like, that can guide us in this further elaboration.

First, a core premise of taking a process perspective is to shift one's horizon from a being to a becoming ontology. Such a shift is not a lightweight endeavour: it requires that we move from having foundations (and losing them) to enacting a reflexive foundationalism (Brown and Stenner, 2009). Many philosophers have been working with process ontology; thus as theorists of process, we are already immersed in a series. For instance, Hernes (2008) creates a series around Whitehead, multiplied by the sociologists Luhmann and Latour and the organizational theorists March and Weick, even if this creates a questionable hierarchy: philosophy, sociology, organization theory. Such hierarchies are not unusual when organization theorists turn to philosophy, as we can see in the comment by Tsoukas and Chia (2011: 4): "the study of organization is inextricably dependent on the *prior* organization of mentalities and modes of thought" (my italics). More of these inventive (and less hierarchical) series need to be created, as organizational theorists seem to tell the usual, yet hardly accurate, history of process metaphysics (Weik, 2011) or pop up the usual suspects of process philosophy: James, Whitehead, Bergson. For instance, a whole series of feminist process thinkers – including Butler, Irigaray, Kristeva, and Braidotti – are rarely included in overviews or accounts of organizational process theorists (Nayak and Chia, 2011). Similarly, we can ask why Deleuze's reading of Bergson is incorporated but not his work on Spinoza (Nayak and Chia, 2011). In my view, these philosophical conceptions are not there to be applied in a hierarchical system; rather they need to be connected to the non-philosophical, so we can invent (new) concepts. That is, as Massumi (2002: 17), puts it,

> If you want to invent or reinvent concepts [. . .]: don't apply them. If you apply a concept or a system of connection between concepts, it is the material you apply it to that undergoes change, much more markedly than do the concepts. The change is imposed upon the material by the concepts' systematicity and constitutes a becoming homologous of the material to the system. This is all very grim. It has less to do with "more to the world" than "more of the same". It has less to do with invention than mastery and control.

In this text, I used the work of Serres to illustrate how he reconceptualized creation through the concept of genesis and developed the notion of stepping aside as a practice of writing multiplicity. Theorizing is thus rhizomatic instead of hierarchical, it creates concepts and invents connections: "Theory, in this sense, is not a process of moving towards a better representation of underlying realities. Processual theory *is not*; instead, it is pure creativity, always moving beyond itself. It *is* not, but it acts, it is not an atemporal and abstract representation of reality but the active, or the useful or more precisely, the creative" (Nayak, 2008: 186).

Second, organizational entrepreneurship is a field of in(ter)vention (Steyaert, 2011), one that practices creativity to add to the world (of movement). Combining entrepreneurship and organization, we rewrite the theme of organizational change as one of change-becoming-change (Lohmann and Steyaert, 2006), thus emphasizing that organizational entrepreneurship consists of organizational becoming (Tsoukas and Chia, 2002) or the joyful production of creativity. This brings us to the core contribution of processual approaches to organizational entrepreneur-ship: it conceives of becoming as a mode of invention and a sense of alive-ness. Organizational entrepreneurship can be seen as an indication that organization studies and entrepreneurship studies are gradually coming together, through their joint interest in processes of creation and creativ-ity. If entrepreneurship takes a relational turn, it turns its focus to social processes of creation, and thus onto organizing creativity. If organization studies, exploring a becoming perspective, follows an interest in creativity and creation, it will inevitably enter discussions that have been prepared in entrepreneurship studies. A process perspective turns organizational entrepreneurship into a neo-vitalist practice of affirmative creativity, one that is oriented toward (the joy of) life itself, and its ongoing creation. This aligns well with Nayak's (2008: 187) argument:

> Process philosophy defines theory by its relation to what does not yet exist. Processual theory does not synthesize something that has been or that is. Instead, it announces what will be and provokes our attention to what is going to be. It is in this sense that processual theory is a way of 'thinking beyond' the human intellect and opening ourselves to the reality of movement and becoming.

Whether a series of images (Hjorth and Steyaert, 2006), a multiplication of speeches (Steyaert and Hjorth, 2002) or a mapping of affects (Lohmann and Steyaert, 2006), the processual theorist becomes a symptomatologist, a cartographer of affect (Beyes and Steyaert, 2012) in search of a people to come.

Third, academic praxis is itself performative: "once the world is consid-ered as productive and processual, then, for academics to become worthy of the eventful nondiscursive world, it demands a refigured academic style; one which recognizes that academic praxis itself is performative" (Cadman, 2009: 5). A lot of that academic work is not worthy, as it is hooked on fads and fashions, aiming to score publications and giving a narrow meaning to the term performative: that which sells or gives status (Lyotard, 1984). Instead of scoping our analysis of organizational entre-preneurship as one that aims to resemble it through academic representa-tions, we have outlined a performative style of researching and writing triggered by the urge to experiment with the thinking which occurs in the interstices between thought and practice (Cadman, 2009). We have introduced a writing based on the ideas and intensive writing style of Deleuze which, according to Braidotti (2005: 307), "spells the end of the linguistic turn, as he releases the subject from the cage of representational thinking" in favour of a performative approach of writing (up) organiza-tional research (Steyaert, Marti and Michels, 2012). Process scholars are thus invited to "an apprenticeship in the art of conceptual and perceptual colouring" (Braidotti, 2005: 307). According to Braidotti (2002: 73), what processual analysis does, is perform a series, a "rainbow of alternative figurations."

NOTES

1. This is our translation for "Le multiple, il faut le faire" (literally: "the multiple has to be made"). With thanks to Helen Snively (Cambridge, MA), language editor of this text.
2. This part is based on Steyaert and Dey (2007).

10 Organizational entrepreneurship: an art of the weak?
Daniel Hjorth

A web of microscopic, capillary political power had to be established at the level of man's very existence, attaching them to the production apparatus, while making them into *agents of production* . . . (Foucault, 2002: 86, my emphasis)

OPENING

It seems to me that the late-modern emblematic subjectivity of industrial economy – the manager – emerged as the emblematic manifestation as well as guardian of these 'agents of production' Foucault mentions in the opening quote. From F. W. Taylor onwards (although inherited from much earlier sources), the manager's agency was constituted by the power to negate disorder, to instigate control, and to say 'yes' to carrying the ever-greater load of adjusting to modifications in the environment for the purpose of greater efficiency. Establishing the manageable organization and employee, central to the industrial age, 'gave rise to a series of knowledges – a knowledge of the individual, of normalization, a corrective knowledge – that proliferated in these institutions of infrapower, causing the so-called human sciences, and man as an object of science, to appear' (ibid.)

How can we think organizational entrepreneurship differently as we are now, at the dawn of postindustrialism, looking for the creative/innovative rather than merely 'manageable organizations' (Taylor, 1911; Mayo, 1923; 1924; 1933; 1945; Simon, 1945; Becker, 1964; Chandler, 1977; Porter, 1980; 1985)? Rather than engaging in a critique of the complex matrix of knowledge/power that has shaped practice and understanding of organizations in late-industrial economy, I want to write *for* a new understanding. Its newness would emerge from using process thinking to develop new knowledge. Why process thinking? Because it makes no sense to continue talking about change and processes as normal, as has been done in management and organization studies for some three decades now, while excluding thinking from how the world becomes. It makes no sense to herald that we live in a world, and compete on markets, in continuous flux, while reserving for thinking a stable island somehow outside this world (Tsoukas and Chia, 2002).

The question of how to think (and analyse and study) entrepreneurship in contexts of organization will then have to be articulated in processual terms. In this chapter, I chose to do so focusing on how becoming-entrepreneur as a process of subjectification is related to creation in organizations. That is, can we understand and describe how the new is achieved when we analyse 'organizational entrepreneurship' (Hjorth, 2005) procesually? I am not interested in *managerial* entrepreneurship; entrepreneurship as a possibility ostensibly communicated in corporate strategies. Such entrepreneurship is tamed and will most likely lead only to quantitative difference (i.e., more). My interest is instead in trying to contribute to an understanding of why we do not see more *entrepreneurial* entrepreneurship in organizations than we do. Entrepreneurship that is not a realization of possibilities articulated in management strategy, but an actualization of potentialities, creations that generate qualitative difference – the new (cf. discussion in Introduction, this volume). The proposal is that process thinking can assist our attempts to develop this understanding.

My interest in how organizational entrepreneurship emerges from within the dynamics of strategy and tactics led me now, when trying to radicalize the processual approach, to use Nietzsche's concept of affirmation (1969). Affirmation is the power of becoming-active that destroys reactive-negative forces and makes difference possible (Deleuze, 1983). The affirmative tactician, creating by transmuting, I describe as practicing an *art of the weak*. Nietzsche helps us understand why the negative-reactive is not a possible route to other than quantitative change (creation as burdening us with more of the same), but how instead affirmation can explain the fact that organizational entrepreneurship *does* happen. The question is how becoming-entrepreneur and organizational creation of the new are related. They are simultaneous and consubstantial, immanently related in the process of organization-creation. 'In other words, they might be seen as differential emergences from a shared realm of relationality that is one with becoming – and belonging.'(Massumi 2002: 71). Understanding how this happens, using process thinking, is the task of this chapter.

The chapter struggles in particular with the question of agency and agent: how to rethink agency in a processual approach to organizational entrepreneurship? Spinoza's ideas of power to affect and power to be affected; of sadness and joy; of passion and action (Deleuze, 1988; Massumi, 2002; Smith, 2007b; Spindler, 2009) provide help and an enriching backdrop to Nietzsche's analysis of will to power (which is either affirmative or negative). Deleuze is the central process philosophical thinker in this inquiry, and also the one whose philosophy relates the thinkers of multiplicity and creation (Henri Bergson, Alfred North Whitehead and William James) with thinkers of force, affect and power (Spinoza and Nietzsche).

This chapter is included in the *Handbook* to represent the inter- and multi-disciplinary entrepreneurship research that goes on in 'our field'. Researching entrepreneurship is itself a multiplicity, a dynamic becoming. This Handbook grasps this particular nature of organizational entrepreneurship, partly reflecting organization studies' vivid engagement with social science and humanities (Zald, 1993; Gagliardi and Czarniawska, 2006). The chapter will progress along the following structure. After the introduction, which develops the problem, I discuss the challenges with thinking the new (representing creation; the dilemma of organizational creativity; and introducing affirmation.) We then need to contextualize process thinking, which is done in the second part of this chapter, discussing the new/difference, multiplicity and event, and by relating the individual, organization and process. Lastly, in the third part, we close in on the question of agency, discussing affect, subjectification, and an art of the weak.

INTRODUCTION

Analysing creation and agency, when committed to process thinking, presents some challenges. Agency, we can understand as an expression of intelligence in needful or useful movement (Massumi, 2002: 128): from the vacuum that receptivity/sensation activates, to the extended action. Agency is traditionally attributed to an agent that is equal to an acting subject that wills and acts but is never itself part of what achieves being. This locks us into a non-dynamic thinking that makes change into a quantitative change of Being. Neither the subject, nor the social world, and indeed nor the natural world can be realistically grasped assuming such stasis (Latour, 1993). Evolution is the term used in biology to grasp dynamism. Ontogenesis or qualitative transformation/transmuting are alternative concepts. We need those when we think processually. Process thinking doesn't stop at the subject, but thinks subjectification as a process that grasps the dynamics of becoming, and this way helps us understand the new and creation in qualitative terms, as difference. We thus move away from entrepreneurs, identifying opportunities, creating products/firms and adding value. Instead, we are interested in organization-creation processes of entrepreneurship, which modifies the charged social field of potentials, opening up new avenues for the world to become, new ways of existing, actualizing new value: difference.

Would practicing the idea of an actor without agency in the traditional sense of that concept be of help for analysts trying to think entrepreneurship and organization processually? This may be a way to tackle the challenge of how to think creation in process studies (Deleuze, 1988; Massumi, 2002). Doing so with Bergson we are urged to resist the habit of giving priority to position and the related, to instead see how movement and relation are primary. Creation, in non-processual thinking (a philosophy of Being; Rorty, 1980; preventing movement and relation from being represented except as in specialized form) seems to signify a start (origin) and call for an agent (the creator). Agency traditionally already includes the idea of an agent that is the grounding of that wilfully acting subject. Both ideas install obstacles to process thinking. A philosophy of becoming stresses instead flow, contingency, relationality, multiplicity, difference, potentiality, intensity, affirmation and actualization (of the virtual, the incipient).

The *actor*, the way I want to propose this concept here, is a way to think subjectification (rather than subject), and this way help thinking focus on the openness of bodies, their capacities. As is the case also with Judith Butler's emphasis on subjectivity (1993), Deleuze shares Foucault as reference point for thinking subjectification (Deleuze, 1995). Admittedly, there are several social science thinkers that use the term actor as concept for analysing our relational constitution. Goffmann (1959) and Burke (1969) place an emphasis on drama and performing in public, which still preserves the problematic self-grounded subject, although socially constructed. Greenblatt (1980) represents somewhat of a bridge to the poststructuralists in his emphasis on discursively ordered cultural-poetic constitutions of identity and meaning in everyday life, and the importance of frames and framing for 'thickness' (nod to Clifford Geertz's paradigmatic work in anthropology and ethnography) to characterize our narration of this life. Bruno Latour has also opted for actors or 'actants' rather than subject (as a presupposition to agency) when he opened up for non-human actors (as part of so-called actor network theory; Latour and Woolgar, 1979; Latour, 1988).

I chose 'actor' rather than subject: (1) because it escapes presupposition of agency (a line of thinking usually referred to Descartes' self-grounded subject), which prevents us from a relational and processual understanding; (2) as it allows us to problematize the subject as preceded by rules, forces, desires that subjectify, i.e., how many today have come to relate to themselves as 'entrepreneurs'; (3) to emphasize the affective and relational constitution of the acting body vis-à-vis the text(s) that embed and contextualize action. I want to examine how we can think organizational entrepreneurship processually by avoiding the stifling category of the *agent* while still affirming the onto-genetic force of the actor, thought from a poststructuralist conception of agency: 'It is an agency, only without an agent: a subjectless subjectivity.' (Massumi, 2002b: xxiv).

The 'actor' is thus not used metaphorically any more than the 'subject' is. There are only subject*ivities* that index modes of agency, ways of existing. There is no subject at the core. The 'actor' is a concept transferred from theatre in order to highlight the dynamic relationship between text/ narrations, stage and subjectivity. This is not Goffmann's theatre of everyday life, where a choosing subject puts on a mask in order to play a role, to perform in public. Instead, the actor is defined as the body (which can also be social, a collective) on which desires and discourses work to increase or decrease capacities. Bodies are always already related though, and 'our awareness is always of an already ongoing participation in an unfolding relation'. (Massumi, 2002a: 231). The actor is the body that has become active by affirming the power to be affected and thus subjectified into the 'actorship' (agency) needed for the narrative (intension, event) to further itself into its nextness. This passionate line is not chosen. We always affirm from within an unfolding relation.

Desire, which is always relational, desires to become active, to create. When the potential for such becomings reaches sufficient intensity, a point of subjectification achieves being. Subjectified into a particular actor, the power to affect is released as an immanent force of this passionate move of creation. Will to power (the genealogical element of force; Deleuze, 2006: 50), we have noted, has the qualities of being affirmative or negative. When affirming the potentiality of what could become new, movement is released and the social field of 'charged particles' is intensified. In entrepreneurship one could see the potential to create an opportunity as a point of subjectification, as when a passionate move is pursued towards increased capacity to create the new.

A body's power to be affected (passion) and power to affect (action) emerges with different strength depending on what narrativization of life-to-come that has gained 'the upper hand'. There is always a crowd of incipiencies that press themselves upon the actual and seek channels of creation through which this or that piece of story could become actualized (Massumi, 2002a). The actor is the body these event- or action-pregnant stories-of-what-could-become (virtualities) need in order to become actualized or created. A body that negates (rather than affirms), simply re-acts, and a re-actor rather than actor is made. Re-acting is negating/denying the passionate move, the lowest degree of a will to power, seeking only power. In organizational contexts this is often for the purpose of instigating control and predictability. Affirmation instead follows the line of passion – a spontaneity (cf. Aldrich and Fiol's, 1994, 'fools' that 'rush in') that makes movement and creates space.

Strategy, often thought as appropriation of a place/position in a market*place*, the basis for 'inside' and 'outside', 'us' and 'them', represents thinking in spatial rather time-based terms. Movement – qualitative transformation underway – is central to our understanding of process, but also to the time-based conception of the relationship between the virtual/incipient, and creation. Process is the 'rolling of the "already more" of the world into a nextness' (Massumi, 2002a: 98) The 'already more' is the potentiality/virtuality of that which has achieved being (the actual), the momentum of expression. Sensation and thought are in excess over experience or the actual as they register potential (the virtual, fabulating power): multiple becomings (heterogenesis) beyond present experiences are thus anticipated, which tells us that it takes a Cartesian 'subject' or organizational 'structures' to think the world as stasis.

Movement, within organizations, is what charges the field and triggers the flash of action "by which it plays out the consequences of its own intensity." (as Massumi, 2002b: xxiv, puts it.) Potential for creation is immanent to organizations through its relations of desires and imaginations. We could think of a strategy as a narrativization (in the genre of management) of life-to-come that is composed and communicated for the purpose of controlling this potentiality of creative desires. Entrepreneurship can in this perspective be described as operating in a landscape appropriated by this ostensive story, strategy, which has delineated a place of its own. Organizational entrepreneurship is then an exercise in tactical readings of such narratives. Such tactics open space for creation in-between ostensive singularity (strategy) and performative multiplicity.

> By an art of being in between, he [sic!, the tactician] draws unexpected results from his situation. [. . .] The space of the tactic is the space of the other. Thus it must play on and with a terrain imposed on it and organized by the law of a foreign power. (de Certeau, 1984: 30; 37)

Organizational entrepreneurship is by necessity tactical since organizations are arresting of potentiality, multiplicity and flow (Tsoukas and Chia, 2002). Opposition cannot change this, for it will always only provoke the instigation of a new arresting (ostensive story, strategy). Instead, it has to be affirmed – tactically – in a transformative move. *It has to be an art of the weak*. This is still resistance to the strategic: against normalizing and individualising ourselves on the basis of managerial knowledge/power, and against fixed and ready-made identities, fulfilling the requirements of an ideal employee subjectivity. When we conceptualise this in processual terms it helps to think in terms of the dynamics of text and actor. No text can escape its belonging to the becomings of language. No actor can found itself outside 'the social script'. Script and actor are always already part of an unfolding relation. The above initiation of organizational creation is elaborated, and implications for describing and theorising are discussed and analysed in the continuation of the chapter.

PROCESS THINKING AND 'THE NEW' IN ORGANIZATIONS

Representing Creation

Christian biblical images are influential inputs to how our thinking of creation has been shaped, what it is to create, and what is required for creation to happen. Indeed, the reader of John 1:1–2 in the Bible (King James' version) experiences this attempt to fold the beginning into a complex inauguration-story that seeks to prevent the idea that something was there before this 'start'. It represents an early attempt to think and write creation, and illustrates the challenge: 'In the beginning was the Word, and the Word was with God, and the Word was God. The same was in the beginning with God.'

This is often described as a complex play (by John) of references to the start of Genesis (and thus a historical reference to the beginning of history) and to the start of universe (in a cosmological sense). The 'word' is a translation of *Logos* and is therefore understood as giving *Logos* an equally divine status as God, but also complicating the relationship: *Logos* and God seem hard to separate but are still in a relation (and thus distinct). Acknowledging there are centuries of debates over interpretations regarding these words (and translations), we may read them as an attempt to deal with the problem of agency by folding the creator, the will or intention to create, and the world: a dissolving of rock-solid agency into the relationality of a folded text–actor emergence. What we read is maybe the echo of the famous words of Heraclitus (who died 475 BC; the gospel of John completed around AD 90–100): *panta rei* (that he most likely never wrote, rather something like *Πάντα ῥεῖ καὶ οὐδὲν μένει* :'in the end there is only flux, everything gives way', or 'everything is in flux and nothing abides', or 'everything flows and nothing stays fixed') (Rehnberg and Ruin, 1997).

Process philosophy, here mainly represented by poststructuralist thinkers (Nietzsche, Bergson, Deleuze), has gradually made clear how this flux can be thought. The implications of this for entrepreneurship-, management- and organization theory are slowly made clear in an emerging body of literature (e.g., Styhre, 2002; Tsoukas and Chia, 2002; Linstead and Mullarkey, 2003; Chia and Holt, 2009; Hjorth and Steyaert, 2009). The purpose here is not to review this literature, nor to provide an extensive overview (see however: Chia, 1999; Langley, 2007; Cooper, 2007; Steyaert, 2007; Steyaert, this volume). Our more specific challenge is to understand how to think organizational entrepreneurship from a process perspective.

It seems rather obvious that process thinking would cater to our needs to describe, study and analyse organizational processes. In the case of entrepreneurship or creativity, however, we do not have organi*zing* as our analytical focus. We have, instead, the problem of 'the new' (Smith, 2007a). This is the interruption of the flow of becoming, so as to force time to start again from a new platform. How can we, by the help of process philosophy, think 'the creation of the new' as an entrepreneurial-organizational achievement? And, more specifically; what is the role of subjectivity in understanding organizational entrepreneurship? In order to understand how entrepreneurship (as organization-creation) is possible at all in organizational contexts, we will conceptualize 'the new' by the help of Gilles Deleuze's philosophy (Smith, 2007a). His readings of Nietzsche and Spinoza will be important, and invites us to think life processually via 'dance' (affirmation of becoming), 'play' (affirmation of chance) and 'laughter' (affirmation of life). We will understand the new as actualized potentiality (Colebrook, 2005; Deleuze, 1983): difference. Actualization results in a multiplicity of organization, which is indeterminate and unforeseeable: 'Without the blueprint of order, the creative process of organization is always an art.' (Hardt, 1993). Organizational entrepreneurship is a movement away from determinate-strategic order (blueprint) towards a multiplicity of organization, an original arrangement, an actualized virtuality.

The Dilemma of Organizational Creativity

The dilemma is indicated by the famous concept of 'creative destruction', described by Schumpeter (Schumpeter, 1942 [1962]) as a mutation that revolutionizes economy from within, 'incessantly destroying the old one, incessantly creating a new one' (p. 83). This signals that the creation of new ideas always means existing ideas become 'old' and most often (need to be) destroyed. Existing ideas are protected mainly by people of power in the established organizational structure/hierarchy (the relation of a dominant to a dominated force, Deleuze, 1983: 7): managers. They have, as already Machiavelli (1513 [1988]) pointed out, little to gain from 'the new' as it brings multiplicity of organization with it, not fitting in the existing order. The classical quote again:

> It ought to be remembered that there is nothing more difficult to take in hand, more perilous to conduct, or more uncertain in its success, than to take the lead

in introducing a new order of things, because the innovator has for enemies all those who have done well under the old conditions, and lukewarm defenders in those who *may* do well under the new. This coolness arises partly from fear of the opponents – who have the laws on their side – and partly from the incredulity of men, who do not readily believe in new things until they have had a long experience of them. (1988: 20–21)

The result is that they – all those who have done well under the old conditions, i.e., managers – mostly try to stop movements from which 'the new' emerges since it challenges the present order (Schumpeter pointed out, 1942 [1962]: 105). Instead, controlling a specific version of the new is preferred, which is achieved by dictating what is possible in a blueprint/strategy. This, however, reduces the new from a differentiating movement (transmuting, or qualitative transformation) to quantitative change. Such controlled change means that the established model of the game, the strategy, the dominant script takes over: managerially sound, entrepreneurially dubious.

How does organizational creativity avoid such control-driven opposition? Opposition from people backed up by strategy and structure; fully legitimate in an efficiency-driven industrial economy, but highly problematic in an innovation-driven postindustrial economy. This is an important question for any theorization of organizational creativity. Process thinking will help us also here to conceptualize an art of the weak as the *tactical* mode of engaging in transformative affirmation – the 'no' of the established (structure, position) transformed into the opposite quality, turned creative (i.e., transmuting; Deleuze, 1983: 191). Here we cross Michel de Certeau's concept of tactics (1984) with Deleuze's concept of affirmation (1983, derived from Nietzsche), so as to conceptualize a way out of Machiavelli's 'organizational creativity dilemma'.

Thinking Organizational Creativity as Affirmation

To conceptualize the 'reply' that can still be creative, we turn to play and dance:

play and dance are affirmative powers of transmutation: dance transmutes heavy into light, laughter transmutes suffering into joy and the play of throwing (the dice) transmutes low into high. [. . .] Dance affirms becoming and the being of becoming; laughter, roars of laughter, affirm multiplicity and the unity of multiplicity; play affirms chance and the necessity of chance. (Deleuze, 1983: 193–4)

Deleuze writes: 'Heraclitus denied the duality of worlds, "he denied being itself". Moreover *he made an affirmation of becoming. [. . .] Return is the being of that which becomes*. Return is the being of becoming itself, the being which is affirmed in becoming. The eternal return as law of becoming' (1983: 23–4, emphasis in original). What Nietzsche discovers – one of his 'great discoveries' according to Deleuze – is negativity as negativity *of the positive*, which is how affirmation works. It resists but only in the service of transmuting. It makes use, but wills difference. Affirmation is the power of becoming active.

This is where Michel de Certeau's concept of *tactics* is helpful. It operates like Nietzsche's 'negativity of the positive' in that it explores conditions from where opportunities might emerge. The conditions are the grid of strategic/dominant power. Tactics also agree with Bergson's emphasis on time: 'At the very least they [strategies] attempt to reduce temporal relations to spatial ones' (De Certeau, 1984: 38). However, Nietzsche (and thus Deleuze) would criticize de Certeau for not trusting affirmation's power enough. De Certeau's thinking remains seated in negativity, and remains reactive to the extent that he makes tactics depend on opportunities as served by strategy (de Certeau, 1984). Nietzsche already pointed at what brings affirmation beyond the tactic's dependence on opportunities: 'Affirmation would never be itself affirmed if negation had not broken its alliance with reactive forces and become an affirmative power.' (Deleuze, 1983: 179, reading Nietzsche)

This means that the reactive-negative that otherwise always precede and follow the active-positive, is broken in the affirmative act, meaning we break away from Hegelian dialectics: 'For the speculative element of negation, opposition or contradiction Nietzsche substitutes the practical element of *difference*, the object of affirmation and enjoyment.' (Deleuze, 1983: 9, emphasis in original). This is thinking that invents and uses concepts 'filled with life and passion through and through' (ibid.) in order to prioritize difference and becoming. De Certeau's concept of tactics is still important as it directs us to the central tension between strategy and tactics in contexts of existing orders. Being focused on discourse and everyday practices, de Certeau is missing the affective, sensation and intensity. For it is on the strategized field of organizational practices that potentiality is sensed and intensity is resulting from movement, movement towards actualizing that organization-creation process (entrepreneurship) that differentiates (makes the new actual).

The struggle between reactive/negative and active forces is the eternal return as the law of becoming. But Nietzsche also stresses that the negative is only defeating itself as part of affirmation. It is only in affirmation that the active defeats the reactive. When defending *being*, the reactive reduces and limits. Deleuze almost bursts out in his own affirmation of Nietzschean thinking as he emphasizes this: 'Nietzsche's "yes" is opposed to the dialectical "no"; affirmation to dialectical negation; difference to dialectical contradiction; joy, enjoyment, to dialectical labour; lightness, dance, to dialectical responsibilities.' (Deleuze, 1983: 9).

According to the Machiavellian dilemma, organizations simply represent too much to defend for people of powerful positions. Organizations are achieved stabilities of human relations and interactions (Tsoukas and Chia, 2002). They master quantitative change, but makes difference by accident. We have found in Nietzsche, Deleuze and de Certeau, a possibility to analyse how the tactical/entrepreneurial is possible as an affirmative power, as *an art of the weak*. In affirmation, life potentializes the relationship to a different life available via becoming, a positivity yet to be actualized. Negativity is not at play here, for that opposes by revealing something hidden or reducing something surplus that it believes to have found – in the style of critique. The eternal return, again, is the being of that which becomes, it is the return of difference and the differential potential is what drives creation, sets up affirmation as creation.

The art of the weak, sensing potentialities on the organizational field of practices, exercising a power to be affected (receptivity), is what opens the entrepreneurial actor to the power to affect, to differentiating action. Entrepreneurship is a mundane art that defies the laws of organizational inertia and its politics of preventing or controlling 'the new'. It is the joy of inventiveness, of affirming the eternal return of a differential force that is creation. We try to think with Nietzsche's emphasis on affirmation as breaking free from the reactive, negative and dialectical. Negativity opposes to confirm the present order and predict the possible. What we have analysed as an art of the weak is affirmation that needs no opposition to be confident about its transmuting intervention. Affirmation affirms difference (has no image to copy, but a virtuality to actualize) and the joy of creation. Maybe Kirzner was on to this with his concept of alertness, which places strong emphasis on dreams and imagination (Kirzner, 1992: 131) as well as images of the future (Kirzner, 1985: 56). We have still named this 'weak' due to the contextualization of such joyous creation in organizations, where the Machiavellian dilemma is present. Creation, in order to find its openings, therefore has to be tactical rather than strategic, based on movement rather than position and opposition. Weak as in receiving, dancing, process, becoming and perishing.

'The actual order of things is precisely what "popular" tactics turn to their own ends . . . here order is *tricked* by an art.' (de Certeau, 1984: 26).

CREATIVITY IN PROCESS THINKING

Having outlined a preliminary conceptualization of how creativity in organizations is at all possible, two problems remains for us: (1) how to understand the conditions of the new in perspective of the problem of creativity in process thinking; and (2) how to understand the role of the individual in organizational creation processes. Whereas the next part will deal with the latter, we are here taking on the task to elaborate how process thinking can support our descriptive and analytical needs as researchers of organizational entrepreneurship.

The New/Difference

Affirmation, although described above as the style of creation in organizations, needs to be understood *not* as something added on to action, not as a technique that serves as an enabler, but as the power of becoming active, as 'the pure creativity with no end or ground outside itself.' (Colebrook, 2005: 8, describing dance). Organizational creativity, as an affirmative action, is easier to understand if we use dancing as metaphor: 'The dance as act is at once fully actual, not the expression of some prior ground [blueprint, order] that it represents only in part, but at each moment fully itself, referring to nothing other than itself: not a signifier of some prior intent, nor the expression of some being before the act, but pure act in and for itself.' (ibid.: 9). The point here is not to suggest that organizational creativity in our tactical-affirmative description is dancing. Rather, affirmatively transmuting is an act that shares the processual character of dancing as described by Nietzsche. Nietzsche philosophizes against the 'higher men', the manager of powerful positions in organizations – and says that: '[T]here are things that the higher man does not know how to do: to laugh, to play and to dance. To laugh is to affirm life, even the suffering in life. To play is to affirm chance and the necessity of chance. To dance is to affirm becoming and the being of becoming.' (Deleuze, 1983: 170).

The dancer is a Nietzchean image of will to power, the full reality of potentiality. The dancer is the actualization of potentiality, or the virtual. *Not* dancing is of course also a power, but a passive one, that Nietzsche called ressentiment. Apart from ressentiment, the reactive-negative includes also bad conscience and nihilism (will to nothingness). As this defines the history of man, according to Nietzsche, conquering it – in affirmative transmutation – represents the 'overcoming and destruction of even the best men' (Deleuze, 1983: 166), also the higher men as described above.

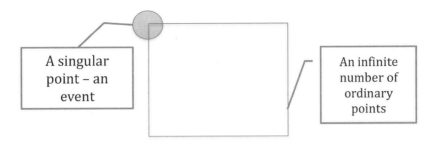

Figure 10.1   Multiplicity, series, event

One would in this sense have to go beyond oneself in order to become other. Play and the dance capture this pure becoming well. This, however, is not an individual achievement. Both leadership research (Thyrstrup, 1993) and entrepreneurship research (Chell, 1985; Gartner, 1988) has ended up with the parallel conclusion: focus on traits are not key to understanding great entrepreneurship/leadership. The key is the dividual, not the *in*dividual; the larvar subject (the subject in becoming), not the self-grounded subject. It is subjectification as individuation we need to understand, not the subject. One needs to think subjectification liberated from the perspective of subjects. Transmuting tactics of affirmation should not be 'referred back to a definitive life, self or subject for whom we could say that the act was expressive of its essence; the existence (or bringing into being) would be the act itself. And, according to Deleuze, this would mean that the only true essences would not be beings as subjects, but infinities, powers to.' (Colebrook, 2005: 10). Deleuze challenges us to think in lines rather than dots, processually rather than structurally.

'Bergson transformed philosophy by posing the question of the "new" instead of that of eternity (how are the production and appearance of something new possible.)' (Deleuze, 1986: 3). The differential relation determines what it relates. Difference here constitutes identity, which can be understood as an assemblage of singular and ordinary points, a multiplicity. 'The singularities are precisely those points where something "happens" within the multiplicity (an event).' (Smith, 2007a: 12) We will come back to the event of subjectification in the next part, noting here only that subjectivity is a multiplicity – series and events related by a line of becoming.

Before we turn to the question of how individuation, subjectification, happens, we will shortly develop how process thinking can conceptualize 'the new' by the help of multiplicity (instead of substance) and event (instead of essence).

Multiplicity and Event

Via Bergson, Deleuze makes a distinction between *extensive* and *intensive* multiplicities. The former is numerical (quantitative) and relates to space, whereas the latter is related to time and is changed as a whole (qualitative) each time there is an alteration to its intensive state. Individuals are then to be thought of as multiplicities in which the actual state of affairs is always related to the virtual as intensity, as power to become. Think again of the dancer here: a multiplicity of a body in actual movement and in real potentiality to move and change. There is no way to take a still position from the flow of the dancing body and make this part of an extensive multiplicity that would explain dancing.

Bergson's cardinal criticism of science concerns precisely its tendency to 'spatialize time, according to which being no longer present anything but differences of degree, of position, of dimension, of proportion. [. . .] this disregard for true differences in kind' (Deleuze, 1988: 23).

Dancing is an intensive multiplicity where it is inseparable from the movement of its actualization (Deleuze, 1988: 43). This intensive or qualitative multiplicity is thus an event, a processual intensity. We sense the registering of potential, of nextness enveloped in action under way, as a sensation, which Massumi (2002: 93) describes as: 'the multiplicity of potential connections in the singularity of *a* connection actually under way'. We can say that it is in the unity of dancing that the multiplicity of the dancer is *singularly* expressed (ibid.) It is in the unity of organization-creation (entrepreneurship) that he multiplicity of 'the entrepreneur' (a subjectivity) is singularly expressed. Wherefore we do understand how the history of Western thinking serves us the image of the entrepreneur as a self-grounded subject of certain traits.

In stasis oriented thinking, process is spatialized and reduced to quantitative change. Bergson problematized this and challenged us to think by multiplicity rather than substance: The arrow in flight is ontologically different from the one that has reached its target, at rest perhaps with its point in the *place* where the shooter aimed it to be. The example highlights that difference and relation, intensity, affect and passage are more important than position and essence when identifying the new. That is, they have ontological priority as constitutive of the new. The arrow differs from itself qualitatively by changing its intensive state vis-à-vis shooter and target, that's how its process of becoming new (an arrow that has hit its target) can be described and analysed.

The key to thinking the new processually is to break away from a habitual focus on what is related, to instead emphasize the relation. We need to analyse a relation from the perspective of duration and actualization, and not simply space. For duration describes how something qualitatively varies from itself whereas space describes quantitative homogeneity (Deleuze, 1988: 31; Hayden, 1998: 42). Concrete newness – actualized in empirical contexts – is a composite of extensive/quantitative and intensive/qualitative multiplicities. Process thinking, opening for such multiplicity, balancing our attention to prioritise relation and duration, makes us see newness happening all the time. Interrupting it is an achievement, often resulting from an urge to control.

The question is now how the agent, traditionally, the subject acting from free will, is to be understood in process thinking. Theorizations of creativity usually re-install the Cartesian self-grounded and self-contained subject on the throne. In process thinking, as suggested earlier in this chapter, the agent may instead be understood in terms of an actor. Let us move into developing this thought.

AFFECT, INDIVIDUATION/SUBJECTIFICATION

Agency, when we want to develop how *process thinking* can conceptualize creation, is all about becoming-active. This is a *first* important step towards a processual theorisation of agency as actorship. A *second* step is the one that follows from our emphasis on the relational. A certain openness or receptivity of bodies are important for their capacities to relate. Massumi (2002) calls this receptivity 'relationality', described as 'the potential for singular effects of qualitative change to occur in excess over or as a supplement to objective interactions' (p. 225). The question of individuation, or subjectification is provided with an important concept here – receptivity, or power to be affected. Actorship, in this perspective, is not about a subject, but about how the productive capacity of the relational forces of desiring-creation is formed. Actorship is collective and compositional. The becoming-active of a body is a process that includes subjectification in a context of specific relations of forces, will to power and movements. The qualities of force are active or reactive, and the qualities of will to power are affirmative or negative (Deleuze, 1983).

Individuation, which is subjectless (it happens precisely as there is no subject), is about passion: 'For such modes [of subjectification] involves subjectless individuations. That may be their main feature. And perhaps passion, the state of passion, is actually what . . . knowing how to breathe, is about.' (Deleuze, 1996: 116). The question of actorship is one we will have to understand from how we make sense of subjectification/individuation as this breathing. We do this by the help of openness, receptivity and spontaneity – passion. Nietzsche suggested that 'feeling of power' is the most important element of human agency (Patton, 2000: 53). Since we operate with individuation as relational, and self as a relation to oneself, as a relation of force to itself, as in breathing, agency is a question of how the feeling of power becomes part of the self *relationally*.

Deleuze's somewhat peculiar phrasing of this describes subjectification as happening in 'a magnetic or electrical field' (1995: 92). We suggested above that the organizational field of practices, when set on a specific order, holds this tension between the strategic and the tactical. When the trace, investment, costs ploughed into the history of action, takes over, spontaneity is separated from what it can do. Structures, institutions, roles, hierarchies, all constructs that relate forces to traces/investments, tend (for reasons Machiavelli made clear) to dominate organizations: 'when the trace takes the place of the excitation in the reactive apparatus, reaction itself takes the place of action, reaction prevails over action.' (Deleuze, 1983: 114).

Reactive forces, in organizations, want to limit action for the purpose of keeping the order, maintaining control. This does not mean that change is prevented. It means that change is controlled. Indeed, the practice of management has been focused on change for quite some time, as has management literature. However, this is *strategic* change in de Certeau's language; change that serves 'the established' by adding another piece to the puzzle, realising a possibility as moulded on the order of the present. Let us call strategic change *realized change*, meaning change that is limited to the possible as defined by the order of the present place. *Actualized newness,* in contrast, emerges from movement and differentiation, organization-creation affirming the new.

Moving in this field, interrupting the established, intensifies, turns a crack into a compression of time, a bifurcation, the exit from which is a shooting off of movement, the event of differentiation. This potentializes the field of practices and the receptive body senses intensities that make virtual what affirmative acts can actualize, taking the organization beyond the established order. The actor is here part of a process of moving beyond oneself in order to become-other. Actorship is suggested here as grasping the dynamics between the actor and the text. There is not a one-to-one relationship between actors and text. 'Actorships' are only limited by the field of potentials that relations between bodies in assemblages give rise to.

Subjectivity does not presuppose identity but is produced in a process of 'individuation, which is always already collective or "populated"' (Deleuze, 1998: 9, in Semetsky, 2004: 325).

Just as there are endless versions of Shakespeare's Hamlet, there are of course endless versions of transmutative organizational actorships.

Reactive forces and negative 'will to power' limit organizational fields of potentials. This is how formal organizations (structures, roles, hierarchies, institutions) work. Organizational entrepreneurship is ontologically different from organising or managing, just like the arrow in flight, in midair, is different from the one fixed in its target.

Subjectivity is never singular (a subject) but takes only the form of multiplicity, a resonance in an assemblage, the result of an ephemeral creation, an intensity manifesting the potential of the body (the latter which is a composition of active and reactive forces). This potential of the body we have previously discussed by the help of two concepts that Deleuze develops from Spinoza's philosophy: the power to affect (spontaneity) and the power to be affected (receptivity) (Deleuze, 1988: 123; Hjorth, 2009). The affect is 'an increase or decrease of the power of acting, for the body and the mind alike' (Deleuze, 1988: 49). Semetsky (2004: 326) are on the same track as she notes: 'The dynamic subject's complex rules of formation are defined by the intensive capacity "to affect and be affected"'. She also stresses that Deleuze defines a body's power as a capacity to multiply and intensify connections. It is characteristic that the entrepreneurial capacity is since long considered actualised as multiplying connections: in entrepreneurship research this is called the personal networking (cf. Johannisson, 1987).

'Affects aren't feelings, they're becomings that spill over beyond whoever lives through them (thereby becoming someone else).' (Deleuze, 1995: 137).

Spinoza called our *striving* towards increased joy – increased power to act – our *conatus*, and said this is our effort to 'augment the power of acting or to experience joyful [active] passions' (Deleuze, 1988: 101). He also connects acting with imagining as he says that our conatus 'is the effort to experience joy, to increase the power of acting, to imagine and find that which is a cause of joy' (ibid.). Research on leadership as well as on entrepreneurship traditionally follows consciousness (the cognitive–psychological), which expresses the relation of forces to the ones that dominate them, and in this sense is primarily focused on the reactive. Entrepreneurship, in process thinking, is oriented towards what bodies – including teams, groups and organizations – can do, what active forces there are, and how to affirm them so as to differentiate, create new value. Consciousness moves downstream, with reactive forces, and makes us focus on results. Process thinking that studies creation needs to move upstream to discover active, differentiating forces (cf. Chia, 1996) that counter the dominance of the trace, investment, the economy of the established (the existing order.)

Subjectification: The Joy of Speculative Affirmation

Deleuze sees a focus on identity as damaging for our capacity to grasp difference and becoming and regards the subject as an imprisoning image. The idea that there is an experienc*ing* one that grounds all experience, a doubt*ing* one that thinks and therefore secures the thinking subject as what cannot be doubted – the Cartesian cogito – is an idea that installs transcendence and totalization; negativity based on judging life with reference to values exterior to it. This corresponds to a will to control that we have problematized by the help of Nietzsche above. Instead, argues Deleuze, we need to see that there is a flow of disordered experiences to which we have responded by creating a concept of an experiencing subject, which in turn – according to the tendency (nihilistic) to prioritise reactive forces – suggest we can control this flow.

The subject is thus abstracted from processes of subjectification. If this subject is not to be the reactive result of dominating forces from the outside, there needs to be a will to power (the genealogical element of force; Deleuze, 1983: 50), an active force, conatus, that also seeks to become-active. Process thinking allows us to see that bodies can be defined relationally, as transitions between movement and rest, as intensive capacities or powers to be affected and affect, as a composition of active and reactive forces. The affected body is then of a different reality than the one at rest; the acting one different from the passive one. Process is of a different reality than its result.

But why have we invented the concept of subject, this relational stabilizer that thinking uses to found a home for the mind (a power of connections, according to Hume)? A moral theory of domination, of the passions/body by consciousness, which Spinoza rejects, has (via Christianity) come to normalize our thinking. Spinoza emphasizes the parallelism between mind and body: the body surpasses the knowledge we have of it, and thought surpasses the consciousness we have of it (Deleuze, 1988: 18). The concept of actor releases this capacity to think the subject in more relational-processual terms. 'Entrepreneur', as actor, is a concept we can use to describe this particular subject*ivity* that fills the function of going beyond oneself in order to affirmatively transmute or create new value, resources, businesses, or industrial logics. Entrepreneur is then an intensified body-mind capacity that has become an actor, creating organization.

In relationship to others that increase your capacity to act, i.e., add 'joy' in Spinoza's terms, a body gets represented as a capacity to act. When such a capacity is endowed with character, it becomes an actor, i.e., a body-mind capacity with qualities, history, desires, life (Latour, 1996). Each mind and body composition is a degree of power corresponding to a

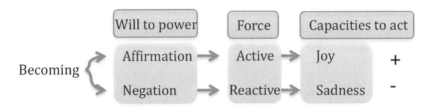

Figure 10.2   Qualities of becoming

capacity for being affected and affect. Affections are actions and passions, where the former is a power to act and the latter a power to be acted upon. Whereas 'opportunity' has featured as the prominent 'object' in relationship to which a capacity is represented as 'entrepreneur', in this chapter we suggest affirmation/transmuting, this art of the weak, to be what characterizes a body/mind capacity as entrepreneur.

'Affirming and denying, appreciating and depreciating, express the will to power just as acting and reacting express force.' (Deleuze, 1983: 53–4). Action/reaction are means of the will to power that affirms and denies. These are genuinely processual concepts: affirmation is *becoming* active; negation is *becoming* reactive: see Figure 10.2 above.

Deleuze, who stresses individuation as an aesthetic practice (1995: 113), artful and creative (Semetsky, 2004), elaborates upon this Spinozist framework. Individuation is thought as exercising power over oneself, 'making force impinge on itself' (Deleuze, 1995). But he immediately clarifies: 'There's no subject, but a production of subjectivity: subjectivity has to be produced, when its time arrives, precisely because there is no subject.' (ibid.: 113–14). Subjectification, or individuation, is intensity that relationally differentiates. Since joy is a result of increased capacity to act, something that happens when we encounter other bodies that agree with us, Deleuze can conclude (1988: 29) that '[E]thical *joy* is the correlate of speculative affirmation.' We recognize this in the 'acting as if' style of entrepreneurial action (Vaihinger, 1952; Gartner et al, 1992; Hjorth and Johannisson, 2008). A capacity for being affected is not a passivity but an affectivity, according to Nietzsche. It is 'a personal intensity corresponding to the passage from one experiential state of the body to another and implying and augmentation or diminution in that body's capacity to act' (Massumi, 1987b: xvii). This is how a feeling of power is crucial for agency or actorship.

Becoming-active depends on affirming. However, '[w]hen reactive force separates active force from what it can do, the latter also becomes reactive'(Deleuze, 1983: 64). The Machiavellian dilemma of lukewarm support for change in organization, partly emphasised by the Schumpeterian notion of entrepreneurship as creative destruction, indicates the general problem with negative forces and status quo. Negative forces can legitimize reactive responses with reference to the economy of the trace, of made investments, to controllable change. Affirmation has the virtually real, a trust in the world, embrace of multiplicity, and potentials of a future missing world as guides for action. It cannot be legitimized in the traditional sense, for that always works with reference to the established and is thus reactive. We have used dance above as the action *par excellence* that manifests affirmation – trust in what movement will release – and increases our joy.

CONCLUDING: AN ART OF THE WEAK

The tactical-affirmative power needs to transmute the established order: 'in transmutation, we are not concerned with a simple substitution, but with a conversion' (Deleuze, 1983: 175). This happens through actors that affirm the transmuting potential of the present, that wants to become-other: typical of subjectivities such as entrepreneurial and artistic. The concept of actor captures the conversion-quality of a relationally constituted agency/ actorship (feeling of will to power) that makes affirmation actual. When managerial strategy is transmuted into entrepreneurial newness, difference passes into action, Bergson's *élan vital* (Patton, 1996).

There are of course false affirmations, affirmations that are not capable of creation. Nietzsche describes this in the form of the ass that says 'Yea . . . ha' but doesn't know how to say 'No'. 'Thus we can guess the meaning of the ass' affirmation, of the yes which does not know how to say no: *this kind of affirmation is nothing but bearing, taking upon oneself*, acquiescing in the real as it is, taking reality as it is upon oneself.' (Deleuze, 1983: 181, emphasis in original). This is *homo oeconomicus,* which, in Gary Becker's sense, is someone that 'accepts reality' (Foucault, 2008: 269) and systematically (rationally, in the economists' sense) responds to modifications of variables in the environment. This results in 'efficient' adjustments, which will only ever lead to reactive behaviour and the triumph of the negative. Affirmation as transmutation is instead: 'not to take responsibility for, to take on the burden of what is, but to release, to set free what lives. To affirm is to unburden' (Deleuze, 1983: 185). Here is where dance/play/ laughter represent such powers, pushing off the nihilistic tendencies of the guardians of the established order – efficiency-maximising adjustments to the modification in the variables of the environment – and creating surprising results from often known ingredients.

Affirmative movement (qualitative transformation underway) within any system of relations is what charges the field and triggers the flash of action 'by which it plays out the consequences of its own intensity' (as Massumi, 2002b: xxiv, puts it). Potential for action/event is immanent to the assemblage (e.g., an organization, or a project) and its relations of productive desires. Simply negating the strategic would correspond to Spinoza's sadness, i.e., decrease our capacity to act and thus prevent creation. The tactical is an *art* since it operates with intensities (Deleuze and Guattari, 1994), i.e., contributes positively to the increased capacity to act that characterise the relation with others. It is *weak* as it needs to 'make use' (de Certeau, 1984) in order to transmute/make new. 'It is a guileful ruse. In short, a tactic is an art of the weak.' (De Certeau, 1984: 37). Registering intensity would correspond to a new understanding of passion, a power to be affected, receptivity, openness. Subjectifications are not there to constitute a subject. We have noted that this is an image (the subject) that thought uses to reduce multiplicity and becoming, to found itself. Subjectifications are about creating new 'ways of existing, what Nietzsche called inventing new possibilities of life' (Deleuze, 1995: 118).

Organizational entrepreneurship, as an art of the weak, as affirmative tactics of transmuting, could then be summarised as: Affirmative-tactical creation, released by the actor we call entrepreneur. This is the result of an assemblage, a system of relations, that an affirmative will to power intensifies so that the capacity to act is increased, and becoming-other is actualised. The joyful assemblage has the capacity to overcome reactive forces, to transmute established orders. The Nietzschean ass, the one who says 'Yea . . . ha' as with Gary Becker's *homo oeconomicus,* is emblematically manifest in the industrial organization's manager, that endlessly burdens him/herself with additional adjustments to modifications in variables of the environment. Entrepreneurship is a force that creates by transmuting this 'burdened life', affirming the virtual capacity to become-other that it holds. Entrepreneurship invents new possibilities of life, makes heavy light.

This subjectivity, thinkable as an actor open to become-other in processes of organizational creation, describes individuated relations of bodies/minds that display exceptional capacity for registering intensities and diagnosing the social so as to decide whether there is passion to spend, whether there is intensity enough to transmute the established order. Movement intensifies the organizational field of practices, makes the new/ difference incipient. It powers up, makes a context magnetic/electric, intensifies and raises the capacity for action (joy). This is how entrepreneurs are subjectified and affect others to join the becoming.

Consistent with both Nietzsche's warning that becomings are dominated by becoming-reactive (negation for the sake of capitalizing on the trace), and Schumpeter's warning that '[e]conomic life, or the economic element in, or aspect of, social life might well be essentially passive and adaptive' (Schumpeter, 1928 [1991]: 60), entrepreneurship in organizations is ephemeral. Organizations are stabilities, ossifications, and movement have to re-charge the particles, magnetizes the field again and again. To accomplish this, the new value created must avoid captures ready and waiting. It must avoid becoming reproduction, being caught by the negative, passive, the Machiavellian dilemma of organizations, the Nietzschean dilemma of the triumphant negativity. Dance (lightness, affirmation of becoming), play (the high, affirmation of chance) and laughter (joy, affirmation of life) are such modes of existing, balancing organiza*tions* as dynamic tensions between established orders and the multiplicity of organisation-creation.

PART II

FIELDS OF RESEARCH, PRACTICES AND POLITICS

11 The entrepreneurial firm
Saras Sarasvathy

INTRODUCTION: A SEMINAL QUESTION

Is the entrepreneurial firm an artefact resulting from markets, or are both firms and markets artefacts resulting from entrepreneurs seeking to create economic organizations?

Classical and neoclassical economic theory assumes the centrality and preexistence of markets. In other words, the world of economics here consists almost entirely of transactions between two or more parties seeking to exchange goods and services through the price mechanism of the market (Simon, 1991). In such a world, the existence of firms becomes an anomaly to be explained. Coase's (1937) thesis offered an explanation based on the cost to use the market – namely transaction costs. As Langlois (1995: 71) summarizes,

> The firm exists, Coase argued, because there is a cost to using the price system. And 'a firm will tend to expand until the costs of organizing an extra transaction within the firm become equal to the costs of carrying out the same transaction by means of an exchange in the open market or the costs of organizing in another firm' (Coase, 1937, p. 395). Inspired by Coase, a school of transaction-cost economics sprung up in which peculiarities in the process of exchange – that is to say, the costs of contracting – explain the firm. Costs of production figure in very little, and the process of production even less. (Winter, 1988)

Yet in the world as we know it empirically, organizations are ubiquitous – not an anomaly to be explained (Simon, 1991). And markets do not always preexist firm formation (Sarasvathy and Dew, 2005b). Nor are they guaranteed to come into existence at all. Even Arrow (1974) acknowledged this, 'Although we are not usually explicit about it, we really postulate that when a market could be created, it would be.' And Coase (1988c) himself once commented that markets – one of the two central institutions of capitalist societies (the other is firms) – had a 'shadowy' existence in the economic literature.

If firms are not simply a rarity arising only when markets fail to work efficiently and markets are not always necessary preconditions to firm formation, how do firms come to be? Practically speaking, of course, firms come to be when entrepreneurs, either on their own or as part of existing firms, start new ventures. In recent years, there have been a series of empirical studies that look into how exactly they do that. Several heuristics, techniques and mechanisms have been identified and a rather interesting picture of the entrepreneurial firm is beginning to emerge. The resulting theory of the firm, it turns out, is more Knightian, than Coasian (Boudreaux and Holcombe, 1989). Knight (1921 [1985]) had argued that the entrepreneur takes on true uncertainty – in other words, they tackle a future that is not only unknown, but is also unknowable.

This means that they cannot rely on predictions about the future to make decisions. Nor can an entrepreneurial theory of the firm assume either firms or markets as givens (Dew et al., 2008). From an evolutionary perspective, entrepreneurial firms endogenize both variation and selection mechanisms. That is why, entrepreneurship would be more amenable to being classified a science of the artificial than a social science (Simon, 1996; Sarasvathy, 2003; Sarasvathy and Venkataraman, 2011; Venkataraman et al., 2012). In order to clarify these statements, we must first examine what we have learned about the process and logic used by entrepreneurs building organizations.

Through a decade long effort to understand how entrepreneurs go about organizing economic activities that result in new firms and markets, my collaborators and I have developed a series of principles, mechanisms and logic that constitute the micro-foundations for theories of the entrepreneurial firm. In the next two sections I will elaborate on these cognitive elements, work out their implications for social, behavioral and evolutionary elements of the entrepreneurial firm, and show how they can form the basis for future research into organizational entrepreneurship.

COGNITIVE ELEMENTS IN THE ORGANIZING OF THE ENTREPRENEURIAL FIRM

According to Knight (1921 [1985]) entrepreneurs are able to act in the face of true uncertainty. His insight consisted in classifying uncertainty into three types: where the future can be described in terms of (a) a known distribution, but an unknown draw; (b) unknown distribution, unknown draw; and (c) unknowable distribution. The third type of uncertainty arises in those contexts in which as Knight (1921 [1985]: 225) explains, 'there is no valid basis of any kind for classifying instances'. To explicate this notion further, he discusses the example of an entrepreneur making founding decisions for a firm and contrasts this with examples of insurance risks and other types of uncertainties with (a priori or statistically) enumerable probabilities. Then he goes on to argue the following (1921 [1985]: 227): 'The essential and outstanding fact is that the "instance" in question is so entirely unique that there are no others or not a sufficient number to make it possible to tabulate enough like it to form a basis for any inference of value about any real probability in the case we are interested in.'

Yet Knight does not offer a clear explanation as to how the entrepreneur deals with this type of 'true' uncertainty. Instead he simply states, 'The ultimate logic, or psychology, of these deliberations is obscure, a part of the scientifically unfathomable mystery of life and mind. We must simply fall back upon a "capacity" in the intelligent animal to form more or less correct judgments about things, an intuitive sense of values. We are so built that what seems to us reasonable is likely to be confirmed by experience, or we could not live in the world at all.' The content of that 'reasonableness' has recently begun to be unearthed through a series of cognitive-science-based studies looking into the black box of how expert entrepreneurs think, decide and act.

Using well-established methods from expertise research, Read and colleagues (2009), for example, identified a set of heuristics and principles that differentiated expert decision-making from that of novices as well as expert managers on marketing in the entrepreneurial firm. Dew et al. (2009) showed how expert entrepreneurs use an 'effectual' as opposed to a 'causal' frame in making decisions in starting new ventures. The issue of logical framing is a really important one in terms of a Knightian theory of the firm because causal logic frames problems in terms of a predictable future, whereas an effectual frame explicitly eschews prediction. Evidence for the use of effectual logic has also been shown in the use of social media (Fischer and Reuber, 2011) and in R&D departments (Brettel et al., 2012). The growing literature on effectual logic has elicited the following cognitive elements in the organizing of the effectual firm.

Non-predictive Control

Entrepreneurs who build organizations effectually have learned several heuristics that together cohere into a logic of *non-predictive control.* In other words, these entrepreneurs have learned through their experience to work with things within their control to try and shape the future or co-create it with stakeholders who self-select into the process. In Sarasvathy (2001) I provided a brief compilation of these heuristics following up with a more elaborate treatment in Sarasvathy (2008) where I worked out their behavioural and philosophical bases as well as outlined connections with and implications for a variety of theories and assumptions from the disciplines such as psychology, sociology and economics. For a pedagogical treatment of the logic combined with numerous case studies and other types of teaching materials, see Read et al. (2011). Here I will provide a very brief description of each principle primarily with a view to deepening the cognitive basis for the entrepreneurial firm.

The bird-in-hand principle

Briefly, effectual entrepreneurs begin with who they are, what they know and whom they know (their means) and choose to invest only what they can afford to lose in ventures they find eminently doable and worth doing. This means they do not first engage in processes of opportunity recognition or discovery based on extensive search and selection. Nor do they always begin with brilliant ideas or a clear vision or well-articulated goals. In many cases, they do not even 'choose' to become entrepreneurs at all. Instead entrepreneurship is intricately intertwined with the normal routines of their lives, its events and their responses to those events. Sears, for example, was started by a railroad station agent who happened upon an unwanted consignment of watches and began selling them up and down the railroad line. KitchenAid and Yahoo! are but two more of innumerable examples that show how great companies can have rather mundane (Shah and Tripsas, 2007) and even serendipitous origins (Dew, 2009).

The affordable loss principle

It stands to reason that when people start ventures in such a mundane fashion, driven mostly by their means (things within their control) and not by grandiose visions of inevitable futures, they are not likely to risk everything they have in building it. Experienced entrepreneurs especially learn to bootstrap new ventures and build them to a point of proven growth potential before they take in major investors, if at all. This is true of high potential ventures in general as well. A survey of Inc. 500 companies, for example, showed that the median startup capital was $10 000 (Bhide, 1992). The guiding heuristic here is one of affordable loss, namely thinking through the downside and assessing whether the venture would be worth building even if unsuccessful rather than envisioning the upside and calculating expected returns.

The crazy quilt principle

Although effectual entrepreneurs start with who they are, what they know and whom they know, they quickly begin working other people, each of whom invests only what he or she can afford to lose. What someone commits to the venture determines who comes on board and the particular terms they negotiate allows them to shape the ventures' goals and its future in varying ways and to different extents. In other words, effectual entrepreneurs stitch together a stakeholder network that grows organically and in unpredictable ways, but always through actual commitments.

The lemonade principle

The effectual process that drives the development of the entrepreneurial firm utilizes not only the means readily available to the founding entrepreneurs and their self-selected stakeholders, but also a variety of contingencies and surprises that occur along the way. Every entrepreneurial venture, planned or otherwise, experiences unexpected events and unanticipated changes in its environment. Effectual entrepreneurship advocates a welcoming rather than a defensive posture toward such surprises.

Pilot-in-the-plane principle

In the final analysis, the effectual process is people-focused and stakeholder-driven. People's choices, often myopic, idiosyncratic and irrational, rather than stable trends with predictable patterns, form the basis for its history. In this sense, effectuation is a technology of foolishness, rather than a matter of rational intelligence (March, 1982, 2006; Sarasvathy and Dew, 2005a). Yet, because of the co-creational aspects of the process, the free choices are not entirely 'free' and the 'market' is not entirely faceless. In other words, variation creation at the individual level is less random and selection is less exogenous than in typical evolutionary models. Each individual is trying to create variation that has value for others they know and care about. And as stakeholders self-select into the process, they act together as selection mechanisms that weed out variations that do not work for them. By the time the effectual firm grows enough to compete *within* an existing marketplace or within the new market it has helped create, the variations it offers are much more aligned with the market than purely or even mostly random.

Please note that the above arguments are specific to *effectual* entrepreneurial firms and not to *all* entrepreneurial firms. Yet, to the extent that effectual logic embodies entrepreneurial expertise, it has important theoretical implications for entrepreneurial firms in general. Put another way, how expert entrepreneurs build organizations based on what they have experienced building them litigates for a different set of assumptions and conceptualizations than conventional wisdom or received theories of the firm advocate. Let us turn to that next.

SOCIAL, BEHAVIORAL AND EVOLUTIONARY ELEMENTS IN THE ORGANIZING OF THE ENTREPRENEURIAL FIRM

From the cognitive elements explicated in the previous section, we can derive alternative conceptualizations for several of the taken-for-granted ideas in organizational theories, ranging from the behavioural theory of the firm (Cyert and March, 1963), resource-based view (Barney, 1991), and new institutional economics (Williamson, 1973), to the more recent dynamic capabilities (Teece et al., 1997). We examine key differentiators that describe the entrepreneurial firm in terms of ideas relevant to organizational studies in more depth below.

Vision and Goals: Emergent Political Conception

In their seminal book, *The Behavioral Theory of the Firm*, Cyert and March (1963) presented a political conception of organizational goals – namely that these reflect the political coalitions within organizations and change as those coalitions change over time. In the entrepreneurial firm, we would expect the same except that these goals are more emergent as they are co-created through stakeholder commitments. Over time these commitments coalesce into embodiments of a variety of different values and aspirations that intersect with the interests and values of the stakeholders involved. Cyert and March suggested bargaining as the process through which organizational goals are formed and evolve. Their notion of bargaining operated through at least two mutual control systems – the budget and the allocation of functional roles (1992 [1963]: 38). In the entrepreneurial firm, the situation may be both more fluid and more rigid than in an established organization – more fluid because the organizational structure (including budgeting and roles) itself is being formulated through the stakeholder self-selection process; and more rigid because a smaller and tighter group of stakeholders get to decide almost all aspects of building and running the new organization.

Moreover, the specific goals that embody the values and aspirations of key stakeholders are driven by the means available to the entrepreneurial firm at any given point in time. These means come from the commitments stakeholders make. Thus in the entrepreneurial firm, both means and ends may be politically construed albeit in an emergent manner. However, as more stakeholders come on board and the firm grows into a more stable organization, Cyert and March's behavioural theory of the firm begins to apply more fully – both organizational structure and goals become more stable and constrained and internal negotiations serve to elaborate and revise these rather than co-create them.

Resources: Proactive Conception

The resource-based view (RBV) of the firm (Wernerfelt, 1984) has long dominated the study of strategic management. In this view, firms are conceptualized as heterogeneous, yet relatively stable bundles of resources. The unique bundle of resource in any given firm, therefore, forms the basis for its sustainable competition in the marketplace. Barney (1991) theorized four empirical indicators of resources – namely that they are valuable, rare, inimitable and non-substitutable (VRIN, for short). This conception of VRIN resources led to a criticism of the resource-based view. Priem and Butler (2001), for example, argued that by positing valuable as a part of the empirical attributes of resources, RBV collapsed to a tautology. All the same, as Barney (Barney, 2001) rebutted, empirical work in the field continued to parameterize and test relationships between resources and sustainable competitive advantage with varying results. Moreover, RBV continued to be theoretically extended to applications in micro- and evolutionary economics. In a decade long reprise of the theory, Barney (2001: 649) summarized, 'Thus, what marks these theories "resource-based" are not these differences in application, but rather, the assumptions they share. These include the assumption that resources and capabilities can be heterogeneously distributed across competing firms, that these differences can be long lasting, and that they can help explain why some firms consistently outperform other firms.'

With some minor quibbling on the duration implied by 'long lasting', a theory of the entrepreneurial firm would definitely be consistent with these assumptions. Yet its conception of what constitutes a resource would be very different from the VRIN attributes argued for in Barney (1991). Here, it might be more useful to revert to Penrose's (Penrose, 1959) more proactive conception in which the value of resources was contingent on what management *did* with them. This view has recently been reimagined through Austrian capital theory (b., 2007), which argues for not taking the value of resources (or 'capital') as exogenous to strategizing within organizations. In other words, attributes that make something a VRIN resource have to be 'created or discovered by means of entrepreneurial action' (Foss and Ishikawa, 2007: 44).

This view from Austrian capital theory, while consistent with the conception of resources in the entrepreneurial firm, differs not only from more familiar static conceptions of RBV (Foss and Ishikawa 2007), but also from Teece et al.'s (1997) conception of dynamic capabilities. In that seminal article, Teece et al. tried to distinguish 'strategizing' from what Venkataraman (1997) and Shane and Venkataraman (2000) would later define as the distinctive domain of entrepreneurship – namely the pursuit of opportunities. Their objective in making the distinction was to attribute the source of sustainable competitive advantage to the latter (1997: 509):

> In short, identifying new opportunities and organizing effectively and efficiently to embrace them are generally more fundamental to private wealth creation than is strategizing, if by strategizing one means engaging in business conduct that keeps competitors off balance, raises rival's costs, and excludes new entrants.

Since then, scholars have struggled to specify what dynamic capabilities are (Eisenhardt and Martin, 2000), delineate them in terms of new ventures and established firms, debate their effects and consequences for firm performance (Eisenhardt and Martin, 2000; Teece, 2007a; Easterby-Smith et al. 2009; Helfat and Peteraf, 2009) and extend their reach to economic systems and industrial leadership (Augier and Teece, 2009). In the final analysis, almost all of these conceptions of dynamic capabilities focus on whether firms have them or not. The entrepreneurial firm, however, has to concern itself with the details of how to acquire and use such capabilities. Again, a more proactive conception is called for.

Furthermore, the entrepreneurial firm poses a challenge for the very notion of a set of capabilities that is essentially capable of providing advantages for very long periods of time. Collis (1994) made the argument in some detail. The abstract to the research note summarizes his arguments well:

> Organizational capabilities, appropriately defined, can meet the conditions, articulated by the resource-based view of the firm, for being a source of sustainable competitive advantage. However, this paper observes that there are limits to the extent of the importance of such capabilities. They are vulnerable to threats of erosion, substitution, and above all to being superseded by a higher-order capability of the 'learning to learn' variety. This suggests that there can be an infinite regress in the explanation for, and prediction of, sustainable competitive advantage. The problem is resolved by arguing that the value of organizational capabilities is context dependent, and by recognizing that the strategy field will never find the ultimate source of sustainable competitive advantage. (1994: 143)

Even without worrying about the existential issue of 'the ultimate source of sustainable competitive advantage' an entrepreneurial theory of the firm argues for the need for firms to die as well form and survive and grow. The entrepreneurial firm, therefore, takes exit seriously and as an important strategic issue. Knowing when to quit and dissolve an enterprise ought to be a more serious topic of interest to scholars of entrepreneurship and strategic management than it currently is (Burgelman, 1996; Sea Jin and Singh, 1999; Mata and Portugal, 2000). And given a world in which the 'sustainable' in sustainable competitive advantage is a more time-limited and context dependent concept, the use of non-predictive and collaborative strategies becomes very relevant to any theorizing about the entrepreneurial firm.

Strategy Making: Non-predictive and Collaborative Conceptions

In a thoughtful, learned and provocative article, Langlois (2007) argued for the insight that entrepreneurship was the answer to Coase's famous question about the existence of the firm that set off and informed all theories of the firm to date. It is useful to ponder Langlois' insight in his own words:

> Why do entrepreneurial firms exist? When I first heard the question, it seemed an easy one to answer. 'Entrepreneurship' and 'firm' were part of the prose I had been speaking all my academic life. After a bit of thought, however, it became clear that this was not exactly the question I had been trying to answer for more than 20 years. My question has really been Coase's question: why does *the firm* exist? For me, entrepreneurship is not part of the question; it's part – or maybe even all – of the answer. *The firm* exists because of entrepreneurship. To put it another way, I have been working on the entrepreneurial theory of the firm, whereas the question posed seems to be calling for a theory of the entrepreneurial firm. These are not the same thing. To assert that there exists an 'entrepreneurial firm' implies that there must also exist non-entrepreneurial firms and that entrepreneurial firms exist for reasons different from those that give rise to nonentrepreneurial ones. (2007: 1107)

Langlois seeks to separate the notion of a separate kind of firm called the 'entrepreneurial firm' with a view to specifying a more general 'entrepreneurial theory' of *the firm*. Again in his own words,

> The entrepreneurial theory of the firm argues that entrepreneurship, properly understood, is a crucial but neglected element in explaining the nature and boundaries of the firm . [. . .] In such a theory, the firm exists as the solution to a coordination problem in a world of change and uncertainty, including Knightian or structural uncertainty.

The empirical studies cited earlier that unearthed a non-predictive and collaborative logic used by expert entrepreneurs provide microfoundations (namely answer the 'how' do firms come to exist question) for an entrepreneurial theory of the firm as conceptualized by Coase and Langlois (namely answer the 'why' do firms exist question). Interestingly both how and why draw upon the perspective of Knightian uncertainty.

It stands to reason, therefore, any theory of the entrepreneurial firm has to take the notion of 'non-predictive' as its core. We have already examined in some detail at least one way to think about non-predictive – that is to think about effectual logic. Effectual logic has the advantage of being validated as the preferred way for expert entrepreneurs to think. The broader literature has argued for at least two other ways to think about non-predictive as well, both of which are consistent with effectual logic. The first one of these is March's ideas about the technology of foolishness alluded to earlier. This idea seeks to disconnect decision-making from consequences. It argues that oftentimes people are not driven by consequences in their decision-making. While that may be considered a bad thing in light of the philosophy of rational choice, such non-consequential decision-making may be ecologically rational – namely, that this type of decision-making may have been adaptive in the sense of biological and sociological evolution (Todd and Gigerenzer, 2003). Even when that might not be the case, even when it might simply be irrational and myopic, there is something very human and perhaps moral about the technology of foolishness. March (1996) points to Quixote as an example of this argument:

> Quixote reminds us
> That if we trust only when
> Trust is warranted, love only
> When love is returned, learn
> Only when learning is valuable,
> We abandon an essential feature of our humanness

Just as effectual logic is both non-predictive and non-consequential and hence consistent with a technology of foolishness (Sarasvathy and Dew, 2005a), it is also consistent with another way to think about non-predictive logic, namely Winter's (2003) notion of ad-hoc problem solving. Winter offers ad-hoc problem solving as an alternative to dynamic capabilities. He defines the idea as follows (2003: 991):

> Whether it is because such an external challenge arrives or because an autonomous decision to change is made at a high level, organizations often have to cope with problems they are not well prepared for. They may be pushed into 'firefighting' mode, a high-paced, contingent, opportunistic and perhaps creative search for satisfactory alternative behaviors. It is useful to have a name for the category of such change behaviors that do not depend on dynamic capabilities – behaviors that are largely non-repetitive and at least 'intendedly rational' and not merely reactive or passive. I propose 'ad hoc problem solving'.

The lemonade principle in effectual logic is particularly coherent with ad-hoc problem solving. Both of these go beyond reactive responses to a more creative approach. In the entrepreneurial firm these types of non-predictive strategy making also have to evoke a collaborative attitude toward external stakeholders simply by virtue of being in markets that are either nonexistent or drenched in Knightian uncertainty. The fact is that without predictions to guide the tackling of multiple uncertainties (Milliken, 1987), resources are likely to be scarce and visions not worth placing big bets on. Additionally, under Knightian uncertainty, since the existence of the market itself is in doubt, a competitive stance is not very useful. Hence in the entrepreneurial firm, non-predictive strategies naturally wind themselves around collaborative initiatives. The literature on strategic alliances is rife with evidence of the importance of partnering as a way to scale up and grow entrepreneurial firms (Steier and Greenwood, 1995; Tan and Tan, 2004; Ferriani et al., 2009; Zhang et al., 2011).

Strategic Focus: Downside and Exit

As can be seen from the literature cited in the previous two sections, the central concern of the bulk of work on strategic management has to do with the performance of the firm. Almost all of that work is focused on a two-factor conceptualization of strategy – namely, success producing and failure preventing (Varadarajan, 1985). Yet relationships between strategy success, failure, learning and capability development are more complicated and interesting than a two-factor model assumes. As discussed earlier, March has called for a deeper understanding of the technology of foolishness (March, 1982, 2006); Levinthal and March (1993) highlighted the imperfections of organizational learning; and Denrell and March (2001) pointed out the pitfalls of overlearning. In a related yet different vein, Barnett and Hansen (1996) pointed out the Red Queen phenomenon whereby learning efforts in one organization trigger competitive responses that lead to the need for more learning to the point where learning no longer had the benefits conventionally attributed to it. Lant and Mezias (1990) used a simulation to identify three different types of learning traps in firms using entrepreneurial strategies.

By its very existence, the notion of the entrepreneurial firm complexifies relationships between strategy and performance. Christensen and Bower (1996) for example, argued that leading firms could fail by following best practices with regard to soliciting and acting on customer feedback. And Knott and Posen (2005: 617) show that failed entrepreneurial firms 'generate externalities that significantly and substantially reduce industry cost'. Moreover, 'on average these benefits exceed the private costs of the entrants'. The study concludes that failure is actually good for the economy. Interestingly, studies of expert entrepreneurs offer a similar conclusion about firm failure for the success of the entrepreneur. By taking an instrumental view of the firm, a serial entrepreneur may construct a temporal portfolio with a view to exploiting contagion effects of learning even from failed firms (Sarasvathy et al., 2012).

In essence, the entrepreneurial firm posits the notion that success-failure is not a Boolean variable and challenges the premise that the upper echelon's job is to keep the corporation alive and thriving at all costs and under all circumstances. Dew et al. (2006) developed a formal model of incumbent behaviour in the face of challenger competition that accommodated complementary assets to predict and describe conditions under which organizational inertia, as subsequent organizational failure, would be optimal. The primary implication of such optimality, of course, is to incorporate exit as a strategy not only under conditions of poor performance, but even under conditions of good performance – a topic virtually unstudied in current management scholarship.

Stance Toward Others: Docile and Intelligently Altruistic

One of the theoretical puzzles concerning how organizations and markets come to be has to do with our fundamental behavioral assumptions. While economic theories are built on assumptions of opportunism, organizational and sociological theories either look for existing structures of trust as ways to overcome opportunism, or emphasize the role of a third-party arbiter.

Opportunism, defined as self-interest seeking with guile (Williamson et al., 1975), is a fact about human behaviour. As is trust, defined as affect-based belief in moral character (Wicks et al., 1999). Yet, taking one or the other as more fundamental and prior in our set of behavioural assumptions has led to a deep rift in our theorizing. On the one hand, management researchers often observe the role trust plays in business relationships, both inside and outside the firm (Adler, 2001). Trust is observed as an important lubricant in inter- and intra-organizational life (Greenwood and Buren Iii, 2010; Hales and Williamson, 2010; Kramer, 2010). On the other hand, economists have built models with powerful explanatory value based on assumptions of opportunism, diametrically opposed to trust (Williamson, 1973, 1993b).

So, while organizational literature provides evidence for the presence of trust and group identification, it has to deal with the existence of opportunism and has to come to grips with transaction costs. TCE in turn has been criticized (Donaldson and Preston, 1995; Ghoshal and Moran, 1996; Moschandreas, 1997) as an anti-managerial theory – treating all individuals as crooks. In sum, it might just be enough to say that the opportunism assumption does not fit well with many managers' actual experience of life in firms.

Sociologists have tried to overcome this logical inconsistency by positing a tertiary gaudens of one kind or another, who through the good fortune of his/her position in a social network acts as an arbiter of trust and legitimacy between two opportunistic parties. James Coleman (1990), for example, identifies three different kinds of intermediaries in trust, one of which is the entrepreneur: 'The entrepreneurial function is one in which the intermediary induces the trust of several trustors and combines these resources, ordinarily placing them in the hands of one or more other actors who are expected to realize gains for the original investors'. (1990: 181) And finally, there are those (Marxists) who trust in the government, as the tertiary gaudens of ultimate resort.

But Simon (1993a) offered an alternative behavioural assumption based on a construct called 'docility'. Docility refers to the idea that human beings like to give and take advice and are both persuadable and persuasive. Simon further showed that, evolutionarily speaking, a docile species tends to evolve into a gradual predominance of *intelligent* altruists – folks who know when to be selfish and when to be altruists (Simon, 1993b). Entrepreneurial firms that leverage this attribute of human beings are likely to build networks of trust and commitment without having to first overcome the threat of opportunism. Like effectual entrepreneurs, they realize that opportunism is something to be worried about only when there is something to be opportunistic about. But the creation of that something, something that becomes viable and valuable, requires the coming together of docile and intelligently altruistic stakeholders who are willing to invest at least what they can afford to lose in the hope of co-creating it.

It stands to reason that the entrepreneurial firm should take docility, rather than opportunism, as its fundamental stance toward both internal and external stakeholders.

Stance Toward Environment: Exaptive and Transformative

Whether we consider the relationship of a firm to its market or think of organizations and their environments, the first word that comes to mind is 'adaptation'. Astley and Van de Ven (1983) provided one early definition of the term in organizational settings as follows:

> Drawing from systems theorists who analyse social organizations as 'complex adaptive systems' (Buckley, 1968) contingency theorists have emphasized that organizations respond to change by modifying or elaborating their internal structures to maintain an isomorphic relationship with the environment. (1983: 253)

They contrasted this with a related definition from population ecology or industrial economics that view organizations as severely limited in their ability to adapt. Instead organizations are at the mercy of their environments, which can select them in or out depending on a variety of structural factors mostly outside the control of managers within firms.

Hrebiniak and Joyce (1985) sought to overcome these two mutually exclusive explanations of organizational adaptation by positing them as independent variables positioned on two continua that yielded a typology of four forms of adaptive strategies available to firms. Today the adaptive view, whether at the proactive or deterministic extreme or anywhere in between, dominates the literatures on strategic management and organizational science. Yet both of these completely ignore an important related notion from biological evolution – that of exaptation (Dew et al., 2004; Dew, 2007; Cattani, 2008). For example, a search for the term 'adapt' yielded 325 articles published in the *Strategic Management Journal* and 264 in *Organization Science*. The term 'exapt' yielded zero in both journals.

In a recent article on the subject, Marquis and Huang (2010: 1442) explain the situation and define exaptation as follows:

> But institutionalized organizational capabilities, developed as adaptive responses to founding institutional conditions, may also be *exapted* for new uses that are different from original uses but made possible by external environmental changes. 'Exaptation,' a concept developed by evolutionary biologists, refers to a process in which *features adapted for a particular purpose in a particular environment are used for another purpose in a subsequent environment* (Gould, 1980, 1991).

And Mokyr described exaptation as 'The basic idea . . . that a technique that was originally selected for one trait owes its later success and survival to another trait which it happens to possess.' (Mokyr, 2000: 57). For a more detailed definition, history and application to strategy and entrepreneurship, see Dew et al. (2004).

The entrepreneurial firm takes a predominately exaptive stance to its environment, especially to the extent that it acts under Knightian uncertainty and therefore cannot search for ways to adapt to an existing, predictable environment. Instead, looking around at existing resources and artefacts within their control, the entrepreneurial firm asks, 'What can we do with these?' and then again, 'What *else* can we do with these?' Exaptive strategies have the benefit not only of innovation on the cheap, but they also allow firms to choose bits and pieces of existing environments to transform them into new ones. The notion of transformation takes us beyond the more familiar notion of 'combinations' due to Schumpeter who defined the entrepreneur as someone who carries out new combinations of existing resources (Schumpeter, 1976). Whereas all combinations are also transformations, not all transformations are combinatorial. As Dew et al. (2011) show, in addition to combinations, expert entrepreneurs use at least ten types of transformations in co-creating new markets and new ventures.

Bringing in an exaptive and transformative stance to studies of the relationship between organization and environment ought to open up interesting new avenues for future research.

CONCLUSION: BEYOND THE ENTREPRENEURIAL FIRM TO THE ENTREPRENEURIAL SOCIETY

I started this essay with the question, 'Is the entrepreneurial firm an artefact resulting from markets, or are both firms and markets artefacts resulting from entrepreneurs seeking to create economic organizations?' Not surprisingly the answer in actual fact may be both. Yet, theoretically speaking, we have underweighted the latter in our research. When we set out to correct that imbalance, we begin to uncover a veritable cornucopia of possibilities including new conceptions of familiar notions such as vision, goals, resources, capabilities and adaptation as well as new frameworks and assumptions for our theorizing about these.

But perhaps the most exciting possibility beckoning us may have to do with using these new conceptions as building blocks in the construction of connective tissue between our theories of micro behaviour in organizations and the macro environments we all live in. When we begin to take seriously the idea that both organizations and markets are artefacts arising out of the entrepreneurial process, we can begin laying the foundations for not merely a *responsive* microeconomics, *given* markets and governments, but a *responsible* one where we have the tools to reshape both.

12 Strategic entrepreneurship: an emerging approach to firm-level entrepreneurship
Nicolai J. Foss and Jacob Lyngsie

INTRODUCTION

The field of strategic entrepreneurship (henceforth, "SE") is a fairly recent one. Its central idea is that opportunity-seeking and advantage-seeking – the former the central subject of the entrepreneurship field, the latter the central subject of the strategic management field – are processes that need to be considered *jointly*. This involves going beyond the overwhelming focus on start-ups, characteristic of the entrepreneurship field, and paying explicit attention to the established firm as a source of entrepreneurial actions. It similarly involves paying explicit attention to the creation of competitive advantages, somewhat surprisingly a weak spot of the strategic management field.

Anticipations of SE can be found in earlier contributions. For example, Penrose (1959) coined the notion of the firm's "subjective opportunity set," that is, the set of opportunities the firm's top-management team perceives and believes it can seize; Baumol (1990) argued that entrepreneurship may be exercised by established firms; and Rumelt (1987) linked entrepreneurship and the creation of competitive advantage. Moreover, work on corporate entrepreneurship (Zahra, 1996) and venturing (Burgelman, 1983); organizational learning theory on the exploration/exploitation tradeoff (March, 1991) and ambidexterity (Simsek, 2009); innovation research (Teece, 1986; Ahuja and Lampert, 2001); work on hyper-competition (D'Aveni, 1994); real options; dynamic capabilities theory (Teece et al., 1997) each in various ways anticipate SE theory. And yet, those streams needed to be explicitly pulled together and focused. Understood as a relatively concerted research effort, SE is a very young field that has existed for only about a decade or so (Covin and Miles, 1999; Zahra et al., 1999; Hitt et al., 2001), the first dedicated journal (the *Strategic Entrepreneurship Journal*) being established as recently as 2007. Not surprisingly, many things, some of them quite important, are still quite unclear in this emerging field, such as the precise nature of the dependent variable (or, *explanandum* phenomenon), which independent variables are primarily relevant, and how the dependent and independent variables are linked (i.e., the nature of the *explanans*).

The purpose of this brief chapter is to explain the emergence of SE theory field in terms of a response to research gaps in the neighboring fields of entrepreneurship and strategic management; describe the main tenets of SE theory; discuss its relations to neighboring fields; and finally describe some research gaps in extant theory, mainly focusing on the need to provide clear micro-foundations for SE theory and link it to organizational design theory. The chapter deals with these points *seriatim*.

WHY STRATEGIC ENTREPRENEURSHIP?

There are several potential explanations of the emergence of a specialized research literature on SE. One is that it represents the takeover of a less developed (entrepreneurship) by a more developed (strategic management) field (Baker and Pollock, 2007). A different explanation, and the one that we here pursue, is that it represents an attempt to fill gaps and do away with biases in the two closely related fields of entrepreneurship and strategic management.

Biases in the Entrepreneurship Literature

Entrepreneurship research has traditionally had three characteristics, even biases that are relevant to understanding the emergence of the SE field, namely an (over-) concentration on start-ups, individuals, and the process of discovery of these individuals (Foss, 2011b; Foss and Klein, 2011; Foss and Lyngsie, 2011).

With respect to the first bias, Gartner and Carter (2003) declare that we "consider the processes of organization formation to be the core characteristics of entrepreneurship," and many appear to agree with them. However, this view would seem to exclude established organizations from the set of agents who can engage in entrepreneurial actions. Consider the general understanding of entrepreneurship as the exercise of ability and willingness to perceive new economic opportunities and to introduce specific ways of seizing these opportunities into the market in the face of uncertainty (Knight, 1921; Wennekers and Thurik, 1999; Foss and Klein, 2011). There is simply no inherent reason why entrepreneurship thus defined cannot be exercised by established firms. And, of course, established firms regularly discover and exploit new opportunities. In fact, Schumpeter (1942 [1962]) in a classic contribution argued that entrepreneurship should be thought of as a firm-level phenomenon. Indeed, he expressed concern regarding the way in which entrepreneurship was becoming subordinate to the R&D routines of the big corporation.

Other scholars have also argued that entrepreneurship can be meaningfully conceptualized at the firm-level (Baumol, 1990). If entrepreneurship researchers have nevertheless often tied together new firm formation and entrepreneurship, one may speculate that this is caused by new firm formation being an important driver of economic growth, as well as by an attempt to define and defend an independent subject for entrepreneurship (entrepreneurship in established firms may be seen as strongly overlapping with, e.g., innovation research).

A second bias in the entrepreneurship literature is the concentration on individuals as the only agents that can exercise entrepreneurship. Thus, entrepreneurs are conceptualized as individuals who believe that they have lower information costs than other people (Casson and Wadeson, 2007), and/or privileged information about, for example, the future preferences of consumers (Knight, 1921 [1985]; Mises, 1949). Organizations enter the analysis simply as instruments of the entrepreneur's vision (Knight, 1921 [1985]; Mises, 1949), and are themselves given very little attention (which also helps explaining the strong focus on start-ups in the literature). This contrasts with the evidence that a substantial number of new ventures are founded by entrepreneurial teams, that is, a group of entrepreneurs with a common goal that can only be realized by certain combinations of entrepreneurial actions (Harper, 2008). It also conflicts with the fact that established firms may mobilize and integrate multiple essentially entrepreneurial skills and action in the pursuit of opportunities.

The third bias in the literature is an over-concentration on *opportunity discovery*. Following Israel Kirzner's work, much management research on entrepreneurship has made entrepreneurship virtually synonymous with opportunity discovery (Busenitz, 1996; Shane, 2004; see Foss and Klein, 2011: Chapters 2 and 3 for a critique). In elucidating his conception of the entrepreneurial market process, Kirzner has consistently emphasized the highly abstract nature of his "metaphor" of the entrepreneur (Kirzner, 2009). As Klein (2008) explains, Kirzner's concept of the entrepreneur is a purely "functional" one – it is simply the device that clears markets. Because Kirzner's conception is extremely stylized, he portrays the discovery, evaluation, and exploitation of opportunities as one *Gestalt*.[1] He is also insistent that the "pure entrepreneur" does not need a firm to seize opportunities, in fact, he doesn't need to own any assets at all (see Foss and Klein, 2011). Adopting Kirzner's views as a foundation for management research on entrepreneurship risks biasing such research towards a preoccupation with discovery at the expense of evaluation and exploitation of opportunities (which Kirzner is essentially silent about) and strengthens the neglect of the established firm as an entrepreneurial agent.

Taken together the three biases in the entrepreneurship literature arguably accounts for the rather systematic neglect of organizational processes, structure and control in this literature: if entrepreneurship is mainly conceptualized as opportunity discovery and the locus of such discovery is the individual, organizational aspects logically becomes at best a matter of organizing the upstart firm. Processes of coordinating acts of discovering, evaluation and exploiting opportunities inside an established firm fall out of the picture. As we later explain, even the SE approach is vulnerable to this critique.

The Creation of Competitive Advantages: Related Approaches

The dependent variable in strategic management research is usually taken to be sustained competitive advantage, that is, a firm's ability to create and appropriate more value than the competition on a sustained basis. This is often addressed in terms of the established economics corpus of applied price theory, industrial organization theory, game theory, and bargaining theory. In fact, most modern strategic management theory (whether resource-based theory or the positioning approach) is based on a logic of "competitive imperfection": ultimately, *some* deviation from the ideal of the perfectly competitive model, leading to imperfect factor and/or product markets, explain strategy's central dependent variable, sustained competitive advantage. Indeed, the latter is very often taken as synonymous with earning rents in equilibrium (Lippman and Rumelt, 1982; Barney, 1991; Peteraf, 1993). Various lists have been compiled of the criteria that resources must meet in order to yield rents in equilibrium (e.g., Barney, 1991; Peteraf, 1993; Peteraf and Barney, 2003). However, there is a retrospective character to such lists: Their main function is to perform a kind of sort among the firm's resources to see if any conform to the criteria.

In contrast, most strategic management theory has until recently been surprisingly silent about where competitive advantage comes from (Rumelt, 1987). However, over the last decade or so, building, accumulating, transforming, managing, learning about, combining and recombining, etc., resources has become a central theme in strategic management. Three distinct research streams exemplify this, namely the hypercompetition, the real options, and the dynamic capabilities approaches. In various ways these developments anticipate the SE view.

Hypercompetition
Whereas the strategic management field in the 1990s emphasized the *sustainability* of competitive advantage, a handful of scholars emphasized,

following Schumpeter (1911), the inherently *temporary* nature of competitive advantages (Eisenhardt, 1989b; D'Aveni, 1994; Wiggins and Rueffli, 2002). This focus has substantial support in the relevant empirical literature, which broadly suggests that firm-specific returns that can be linked to specific competitive advantages regress to the industry mean, and that, moreover, the pace of regression has accelerated over the last few decades (Pacheco-de-Almeida, 2010). In those hypercompetitive environments in which both the rate of innovation and imitation are high, "advantages are rapidly created and eroded" (D'Aveni, 1994: 2). As Pacheco-de-Almeida (2010) shows, a tradeoff arises under these circumstances, because on the one hand, hypercompetition provides incentives to accelerate investments in discovering new entrepreneurial opportunities that can be turned into temporary advantages, while on the other hand driving investments costs up (because of time-compression diseconomies). An implication is that firms may rationally choose to be displaced by competitors. This interesting analysis thus directs attention to the costs of entrepreneurial firm-level strategies.

Real options theory
Real options theory has been developed from financial options theory in which the value of options on uncertain financial assets is assessed (Dixit and Pindyck, 1994). Myers (1977) realized that many of the characteristics of financial options carry over to real investment issues, and following his work researchers have started using financial option pricing methods. Strategic management scholars got involved with real options thinking in the beginning of the 1990s (Bowman and Hurry, 1993). The reason is not difficult to understand: strategic management has choices between flexibility and commitment at its very core (Ghemawat, 1991). Real options allow strategic managers to take specific actions now or postpone them to a future point in time. They thereby provide flexibility in uncertain markets. Strategic managers may invest in a host of different real options to accommodate speedy and flexible reaction to changes in the environment. They may, for example, defer the allocation of resources in order to learn how external conditions develop, expand existing resources or reduce the scale of existing projects if environmental conditions require these steps. Coupled with methods of forecasting (e.g., scenario analysis) real options theory offers a dynamic approach for assessing firms' strategic flexibility in reacting to future changes in the environment.

The link to firm-level entrepreneurship and competitive advantage is straightforward: As environments change, so do competitive advantages. Given that future competitive advantages are highly uncertain, it may pay to keep developing and keep several options open. Internal corporate venturing is a means to such option-creation. When uncertainty resolves, the firm can then call the option most likely to lead to an advantage in the relevant environment.

Dynamic capabilities

The perhaps most direct precursor of SE may well be the "dynamic capabilities view" (Teece et al., 1997). This view argues that superior performance comes from a firm's capacity to change its resource base in the face of Schumpeterian competition and environmental change. Dynamic capabilities are defined as the firm's ability to integrate, build, and reconfigure internal and external competences to address rapidly changing environments (Teece, et al., 1997: 516). Importantly, dynamic capabilities reflect past learning processes, as they are a learned pattern of collective activity through which the organization systematically generates and modifies its operational routines in pursuit of improved performance.

This basic definition has been subsequently refined and extended (e.g., Eisenhardt and Martin, 2000; Winter, 2000; Zollo and Winter, 2002; Teece, 2007b; Di Stefano et al., 2010). What unites different approaches and definitions is the insistence on an organizational ability to alter its resource base. Thus, Helfat et al. (2007: 4) synthesize prior conceptual work by defining a dynamic capability as "the capacity of an organization to purposefully create, extend, and modify its resource base". Accordingly, dynamic capabilities may perform different tasks that alter the resource base, such as new product development, alliance formation, or post-acquisition integration (Eisenhardt and Martin, 2000). According to the dynamic capability (DC) approach, a firm's capacity to alter its resource base indirectly influences economic profitability (Helfat and Peteraf, 2009). Superior dynamic capabilities enable firms to adapt more quickly and effectively to a changing business environment, creating a stream of temporary competitive advantages over time (Teece et al., 1997; Zott, 2002; Helfat et al., 2007).

Recent work on dynamic capabilities has increasingly stressed the role of organizational processes for understanding how firms alter its resource base. Teece (2007) opens up the black box of dynamic capabilities by relating the concept to organizational processes of sensing and seizing business opportunities and the constant (re)alignment of resources (cf. Helfat and Peteraf, 2009). A firm's sensing ability critically depends on the organizational systems and individual capacities to learn and to identify, filter, evaluate, and shape opportunities. Once a business opportunity is identified, the organizational structure, procedures, and incentives influence whether and how a firm seizes the opportunity and creates a new strategic path. What is more, governance and organizational structures shape how firms align their specific resources over time. As we shall see, the dynamic capabilities view is quite akin to SE theory.

THE ROAD TRAVELLED: THE STRATEGIC ENTREPRENEURSHIP LITERATURE

The Domain of Strategic Entrepreneurship

SE is still emerging as a distinct research field with well-defined characteristic research questions. The official birth certificate of the field may be the 2001 special issue on "strategic entrepreneurship" of the *Strategic Management Journal* (Hitt et al., 2001), although, as we have seen, related and anteceding work was done prior to 2001. In spite of its short period of existence, significant progress has been made in defining the SE research agenda as placed in the intersection of the opportunity seeking perspective of the entrepreneurship literature and the advantage seeking perspective of strategic management. The development of a research agenda has been aided by mainly two aspects of SE. First, defining the phenomenon of interest, the dependent variable, if you like, as *firm-level wealth creation* and examining various antecedents of such wealth creation allows researchers, with little difficulty, to capitalize on existing research. Placed at the firm-level, main antecedents have mainly been examined in terms of existing variables from related research streams like entrepreneurial orientation and other variables capturing the firm's motivation and ability to engage in discovery and exploitation of those opportunities that are highest in wealth creation. Second, focusing on wealth creation has the advantage that SE research is not committed to the strategy scholar's emphasis on sustained advantage; wealth creation may be a matter of discovering and exploiting a few massive, but short-lived opportunities, or it may be a matter of many small, long-lived ("sustainable") opportunities (Lippman and Rumelt, 2003). Competitive advantages may thus be fleeting and need to be created and created anew. Thus, firms' strategic intent must be to continuously discover and exploit entrepreneurial opportunities, in order "to continuously create competitive advantages that lead to maximum wealth creation" (Hitt et al., 2002: 2). Thus, broadly defined SE is taken up with *how* firms used strategic intent to *continuously* leverage entrepreneurial opportunities for advantage seeking purposes (Ireland et al., 2001, 2003). Table 12.1 highlights some of the fundamental as well as representative recent contributions to the SE literature. The table illustrates the intersecting position of SE research and the direct impact of both entrepreneurship and strategic management.

Table 12.1 Key contributions to strategic entrepreneurship

Contribution	Dependent var.	Independent var.	Level of analysis	Key argument	Key findings
Covin and Slevin, 1989	Firm performance	Organizational structure, environmental hostility and entrepreneurial strategic posture	Firm-level	Contingency perspective where optimal firm practices and organizational design are dependent on the competitive environment.	An organic organizational structure and an entrepreneurial strategic posture have a positive effect on firm performance in high hostility competitive environments.
Dess et al., 1997	Firm performance	Entrepreneurial strategy making, strategy and environmental conditions	Firm-level	The match between strategy and varying environmental conditions affects firms' entrepreneurial strategy making.	Entrepreneurial strategy making has a stronger positive effect on firm performance when combined with both an appropriate firm strategy and environmental condition.
Barringer and Bluedorn, 1999	Corporate entrepreneurship (EO)	Scanning intensity, planning flexibility, planning horizon and locus of planning	Firm-level	Empirical test of the relationship between firms' entrepreneurial intensity and strategic management practices	Scanning intensity, planning flexibility and locus of planning all positively affect firms' entrepreneurial intensity. However, planning horizon does not affect entrepreneurial intensity.

Table 12.1 (continued)

Contribution	Dependent var.	Independent var.	Level of analysis	Key argument	Key findings
Ireland et al., 2003a	Wealth creation	Entrepreneurial mindset, culture, leadership, resource management, creativity and innovation	Firm- and individual-level	Firms pursuing either an opportunity or advantage seeking strategy are unlikely to be able to achieve sustained competitive advantage. Hence, firms must be both opportunity and advantage seeking. Strategic leverage of entrepreneurial opportunities requires firms to be pro-entrepreneurial in all dimensions.	The authors construct a SE model defining four key dimensions and delineating direct and indirect effects between these and wealth creation.
Ketchen et al., 2007	Wealth creation	Collaboration and innovation	Firm-level	Large and small firms differ in terms of operational effectiveness. Large firms are more skilled at establishing competitive advantages. On the other hand, small firms have stronger opportunity-seeking skills.	Building on network, learning, resource-based, and real option theories, the authors argue that collaboration between small and large firms may enable integration of advantage- and opportunity-seeking abilities across firm boundaries.

Kuratko and Audretsch, 2009	n.a.	n.a.	Firm and individual-level	Essentially the authors recapitulate the dominant logics of integrating strategic management with entrepreneurship.	The authors point to numerous avenues for future enhancement and development of strategic entrepreneurship at the intersection of strategic management and entrepreneurship research.
Monsen and Boss, 2009	Job stress and employee retention	Risk-taking, innovativeness and proactiveness	Individual-level	Empirical examination of the intra-firm effects of strategic entrepreneurship on employees.	Strategic entrepreneurship negatively affects role ambiguity and employees' intention to quit. Also, employees and managers react differently to strategic entrepreneurship.
Hitt and Ireland, 2000	Competition capability and strategic repositioning	Environmental conditions, individual entrepreneurial cognitions and organizational architecture	Multi-level	Construction of a detailed model placing firms' entrepreneurial strategic vision at the interlink of the reciprocal effects of environmental conditions, entrepreneurial cognition and organizational architecture.	First, proposes a model of inter-linkages between environment, entrepreneurial cognitions and organizational architecture. Second, points to numerous avenues for future empirical research.

Table 12.1 (continued)

Contribution	Dependent var.	Independent var.	Level of analysis	Key argument	Key findings
Anderson et al., 2009	Strategic learning capability	Entrepreneurial orientation, structural organicity, market responsiveness and strategy formation mode	Firm-level	EO positively affects firms' strategic learning capability. Also, this relationship is mediated by structure, market responsiveness and strategy formation mode.	Finds a positive, relationship between entrepreneurial behavior, generation of strategic knowledge and strategic change. Also, this relationship is fully mediated by structural organicity, market responsiveness and strategy formation mode.
Ahuja and Lampert, 2001	Breakthrough inventions	Novel technologies, emerging technologies and pioneering technologies	Firm-level	The familiarity, maturity and propinquity traps inhibit established firms in developing breakthrough inventions.	Firms may overcome the negative effect of the familiarity, maturity and propinquity traps by enacting entrepreneurial strategies focused on novel, emerging or pioneering technologies.

The Search for the Entrepreneurial Recipe: Firm-level Antecedents of Entrepreneurship

In one of the earliest conceptualizations of SE, Hitt and Ireland (2000) propose six domains where strategic management and entrepreneurship intersects: innovation, organizational networks, internationalization, organizational learning, top management teams and governance, and growth, flexibility, and change. Building on these intersecting domains, Ireland et al. (2003a) proposed a strongly influential model of SE containing four strategic dimensions needed to achieve competitive advantage by virtue of entrepreneurial acts: an entrepreneurial mindset, entrepreneurial culture and leadership, managing resources strategically, and applying creativity and developing innovation. Basically, an entrepreneurial mindset refers to the ability to notice new opportunities, being alert (à la Kirzner, 1973, 1997b), as well as possess capabilities for successfully exploiting opportunities (Ireland et al., 2003a). An "effective entrepreneurial culture is one in which new ideas and creativity are expected, risk taking is encouraged, failure is tolerated, learning is promoted, product, process and administrative innovations are championed, and continuous change is viewed as a conveyor of opportunities" (Ireland et al., 2003a: 970). Delineation of how the strategic dimensions exert a positive influence on entrepreneurial wealth creation has largely been carried over for the existing entrepreneurship literature. For example, Dess and Lumpkin (2005: 149) note that "champions are especially important after a new project has been defined but before it gains momentum." This means that in a firm-setting product champions carry out an important entrepreneurial role by scavenging for resources and encouraging others to take a chance on promising new ideas. As with the importance of champions, many of the notions of SE obviously hark back to the older corporate venturing literature.

Although many of the conceptual building blocks used in SE have been operationalized and used empirically in either the entrepreneurship or strategic management literature, as a distinct research field SE has yet to produce its own robust literature of empirical tests of dominant conceptual models and their main mechanisms. Conceptually SE has been rather quick to converge on an overall theoretical model with wealth creation as its dependent variable (e.g., Ireland et al., 2003a, 2009; Ireland and Webb, 2007a); however, lower-level causal mechanism underlying this relationship are not clearly defined and operationalized.

Entrepreneurial orientation

A primary focus of entrepreneurship research is the explanation of entrepreneurial wealth creation stemming from opportunity discovery, and the SE view borrows heavily from entrepreneurship research on opportunity discovery. An example of a borrowed construct that antedates the SE view (e.g., Covin and Slevin, 1991b) is the highly influential concept of a firm's "entrepreneurial orientation" (EO) (Lumpkin and Dess, 1996; Wiklund and Shepherd, 2003). EO "refers to the strategy-making practices that businesses use to identify and launch corporate ventures" (Dess and Lumpkin, 2005: 147). A firm's entrepreneurial orientation is measured by five key entrepreneurial antecedents: autonomy, innovativeness, risk taking, proactiveness and competitive aggressiveness (Dess and Lumpkin, 2005). Although some firms may naturally have high levels of all or some of the dimensions of EO, continuously leveraging entrepreneurial opportunities requires firms to deliberately enact an entrepreneurial orientation (Ireland et al., 2003b). Innovation is perhaps the most examined dimension of entrepreneurial orientation. However, innovation by itself does not make a firm entrepreneurial (Covin and Miles, 1999). Instead, firms must have high levels of both the opportunity seeking as well as the advantage seeking dimensions in order to create sustained competitive advantage.

The clear overlap between the strategic and entrepreneurial dimensions of EO explains why EO has been one of the key concepts of SE. In a recent meta-analysis of the entrepreneurial orientation concept Rauch et al. (2009) found that the EO had been used in more than a hundred studies and that the relationship between EO and firm performance was robust across studies. Nevertheless, inheriting or borrowing explanatory variables and constructs from the extant entrepreneurship and strategic management literature raise critical concerns regarding whether or not firms' *continuous* leveraging of *entrepreneurial* opportunities is actually being empirically captured by the explanatory variables. Appropriate tests of the underlying mechanisms of SE would appear to require longitudinal examination of how exactly firms' strategic intent affects their ability to transform the discovery of opportunities into wealth creation. What are the underlying mechanisms? Specifically, what is the interplay between organizational members with specific abilities and skills, interacting within an administrative framework (broadly conceived) that makes some firms capable of continuous wealth creation? This calls for an approach to SE that highlights organizational design and behaviors in a multilevel framework. We view the absence of such framework as the major gap in extant SE research.

THE ROAD AHEAD I: MICRO-FOUNDATIONS AND THE DIVISION OF ENTREPRENEURIAL LABOUR

A direct relationship between firms' strategic entrepreneurial intent and firm performance has been the implicit foundation of most prior SE research. However, there are strong reasons to believe that individual-level heterogeneity plays an important role in explaining firm-level outcomes (cf. Felin and Hesterly, 2007). Moreover, research on corporate venturing, skunkworks, emergent strategy processes, employee entrepreneurship, etc., indeed indicate that entrepreneurial initiatives may emerge from lower levels than the firm level. Understanding how variables at the firm-level affect entrepreneurial outcomes require understanding the micro-aspects of this link. SE theory implicitly agrees. For example, in the influential model by Hitt et al. (2003) determinants of firm-level entrepreneurial outcomes are placed at different analytical levels; similarly, in Monsen and Boss' (2009) recent examination of the micro-level effects of firms' strategic entrepreneurial intent.

Kuratko and Audretsch (2009: 13) "strongly support the idea that Strategic Entrepreneurship – like entrepreneurship in general – is a phenomenon that has antecedents and outcomes on many levels of analysis, and hence can and should be studied on these different levels." There are several reasons that SE research stands to gain from paying more attention to micro-level issues. First, the micro-level is literally where the action is: organizational members are surely the discoverers, evaluators and exploiters of new opportunities. Or, as Burgelman (1983a: 241) argues: "the motor of corporate entrepreneurship resides in the autonomous strategic initiative of individuals at the operational levels in the organization." Second, organizational members are different in terms of skills and experience (Felin and Hesterly, 2007). Such heterogeneity can in itself impact, for example, opportunity discovery; the proper management of this diversity is therefore an important issue. Third, the effects of firm-level variables on entrepreneurial outcomes are mediated through these actions. Thus, attempts to influence firm-level entrepreneurial outcomes by means of firms' strategic intent should be based on such mediation. Delineating how SE enables firms to achieve continuous wealth-creation should first and foremost be a question of understanding: "[t]he processes through which the belief, goals and strategies of would-be entrepreneurs are expressed and furthered by the organizations they build" (Baker and Pollock, 2007: 299).

The Entrepreneurial Division of Labour

In their very influential statement, Shane and Venkataraman (2000) defined entrepreneurship as the study of the discovery, evaluation and exploitation of opportunities. Their definition has become the common reference point in regards to examinations of entrepreneurial behavior within SE as well as in the entrepreneurship literature at large, for example, the closely related literature of corporate entrepreneurship. Broadly defined, discovery represents the noticing of hitherto undiscovered opportunities. Entrepreneurs are discoverers; they discover new resource uses, new products, new markets or new possibilities for arbitrage – in short, new possibilities for profitable trade. Within the economics and management research literatures on entrepreneurship, much effort has been devoted to delineating why some individuals and not others discover new opportunities. However, SE research has not placed much emphasis on this first action of entrepreneurial wealth creation. Opportunity evaluation involves "a comparison between the discovered opportunity and other alternatives to entrepreneurship that the entrepreneur faces" (Shane, 2000: 467). *Post* evaluation firms may engage in exploitation of the opportunity (Alvarez and Barney, 2004).

However, in much of the entrepreneurship literature, and specifically the economics of entrepreneurship (e.g., Knight, 1921 [1985]; Schumpeter, 1934 [1983]; Kirzner, 1973b), these three actions of entrepreneurship are not explicitly separated. In fact, Kirzner's classical contribution explicitly treats the discovery, evaluation and exploitation as activities that are essentially taking place simultaneously and are undertaken by the same person. As we argued earlier in this chapter, this bias can be found in much of the contemporary entrepreneurship literature. However, unlike individual entrepreneurs starting up a new business, firms have access to a base of entrepreneurial skill sets: some organizational members are higher in discovery skills, some higher in evaluation skills, and some higher in exploitation skills. (Foss and Lyngsie, 2011). Accordingly, not only are discovery, evaluation, and exploitation conceptually separate actions, but within firms each action may be undertaken by different organizational members relying on different skill sets. In other words, there is an entrepreneurial division of labor which can be defined, mobilized, and coordinated by firms (Foss, 2011a). Efficiently utilizing different entrepreneurial skills requires coordination. This places organizational design, specifically, the design of organizational structure and the means of organizational control, at the core of SE research.

THE ROAD AHEAD II: ORGANIZATIONAL DESIGN FOR FIRM-LEVEL ENTREPRENEURSHIP

Organizational Design for Entrepreneurship

In a recent paper, Sørensen and Fassiotto (2011: 1) rightly point out that "it is natural to expect that our understanding of the entrepreneurial process would be informed by the vast literature on organizations and organizational processes," but note that there is a "rather distinct separation" between the literature on entrepreneurship and the literature on organizations. We concur. However, it is clear from their discussion that they, too, think of entrepreneurship in terms of startups. Established firms may serve as "fonts of entrepreneurship," but only in the sense that they supply knowledge and skills, beliefs and values and social capital that entrepreneurs can exploit when they start a new firm. We argue that established firms may be fonts of entrepreneurship in the broader sense that they may stimulate entrepreneurship within their corporate hierarchies (for a fuller and more complex statement, see Foss and Lyngsie, 2011; Foss, 2011b).

The need to understand the division of entrepreneurial labor is closely intertwined with the need to examine the impact of organizational designs on entrepreneurial actions. Prior entrepreneurship research has examined what skills or abilities are associated with distinct entrepreneurial actions. For example, individuals discover opportunities related to information they already possess (Amabile, 1997; Venkatraman, 1997; Shane, 2000; Shane and Venkatraman, 2000). Hence, acquiring new information about resource uses is fundamental for firms' opportunity discovery (Casson and Wadeson, 2007).

How well firms succeed in acquiring such information critically depends on firms' organizational design. For example, a high degree of decentralization and delegation of decision authority to organizational members may prompt more opportunity discovery because such an organizational design promotes the motivational drivers of such discovery (e.g., it stimulates intrinsic motivation) and because it co-localizes decision rights with local knowledge (Hayek, 1945). Organizational designs that strengthens lateral communication and combines this with the delegation of decision rights to lower-levels in the hierarchy may drive Schumpeterian, new combinations of existing resources in the pursuit of new opportunities. On the other hand, more hierarchical structures with a strong emphasis on coordination may ease the exploitation of opportunities, suggesting an interesting tradeoff in the effect of organizational design on firm-level entrepreneurship.

Another fascinating, but unexplored, area is the separation of those effects on entrepreneurship that stem from hiring, promoting, retaining, etc., particularly talented individuals (i.e., selection and matching processes) from the effects of the organizational design itself (e.g., certain reward systems may call forth entrepreneurial initiatives, e.g., discovery of opportunities, even from employees that do not possess particular entrepreneurial talent to begin with). In a sense, certain organizational designs may compensate (in terms of firm-level entrepreneurial outcomes) for a relative lack of entrepreneurial skills. However, because the impact of organizational design has not yet been examined in the research literature, we know very little about the relative contributions of individual entrepreneurial skills and organizational design. The relation between these two sets of variables could be one of complementarity, so that entrepreneurial skills need to be embedded in the appropriate organizational architectures to become effective.

Recent SE research has begun to acknowledge the importance of applying both an individual-level perspective and include organizational design when examining how entrepreneurial firms' discover and leverage opportunities to create sustained competitive advantage (e.g., Ireland et al., 2009; Monsen and Boss, 2009). Although this early research is promising, organizational design variables still need to be explicitly highlighted in the SE field. Adopting a micro-focus emphasizing individual (entrepreneurial) actions and examining how firms' organizational designs assist in sourcing, coordinating and leveraging entrepreneurial skills, will without a doubt provide much added insight on how firm-level entrepreneurial capacity and outcomes emerge from intra-firm behaviors.

The Organizational Loci of Entrepreneurial Actions

Different entrepreneurial actions are likely to be undertaken by different organizational members dispersed across different organizational levels (Kuratko et al., 2004). Extant entrepreneurship literature has typically focused on three distinct levels of organizations, namely top management, middle management and operational management. Within SE research the discovery, evaluation, and exploitation of opportunities are most frequently conceptualized in a sequential manner: the discovery of a new project, essentially a new opportunity for wealth creation, is followed by project definition and project impetus and lastly exploitation (Dess and Lumpkin, 2005). In this sense, continuous wealth creation must be achieved by firms performing continuous cycles encompassing all three entrepreneurial actions. Coordinating the internal division of actions by virtue of organizational design necessitates a clear conceptualization of at what organizational level each actions is in practice undertaken. Furthermore, neither organizational level nor action is necessarily identical between each entrepreneurial cycle. For example, prior knowledge plays a critical role in discovery of new opportunities, but is at the same time distrusted across the entire organization. Hence, discovery of opportunities can occur at any specific organizational level or among a specific group of organizational members. Indeed, discovery actions are likely to be undertaken by all organizational members endowed with the "right" prior knowledge; what Burgelman (1983) refers to as "spontaneous initiatives." Furthermore, firms' strategic intent may predispose specific individuals or groups to engage in discovery. Accounting for this micro-level heterogeneity is surely an avenue of SE that warrants more emphasis in the future.

CONCLUSIONS

SE has emerged over the last decade as a new focus in the intersection between the individual-centric and upstart-focused entrepreneurship field and the strategic management field with its traditional emphasis on established firms and firm-level performance variables. The defining characteristic of the field is a sustained attempt to link opportunity-seeking (i.e., opportunity discovery and evaluation) with advantage seeking; an endeavor that is related to work on dynamic capabilities, hypercompetition, and real options. Like these research streams, SE appears to have dropped strategic management's search for the conditions of sustainability of (any single) competitive advantage, and instead focused on the entrepreneurial pursuit of a string of temporary advantages, often encapsulated under the label of "wealth creation." SE research has identified a large set of variables that may drive such firm-level entrepreneurship, for example, borrowing (from strategic management) notions of "strategic intent" or (from entrepreneurship) "entrepreneurial orientation."

We have argued, however that SE is still mainly a rather loose amalgam of a number of insights from strategy and entrepreneurship. Whether it will morph into a distinct and cumulative research stream seems dependent on the development of clear(er) research models around which research can build, and also on gradually building a body of distinct SE empirical knowledge. We have argued that organizational design variables and explicit micro-foundations are important components of such a development.

NOTE

1. A favorite example of Kirzner's is discovering a bank note on the pavement and picking it up, a situation in which the three phases are indeed near simultaneous.

13 Corporate entrepreneurship
Donald F. Kuratko

INTRODUCTION

Since innovation is such a critical issue for companies today, corporate entrepreneurship (CE) is being embraced today by executives as more than simply a component of a company's strategy, but rather as the focus of an organization's success. As Hamel (2000) advised, "In these suddenly sober times, the inescapable imperative for every organization must be to make innovation an all-the-time, everywhere capability." Firms that are more adaptable, aggressive, and innovative are better positioned not only to adjust to a dynamic, threatening, and complex external environment, but to create change in that environment. They do not take the external environment as a given, but instead define themselves as agents of change, leading customers instead of following them, creating new markets, and rewriting the rules of the competitive game (Morris et al., 2011).

Corporate entrepreneurship researchers have emphasized the importance of CE's potential as a growth strategy (Zahra et al., 1999). Dess et al. (1999) noted that, "Virtually all organizations – new start-ups, major corporations, and alliances among global partners – are striving to exploit product-market opportunities through innovative and proactive behavior" – the type of behavior that is called for by corporate entrepreneurship. Barringer and Bluedorn (1999) suggested that in light of the dynamism and complexity of today's environments, "entrepreneurial attitudes and behaviors are necessary for firms of all sizes to prosper and flourish." Developing organizational environments that cultivate employees' interest in and commitment to innovation contribute to successful competition in today's global economy. Ireland et al. (2006a, b) pointed out that to simultaneously develop and nurture today's and tomorrow's competitive advantages, advantages that are grounded in innovation, firms increasingly rely on corporate entrepreneurship.

However, despite the espoused and observed positive effects of CE, there are issues to explore if we are to fully understand this construct's promise (Zahra et al., 1999; Hornsby et al., 2002; Dess et al., 2003; Hornsby et al., 2009). The theoretical and empirical knowledge about the domain of CE and the entrepreneurial behavior on which it is based are key issues warranting greater attention. Moreover, outcome factors that influence an organization's willingness to continue implementing a CE strategy as well as managers' willingness to continue engaging in entrepreneurial behavior are now being integrated to enhance our understanding of CE practices (Kuratko et al., 2004). Even so, it has been argued that a fundamental ambiguity exists in the literature concerning what it means, in a theoretical sense, to have CE as a firm's strategy (Meyer and Heppard, 2000). The existence of a corporate entrepreneurship strategy implies that a firm's strategic intent is to continuously and deliberately leverage entrepreneurial opportunities (Shane and Venkataraman, 2000) for growth- and advantage-seeking purposes. Covin and Miles (1999) contended that innovation was the single common theme underlying all forms of corporate entrepreneurship.

While there is a broadly held belief in the need for and inherent value of entrepreneurial action on the part of established organizations (Hitt et al., 2001; Kuratko, 2009; Morris et al., 2011), much remains to be revealed about how CE strategy is enacted in organizational settings. Fortunately, knowledge accumulation on the topic of CE has been occurring at a rapid rate, and many of the elements essential to constructing a theoretically grounded understanding of CE can be readily identified from the extant literature over the last four decades. This chapter begins with an evolution of the academic field of corporate entrepreneurship (CE) and then examines some of the key research elements in the field today. By focusing on how corporate entrepreneurship is configured as a strategy, the elements of an organizational architecture conducive to CE and the managerial roles within that architecture are explored. The intention is to formulate a more complete understanding of the concepts behind a corporate entrepreneurship strategy. The chapter concludes with the future challenge of corporate entrepreneurship leadership that confronts organizations today.

THE EVOLUTION OF CORPORATE ENTREPRENEURSHIP

The concept of corporate entrepreneurship (CE) has evolved over the last four decades and the definitions have varied considerably over time. The early research in the 1970s focused on venture teams and how entrepreneurship inside existing organizations could be developed (Hill and Hlavacek, 1972; Peterson and Berger, 1972; Hanan, 1976).

In the 1980s, researchers conceptualized CE as embodying entrepreneurial behavior requiring organizational sanctions and resource commitments for the purpose of developing different types of value-creating innovations (Schollhammer, 1982; Burgelman, 1983a, b, 1984; Pinchott, 1985; Kanter, 1985; Alterowitz, 1988). CE was defined simply as a process of organizational renewal (Sathe 1989).

In the 1990s researchers focused on CE as re-energizing and enhancing the firm's ability to develop the skills through which innovations can be created (Jennings and Young, 1990; Zahra, 1991; Merrifield, 1993; Borch et al., 1999). Also in the 1990s more comprehensive definitions of CE began to take shape. Guth and Ginsberg (1990) stressed that CE encompassed two major types of phenomena: new venture creation within existing organizations and the transformation of on-going organizations through strategic renewal. Zahra (1991: 261) observed that "corporate entrepreneurship may be formal or informal activities aimed at creating new businesses in established companies through product and process innovations and market developments. These activities may take place at the corporate, division (business), functional, or project levels, with the unifying objective of improving a company's competitive position and financial performance." Sharma and Chrisman (1999: 18) suggested that CE "is the process where by an individual or a group of individuals, in association with an existing organization, create a new organization or instigate renewal or innovation within that organization."

With all of these various definitions taking shape, the twenty-first century linked CE to firms' efforts to establish sustainable competitive advantages as the foundation for profitable growth (Kuratko et al., 2001; Kuratko et al., 2005; Hornsby et al., 2009). In this regard, Morris et al. (2011) described Corporate Entrepreneurship (CE) as being manifested in companies either through *corporate venturing* or *strategic entrepreneurship* (see Figure 13.1).

Corporate venturing approaches have as their commonality the adding of new businesses (or portions of new businesses via equity investments) to the corporation. This can be accomplished through three implementation modes – internal corporate venturing, cooperative corporate venturing, and external corporate venturing. By contrast, *strategic entrepreneurship* approaches have as their commonality the exhibition of large-scale or otherwise highly consequential innovations that are adopted in the firm's pursuit of competitive advantage. These innovations may or may not result in new businesses for the corporation. With strategic entrepreneurship approaches, innovation can be in any of five areas – the firm's strategy, product offerings, served markets, internal organization (i.e., structure, processes, and capabilities), or business model (Morris et al., 2011).

Corporate venturing is the first major category of corporate entrepreneurship and it includes various methods for creating, adding to,

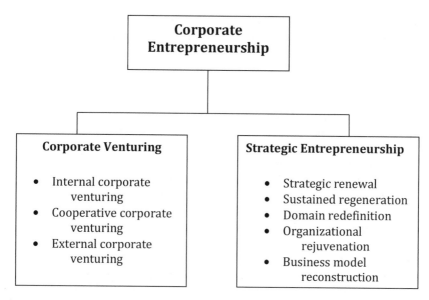

Source: Morris et al., 2011: 88.

Figure 13.1   Defining corporate entrepreneurship

or investing in new businesses (Covin et al., 2003; McGrath et al., 2006; Kuratko et al., 2009). With *internal corporate venturing*, new businesses are created and owned by the corporation. These businesses typically reside within the corporate structure but, occasionally, may be located outside the firm and operate as semi-autonomous entities. Among internal corporate ventures that reside within the firm's organizational boundaries, some may be formed and exist as part of a pre-existing internal organization structure and others may be housed in newly-formed organizational entities within the corporate structure. *Cooperative corporate venturing* (aka joint corporate venturing, collaborative corporate venturing) refers to entrepreneurial activity in which new businesses are created and owned by the corporation together with one or more external development partners. Cooperative ventures typically exist as external entities that operate beyond the organizational boundaries of the founding partners. *External corporate venturing* refers to entrepreneurial activity in which new businesses are created by parties outside the corporation and subsequently invested in (via the assumption of equity positions) or acquired by the corporation. These external businesses are typically very young ventures or early growth-stage firms. In practice, new businesses might be developed through a single venturing mode, any two venturing modes, or all three venturing modes. A firm's total venturing activity is equal to the sum of the ventures enacted through the internal, cooperative, and external modes. With corporate venturing, creating an entirely new business is the main objective (Covin and Miles, 2007).

It is impossible, however, to evaluate the success or failure of corporate venturing initiatives unless it is clear what management's goals were in the first place. Companies must create venture evaluation and control systems that assess venture performance on criteria that follow from the venture's founding motive. Tidd and Taurins (1999) concluded that there are two sets of motives that drive the practice of internal corporate venturing: leveraging – to exploit existing corporate competencies in new product or market arenas; and learning – to acquire new knowledge and skills that may be useful in existing product or market arenas. When the overall motive is leveraging, some of the specific reasons that firms engage in corporate venturing include: to exploit under-utilized resource; to extract further value from existing resources; to introduce competitive pressure onto internal supplier; to spread the risk and cost of product development; to divest non-core activities. The learning motives can also be broken down further as well. Three major types of organizational learning tend to receive the greatest emphasis: to learn about the process of venturing; to develop new competencies; to develop managers.

In another study of corporate venturing practice – this one including firms engaged in both internal and external corporate venturing – Miles and Covin (2002) reported that the firms pursued venturing for three primary reasons: (1) to build an innovative capability as the basis for making the overall firm more entrepreneurial and accepting of change; (2) to appropriate greater value from current organizational competencies or to expand the firm's scope of operations and knowledge into areas of possible strategic importance; and (3) to generate quick financial returns.

Strategic entrepreneurship constitutes a second major category of approaches to corporate entrepreneurship. While corporate venturing involves company involvement in the creation of new businesses, strategic entrepreneurship corresponds to a broader array of entrepreneurial initiatives which do not necessarily involve new businesses being added to the firm. Strategic entrepreneurship involves simultaneous opportunity-seeking and advantage-seeking behaviors (Ireland et al., 2003a). The innovations that are the focal points of strategic entrepreneurship initiatives represent the means through which opportunity is capitalized upon. These are innovations that can happen anywhere and everywhere in the company. By emphasizing an opportunity-driven mindset, management seeks to achieve and maintain a competitively advantageous position for the firm.

These innovations can represent fundamental changes from the firms' past strategies, products, markets, organization structures, processes, capabilities, or business models. Or, these innovations can represent fundamental bases on which the firm is fundamentally differentiated from its industry rivals. Hence, there are two possible reference points that can be considered when a firm exhibits strategic entrepreneurship: (1) how much the firm is transforming itself relative to where it was before (e.g., transforming its products, markets, internal processes, etc.) and (2) how much the firm is transforming itself relative to industry conventions or standards (again, in terms of product offerings, market definitions, internal processes, and so forth). Strategic entrepreneurship can take one of five forms – *strategic renewal, sustained regeneration, domain redefinition, organizational rejuvenation*, and *business model reconstruction* (Covin and Miles, 1999; Ireland and Webb, 2007b).

The major thrust behind corporate entrepreneurship is a revitalization of innovation, creativity, and leadership in corporations. It appears that corporate entrepreneurship may possess the critical components needed for the future productivity of our organizations. If so, then examining the range of research that has focused on the various aspects of the corporate entrepreneurship process is most important for scholars to move the field forward.

CORPORATE ENTREPRENEURSHIP STRATEGY

Corporate entrepreneurship (CE) and the behavior through which it is practiced has been initiated in established organizations for a host of purposes, including those of profitability (Zahra, 1993; Vozikis et al., 1999), strategic renewal (Guth and Ginsberg, 1990), innovativeness (Baden-Fuller, 1995), gaining knowledge to develop future revenue streams (McGrath et al., 1994), international success (Birkinshaw, 1997), and the effective configuration of resources as the pathway to developing competitive advantages (Borch et al., 1999; Covin and Miles, 1999; Covin et al., 2000; Ireland et al., 2003b; Kuratko et al., 2009). Regardless of the reason the firm decides to engage in CE, it has become a major strategy in all organizations (Narayanan et al., 2009; Morris et al., 2011).

A strategy for corporate entrepreneurship is a set of commitments and actions that is framed around entrepreneurial behavior and innovation in order to develop current and future competitive advantages that are intended to lead to competitive success. (Ireland et al., 2003b). The choice of using a strategy for corporate entrepreneurship as a primary means of strategic adaptation reflects the firm's decision to seek competitive advantage principally through innovation and entrepreneurial behavior on a sustained basis (Russell, 1999).

Increasingly environmental triggers are interpreted by today's decision makers as ones that call for the formation and use of corporate entrepreneurship as the core of the firm's efforts to adapt strategically. Lumpkin and Dess (1996) suggested that organizations facing a rapidly changing, faster-paced competitive environment might be best served by implementing corporate entrepreneurship behaviors as an adaptation mechanism. Labels have been attached to organizations relying on entrepreneurship actions as the core of their commitments, decisions, and strategies. Examples of these labels have included entrepreneurial firms (Mintzberg, 1973), prospectors (Miles and Snow, 1978), and adaptive, innovative, and impulsive firms (Miller and Friesen, 1980).

The operational essence of using a strategy for corporate entrepreneurship as the foundation of a firm's adaptation responses is the call for an organization's employees to rely on entrepreneurial behavior as the source of adjustments required to assure current and future marketplace success. In this context, a corporate entrepreneurship strategy encompasses the full set of commitments, decisions, and entrepreneurial behavior required for the firm to improve the likelihood of achieving current and future competitive success. When using corporate entrepreneurship as the source of strategic adaptation to the realities of a firm's external environment, the intention is to rely on innovation as the foundation for creating new businesses or reconfiguring existing ones. In general, corporate entrepreneurship calls for firms to innovate boldly and regularly and to be willing to accept considerable, though reasonable levels of risk in doing so (Miller and Friesen, 1982). To Sykes and Block (1989), reasonable risks are "affordable" to the organization in terms of its current and future viability as an operating entity. Resulting from successful use of corporate entrepreneurship firms may deliberately reposition themselves within their environment, including the main arena(s) in which they compete (Covin and Slevin, 1991a).

For success to be recorded by using corporate entrepreneurship, those within the firm must be aware of it and encouraged and nurtured in their use of it. Without awareness, encouragement, and nurturing, the entrepreneurial behavior that is linked to use of corporate entrepreneurship will not surface or be used consistently throughout the firm (Kuratko, et al., 2001). Furthermore, an awareness of what corporate entrepreneurship calls for in terms of behavior on the part of individuals permits an analysis of choices. Typically, organizational members compare and evaluate the opportunity cost of engaging in entrepreneurial behavior with those of either not doing so or displaying still other behaviors. Lower opportunity costs, relative to the costs of other behavior, engender a commitment to engaging in entrepreneurial behavior (Reynolds, 1987; Amit et al., 1995; Shane and Venkataraman, 2000).

In comprehensive arguments, Burgelman (1983a, 1984) and Burgelman and Sayles (1986) argued that organizational innovation as well as other strategic activities surface through two models – induced strategic behavior and autonomous strategic behavior. Of the two models, induced strategic behavior occurs more frequently in organizations. Comparatively, induced strategic behavior captures formal entrepreneurial behavior while autonomous strategic behavior is concerned with entrepreneurial behavior that surfaces informally in the firm. The more resource rich is the firm the greater is the likelihood that autonomous strategic behavior will emerge.

Burgelman's (1983b) induced strategic behavior approach is a top-down process whereby the firm's strategy and structure provide the context within which entrepreneurial behavior is elicited and supported. The responsibility for establishing a strategy and forming a structure that can induce entrepreneurial behavior rests with top-level managers. Thus, induced strategic or entrepreneurial behavior can be shaped by the firm's structural context.

While Burgelman's (1983b) analysis focuses on induced strategic behavior, it does not suggest ignoring the importance of autonomous strategic behavior for successful corporate entrepreneurship actions. Indeed, both induced and autonomous strategic behavior are important to a firm's corporate entrepreneurship efforts, whether they are oriented to creating new businesses or reconfiguring existing ones. In the induced strategic behavior model, top-level managers oversee, nurture, and support the firm's attempts to use entrepreneurial behavior as the foundation for product, process, and administrative innovations (Heller, 1999). A corporate entrepreneurship strategy that is intended to elicit and support induced strategic behavior should also include degrees of flexibility through which autonomous strategic behavior is allowed and indeed encouraged to surface. Properly viewed as a formal tolerance of autonomous strategic behavior, an intentional commitment of this type is a conscious strategic decision on the part of the firm's upper-level decision makers to foster the surfacing and use of innovative entrepreneurial behavior, regardless of whether its origin rests with formal or informal processes (Bird, 1988).

Ireland et al. (2009: 21) define CE strategy as "a vision-directed, organization-wide reliance on entrepreneurial behavior that purposefully and continuously rejuvenates the organization and shapes the scope of its operations through the recognition and exploitation of entrepreneurial opportunity." Morris et al. (2011) contend that when the actions taken in a large firm to form competitive advantages and to exploit them through a strategy are grounded in entrepreneurial actions, the firm is employing an *entrepreneurial strategy*. Further, when establishing direction and priorities for the product, service and process innovation efforts of the firm, the company is formulating its *strategy for entrepreneurship*.

ORGANIZATIONAL ARCHITECTURE FOR CORPORATE ENTREPRENEURSHIP

Much of our understanding of the impact of organizational architecture on individual-level entrepreneurial behavior is based on the empirical research of Kuratko and his colleagues (Kuratko and Montagno, 1989; Kuratko, Montagno, and Hornsby, 1990; Hornsby, et al., 1993; Kuratko, 1993; Hornsby et al., 1999, 2002; Kuratko et al., 2004; Kuratko et al., 2005a, b; Hornsby et al., 2009). In the Kuratko et al. (1990) study, results from factor analysis showed that what had been theoretically argued and hypothesized to be five conceptually distinct factors that would elicit and support entrepreneurial behavior on the part of first- and middle-level managers (top management support for CE, reward and resource availability, organizational structure and boundaries, risk taking, and time availability) were actually only three in number. More specifically, based on how items loaded, Kuratko et al. (1990) concluded that three factors – management support, organizational structure, and reward and resource availability – were important influences on the development of an organizational climate in which entrepreneurial behavior on the part of first- and middle-level managers could be expected. Although this study's results did not support the hypothesized five-factor model, the findings established the multidimensionality of antecedents of managers' entrepreneurial behavior.

To extend this earlier work (Kuratko et al., 1990), Hornsby et al. (1999) conducted an empirical study designed to explore the effect of organizational culture on entrepreneurial behavior in a sample of Canadian and US firms. In particular, Hornsby et al. (1999) wanted to determine if organizational culture creates variance in entrepreneurial behavior on the part of Canadian and US managers. The results based on data collected from all levels of management showed no significant differences between Canadian and US managers' perceptions of the importance of five factors – management support, work discretion, rewards/reinforcement, time availability, and organizational boundaries – as antecedents to their entrepreneurial behavior. These findings partially validate those reported by Kuratko et al. (1990) and extend the importance of organizational antecedents of managers' entrepreneurial behavior into companies based in a second (albeit similar) national culture.

Hornsby et al. (2002) developed the Corporate Entrepreneurship

Assessment Instrument (CEAI) to partially replicate and disentangle previously reported findings. The instrument featured 84 Likert-style questions that were used to assess antecedents of entrepreneurial behavior. In this study, only middle-level managers, from both Canada and the United States, were surveyed. Results from factor analyses suggested that there are five stable antecedents of middle-level managers' entrepreneurial behavior. The five antecedents are: (1) *management support* (the willingness of top-level managers to facilitate and promote entrepreneurial behavior, including championing of innovative ideas and providing necessary resources), (2) *work discretion/autonomy* (top-level managers' commitment to tolerate failure, provide decision-making latitude and freedom from excessive oversight, and delegate authority and responsibility), (3) *rewards/reinforcement* (development and use of systems that reward based on performance, highlight significant achievements, and encourage pursuit of challenging work), (4) *time availability* (evaluating work loads to assure time to pursue innovations and structuring jobs to support efforts to achieve short- and long-term organizational goals, and (5) *organizational boundaries* (precise explanations of outcomes expected from organizational work and development of mechanisms for evaluating, selecting, and using innovations).

In summary, the literature on the organizational antecedents to CE is vast and expanding. The literature reviewed in this section is meant to demonstrate the growing importance in identifying the attributes of a pro-entrepreneurship organizational architecture.

MANAGERIAL ROLES IN CORPORATE ENTREPRENEURSHIP

Managers at all organizational levels have critical strategic roles to fulfill for the organization to be successful (Floyd and Lane, 2000; Ireland, Hitt, and Vaidyanath, 2002). According to Floyd and Lane (2000), senior-, middle-, and first-level managers have distinct responsibilities with respect to each subprocess. Senior-level managers have *ratifying, recognizing,* and *directing* roles corresponding to the competence definition, modification, and deployment subprocesses, respectively. These roles, in turn, are associated with particular managerial actions.

In examining the role of senior-level managers, Burgelman (1984) contends that in successful corporate entrepreneurship senior-level management's principal involvement takes place within the strategic and structural context determination processes. In particular, senior-level managers are responsible for *retroactively rationalizing* certain new businesses into the firm's portfolio and concept of strategy based on their evaluations of those businesses' prospects as desirable, value-creating components of the firm. Senior-level managers are also responsible for *structuring* the organization in ways that accommodate and reinforce the business ventures embraced as part of the firm's strategic context. Overall, Burgelman (1984) sees senior-level managers as having a *selecting* role in the corporate venturing form of CE.

Ling et al. (2008) examined 152 firms in regard to "transformational" CEO's impact on corporate entrepreneurship. Their research demonstrated that the transformational CEOs had a significant role in directly shaping four salient characteristics of top management teams: behavioral integration, risk-taking propensity, decentralization of responsibilities, and long-term compensation. This study provided impetus to the importance of the "directing" role that top management must embrace.

In summary, senior-level managers have multiple and critical roles in CE activity. These managers are responsible for the articulation of an entrepreneurial strategic vision and instigating the emergence of a pro-entrepreneurship organizational architecture. Moreover, through specific manifestations of entrepreneurial actions, senior-level managers are also centrally involved in the defining processes of both the corporate venturing and strategic renewal forms of CE, and they proactively respond to various entrepreneurial imperatives.

In examining the role of middle-level managers, research highlights the importance of middle-level managers' entrepreneurial behaviors to the firm's attempt to create new businesses or reconfigure existing ones (Floyd and Wooldridge, 1992; Ginsberg and Hay, 1994; Kanter, 1985; Pearce et al., 1997). This importance manifests itself both in terms of the need for middle-level managers to behave entrepreneurially themselves and the requirement for them to support and nurture others' attempts to do the same. Middle-level managers' work as change agents and promoters of innovation is facilitated by their organizational centrality.

Kuratko et al. (2005) proposed a model of middle-level managers' entrepreneurial behavior. They contend that middle-level managers *endorse*, *refine*, and *shepherd* entrepreneurial opportunities and *identify, acquire,* and *deploy* resources needed to pursue those opportunities. Regarding the *endorsement* of entrepreneurial opportunities, middle-level managers often find themselves in evaluative positions vis-à-vis entrepreneurial initiatives emerging from lower organizational levels. In an induced sense, middle-level managers endorse CE perspectives coming from top-level executives and "sell" their value-creating potential to the primary implementers – first-level managers and their direct reports.

Their *refinement* behaviors characteristically involve molding the entrepreneurial opportunity into one that makes sense for the organization, given the organization's strategy, resources, and political structure. It is characteristically the job of middle-level managers to convert malleable entrepreneurial opportunities into initiatives that fit the organization. Through the *shepherding* function, middle-level managers champion, protect, nurture, and guide the entrepreneurial initiative. These behaviors assure that entrepreneurial initiatives originating at lower organizational levels are not "orphaned" once their continued development requires support beyond what can be given by individuals at those lower levels. The pursuit of entrepreneurial opportunities necessitates the *identification* of resources needed to convert the entrepreneurial concept into a business reality. Knowing which resources will be needed to pursue any given entrepreneurial opportunity will be difficult inasmuch as entrepreneurial initiatives tend to evolve in their scope, content, and focus as they develop (McGrath and MacMillan, 1995). While the resource identification function relates to middle-level managers knowing what resources are needed to pursue the entrepreneurial opportunity, the resource *acquisition* function relates to them knowing where and how to get those resources. Middle-level managers are often most responsible for redirecting resources away from existing operations and toward entrepreneurial initiatives appearing to have greater strategic value for the firm (Burgelman, 1984). In short, it might be argued that the middle management level is where entrepreneurial opportunities are given the best chance to flourish based on the resources likely to be deployed in their pursuit.

In summary, evidence shows that middle-level managers are a hub through which most organizational knowledge flows (Floyd and Wooldridge, 1990, 1994; King et al., 2001). To interact effectively with first-level managers (and their reports) and to gain access to their knowledge, middle-level managers must possess the technical competence required to understand the initial development, subsequent shaping, and continuous applications of the firm's core competencies. Simultaneously, to interact effectively with senior-level executives and to gain access to their knowledge, middle-level managers must understand the firm's strategic intent and goals as well as the political context within which these are chosen and pursued. Resulting from these interactions is the ability of middle-level managers to champion strategic alternatives from those below (i.e., first-level managers and their reports) and to make them accessible to those above. Through interactions with senior- and first-level managers, those operating in the middle of an organization's leadership structure influence and shape their firms' CE strategies.

In Floyd and Lane's (2000) model, first-level managers have *experimenting* roles corresponding to the competence definition subprocess, *adjusting* roles corresponding to the competence modification subprocess, and *conforming* roles corresponding to the competence deployment subprocess. For example, first-level managers' experimenting role is expressed through the initiating of entrepreneurial projects. The adjusting role is expressed through, for example, first-level managers' responding to recognized and unplanned entrepreneurial challenges. Finally, the conforming role is expressed through first-level managers' adaptation of operating policies and procedures to the strategic initiatives endorsed at higher organizational levels.

Thus, organizations pursuing CE strategies exhibit a cascading yet integrated set of entrepreneurial action at the senior-, middle-, and first-levels of management. At the senior level, managers act in concert with others throughout the firm as well as with key stakeholder groups to identify effective means through which new businesses can be created or existing ones reconfigured. CE is pursued in light of environmental opportunities and threats, with the purpose of creating a more effective alignment between the company and conditions in its external environment. The entrepreneurial behaviors expected of middle-level managers are framed around the need for this group to propose and interpret entrepreneurial opportunities that might create new business for the firm or increase the firm's competitiveness in current business domains. As recipients of these interpretations, first-level managers then work with their people to fashion the entrepreneurial behaviors through which the firm's core competencies can be used daily to exploit entrepreneurial opportunities that others have not observed or have failed to effectively exploit.

In one empirical examination of managers' relation to employees in the corporate entrepreneurship process, Brundin et al. (2008) studied the entrepreneurial behavior of employees in entrepreneurially oriented firms and found a direct relation to manager's emotions and displays. The employees' willingness to act entrepreneurially increased when managers displayed confidence and satisfaction about an entrepreneurial project. It was also shown that the employees' willingness to act entrepreneurially decreased when managers displayed frustration, worry, or bewilderment about an entrepreneurial project.

In an effort to study entrepreneurial actions within the context of CE at different levels of management, Hornsby et al. (2009) conducted an empirical study of 458 managers at different levels in their firms. They found that the relationship between perceived internal antecedents (as measured by the Corporate Entrepreneurship Assessment Instrument – CEAI (Hornsby et al., 2002)) and corporate entrepreneurial actions (measured by the number of new ideas implemented), differed depending on managerial level. Specifically, the positive relationship between managerial support and entrepreneurial action was more positive for senior- and middle-level managers than it was for first-level (lower level) managers, and the positive relationship between work discretion and entrepreneurial action was more positive for senior- and middle-level managers than it was for first-level managers. The few studies that have explored managerial level (primarily conceptual studies) have emphasized the role of first-level managers in a "bottom-up" process of corporate entrepreneurship (Burgelman, 1983a, b, 1984). This study offered a counter-weight to this "bottom-up" process with arguments and empirical support for the notion that given the specific organizational antecedents necessary for corporate entrepreneurial activity (as measured by the Corporate Entrepreneurship Assessment Instrument- CEAI), senior managers demonstrated a greater ability to "make more of" these specific conditions (such as work discretion, time availability, organizational boundaries, and managerial support) to potentially implement more entrepreneurial ideas than do first-level managers.

Even with the differences found with levels of management in the Hornsby et al. (2009) study, it reinforced the belief that working jointly, senior-, middle-, and first-level managers are responsible for developing the entrepreneurial behaviors that could be used to form the core competencies through which future competitive success can be pursued.

THE CHALLENGE OF CORPORATE ENTREPRENEURIAL LEADERSHIP

The true value of entrepreneurship as a corporate concept lies in the extent to which it helps organizations create *sustainable competitive advantage*. In order to maintain this "entrepreneurial mindset," managers must assume certain ongoing responsibilities (McGrath and MacMillan, 2000). Managers must exhibit "entrepreneurial leadership" for their organization (Kuratko, 2007; Ling et al., 2008). The first responsibility involves "framing the challenge." In other words, there needs to be a clear definition of the specified challenges that everyone involved with innovative projects should accomplish. It is important to think in terms of, and regularly reiterate, the challenge.

Second, leaders have the responsibility to "absorb the uncertainty" that is perceived by team members. Entrepreneurial leaders make uncertainty less daunting. The idea is to create the self-confidence that lets others act on opportunities without seeking managerial permission. Employees must not be overwhelmed by the complexity inherent in many innovative situations.

A third responsibility is to "define gravity" – that is, what must be accepted and what cannot be accepted. The term *gravity* is used to capture limiting conditions. For example, there is gravity on the earth, but that does not mean it must limit our lives. If freed from the psychological cage of believing that gravity makes flying impossible, creativity can permit us to invent an airplane or spaceship. This is what the entrepreneurial mindset is all about – seeing opportunities where others see barriers and limits.

A fourth responsibility of entrepreneurial leadership involves 'clearing obstacles' that arise as a result of internal competition for resources. This can be a problem especially when the entrepreneurial innovation is beginning to undergo significant growth. A growing venture will often find itself pitted squarely against other (often established) aspects of the firm in a fierce internal competition for funds and staff. Creative tactics, political skills, and an ability to regroup, reorganize, and attack from another angle become invaluable.

The fifth responsibility is for entrepreneurial leaders to understand the "grief" that may be associated with project failures (Shepherd et al., 2009). Although failure can be an important source of information for learning, this learning is not automatic or instantaneous. The emotions generated by failure (i.e., grief) can interfere with the learning process and grief recovery may be an important component for individual innovation to continue. Recognizing the grief process and how it can be managed by individuals and organizations for enhanced learning (Shepherd and Kuratko, 2009) will be critical to the grief recovery process. Thus, having failed innovators recover more quickly from the emotions of grief, learn more from their project failures, and remain committed to future innovative endeavors likely to enhance the organization's sustained innovative output.

A final responsibility for entrepreneurial leaders is to keep their finger on the pulse of the project. This involves constructive monitoring and control of the developing opportunity (Morris et al., 2011).

CONCLUSION

The evolution of research in corporate entrepreneurship has changed the view of innovative activity in organizations dramatically. In the 1970s, the word entrepreneurship was simply not associated with large corporate environments. During the 1980s, many argued that it was difficult if not almost impossible for people to act entrepreneurially in bureaucratic organizational structures (Morse, 1986). At the same time, a few researchers began to suggest that entrepreneurial actions were possible for companies of any size, should be encouraged, and might be expected to enhance firm performance (Burgelman, 1984; Kanter, 1985). During the latter part of the 1980s and throughout the 1990s, there was a veritable revolution with respect to the perceived value of entrepreneurial actions. This significant change paralleled the profound adjustments companies were making in terms of how they defined their business, utilized their human resources, and competed in the global economy. Zahra et al. (1999) noted that:

> Some of the world's best-known companies had to endure a painful transformation to become more entrepreneurial. They had to endure years of reorganization, downsizing, and restructuring. These changes altered the identity or culture of these firms, infusing a new entrepreneurial spirit throughout their operations . . . change, innovation, and entrepreneurship became highly regarded words.

The twenty-first century is now a time when entrepreneurial actions are recognized widely as the path to competitive advantage and success in organizations of all types and sizes (Covin et al., 2000). Moreover, a lack of entrepreneurial actions in today's global economy is a recipe for failure.

A sustainable corporate entrepreneurship strategy will drive organizations through the challenging global economy (Kuratko, 2009). As Baumol (2004) states, "The outlook is, indeed, that there will be no break in the acceleration of innovation, and that the innovations in prospect will be as difficult for us to comprehend as those now thoroughly familiar to us would have been to our ancestors." Corporate entrepreneurship is a risk and it has to start somewhere – sometimes small and corporate controlled. But if it starts, there is the likelihood of greater success. Managers become more comfortable with the idea, confidence builds, results occur, and soon the first corporate assigned projects evolve into more autonomous ventures that reach farther out before being required to report into administrative structure.

The major thrust behind corporate entrepreneurship is a revitalization of innovation, creativity, and leadership in today's organizations. It appears that corporate entrepreneurship may possess the critical components needed for the future productivity of all organizations. If so, then recognizing entrepreneurial strategies in contemporary organizations will be critical.

In summary, this chapter provides insights from the current research on corporate entrepreneurship strategy in order to establish a stronger frame from which researchers and practitioners can find what ultimately impacts organizational success. It is clear that organizations are choosing to pursue corporate entrepreneurial strategies and as the research on corporate entrepreneurship continues to expand there will be greater understanding of the entire concept.

14 Overcoming inertia: the social question in social entrepreneurship
Ester Barinaga

INTRODUCTION

During the last 10 to 15 years, social entrepreneurship has gained ground as part of a solution to mitigate the crisis of the welfare state. Social scientists, politicians, civil servants, and practitioners in the field, all agree in giving social entrepreneurial initiatives a central role in alleviating the failures of the welfare state (Leadbeater, 1997; Thompson et al., 2000). Some go even further to argue that non-profit organizations and social enterprises are contributing to social innovation, developing new strategies, products, services, and organizational forms that meet previously unmet social needs (Dees and Anderson, 2006). The increase in number and variety of social entrepreneurial initiatives has acquired such a scale that scholars are starting to talk of a "welfare society" (James 1992; Rodger, 2000; Laratta, 2010), policies to regulate and support social enterprises are being developed, foundations are refocusing their funding towards social entrepreneurial initiatives and social entrepreneurs are elevated to the status of heroes in business schools.

Much of the allure of social entrepreneurship and social entrepreneurs lies in the belief that introducing market rationalities and modes of operation into the civil society sector will make that sector more effective thus bringing democracy, social progress and social change (Fowler, 2000; Prahalad, 2005). Telling of the entrenchment of this belief is the actual choice of term – "social *entrepreneurship*" – often reformulating traditional civil society initiatives – from women's groups and ethnic minorities associations to initiatives for the homeless – into "the *business* of doing good." Accordingly, foundations that have traditionally funded non-profit organizations are introducing market-based criteria – such as return on investment and the potential to scale up – to decide what initiative to fund, enforcing competition and closely supervising the organization supported (John, 2006).

And yet, although social enterprises are given a key role in the innovation of our societies and in promoting social change, the social dimension itself remains un-explored. Often building on anecdotal observations and social entrepreneurs' autobiographical descriptions (Hockerts, 2006), studies remain poor in their understanding of what constitutes the social as well as in their comprehension of the dynamics of social change.

Arguably, recent articles have emphasized the relevance of considering the embeddedness of social entrepreneurial initiatives in their socio-economic contexts (Mair and Martí, 2006; Seelos et al., 2011). In such a line, the notion of social capital has been introduced to understand the centrality of networks to the establishment, support and progress of such initiatives. That is, the notion of social capital has been mobilized to grasp the role of networks in the formative stage of the social enterprise (Hulgård and Spear, 2007); however, not to understand the initiative's role in developing social capital to ignite social change. In other words, when introducing sociological notions in the study of social entrepreneurship, these are used to understand the organization itself, ignoring the social change it aims at. Questions concerning the level of change aimed at (individual or structural), the aspects addressed by the changing efforts (material or symbolic), or the sociological processes introduced that may contribute to overcome the inertia of socio-economic inequality, seem to have been left outside the research agenda. This essay is a first effort to take a step in that direction.

Understanding the dynamics behind the social changes induced by social entrepreneurs is essential to formulate thoroughly advised and effective policies to support the sector as well as to design effective social entrepreneurial intiatives. After an overview of the state of the art in the social entrepreneurship research field, the chapter argues that by focusing on the "entrepreneurship" question of "social entrepreneurship," research has forgotten the "social" dimension of the phenomenon. To address this shortcoming, the essay introduces the "social change matrix" suggesting that the matrix may help us take a first step into analysing social change within the framework of social entrepreneurship.

SOCIAL ENTREPRENEURSHIP: THE RESEARCH FIELD

Although still at its beginnings, it is already possible to discern a few key features in the research field of social entrepreneurship. These have to do with the two elements of the term, "social" and "entrepreneurship," as well as with the contrast between how it is being defined and how it is being studied. While the social mission is put at the heart of definitions of social entrepreneurship, research is focusing in its entrepreneurial management, surprisingly ignoring the social dimension. After reviewing the research field in this section, the essay moves on to address this lack of congruency.

The Quest for a Definition: The Social Heart

Social entrepreneurship is troubled by the hurdles common to all nascent research fields: a difficulty in defining its research object. The term "social entrepreneurship" is used by some to refer to traditional non-profit organizations starting for-profit activities to fund their daily operations; some make reference to community-based social ventures (Haugh, 2007), whereas others include traditional businesses acting socially responsible in cross-sectoral collaborations (Tracey et al., 2005); still some refer to the process of starting up a non-profit organization (Dees, 1998; Mair and Martí, 2006). Research focus also varies from the individual level of the social entrepreneur, to the organizational level of the social enterprise or the interorganizational level of network support made available to social ventures. Further still, many struggle with setting the boundaries defining social entrepreneurship apart from related fields such as commercial entrepreneurship (Austin et al., 2006b; Trivedi and Stokols, 2011), social activism and social service provision (Martin and Osberg, 2007). As a result of the vagueness of the term and the blurry boundaries of the phenomenon, most efforts are being addressed to put some clarity into what social entrepreneurship is and what a social entrepreneur does – conceptual papers outnumbering empirical ones (Short et al., 2009; for a recent review, see Hoogendoorn and Pennings, 2010).

Probably the most often quoted definition of a social entrepreneur, and by extension, of a social entrepreneurial initiative is given by Dees (1998):

> Social entrepreneurs play the role of change agents in the social sector, by:
>
> 1. Adopting a mission to create and sustain social value (not just private value),
> 2. Recognizing and relentlessly pursuing new opportunities to serve that mission,
> 3. Engaging in a process of continuous innovation, adaptation, and learning,
> 4. Acting boldly without being limited by resources currently in hand, and
> 5. Exhibiting a heightened sense of accountability to the constituencies served and for the outcomes created.

That Dees' is one of the most cited definitions may be because it succeeds in including the elements that most researchers seem to agree upon while excluding those that are the subject of contention.

Independently of whether definitions come from the academic world or from the world of practice, as well as from either side of the Atlantic, consensus on definition rests on two elements of social entrepreneurship:

First, a focus on achieving social change: social enterprises, it is argued, give primacy to the social mission over other economic and organizational objectives. That is, an explicit social mission – point 1 in Dees' definition – is central to the social entrepreneurial initiative, guiding its choice of partners, the process of scaling up, its relation with those it serves and the way in which value creation is evaluated – point 5 in Dees' definition. Practitioners praise social entrepreneurs for their capacity to catalyze social transformation; politicians promote social enterprises for it is seen to address both market and government failures to address socio-economic inequality; while scholars approve social entrepreneurship for its potential to change underlying social dynamics leading to inequality. In other words, this element relates to the "social" aspect of "social entrepreneurship."

Second, the relevance of innovation to satisfy previously unmet social needs: in striving towards social change, it is argued, these initiatives do not replicate previously tested methods. Rather, such initiatives engage in innovation processes – Dees' point number 3 – through which they make a creative use of resources to address a social problem – Dees' point number 4, and resourcefully identify and pursue opportunities to serve their mission – Dees' number point 2. Scholars particularly emphasizing this aspect of social entrepreneurship have acquired such a weight that it has already been labelled as the "Social Innovation School" (Hoogendoorn and Pennings, 2010). To put it differently, this element relates to the "entrepreneurial" aspect of "social entrepreneurship."

The main contentious aspect, which Dees deliberately leaves outside his definition of the social entrepreneur, is that of the extent to which market dynamics are central to understanding social entrepreneurship. Dees' argument is that "markets do not work well for social entrepreneurs" for "they do not do a good job of valuing social improvements" (Dees, 1998: 3). Those in favor of including a market orientation within the definition of social entrepreneurship do it out of social enterprises' concern to decrease dependence on donors by generating own revenue (Fowler, 2000; Dorado, 2005; Nyssens, 2006). At the heart of their argument, that is, is a preoccupation with the long-term economic sustainability of social entrepreneurial initiatives as this is pivotal if they are to achieve long-term social change. The underlying assumption is that economic sustainability is only possible when left to the market. And yet, many a social entrepreneurial initiative does aim at transforming the capitalist system of the market. Including a market-orientation within the definition of social entrepreneurship would leave such initiatives outside.

For the purpose of this essay, social entrepreneurship will be seen as organized, bottom-up efforts aiming at social change. And, although I am aware this definition may include closely related phenomena such as social movements, it is an intentional consequence. After all, Banks, who first coined the term "social entrepreneur" did it within the sociology of social movements to distinguish between those "whose endeavors had social implications" from those who "saw the possibility of using managerial skills directly for socially constructive purposes." For Banks, the first, the "social engineers," tinkered with social systems, whereas the second, the "social entrepreneurs," radically changed them (Banks, 1972: 53). It is to this use of managerial skills that Banks pointed to that research on social entrepreneurship has mainly turned its attention.

Research Areas: A Focus on Entrepreneurial Management

Mainly three levels of analysis have so far been used when studying social entrepreneurship: the individual level of the social entrepreneur; the organizational level of the social enterprise; and the interorganizational level of networks of collaboration and support. All have at its core an interest on the management aspects of social entrepreneurial initiatives – in terms of personal skills, organizational strategies, support networks, and processual stages – and seem to forget the social aspects addressed by those initiatives.

First, the social entrepreneur. A desire to identify potentially successful social entrepreneurs has instigated research on the traits characterising such a breed. Bornstein (2007), for one, looks at the strategies and personal qualities explaining social entrepreneurs' success. Others have studied their capacity to recognize opportunities for creating social ventures and developed a typology of social entrepreneurs based on how they define opportunities, view their missions, acquire resources, and address social ills (Zahra et. al., 2009). Still some have focused on the heightened sense of social justice driving them (Thake and Zadek, 1997; Hemingway, 2005) or their previous experiences and motives for starting-up a social venture (Sharir and Lerner, 2006).

Prolific as this line of research seems to be, it is a contended one. It follows the same line of argument as that made within research on entrepreneurship in their attempt to define successful (business) entrepreneurs and it is, consequently, permeated by the same flaws. First, how does one evaluate success? This is particularly difficult in social entrepreneurial initiatives as their goal is not a purely economic but also a social, political, and cultural one. Second, in the effort to distinguish general traits, these studies often de-contextualize the initiatives studied and the individuals leading them, with the risk of ignoring factors that may prove relevant for initiatives and entrepreneurs in other places and times. Finally, although the ever-present discussion on whether an entrepreneur is born or is made has not been answered satisfactorily by traditional entrepreneurship research, it influences this type of research – with the consequent bias towards finding distinct traits where there might be none.

The second level of analysis in social entrepreneurship research is the social enterprise. The Social Enterprise School does typically address this level as it focuses on the management, financing, and growth of social entrepreneurial start-ups and of small non-for-profit organizations. It is here that students of social entrepreneurship have focused on successful organizational strategies for scaling-up the social venture (Alvord et al., 2004; Bloom and Sklot, 2010), on the risk-taking inclination of its management (Mort et al., 2003; Weerawardena and Mort, 2005), or on key managerial, finance and marketing aspects for attaining financial sustainability (Zietlow, 2001).

The reasoning in this stream of research is that business methods should be used for improving the effectiveness of non-profits and other social ventures (Hoogendoorn and Pennings, 2010). Underlying is the assumption that business methods make organizations more entrepreneurial, and thus ready to address the complex problems they are set to solve as well as more flexible to adapt to the change of their contexts as they intervene in them.

The third level of analysis is the interorganizational level. Accordingly, studies highlight social venture philanthropy not only as provider of economic capital for non-profit organizations in its start-up or scaling up phases, but as a highly engaged actor in the management and strategic direction of the recipient organization (John, 2006). Others recognize the involvement of external stakeholders as decisive for the development of social entrepreneurial initiatives (Spear, 2006; Dixon and Clifford, 2007). Two types of networks or interorganizational collaborations supporting the social venture throughout its growth stages have been identified: a formal support network of actors such as central government, and local authorities; and a tailor-made support network that contributes to refining and operationalizing the organization's purpose (Haugh, 2007).

In other words, this strand of research approaches networks and collaborations as key aspects to create and develop the social venture. These networks and the way they are mobilized in service of the social entrepreneurial initiative are conceived as the mobilization of social capital for organizational development.

In sum, empirical studies of social entrepreneurial initiatives focus on either the individual entrepreneur, the social entrepreneurial organization or the networks of support for the development of the organization.

Voices are starting to be heard on the need to pay attention to what would amount to a fourth level of analysis: the social entrepreneurial *process* (Mair and Martí, 2006; Seelos et al., 2011). That is, the process through which the initiative is embedded in the local community, a key aspect for succeeding in attaining these initiatives' social mission. This is, as it were, a strand for future research.

Research Silence

All in all, an overwhelming proportion of research has investigated the varied management aspects of social entrepreneurial ventures, a focus that is indeed necessary for a professionalization of the sector. Surprisingly though, silence has befallen on that which, as we saw, was placed at the heart of the definition of social entrepreneurship: A focus on achieving social change.

Although definitions agree on granting social change a central position in social entrepreneurial efforts, research seems to have focused on the entrepreneurial and managerial aspects of those efforts, leaving the social element aside. We have learnt much about the social entrepreneur, the management challenges of a non-for-profit organization, the development of the idea and the identification of the opportunity; we know about the difficulties of scaling up, about cross-sectoral collaborations, and support systems. Yet we have much to learn about the social dynamics set in motion by social entrepreneurial initiatives, and how these contribute (or not) to ignite social change. More needs to be understood of how the tools, methods and strategies that social entrepreneurs apply do indeed work in practice. For instance, the extent to which the symbolic and material aspects of a given social problem are interrelated and how these may be addressed to achieve impact. To put it differently, to better understand the way in which social entrepreneurs ignite social change, it is first necessary to understand the social aspects that make up that which is to be changed, as well as to evaluate the potential of the methods and strategies social ventures implement to address them. That is, we need to understand the dynamics towards social change set in motion by social entrepreneurial intiatives. With that purpose in mind, let me develop the "social change matrix."

SOCIAL CHANGE MATRIX

From the previous review, it follows that probably one of the most crucial challenges in the field of social entrepreneurship lies in acknowledging the "social" aspect of social entrepreneurship. The following is an invitation to address the social aspect by bringing sociological notions into the study of social entrepreneurial initiatives' efforts to ignite social change. Sociology's focus on understanding the means and processes by which human society is organized can help us appreciate the methods and strategies used by social entrepreneurs to change the current organization of our societies.

Sociology, however, has traditionally been divided.[1] On the one side, the so-called "objectivists," who emphasize the extent to which material constraints and impersonal structures coerce and impose limits upon people. Structural functionalism and Marxism are schools taking this approach. These approaches take a macro-sociological level of analysis, studying social structures determination of individual and group behaviour.

On the other side the so-called "subjectivists" stress the ways in which individual agents construct their world through purposive and meaningful activity. Phenomenology and ethnomethodology are typically placed under the subjectivist heading, as both schools take a micro-sociological perspective that highlights the centrality of individual agency in the enactment of the social world.

Both sides of the sociological divide are, as it were, most often seen as two antagonistic paradigms, wherein the strengths of the first are the weaknesses of the second and vice versa. Objectivism recognizes structural necessity, a quasi-deterministic mechanism steering the behaviour of social groups. While this line of thought contributes to undermine the illusion of the transparency of the social world, it is, however, unable to explain the origin of those structures. Objectivism is a sort of social physics that is able to decode the unwritten laws by which individual agents organize (even if unconsciously) their actions. Yet, its very strength – its focus on the hidden macro-structures that give the social world its inherent regularity – is also its main weakness, as it is unable to recognize that the interpretations, meanings, and typifications held by individual agents are essential elements of the social world. Moreover, by making social structures its starting point, objectivism reifies those very structures, reproducing the reality that it claims to be observing. As social entrepreneurs aiming at changing those structures, the challenge is to recognize the structures limiting action while all the same acknowledging the role of individuals in recreating those structures. As scholars trying to understand the intellectual and practical tools used by social entrepreneurs to ignite social change, the challenge is to look at the structures aimed at without reproducing them in the very process of discussing them.

Subjectivism, for its part, focuses on individual agency, on how free actors use or choose not to use the norms implicit to all social interaction. Scholars within this paradigm are not concerned with social organization and social structures, but rather with the way in which individuals respond to each other in saying and doing at a particular moment of time. The interpretative paradigm, thus, emphasizes the role played by mundane knowledge, practical competency, and subjective meanings in the continuous everyday construction of social reality. Similarly to the former line of thought, its very strength – its recognition of the key role played by the classifications through which individuals endow their world with sense – is its major weakness as it cannot account for the origin of those classifications. Their focus on the symbolic aspects guiding face-to-face interaction ignores relevant material aspects that could account for the origin of those categories. Further, by introducing agency back into the analysis through a focus on the micro level of face-to-face interactions, scholars within this paradigm conceive social structures as the sum of individual acts of classification, and are thus unable to explain the resilience of those structures. The challenge this paradigm sets to the social entrepreneur is to address the generally held symbolic classifications and subjective meanings that construct the social order they aim to change without ignoring the material conditions that are at the origin of those classifications in the first place. In turn, as scholars in the field of social entrepreneurship, we are challenged to consider the micro-processes set in motion by social entrepreneurial initiatives from both the material and symbolic perspectives.

In sum, on the one side of the sociological schism, we find structures, determinism and a macro approach; on the other meanings and classifications, ongoing construction of reality and a micro-level analysis. These are, so to speak, two distinct approaches to the social world with direct consequences for both how we act to change that social world and how we study those change undertakings. Efforts have been made to transcend the divisions between these seemingly incompatible paradigms, most notoriously Giddens' structuration theory (Giddens, 1984) and Bourdieu's theory of practice (Bourdieu 1977; 1990). Another reading of these efforts is that subjectivism and objectivism are not so much incompatible paradigms as they are perspectives capturing different aspects of the same social reality (Mouzelis, 2000). Building on this reading allows the field of social entrepreneurship to engage in the aspects of both paradigms of particular relevance for understanding bottom-up efforts, techniques, strategies, and methods aiming at social change.

By way of illustration, let's look at homelessness – a social condition that shapes individual identities (Snow and Anderson, 1987); a social category stigmatizing a group of people and having an impact on attitudes towards those so categorized (Phelan et al., 1997); the expression of a community's poverty of social capital (Rosenheck et al. 2001); a position at the margins of society that inhibits individual possibilities.

To thoroughly comprehend homelessness we need to understand both its macro-structural dimension and its micro-sociological expressions. Further, we need to grasp not only its material aspects, but also the extent to which its symbolic elements work in detriment of individual self-esteem and in favour of group categorizations that perpetuate the exclusion of those so classified. This is particularly relevant for efforts aiming at social change, for to change society one needs to comprehensively tackle the problem addressed, the material and symbolic facets of a many-sided social condition. See Figure 14.1.

Building upon the example of homelessness in a developed welfare state, the matrix can be used to analyse the multilayered reality of the homelessness condition – the material difficulties at both the individual level (quadrant #2) and the group level (#1) as well as the symbolic dimension that subjects the individual homeless (#4) and stigmatizes the group (#3).

Once the particular social problem being addressed by a social entrepreneurial initiative is comprehended in its full complexity, the matrix may be helpful in understanding the tools being used to address it. At what level does the tool work? And what aspect of the problem does it focus on? Aluma, for instance, one of many local monthly magazines about the homeless sold in the streets by homeless people, this time in southern Sweden, would be placed in quadrant 2. "The street magazine creates employment for homeless people who, through Aluma, get help to get back into society again." It could also be argued that by offering employment to the individual homeless, Aluma is also contributing to improve the particular individual's self-esteem; that is, improving the person's material conditions improves her symbolic perception of herself (Hjorth and Bjerke, 2009). Soup kitchens are other initiatives working at the individual-material quadrant; their effect at the symbolic level is however more questionable. Initiatives working at the structural level would be welfare policies such as the basic guaranteed income, which proposes a social security system providing each citizen with a regular sum of money unconditional to their situation (van Parijs, 1995). At the symbolic level we could find measures attempting to influence public opinion and general conceptions of the homeless, advocacy efforts trying to reframe homeless people from social misfits that indulge in drugs and alcohol into people that value their freedom and have ended on the streets due to reasons out of their control (Kisor and Kendal-Wilson, 2002).

Another Example: Aiming at Overcoming Ethnic Inertia

Or take the issue of ethnic segregation. Ethnic and race studies have made us all too aware of the extent to which cultural and ethnic

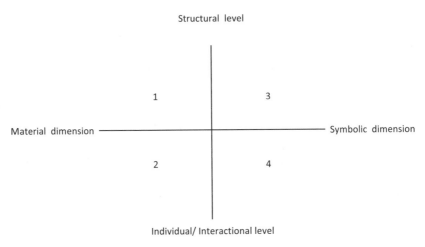

Figure 14.1   Social change matrix

boundaries organize our societies and shape our individualities. To be
sure, at the structural level studies reveal the unequal material privileges
granted to those seen as ethnic others (quadrant #1) – denouncing the
double standard of the judiciary system (Albrecht 1997; Mustard 2001),
the biased curriculum of university education (Carr and Lund 2007),
the differentiated participation in the labor market (Wilson and Portes,
1980; Reimers, 1983), the injustices of regional economic development
processes (Pitti, 2004; Zlolniski, 2006; Barinaga, 2010), the correlation
between one's origin and the quality of health-care received (Sundquist,
1993; Fiscella et al., 2000; Weinick et al., 2000) – along with the divisive
symbolic categorizations that suffuse a broad group of persons with specific attributes and meanings (quadrant #3) – reducing people of immigrant background to disinterested at best (Huss-Keeler, 1998) or social
parasites at worst, and expressing in intergroup bias across ethnic groups
(Hagendoorn, 1995).

The structural organization of our societies along the ethnic boundary finds its expression at the micro-sociological level of unequal individual access to material comfort (quadrant 2) together with articulations
of symbolic categorizations into crucible identities and subordinated
subjectivities (quadrant 4) (Rumbaut, 1994; Barinaga, forthcoming).

In other words, ethnicity is a multifaceted social phenomenon.
Established categorizations of the ethnic other give legitimacy to unequal
socio-economic relations, thus rendering invisible the ongoing reproduction of inequality based on the ethnic boundary. Put differently, the

construction of ethnicity is the result of both structure and agency, "a dialectic played out both by ethnic groups and the larger society" (Nagel, 1994:152).

Initiatives addressing the inertia of ethnic relations, consequently, are just as multifarious as the social reality they aim at (Wimmer, 2008). From micro-finance programs to attend to people of immigrant background's lack of access to established financial institutions (quadrant #2 – Barinaga, under review), to advocacy groups working toward redefining the immigrant other from a social parasite to a group of resourceful individuals contributing to economic growth and conducive to a more cosmopolitan society (quadrant #3 – Lakoff and Saxenian, 2002; Ferguson, 2006). From ethnically defined civil society organizations and movements fostering a politics of identity that encourages individual pride for being, precisely, immigrant others (quadrant #4) to positive discrimination regulations facilitating university access to otherwise marginalized groups (quadrant #1).

The two previous examples illustrate the degree to which the social change matrix may be a first step into introducing the social in an analysis of social entrepreneurship. As an analytical tool, it develops our understanding of the way in which the tools and strategies used by social entrepreneurial initiatives work, as well as it gives nuance to the language we use when describing efforts aiming at social change. As a strategic tool, social entrepreneurial initiatives may be able to use it to evaluate the congruency (or lack thereof) between their stated goals and the tools mobilized for their pursuit, thus strengthening their initiatives.

FURTHER RESEARCH: OVERCOMING INERTIA

A literature review of the research field of social entrepreneurship revealed that although most scholars agree on placing the aim to achieve social change at the heart of the definition of social entrepreneurship, research has practically ignored the dynamics towards social change put in motion by social entrepreneurs. Research in the field primarily focuses on the entrepreneurial dimension of social entrepreneurial ventures, discussing its management, financial and marketing aspects. The social dimension, however, has largely been neglected.

As a first step to remedy this omission, the chapter turned towards sociology. Bourdieu argues that the task of sociology is "to uncover the most profoundly buried structures of the various social worlds which constitute the social universe, as well as the 'mechanisms' which tend to ensure their reproduction or their transformation" (Bourdieu, 1989: 7). Elaborating on Bourdieu's insight, I argued that the task of the social entrepreneurship scholar is to uncover the mechanisms that ensure the reproduction or transformation of the structures of the social world, as well as to understand the methods and strategies used by social entrepreneurs to overcome the inertia of those structures.

It is in this spirit that I proposed the social change matrix, as a first effort to understand the social aspect addressed by social entrepreneurial initiatives. Further, I argued that applying the social change matrix may allow us to capture the social dynamics set in motion by the methods and tools applied by social entrepreneurs to particular social problems. That is, I suggest that the social change matrix can be regarded as an instrument through which to look at the enormous varying patterns of social entrepreneurial initiatives, and analyse the diversity of methods, tools and strategies put at work to ignite social change.

These are, however, only preliminary thoughts and further research is indeed needed if we are to develop our understanding of the social dimension of social entrepreneurial efforts. Evaluating a social entrepreneurial venture's potential for social change may be one area for which the social change matrix may be a valuable tool. Another, assessing the extent of social change aimed at. In this line, some very initial remarks follow.

Extent of Social Change: A First Tentative Application of the Social Change Matrix

Many are the appeals for methods and tools to evaluate the degree to which an initiative, in actual fact, performs, or has the potential to perform, social change (Emerson, 2003; Bell-Rose, 2004). Some have been proposed; namely "Social Return on Investment" and "The Most Significant Change Model" (Dart and Davies, 2003). The social change matrix proposed in this chapter can be used as a supplement to such tools by facilitating an understanding of the extent of the social change aimed at, as well as the dimensions being addressed.

To begin with, three degrees of social change can be distinguished:

1. System maintenance: Interventions in a particular social sphere that result in the provision of services to those left behind by society. Social change is here minimal as these initiatives merely soothe the negative consequences for particular individuals of a social ailment, without changing the system that leads to those consequences. Examples include hostels for the homeless and safe houses for battered women.

2. System expansion: Efforts that result in extending the established system to include groups that are left behind by that very system. Job training programs addressed to long-term unemployed are typically found here, as they expand the existing labor market to include a group that otherwise falls in the interstices. These efforts find solutions to mend the existing social system without, however, questioning the system itself.

3. System transformation: Initiatives that question the social system they deem at the root of the problem and offer a radical new way of organizing society. That is, such efforts aim at developing new political and economic structures. Eco-villages and off-the-grid communities are examples of this approach (Beit-Hallahmi and Rabin, 1977).

Applying the matrix to efforts aiming at social change may help us evaluate the extent of their potential for social impact. For a radical social change to happen, the particular social problem needs to be addressed from all directions, embracing the many stakeholders directly and indirectly involved in it. Because this often requires the coordinated efforts of the various actors involved in the particular problem, Kania and Kramer refer to it with the term "collective impact" (Kania and Kramer, 2011). Put differently, system transformation requires to act in all four quadrants of the matrix – working both on the objective divisions of the social world as well as on the symbolic divisions that agents apply to it.

Alternatively, system maintenance initiatives do focus in a single quadrant of the matrix, often one of those at the individual level. Without underestimating such efforts, their work focuses on relieving some of the negative consequences of a social condition – from lack of a nutritious diet to lack of self-esteem – and are a humble reminder of the capacity of all of us to intervene in our immediate social environment. Finally, efforts aiming at extending the current system to excluded groups often work both on the material conditions of individuals included in the target group as well as on the symbolic categories applied on them (quadrants #2 and #4).

Further research is certainly required. If nothing else, however, the social change matrix can work as a reminder to social entrepreneurs as well as to social-entrepreneurship scholars of:

- The need to comprehend the multifaceted nature of the social problem addressed.
- The merits of humility concerning the extent to which one initiative, alone, can tackle a specific social problem.

- The benefits of developing broad collaborations with other initiatives addressing the problem from other angles, in an attempt to truly achieve collective impact.
- The demand to evaluate a particular tool or method in its potential to ignite the desired change.
- The urge to understand the way in which a particular sociological notion – such as social capital – may be relevant in understanding efforts aiming at addressing specific social problems.

Social entrepreneurial efforts are a call to bring agency back into the spaces carved for us by extant relations of power, and in that doing, reshape those spaces. Taking the study of those efforts seriously demands understanding those spaces, the ways in which they are continuously carved, and our own agency in reproducing, or transforming, them. The social change matrix, I suggest, is a very first step to situate the agency of efforts aiming at overcoming the inertia of the existing spaces.

NOTE

1. Many have written about this divide in the social sciences. It is not the goal of this chapter to develop it. I will only describe the main tenets of each to the extent that these are relevant for the purpose of this essay. That is, to take a first step into developing a set of sociological tools that may help us further understand the methods and strategies used by social entrepreneurial initiatives in their efforts to ignite social change.

15 Entrepreneurship in public organizations

Anne Kovalainen and Elisabeth Sundin

INTRODUCTION

In much of the public and policy discussions, entrepreneurship and the public sector are opposed as contradictory terms. The public sector, its organizations and public sector employees are framed as bureaucratic and in need of change in many dimensions. Bureaucracy has come to mean inefficiency, rigidity, a formal way of handling issues and an organizational life that resembles 'still water'.[1] Entrepreneurship has been seen as the reverse image of the public sector; indeed, entrepreneurship is often framed as a synonym for the innovative free spirit, the manifestation of free markets and a 'natural' outcome of the creative destruction. The public sector 'discourages entrepreneurs' states Wickham (2008: 162) in a book frequently used by students studying entrepreneurship. 'First, the public sector must be paid for, and that means taxation. High levels of taxation are likely to demotivate entrepreneurship. Second, if the public sector is delivering service (over which it usually claims monopoly rights) then the entrepreneurs are crowded out.' Therefore, it is no surprise that entrepreneurship and the public sector are seen as far from each other as possibly can be. It could be argued that it was first through the growth of entrepreneurial studies as an upsurge of the disciplinary field of entrepreneurship, coinciding with developments in the global economies, that the public sector and entrepreneurship became closer; if not in acts, more so in speech.

Originating from this assumed difference the claim has been – for example, as argued by Zampetakis and Moustakis (2007: 415) – that, 'the public sector really needs entrepreneurs and entrepreneurial management'. They quote Drucker by writing that bringing entrepreneurship into the public sector is the 'foremost political task of this generation'. The public sector is spoken of and treated as 'the ugly sister', as expressed by Barbara Czarniawska (1985) already 25 years ago. It is no wonder that the individuals working in the public sector today have, as a group, low self-esteem (Tullberg, 2002). 'Bureaucracy has come to take on a symbolic role in discussions of the reform or modernization of public services. Viewed as the source of waste and inefficiency, rules and 'red tape', and a barrier to the flexibility and entrepreneurialism required in the modern world,

successive waves of reform have taken place in the name of eradication'
(Newman, 2005: 191). These negative descriptions of the public sector are
not unchallenged and neither are the needs for entrepreneurship (du Gay
2000, 2005).

The distancing of these two activities, entrepreneurship and public
sector activities, from each other partly stems from the very different
economic and societal functions originally designated by the State and to
the markets. Today, the question of keeping these two activities, entrepreneurship and public sector apart, or bringing them closer together or
merging them as activities is also very much a political question, illustrated
by the citations above. This calls for paying attention to the methods
through which these activities are organized, delivered, and managed. The
ideological-political discussion is also reflected in the research literature
– both in the methods for how the research questions are formulated and
how the answers are found and presented.

In the following we discuss some of the research on entrepreneurship
and the public sector, with different perspectives on entrepreneurship
and public sector activities. In addition, we provide some examples of
the distant nature relating entrepreneurship to the State's activities. Our
approach to handling the topic 'Entrepreneurship in public organizations'
follows the assumption that the research findings from very different disciplinary fields are of relevance. Both research taking its starting point in
entrepreneurship theory and research in politics and policy analyses are of
relevance, as the topic itself is multidisciplinary by nature, and deals with
real life politics and policies. The aim of the chapter is not to provide a
fully comprehensive list of all the research literature dealing with the public
sector and entrepreneurship, but to present research fields that explicitly
deal with the relationship between entrepreneurship and public organizations. The fields emanate from different disciplines and research traditions
and take very different starting points – in entrepreneurship, in the public
sector or in organizations. Implicitly, and sometimes even explicitly, the
different fields are biased by ideological standpoints concerning the public
sector or entrepreneurship. This is especially expressed in the discussions
on New Public Management, which will be presented below. Our aim is
to both widen the discussion and approach different views on the question
of entrepreneurship and the public sector. This makes it also relevant to
discuss the entrepreneurship in public organizations before and after the
NPM-regime, which we do in the penultimate section of the article. In the
next section we will present some key ideas of entrepreneurship that are
relevant to the topic, followed by some key ideas concerning the public
sector, and finish with a presentation of entrepreneurship in relation to the
public sector, especially public sector organizations.

KEY IDEAS OF ENTREPRENEURSHIP

Much of the entrepreneurship literature derives the definition of entrepreneurship and quotations from Schumpeter and other classic works on the subject. Schumpeter emphasized innovative individuals, rather than institutions or structures, creating innovative processes. For Schumpeter, the difference and the change in society came through the activities of innovative individuals, persons who combined existing resources in new ways (Schumpeter 1934 [1983], 1950). But not all entrepreneurship grows from individual acts: there are many facets to entrepreneurship that have been identified as taking place at the organizational level, thus leaving room for a multitude of definitions for 'corporate entrepreneurship' that, among other things, argues for the adaptation of structures and cultures of large enterprises and organizations (so-called entrepreneurial transformation, see, for example, Burns, 2008: 14) to an ever-changing environment. This was also Schumpeter's take on the innovativeness of large firms: he saw them as the ideal environment for innovation, claiming that the modern corporation had 'routinized innovation', making it possible for large firms to innovate constantly (Schumpeter, 1950).

There are many competing definitions of entrepreneurship, ranging from the Schumpeterian approach, with its emphasis is on the entrepreneur as an innovator (Schumpeter, 1949; Casson, 2004), to the Austrian approach, with its emphasis on market exploitation (Casson, 2004). These differences of emphasis are not necessarily empirically distinguishable, but they do shed light on the differing ways of understanding entrepreneurship in the public sector discourse.

Social entrepreneurship today, it is argued, focuses on the 'soft side' of entrepreneurial activities á la Schumpeter, instead of clear-cut profit making á la Kirchner (e.g., Mises, 1978). Social entrepreneurship, located in the nexus of sociality, markets and innovations, further shifts and blurs the boundaries between publicly organized activities and privately run activities, those activities that seek profit and those that do not seek profit (e.g., Nicholls and Cho, 2006).[2] The idea of 'civic-regarding entrepreneurship' (Bellone and Goerl, 1992) has been introduced to bring democratic policies and principles closer to entrepreneurial policies and principles. In this aim we have a famous supporter. Schumpeter himself in 1949 presented such an example from the ministry of agriculture.

That entrepreneurship is a broad context is also argued by others. Among these, Steyaert and Hjorth (2003: 17) refer to the concept and the phenomenon to social, cultural, ecological and political dimensions – that is, to the creation of society. Entrepreneurship has many faces demanding multidisciplinary approaches and a different focus that includes individuals, groups and processes. In this short chapter, we will not deal with the historical developments of entrepreneurship as a multidisciplinary research field (e.g., Swedberg, 2000; Alvarez et al., 2005), nor do we deal with specificities of entrepreneurship concerning economic growth, innovations or the developments of new fields such as cultural and technological aspects of entrepreneurship. Many of these are covered thoroughly in encyclopaedias, books and articles, too many to be named here, apart from a few which represent the mainstream views on entrepreneurship and reflect well the variety of approaches (e.g., Shane, 2004; Casson et al., 2006).

KEY IDEAS ABOUT THE PUBLIC SECTOR

The concept 'the public sector' is used all over the world although it has different meanings. In general, 'the public sector' has come to mean that the State provides for its citizens, either fully without pay or against a minimal pay, basic services, which can range from common goods to individualized and personalized services. Common to these services provided by the public sector is that they are non-commodified, that is, they are not market driven, borne, and priced. The composition and the width of the public sector varies by country, but in most countries the public sector includes such institutions ranging from legislative bodies to education and health care, and the services provided by these institutions, such as the police, military, public roads, public transit, primary education and basic health care. Access to public services is based on citizenship and on residence. The public sector might provide services that a non-payer cannot be excluded from (such as street lighting), so-called public goods, and services which benefit all members of society rather than just the individual who uses the service, such as public education.

The key issue in the public sector is that much of its functions stem from the legal obligations of the governing State. Taxation, judicial functions, health care, education, etc., are handled by institutions and organizations based on and established by State governance, through and with the help of legislation. These institutions, through which the State works to provide public goods and services to all citizens, also create and re-create a strong equalizing structure in society, provided that they function on a democratically selected and organized basis. Although there are some common public sector characteristics throughout the world, there also exist great differences from a global perspective. The size and ambitions of the public sector are often discussed, depending on ideology or political philosophy.

The sociologist Esping-Andersen (1996) makes a distinction between different welfare regimes which focus on those services that are related to citizenship. Thus Esping-Andersen and other welfare theorists seldom touch upon the issue of public goods or infrastructure such as roads, pavements and prisons. More so, they argue that the service structure of the state formulates the State – which services are universal and based on citizenship, which of them are provided by the State or by the family, which services are accessible by all, and which of them are only available through means-testing or other formative criteria. The markets can provide some of these services when the State or the family fails to provide them.

Esping-Andersen, as well as most welfare state researchers, restricts himself to advanced capitalist states and divides them into three models: the liberal, the conservative and the social democratic (Scandinavian or Nordic) welfare state. The three welfare regimes differ in how the responsibilities between families, markets and the State are divided when it comes to, for example, the care of the elderly and children. Even if the models are ideal models, they reflect the service provision by the State, the non-commodified nature of the services provided by the State to its citizens. The commodification versus non-commodification of the services is thus one key feature of the State that distinguishes it from the markets. But entrepreneurial activities do not necessarily take place only on the markets, but they are to be found in the public sector, and operating inside the State, in the public sector. This means that entrepreneurial activities range from traditional market, commodified services to non-commodified services. This is most visible in the social entrepreneurship discussed earlier. The public sector is, as mentioned at the beginning, representing bureaucracy, slandered but also defended – a discussion we will come back to in the discussion on New Public Management.

KEY IDEAS ABOUT THE PUBLIC SECTOR WITH ENTREPRENEURIAL PROJECTS

The interest in an individual who is capable of making a change has long been a pervading idea throughout the literature dealing with entrepreneurship. As the public sector is built legislatively around the ideas of equality, full citizenship rights, and the stability of the State, and its basis formally and ideologically rests on criteria other than individual achievements, its entrepreneurial achievements do not necessarily function according to the individual logic, as assumed in classic entrepreneurial theories (Schumpeter, Kirzner, von Mises). The traditional position of the public administration, the bureaucracy, was that its way of working was a safeguard against clientism and corruption and to further an unbiased implementation of legislation (also see du Gay, 2000). The continuity of structures, the impartiality of the ideal bureaucracy servicing people, the representativeness of the governance, and the stability of the public administrative machinery laid the foundation for trust. This was what built trust – of course, not contradicting efficiency but efficiency 'is not necessarily the dominant value' (Peters and Pierre, 2008: 8). Consequently, the achievements of the public sector cannot be measured through its entrepreneurialism if that is defined as individual achievements making a difference.

Policy Entrepreneurs

Still, we can argue that the public sector, as well as public organizations and public sector employees, is no stranger to activities and actions that can be classified or labelled as entrepreneurial. Before elaborating on this point we will maintain and illustrate the position that the construction of the public sector, i.e. public organizations, can be seen as entrepreneurial projects created by policy entrepreneurs. Let us use Finland and Sweden, the countries we the authors come from, as examples. One hundred years ago, Sweden was a poor country compared with, for instance, Western European countries of that particular time, such as England and France. In the period 1901–10, Swedish life expectancy was 54.5 years for men and 58.4 years for women. Swedish infant mortality (death before the age of 1 year) in 1901–10 was 10.1% for boys and 8.0% for girls.[3] Voting rights introduced in 1918 (for men) and 1921 (for women) meant a new political landscape developed in cooperation with the transformation of the economy from agrarian rural to an industrialized urban country. One important part of the modernization process was the living and housing conditions, which were very bad. An alarming report with the telling title 'Dirt Sweden' (Lort-Sverige) was published in 1938 (Nordström).

The World War II meant many reforms were stalled. While living conditions improved the change it was not fast enough. To really make a difference the Swedish Parliament decided to build one million new homes in ten years to improve the living conditions of the then seven million inhabitants of the country (Nationalencyclopedin, 1994). We consider this process as an entrepreneurial process. The key politicians saw a problem that they found absolutely necessary to solve. They constructed the knowledge needed for an adequate decision, made a decision, and implemented it. Other parts of society and the lives of ordinary people were arranged in the same way: child benefits, pensions, a system for opening up higher education for everyone, etc. The systematic manner employed for handling these issues has been described 'to organize life' (Att lägga livet tillrätta. Hirdman, 2002).

In Finland, events similar to those described for Sweden took place, but on a smaller scale. The productivity of work in Finland started to increase after World War II, due to the rapid development of the Finnish social state after the war, and the widening of universal services to cover not only those enabled citizens who worked but also those citizens who were not in productive work but were handicapped, retired or even prisoners. Large policy areas, such as family policy and other societal aspects such as housing policy and other fields of societal activities, were included in the State's activities, which promoted the well-being of the nation and thus grew rapidly through rather unitary parliamentary decision-making and governance (Waris, 1961). The development of the nation-state took place through systematic policy development and the creation of a cor-poratist three-partite mechanism, where common agreements concerning industrial salaries and the State's social policy packages were created between employees' unions, employers' unions and Parliament. Many of these changes were planned, implemented, and executed through innova-tive ideas and the kind of determination which would today be called entrepreneurial projects.

These pervasive changes in the Swedish and Finnish societies could be described as entrepreneurial projects of a necessity type (cf. Gawell, 2006[4]), although seldom presented that way in the literature. The explanation behind this may be that the history of the establishment of Scandinavian welfare states is written by politicians themselves and by researchers in history and political science or social policy. The concept of entrepreneur-ship is not a part of their research vocabulary. It belongs to the private sector and the historians specializing themselves in their stories. Indeed, the resistance to entrepreneurialism among public sector researchers is justified, for example, from the perspectives of continuity and democracy: citizenship rights and democratic decision-making set the pace for changes with, for example, the idea of majority vote democracy. The legitimacy of democracy is based on this continuity and contingency, in other words, slowness, and therefore very quick and unexpected changes that would be called agile changes call for legitimacy. Such changes take place through the voting mechanism though.

But entrepreneurship is not necessarily about agility, drastic moves, quick changes, innovations and invasions into unknown territories. It can mean, as is exemplified by Schumpeter, new types of solutions to old prob-lems. Therefore it can be argued, given the examples we provided earlier in the chapter, that the Scandinavian welfare regimes are, to a large extent, the result of entrepreneurial visions and projects – but so are also other welfare regimes. The point we want to make here is that the construction of the public sector and its organizations is the result of entrepreneurial decisions and processes. These processes are still ongoing. Society is never finished. In a democracy the rules for these entrepreneurs and these entrepreneurial processes are established. However, what comes out of the decisions is not at all clear as they are handled in a system of established and sometimes also new organizations. This is a well documented fact sometimes described by concepts such as 'resistance' or 'implementation problems' and sometimes, as below, the result of the transactions conducted by street-level bureaucrats (e.g., Czarniawska and Sevón, 1996; Peters and Pierre, 2008).

The concept of entrepreneurship has, during the last couple of decades, also been used in connection with policy and politics (e.g., Meydani, 2010; Minstrom, 1997; Secchi, 2010). This has taken place with insufficient discussion on the characteristics of the public sector, leading to simplified concepts such as 'homo economicus politicus' (e.g., Shockley et al., 2002). Policy formation in the public sector is sometimes described as the result of 'policy entrepreneurs' who recognize a problem (the problem stream) and through adequate political arenas and arguments (the politics stream) can turn it into an accepted policy (the policy stream) (e.g., Kingdon, 1995; Guldbrandsson and Fossum, 2009). The consequences of these policies are, however, not seen until they are put into practice, and often the consequences can be very complicated. In the words of Peters and Pierre (2008: 2) they are 'implemented when they are formulated and formulated when they are implemented'. In addition to politicians, other actors can also be policy entrepreneurs, as shown by Secchi (2010) in his study of administrative reforms in three municipal governments in very different parts of the world. This could be interpreted as emphasizing the importance of public organizations. It is in and through these organizations that the public sector works.

PUBLIC ENTREPRENEURSHIP AND ENTREPRENEURSHIP IN PUBLIC SECTOR ORGANIZATIONS

There is an increasing number of comparisons between private and public entrepreneurship. As one point of departure, Klein et al. (2010) state that the main impression is similarity, although the definition and measurement of objectives is not the same and nor is the nature of the selection of environment or opportunities for rent seeking (also see Sadler, 2000; and Kim 2010). However, in practice the distinctions between the private and the public are less clear as the distinctions between what is private and what is public concern ownership, financing, rules and regulations and performers (Christensen and Laegreid, 2005; Sundin and Tillmar, 2008). An organization can have private owners, all incomes can come directly or indirectly from taxes and it can be regulated by laws– but is it private or public? Another organization may have private owners, all income may come directly or indirectly from taxes but it is not regulated – is it private or public?

We need to be clear about the boundaries we define when we use the concepts of public and private, and on what grounds conclusions are drawn. It also challenges some of the common prerequisites that are used in established definitions of public and private (e.g., Hjorth and Bjerke, 2006).

An often used, and rather problematic, definition for public entrepreneurship is that public entrepreneurship is 'in the public interest' (Klein et al., 2010). This is a definition similar to those stating that 'social entrepreneurship' depends on the intentions behind the actions (e.g., Austin et al., 2006a, Leadbeater, 1997). Another view concerning the underlying position of the intentions of an individual follows from the definition presented by Shockley et al. (2002: 1): 'Public sector entrepreneurship occurs whenever a political actor is alert to and acts on potential profit opportunities, thus moving the system in which the actor is embedded towards equilibrium.' However, can an individual have a decisive role as a public sector agency? The very expression 'public sector entrepreneurship' was used by Osborne and Gaebler in 1993 and developed by Bartlett and Dibben (2002) by relating innovation and entrepreneurship together in a public context. They use the terms 'the public champion' and 'the empowered champion' for the public sector entrepreneurial roles, based on their evidence from 12 local communities. The public champion was driven by the needs of the public and the empowered champion also by his/her own personal ambitions. Morris and Jones (1999) discuss the different conceptualizations and interpretations of entrepreneurial roles in the public sector. They start with the 'pioneering trailblazer' introducing innovations to increase efficiency and stated goals. Second is the by-product of private sector norms and practices concerning management and leadership. Several other classifications have also been presented, but most of these tackle specific characteristics and normative ideas of the actions of individuals.

That the reorganization of the public sector and its institutions is a political project is most often not made into an issue, although sometimes mentioned. Klein et al. (2010) argue that innovation and entrepreneurship may also be used to update public organizations and institutions and that entrepreneurship is developed and excavated in the frames constituted by the political system and institutional context. This way of looking at entrepreneurship in the public sector shifts the view away from the individualistic approach towards groups, activities, and institutions.

In new political situations one stream of public entrepreneurship is established to create new and innovative combinations of the public and the private (Klein et al., 2010), and we would add, also a third sector of initiatives and organizations. The third sector refers to those activities and organizations that work as non-profit, grass-roots level organizations, outside of the public sector, and often voluntarily complementing public sector services and collaborating with the public sector as well, such as in child care, etc. The Red Cross could be classified as a third sector organization, as well as environmental movements.

Whether public sector entrepreneurship is defined as innovative or not, the similarities concerning how to run economic activities concern both, often in much the same way as in the private sector. Public sector entrepreneurs have to marshal their resources in a different way to those in the public sector, writes Klein et al. (2010) with reference to Elinor Ostrom, the Nobel Prize winner in economics. They also have to look for opportunities and use innovative decision-making. They have to use an entrepreneurial approach and bring together resources from the private, the public, and the social sector (Morris and Jones, 1999). This was also found by Zerbinati and Souitaris (2005) in their study on initiatives by local governments applying for European Union structural funds. The professional contacts and knowledge of internal processes and structures were of the uttermost importance. That risk-taking is a concept of relevance also for public entrepreneurs is shown by Vestrum and Borch (2006).

PUBLIC AND PRIVATE SECTOR ORGANIZATIONS TODAY: ENTREPRENEURSHIP AND BUREAUCRACY MINGLING

In all types of welfare regimes governments work through their institutions and organizations. The construction and activities of these organizations, as well as of other organizations, vary for many reasons. The size of the State measured by population, and the size of GNP or similar figure are important factors as well as the advancement of the economy. Sometimes the public sector executes its duties through the decentralization of its activities mainly to regional and local levels. In the case of providing services to citizens, such decentralization is adequate – the organization structure then follows the distribution of the population. These kinds of services, such as health care and social welfare services, have professions and semi-professions among the employees. The same can be said about fire brigades and the military, but they are still very different. The public sector might be united in its principled tasks but it is diversified in terms of its service production and the nature of services. Services are being produced on State-based terms, market-based terms and, very often, quasi-market based terms.

A common prerequisite for all public sector organizations is that budgets are funded through taxation and/or additionally through compensated fees decided by politicians. Other characteristics are that public organizations are non-profit organizations, that they work for the benefit of citizens, and that the democratic function means that different opinions persist even after the necessary decisions are made, and that they are most often based on majority decisions and some form of transparency is required. These are differences that sometimes are not understood in public debate where the private sector organizations are, ever since the 1980s (Osborn and Gaebler, 1993), presented almost as a functional norm also for public sector organizations with the claim that the democratic system is working slowly and inefficiently.

The shortcomings attributed to public organizations seem to be connected to size and professions rather than to sector. That big organizations are often hierarchical and hard to control and change is a well-known phenomenon both in theory and practice. To meet these characteristics corporate entrepreneurship is presented as a way of encouraging entrepreneurial behaviour (see Burns, 2011). Organizational size, or rather working for big organizations, has proven to make employees less entrepreneurial than individuals working in small organizations (Sørensen, 2007). Size was also the variable presented as the main reason behind the findings that public organizations are less entrepreneurial than private organizations.

The size dimension is relevant when it comes to corporate entrepreneurship as it is often discussed in connection with the need to create an entrepreneurial organization – even when they are big (Honig, 2001; Thornberry, 2002). Another need expressed is to manage a big organization and control creativity. Corporate entrepreneurship is a concept that holds many meanings, such as corporate venturing, intrapreneurship, bringing the market inside or entrepreneurial transformation (Burns, 2011). 'Managerial entrepreneurship' and 'managerialism' are concepts used from a critical standpoint by Hjorth (2005) to classify these strategies, while Peters and Waterman (1982) call for corporate entrepreneurship as a means to manage and control chaos. Management is a key concept, which we will come back to when New Public Management is presented.

THE UMBRELLA OF NEW PUBLIC MANAGEMENT

For the last three decades, public sectors all over the world have been transformed in line with an international operating model and globally travelling ideology; features that are jointly and loosely labelled as New Public Management (NPM) (Sehested, 2002; Sahlin-Andersson, 2006). A number of reasons behind the necessity for reforms of the public sector were (and still are) discussed – the public sector was usually described as too large, too inefficient and too bureaucratic in the most negative meaning of the word. The various ways of making the public sector 'leaner and more manageable' was seen as the answer to these inefficiencies. The different features classified as NPM show, on the one hand, the changes pointing in the same direction, while, on the other hand, the evolving and contextual nature of the changes taking place. The reasons for the adoption of NPM types of reform have been explained in different ways, ranging from the response to external pressures articulated by international organizations such as the OECD, to national historical–institutional reasons (e.g., Christensen and Laegreid, 2006). Other researchers of NPM present similar arguments referring to 'different constitutional features and political–administrative structures'. These findings explain why so many different practices can be found under the common umbrella of New Public Management, as well as some of the problems sometimes related to NPM as the main reform ideas as here is 'a lack of compatibility between the reform content and national norms and values' (Brunsson and Olsen, 1993: 5–6).

NPM has many faces and Ferlie et al. (1996) classify them in four different models: the efficiency drive, downsizing and decentralization, 'in search of excellence' and public-service orientation. There are several other classifications, which all share some commonalities, such as the growth of privatization and quasi-privatization in the domains of the public sector (Hood, 1991). The introduction of professional and private-style management, measures of performance, greater emphasis on output controls, the shift to the disaggregation of units, the introduction of internal competition, and, overall, greater discipline and control over activities (e.g., Hood, 1991: 4–5; Almqvist, 2006), all discuss streamlining and slimming down the public sector.

What is interesting is that the concepts 'entrepreneur' and 'enterprise' are not mentioned in the early analyses of NPM. Some researchers later translated the characteristics above into a demand for entrepreneurs and entrepreneurship and even for enterprising bureaucracies (du Gay, 2005: 4). Some political scientists underline the negative consequences of NPM for power and democracy, and 'from government to governance' is an oft-used expression in explicating how the overall governance steps inside public activities, leading sometimes to increased micro-management, increased control and quasi-efficiency. Entrepreneurial Government and Public Governance are often mentioned as models in close relation with NPM (Secchi, 2011). In practice, New Public Management means that many individuals have to change and many positions in the public sector as well. One of the new roles implicitly or explicitly expected by employees is to be entrepreneurial (Halligan, 2008). The entrepreneurial intentions of NPM are understood and interpreted in different ways. Klein et al. emphasize that 'in short, private entrepreneurs are increasingly charged with serving public ends, while at the same time government action is becoming more entrepreneurial' (Klein et al., 2010: 1). We can find many examples of new organizations created in the wake of NPM reforms, and even aiming to support entrepreneurship. It can even be argued that public organizations are, and have always been, the main tool for policy and political entrepreneurs (e.g., Borch et al., 2008). They work through organizations to implement their visions.

New Public Management as a Political Project

New Public Management has been described as a neoliberal attack on the welfare state. In neoliberalism, no such idea as entrepreneurialism in relation to the public organization is adopted as such, but it is related to other phenomenon, such as downsizing, greater flexibility of work, increasing effectiveness, privatization and the streamlining of the public sector 'inefficient' activities. Despite all of this, entrepreneurship is connected with these characteristics by some researchers (e.g., Morris and Jones, 1999; Kearney et al., 2008).

It is interesting to note that even though research has thoroughly demythologized the inefficiency of the public sector in several ways, the message does not get delivered within public sector management; some of research has looked at the input–output efficiency of the monetary spending of the public sector, ranging from health care to prisons, and some of the research has analysed the difference, also in terms of rhetoric analysis (e.g., du Gay, 2000). Still, the managerial aspects and governance, as the control and exercise of power, seem to keep NPM in place. The sociologist Paul du Gay discusses some of the critics of the public sector and accuses many of them of ignorance concerning working conditions and also for neglecting the demands of democracy. 'Bureaucracy may be more expensive than other types of organizations, but that is not surprising when democracy is not necessarily the cheapest form of government' (du Gay, 2000: 95). Du Gay examines the key concepts of NPM and issues a warning against simple solutions to complicated structures and problems. In his work 'In praise of bureaucracy' he refers to entrepreneurship and enterprise in different terms, such as 'entrepreneurial government' and 'entrepreneurial governance'.

NPM AND ENTREPRENEURSHIP IN PUBLIC ORGANIZATIONS

Reforms inspired by New Public Management aim to change the public sector at large – that is, its organizations – towards more entrepreneurial practices. Entrepreneurship and enterprises are therefore related to NPM in several ways. The ambition to diminish the size of the public sector and let private organizations, i.e. private enterprises, produce services is one of the practical outcomes of NPM as a solution for an overly large public sector and monopolistic service production. Another, discussed by Klein et al. (2010), is to establish new public organizations to replace the old and large organizations. The new and also the old organizations should then work in 'more creative and entrepreneurial ways'. Related to this, the aim to make public organizations use private sector strategies is often assumed. In addition, NPM pervades all levels of public organizations, ranging from managerial to street-level levels. In the following, some aspects of NPM and entrepreneurship in public organizations are related to the different levels of functions.

The Management Level

As seen from the presentation of the characteristics of New Public Management, management comes to represent the new organization, while the old bureaucracy with faceless bureaucrats is replaced with managers. Salaman (2005: 148) says 'the manager is the cornerstone of the new organization' and Sehested (2002) uses the expression 'a managerial revolution'. So does that revolution make managers more entrepreneurial and/ or do entrepreneurs get recruited as managers according to NPM logic? Research findings are far from clear on these points, although many NPM studies do focus on managers. Researchers using concepts like 'policy streams' and 'political streams' in connection with problem streams (Kingdon, 1995, Guldbrandsen and Fossum, 2009) have politicians or top managers in mind, even if implicitly. Top managers are those who realize ideas and make organizations and employees work along those lines. They communicate the stated goals and demand output and control systems. In a way, public entrepreneurship is, in the words of Klein et al. (2010), a management phenomenon which emphasizes the points made earlier by Hood (1991) – that is, 'hands-on-professional management'. This is the conclusion of studies on enterprise discourse by entrepreneurship researchers of the European school (see e.g., Hjorth, 2003). The assumed entrepreneuralization of society is in effect a managerialization. Some would call this increasing and overarching governance (e.g., Rose and Miller 2008).

Currie et al. (2008) argue there is a special entrepreneurial leadership that exists in the public sector. According to Currie et al, as the number of stakeholders are many and often demanding, and as the political context is strongly present, management and leadership practices differ from the private sector, bringing them closer to entrepreneurial practices. Although public sector managers work in public organizations they have to identify opportunities, estimate risks, etc. They have to manage the co-existence of centralized control and the newly earned autonomy. One of the main strategies in identifying opportunities is to listen to their co-workers and support their innovative and creative solutions, in order to maintain their status. Currie et al. (2008) label this strategy as 'enabling entrepreneurial activities' and present examples of these successful strategies. Most often the very top of these organizations is emphasized but the study of Borins (2001) shows that entrepreneurial ideas in public organizations often came from middle managers.

The problem with the focus on managers as public entrepreneurs is that it conflates public sector activity into one person only, highlighting his or her activities as entrepreneurial, and so the idea follows the ideology of the individual entrepreneurial person. In a modern society it is often the case that top managers are the only ones in organizations who enjoy the manoeuvring space for creation and stimulation. When it comes to creating and implementing change, they are thus the key actors. However, Metcalfe (2009: 80) states that 'management is everything that entrepreneurship is not'. Management takes the frame of action as given, which entrepreneurs do not; managers calculate rationally, which entrepreneurs do not; and managers are anxious to reduce uncertainty, which entrepreneurs are not. Entrepreneurial competence does not follow from management competence. So, management and entrepreneurship are here articulated as complementary with each other (Metcalfe 2009, 83; Hjorth et al. 2003). The very idea of 'entrepreneurial managerial reform' is challenged by du Gay (2008) as it is problematic at the very least from the democratic perspective, but also from the perspective we mentioned earlier, the emphasis on individual agency. These tensions between 'the stewardship model' and the new 'transformational' and 'entrepreneurial model' are developed and described in Denis et al. (2007) as an illustration of a vivid discussion on the consequences both of NPM and of the emphasis on leadership and management – with or without connections to entrepreneurship.

Professions

Many public organizations are by tradition dominated by professions, and some are even run by professions (the Ministry of Justice, legal institutions, health care institutions, etc.). The medical profession dominates the health sector and is the most frequently cited example, but there are also others; some of these are called semi-professions. Also, by tradition, these professions govern the management positions in their own sectors. 'The trend of New Public Managements challenges the role of professionals in public organizations' (Sehested, 2002).

NPM has meant changes not only in management but also in the practices of how the work is done by professionals in public sector professions – but the interpretations of what it has meant are shifting. As one example, the demand for effective work-orientation is a dilemma for persons working with the mentally disabled and the handicapped (Saario and Raitakari, 2010). The methods for introducing effective work-orientation among professionals in mental health has, among professionals, changed the ways of working and the ways of thinking about the work and themselves. Instead of the client perspective, they have had to adopt effectiveness and productivity discourse and think about their work through the lens of NPM. Similar conclusions on the effects of NPM on the work of child welfare professionals are presented also by Wastell et al. (2010).

Organizational change sometimes has the character of policy change. This is obvious when the decisions concern professions and semi-professions. A number of studies have been conducted on the implications for professionals in public organizations of reform (see a review in Ferlie et al. 2007). The amount of interest is due to the fact that 'New Public Management reforms challenge professionalism as a governing principle, but also depends on professionals for their implementation' (Ferlie et al. 2007, 423). Ferlie et al. take most of their examples from the medical profession and emphasize the importance of the context and of the political intentions as well as the professional strategies.

Lower Hierarchical Levels

NPM is most often connected to management and the managerial levels, not to street-level work. The outcomes of NPM, however, spread throughout the complex levels of organizations so that even researchers emphasizing the importance of managers admit that lower level employees are also very important members of organizations – also when it comes to organizational entrepreneurship (see e.g., Hjorth 2005). Top leaders presented by Currie et al. (2008) realize their entrepreneurial intentions mainly through others – lower level employees are sometimes the tools of public entrepreneurs in higher organizational levels.

The resistance or the changes in practices against orders by workers have been interpreted as being entrepreneurial (Guldbrandsson and Fossum 2009). Currie et al. (2008) presented examples of entrepreneurship in low hierarchical levels that had been 'enabled' by managers with 'an eye for entrepreneurship'. A conviction that there are entrepreneurial employees everywhere lies behind the programmes on 'employee-driven innovations' developed at the EU level (Hull, 2009). These address small and medium sized firms as many big companies have developed programmes to take advantage of the competence and creativity of their employees. The idea of looking for innovators and entrepreneurs at the bottom of organizations is now taken up in public sector organizations such as health care. As expected, entrepreneurs are also found there; they seem to be everywhere (Nählinder, 2010).

To illustrate entrepreneurship at lower or non-managerial levels, the street-level bureaucrat concept, first proposed by Lipsky in the 1980s, can be used. Lipsky's studies in the United States concerned bureaucrats working in the police force, teachers and social workers. Lipsky presents a number of dilemmas to illustrate the complexity. The main reason behind the dilemmas is that the individual bureaucrats find that they cannot do all they want to and what they believe is their mission. In order to survive they can change their own preferences to be more in line with what is possible. These changes sometimes turn into cynicism. A more active strategy is to try to change the organization and working conditions.

According to Meyers and Vorsanger (2008), research done on the working conditions of street-level bureaucrats after Lipsky is contradictory. Some researchers state that bureaucrats nowadays are helpless and 'sandwiched' in between, while others believe that they can still find ways of handling situations and exercising some discretion. They are embedded within interacting politics, in organizations, in professional communities – but do 'not just do what they are told to do – they do what they can' (2008: 155).

New Public Management and Entrepreneurship in Public Organizations

So far we have engaged in a discussion on entrepreneurship on non-managerial positions without explicit reference to NPM. But, of course, NPM components are of importance also for these groups of employees;

something we will illustrate with examples. A number (ten) of entrepreneurial employees in a Swedish municipality are presented by Sundin (2004). These employees work in different parts of a municipality and a county council. What they have in common is that they see something they want to change or they miss something that they start to create. The author argues that it is probable that this part of the country is not exceptional at all. What is exceptional is that the researchers observe what is going on. Two of the entrepreneurs were later presented in an article in the *Scandinavian Journal of Management* (Sundin and Tillmar, 2008). These two are going on and feel quite satisfied with what they have done and are also appreciated by their employers. A less happy end is described for others among the number (Sundin, 2010), who felt their entrepreneurial strategies were spoiled by new organizational strategies.

The hierarchical division of work does seem to remain surprisingly rigid after the introduction of NPM in organizations; it is the upper level that defines the work and the salaries paid for that work, evaluates the outcomes, and reports higher up, often in the form of economic performances. Added to this, the forms of work intensification – for example, through task restructuring, internal markets, greater external assessment, and high surveillance environments – burden the core workforce of such organizations. This effect is not without tensions. The break-up of traditional bureaucracies – both in public sector organizations and private sector organizations – into a complex web of smaller units, profit centres and internal markets could be interpreted as a manifestation of entrepreneurship. More accurately, however, this is also a manifestation of a new corporate structure which does not necessarily decentralize power. Research into privatized public sector services in many Western countries often shows a large gap between the rhetoric of 'autonomous entrepreneurial units' transacting with each other, and a reality where profit centres are most often monopoly providers to each other, closely monitored through an auditing culture (e.g., Thompson and McHugh, 2002).

So let us end this section with some experiences from studies on organizations created 'in the wake of' NPM. Paralleling the effects of the quick changes are the results showing the conflicts between professions that have been set off by the change processes. Mulholland (1998) identified a struggle between the 'public sector survivors' and the 'movers and shakers'. The study concerned newly privatized utilities in the UK, where older managers were engineers with water and electricity industries, and new managers were younger and from the private sector, running the business with efficiency drives. Mulholland's study shows how the older engineers were no longer preferred, and their competencies were marginalized and their status diminished. In contrast, the younger managers with entrepreneurial attitudes became the admired and wanted group from the owners' perspective, even if not from the employees' perspective. Studies by Kovalainen and Österberg-Högstedt (2011) of small firm owners in care and social services who work in close collaboration with the public sector show how trust is being built during previous employee positions, and utilized as a resource when changing position. The reciprocity of power in that close relationship remains entangled, and many of the former public sector employees work for less pay and longer hours as entrepreneurs, and enjoy it more. The studies of Lindgren and Packendorff (2008) discuss enthusiastic teachers using the possibility to start schools of their own. These few examples illustrate the different experiences found in both research and the public and political debate. Together the importance of the context is emphasized, and as stated before new organizations and contracting out is not always proof of creativity and entrepreneurship – it could also be a proof of deviance or proof of rule-following and obedience.

With the changes in the public sector, there is no single perspective, as most of the studies we have referred to do not aim to describe the only or single truth. It seems that many of the changes relate to changing working conditions, to power positions, and the ability to break free of earlier patterns. While individuals make choices, the adaptation of institutions follows, or it might be the reverse: institutions change and individuals adapt. What is rather clear is that the political processes and discourses evoking and pushing forward entrepreneurial activities throughout the different functions of the public sector all have one thing in common: rhetorical power.

CONCLUDING DISCUSSION

As stated at the beginning, 'entrepreneurship' and 'the public sector' are opposed as contradictory terms in the public and political debate as well as in mainstream research in both the entrepreneurship field and the public administration field. This is explained by the focus of these fields, including the implicit and explicit understandings of common attributes and relations and also by the difference in theoretical explanations. The mainstream ways of analysing the public sector and entrepreneurial activities have rather limited views of the central concepts. Entrepreneurship, defined as an action and a change, is, however, practiced in 'multiple sites and spaces' (Steyaert and Katz, 2004, p. 182), and it can consequently be found in different kinds of organizations, both inside and outside the commercial markets (e.g., Hjorth et al., 2003). Public organizations are also sites for entrepreneurship. In this chapter this statement is analysed and illustrated through the construction of the public seen as the outcome of public entrepreneurship when the combination 'public entrepreneurship' is used as emphasizing sociality as argued for by Hjorth and Bjerke (2006). On the other hand, the context matters, so that not all incidences of sociality are to be interpreted as entrepreneurship.

The specified task of this chapter was to deal with entrepreneurship in public organizations. This task has to be handled in two parts, with the introduction of the international concept for the reorganization of the public sector: New Public Management (NPM). The public sector and its organizations were regulated according to the characteristics of fairness, justice, and the equality of treatment, which also had its disadvantages from other perspectives as elaborated in the models of NPM and in earlier models following the idea of 'public choice'. Even in 'the old systems' there was space for entrepreneurial acts. Employees in the public sector at lower hierarchical levels more or less had to act as described by Lipsky (1980) and many others. The greatest discretion for acting was, however, given to professional groups. Discretion does not guarantee entrepreneurship and power disputes are aligned in new ways in relation to entrepreneurship. Some semi-professions, such as nurses, claim that the medical profession systematically stopped entrepreneurial initiatives to protect their privileged position.

New Public Management (NPM) is without doubt an international phenomenon, although constructed and deconstructed in different ways in different national and political contexts. NPM cannot, however, be blamed for, nor can it take credit for, all the possible changes presented in its name. The same holds true for the connections between globalization and NPM. As Pierson rightly points out, 'many of the pressures on the welfare state are wrongly attributed to globalization; they are actually generated primarily within affluent democracies' (Pierson 2001: 4). To use globalization as an argument makes it politically possible to introduce the reforms of neo-liberalism with its demands for changes in the public sector, the contradiction of the public sector, etc. It is, to quote Gregory (2006), hard to describe and analyse the consequences of NPM. 'There can be no objectively true and accurate evaluation of the reforms. NPM theory itself is heavily ideological' (Gregory 2006: 236). Despite this we can state that even if NPM is by no means simple or one-dimensional conceptually, the political intentions behind NPM were, among other things, to create change in the public organizations and in society.

Reforms and changes to NPM intend to change organizational practices and the behaviour of employees. Entrepreneurship is a phenomenon often desired and admired. Entrepreneurship or entrepreneurial thinking is one of the positive buzzwords often used in relation to NPM. We will come back to that at the very end of the chapter and relate and repeat the studies concentrating on the consequences of NPM for members of public organizations. These studies more often concentrate on new systems of control and new managerial principles than on actual entrepreneurship. The related consequences are of different types and scopes. The commodification of emotions is emphasized as one consequence of both the output control and of the standards (Hochschild, 1983; Putnam and Mumby, 1993). According to Thompson et al. (2000), the capacities and attributes valued of employees are another consequence closely rooted in NPM. In our own studies, we found that the possibilities to be creative in work, doing that 'little extra', decreased (Sundin 2010) as the demand for efficiency and cost-control gave little room for other values such as caring for workmates.

Many researchers have stated that the implementation of NPM is, to a large extent, a management and managerial project. We have, in both research and in public debate, found examples of top managers in public sector organizations who have made their organizations more efficient. Standards can be used for the benefit of an organization, and the output can be controlled. Managers can both control and be themselves controlled (Bourgault, 2011). The new control systems make comparisons with other public and private units possible, which could be stimulating, and even remove the label of inefficiency from public organizations. In the 'old' system, professionals were managers in their own sectors, in a silo-style manner. Among the most important perspectives discussed here, managers are also recruited from the outside. Professions are led by professional managers, not by professionals without managerial training. In the literature referred to, these consequences are often presented. The NPM components, giving power and discretion to managers, could mean more control and less freedom for individuals lower down in the organizational hierarchies. They are the ones that have to follow the standards and whose performance is being measured, they have to work with greater discipline, which means that the street-level bureaucrats as well as the professionals cannot or are not allowed to use their own judgment in new situations. The combined result, all in all, is hard to determine as are the consequences for citizens – the owners and the 'shareholders' of public sector organizations.

As mentioned previously, the principles of control and management are part of the demand to act like private organizations. The actual research findings are nuanced on this demand. Zampetakis and Moustakis (2007) represent a case in point where the conclusions are that findings on corporate entrepreneurship cannot be exported to the public sector. Sensitivity to the context is another way to express these findings as formulated by Currie et al. (2008), meaning that, in the words of Gregory (2006), 'there are problems at the heart of government that have no parallel in the work of corporate affairs' (p. 240). To manage and to control these, leads to a use of 'huge amounts of time and money' (p. 240).

So what then of entrepreneurship? We argue that NPM gives power to managers, sometimes followed by a demand to act in an entrepreneurial manner. The mission often includes the construction of an entrepreneurial bureaucracy and managerial enterpriser. The politics here are discussed and elaborated on, and even criticized by several authors (e.g., Hjorth, 2005), especially for the use of managerial entrepreneurs as a solution to many problems. In practice, the outcomes often seem to be more of managerialism and less of entrepreneurship. This is one of the reverse effects often noticed when organizational change is implemented. However, these change processes are going on. Maybe entrepreneurs and the entrepreneurial processes will find new ways.

Our review and discussion on public entrepreneurship supports those researchers stating that public entrepreneurship can be a way of creating and understanding political change (Minstrom and Norman, 2009), but also a way of understanding entrepreneurship as a phenomenon. Entrepreneurship is a part of social and societal change, like that here which aims to describe changing the public sector and its mechanisms. This conclusion, of course, depends on how we define entrepreneurship. Our conclusion is also that theories on entrepreneurship can make a contribution to our understanding of institutional and organizational change (see Hederer, 2007). Theories from one area should not be implemented naïvely, that is, as taken-for-granted ideas, such as the Schumpeterian legacy often is (where the approach of innovative individuals is emphasized). Minstrom and Norman (2009) show the importance of both the grass-root level of analyses, the contexts, and institutional studies simultaneously, in order to understand the complexity of changes. These conclusions concern all organizations. In this case, concentrating on entrepreneurship in public sector organizations, the conclusions and demands are two-fold: that institutions matter more than is assumed in entrepreneurship studies and that NPM demands an entrepreneurial public sector, are foremost political, not market or internally driven demands.

NOTES

1. Originally, bureaucracy meant efficiency and expertise combined with functional agility and 'collegiality', as described by Weber (1947).
2. Due to the lack of space we leave undiscussed social entrepreneurship, but call for the boundary work necessarily needed between the concepts of 'social enterprise' and 'public sector'. According to one definition, social enterprise differs from public sector service

providers as being a more 'non-traditional' activity (Nicholls and Cho, 2006: 102). As the definition of 'non-traditional' is contextual and changing, these might not be sufficient criteria. It seems that as the concept and idea of 'social entrepreneurship' is gaining popularity, it means very different things, ranging from 'not-for-profit' to 'social responsibility', thus leaving much room for maneuvering the 'social'.

3. Statistics Sweden. Historisk statistic för Sverige. Del 1. Befolkning. http://www.scb.se/Grupp/Hitta_statistik/Historisk_statistik/_Dokument/Historisk%20statistik%20för%20Sverige_%20Del%201.pdf. WHO's statistical information system. World health statistics. 2010. http://www.who.int/whosis/whostat/EN_WHS10_Full.pdf

4. Necessity entrepreneurship is a concept mainly used for individuals starting firms as a way to earn a living. Malin Gawell uses the concept in her thesis on the construction of the Swedish Attac movement, as the persons she interviewed used the term 'necessity' when describing why they established the organization.

16 Collective creativity: E-teams and E-teamwork

Shannon O'Donnell and Lee Devin

PART I: INTRODUCTION

Increasingly, groups do the business work of entrepreneurship and innovation (Stewart, 1989; Bennis and Biederman, 1997; Hjorth, 2003b; Sawyer, 2007). And these groups increasingly resist conventional, hierarchical, industrial command and control management (Reich, 1987; Sutton, 2001; Florida, 2002; Hackman, 2002; Klein et al., 2006; Carson et al., 2007; Austin and Nolan, 2007). In many lines of contemporary work Frederick Taylor has had his day.[1] Accordingly, business practitioners seek to understand the new conditions in which work gets done: increasingly dynamic and competitive work, frequently enabled by creative use of emerging technologies, more and more often placed in a global rather than local or even national context, and more and more focused on innovation (Friedman, 2005; McAfee, 2006). In a creative economy (Howkins, 2001), adapting to these conditions, exploiting them to create value, requires a shift from mobilizing individuals to mobilizing the group (Reich, 1987; Hjorth, 2005). To do this, entrepreneurs and managers need to understand how collaborating groups best work and how to organize them.

In this chapter we take a look at an increasingly important segment of business work: the creativity of special teams working iteratively to create a product that emerges from the activity of producing it. Such teams characteristically do more and better work than seems likely; they exceed the sum of their parts. In the theater we call such a team an ensemble, and for this essay we borrow the concept. We call a non-theater ensemble an E-Team. The work of an E-Team we call E-TeamWork. An E-Team does E-TeamWork; E-TeamWork is what an E-Team does. With this tautology we isolate E-Teams and their work from other activities.

To accomplish a presentation of the E-Team concept we first establish the boundaries of the topic by referencing some elements of the conversation on creative teams so far. We note the difficulties of observation and discussion: (1) a process will be hard to observe: it disappears when you're not doing it; and (2) sloppy usage has debased the language thinkers and practitioners alike use to talk and write about the workers and work we call E-Teams and E-TeamWork. We proceed, then, with some considerations on language as a tool for productive thought and conversation. We use that language to present for your consideration a template for collective creativity. Our experiences as working artists, combined with a multi-year study of a wide range of makers, provide our data. We refer now and then to thought leaders who have contributed to theoretical understanding of E-TeamWork (however named) but we rely principally on research we've conducted and experiences we've had. We intend this template as an aid to observation and conversation. It's our hope that by organizing precise language we will help implement newly productive thought and practice among scholars and makers.

Researching Collective Creativity

In their review of the literature on work team effectiveness, Kozlowski and Ilgen (2006: 115) acknowledge that much investigation into group work focuses surprisingly on individuals and individual skills, behaviors, incentives, and development. Studies of creativity, while addressing social influences and group context, tend similarly to focus on individuals (Amabile, 1996; Csikszentmihalyi, 1997). Meanwhile, much remains to be understood about group creativity. Such understanding needs in-depth, qualitative – ideally ethnographic – studies, and given the complexity of interaction, requires either immersion in the process itself, and/or a team of researchers engaged in lengthy, deeply informed, and intimate observation. Given this difficulty, researchers who study collaborative teams often rely on retrospective reports by informants, or on surveys designed to capture the effects of certain behaviors or conditions on group creativity (e.g., Murnighan and Conlon, 1991; Gratton and Erickson, 2007). These contributions advance our understanding of the organizational *conditions* that support effective teams, such as team member selection, size of work group, worker autonomy, attitudes towards conflict and knowledge sharing, and the design of task and reward systems (Wageman, 1995; Hackman, 2002; Gratton and Erickson, 2007); they do not necessarily address the *processes* of collective creativity. Leadership is another popular focus in the study of creative teams, perhaps because the focus on an individual's traits and actions makes for a more manageable unit of study and analysis than collective making processes, or because incumbent and prospective leaders dominate readership. This research again investigates conditions and behaviors, with a focus on the leader's role in creating conditions in which group work can thrive (Hackman, 2002), and on the leadership behaviors that support entrepreneurship and creativity in teams (Gartner, 1989; Amabile et al., 2004).

The study of collective processes of creativity is becoming more interesting to scholars. An emerging group of researchers apply a process-oriented approach to studying entrepreneurial and creative activity in groups (Steyeart, 2007). They focus on *relationships* rather than on individuals (Hjorth and Johannisson, 2003; van der Haar and Hosking, 2004), on the continual emergence of the new as a result of the situated, corporeal, social and creative nature of human action (Joas, 1996; Hjorth, 2005), and on organizational becoming based on this evolving human action (Tsoukas and Chia, 2002). Motivated in part by a surge in interest in the innovation potential of "creative work" – for instance, in "design thinking" approaches to value creation (Brown, 2008) – case studies increasingly describe *how* creative groups work together (Nussbaum, 2004; Catmull, 2008). Micro-level studies of creative work aim to understand the processes by which groups generate and evaluate new ideas, organize and manage work that proceeds iteratively rather than sequentially, and develop products that emerge from the processes of making rather than products made that fulfill preconceived goals conceived by people who don't themselves do the making work (Austin and Devin, 2003). Studies of the improvisational practices of theater groups and jazz ensembles offer detailed descriptions of work practices inherent in that form of group creativity, while gathering evidence of organizational creativity as situated in social interactions (Weick, 1993; Barrett, 1998; Hatch, 1999; Tsoukas and Chia, 2002: 576; Sawyer, 2007). It is to this endeavor that we add our contribution, grounded in our unique access to data that are difficult to obtain, and our perception that the *processes* by which creative teams make innovations remain mysterious.

As mentioned, we base our discussion of collective creativity on two primary sources of data. First, we have, in company with Robert D. Austin, for many years investigated creative making processes and the management principles implicit in these processes. Our inductive, "grounded theory" study includes analysis of 35 detailed case studies, and makes use of widely accepted methods for developing theory from case analysis (Glaser, 1978; Yin, 1984; Eisenhardt, 1989a; Miles and Huberman, 1994; Strauss and Corbin, 1998; Edmondson and McManus, 2007). Each case consists of videotaped, semi-structured interviews with expert innovators, grounded, whenever possible, in observation of their process. All cases present people who make things: art, pharmaceuticals, software, airplane cockpit controls, graphic design, home entertainment systems. Cases offer comparisons and contrasts among organizational size, number of people at work, and resources available. A team of half a dozen researchers analysed these data, according to 37 inductively derived categories (21 numerically coded), the process subjected to rigorous protocols to avoid bias. A series of Harvard Business School teaching cases made further use of these materials. We found, to our surprise, many cases in which a business team's approach to making something new looked a lot like an artist's approach, and, conversely, a number of business-like artists (Austin and Devin, 2010). In this chapter, we draw on these cases for examples.

The multi-case study provides us with a vast store of detailed information that supports and extends our second major source of data: our own professional experience as artists who do professionally the kind of collaborative team work addressed in this chapter. We have found that the work methods of theater production, refined more or less continually for about 2500 years, provide an excellent model for team work in business innovation (Austin and Devin, 2003). Shannon worked as a resident director, producer, and dramaturg at the People's Light and Theatre of Malvern, Pennsylvania[2]; Lee worked as an actor, director, playwright, and dramaturg in a variety of venues, including People's Light, and in addition taught theater in colleges and universities for 40 some years. We've each spent our "10 000 hours" developing expertise in observing and understanding actions taken in the context of collective creativity, skills and methods we apply to our research practice. This means that we support findings from our research with our direct experience, and support descriptions from our experience with cases from our research, and, here and there, point you to sources that can provide further reading and discussion, or that apply insights from art practice directly to business situations.

Drawing on these sources, we want in this chapter to take a step toward understanding the kind of team-based work processes that will naturally create innovations. But in order to understand how groups innovate together, and how to create conditions for such collaborative action in organizations, we first need to clean up our language. Promiscuous overuse has devalued many terms we need in order to achieve this understanding; terms that used to mean one thing now mean every thing. On our way to addressing this difficulty, let's look at two of the most egregious examples.

Collaboration

Here's a typical "collaboration" often described in accounts of work: A leader has a vision for what s/he wants made. S/he chooses team members according to the skills each has, whether co-located or geographically distributed, and each team member works on the parts of the project that require those skills. The success of the project depends on them, and on the skill of the leader in planning, directing, organizing, and unifying their work in accordance with his/her vision. The team leader has a good understanding of the work necessary to the project, though not necessarily at skill levels equal to the team members. S/he makes sure that the group has the resources they need and helps them stay on target. At the end of the process, the leader congratulates the members and reports to the Big Boss: "It was a collaborative effort. Everyone contributed, and it really worked well."

And, here's another, from one of our research cases: A product design team including a CEO, a marketing director, an art director, an engineer, and a textiles designer come together and decide it would be nice to make a soap dispenser that complements their popular trash bin. They talk about what kinds of values and feelings should be associated with the soap dispenser, then go about their individual work in a shared office setting that stylishly expresses their brand. The textiles designer digs through her collection of interesting samples, the engineer sketches ideas and uses 3-D printing technologies to craft a few prototypes, the art director begins to plot the story-concept that links the soap dispenser to the trash bin. As they work, they share ideas and challenge each other to go further. The group meets again and evaluates ideas, incorporating input on manufacturing costs and marketing possibilities, then reconceives the focus of the product's further development. After several such cycles, they achieve closure on a final concept that all agree expresses the "DNA" of the company (Austin and Beyersdorfer, 2006).

In the first example, people cooperate nicely to achieve an outcome that was determined from the start. Innovation takes place in the conceiving and planning stages, and in a few instances in which a team member improvises during the process, probably in response to an unexpected problem. Should the user's needs change over the course of the project, or should an unanticipated insight or opportunity arise, it's unlikely that the team would diverge much from the original plan, unless resources allowed them to go back to scratch. In the second example, people work together to develop their ideas in relationship with one another towards an emergent outcome that they cannot predict in detail when they start. Innovation takes place throughout the process, as the team members interact with one another and incorporate new information and ideas into their work. They agree at stages on an overall "direction" for the work, but that direction evolves along with everything else. The interactions of team members resonate with each other, producing outcomes that could not be achieved by any team member working alone. To use the same word to denote these two processes – as well as the myriad other processes folks describe as "collaboration" – merely tortures language, and makes it difficult to increase our understanding of the work practices and management approaches most suitable to each process.

Ensemble

Ensemble as a term interests us because we think that, when used appropriately, it names a group that practices the special type of collaboration that produces innovation. Yet, varying usage shows how this word too can lose its value for clear communication: In his review, a music critic praises a string quartet for their "quality of ensemble." By which this particular critic means that the four musicians achieved an impeccable precision and unity in their playing together, to the point that the individual voices blended into the whole. Another critic responds to the same performance by faulting the quartet for such a blend, arguing that a quality of ensemble is better served when the four musicians are unified but dynamically engaged in a conversation in which distinct voices can be heard.[3] In this case, there's no agreement, even among two professionals observing the same performance, about what an "ensemble" is, does, or means. Additionally, these uses of the word ensemble provide no evidence of how this group worked together or how they achieved such unity of performance, blended or not. We have, in other words, no idea what these guys are talking about.

In 1953, T. D. Weldon, writing about politics, formulated a distinction between problems and difficulties. Problems, he wrote, have solutions. Identify them, figure them out, and solve them. They go away. Difficulties, on the other hand, require continual address. They don't go away (pp.75ff). There's a problem with the bridge at 1st Street: it needs new pavement. Pave it. Problem solved. Parents aren't satisfied with the school system. There may be many solvable problems associated with this dissatisfaction, but overall the school isn't a problem. It's a difficulty. Different groups must differently and continually address their concerns to achieve *and then continue to maintain* the level of quality they need.

We doubt that Professor Weldon anticipated the value his work would have for management and management studies. But the increasing need for group work leads inevitably to work issues that can't be solved and won't go away. For instance, innovation by a team routinely puts team members into ambiguous and scary situations. That's not a solvable problem; it's a difficulty that's part of the job (Devin and Austin, 2004). Group work requires methods that address ongoing difficulty in creative and satisfying ways, accepting the long term as an appropriate time frame and reconceiving our ideas of efficiency and success in the management of entrepreneurship and, especially, innovation. To capitalize on emerging opportunities and fully to exploit the potential of team work, managers and workers alike must learn to achieve productive competence in complex and ambiguous work situations. A creative economy will require teams with various knowledge and capabilities, teams that, like it or not, will produce innovation.

Presently the sloppy language of our professional vocabulary constitutes a difficulty: each conversation must begin with "Well, for me collaboration means . . ." and in case of difference, the parties must negotiate the differences away. We're going to propose another approach: we're going to declare this difficulty a problem and solve it. (Don't try this at home. Most of the time treating a difficulty as a problem leads to frustration, failure, and cynicism.) We'll do that by assigning to teams and team work names that denote one thing and one thing only. Remember our tautology. We use the name "E-Team" for a team that collaborates to create innovation. We use the name "E-TeamWork" for innovation work done by an E-Team. In this essay these terms refer only to the thing and activity to which we've assigned them. We'll now devote the bulk of this chapter to descriptions and accounts of E-TeamWork, and the kind of creature, an E-Team, that can do it.

PART II: E-TEAMWORK AND E-TEAMS

Let's start with a brief description of E-TeamWork, built on findings from our case study research and supported by experience, a description that will serve also to present the outlines of an E-Team. Then we'll examine the parts of each in greater detail.

An E-Team works iteratively towards an emergent outcome. Each iteration becomes part of the given circumstances for the next iteration. As this happens, the E-Team reconceives the project, leading to an evolution of the emerging outcome. The team reaches closure through consensus, and arranges the overall process to create coherent, innovative outcomes, relevant to the given circumstances. To achieve this, an E-Team must do the tasks and have the features we describe below. This isn't to say that other groups don't do many or most of these things; just that *all* of them combine *all the time* to create an E-Team doing E-TeamWork.

Now let's examine the parts.

Preparation

To work iteratively in this way first requires an appreciation of the difference between planning and preparation. Planning of the sort that involves designing a product or determining an outcome in advance of the process of making it belongs to industrial work, and not to the iterative work of special teams (Austin and Devin, 2003). An E-Team plans in order to get what they need to accomplish the assignment. Plans include arrangements for space, time, supplies and equipment, personnel, and an idea of how to proceed. Planning relates to a particular assignment.

Preparation, on the other hand, means activities that E-Team members engage in to master their craft in order to become expert collaborators. It involves learning and practicing what you need to know and do in order to be ready to learn whatever needs to be learned and to do whatever needs to be done. E-Team members build skills through repetition and experiment with tools and techniques that push their limits. They extend their craft, discover new methods, and acquire new capabilities that don't apply to a current assignment. In preparation, E-Team members discover how to work so that the work provides its own reward, quite apart from any commercial purpose or constraint. The artists in our research study asserted time and again, "I do this for myself; I don't do it for sale." Musician lore instructs us here. A teacher will tell a young violinist, "You're not in command of the instrument until you've put in at least 10000 hours of practice." Here's the math: 10000 hours is 1250 8-hour days, 250 weeks, 5 years with an annual 2 week vacation. And if you don't think it's worth doing for its own sake, if you don't *like* to practice, you'll never be able to hang in.[4]

Not all E-Team preparation need be quite *that* rigorous, but the 10000 Hour Rule is an excellent guiding idea. And it sorts with another useful tautology: an E-Team member prepares in order to be prepared. We spoke to a senior software developer at a business school who regularly prepares by learning and practising. She works as a member of a team that uses an agile, or iterative, approach to develop custom software for business school clients, such as recruiting and event planning tools. Though software solutions emerge over the months dedicated to a project, careful planning goes into the team's work: Time and resources are allocated to tasks at the level of hourly detail, deadlines agreed upon, and daily team meetings organized to include client updates and input. On a daily basis, our senior software developer manages a full schedule, communicating at regular intervals with a team of people whose work depends on hers, and functions within a competitive industry characterized by rapid change. New applications and new functionality intrude, and skills needed for the last project become obsolete. Our developer's ability to come up with novel and relevant solutions depends on her commitment to carrying on preparations outside the immediate task. So she talks to other people in her field to learn what others are doing, reads technical magazines, researches new trends and tools, and makes time to play with these new ideas by, for instance, building code "for fun." She faithfully keeps a list of these ideas as her "toolbox," without knowing if and when the ideas may apply usefully to a work task, yet reports that many times these ideas do in fact "come in handy." In combination with unpredictable current need, they often save the day.

E-Team members prepare by doing exercises that build fundamental skills when the task calls for extreme mental or physical stamina and agility, and must be performed with spontaneity and grace. Think for instance of the muscular strength and control required of gymnasts, ballet dancers, even golfers, for whom training is a full time job. Indeed most other activities in an athlete's daily life (nutrition, sleep, physical therapies) are organized to ensure they can optimize their training time: "The champ is always in the gym." Should business innovators be less well prepared than the athletes? Musicians show us how physical and mental stamina and agility work hand-in-hand. They need physical dexterity to play an instrument, and mental dexterity to hold entire complex compositional structures in mind, even as they respond to the rest of the group in performance. Yet none of these tasks should be evident as effortful. The fiddle player who lets you know how hard he's working is, reliably, a second rate player.

In the first 16 years of their 35-year career, the musicians in the Medici String Quartet rehearsed as a group 4 to 6 hours daily, on top of 3 to 4 hours of individual practice, nearly 365 days of the year. Rehearsals happened whether or not there was an impending performance scheduled. Under the mentorship of the legendary pianist Sir Clifford Curzon, the Quartet learned an extreme approach to preparation that they could apply to any task. They invested hours upon hours rehearsing a composition until they could perform difficulty with ease. They began by rehearsing in perfect time to a metronome, getting comfortable with the structure of the piece as it was played "correctly," until the task was relatively easy to achieve, nearly automatic. Then, they invested even more hours playing the piece *out of time* with the metronome, making it as difficult as possible – even "torturous" – to play, given that there are infinite ways to play a piece of music *out* of time. Only after they had exhausted the boundaries of this exploration could they achieve what Curzon called "second innocence," a state of grace that first violinist Paul Robertson described as having an extremely pleasing effect on the listener. With this kind of preparation invested, Robertson said he could "come on stage and play with no conscious complexity present at all, but a great deal of unconscious information informing the simplicity" (Austin and O'Donnell, 2007: 7).

Martha Graham, a dancer, summed up preparation in these words:

"Technique is the dancer's freedom." That is, the better you are at the fundamentals of your work, the more creatively you can use them to make something new. For E-Team work, the fundamentals include training both body and mind to their highest pitch of skill and stamina. An E-Team member accepts a professional obligation to be ready each day to work at peak performance levels. People working in business may not think of themselves as athletes, yet like athletes they use their bodies to lead, motivate, communicate with, and otherwise engage colleagues, clients, and other stakeholders. They need conditioning to raise their base level of energy, stamina to apply that energy to a task for as long as necessary, and dexterity to direct that energy with productive intention. Again, why should s/he be less well prepared than an athlete or artist?

Vocal training rarely figures in preparation for E-TeamWork, but in fact a clear, centered speaking voice, supported from the diaphragm, can work wonders. E-Teams communicate constantly and with a certain intimacy, using, among other things, voice to express a range of ideas and to motivate each other, or one another to take action. Certain speaking habits get in the way of the work: a squeaky unsupported voice can dilute or distort meaning. A voice full of tension will communicate tension, not insight.

Mind fundamentals are less routinely known and demonstrated than body fundamentals. At their most abstract they include Concentration and Release. Until they learn otherwise, most people regard an ability to concentrate as a talent, unteachable, unlearnable. It's not. It's a skill that anyone can learn, practice, and get better at.[5] Meditation is the place to practice, and the skill we (and many other performing artists) call "deep listening" is the practical outcome of this preparation. By deep listening we mean attending so as to grasp, not only the discursive meaning, but to understand, with empathy and sympathy, the underlying action of the speaker. To know, for instance, if the speaker has confidence in the idea, or feels tentative about offering it to the team. Also, to track how the speaker is developing an idea in the context of articulating it, and what potentially important contribution the speaker may be leaving unsaid (and what prompts them to edit themselves). In many of these cases, a deep listener can support and encourage a fuller expression.

Release, a skill/attitude well known to athletes and great leaders, can be counterintuitive until learned and practiced. Beginning actors, for instance, often fear that if they release into the emotional state of a character they'll "never get back." They overcome that fear by practice.[6] Beginning E-Team members will need practice at releasing into a state of receptivity, reflexive reaction to new ideas, and willingness to see their own brilliant and precious ideas disappear into the group effort. Anyone who has done this knows how scary it is. E-TeamWork requires body release to get rid of the muscular tension that robs team members of energy and stamina; team members need mind release to get rid of the inhibitions they feel toward the impulsive, reflexive action that drives so much of E-TeamWork, and accounts for the conceptual leaps routinely made by E-Teams. Team leaders and other managers benefit by approaching control through the practice of release. Creative work proceeds by fits and starts in unpredictable directions and is easily thwarted by thoughtless constraint. Good managers aim, they don't direct. We'll return to this point later.

Once given an assignment, E-Team members will engage in additional preparation targeted on the task at hand. These preparations may include mastering technical requirements specific to the formal structure of the work: for instance, dancers learn the choreography of *Swan Lake* to the point that they no longer need to think of what move comes next; product designers learn the parameters of a specific assignment; or musicians learn the idiosyncratic notation of a new composition. An E-Team making software may not use choreography or parameters; they'd use consultation with the client or other forms of research. Still, the objective is the same: to learn and practice what you need to know and do; to be ready for whatever comes up as an assignment and its outcome evolve in unpredictable ways.

While individuals can do some preparation in advance of project work, in E-TeamWork, tasks are interdependent and contextualized, meaning the work of one directly depends on the work of another, as well as on the conditions in which the work takes place.[7] It is only when the group gathers together and begins to interact over the task that they come to understand what will be required of them. Often, E-Team members report needing a first run at the assignment in order to understand what the problem is, or how best to conceive of the problem, so that they can learn what further preparation and research they need and how they ought to proceed.

To return to our musical example, the Medici String Quartet committed to work on a new, never-before-tried composition in partnership with three other quartets as a four-quartet entity, which was itself a never-before-tried team structure. First violin Paul Robertson described the early meetings, in which the four quartets gathered to work together, as "pre-rehearsals," or preparation for later work. Given that working as a group of 16 musicians cannot in any way be tried out by one (or even one group of four) in advance, the only way for the group to understand what the work would be was to meet and try it out. They needed to hear how they interacted as a larger ensemble, and to hear the challenges of working together on that score. Only then could the four groups understand the task well enough to determine how best to proceed with preparing and with working together.

We can consider this phase of the work in design processes as well. When teams from the design giant IDEO gather around the task of designing a better consumer experience, they begin with a phase of anthropological research through observation and interaction with end users (Nussbaum 2004). They aim to understand better the context in which the client framed the problem; they seek to understand how best to address that problem. In some cases they help the client re-frame the problem in a more innovative way or re-define the boundaries of possible solutions. When asked to design a new high-end casual bicycle for Shimano, for example, IDEO engaged in an extensive research phase that led them to propose the concept of a "coasting" bicycle (Brown 2008). They aimed to design a holistic experience, to make biking fun and easy for a generation of people who had come to feel the sport had grown inaccessible to them. When designing a new visual identity for a company, a graphic designer at e-Types, a cutting edge Danish design firm, will do a lot of research talking to clients about their business and finding out about their history, their customers, and their competitors before beginning a design (Austin et al., 2006a). They gradually master the conditions in which the new thing will exist: they start work even as they begin to learn the scope of the work.

Discovering and Creating Given Circumstances

It is famously true that in work toward an emergent outcome plans become obsolete the moment the work begins. (No military genius has ever failed to remark this in his memoirs.) When you must jettison plans in the heat of work, what do you replace them with? With preparation in the form of "given circumstances." We borrow this term from the theater, where it means "Everything you can discover or invent about the character you play." For an E-Team member, it means "Everything you can discover or invent that bears on the assignment." Unlike plans, given circumstances do not become obsolete. Each team member contributes them to each iteration of the work.

As team members interact, given circumstances function in two main ways. First, they form the database that E-Team members use to respond to each other reflexively, out of deep listening, before taking time to figure out what they want to do, before wondering what would be best for them to do, or guessing what the others might think they should do. This response, before and beyond thought or editing, is the source of the innovations that E-TeamWork naturally produces. Second, each iteration of the team's work becomes part of everyone's given circumstances, becomes the database out of which the team reconceives the evolving project at each iteration. The operating limit for given circumstances is, "More!" The boundaries of what might be useful are, "None!" When the Medici String Quartet worked with pianist Sir Clifford Curzon, he showed them a new emphasis on given circumstances in preparation for playing Elgar's piano quintet. Paul Robertson told us:

> And it was when we worked with Curzon on the Elgar piano quintet – which we spent months together, just he and I, working on – which was a wonderful revelation to me about the process of what really music making is all about, which is an exploration of the [composer's] psychology, his relationships, his social and cultural history, the context, everything. So we actually knew everything about Elgar with an intimacy before ever we really played a note. Then the music becomes a revelation. That's what music is, sort of a map of somebody's psychological line or psyche.

And what do Elgar's psychology, relationships, social and cultural history, etcetera have to do with playing the notes of his piano quintet? Nothing, of course. And everything. You have no way to know what bit of research is going to influence what bit of E-TeamWork. Hence the limit, "More!" And hence the need to reconceive your idea of efficiency from a predictable one-to-one ratio between input and product, to outcomes more nuanced, and (very important!) unpredictable.

Reconceiving

Because each iteration toward closure includes new material, and because an E-Team uses as much of that new material as possible in the next iteration, an E-Team project undergoes constant reconceiving. That's to say, the product itself emerges from the processes of making the emergent product.[8] This injects a note of ambiguity into E-TeamWork. E-Team members must learn to be, not placidly comfortable, but open to the changes that E-TeamWork requires of them. This openness is a product of release and of each team member's confidence in the quality and quantity of preparation (skills, energy, stamina, and given circumstances) s/he brings to the table.

Central to the process of reconceiving, deep listening requires an E-Team to listen to each other in new and scary ways. Deep listening requires you to attend to the discursive meaning of words, but also to the speaker's inner state, motives, and desires. Deep listening means that you histrionically replicate, in your own brain, the brain activity of the person you're listening to. Deep listening means that you feel empathy with ideas and discussion so that the materials enter your mind, not as propositions for debate, but as material for new thoughts and actions.[9]

By reconceiving we mean exactly that: beginning each new iteration as if for the very first time, combining experience and new ideas to *discover* what will happen next. This requires imagination, and a mastery of release that can set it free. We don't mean free to do just any old thing. The freedom here is freedom from pre-conceived notions,[10] freedom to use past experience in new ways, and freedom to follow an impulse. Here's a theater story to illustrate what we mean.

We watched a rehearsal at People's Light, a difficult scene in which a husband and wife attempt to come to an agreement, full of love and hostility, defense and aggression. We saw a clinic on iterative making: The actors ran the scene. The director joined them on the set at the kitchen table. The three artists talked intensely, actors scribbling furiously in their notebooks. The director left the stage, the actors began again. The scene played differently, slightly. Again the intensive conversation, scribbling, etcetera. Then, in the midst of the third iteration, the director left her seat in the house and came to the front of the stage. "Excuse me." A smart director, she paused for a moment to let the actors release from their intense concentration. "I'm sorry to interrupt. But, David, if you'll just go around the table the other way when you jump up?"

David looked at her for a long moment. We could almost see the click in his head. "Yes," he said.

"From the top, please," said the director. "Whenever you're ready." The scene began. David jumped up, went the other way round the table. We had no idea what happened to him or to Joyce, playing his wife, but the scene exploded in a new direction, bringing with it all that had gone before, but gaining a new energy and urgency that grew as the actors felt it, recognized it, welcomed it, and exchanged it in a dance of mutual creativity. Wow! When the scene ended both actors scribbled madly in their books. They were making notes about all the places before and after this scene in which what they learned just now would figure.

We asked the director later, "What happened?"

"I have no idea," she said. "An impulse."

This is an E-Team doing E-TeamWork at its best and most mysterious. Among them these artists had maybe a hundred years of experience, 10 000 hours and then some; all had done months of work researching and inventing given circumstances for this project. As the source of their absolute confidence in themselves and each other, this experience and research supported their willingness to trust the director's "impulse" and act upon it with utter conviction. In this context, what this director called an "impulse" was the polar opposite of unconsidered; it was, rather, a reflexive burst of creative inspiration set free by her hard-won skill at release. The content, "go around the table the other way," issued from 20 plus years of experience directing plays, training as an actor and scenic artist, and a year of intense preparation on given circumstances for this particular play. This was by no means the "impulse" of daily life. This kind and quality of preparation accompanies and supports any creative person, artist, or entrepreneur.

In business, we're not always dealing with outcomes as immediately pliant as live performance. It costs a theater or musical group little to try again, but differently. In creative businesses, ideas, pliable but abstracted from their application, are often the material of brainstorming processes; reconceiving in this case would describe instances in which one team member "builds on" the ideas of others (Sawyer, 2007: 54). Reconceiving functions best when E-Teams find ways to demonstrate their ideas in form or action, rather than abstraction. Engineers at The Boeing Company – yes, we're talking now about making airplanes – call their reconceiving process "trystorming." Trystorming is a clever coupling of brainstorming and prototyping; ideas – even the most outrageous ones – are tried quickly and cheaply, using materials at hand, in physical form. The Boeing Company has even devoted a group of a dozen top-performing mechanics to this task, calling them "The Moonshine Shop." This group has put trystorming to use to help the company, for instance, transform their production process from batch-and-queue to moving assembly lines, resulting in enormous savings. An example of the kind of reconceiving that happens in this group: "How might we use this piece of farming equipment to load airplane seats faster?" (Austin et al., 2007).

Managing collective divergence and convergence, towards closure

As they work iteratively, E-Teams try out a range of ideas in the process of choosing some "keepers." This involves managing processes of divergence and convergence. It means always being willing to try out an idea proposed by a member of the group, and always being willing to let an idea go as it's sifted out or modified. In fact, this rarely happens, as the obsolete idea doesn't exactly disappear. Usually it mixes into the given circumstances and so is still part of the emerging outcome.

E-Teams understand that divergence, or working through many possible ideas, isn't random, and it isn't a "quantity equals quality" game. As opposed to some popular brainstorming theories, the goal here isn't to come up with the most ideas. Rather, the E-Team generates an ongoing stream of ideas out of deep consideration of the project's given circumstances; they seek ideas that contribute to the emerging form. E-TeamWork doesn't make judgments before including an idea; the team assumes that any idea that came up through the given circumstances is a result of deep listening, and of the inherently situated, social nature of their creative actions. The idea's value will become apparent during convergence. The principle here is: all ideas will become part of the final outcome in one way or another. One idea may be prominent at closure, but it includes everything that went before. This is both a difficulty for and a gift to the manager or team leader. As a difficulty it requires constant address to the integration of the team's thought into a coherent whole. The director in our last example took home a sheaf of notes to guide her in accommodating and arranging everything that the new move had affected. As a gift, it means that in an E-Team everyone shares all credit: usually no one can tell to whom an idea originally belonged. The manager does everything s/he can to maintain that state of affairs. "That was my idea," has no place in E-TeamWork.

E-TeamWork, being iterative, involves cycles of divergence and convergence. Over time, an E-Team will (often tacitly) converge on a shared agreement that further innovation will degrade rather than improve the product.[11]

We've mentioned the need for E-Team members to prepare themselves to work in uncertain conditions. As they become experienced in this kind of work, the form of the process begins to help them adjust to ambiguity. First, the team internalizes the fact of working toward an emergent outcome. They develop an attitude of curiosity, rather than anxiety, about outcomes. And as they complete a few projects they begin to reconceive their ideas of efficiency and success. Looking back on a successful process, they see that the outcome, while unpredictable in process, turned out to be inevitable. We can turn again to athletes for wisdom: Contemplating a win or a loss they know that "What should have happened, did."

Producing Innovation (Like It or Not)

It should be clear by now that E-TeamWork produces innovation as a natural outcome. The difficulty here is that no one can tell exactly what the outcome will be. After all, if you can predict it, how new is it? If there's a designated customer, the best way to ensure customer satisfaction is to include the customer on the team. If an E-Team seeks new products, it may be wise to include an engineer and a marketing specialist on the team, not to limit the scope of team work, but to keep their departments abreast of what's happening. Their experience with the E-Team becomes given circumstances out of which they can develop ideas about what to do with new things in the pipeline. And, they too must reconceive the idea of efficiency, as there's no telling what will emerge, and how much new thinking it will require.

On the other hand, there are plenty of business situations in which unpredictable innovation is contra-indicated, in which a lack of coherence among intention, input, and outcome is potentially harmful. Or, an innovation may not find an immediate use or viable market. So what if it's beautifully made and greater than the sum of its parts: either the firm or the market may not be ready. At this point, more new concepts of efficiency come into play. Team leaders, managers, and budget makers must learn to take a long view, and the firm must find ways to accommodate a stockpile of not-quite-ready for the market products that might come in handy some day.

E-Team Leadership

Leading E-TeamWork requires special practices. E-Teams do not achieve the perfect creation as a result of being directed by a solo vision, but by creating harmony out of many visions. Leaders of E-Teams hold a vision for the perfection of the process rather than the perfection of their own (or the boss's) idea.

To return to the practice of release, a good leader will direct energy and attention rather than specify outcomes. Like the theater director from our example, a good leader aims, then "steps back" to see what happens, and carries on with another E-Team practice, deep listening. Jazz legend Miles Davis offers an elegant example of this. He leads groups of musicians by aiming their attention, through the focused energy of his own attention, reinforcing choices as they are made and creating space for others to take the lead (Austin and Størmer, 2008).

Working with quite different materials – time-sensitive and expensive molten glass – artist Dale Chihuly practices release while directing teams of artisans to make complex, large-scale sculptures. Chihuly begins a making process by sketching his idea on paper and presenting it to the team as an inspiration, not a blueprint, for the sculpture. (You can watch videos of this process online.[12]) The self-directed team interprets the sketch in their own way, expands or contracts in membership to suit the task, and sets to work. Everyone is exactly where needed at the right time, responding in the moment to the dictates of the glass form as it emerges, and reacting quickly in moments of near-crisis to keep the process on track. Chihuly meanwhile observes from the edges, sometimes interjecting direction, often making drawings in response to the team's work, but rarely interfering with the work. When a master craftsman on the team makes a decision mid-process to veer from the original drawing, Chihuly stays out of his way. The result: a one-of-a-kind sculpture emerges, a thing beyond Chihuly's sketched anticipation. And he, by now, has a new sketch ready.[13]

E-Team leaders don't just get out of the way of their team. They also help clear the way for the team to do its work, whether that means providing needed resources or protecting them from un-useful constraints. E-Team members might take on leadership tasks to free up their colleagues to do more important or difficult work in the moment. For instance, if a colleague's total attention is required to perform a technically complex task, or if s/he's working at the edge of known abilities to try something new, the best leadership response is to free up as much of that team member's capacity as possible.[14]

Leadership within an E-Team may not be an assigned role, as this last practice suggests. Sharing and spontaneously passing leadership among members, as the expert ensemble musicians do (Blum, 1986; Austin and O'Donnell, 2007; Austin and Størmer, 2008), has two effects beneficial to E-TeamWork: (1) every member expects, at any moment, to take the lead; this raises the quality of their preparation and attention; (2) in line with the process of reconceiving, no one goes on autopilot, following a fixed leader, but rather responds to each leadership action with a new action that in itself can "lead" the group to a next action. In this way, E-Teams achieve that second critic's definition of "ensemble" – a set of dynamic voices in conversation with one another; "harmony, not homogeny."

PART III: CONCLUSION

E-Teams collaborate to create innovation. To "collaborate," they use the particular methods that make up E-TeamWork, methods we've practiced for years, and recently, in a multi-case research project, observed in use by groups such as performing arts ensembles, product design teams, software developers, and production process engineers. Because they rely on their given circumstances and deep listening to each other to generate new ideas, E-Teams respond adeptly to new information in their environment, be it customer input, new resource constraints, or commercial opportunities. Everything serves as a source of ideas and inspiration. The work of an E-Team is highly interdependent, and its actions emerge from the collective context, giving products a high degree of internal coherence and outward appeal, whether or not the world is ready for the innovation. E-Teams offer us a new concept of "efficiency" as well: while there may be no end of preparation, special capabilities enable team members to get right down to work and to converge around a "perfect" outcome, often, amazingly, on time and under budget (Austin and Devin, 2003).

With our new terminology in mind, we can next refine our understanding and search out the boundaries of E-TeamWork by looking for examples of E-Teams in other industries than those we've studied so far, in other constellations, and at other levels of the organization. Researchers at Harvard Business School, for instance, are investigating how entrepreneurs in the sustainable cities industry engage in collective processes of strategy making in groups that look to us mighty like E-Teams: In the case studied, goal formation emerges from a social, iterative process in which group members pool their experiences and resources to identify opportunities, build on one another's ideas, and continually reconceive the best way forward (Zuzul and Edmondson 2011). Other questions to occupy us: How do E-Teams form? Can we find examples of E-Teams operating in geographically distributed or networked conditions? What about open innovation communities or cases of crowdsourcing? And reflecting back on our need for a better language for talking about the ways in which teams of people work together, are there other degraded terms we might declare as solvable problems?

NOTES

1. For an overview of this progress, see Austin and Devin (2010).
2. People's Light is a medium sized regional theater that employs 50 or 60 full time artists and others, together with about 200 guest artists in a year, and reaches an audience of about 65 000 on an annual budget of US$5.5 million.
3. We condense these two examples based on the opinions of case informants; the second example is based on the collaborative approach of the Guarneri String Quartet, as described by members in David Blum (1986: 3–4).
4. Lee experienced an interesting occasion of this principle, about a hundred years ago when he was in high school. Listening to the rest of the cast whine about boring rehearsals and wish impatiently for Opening Night, he suddenly realized, "What are they bitching about? I *like* rehearsing." Not long after he took this as a suggestion about a career choice.
5. Mind fundamentals are synonymous with the concept of "mindfulness" from social psychology (Langer, 1989), which includes bringing one's complete attention to the present moment and being sensitive to the context in which one thinks and acts. The Western practice of mindfulness is inspired by Buddhist teachings.
6. Shannon has worked with a particular method for practicing this, taught by resident members of the Shakespeare & Company in Lenox, Massachusetts. Actors are asked to begin by identifying their own emotional state in the moment (itself a challenging task), and rather than determining the emotion is irrelevant to the work and blocking it, allowing that emotion – sadness, anger, joy, desire – to be a departure point for the work. Actors who engage in this practice commonly discover that once the emotion is expressed as part of the work, the experience introduces new opportunities, and the emotion quickly transforms into other relevant emotions as the work proceeds.
7. See Weick's theory of organizing (1979) for further discussion of this phenomenon.
8. We consider our description of the situated action involved in reconceiving and the emergent nature of the outcomes of E-TeamWork related to the process-oriented descriptions of organizational becoming. For instance, Tsoukas and Chia (2002) argue that organizations continually emerge from processes of organizing. Orlikowski

(2002: 249) describes organizational knowing as "an ongoing social accomplishment, constituted and reconstituted . . . in practice."

9. The current research into "mirror neurons," that area in the brain where this histrionic replication takes place has a good deal to teach E-Team members and managers. See Rizzolatti and Craighero (2004) for an overview.

10. Keith Sawyer also reports that improvisational performers describe the practice of "close" or "deep" listening as listening free of pre-conceived ideas regarding the outcome (2007: 46–7).

11. Lee once acted in a commercial shot by a collaboration between a cameraman and a director. The two worked out an elaborate tracking shot full of swoops and curves for the 30 second bit. The Robert Altmans of commercials. Together they made take after take, each iteration the result of conversation and careful tinkering. The actors were not a part of this collaboration: their job was merely to be perfect every time. Thirty seconds is a long time to be perfect. Finally, after about 4 hours, this dialogue:

DIRECTOR:	I can't think of anything more to do with this sucker. Can you?
CAMERAMAN:	Nope. We'd just mess it up.
DIRECTOR:	All right. *To the actors.* Thank you all, that's if for today. Let's work together again, sometime.
ACTORS:	Phew!

12. See, for example, 'Masters of Venice,' 'Potatoes + Bamboo' and 'Working with Pino', available at http://www.chihuly.com/video-putti-interview.aspx (accessed 10 June 2011).

13. Shannon O'Donnell further described this process in, 'Organizing the Creative Crowd for Innovation', *Advisor*, Boston: Cutter Consortium, 2010. Note the similarity with the theater work: the director doesn't do any acting; she leads people who do something she can't. Chihuly doesn't dash around doing the ten things at once it takes to make a piece of glass.

14. This kind of leadership is described by the Guarneri String Quartet violinist Arnold Steinhardt in Blum (1986).

17 Organizing reality machines: artepreneurs and the new aesthetic enlightenment
Pierre Guillet de Monthoux

FROM ENTREPRENEURS TO ARTEPRENEURS

How do contemporary artists act as entrepreneurs? How do they accomplish the practical tasks involved in undertaking art projects and how do they organize in order to insure success for their enterprises? This chapter listens to contemporary artists to identify how they navigate in the art world as organizing entrepreneurs. In addition it examines the change in the world's perception of artists when they step into the role of entrepreneur.

Many have explored the role of entrepreneurs who make art work as an enterprise. A common view is that we have artists to thank for putting some play, reverie, and pleasure into our deadly serious everyday world! Their enterprises inject the unexpected, the spontaneous, the poetic, and the graceful into the normally dull seriousness of our orderly realities. That is why using the terms entrepreneur and artist together is no longer considered ambiguous, contradictory or even absurd to those who earlier looked upon art as something exotic and marginal to economic development.

Some managerial gurus of corporate worlds look at artists as entrepreneurs of irrationality and the silly enterprise of art as a profitable escape from the dull bureaucracy that bogs down corporate creativity (Gustafsson, 2011). During the past decade especially, terms like "experience economy" and "creative class" have helped shape a new corporate awareness, one where artists are the ones untangling the red tape inhibiting profitable take off into the visionary skies of real success. As a consequence, well-known artists who used to be commissioned to decorate corporate headquarters are now invited to serve on company boards (Ullrich, 2000). This corporate habit of seeing artists as entrepreneurs, similar to the custom of feudal kings' appointing artists to their courts, is primarily motivated by the desire to inject artistic passion into businesses to make them tick faster, better, and bolder. The hope is that an artist-entrepreneur can lubricate old corporate organizations to deliver more of the same but at a considerably cheaper and faster rate. Surely an artist will be more fun to work with and certainly cheaper than advertisers or other creative professionals. Such artist-entrepreneurs should make "the experience economy" boom: they are the "creative class" adding value as "product designers" in globalized "creative industries." And besides, if the state cannot provide artists with grants and commissions, artists had better quickly transform into self-supporting entrepreneurs.

So goes the mainstream capitalist discourse of how art and economy interact when artists are entrepreneurs. If this account is correct or incorrect, if it is good or bad, is of no concern to this chapter. We are after another story, the story of entrepreneurs told by the artist and circulated in the art world.

Many young artists seem increasingly engaged in the construction of new organizations less geared to applying art to business than making new organizations serve art; such artists are more *artepreneurs* than entrepreneurs. They take charge of their own instrumentality in the service of self-selected goals. Let us explore the genesis of *artepreneurship* and see how organizational awareness makes a radical difference to the old artist-entrepreneur figure.

THE WAKE OF ARTEPRENEURSHIP

Art as Organizing

Here is not the place to analyse the complex economic–political context of the last decade of the last millennium that began to accommodate the marriage of art and enterprise in mainstream capitalism. The late Swedish pop art collector and businessman Torsten Lilja, one of the early and passionate spokesmen for the artist-entrepreneur, recalled that his artist friend Christo Javacheff was originally resistant to being labeled an "entrepreneur." Lilja was a hardcore businessman while Christo, with roots in the anti-commercial Soviet avant-garde, had seen the backside of communist Romania. Christo therefore was far from coveting a place among the heroes of capitalism, a designation assigned to "entrepreneurs." When during the late 1980s Christo became more at ease with being called an "entrepreneur," he began to adapt the raw idea of a capitalistic entrepreneur to a novel ethos of artepreneurship. Christo's whole rhetoric since the wrapping of the Berlin Reichtag in 1995 transcends simplistic entrepreneurship. He prides himself on being the authentic self-made artist, one who organized a self-financed piece of public art completely independent of tax money. He repeatedly emphasizes that he paid helpers regular market wages and never exploited voluntary work. And up to this point what he does appears to be textbook entrepreneurship.

His inclusion of ecological arguments, however, makes his work far more socio-politically correct (Guillet de Monthoux, 2008). Waste was to be avoided, for example, and all wrapping material was recycled. Eventually he promised never to institutionalize his project and to terminate his temporary installation at a stipulated date. Christo's discourse is always geared to the public good. The hardware content of his enterprise was to give "a pure aesthetic experience" with "no strings attached" to the general public (Guillet de Monthoux, 2006). The context, or the software as Christo put it, was his and his partner Jeanne Claude's ability to lobby and convince audiences, critics, politicians, technicians, and the media of the public necessity to let their visions come true materially as a public event for a short moment. Christo always presents himself as totally sensitive to political organizing. He has always been an artepreneur in the bud!

In the mainstream story of art and economy told and retold during the 1990s, artists like a Jeff Koons, Andy Warhol, or Damien Hirst starred as heroic entrepreneurs cleverly providing better motivation for business activities. In Lilja's case the Christos' success story certainly helped boost the value of the Torsten Lilja collection of pop art. This also seems to be the dominant motivation for the majority of chatters on the art and aesthetics website Aacorn, an initiative evolving from the time when artists caught the interest of business as hero-entrepreneurs early in this millennium.[1] Still neither Christo, Warhol nor Hirst completely fit the entrepreneurial ideology of the invisible hand. They were hardly children of the libertarian market. What was instead admired and reported was their skill in organizing for art to work as they really wished. Performing arts such as symphonic music, classical theatre, and the ballet had always been a matter of organization, but now visual artists like Andy Warhol, ex-commercial advertising artist, gained celebrity status in the art world as the charismatic manager of a "factory" and a smart organizer of its "public relations" and "communication strategies." Christo's systematic ways of managing the physical constructions of his installations became as famous as his wrappings. From the vague idea of the individual artist entrepreneur slowly emerged an awareness of artepreneurs as solid constructors of social communication and art organizations.

Andy Warhol with his early affirmation of "business art" (Danto, 1981) and Joseph Beuys with his provocative "Art=Capital" (Beuys, *1992)* were pioneers of an artepreneurial movement that gained momentum in the shadow of the dot.coms and start-ups of the "new economy." Flexible software enterprises on the volatile markets of creative economies replaced the heavy hardware factories run by unimaginative and hopelessly materialistic managers (Austin and Devin, 2002). Artists with a special skill in pitching a new science fiction to investors found employment as vendors and advisers. An army of artists joined forces with other financial trick-sters in pumping up values as big business balloons. By the millennium shift, economic actors hailed as artist entrepreneurs and management, business and leadership were all redefined as the noble art of making something out of nothing.

Artists as Realists

After the bubble burst – when a Christo painting hit the million dollar col-lectors' mark in 2004 during the Gates show in Central Park, New York – some artists became the few surviving profiteers of a dead new economy. In short time most artists hired by the telecom start-ups and IT dot.coms to dream up new applications for existing technology became redundant. The climate switched from "vision, vision, vision" to new harder times of "hunt, kill, and eat."

Inside the art world, ironically tainted commentary about the imagination-fetishism of artist-entrepreneurs emerged. It was an observa-tion heralding the rise of the artepreneur out of the ashes of the bankrupt artists-entrepreneur. In 2003 artist Alexandra Mir published her complete documentation of this critical movement from the entrepreneurial to the artepreneurial (Mir, 2003). Mir accounts for several artworks heckling the corporate mentalities dominating the relation of art and business during the 1990s. They poke fun at all the talk of business enterprises as art of creativity, vision and newness. As Mir was investigating art as enterprise, she also discovered a critical movement having little in common with traditional anti-capitalism. What she documents brilliantly is a subversive avant-garde irony targeting the discourse of creative industries and experi-ence economy. Mir lines up several artists who invent business structures and then puts their virtual corporations on display. We see brands like Ingold Airlines, an airline that never flies, or Bonk Business, Inc. (Guillet de Monthoux, 2003), a firm with an impressive but completely fictitious centenary business history documented in fake photos, product models, films, and letters displayed in contemporary art museums. This movement was full of aesthetic humor in the spirit of Marcel Duchamp's imaginary but typical bourgeois lady Rose Sélavie. Dada made funny statements about the absurdity of bourgeois seriousness, Cubism made crystal clear the square flatness of representation, and Surrealism turned the Freudian subconsciousness behind human action into colorful cartoons! In the old tradition of creating poignant puns about bourgeois existence, the artwork of the "corporate mentalities" now poked fun at the new dematerialized economy escaping reality into the dream worlds of empty symbols and void brands. These irony-enterprises were practical jokes to be exposed at art shows. They mirrored capitalist formalisms, poses, and attitudes, all sorts of immaterial value making that corporations had hired artist entrepreneurs to help them out with during the "new economy."

Where the old avant-garde, like Bolshevik Constructivism, anarchist Situationism or fascist Futurism, would have agitated for subversive assaults on capitalism, the irony-enterprises' attack of "corporate mentalities" emerged inside an entrepreneurial capitalism. Now there seemed to be no outside position from which to wage a radical war on capital. The only remaining utopia was the same capitalist dream world for which some artist entrepreneurs had acted as top management consultants. This occurred of course not long after 1989 when the Berlin wall, the main symbol of a possibly clear frontier between culture and commerce, crumbled, and in the shadow of this Big Bang of Communism the idea of a final victory of global capitalism still enjoyed the benefit of the doubt! In this situation Mir spots the only critical position left: that of the candid kid in Hans Christian Andersen's tale about the Emperor's new clothes. To exclaim "But he is naked" becomes an aesthetic-ethic gesture, a radical turn to the real as the core of the artepreneurial.

Incorporated Art Firms

The new millennium opened with the 9/11 Big Bang of Capitalism. In 2003 during an art show in Zurich, Dr Dagmar Reichert and artist Michelangelo Pistoletto made an intuitive attempt to grasp what is here called an artepreneur.[2] They explicitly addressed a dilemma at the heart of the irony-enterprise movement. Their show "Critique is not enough" pointed to the need to breach the traditional avant-garde outsider attitude. Pistoletto had long been experimenting collectively with ways of organizing "socially responsible art." His oeuvre as well as that of his friends Christo, Warhol, and Beuys grew out of dissatisfaction with art isolated in art institutions or used as occasionally witty poignant puns about society. From the outset Pistoletto's experiments took a distinctly artepreneurial route. He contended that artists had to tear down the illusion of their comfortable outside position and realize their projects in society. As impressionist painters left their ateliers for real nature, artepreneurs of the new millennium should move out of their isolated institutions and reconnect to society. This conviction even led Pistoletto to abandon the successful pop artist crew in New York and return to Europe to stage street art and collective performances with neighbors and friends in the communities where he lived.

This was art in a completely different spirit than that of the 1990s when artist entrepreneurs offered dreams and visions in service of blowing hot air into the IT bubble. A decade later, it does not seem that artists, maybe with the exception of Damien Hirst who allegedly made an insider attempt to rig market values for auctions of his own pieces (Lewis, 2009), have been any more instrumental in recent financial bubbles.

Since the 1990s, however, artepreneurs have gradually discovered ways to take part in economy without being instrumentalized. They have gained an awareness of art as an enterprise in its own right, an insight that also entails a reflective reassessment of the artists' traditional focus on the market success of their single pieces of art. Now painting, sculpture, or drawing turn from being the output of art as a craft into being the artepreneur's tool to organize art firms. This shift in focus also implies a much more subtle mix of the public and the private.

To Christo for instance the aim is to realize his wrappings. The preparatory work, drawings, models and paintings sell as shares in the temporary installation they represent. The holders of such art work/shares find their private capital increasing as an effect of the public impact of its respective installation. All value created in each single piece of art is thus directly tied to the success of the installation, the performance, the show, or the event to which it refers.

This art firm strategy was already obvious in the way Christo early operated, and Torsten Lilja, then CEO of a company selling plastic, became so impressed that he reinvested his whole fortune in pop art. In the 1970s Lilja had already been deeply impressed by Andy Warhol's business art and had, of course, commissioned a collection of Warhol's Polaroid screen-print portraits.

Subsequently Lilja made friends with Christo and early in the new millennium, his son Bob, now firmly established as a Swiss private banker, took over as his financial advisor. Lilja realized that the market value of his private art collection depended on the public success of the art firm called Christo Corporation.

Pistoletto, another artepreneur pioneer, started out as the only European painter in a group of US pop artists made world famous by the legendary Sonnabend Gallery in New York. When he returned to Europe in the 1970s, he freed himself from the gallery and engaged in a new career as an independent artepreneur. For a while he was a professor at the Vienna Art Academy, and then he and his partner, artist Maria Pioppi, began to establish their version of the art firm. They bought and renovated rundown textile mills in Biella, Italy, and created the Cittadellarte Pistoletto Foundation, which performs a mix of art education and experimental work actively involving not only young artists but also urban planners, philosophers, managers, curators, consultants, and politicians.

While Christo's installations involve the audience, technicians, and critics as actors in the final art show, Pistoletto's Cittadellarte houses a multitude of self-financed activities and works year round. Cittadellarte is light years away from just being an ironic artist's funny blueprint of a crazy business. He has created his own art firm in Biella and makes every effort day in and day out to secure support for it from a multitude of sources. He seizes every opportunity, expected or unexpected, to generate changes inside constantly evolving networks. Cittadellarte cooperates in projects ranging from Venice Biennales to Illy coffee campaigns, and Pistoletto arranges encounters between Milano fashion and Biella textile industries. He attracts students sponsored by their respective ministries of culture worldwide and stimulates local Biella manufacturers to market their products globally.

Such art firms seem to develop in non-linear ways over many years, and it is far from a trivial or easy step to move from the back of the easel as an artist entrepreneur into the role of an artepreneur heading a multitasked organization with global operations like Fondazione Pistoletto or Christo Corporation (Guillet de Monthoux, 2004).[3] The organizing of an art firm is a constant struggle to secure new independence from unmet and new dependencies. This makes artepreneurship seen from the inside a windingly obscure and social creative process far from the naïve and simplistic success stories of artists as entrepreneurs. As we shall see, being an artepreneur is not an explicit choice but a process of slow evolution.

BECOMING AN ARTEPRENEUR . . .

. . . By Coincidence

Autobiographical narratives of how single artists navigate provide us with an honest inside account of this process (Scherdin, 2007).[4] A Swedish art student, landing in art school after dropping out of a PhD program in management, for instance, gets excited about managing visual experiments with video cameras and TV screens in the media lab of his school. This story starts back in 1996, when broadband and streaming were still pretty unheard of in Scandinavia. While our student is hooked on performing his video art experiences à la Nam June Paik, he also realizes the urgent need for better tech resources to scale up his small experiment. His ambition is clear. He wants "doing digital art" immediately real-time online to a big audience on big public screens. However, he can neither communicate nor sell his idea to those who have not experienced the same intensive "flow" of doing video art. He has to make people experience what he feels, for his project is inherently presentational and not discursive (Ramirez, 1991). As he puts it, to make a dream real you have to embed the idea in an organization of kindred spirits.

This single artist then depicts his project as upscaling his playful school experiment for wide public use. His dream is to lease big screens for online real-time video art to all public art museums and maybe even to other state schools throughout Sweden. He toys with cool logos and brands like "BeeOff," "Radomstudio," calling his vision "a cultural portal," a "DCP, digital content provider," a "Test spot," or "Free channel for art and music." Finally and reluctantly – for artists in business were then mostly frowned upon in art circles – he registers as a Swedish limited liability stock company under the name of "Splintermind, Inc.," and his art firm is incorporated.

A question still remains, however. Is it his good European artist-identity, firmly rooted in the Kantian idea of art as the maker not of markets but of public organization, that makes him totally focused on securing public partnership and tax-financed resources? Is it this traditional artist's ambition that brings him into endlessly winding corridors of Swedish public cultural administration? Even though he asks for official help to put his ideas at the service of the general public, he cannot help feeling exploited. He understands that in reality he is just an unpaid keynote entertainer at the public seminars he gets invited to. He spends most of his work hours presenting ideas to public IT committees led by bored civil servants without a clue about what IT is about. They seem to enjoy his pitches, but much to his despair they postpone and ignore his applications. After two long years of analysis paralysis, the Swedish administration refuses to supply the money necessary to match the big sum of money granted to him in 2003 by the European Commission in Brussels – on the condition of just such a match. The very same public agency that tipped him off about the Brussels grant ultimately deep-sixes his idea by rejecting his application. In 2005, nine years after he originally got hooked on video art at school, his company Splintermind, Inc. went bankrupt. The student left art and quite fortunately receives a scholarship to pursue a doctorate at his old business school.

A couple of years later he completes an auto-ethnographic art practice-based dissertation that primarily focuses on his bitter experience with public agencies that kick out artists who take the public demand for artists-entrepreneurs seriously. It is a fascinating story, but mostly for its blind spots. While making visible the public "invisible foot" that kept kicking him out, he strangely misses the private "invisible hand" that actually helped. This artist might have failed as an entrepreneur, and a lot of data would support that, but it takes some close reading to reconstruct the information of another story, one pointing out how hard it might be to gain awareness and face the facts of artepreneurship.

The dissertation also candidly relates how in 1998 engineers from a Swedish public Telecom Administration research lab approached him. And here the irony sets in. As difficult as it was for him to get public money when he sought it, how easy it was now to obtain development orders from the Telecom engineers! They brought him expensive equipment, all the time expressing an active interest in the art events staged in the factory building he got gratis from the city of Stockholm on the recommendation of these engineers. When he received an explicit request from the Telecom accountants he founded his company to legally keep track of the resources poured into the art project, and the engineers seemed honestly interested in his ideas of "online" art. It was, he suspects, less for the cool crowded space always full of arty geeks than for the real life testing ground for their new technology. The endeavor did seem to have worked well both as an art studio and a science lab. Through its international connections the studio also helped them keep track of what happened with similar art applications for new cable technologies throughout the world.

Had it not been for the IT industry the idea would have remained in art school. When the IT bubble burst, however, it was not immediately over for the project. For five more years it dragged on in increasingly desperate attempts to make public agencies assume their alleged responsibility and take over financing. Since they had never supported the project in the first place, they now refused to back it up when the private partner backed out. All of this testifies to the point brought out about the strange and mysterious ways state and local bureaucracies block well-intentioned attempts to offer good art to the people.

On the surface this tale resembles the disheartening story of a poor artist Josef K. in the Kafkaesque Castles of national and European Cultural Politics. These struggles in fact seem typical for artists traditionally defining their audiences as the "people," and it just as typically ends in disappointment with "public" institutions that hypocritically pay only lip service to their good ideas. As his dream to become a "hero-entrepreneur" was crushed, our artist might have dressed his project up as an "irony enterprise." Maybe self-pity prevents him from seeing his story from the funny side, so here it is: "end of the entrepreneurial story."

. . . By Education

While the "Splintermind" project survived for almost nine long years from 1996 to 2005, it is important to note that other things were happening as well. The scattered bits and pieces of a different arteperneurial story were

largely left untold in the wake of the eloquent complaint about the entrepreneurial failure. Christo, once asked to comment on his many failed
wrapping projects, simply muttered that he regretted not being "intelligent
enough."

A knowledge and awareness of what is involved in becoming an
artepreneur requires deliberate reflection, and increasingly this type of
reflection is supported by the contemporary art schools that switch from
promoting the oversimplified cliché of artists as misunderstood entrepreneurs to investigating the practical implications of what we here label
artepreneurship.

In 2004 a Harvard Business Review article by Daniel Pink claims the
new MBA to be a Master of Fine Art, and understandably this immediately caught the attention of both the business and the art worlds. At
Harvard Business School, Professor Robert Austin had just been given
the specific assignment of creating a MBA teaching module based on cases
from the arts and crafts. Some effective art cases, including those about
Christo, already existed at HBS, but they had no explicit focus on art and
artists. Austin now directed his attention to what he called "organizational
art," and in some mindful business schools, similar ideas helped roll the
ball even faster and in rather different directions in the art world. Artists
themselves were now slowly forming new identities as artepreneurs!

In 2002, in the aftermath of the new economy, US art professor Ronald
Jones pointed out that real change might best be stimulated by smaller
European art schools (Artforum, 2002). A book documenting Germany's
Städel Schule, specifically mentioned by Jones, provides insider details for
roughing out a tentative self-portrait of this new artepreneur.

Städel professor and American artist John Baldessari begins the insider
look by pointing out that tuition-free European art education makes
students less burdened by debt and therefore more open to risk taking
(Belzer and Birnbaum, 2007). Also worth emphasizing here is the fact that
Städel Schule, funded mainly by the city of Frankfurt-am-Main, opted
out of the Bologna University system that threatens to make European
higher education conform to a US model of "income maximization"
under a new banner of "employability." At the Städel neither "exchange"
nor "transactions" nor even "art prices," classical terms associated with
the artist-entrepreneur, were perceptible. The Städel seemed more interested in how "gifts" or "hospitality" could be performed and enacted as
artwork. Rector Daniel Birnbaum, an international curator-critic and also
the author of a philosophical thesis on Edmond Husserl, "The Hospitality
of Presence" (Birnbaum, 1998) provided "good life" reflections, and art
students began asking how can art make "a good life" come true instead
of the standard "what is art" or "what is beauty."

. . . By Curating

Further consideration of the path to artepreneurship now made clear that wellbeing and welfare should not be confused with vague "feel-good" responses or "wellness." Artepreneurs do not share dated hippy dreams of art schools as "alternative" utopias of freedom or tolerance. Instead a real art school encourages students to get inside the real world and face all of its constraints and conflicts. Rector Birnbaum makes it clear that he dreams of a school that is a mix of monastery and bazaar, one that provides the practical skills necessary for intelligently navigating the deep shark-filled waters of art worlds. How should an artepreneur react when collectors want to put her under their long-term contracts? To what extent is it worthwhile to follow all the whims of curators and gallerists? How can artepreneurs negotiate their positions in worlds where freedom is always relative and contingent?

These practical questions imply no theoretical shortcuts. For example, students must familiarize themselves with real-world practices of curating. And to that end, the Städel houses Porticus, one of Frankfurt's most famous small galleries. Art students are given a chance to experience the practice of making and curating real art shows, and thanks to the international reputation of Porticus, they also have the opportunity of exchanging ideas with the many established artepreneurs hanging out at the school while they are preparing exhibitions. What artist entrepreneurs usually left to gallerists and art dealers must be mastered and integrated in arteprenurial practice.

Art critic Pamela M. Lee cites a 2004 Porticus show where contemporary artists Pierre Huyghe and Rirkrit Tiravanija staged an encounter with some of Gordon Matta-Clark's legendary work from the early seventies (Lee, 2007). Students here got to participate in and gain direct inside experience with the complex organizational exercise involved in performing art and releasing its impact on audiences and critics. How is creation interwoven with interpretation? Young artepreneurs get this insight into a kind of plurivocal hermeneutics of action by participating in curating.[5] What Joseph Beuys prophetically alluded to when talking about art as "social sculpture" has now, almost half a century later, also found its philosophical articulation in Nicolas Bourriaud's "relational aesthetics" (Bourriaud, 2001). Students at Städel experience this in their artepreneurship laboratory Porticus. In the case of the Matta-Clark show, they do it under the curating leadership of an artist that inspired Bourriaud's work, Rirkrit Tiravanija. Lee plays up the fact that such an experience conveys an understanding for "the conceptual impossibility of an unmediated aesthetic translation from the past . . . acknowledging that the repetition of an artistic gesture over time constitutes an act of difference, not sameness" (Lee, 2007: 244).

. . . By Socializing

The exercise of remaking and reenacting old projects sensitizes artepreneurs in a way similar to what copying the old masters did in the old art curricula. To copy a work of art raises awareness about its original meaning and forces students to insert the piece into a contemporary framework in order to have it make sense. Today it is not the piece of art that is copied but its process. The organizational reenactment of a performance or installation makes it clear

> that a community involved in the production of a work of art is always social and socializing but in itself *inessential*. Now when I use the word "inessential" to describe these social operations I do not mean negligible or irrelevant, but indeterminate. . . . The question is how a work of art emerges out of this constellation of inessential social forces. (Lee, 2007: 245)

As art and society penetrate each other and then intertwine, such problems become points of departure for reflections on an artepreneurship now also taught differently.

At one time, art academy students began by sharing a crowded common studio, and it was only after years of study that the studio got less and less crowded. Finally upon graduating they were told they had reached the top. And while this was the classical way to prepare the artist as entrepreneur, the individual – though at the top – felt more as if she were at the bottom of society. Artists believed they were loners lost in a hostile and alien world and had been kicked out of an academy to which they longed to return.

This process has long been criticized, and Birnbaum suggests that this individual model blocks the social knowledge needed for artepreneurship. Such knowledge cannot be transferred by assigning "passwords" to students. Contrary to monetary capital, the social capital that helps integrate art with society will be destroyed if it is managed as individual property, for it is both produced and shared in a cooperative experience. Art critic Jan Verwoert expresses this fundamental insight for artepreneurs: "Experience and knowledge . . . ought to be understood not as possessions and capital but primarily as social relations. And the mission of the academy would be to produce experiences by provoking illuminating relations" (Verwoert, 2007: 102).

At the core is the idea of experience and its meaning. Respect for this kind of knowledge can only be conveyed if teachers share their experience and leave behind the model of knowledge as information to single individuals. Such considerations also make an artepreneur respectful of the embodiment of knowledge and the importance of sensual knowledge (Strati, 1999). The implication of course is that learning about "aesthetics" is only possible in social interaction.

. . . By Singularity

The artepreneur must also distance herself from both the heroic and ironic postures of the old idea of art as enterprise. It is no wonder that to artist Tobais Rehberger the first task of a Städel professor is to deconstruct new students' obsolete clichés of artists (Belzer and Birnbaum, 2007). The hero-entrepreneur role model he once received from his own master Martin Kippenberger is obsolete. Without a doubt Kippenberger was generous and engaged, but his "presence" was so strong that the class became "sect like," with everyone trying to imitate the master who taught "by constantly trash[ing] everything and tell[ing] you how stupid you were." That kind of eccentricity verging on egocentricity resonates with the old myth of the artistic genius, one having no place in a contemporary art school.

The Städel debate is utterly critical of seeing individual creativity as the main competence of "good life" artists. However this is not a plea for collectivism or compromised consensus. Instead Jan Verwoert suggests we develop a fine feeling for the difference between good and bad bohèmes.

> With respect to the good life, the good Bohème differs from the bad one perhaps precisely in that the good one involves humor, and the pose is truly cultivated and celebrated as a means of social exchange, while in the bad one everyone attempts to assert his own pose, with great seriousness, as the only authentic one against those of the others. This humor, which implies an intuitive awareness of how I use my pose to set up a stage on which others can present themselves in an equally singular fashion, is perhaps the principle of urban attitude in general. (Verwoert, 2007, p. 102)

Artists are of little use as artepreneurs if they are isolated single heroes, even if they are able to survive hard competition. What happens to the artepreneur is less important than what she makes others do. The old entrepreneur is more of a Darwinian survivor while the artepreneur is someone who triggers processes by boldly

> putting a claim on the table, a provocation that puts out for anyone to see what might be at stake in this social situation. In the good pose, it is not merely an ego that is exposed but equally the spirit of the moment; the mood of the evening as well as the philosophy of those that have congregated. The bad

social pose lacks the social intuition. It is arrested in obtuse self-reference. (Verwoert, 2007, p. 102)

The hesitance towards simple subjectivity and the hope of developing an education fostering singularities of artepreneurship seem central to the new art school.

One of Pistoletto's projects is the creation of a party called "Love Difference," which is a sort of singularity campaign that acknowledges singularity as training one's sensitivity to differences. It could be about our perceptions of time, for instance, or our varying rhythms of work. Artists believing in universal ways of being and working are easy prey to paralyzing paranoia when they witness the creativity of others and lack their own inspiration. Not only must there be a tolerance for many different ways of working, but at Städel the old idea that artist-entrepreneurs must necessarily focus on one project at a time is also questioned. Städel sees the relevance of artepreneurs' learning from architects who constantly juggle many projects at a time and develop a strange competence Professor Mark Wigley defines as the ability to

> combine many, many things that don't belong together. That's the only thing we do as architects. We are simply able to look extraordinary complex problems in the eye and come up with the singular form that can sort of happily accommodate variables that simply don't belong together. (Bettum and Wigley, 2007: 267)

This singular focus also marks an artepreneur's view of art techniques and instruments. The case of the video artist cited earlier shows how an artist might be promoted but is also captured by one single technological development. At Städel there is an ingrained skepticism of ideas of linear technological developments that dictate a rush to the most recent technology. There are, so it goes, no rational reasons for discarding old techniques as obsolete to art. Old techniques might at any time resurface as refreshing means for new ends. How could one otherwise explain the return of good old oil paintings after long periods of concept, performance and installation art, asks Professor Thomas Bayerle. In the same way, a hopelessly locked situation with a series of depressing failures might in the arts unexpectedly emerge in surprising creativity due to mere chance. In consequence then the relevance of "individual creativity" and "newness" and "innovation," the three super-mantras of the old entrepreneurial paradigm, fade away. No technique can be discarded as passé, and no art abandoned to dusty archives can be declared dead, for the artepreneur is trained as a situationist-bricolleur. All instruments are potentially good instruments, and the dusty archives are historical treasure chests for surprising future work.

... By Realism

The old heroic and ironic "art and enterprise" postures were easily co-opted by capitalist and anti-capitalist discourses. Artist heroes like Christo, Andy Warhol, and Joseph Beuys helped forge popular images of entrepreneurs more colorful and cool than those in economics textbooks. "Irony art" was for sure more subtle and bitingly critical than that of old leftist pamphlets. Old "art and enterprise" basically worked as instrumental "attention-grabbers" while the emerging artepreneur helped engage in deeper action-oriented reflections on how art as organization might contribute to society in its own right.

As pointed out earlier, artepreneurs are leaving the dream to reclaim and reconstruct reality. This makes them close to the intellectuals who tackle questions of how ideas get materialized. The old art-and-enterprise heroes preferred to touch only occasionally upon philosophical issues. Sometimes as in the case of philosopher Arthur Danto's prolific writings on Andy Warhol (Danto, 1981) this worked marvels as a trick attracting critics to market art by using it as a vehicle for their own ideas. In the case of Joseph Beuys' anthroposophic roots in German idealism we have an artist almost consciously dissimulating his intellectual references, in part to enhance the strange making effect of art partly hiding away politically incorrect ideas in his time. The artepreneur however is much more explicit about philosophical foundations (Guillet de Monthoux and Sjöstrand, 2003).

The Städel is a good example of a close and productive relationship between philosophers and artists. Here young artepreneurs are exposed to an educational system integrating lectures, round tables, and seminars with regular studio work. Over the years the intellectual side has fused with the more traditional so that critics and philosophers could be considered as coworkers of arteprises in the same way as audiences, technicians and curators fall into position in "art firms" (Guillet de Monthoux, 2004) our art-organizational model in the spirit of Howard Becker's "art worlds" (Becker, 1982). The ground had been well prepared, for rarely did any art show in the 1990s refrain from arranging seminars as intellectual appendices to the main show. Sometimes intellectuals expressed their envy with artists able to aesthetically tackle issues hard to approach by means of traditional texts only (Bourdieu and Haacke, 1995). Many contemporary philosophers, Bruno Latour, Jacques Derrida, and Francois Lyotard to mention the most famous, also opted for the art show as a medium for materializing their ideas into physical reality. Sociologists might have preached social constructivism, but artists made their points load and clear in art practice (Sullivan, 2005).

. . . By Reflection

At Städel this intellectualization of the arteprise is pushed even further by regularly exposing students and faculty to a steady stream of intellectuals (Birnbaum and Graw, 2008). When speaking to students, for example, Luc Boltanski notes that "artistic criticism" of societal problems within capitalism counts even more than "social criticism" did decades ago. Yesterday's managers or politicians talked to social scientists; today they experience criticism in art shows. In his work with Eve Chiapello on "the new spirit of capitalism" (Boltanski and Chiapello, 2006), which soon became a favorite reading of Städel students, Boltanski ascribed contemporary artists an eminent role in influencing new developments of economy and management. No one can ignore the artepreneur's impact on opinion through the media as they capture and amplify the negative "indignation" around social issues as efficiently as the old hero entrepreneur "celebrated" the nice and beautiful sides of a society whose devoted and apologetic servants they were.

To another guest speaker Paulo Virno, workers in contemporary economies are like artist entrepreneurs; some even claim to be laborers of a new "creative class" contributing to "creative industry" capitalism. How then could artists avoid becoming a new proletariat? How could they take their collective destiny in hand as artepreneurs? Focusing on performance artists and the way in which art today is more a process than a product Virno claimed that artists actually have an inherent ability to carve out a niche of new reality in modern economy and work life (Virno, 2002).

A third Städel speaker deeply sensitive to the philosophical turn of contemporary art was Jacques Ranciére (2004b). Artists in Ranciére's argument are active as aesthetic agents who clear the ground for new fields of attention. The main task of artepreneurs can thus be seen as a way to introduce new issues, giving them a voice and a treatment otherwise impossible because of their vagueness and lack of form necessary to be granted attention on a political agenda.[6]

The question of what is special in aesthetic action was explicitly addressed when Georgio Agamben was asked to participate. Agamben offers a slightly different take on the problem of how arteprises can bring new political issues to the agenda. Agamben seemed to position artepreneurial action in a third category situated between the two other instrumental and intentional actions treated by traditional action philosophy. The third kind of action then does not figure out ends, as in intentional acting, or implement tools to realize intended goals. Agamben calls this third non-instrumental and non-intentional action a "Gesture" (Agamben, 2000). What arteprenurs do then is to perform Gestures, thereby making a philosophical commitment to lead the way into realms previously inaccessible in common communication. It is a point common to Giorgio Agamben, Jacques Ranciére, and Nicolas Bourriaud. For Bourriaud the message about "relational aesthetics" can be read as another take on an overall arteprenurial task to organize the real making the tacit, hidden and unarticulated perceptible (Bourriaud, 2001). While the artist entrepreneur makes us dream, the artepreneur wakes us up to new life.

CONCLUSION: ENLIGHTENED ARTEPRENEURS ORGANIZING REALITY MACHINES

This chapter is called "Organizing reality machines," thanks to something Danish artist and artepreneur Olfur Eliasson said in a 2011 lecture. He saw the aim of his artwork as putting the audience in the position of an active observer physically experiencing his installations. The physical experience reveals a sensible reality in sharp contrast to the virtual, the special effects, the symbols and all other artefacts of the capitalist dream factories. Thus what happens in contemporary art museums is much more real than most of what surrounds us in everyday life. The museum is, in Olafur Eliasson's words, a "Reality Machine" where the artepreneur takes on the task of making us return to and rely on our senses. Does artepreneurship then not have a ring of enlightenment?

The old enlightenment according to Immanuel Kant carved out the role of aesthetics in the shaping of a "public realm" (Kant, 1991). Artepreneurship surely wants to open up a public art space; this was the overarching ambition of the Splintermind artepreneur, for example. It is to the extent that artepreneurs aim at aesthetically reclaiming a lost "sensus communis" that they work for enlightenment, and it is important to emphasize that it is a "new" kind of enlightenment.

The newness of aesthetic enlightenment resides in its deletion of the old enlightenment's transcendence according to which the aesthetic reality can help in approximating a sur-real or sub-real truth behind or above what our senses reveal. Senses were only good as ladders to higher truth, and concrete reason was fine as long as it led to abstract rationality in theories or dogmas. If senses were useless as instruments of rationality, they were easily discarded as feelings or affects.

In the old enlightenment there was little room for artepreneurs' organizing reality machines. Artists were regarded as irrational, immature and even irresponsible. This is the purpose of stories of a lazy and dreamy Marcel Duchamp playing chess, a beastly playful Pablo Picasso hanging out at the Corrida, or a lustfully carnal Salvador Dali masturbating behind his easel. The sensual and somatic elements were simply left out, for then dream, play and pleasure were hijacked by the transcendental and raised to the realm of the sacred "fine" arts.

Modern art history is deeply imbued with the idea of a transcendental enlightenment. We see it in the popular accounts of the low, irrational, and crazy avant-garde. Art became reduced to a sentimental safety valve for modern man harshly disciplined by rational order. And this in turn made artists adapt and survive as the last eccentrics elegantly balanced on a dangerously sharp edge between reason and madness. Of course, it would not be long before Freud had to invent therapies to treat the effects of the reappearance of suppressed forces in the lives of well-behaved bourgeoisie. And from the modern perspective, it also makes sense that Freud was an art collector and connoisseur! Art became the irrational leftover of a rational society where artists as entrepreneurs occasionally find cracks in the walls of reason through which they can pollute the world order with their flipped-out ideas.

So let us summarize. Investigating artists as entrepreneurs led to the discovery of the artepreneur living in the aftermath of modernity. The artepreneur has to navigate both public and private waters and must cope with new dependencies in order to negotiate his independence. The visit to the art school reveals questions that preoccupy artepreneurs, and the brief portrayal of the intellectuals they communicate with shows an ongoing intellectual reflection of artepreneurship as far more than just ironic safety valves or exceptional events by star-artists. Following the artist entrepreneurs we enter the era of artepreneurs. So let us finally pinpoint some differences between the artist as entrepreneur and artepreneur by means of the following Table 17.1.

Art is today as omnipresent as the raw materials for making products

Table 17.1 From entrepreneur to artepreneur

From ENTREPRENEUR	to	ARTEPRENEUR
Expectation		Experience
Subjectivity		Singularity
Intention		Gesture
Exchange		Event
Art		Aesthetics
Firm		Foundation
Vision		Reality
Creation		Construction
Cash		Capital

and processes. Old avant-garde art might have been the fruits of odd experiments by individual outsiders, but today it is as institutionalized as any official art ever was in the past. Works of Duchamp, Picasso, and Dali are heavily guarded relics in the ever-increasing number of world-wide public art temples. In museum bookstores, as well as in the media, we are today submerged in explications of what we see and experience in art spaces. An army of scholars, journalists, critics, curators, and even management consultants makes a living out of making art increasingly meaningful in its own right. And it is not only audiences that learn to make sense of art. Artepreneurs are also brought up and trained to make use of those explications in their own arteprises. Art not only makes sense; it actually is made reasonable as the emerging new aesthetic enlightenment where artepreneurs are the true ambassadors of reason. In other words the vision of John Dewey of art as experience will come true by artepreneur-ship while the classical entrepreneur was keen on raising expectations for something visionary (Dewey, 1958).

The old individual bourgeois seems long dead in the contemporary art world, and his transcendental heritage from the old enlightenment has exploded and spread into new scattered faiths, beliefs, and fanatic mys-ticisms. Economic models made room for single spontaneous subjects acting as entrepreneurs and that was how artists were cast in parts to play in the big market game (Scherdin and Ivo Zander, 2011; Schiuma, 2001). The artepreneur however is in constant flux inside a society where her singularity is evolving. The belief in the creative individual acting out her intentions is hardly trustworthy in a world where artepreneurs construct organizations as events. Instead of inventing new pieces of art, as a firm might innnovate new products, the artepreneur takes art as the technical tools and financial instruments to provide new foundations for a sensible, perceptible and observable – in short, an aesthetic – reality. Finally we note an important difference in the relation between art and economy. The artists entrepreneur seems focused an somewhat naïve idea of the cash value of art pieces; remember for instance how Pablo Picasso prided himself of being the most successful counterfeit artists and Yves Klein's obsession with gold or Salvador Dali's dollar fetishism. When Joseph Beuys posed by claiming "Art =Capital" he heralded a much more sophisticated awareness of economic value as an organizational instead of physical phenomenon. As arteprises and artepreneurs offer reasonable resistance through a new aesthetic enlightenment we may ask if we have gone full circle. Artists as artepreneurs help us face and see social reality in the same way that impressionists once inspired the scientific positivist in their quest to physical reality behind veils of old prejudice.

NOTES

1. Aacorn is the acronym for a webgroup called arts, aesthetics, creativity, and organization research network.
2. "Critique is not enough," art show at Cittadellarte Fondazione Pistoletto, Biella Italy, 2002; Schedhalle, Zürich, Switzerland, 2003. Catalogue: La nuova agora: Critique is not enough, Torino: Mariogros, 2003.
3. See www.cittadellarte.it or Guillet de Monthoux (2004: Chapter 10).
4. The one we refer to here is Michael Scherdin, "The invisible foot: survival of new art ideas on the Swedish art arena," Doctoral thesis in Business Administration no. 127, Uppsala, 2007. But during the past decade artists have been given the opportunity to transfer their experiences as and reflections on artepreneurs in form of practice-based PhDs: see e.g., Mathias Bejean, "Le Management des entreprises a prestation artistiques, activites de conception, regimes de signification et potentiel de croissance," These des docteur de L'ecole des Mines de Paris, 2008; Armin Chodzinski, *Peter Behrens, Emil Rathenau und der dm-drogerie markt*, Berlin: Kadmos Kulturverlag, 2007; Henrik Scharder, "Meanwhile Wham, comic and its communication value in organizational context," Doctoral thesis University of Essex, 2010.

   Amongst recent inside research of how artists maneuver as both entrepreneurs we recommend the following detailed accounts; Lindqvist, Katja, "Exhibition enterprising," PhD dissertation, School of Business, Stockholm University, 2003; Thornqvist, Clemens, *Artistic direction: the ways of Robert Wilson*, Borås ,Textile Research Centre, The Swedish School of Textiles; Piras, "La routinizzazione della passione et la passione nelle practice organizzative. Etnografie di una fondazione d'arte contemporanea," Doctoral Dissertation, Trento 2005.
5. The awareness of the social play of many actors making art work has been increased by works on practical aesthetics: Guillet de Monthoux's *The Art Firm*; Guillet de Monthoux, Gustafsson and Sven-Erik Sjöstrand, *Aesthetic Leadership*, Houndsmills, UK: Palgrave Macmillan, 2007, and Guillet de Monthoux, "Hermeneutik des Handelns" in Marc Markowski and Wöbken Hergen, eds., *Oeconomenta-Wechselspiele zwischen Kunst und Wirtschaft*, Berlin: Kadmos Kulturverlag, 2007.
6. For an artepreneurial perspective on Jacques Ranciére, see Timon Beyes' article in Aesthesis 2008, "Reframing the possible, Rancièrian aesthetics and the study of organization".

18 Organizing the entrepreneurial city
Timon Beyes

INTRODUCTION: "NOT IN OUR NAME, BRAND HAMBURG!"[1]

A spectre has been haunting Europe since US economist Richard Florida predicted that the future belongs to cities in which the 'creative class' feels at home. (. . .) Many European capitals are competing with one another to be the settlement zone for this 'creative class'. In Hamburg's case, the competition now means that city politics are increasingly subordinated to an 'Image City'. The idea is to send out a very specific image of the city into the world: the image of the 'pulsating capital', which offers a 'stimulating atmosphere and the best opportunities for creatives of all stripes'. (. . .)

We say: ouch, this is painful. Stop this shit. We won't be taken for fools. Dear location politicians: we refuse to talk about this city in marketing categories. (. . .) We are thinking about other things. About the million-plus square metres of empty office space, for example (. . .). That the amount of social housing will be slashed by half within ten years. That the poor, elderly and immigrant inhabitants are being driven to the edge of town (. . .). We think that your 'growing city' is actually a segregated city of the 19th century: promenades for the wealthy, tenements for the rabble. (. . .)

You obviously consider it a matter of course that cultural resources should be siphoned 'directly into urban development', 'to boost the city's image'. Culture should be an ornament for turbo-gentrification. (. . .) We get the picture: we, the music, DJs, art, film and theatre people, the groovy-little-shop owners and anyone who represents a different quality of life, are supposed to function as a counterpoint (. . .). We are meant to take care of the atmosphere, the aura and leisure quality, without which an urban location has little chance in the global competition. (. . .) But then, tragically, your proposed solutions never venture one iota beyond the logic of the entrepreneurial city. A freshly printed document from the Senate announces its plan to 'develop the future potential of the creative economy by strengthening its competitiveness.' (. . .) There could not be a more unequivocal definition of the role that 'creativity' is supposed to play: namely of profit centre for the 'growing city'.

And this is where we draw the line. (. . .) We say: a city is not a brand. A city is not a corporation. A city is a community. We ask the social question which, in cities today, is also about a battle for territory. This is about taking over and defending places that make life worth living in this city, which don't belong to the target group of the 'growing city'. We claim our right to the city – together with all the residents of Hamburg who refuse to be a location factor.

Penned by local artists and activists in the late summer of 2009, shortly after around 200 artists began squatting the *Gängeviertel*, an old inner-city block already sold to an investor and about to be demolished and turned into office space, the "Not in our name"-manifesto was circulated, signed and commented upon widely; it was reprinted in the national press and discussed on TV. Suddenly, the debate on the entrepreneurial city had entered the German public discourse. A concept like 'gentrification' became an everyday term, at least for urban dwellers. And a broad informal coalition of local inhabitants supported the squatters and forced the local government to renege on its decision and buy back the property from the investor. In the meantime, Richard Florida, author of the best-selling *The Rise of the Creative Class* (2002) and alleged inventor of the spectre haunting Europe alluded to in the manifesto, intervened into the debate in style. In a televized interview on a national cultural show, he, too, applauded the squatters, called for a dialogue and encouraged the city politicians to formally let artists and cultural producers have their say in urban development – and to offer them ownership stakes in quarters and buildings. Hamburg, he said, could become a worldwide model (Spiegel Online, 2009).

As if under a burning glass, the manifesto and its story bundles and presents the theme of this chapter: organizing the entrepreneurial city. It gives testament to – and brings a polemical charge against – the potent discourse and practices of urban entrepreneurialism and its contemporary adjunct, the 'artistic mode of production' (Zukin, 1989: 176). It illustrates what organizing the entrepreneurial city might entail and points to a knot of conflicting opinions and arguments about its operations. In the following, I attempt to disentangle this knot by tracing the scholarly debates around and definitions of the entrepreneurial city and by somewhat schematically mapping two narratives of its organizational force: a celebratory narrative of urban creativity and economic redemption, and a counter-narrative of urban entrepreneurialism's detrimental effects. Going beyond what seems to amount to a dominant, consensual image of the entrepreneurial city, which is either affirmatively hailed or critically scrutinized, I offer a third, prosaic mode of narrating the entrepreneurial city (Steyaert and Beyes, 2009). Here, cities are seen as sites of a diversity of organizational forces and thus as constituting heterotopic spaces of potential and innovation too easily overlooked in dominant accounts of urban entrepreneurialism.

This chapter pursues these issues as follows. First, I engage with organization theory's 'urban problematic' (Lefebvre, 2003), i.e., with the city as a site of organization and entrepreneurship. Departing from Harvey's (1989) seminal article on the rise of urban entrepreneurialism, I secondly outline a brief history of the notion of the entrepreneurial city – from the entrepreneurial turn in urban governance to the more recent emphasis on the 'artistic mode of production' and cultural consumption. On this basis, the third section is dedicated to the celebratory narrative, with Florida's widely discussed *Rise of the Creative Class* (2002) as symptomatic text. The critique of Florida's theses directly and fourthly connects to the counter-narrative, the discussion of which again builds up on Harvey's work. Finally, arguing that such 'dark' accounts of the entrepreneurial city tend to reproduce a dominant conception of urban entrepreneurialism translates into the need for a different imagination of the entrepreneurial city. In the fifth section, I therefore call for scholars of organizational entrepreneurship to adopt an 'urban sensibility' and to provide prosaic accounts of the emergence of alternative visions of urban life and novel forms of organizing. There is a brief conclusion.

ORGANIZATION THEORY'S URBAN PROBLEMATIC

[W]e are all urbanists now. (Soja, 2003: 280)

Cities, we can take from Benjamin (1982), are deeply ambiguous; they are not only organizing, but also dis-organizing machines full of uncertainties and unexpected encounters and, perhaps, possibilities of redemption. In this sense, classic scholars of urban conditions and the urban situation such as Benjamin, Weber, Simmel and Lefebvre have a lot to say about organization. They treat the city as an organizational form, which attests to and produces the organizational dynamics of our (urban) lives: 'What differentiated the city from other social forms was not simply its size, or its geography, its identity or its economic power, but the very nature of organization that it manifested' (Knox, 2010: 186).[2]

While organizational theory has traditionally shown only scant interest in the processes of organizing urban forms, this seems to be about to change (e.g., Czarniawska, 2000; Pipan and Porsander, 2000; Clegg and Kornberger, 2006; Knox, 2010). For one, that the city has recently begun to make its presence felt in the study of organization and entrepreneurship is connected to what Lefebvre (2003) called the dominant question of our time, namely the 'urban problematic'. A few decades ago a seemingly neglected issue in the academic world, the spectres of the urban (Lefebvre, 1996: 142) now haunt the theoretical imaginations of the humanities and social sciences; 'even, perhaps, as one of the speculative horizons of their transdisciplinary convergence' (Cunningham, 2005:14).[3] For Lefebvre, the urban problematic posits a crucial challenge for an engagement with contemporary and future society: the contradictions of capitalist development play themselves out within – *and simultaneously produce* – the urban itself (Lefebvre, 1996, 2003). The city is not only 'everywhere and in everything' (Amin and Thrift, 2002: 1); '[i]n fact, the city itself functions as an ecological body, one that facilitates the circulation of particular socio-economic and cultural discourses while also thereby delimiting them" (Whybrow, 2010: 3). It follows that a city should be apprehended not as *an organization* but as simultaneously produced and producing, as genera-tive and generated (Kaulingfreks and Warren, 2010) and hence as a *site of organization*.[4] Accordingly, probably the most basic definition of cities is that they organize people, things and affects in manifold constellations (Thrift, 2005: 140). They are sites of the coming-together of a manifold set of organizational forces, of 'stuff' – 'technologies, texts, people, animals, computers, plants, words and images – (. . .) in more-or-less expansive networks of connection' (Hubbard, 2006: 248).[5]

Conceptually, such a notion of the city relates well to attempts to move the study of organization from a focus on formal organizations to pro-cesses of organizing that take place outside and across the boundaries of conventional organizational entities (e.g., Chia, 1999; Jones and Munro, 2005; Czarniawska, 2008a). If to think 'organization' entails, in Cooper's words, the recognition of 'a more general force which includes us in its per-petual movement between order and disorder, certainty and uncertainty' (in Chia and Kallinikos, 1998: 154), then today such thinking of organiza-tion is bound to encounter and get immersed in urban settings.

Moreover, to view the city as a productive or performative concatena-tion of organizational forces and thus a generative site of organization should be home turf for scholars of organizational entrepreneurship. That cities are laboratories of the new is a well-worn trope, of course. In his magisterial *Cities in Civilization*, Hall (1999) traces the emergence of creative urban milieux by way of an expansive overview of cases that seek to demonstrate how cultural-artistic and entrepreneurial innovations – connected to phases of great social tensions and intellectual turmoil – are located in specifically urban contexts. It is these contexts, then, that effect creativity and entrepreneurship. The complex constellation of 'stuff' that is the city harbours the potential of novel forms of organizing. Lefebvre, who was well aware of the intensity of social control and repression at work in urban life, nevertheless called the urban a 'differential field' that would bring together contrasts and contradictions, that would unite an ensemble of differences, encounters and simultaneity (Lefebvre, 2003: 156ff). 'As a place of encounters, focus of communication and information', he writes, 'the urban becomes what it always was: place of desire, permanent disequi-librium, set of the dissolution of normalities and constraints, the moment of play and of the unpredictable' (Lefebvre, 1996: 129).

For sure, then, this arena for entrepreneurship is a societal rather than a purely economic phenomenon; it surpasses technology and economy (Hjorth et al., 2003) and the managerial focus so often at work in enterprise discourse (Hjorth, 2003b). It cultivates manifold forms, practices and concepts of entrepreneurship (Beyes, 2006). Following Steyaert and Katz (2004: 182) the city is a site of organizational entrepreneurship 'across a broad range of settings and spaces and for a range of goals such as social change and transformation far beyond those of simple commerce and economic drive'. As we will see, however, narratives of the entrepreneurial city are dominantly framed or couched in fairly simple commercial-cum-economic terms.

THE RISE OF THE ENTREPRENEURIAL CITY

Consider Manchester, which 'has long been seen as the definitive entrepreneurial city' (Mace et al., 2007: 60; see also Quilley, 2000; Williams, 2003). Or consider Barcelona, which seems to convincingly connect the spectacle of new and old architecture with economic dynamism (McNeill, 2001; Marshall, 2004; Luna-Garcia, 2008). Or consider Berlin, 'a text frantically being written and rewritten' after the wall came down (Huyssen 1997: 57; Cochrane and Jonas, 1999; Lange 2005; Beyes, 2009). Or Stockholm (Pipan and Porsander, 2000; Dobers, 2003). Or Amsterdam (Oudenampsen, 2007). A sprawling list of cities has been called 'entrepreneurial', usually in tandem with having been given a 'creative label'. While scholars of organization and entrepreneurship have been mostly silent about these developments, they have been at the forefront of debates in urban studies and human geography for the last two decades. Diagnosed as 'a key feature of neoliberal capitalist societies' (Hetherington and Cronin, 2008: 1), today the notion of cities acting and being run in an entrepreneurial manner is widely subscribed to, serving as a regular part of local politicians' and public administrators' semantics.

To trace the rise of the entrepreneurial city, it is helpful to turn to Harvey's seminal article 'From managerialism to entrepreneurialism' (1989), and to roughly distinguish between two stages, the first ranging from 1970–90, the second from the nineties to the present. Harvey's article, perhaps the single most influential text on the entrepreneurial city (Wood, 1998), situates the advent of the 'new urban entrepreneurialism' from the early 1970s onwards.[6] It arose when the economic and fiscal base of many large cities started to erode, especially in industrial cities, where new and innovative models of governance were called for. It thus denotes a shift in urban politics away from a managerial-administrative regime of public services and local welfare provision 'towards the promotion

of economic competitiveness, place marketing to attract inward investment and support for the development of indigenous private sector firms'
(Painter, 1998: 261). Harvey identifies four basic tenets, which in combination underlie the new forms of governance in capitalist cities (ibid.: 8–11):
First, responding to international competition based on local advantages,
investments, new technology and tax breaks; second, developing a local
service-oriented economy with an emphasis on tourism, retail as well as
cultural events and place-marketing; third, assembling a wide range of
supportive services in finance, media, education and government; and
fourth, making central government support and funding available region-
ally. Importantly, moreover, Harvey underscores what he calls 'the up-
grading of the image' (ibid.: 7) of cities and the emphasis on appearance,
style, spectacle, display and imagery. 'Above all', he writes, 'the city has *to
appear* as an innovative, exciting, creative, and safe place to live or to visit,
to play and consume in' (ibid.: 9; my emphasis). Under the rubric of the
entrepreneurial city, the battle between cities has evolved into a process of
multiplying ever-new images and variegated stories of urban attractive-
ness and success. The speculative is not limited to engineering and curating
a city's image, however. In what is perhaps the last twist in the development of urban entrepreneurial governance so far, after the dot-com crash
of 2001 cities became more open to – and thus dependent on – the financial
markets and debt-financing models of urban development on a global
scale (Harvey, 2008; Mayer, 2010).

From the 1990s until today, furthermore, the notion of the entrepreneurial city has become attached to the call for cities to regain and groom
their creativity (Chatterton, 2000) and the connection between cities,
creativity and economic success became a dominant formula (Hjorth and
Steyaert, 2003). 'Within the space of little more than two decades, the initiation of culture-driven urban (re)generation has come to occupy a pivotal
position in the new urban entrepreneurialism' (Miles and Paddison, 2005:
833); consequently, 'culture is more and more the business of cities' (Zukin
1995: 2) and 'contemporary debates about urban policy are littered with
culture and creativity' (Pratt, 2008: 107). Moreover, related discussions of
the 'experience economy' (Pine and Gilmore, 1999; Hjorth and Kostera,
2007) or the 'symbolic economy' (Zukin, 1995) show how post-industrial,
entrepreneurial cities are organized around issues of consumption rather
than production (Cronin and Hetherington, 2008).

While Harvey (1989: 12–13) was already relating entrepreneurial urbanism to the tendency of mobilizing urban cultural resources, he might not
have fully foreseen the increasingly prominent role of culture, creativity,
aesthetics and consumer spectacle in shaping the symbolic economy of
the entrepreneurial city. To make these linkages clearer, it is helpful to

turn to urban scholar Sharon Zukin's observations of what she called the 'artistic mode of production' in New York (1989: 176). The artistic mode of production denotes urban redevelopment strategies responding to 'greater "leisure" time and more "sophisticated" patterns of consumption' (p. 176) and focused on the art and heritage sectors. Art's growing value also increased the value of connected factors: 'the urban *forms* that grew up around it, the activity of *doing* it, and most important, the status of *consuming* it'. Zukin thus identifies the emergence of a close relation 'between *accumulation* and *cultural consumption*' (p. 177; orig. emphasis). Based on intensified efforts of place promotion, image building and city marketing as well as investments in cultural forms, which prominently include the promotion of artistic and cultural lifestyles, images and entertainment options (Hetherington and Cronin, 2008), contemporary urban development can therefore be interpreted as a 'cultural performance' (Amin and Thrift, 2007: 153).[7]

As this brief history of the rise of the concept of the entrepreneurial city indicates, the notion of urban entrepreneurialism has not only made a lasting impact on the semantics and practices of urban policy makers, it has also kept urban scholars busy and alert. In the following, I will switch to a broad juxtaposition of two different scholarly stances and strategies: celebratory narrative and counter-narrative. That the narrating of urban entrepreneurship can raise very different images and discourses of urban life will help me to set up a tentative critique of not only the celebratory but also the 'conventionally critical' take on what has been said to constitute 'a new diktat on the organization of urban space' (Ward, 2003: 203). Through outlining a third, 'prosaic' mode of encountering the entrepreneurial city, I will argue towards the awareness of the gaps and silences in the dominant script of urban entrepreneurialism, which might constitute a different entrepreneurial city (Steyaert and Beyes, 2009).

CELEBRATORY NARRATIVE: 'A WHOLE NEW WAY OF LIFE'?

What I suggest calling the celebratory narrative reaffirms the ideas and potentials of the entrepreneurial city in general and the nexus of urban culture and urban economy in particular. In fact, combining urban development with entrepreneurship, creativity and culture has become fashionable, if not a hype: how-to books provide readers with tools to develop their cities as entrepreneurial (Goldsmith, 1999) or creative (Landry, 2000). Moreover, as Latham et al. (2009: 171) point out, 'as opposed to earlier versions of the "culture industry" (. . .), [recent] academic studies of the influence of cultural industries are increasingly upbeat'. There hardly seems to be a more upbeat treatment of urban entrepreneurialism than 'the most popular book on regional economies in the last decade' (Glaeser, 2004: 1; quoted in Peck, 2005: 741): Florida's influential and widely discussed *The Rise of the Creative Class* (2002) – the spectre haunting European cities, as the re-printed manifesto at the beginning of this text has it. The book expounds and explores an intriguingly simple hypothesis: if cities attract creative people, then they are economically more successful and their regeneration is accelerated through the creativity created by these people. Urban economic development thus emerges from a cocktail of entrepreneurship, creative life styles and a diverse, creative class. Florida (once an urban planner, now a professor of business and creativity in Toronto) was able to elevate this 'new credo of creativity' (Peck, 2005: 740) to a wide acceptance in circles of (urban) policy makers as a kind of "*new* new economy" (ibid.: 743) by promoting an upbeat belief in, and image of, urban policy making and its beneficial effects for the urban populace.

What Florida (2002) sees as the rising creative class is a group of so-called creative professionals – from artists to scientists, from entrepreneurs to venture capitalists – who turn their lifestyles, tastes, values and relationships into an attractive combination of work, leisure and living. In doing so they seem to complement such traditional classes as the working, service and agricultural classes. Creativity thus gravitates to specific locations, as creative people tend to 'cluster in places that are centers of creativity and also where they like to live' (p. 7). For Florida, this is not a small change, but a 'sea-change'; indeed, 'it is the emergence of a new society and a new culture . . . a whole new way of life' (p. 12).

In addition to attracting talented professionals, then, Florida advises cities to seek technological prominence and to encourage a multicultural environment. These three elements are combined in a formula of 3 Ts: talent is connected with technology and tolerance. Art is seen as the close associate that combines well with technological nerds and with cosmopolitan and queer lifestyles. In an interview given as he launched his book in 2002, Florida summarized his view by stating that 'cities must attract the new "creative class" with hip neighborhoods, an arts scene and a gay-friendly atmosphere – or they'll go the way of Detroit' (Dreher, 2002: 1; quoted in Peck, 2005: 740).

As a consequence, Florida inscribes a mixture of figures into a narrative of mega-optimism and elitism. Artists, nerds and homosexuals are needed to enact the urban imagineering projects and to play a prime role in aestheticizing the urban landscape and concocting spectacles and events. His emphasis on the gay and lesbian community has been contested both by conservatives who find that it undermines the values of family life so central in conservative narratives (Peck, 2005) and by the gay and lesbian community which finds itself staged in a spectacle of creativity where 'queer difference is now exploited as a material and semiotic resource in the commodification of the city' (Grundy, 2003: 4).

In sum, '[t]he script of urban creativity reworks and augments the old methods and arguments of urban entrepreneurialism in politically seductive ways' (Peck, 2005: 766). The success of Florida's recipes in terms of their effects on the discourse of the entrepreneurial city and narratives of urban policy making is as impressive as scholarly critique of his assumptions and theses is fierce (e.g., Peck, 2005; Pratt, 2008). For instance, the idea of instrumentally breeding 'authentic' local cultures by way of public policy interventions is at odds with decades of rather sobering experiences with attempts of steering urban development to desired ends. Then there are methodological issues, like a troubling linkage of causality between creative class and urban change that disregards a city's complex interdependencies (Pratt, 2008). An international comparative analysis of urban creative industry policies and their effects shows disappointing results and diagnoses an over-reliance on either unproven or hardly transferable policy models, which is partly traced to unfounded or unreliable notions of innovation and the creative class, on which growth predictions have been based (Evans, 2009). Conceptually, there is the rather undeveloped but 'distinctly positive, nebulous-yet-attractive, apple-pie-like' notion of creativity (Peck 2005: 765), limiting an understanding of creativity 'to the bodies – or perhaps more accurately, the souls – of creative individuals' (ibid.: 765). Furthermore, Florida's framework shows scant – or only gestural – regard for social issues such as inequality and the division of labour, for instance with regard to the working poor who provide the basic services for members of the creative class. (As Peck points out, in the United States the so-called creative capitals are actually producing more inequality than the rest.)

In fact, a class analysis that knows of no class divisions is a profoundly strange one. Halls' afore-mentioned epos on *Cities in Civilizations* (1999) repeatedly shows how a fluid class structure, for instance based on an influx of immigrants, and the tensions and social struggles *between* classes provoke creativity and innovation. In this sense, Florida's consensual dream defies historical urban experience, and "the notion of 'creative class' as an emergent social subject is absolutely useless because it articulates a friction-less and conflict-less notion of agency, described only on the basis of a 'positive' or 'progressive' paradigm" (Pasquinelli, 2008: 135). In the context of this chapter, then, the biggest caveat is this: if the creative class-hypothesis makes sense at all, about which there is considerable doubt, then it is only 'within the narrow context of enterprise and competition' (Pratt, 2008: 114). Organizing the entrepreneurial city à la Florida, its emphasis on culture and creativity notwithstanding, falls back on a simple logic of enterprise discourse which inscribes culture and creativity into an economistic logic of the means and ends of urban competitiveness. It does not live up to the diversity of organizational forces that produce the city and the manifold entrepreneurial possibilities, 'the myriad experiments that set out to invent flexible models of imagination and narrative outside the enforced routines of consumption' and capitalist accumulation (Thrift, 2007: 22).

COUNTER-NARRATIVE: SAMENESS, SOCIAL COSTS, STATE INTERVENTION

As the debunking of Florida's endeavour shows, the celebratory narrative of the entrepreneurial-cum-creative city has not remained uncontested. Generally speaking, 'crisis' is a reliable, perhaps even overwrought, theme in the scholarly literature on the city and urban development (Lake, 2005). Correspondingly, the entrepreneurial optimism that brings forth 'a futuristic vision of a visually enticing city of dreams' is 'entwined with a post-apocalyptic scenario of urban unrest, deprivation and despair' (Hubbard and Hall, 1998: 1). Researching the organizational forces that make and unmake the city can therefore counter the claims of entrepreneurial betterment and redemption with images and narratives of the 'dark side' of urban entrepreneurialism. As Latham et al. (2009: 143) point out, the critical potential of research into urban entrepreneurialism has been met with enthusiasm by critical geographers engaging with the 'geographies of "actually existing neoliberalism"' (Brenner and Theodore, 2002: 368). In the following, I distinguish between four main and themselves interrelated critical arguments: the similarity and thus exchangeability of urban development strategies, their social costs, their tight coupling with intensified regimes of control and the emergence of new forms of commodification of urban space.

First, what Harvey (1989) in his path-breaking paper on urban entrepreneurialism finds most striking is the unanimous consensus about the idea of positive effects to be gained for cities by becoming more entrepreneurial. Instead of being unique or innovative, cities seem to look more and more the same: 'How many successful convention centres, sports stadia, Disney-worlds, harbour places and spectacular shopping malls can there be?' (p. 12) Almost 20 years later, Zukin (2008: xii) echoes Harvey's question with regard to the entrepreneurial city's 'cultural and consumerist turn': 'Like brands (. . .), most cities develop the *same* market-ing tools. They *all* have tall towers and modern art museums. They *all* hire the same famous architects from overseas. They *all* offer lattes at sidewalk cafés. They are *all* "creative".' (orig. emphasis).

Second, Harvey (1989, 2008) warns of the social costs of urban entrepre-neurialism, like increasing disparity in wealth and income and processes of urban impoverishment, dispossession and displacement. As scholars of entrepreneurship very well know, 'the creative' might be intertwined with 'the destructive', so the notion of 'creative destruction' might be apt to make sense of the development of entrepreneurial cities (Brenner and Theodore, 2002). Zukin's (1989) pioneering work on New York quoted above already showed how the artistic mode of production leads to displacement and gentrification. In this sense, it can be argued that the artistic mode of production 'has innervated the economy of European cities, but more for the sake of gentrification than for cultural produc-tion itself' (Pasquinelli, 2008: 16). These organizational effects are often far removed from images of benign urban revitalization; they involve 'the wholesale, and frequently shockingly brutal, "cleansing" and "pacifica-tion" of inner-city areas to make them "safe" for middle class residents' (Latham et al., 2009: 182). Smith (1996) diagnoses an evident 'revanchism' in contemporary cities, where entrepreneurial measures of urban policy go hand-in-hand with draconian policing tactics to exclude the 'undesired' ones from (parodies of) public spaces. Moreover, where urban develop-ment has been debt-financed via the financial markets, the recent financial crisis is having disastrous consequences for municipal finances, further exacerbating social polarization (Harvey, 2008). Whether the celebratory narrative of urban entrepreneurialism as unmistakably economistic and unambiguously beneficial has suffered from the recent crisis remains to be seen (Mayer, 2010).

Third, it therefore has been argued that – contrary to claims of refrain-ing from state interference – urban entrepreneurialism is complicit with 'a dramatic intensification of coercive, disciplinary forms of state interven-tion' (Brenner and Theodore, 2002: 352). Turning cityspace into land-scapes of consumption is not an innocent, apolitical activity, because such space is increasingly observed and discussed on the foil of security and order, thus provoking rhetorics of social warfare about missing safety, urban poverty, inner-city decay, drugs and organized crime, as well as private and state measures of surveillance and control (Ronneberger et al., 1999; Beyes, 2006).

Fourth, and finally, the increasing importance of matters cultural and aesthetic seems to herald new forms of 'heterarchic' manipulation and control, which go beyond manifest measures of policing urban space and work through the (conceptual, affective, physical) ordering of everyday space-times in order to perform 'powerful new geographies of organization, belonging and attachment' (Amin and Thrift, 2005: 226). According to Thrift (2009), social realities in Western cities are turning into aesthetic projects through the mass deployment of artistic techniques which modulate, mobilise and manipulate the affective background and which foreground an ethic of entrepreneurial inventiveness. Therefore, urban commercial spaces have ceased to merely display goods in favour of being actively entertaining; people are no longer seen as passive consumers but are encouraged to actively perform their presence. In what can be called a theming of experience, urban spaces become a vital part of the commodity to be sold:

> These spaces have a number of characteristics. To begin with, they are highly interactive. (. . .) Second, (. . .) [t]he spaces are theatrical, intended to stimulate the exercise of certain forms of imagination through carefully scripted performances. Third, they are omnisensory. Because they tend to rely on a multitude of media, they tend to reach across the senses, using not just vision but also touch, smell, taste, hearing and kinaesthetic (movement) senses in order to produce strong bodily reactions. Finally, theses spaces are adaptive; that is, they are spaces which are constantly monitored and adjusted to data gathered on audience reaction. (Amin and Thrift, 2002: 124–25)[8]

In sum, while the discourse of creativity has increasingly been appropriated into optimistic tales of urban entrepreneurship, there has been no shortage of critical voices, which question and reject these tales by documenting the dystopian side of the entrepreneurial city. The counter-narrative thus responds to the tendency to reduce the organizing effects of urban entrepreneurialism to myth making and spectacle styling. Nevertheless, it should be noted that these voices seem to be far less successful in making policy makers think twice about the entrepreneurial city as a preferred script.

BEYOND PLEASANTVILLE AND PANICVILLE: TOWARDS PROSAIC NARRATIVES

While the author of these lines holds the opinion that the critical writings – heterogeneous in themselves – are both necessary and convincing, critical strategies of disapproval, rejection or even ridicule might not be enough. For one, *both* the optimistic narrative and the more or less dystopian counter-images tend to present the relationship between the urban and the entrepreneurial as self-evident. In this respect, both 'camps' eschew the same trope of the unavoidability of entrepreneurial urban development as we know it, either following a celebratory mission or 'indulging in the necrophilia of global capital and the police state (as a dominant criticism and even a certain fatalistic Marxism)' (Pasquinelli, 2008: 134). Perhaps, this scenario offers the scholar a too comfortable, pre-decided position of mastery vis-à-vis his or her object of inquiry (Ranciére, 2004a). But if the city is a site of a diversity of organizational forces, then the everyday urban mess constitutes a field of potentiality, of experiments and connections too easily overlooked in the grand scheme of things (Amin and Thrift, 2002).

To do justice to the diversity of organizational forces at work in the city and to 'the moment[s] of play and of the unpredictable', to re-quote Lefebvre (1996: 129), the relationship between entrepreneurship and the city has to become more ambivalent. In other words, there is a need to invent alternative forms of critique that can not only document how the styles of seduction and control have altered but also affirm other imaginations, appropriations and inventions of cityspace. To oversimplify for a moment, the question thus becomes how to move beyond the representation of city life as either Pleasantville or Panicville (Virilio, 2005), as either urban dream or metropolitan nightmare, as the site of either an 'experience economy' of play and passion (Hjorth and Kostera, 2007) or a 'fear economy' of surveillance and security (Davis, 2002; Thrift, 2005). In a spatial vocabulary, this would imply to add to the utopian and dystopian imagination a heterotopic one (Soja, 1996). It would direct scholars of organizational entrepreneurship towards '"specific", "potential" or "other", spaces and timings, which (. . .) allow transition and transformation' (Steyaert, 2006: 248; Beyes and Michels, 2011).

A minor yet symptomatic debate within the field of urban studies might help to make this clearer (Latham, 2006a, b; Cochrane, 2006). In the *Journal of European Urban and Regional Studies*, the geographer Alan Latham staged an intervention into what he perceives as the 'limitations' of Anglophone urban studies (2006: 88); his example is studies of the (development of the) city of Berlin. Latham identifies a consensus at work in current discussions in English-language urban studies: an implicitly shared understanding of what is 'driving' the development of the European city, of what processes call for scholarly attention and, therefore, of what is seen and what is left out. This consensus broadly concurs with the counter-narrative of the entrepreneurial city as geared towards an intensified entrepreneurialism. Latham (2003, 2006a) traces several widely shared and interrelated propositions: an intensified orientation towards consumption, a '"hyper-aestheticisation" of the everyday' (Latham, 2003: 1701) and neoliberal governmental strategies go hand-in-hand with a globalization of urban landscapes and an increasing polarization by wealth and income as well as social exclusion.

The counter-narrative has itself become a compelling and dominant narrative of Anglophone urban literature, which according to Latham is applied to Berlin. Apart from studying how Berlin has been re-imagined through place-marketing 'and the symbolic spectacle of global architecture' (Cochrane and Jonas, 1999: 152), the reinvention of the Potsdamer Platz is regarded as the obvious case that demonstrates the dominance of economic power and consumerist urban development (e.g., Allen, 2006). For sure, the reconstruction of Potsdamer Platz is a particularly apt example of the 'potential tragedy (. . .) that the menu from which big cities seem to be permitted to choose their futures appears to remain so limited' (Cochrane and Jonas, 1999: 161). The question, therefore, is not whether such analyses might miss the point; in fact, they vividly reveal the power of urban entrepreneurialism at work, so to speak. Rather, the question is what this agenda of Anglophone urban studies does *not* permit us to see. One risk is that this particular discourse may fail to notice the diversity *between* (European) cities. As Latham points out, Berlin has a distinct history of urban planning and renewal that, even now, continues to deviate from the clear-cut neoliberal or 'entrepreneurial' model which apparently determines urban development in larger (Western) cities.

In the context of developing an agenda of 'affirmative critique' of the entrepreneurial city through prosaic narratives, an equally important and related danger lies in overlooking the plurality of organizational trajectories that produce the city. This is not limited to the example of Berlin, of course. But it is somewhat ironic that during the same period when the Potsdamer Platz was being conceived, built and put to use, Berlin was becoming an object of inquiry as a hotbed for experimental, 'autonomous' and often minor spaces, for so-called 'counter-urbanities' in multiple expressions (e.g., Latham, 1999; Oswald, 2000; Cupers and Miessen, 2002; Groth and Corijn, 2005; Beyes, 2009), including a host of endeavours to resist or playfully parody consumer culture and the privatization of space.

Thus, through dominant critical patterns of thinking, 'we end up with accounts of Berlin which (. . .) miss many of the more interesting and exceptional phenomena which are shaping Berlin' (Latham, 2006b: 377). Both Latham's diagnostic reading of urban theory's dominant (counter-) narrative and his call to open up to the plurality of urban trajectories chime well with the broad distinction between celebratory narrative, counter-narrating and the prosaic narration of spatial performances that moves beyond orthodox theoretical orderings. Perhaps not surprisingly, artistic performances and interventions and their potential to reconfigure what we can perceive and express are of considerable interest here (Rancière, 2004b; Beyes et al., 2009).

And yet, the notion of performance leads beyond the realm of art, into very practical imaginations and creations of encounters, affects, unforeseen relations, play, liminality, protest and transformation (Thrift, 2000; Thrift and Dewsbury, 2000). From serious or carnivalesque performances of resistance (Lyle, 2008; Beyes, 2010) to the affective enactments and reorderings of urban geographies by homeless people (Cloke et al., 2008); from the reclaiming of the urban agenda by informal actors reanimating indeterminate spaces (Groth and Corijn, 2005) to the emergent (self-) organization of 'inoperative communities' through mobile clubbing and flash mobs (Kaulingfreks and Warren, 2010) to indeed the disorganizing potential of site-specific art interventions, which 'reroute' or add to the multiple trajectories that organize urban life (Beyes et al., 2009): the urban fabric produces manifold manifestations and new forms of expression which allow change to happen.

This is not to gloss over the oppressive and damaging consequences of entrepreneurial urbanism, which the critical counter-narrative lays bare. But it seems all the more urgent to add to our understanding of cities in neoliberal times by exploring stories that present alternatives to the dominant critique of urban entrepreneurialism, because it is here that we might 'imagine possible futures beyond the narrow confines of a globalized, neoliberal, free-market model' (Latham, 2006a: 91). Following Lefebvre's notion of 'the right to the city' (1996) and Amin and Thrift's articulation of a 'politics of the common' (2002), I therefore suggest enriching the study of how the entrepreneurial city is organized with the notion of 'the city as a site of politics in motion' (Amin and Thrift, 2002: 155). 'The ideal city (. . .)', writes Lefebvre (1996: 173ff; orig. emphasis), 'would be the *ephemeral* city, the perpetual *oeuvre* of the inhabitants, themselves mobile and mobilized for and by this *oeuvre*. (. . .) The right to the *oeuvre*, to participation and *appropriation* (clearly distinct from the right to property), are implied in the right to the city'. It is precisely this notion of the right to the city that the Hamburg manifesto positioned at the beginning of this chapter refers to and that has currently become a shared credo and rallying cry for a loose network of urban activists around the world (Woessner, 2009: 474; Mayer, 2010). Researching this 'kind' of urban entrepreneurship, of organizing the entrepreneurial city, entails tracing the reorderings of the manner in which everyday urban space lends itself to participation and appropriation, to moments of play and of the unpredictable, to reorganizing the established and crafting the new.

CONCLUSION

Big-city space is in no way analogous to the space of a company town – and it is for this reason that a city cannot be run on such a model, not matter how big a company one envisages. (. . .) Whereas businesses tend towards a totalitarian form of social organization, authoritarian and prone to fascism, urban conditions, either despite or by virtue of violence, tend to uphold at least a measure of democracy. (Lefebvre, 1991, p. 319)

This chapter has sought to demonstrate how the city as site of organizational dynamics is – or should be – of the utmost importance to scholars of organizational entrepreneurship. As the introduction in the form of an urban manifesto against the conditions and effects of the entrepreneurial city illustrates, the city is a highly relevant and contested space of organization and entrepreneurship. Largely ignored in the literature on organization and entrepreneurship, the concept of the entrepreneurial city has been at the forefront of urban studies and urban policy making for the last 30 years, denoting a complex knot of developments in the imagining, representation and governance of the city. More recently, matters of culture, creativity and consumption have been inscribed into the discourse of entrepreneurial urban development, placing an emphasis on the creation of cultural buzz, the artistic mode of production and the mobilization of urban cultural resources in general.

Differentiating three narrative clusters of urban entrepreneurialism – celebratory narrative, counter-narrative and prosaic narration – I have tried to juxtapose different and partly conflicting scholarly strategies and political stances in making sense of the 'entrepreneurial turn' in urban politics and urban culture. While each of the three broad narratives offers ample room for future research on organizational entrepreneurship, I have argued in favour of a strengthening of prosaic narratives of urban change and transformation. After all, it is not only developers, investors and marketers that create narratives and images of and for 'their' entrepreneurial cities. Scholars of organizational entrepreneurship, too, make visible and enact images and imaginations of (in this case) urban entrepreneurialism. This way, research contributes to the development and circulation of images and imaginations of the urban condition and its possible futures. In other words, it can itself have political effects (Beyes and Steyaert, 2011). Going beyond the celebratory and the conventionally critical helps to open up the discourse of the entrepreneurial city to other kinds of stories, ones that (re-)enact the city as a heterotopic space of potential and invention. Rather than assessing the entrepreneurial city as 'mere' terrain of economic production or as an object of governance, then, urban spaces may be regarded as potentialities for reorganizing the established and enabling the new.

'Becoming-urbanist' therefore entails viewing the city as a site of organization, which is made up of a multitude of organizational forces and ongoing processes of encounter through which urban spaces are continuously assembled and organized. It follows that for instance the emergence of alternative visions of urban life and novel forms of organizing resembles a struggle 'to name neglected spatialities and invent new ones' (Amin and Thrift, 2002: 4). Thus, research into organizational entrepreneurship would benefit from an 'urban sensibility' – one that is not limited to questions of how cities are organized in the potentially hegemonic interest of the powerful but open towards the complex meshworks of urban trajectories that harbours other geographical imaginations, new solidarities and new collectivities (Latham, 2003).

NOTES

1. The original version of the manifesto can be found here: http://www.buback.de/nion/ (accessed 20 February 2011). The English translation used here – with minor amendments by myself – can be found at http://www.signandsight.com/service/1961.html (accessed 20 February 2011). Another translation with the title 'Not in our name! Jamming the gentrification machine: a manifesto' has been published in the *City* journal (NION, 2010: 323–325).
2. In brief, for Weber the existence of commerce and trade as well as associated activities such as the establishment of markets and exchanges account for the rise of modern cities. The city basically is a market settlement, complemented with a certain degree of political and administrative autonomy (Weber, 1980). In Simmel's seminal essay 'The metropolis and mental life', the modern metropolis's forms of organization allow for such a high concentration of capital that the integration of space, time and social actors reaches a hitherto unheard-of complexity. The speed and intensity of interactions in the city has led to the advent of a new, modern society – and its corollary, a transformed, metropolitan type of personality, the comparably rational and intellectual urban dweller able to protect him- or herself from the frenzy and fluctuations of the urban mess (Simmel, 2002). In this context, Benjamin serves as a timely reminder that more or less grand claims about the city's (in the singular) organizational force tend to overlook that cities (in the plural) are specific relational constellations. As such, they are haunted by the ruins of their respective pasts and the collective hopes and dreams that cannot be put to rest (Benjamin, 1982).
3. 'In fact, it may not be exaggerating the matter to say that the question of the city has superseded the preoccupation in recent decades of arts and humanities critical discourse generally with the signifying body as implicated and expressive, indeed performative, locus.' (Whybrow, 2010: 3)
4. Therefore, the notion of 'site' does not denote 'only a physical arena but one constituted through social, economic, and political processes' (Kwon, 2004: 3). The urban site therefore becomes 'an active and always incomplete incarnation of events, an actualization of times and spaces that uses the fluctuating conditions to assemble itself' (Thrift, 2007: 12).
5. For a recommendable introduction to concepts of the city and contemporary challenges to urban studies see Hubbard (2006); for a more in-depth engagement with the kind of urban thinking alluded to here see Amin and Thrift (2002).
6. Often presented as 'new', this shift can be seen as part of a wider 'entrepreneurial turn' which has been in the making over the past decades (Locke and Schöne, 2004).
7. And echoing Simmel's and Benjamin's metropolitan types of calculating individual and flaneur, respectively, the entrepreneurial city's everyday spectacles of imagineering and consumption summon 'a new urban sensibility (. . .): that of the twenty-first century

flaneur, who is in equal parts shopper, tourist and entrepreneur' (Zukin, 2008: xiii; orig. emphasis).

8.   There are larger methodological issues at stake here, which I can only briefly hint at (see Steyaert, 2009; Beyes and Steyaert, 2012). For instance, Benjamin's writings – his experiments with different forms, such as montage, aphorism, memoir, essay and journalistic reportage – confront us with the problematic of how to 'write cities', how to apprehend their complex textures and how to organise our texts in order to do justice to this complexity and ambiguity (Savage, 1995). The progressive involvement in what has been called an immaterial capitalism that increasingly valorizes the expressive and the experimental requires an organizational theorizing that experiments with ways of apprehending the everyday enactments of such formative spaces. It entails a move from representational strategies of extracting representations of the world from the world to embodied apprehensions of the everyday performing of the city, to different enactments of organizational geographies (Thrift, 2007). Going beyond conventional representational strategies thus means experimenting with 'different and as yet unformulated modes of expression (. . .), ones that *apprehend* rather than *represent* the world, modes that employ the full range of senses and evoke the kinaesthetic character of being in a world that is always becoming' (Rycroft, 2005: 354; orig. emphasis).

19 Management as farce: entrepreneurial subjectivity in the creative industries
Bent Meier Sørensen

INTRODUCTION

The managing director of Lars von Trier's production company Zentropa, Peter Aalbæk, is walking around in the offices and corridors of the organization, greeting and kissing the employees. We are watching a short documentary, *One Day with Peter*, released by Zentropa in 2004. Working his way through the barracks of the company, he finally strips naked in one of the offices in which a (male) employee is still working, talking on the phone. Directed towards the camera, Peter enthusiastically grabs his penis and shakes it, smiling. The employee keeps talking on the phone. Peter leaves, heading for the outdoor pool and sauna, wearing a colourful, perhaps African, long shirt. As he leaves, the employee picks up some of the clothes that Peter has dropped to the floor, and puts it on a hanger in the closet. In the hall, Peter shouts at an employee for a towel, which he wears around his neck walking towards the pool. Now his appearance is not unlike a boxing champ. As he approaches the pool, he teasingly threatens a group of (female) employees with exposing himself. Meanwhile, Peter is also the voice over on the documentary. At this time he says the following: 'We have a company that is totally controlled by women. All our best directors are women and so are all our best producers. . . . *We are a matriarchate*'.

At the pool he finally drops his shirt, and dives naked into the water. In the background, some employees pass by. They don't seem to pay any notice. Yet, the naked manager seems to be an important part of what produces their possibilities for self-expression and professional/personal subjectivity. This chapter will seek to analyse some of the aesthetic aspects of this production. So while the chapter at a first level focuses on the manager's activities, it aims to discuss which possibilities this gives for the production of various entrepreneurial subjectivities available to the employees.

This chapter, on its side, is structured as follows. After an introduction to the method of juxtaposition, in which various images can become unfolded, the basic concept of the 'fold' as it is found in Gilles Deleuze's philosophy is presented. This paves the way for seeing the organizational member as a 'fold' folded through aesthetic performance; indeed, one important entrepreneurial benchmark gauges the ingenuity and adequacy of this perpetual folding. An aesthetic analysis proves then to be a fruitful way of conceptualizing how an organizational pathos, working directly through the member's affective registers, is constructed on order to produce, that is, to fold, the 'ideal worker' (Weiskopf and Loacker, 2006). Before venturing into the empirical analysis, the chapter contextualizes the aesthetic framework in the current debate regarding subjectivity and entrepreneurship. The method deployed in the empirical analysis implies that images from the organization, in our case a still from the short movie *One Day with Peter*, are juxtaposed with other images that are familiar to the original image, but different from it. The juxtaposed images can be said to originate from the same 'archive' (Deleuze, 1998a), or what Taylor (2004) refers to as 'social imaginaries' that feed our joint horizons of expectation, and this way be telling for which kind of employee subjectivity the actual image is able to construct. This particular procedure provides material for understanding how an employee's subjectivity can be understood as a fold, with, as it were, one 'bureaucratic' side and one 'post-bureaucratic' or entrepreneurial side to it. Having carried through a number of 'foldings' and 'unfoldings' of such folds, the chapter will finally discuss the implications this research has for our understanding of the possible farce of contemporary management as it engages with creating worker subjectivity and entrepreneurial selves.

AESTHETIC ANALYSIS AS JUXTAPOSITION AND FOLDING

The method of juxtaposition that I put forward in this chapter is inspired by Michel Foucault,[1] but is actually quite straightforward: juxtapose two images with each other, describe their similarities and differences, and connect these observations back to the case in question. Such juxtaposition could as happens in Sørensen (2010) compare Caravaggio's two versions of *The Conversion of St Paul* (1601) with organizational models from Mintzberg (1983) and Deleuze and Guattari (1988) respectively, and analyse the consequences of their similarities, this way identifying two very different models of entrepreneurship. King (2003: 195) deployed a similar method when he juxtaposed a Mondrian painting and a model of a matrix organization drawn from Mary Jo Hatch. He admitted that the procedure may be considered ridiculous, but maintained that it also may be revealing. In this case I intend to analyse which kinds of 'archives'

(Deleuze, 1988a) the organizational aesthetic construction of subjectivity in Zentropa draws from. As indicated, the archive is seen as that imaginary or simulated resource from which the employees use material to fold their subjectivity.

As such, any juxtaposition can be considered a potential *fold* (I shall return to this concept in more detail below). When one folds two juxtaposed images in the middle where they meet, a front side and a back side is produced, with a hollow middle. The argument of this chapter runs as follows: to be an employee (or a manager) in any organization, calls for an employee that *fits* the organization, i.e., demands of the individual to constantly fold various images into a fold of the *suitable* employee, what Alvesson and Willmott (2002) call the 'appropriate individual'.

While the aesthetic regime deployed by Zentropa by definition has strategic ideas about which type of subjectivity is going to be produced, there is less trace of delimitations of such subjectivity; rather, as Maravelias (2009) has pointed out, the regime is a generator of a vast potential space in which there are ample opportunities for individual subjectivity formation – not least, of course, for the opportunists.

Through aesthetic landscaping (Gagliardi, 1996) this subjectivity is constructed via (simulated) images that are made available to the employee. These are both images produced 'in real time' through for instance managerial practices, but also, as in the present analysis, images that are, as it were, re-produced in the company imagery: marketing material, movies, art. These images become a 'source of identification' in a very material sense: they become folds potentially expressing the subjectivity of the employee.

The images that are juxtaposed in the analysis form a number of constructed archives, which all are part of an ideal, simulated dimension, a common fantasy or social imaginary, activated by the aesthetic regime deployed in Zentropa, when images and stills are produced in the short movie. Through such sensuous activation, then, the forces of the archive, as Massumi (1987a) explains, folds the archives' ideals 'back down onto bodies and things', in order to produce recognizable, appropriate individuals. In order to understand this procedure, the body is perhaps best understood, with Harding (2002), as split into a physical body and a 'thought body', the latter conveying the archive's images and discourses onto the body physical: 'hence the material body is revealed to be a "thought body" whose particular locale in a technical, cultural and scientific history provides it with the ideas through which it is thought into being'.

The archives which are folded back onto the body are then the material making up such 'technical, cultural and scientific history', archives which also include, of course, images. With such a conceptualization, subjectivity is not supposed to be an inner quality of the human, but a configuration

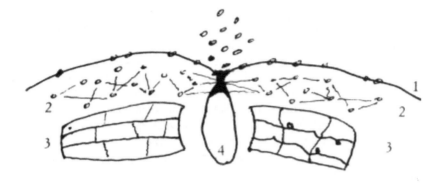

1. Ligne du dehors   2. Zone stratégique   3. Strates   4. Pli (zone de subjectivation

DIAGRAMME DE FOUCAULT

Figure 19.1   The fold ('Foucault's diagram')

imposed onto the subject through the 'thought body' and its historical archives. In mainstream organizational research, the formation of subjectivity is normally traced *inwards*, into the 'core' of the person, his or her inner or indeed 'true' and authentic self (Ladkin and Taylor, 2010). The aesthetic method of juxtaposing and unfolding goes the reverse direction, tracing the imagery's archive and projecting it onto a 'geographical, historical, and political *map* of the world' (Deleuze and Guattari, 1986: 10), that is, contextualizing it in its material and political significance.

The method is sought illustrated by reproducing Deleuze's (1988: 120) diagram above. Figure 19.1 illustrates the fold, and shows how the subject's fold (no. 4 in Figure 19.1) is 'a folding of the outside' (the area above the line of the fold, opposing the fields of the so-called 'strata'). This way, the outside gets folded into an inside: you don't so much bring your subjectivity into the organization as you fold the organization unto and into yourself. Yet, 'the outside', that is, free thought, is always the force that opens up other ways of becoming a subject, than those prescribed by the strata. The expression 'the outside' is one Deleuze has picked up from Foucault, and it serves to indicate that there always remains an amount of freedom and resistance in how the actual, material folding takes place. The 'outside' signifies a thought practice, a reflective position vis-à-vis one's own formation of subjectivity. Yet, as Deleuze (1988a: 98) argues, 'I do not encounter myself on the outside, I find the other in me . . .' The fold, he continues, 'resembles exactly the invagination of a tissue in embryology, or the act of doubling in sewing: twist, fold, stop, and so on.'

The two sides of the fold, each side facing a specific set of strata, may then be unfolded again, and juxtaposed with other images from the same stratum. This procedure is as such indefinite; each unfolding, however, should be assessed on its relevance and the ideas that it produces: a virtual map of possibilities.

Folding does not, in other words, take place in a vacuum. Any notion of a decontextualized 'free will' is primarily and ideological exercise, much like 'the free market' is. The strata are closing in on the fold, which is to say that the stratified archive of available material (images, ideologies, organizational cultures, language games, mediatized imagery, human resource technologies, Facebooks of various kinds) from which the employee draws the material with which to produce 'myself as a subject' as Deleuze says, is becoming a more and more set game, and an intimate part of a smooth set of control technologies. You may be folding yourself, but you are, meanwhile, being folded. As you are explicating who you are, it is already implicit who you are supposed to be. Yet in the creative sector's post-bureaucracy, limitations and delimitations have receded, and the managerial efforts are directed towards creating a potential multiplicity, an infinite number of folds, in which subject formation can happen. This multiplicity is then what we may refer to as 'freedom'.

While the inside of the fold may be what we usually refer to as subjectivity (traditionally referred to as identity or personality), its character as a substantive given has been heavily exploited in organization studies. But this central essence is rather to be conceptualized as a void. Deleuze (1988a: 121) reads Melville on the possible core matter of the person: 'we look for a central chamber, afraid that there will be no one there and that man's soul will reveal nothing but an immense and terrifying void'.

As it etymologically speaking is significant to talk about the employee as a fold, this void becomes especially precarious for the *un*employed. The word 'employee' dates itself back to the fifteenth century and stems from Middle French *employer* (see Sørensen, 2009b), a word which is derived from the Latin *implicare*, to enfold, involve, implicate. To be employed is to be implicated, from Latin *in-* + *plicare*, in a com-pli-cated multi-pli-city, a manifold. This logic is, in Deleuze's (1993) baroque vision, of course not restricted to employees. It goes for all matters, living or non-living. What the parallel denotation between employer (Fr. *employer*) and fold (Fr. *pli*) shows, rather, is how a certain, stratified fold, the employee, has become the signifier and subjectifier of capitalism, a social imaginary that 'channels our desire so that desire desires its own repression' (Carter and Jackson, 2004: 112). No surprise that un-employment today is a death sentence, economically, socially, existentially and, of course, aesthetically.

The present analysis will, as already indicated, focus on the outside, that is, the images that practically construe the fold. The analysis is then formed as a series of *un-foldings*, in which the im-plicated imagery in this aesthetic landscaping is ex-plicated and made accessible for critique. This unfolding focuses on the body and its presence in organizational practice.

THE BODY AND AFFECT

In their detailed study of organizational performance, Hancock and Tyler (2007: 514) point out that the expressivity of the organizational member implies this member's embodied presence and that: 'the presentation, maintenance and performance of a mode of embodiment that is specified or compelled by their employing organization has become a central component of the work performed by many employees'.

When Peter Aalbæk in the short movie's voice over declares that Zentropa is a 'matriarchate', while at the same time performing his own body like a boxing champ (if not quite at his fighting weight), there is a short circuiting of the cognitive faculties, and the performance acts directly upon the sensuous, non-cognitive faculties of the recipients. This way the individuals in question, the employees to be precise, are incorporated into an 'aestheticized regime of meaning or *pathos*' (Hancock, 2005: 35), which 'influence [the subjects'] *perception* of reality, to the point of subtly shaping beliefs, norms and cultural values' (Gagliardi quoted in Hancock, 2005: 35). The spectacle we are about to confront, Aalbæk's spectacle, cannot be fully comprehended by reducing it to its representational content; what becomes important is the spectacle's *production of affects*. The posing of the naked body produces affects.

Affects, however, should not be confused with feelings (Massumi, 2002). Whereas feelings are personal, affects are pre-personal: the affect is the feeling freed from its object and the subject that experiences it (Colebrook, 2002: 21ff). Affects occur prior to the subject that experiences feelings. The charismatic leader uses, in practice, affects. Her trick is that despite the fact that we might despise her, she nevertheless elicits affects which pass our cognitive and emotional filters and, often against our intentions, forces us into an affected state for which we cannot entirely account. One may here think of Sarah Palin (Massumi uses the former US president Ronald Reagan as example, Massumi, 1996). Palin's force lies in particular in the communication of affects that amounts to a whole 'pathos of America', rather than strict communication of meaning. A regime of pathos is concerned about its production of affects. Aesthetically speaking, it is the affects released by today's image bombardment, argues Massumi (2002: 42), that 'holds a key to rethinking power after ideology'.

Concretely, 'organizational bodies' like Peter Aalbæk's own, but also the bodies of his employees become elicitors and receptors of affects, or 'material signifiers of an organizational pathos' (Hancock and Tyler, 2007: 514). Such aestheticized regime of pathos, observe Weiskopf and Loacker (2006: 397), continuously 'produces images of the "ideal worker" or employee'. By the force of these images, we are all fundamentally subjected to regimes of work as this way of deploying pathos may develop into what Gagliardi (2006: 713) calls 'an extraordinary resource for coordination', in the sense that the individuals themselves contribute by creating, that is, folding, a subjectivity that corresponds to this particular aestheticized regime of pathos. Failing to do so, they will not be recognized by the organization and they will soon, especially in the creative sector's project based work, find themselves expelled from the organization: insecurity becomes a premise in subjectivity formation at work (Collinson, 2003). Yet an informed aesthetic analysis should be able to decode or uncover the organization's in- and excluding aestheticization of meaning (a subjectivity dependent on style and affect rather than values and relation), thus paving way for 'an alternative and potentially critical way of knowing organization' (Hancock, 2005: 35). In the present case, the critical knowledge pertains to the subjectivity of the organizational members and how their bodies are inscribing and inscribed in various figures of entrepreneurship.

SUBJECTIVITY, ENTREPRENEURSHIP AND THE BODY

While I until now have sought to explicate how subjectivity ontologically can be considered a fold, and how the practice of folding can be analysed aesthetically, I want, before proceeding to the empirical analysis, briefly to contextualize this analysis in organization studies' current theorizing. The rather excessive practice in Zentropa by CEO Peter Aalbæk depicted in the documentary *One Day with Peter* does, with its kissing and caressing, skinny-dipping and somewhat forced colloquialism, appear out of the ordinary. Yet in its extraordinariness it captures key points of what contemporary work-life is about. It may, after all, not be so terrible extraordinary. Stripped of its pomp and circumstances, in, perhaps, its sheer dullness and conventionality, it offers us some strong inroads subjectivity and entrepreneurship. The case has from one point of view the emperor, Peter Aalbæk, at its centre. However, as this figure become 'unfolded' it will offer images of creative subjectivity and entrepreneurial selfhood that to a critical degree pertains to the employees in the creative industries.

From such a 'shop floor' point of view, the case also produces images of a less expressive, 'bureaucratic' subjectivity, that exists vis-à-vis the expressive, entrepreneurial figure.

With this intent, the study places itself in the middle of organization studies, as well as modern management. The attempt to capture subjectivity is, argue Costea et al. (2008), today's general agenda for management. This agenda must be connected to the likewise dominant trope of the literature that entrepreneurship is the *sine qua non* of work in high capitalism, indeed, its Prince and hegemonic actor (Levy and Scully, 2007).

At bottom, the entrepreneur and the concept of subjectivity come together in what has been termed 'the entrepreneurial self' (du Gay, 2000; Kelly, 2006), characterized by a subjectivity that constantly senses and measures the potential opportunities in a given situation. The entrepreneurial self appears most pedagogically in its difference from the subjectivity of the bureaucratic worker. The bureaucratic organization would allegedly delimit the 'personal' subjectivity from becoming entangled in work, less for the sake of this subject's privacy, but in order to live up to its Weberian ideal of performing work *sine ire et studio*, that is, 'without anger and fondness'. The post-bureaucratic or entrepreneurial organization of today on the contrary includes subjectivity as its very core site of production. Here the organization is supposed to prosper from the inherent creativity of the worker's personal and affective capabilities, whereas the worker's self is supposed to prosper from radically enhanced possibilities for self-creation: post-bureaucratic work 'provides the opportunity to enhance personal value, to realize previously latent capabilities in the service of self-affirmation and self-realization' (Costea et al., 2008: 675). Evidently, this intensification of work and permanent crossing of limits between work and self cannot be understood entirely as subordination under corporate power (Knights and Willmott, 1989) or entirely as labour's 'dressage' (Jackson and Carter, 1998), but must as Maravelias (2009) shows, be understood in its precarious relation to freedom. Whereas freedom in a bureaucratic organization is constructed as the tension between a set of external limitations and demands which balances the 'autonomy' of the self, the post-bureaucratic organization reconfigures freedom in the form of 'potential' (Maravelias, 2009). In order to live up to this expected potential, the self becomes the very device that senses and measures potential opportunities:

> Rather than as a slave or a silent rebel the post-bureaucratic worker hereby emerges as an *opportunist* who must constantly fight against any form of subordination, even the subordination of his or her self. (Maravelias, 2009: 568)

The opportunities thus seized are doubled, as they both open creative vistas for the corporate production as well as for the existential realization of this self, a self which becomes constructed as an infinite resource of performativity (Costea et al., 2007: 247). Weiskopf and Loacker (2006) see the 'post-disciplinary' mode of organizing as a continuous 'process of subjectification that contains both possibilities for increased subjection and for self-creation.' The corporate catchphrase 'Just be yourself' (Fleming and Sturdy, 2009) encapsulates this double movement of the self as the site of corporate production as well as the agora of a self-expression. The very junction between the self as the personal site of expression and the self as the entrepreneurial engine of current capitalism is motivated by a neoliberal ideology that ties subjectivity down to the image of an individualized, psychological actor who must obey the law of opportunism (Styhre, 2005; Kelly, 2006).

Historically, the entrepreneur emerged as a distinct figure under the pressure of a deregulated and liberalized economy, in which the state's ability to intervene was shrinking; as we know from Margaret Thatcher, *'there's no such thing as society*. There are individual men and women and there are families' (Thatcher, 1987). This individual becomes the primary locus for the action capability of that emerging entrepreneur who during the last four decades has attained mythological powers, hitherto ascribed other historical figures (Ogbor, 2000; Deutschmann, 2001). He – much less often she – rises up from within the creative class with nothing less than the power of a saviour (Bill, 2006; Sørensen, 2008), as a potential Superhuman (Townley, 1999). Unsurprisingly, the actual entrepreneur tends to be unable to live up to such mythological expectations and remains curiously sublime (Jones and Spicer, 2005). In the present case, it is the CEO Peter Aalbæk whose body performs (somewhat) superhumanly and (in certain measures) sublimely, and it is this performance that calls forth or interpellates the employees' performance in a vast potential space. Or, conversely, Aalbæk's imperial décor can be seen as being interpellated by the employees' expectations and projective urge for identification. This is a methodological tension to which I will return.

As the worker's subjectivity, if not the worker's entire life (Lazzarato, 2006), is being integrated into the 'expressive organization' (Schultz et al., 2000) and becoming part and parcel of productivity, expressiveness becomes a set requirement for each and everyone. *Perform, or else!* as McKenzie's (2001) suggestive book title has it. With the rise of self-management, where the responsibility of a number of previously managerial obligations like planning and surveying is becoming a part of the worker's own portfolio of tasks, expressivity on the level of the worker becomes important: the employee has to become visible through his or her own account, and actively create him- or herself as a branded resource with unique capabilities: as a true, authentic subject (Fleming and Sturdy, 2009; Johnsen et al., 2009). In this case, the indispensability of the body as an entrepreneurial token and at the same time as a topology sexualized in precarious ways comes to the fore. This was also confirmed in my recent study of the performance artist Miss Black Rose who in her act undressed, bathed in milk and distributed the milk to the spectators in a solemn communion: her naked body worked as a site of entrepreneurial transformation of both her subjectivity as well as of the subjectivity of the crowd (Sørensen, 2009a). Hazard and Elita's (2008) book *The Naked Entrepreneur* (intriguingly subtitled: *A Millionaire's Journey from Fear to True Wealth*) is not just a mainstream story of entrepreneurship, but also an indicator of the centrality of embodiment (and, as it were, nakedness) in entrepreneurship studies. The body is an agent of expression, but this at the same time puts pressure onto the same entrepreneur – not least his fear of being 'found out' (Sørensen, 2006: 139). The aestheticized body is indeed a site of power struggle and an important place where entrepreneurship shows its intimate relation to politics (Steyaert and Hjorth, 2002; Hjorth and Steyaert, 2009).

FOLDING YOUR SUBJECTIVITY IN ZENTROPA

Zentropa is a Danish film production company founded by film director Lars von Trier (*Breaking the Waves*, *Dancer in the Dark*, *Antichrist* and more) together with its producer (and managing director) Peter Aalbæk in 1992. Trier and Aalbæk own 25 per cent of the company, 25 per cent is owned by the employers and 50 per cent was bought by another Danish film company, Nordisk Film, as of February 2008. Since then, economic crisis has hit hard, and Aalbæk is no longer formally managing director. The homepage of Zentropa, however, still informs us that Trier is the 'creative brain behind Zentropa', while Aalbæk is the 'visible leader'. According to Aalbæk, Zentropa is based on three distinct values: Christianity, Communism, Capitalism. This triplet is a suitable background on which to consider the documentary *One Day with Peter*, a 16-minute documentary directed by Pablo Tréhin-Marçot (2004). In it, we follow producer and Managing Director Peter Aalbæk for what is ostensibly one day. Peter Aalbæk is known in the company by his first name, and Peter begins every day by greeting 'everyone' in the company: he will kiss the women and shake hands with the men. The issue of gender is confronted straight away in the voice over. Regarding the kissing says Peter: 'There is no system there . . . but I do not kiss the men. I think that's disgusting.' One man does seem to get a hug, though, but he turns out to be Peter's son, who is working as a handy man in the company.

The female employees are then, in various ways, kissed and hugged. In an opening scene Peter refers to himself as 'a preacher man's son', and declares, while holding up both his hands palms outward, that he sees himself much as a 'priest' in the company, 'blessing' its members. Some of the women, the not so tall ones in particular, are even blessed in the more old-fashioned style where the minister lays his hands on their heads. And indeed, the movie both opens and ends with the Friday company gathering, in which everybody sings. It's not really 'songs' that are sung. It is hymns. In the current case, it is a well-known Danish hymn *We Plough the Fields and Scatter* by Jakob Knudsen.

Back at the greeting spree, most of the women appear slightly taken aback by the kissing and hugging, though some accept it more readily. For a great part of both the women and the men, the greetings seem to come as an interruption of their work. Some men, for instance, greet their boss without really taking their eyes of the computer screen.

During the movie, Peter's voice over commentary expounds on what we see, but also on Zentropa, life and business in general. Peter says this about his own role in the company: 'I like being a pain in the ass to Lars [von Trier] and Vibeke [Vindeløv, a prominent Zentropa producer] . . . that's the part I play.' He further philosophizes about business: 'I think business is more pure [compared] to other things in life. You talk about the hidden agenda is money. But with business it's clear for everyone that here it's money.'

Then we are invited inside Peter's 'office', which is really furnished as a living room. Peter Aalbæk explicitly, in the voice over, abolishes any distinction between his spare time and his working hours. Of course he has his 'own family', but Zentropa is a family with which he spends 'much more time'. He has a conversation with a (female) producer on his sofa, after which he falls asleep there. The conversation is about a pay raise that the producer has asked for. Peter is halfway lying with his feet on the table and with his legs parallel to the sofa, in effect pushing the producer deep into the corner of the sofa. The game seems set from the start, premised on what Butler (1993) names 'the heterosexual matrix', in which the male position is assumed dominant. Unsurprisingly, the producer did not get the raise she came for. As is becoming apparent, perhaps also unsurprisingly, in Zentropa it is far from 'clear for everyone that here it's money'.

During the movie, Aalbæk of course also attends to what we may call more traditional 'real business', as was the case with the producer's salary negotiation. But on each occasion, just as with the pay-raise conversation, the scenes where it should be 'clear for everyone that here it's money',

Figure 19.2   Unfolding #1

this is never entirely clear. In one scene, Peter is signing bills and budgets. The voice-over informs us that he (Peter) was always fond of invoices: he would as a child write them out to his father (the reverend). Strikingly, at Zentropa, he enters the same activity with what seems to be much less seriousness than reportedly was the case back in the rectory. Again, we see his feet on the table as he hurries through the invoices that his assistant hands him, not even glancing on each sheet, rather just putting his signature on the dotted line, saying 'I trust Marianne [an accountant] on this . . .'. Indeed, as he informs the viewer, 'I could [as well] be selling pigs.'

The closing event of this short movie depicts the typical end of the week: Aalbæk in the sauna and bathing. The sequence begins when Aalbæk has just stripped naked in the office of one of the employees.

This image will be the focus of the empirical analysis. At a recent conference, I had shown (excerpts of) the movie, and had then put up this still for the audience to discuss. Stating my pedagogical question, 'What is this?', I got an answer far better than the stale question deserved: 'It's the cover of a management guru book!' This answer epitomized the core of the insight that I find in this picture. Admittedly, such a claim has to be unpacked to make sense. But imagine folding the picture along the (imagined) dividing line down through the middle of the image, and appreciate how one half-part of the image becomes the front and one half-part becomes the back of the book. As we fold the image around such a management guru book, we will, as attention seeking publisher, of course put the naked entrepreneur and founder on the front cover, and the old school knowledge-worker seen to the right on the back.

If we consider this still to be a part of the aesthetic landscaping, out of which the appropriate individual folds his or her subjectivity, this fold is suitable: one side being the knowledge-worker at his desk, the other side being the naked boss. We may further say that two specific strata or archives are implicated in this multiplicity, that is, two strata have provided the necessary material for the folding, one being a stratum containing 'images of knowledge-workers', another being a stratum containing 'images of nakedness'. We could of course construct numerous other strata, but must choose which ones to construct strategically in relation to the folding procedure we want to analyse: what do we want to unfold? The intention here is, in other words, to reveal the kinds of 'archives' (Deleuze, 1988a) that the organizational aesthetic construction of subjectivity in Zentropa draws upon. Such archive is seen as the imaginary or simulated resource from which the employees use material to fold their subjectivity. The analysis experiments with which juxtapositions may be productive in identifying the opportunities the employees have for folding their entrepreneurial subjectivity.

Any juxtaposition can be considered a potential fold. When one folds two juxtaposed images in the middle where they meet, a front side and a back side is produced, with a hollow middle. The argument runs as follows: to be an employee (and a manager) in any organization, an employee that *fits* the organization, i.e. demands of the individual to constantly fold various images into a fold of the suitable employee, what Alvesson and Willmott (2002) call the 'appropriate individual'. Through aesthetic landscaping this subjectivity is constructed via simulated images that are made available to the employee.

While 'the aesthetic regime deployed by Zentropa' by definition gives strategic ideas about which type of subjectivity is going to be produced, there are no traces of delimitations; rather, as Maravelias (2009) has pointed out, the regime is a generator of a vast potential space in which there are ample opportunities for individual subjectivity formation – not least, of course, for the opportunists.

This simple procedure now allows us to see the image in Figure 19.1 as the – now unfolded – fold of a modern, creative knowledge worker: on the one side we see the bureaucratic, knowledge-creating and -exchanging employee, and on the other side we see this knowledge worker's creative plane, his raving, orgone-charged and, indeed, sexually aroused desire and urge for freedom. While the right side expresses the knowledge worker's 'bureaucratic' component, the left – and somewhat noisier – side expresses this knowledge worker's 'entrepreneurial' component. The image is in total a part of a vast 'geographical, historical, and political *map* of the world' (Deleuze and Guattari, 1986: 10), which can be explored: what are the images that feed into this double component, on each side of the divide?

These questions are pursued in Unfolding #2 (Figure 19.3). The image of Peter has been juxtaposed with an image of four (un-identified) Nigerians at a 1944 traditional Durbar festival (Levine, 2008: 214). The Nigerians were to appear for the colonial governor, and had dressed accordingly, that is by mocking the ceremonials and the colonial Western gaze: they had painted themselves white and equipped themselves only with white penis sheaths and odd head gear: the crowd, it was observed 'laughed heartily in appreciation' (Levine, 2008: 214). This stratum, 'images of nakedness', of course contains a lot of more straightforward images of 'savages' without clothes, which could more readily have been juxtaposed to the naked Aalbæk. But many of these images that mirror Aalbæk more 'precisely', mirrors him exactly because they themselves are exemplary of the 'colonial imagination' (Levine, 2008: 214).

In the image of the four Nigerians that I have chosen as an unfolding of Aalbæk's posture, the imagery is itself staged and ironic, much like Aalbæk's image is staged and (at least possibly) ironic. Both Aalbæk and the Nigerians are *simulating* being 'Aalbæk' and 'Nigerians'. This neither subtracts nor adds to their 'realness', as simulation is the engine of any multiplicity, but it does expose the strategic pose that the camera calls forth. It also gives both images a certain character of 'commentary'. Such archive of commentary remains a part of the fundamental monument of the juxtaposition. They comment on the relation between nakedness and clothing in a colonial setting and a creative industries setting, respectively.

There is a likeness between Aalbæk's pose and that of the Nigerian in the middle. They have both caught the camera's eye, and they both tease the audience; they show off. Their gesture and pose directs the attention towards the genitals, and while the Nigerian is not holding his (own) penis, as Aalbæk is, he is holding so much more, in a gesture of victory, a stick which practically has a tag attached to it: This Is A Phallus! The humor wasn't lost on the crowd in Nigeria, neither is it lost on the crowds that I have shown the movie: they always laugh when Aalbæk waves his penis. There may be, in the applause, an acknowledgement of the normally

Figure 19.3   Unfolding #2

352

unacknowledged fact that the penis always seems to be in need of *technologies of extension* to become a phallus: the penis, in its flaccid and sagging, 'natural' stage, is an embarrassment. The men in the pictures need penis sheaths or, lacking that, a helping hand in order for the penis to appear before the gaze. The penis as it appears as part of a body is potentially a sign of weakness, at least when faced with the gaze that craves the African libido or the Manager's management, or where the two come together, in modern, fun-loving and creative companies. One may sharpen the point: *the penis appears always to be in need of management*. This jibes well with the etymological root of the term manager, *manus*, Latin for hand, which became established through the Italian *maneggiare*, a term directly connected to handling things, especially horses (Wensley, 1996). The horse is often, in Greek folklore, depicted as one of the prime phallic animals (Keuls, 1993), and management's close connection to and need of such a powerful phallus can be understood through this connection. In order, then, to appear as phallus, one has to *maneggiare* the penis, either by hand (as Aalbæk does) or by penis sheaths, where the hand in the Nigerian case handles the penis substitute, namely a real and functioning, that is, *erect*, phallus.

The facial expressions and the staging suggest that the 'real' phallus, the historical *Citizen Cane* style entrepreneur (the Chief Executive Officer and the Colonial Governor, respectively), has returned as a post-bureaucratic, soft and all-encompassing entrepreneurial manager, although this time as farce. Marx (1972) famously suggested (mocking Hegel) that great historical events appear twice, first as tragedy, second as farce. In our case, the first appearance of the phallus of management certainly draped itself tragically in the industrial alienation and the colonial zeal, respectively. Confirming Marx's mockery, both these proud, Western phalluses have returned as farce: a soft, inviting yet unpredictable entrepreneur. This farcical appearance is epitomized in Aalbæk's post-modern, creative industries manager: we can all shake our dicks and express ourselves, and there should be no shame attached.

Connected to this shamelessness is another significant farcical return, the return of the faltering, imperial gaze of Africa, in 1944: "We are the savages!", the Nigerians suggest as they laugh, painting themselves white, and managing their phallus as the ever so fallen European kings' sceptres. The nakedness of the savage is in itself a significant emblem. Some of my students have suggested that Aalbæk's nakedness is a sign of his creativity, an idea supported by mainstream literature on the subject of entrepreneurship and creativity. Po Bronson's bestseller *The Nudist on the Late Shift, and other Tales of Silicon Valley* (1999), reports on: 'the programmer community [in which] eccentricity is de rigueur, and when [the entrepreneur]

David Coons and his wife held skinny-dipping parties, he invited his friends from work. So nobody made much of it that he took his clothes off at the office after 10 p.m.'

This is, as it were, also the case with the CEO of *American Apparel*, Dov Charney (see Moor and Littler, 2008), who entertains a practice of walking around in his Los Angeles clothing factories in his underwear or even less (none of the corresponding lawsuits against Charney have, however, led to verdict). He connects his practice to nature and to a philosophy that will let the immediate desire rule the day. Likewise, at Zentropa, Aalbæk's skinny dipping now occupies ordinary office hours.

But nakedness and savagery is not just an indicator of creativity. It also occupies the Victorian bourgeoisie's repressed dream of freedom. It remains, though, a dream. Historically, as the history of Nigeria attests, this Victorian fantasy amounts to a colonial nightmare of projective imagery. In early Western history the clothed body became, with background in for instance Mark. 5:15: 'Clothed and in their right mind', connected to salvation and sanity: 'People displaying no shame at being naked, then, were people whose souls were in danger' (Levine, 2008: 191). These naked individuals were, obviously, endangered by their proximity to the animal, to sexuality and to a potent, savage monstrosity; in some ways, the naked body signals its intimate relation to the original creation before civilization. The nakedness only becomes real sin when confronted with Civilization, that is, clothed (and white, etc.) people. Here it becomes obvious that man actually has a (moral) choice to make, and can become clothed. Zentropa's triumvirate 'Christianity, Communism and Capitalism' has an obvious predecessor in the missionaries' triumvirate 'Christianity, Civilization and Clothing'. In correspondence to this last value, the colonial gaze would often when photographing place clothed colonialists together with unclothed savages (also this way exposing the superior height of the Europeans/Arians). Insofar as the natives had not yet been taught Christianity, their creativity was still innocent, and it would allegedly still connect to an orgone freedom, also sexually. Indeed, as Levine (2008: 210) argues, circulating images of colonialized natives were by default oversexualized: 'The non-Western body, with its absence of shame and its apparent normalizing or incomprehension of nudity, re-mapped that violation [of taboo], creating a safe space for observing naked bodies belonging to nameless, over-sexualized people to whom shame could not, allegedly, attach.'

Yet, the second return of nudity is not *over*-sexualized, rather, in Aalbæk's case, *under*-sexualized: it comes not as tragedy but as farce. This is, on the other hand, what gives Aalbæk the possibility to stage his body as a decoded, smooth surface for anyone to code for him- and herself: the manager disappears in order to create a potential space for the entrepreneurial, self-managing employee.

Moreover, as we noted earlier, an aesthetic regime of pathos is directed at producing *affects*, a production which forges a link between the intended effects and a pre-personal plane; Peter Aalbæk is not 'ideological', setting a clear programme for the conduct and the production at Zentropa, but *affectual*, which works all the better by being, really, impossible to cognitively 'accept'. Aalbæk this way affords the serene knowledge worker with a sense of urgency and excitement (if only directionless). There is, then, another important side to the expressive subjectivity that Aalbæk explicitly conditions: a side represented by the knowledge-worker to the right in the picture. Without the ado of his manager, this character nevertheless is the necessary other side of the suitable employee of Zentropa; the real difficulty in producing one's entrepreneurial subjectivity in the creative industries is that you must be in command of both. This calls for an unfolding of this other character.

THE LESS NOISY ENTREPRENEUR AND THE SOLEMNITY OF KNOWLEDGE WORK

While Aalbæk at work appears as a pure celebration, the other side of the still calls for an entrepreneurial subjectivity of no less importance, if of a less noisy style, a subjectivity bent on *production*. In the original still, the knowledge worker appears entirely undisturbed by Aalbæk's performance. He only takes notice when there is an actual task at hand, namely to pick up Aalbæk's dropped clothing and put it on a hanger in the closet. Contrary to the expressiveness of Aalbæk, the knowledge worker (or *this side* of the knowledge worker, as opposed to his expressive and entrepreneurial, *naked* side) is highly functional, fitting like a Weberian cog in the machine, installed as he is as an intermediary in the circulations of knowledge and its categorization in the archive, as the archive covers the wall behind the employee. This is an ordered world, in which each thing has its place.

The production of knowledge is connected to networks of information technologies, but is also, specifically, bathed in light, a light that is itself invisible, but lights up the world. The tradition for connecting knowledge to light and to the process of becoming visible is long, marked in Plato's cave myth, but also among artists and religious mystics, as for instance seen in the church father Nicholas of Cusa (Debrix, 1999), for whom vision and light is the essence of God's (and the mystics) true essence, an essence one comes to partake in through *gnosis*, knowledge (Rossbach, 1996;

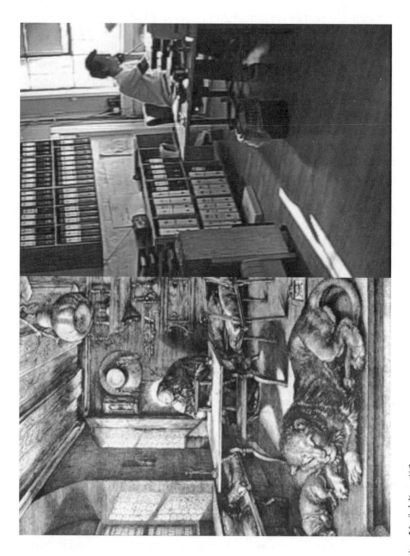

Figure 19.4   Unfolding #3

Kaulingfreks and Bos, 2005). We may, as in the unfolding of the 'images of knowledge workers'-stratum below, unfold the imaginary that is implicated in today's understanding of an entrepreneurial knowledge-worker.

The engraving which in the Unfolding #3 (Figure 19.3) has been juxtaposed with the knowledge worker is 'the scholar-saint at work' as the work is referred to at British Museum: Albrect Dürer's *St Jerome in His Study* (1514). The figure can be identified as St Jerome (AD 347–420) via for instance the cardinal hat, the lion and the dog – the latter signifying loyalty. Jerome was an extremely productive scholar of the early Christian church, and it is fair to see him as the leading Christian entrepreneur of the early church (rivaled only by Augustine). Jerome remains patron saint of translators, librarians and encyclopaedists. We see him, just as we see the knowledge worker on the right, deeply immersed in his work, untouched by the surroundings, be it naked bosses or lions. They are also both untouched by 'the viewer', be it the artist/the viewer of the art work, or, as is the case with the other side of the fold, the naked boss and his camera crew. Jerome may be translating the bible into Latin in this picture (the *Vulgata* edition is based on Jerome's work), just as the employee on the right may be 'translating' his knowledge from the archive behind him into understandable data for the person with whom he is talking on the phone. While the immediate focus in the original still remains with Aalbæk's naked body and shaking penis, there is at the same time a strange relation between him and his employee: a distance created not by Aalbæk, but by his employee. This third unfolding suggests that the distance is created through the communality that the employee shares with other (seemingly lonely) knowledge workers. Knowledge workers are, as Jerome in fact was, monks or, with Leibniz, *monads* – the words enjoy the same Greek root, *monos*, alone (Serres, 1995a: 96) – whose loneliness only constitutes an entire world because the monks, as Serres further points out, continuously communicate with God. This is the way, possibly, to appreciate the apparently absurd practice of monks in a monastery praying. Today, where faith-intensive organizations have been replaced with knowledge-intensive organizations, this practice has been reinforced through communication technologies, which in turn create a variety of worlds in which the knowledge workers partake. None of these worlds, however, seems to include their manager, Peter Aalbæk. Perhaps he is too ignorant or noisy, his spectacular embodiment excluding him from experiencing *gnosis*. The suitable entrepreneurial employee subjectivity in Zentropa is, then, very dynamic and manifold, and must encompass both the expressive side and the knowledge side. If one only encompasses the expressive side, one is in effect usurping Aalbæk's position. If one only encompasses the knowledge side, one is in effect a subcontractor. The discussion will reflect on how such a dilemma is managed through the production of paradoxes and ambiguities.

DISCUSSION

While Aalbæk through his affective pose appears to express a creativity that existed prior to both civilization and organization, he also opens a paradoxical space in which the entrepreneurial subjectivity of the worker may be reshaped (Jones, 2002; Jones and Spicer, 2009; Knights, 2002; Kelly, 2006; Townley, 1993). In this space he is a colloquial character with an office designed as a living room, and a habit of penis shaking and skinny dipping during office hours: a soft man, round and affectionate. In short outbursts, however, he is also able to 'make hard decisions' (as he says in the movie). A classical psychoanalytical reading would divide Aalbæk's performance into the visible and the repressed, respectively, and read the repressed from the visible. Zizek (2008: 202) is the best-qualified position here:

> A 'postmodern' boss insists that he is not a master but just a coordinator of our joint creative efforts, the first among equals; there should be no formalities among us, we should address him by his nickname, he shares a dirty joke with us . . . but during all this, he *remains our master*.

The motivation behind the fact that the knowledge-worker ignores Aalbæk may then be, as Zizek further argues, that in such a social link, 'relations of domination function through their denial: in order to be operative, they have to be ignored'. Yet while this is a possible reading, it is still subjected to reiterating a master–slave dichotomy – if now only now with the 'anal' and 'impotent' father, rather than the capitalized Father as the master (Zizek, 2001, p. 127), much the same way as Harding (2002) sees the manager's uniform way of clothing (with a 'phallic' neck tie) as a way of disguising his body; a body which expresses his more human, or, with Ladkin and Taylor (2010), *authentic* self. The only difference is that Zizek (as usual) has reversed the codes, so that what we see is the soft humanism, and what is hidden is the actual (and hence somewhat authentic) agent.

Such psychoanalytical readings are challenged by the method of juxtaposition, in which only what can be seen and felt, that is, only what has a material base in the empirical assemblage is part of the analysis. The hierarchy of master and slave is, I want to conclude, more ambiguous than just a reiteration of this ancient form. The ancient had, as one may remember, different brotherhoods (and sisterhoods) that stood aside those of 'the world': the knowledge worker in the still turns away, redraws and holds back, performing a subjectivity that, in Heidegger's (1962) words, shelters and spares the ground where he sits. The corona that surrounds St Jerome protects him from the lion, just as the knowledge-worker in the still is protected from Aalbæk's expressive demands, since this figure partakes in another form of communication: the stratum containing 'images of knowledge-workers' is an active resource in the Zentropa-worker's tactic of folding a viable subjectivity. While this subjectivity is less marketable than the one Aalbæk's performance offers, it is not entirely disconnected to desire. We may indeed see it as another way of producing desire. This side of the juxtaposition is 'bureaucratic man' only insofar as we link bureaucracy directly to desire, as Deleuze and Guattari (1986: 56–7) wants us to do: while there 'isn't a desire *for* bureaucracy, to repress or to be repressed', there exists, they argue, 'bureaucracy *as* desire'. This is a production that is present when the bureaucrats caress their computers and documents, fondle their books and eagerly look forward to their daily comic: 'a bureaucratic perversion, a permanent inventiveness or creativity practiced even against administrative regulations' (Deleuze and Guattari, 1988: 214). This is another creativity, an immanent one rather than the expressive and noisy creativity placarded by Aalbæk.

This, finally, points to what I have referred to as 'folding' as a practice of *connecting* and *conjoining*, rather than a practice of separating. Mainstream management and not least entrepreneurship studies are to a high extent characterized by producing polarizing distinctions (Borgerson and Rehn, 2004). Entrepreneurship studies distinguish between male and the (unmentioned) female entrepreneur, between the successful and the (unmentioned) unsuccessful entrepreneur, between the entrepreneur and the (unmentioned) bureaucratic man, etc. As Peter Aalbæk produces a vast, virtual or potential space for the employee to project her or his personal images of entrepreneurship, its strength is precisely its ambiguity or fluidity: the potential unfoldings are indefinite and show analytically the fluid possibilities that the employees have for constructing themselves in the entrepreneurial spirit produced by their supposed manager (Bruni et al., 2004; Linstead and Brewis, 2004).

Folds and foldings of course also do not have to follow the naturalized, mathematical lines in the frame – other folding could presumably focus on the expression of direct, sexualized connections between Aalbæk and the male employee. The voice-over assures us as referred above that 'There is no system there . . . but I do not kiss the men. I think that's disgusting.' Yet the visual material shows a man showing off his penis in the employee's office, and the voice over seems on the contrary to actually express the 'system' in its (failed) attempt to freeze the potential and dangerous fluidity of (not least homoerotic) sexuality (Linstead, 2000; Fleming, 2007).

The modern employee in the creative sector is faced, as this alternative folding suggest, with another precarious balancing act: the order to express his or her sexuality is constantly expressed, but at the same time one must display a minute control over such balance (Fleming, 2007).

CONCLUSION

This chapter has addressed what appear as pertinent questions in the knowledge economy of late capitalism: what is the relationship between the 'social imaginaries' that create our joint horizons of expectation (Taylor, 2004) and our subjectivity as expected entrepreneurial knowledge workers? How is it that we make use of the visual sphere of organizations, so permeated by images that are conspicuously designed to capture our attention in a visual economy where attention is the scare resource, and at the same time has to progress with a production of knowledge that is more introvert and repetitive?

Via a 'method of juxtaposition', current images, or, to be precise, *one* such current image from Zentropa was related to other visual sources and two archives were sketched: one containing 'images of nakedness', another containing 'images of knowledge-workers'. It was argued that the construction of these archives did not entirely determine the subjectivity of the modern, creative and entrepreneur employee, but that such archives incite certain figures to become prominent: on the one hand creativity, orgone energy, 'freedom'; on the other hand secluded seriousness and incrementally increased knowledge. We further saw that the stratum containing 'images of nakedness' today has been reduced, as the Nigerians effectively dramatize with their sarcasm, to mere farce. The Western body, so admired and exposed in early twentieth century totalitarian ideologies (see Falasca-Zamponi, 1997), appeared truly tragic in its manifestation at the time, and truly farcical in its contemporary return. At the same time the solemn inwardness of the bureaucratic, labouring knowledge-worker may point to another, more creative view on labour, one which Guattari and Negri has promoted, by which we come to 'consider "labour" as a source of inspiration and stimulation' (Guattari and Negri quoted in Parr, 2005: 328).

This, then, points to new figures of the corporate employee's entrepreneurial subjectivity: potential and affective spaces for expressionism that exceeds the (farcical) command of management as well as the alleged limitations of bureaucracy. Rather than actual limitations, Aalbæk's passage through the company creates a potential space into which great resources of identification are drawn, and in which the employee must experiment with his and her own entrepreneurial subjectivity. The case also seems to attest that navigating even a farce is nonetheless dangerous, as any Sun King himself is caught between absurd superpowers and as absurd courtly rules. Folding your subjectivity is the eminently human and, as it were, corporate struggle. This fraught life of multiple folds is where Deleuze (1988a: 105–6) identifies spaces of resistance: 'The struggle for modern subjectivity passes through a resistance to the two present forms of sub-jectivation, the one consisting of individualizing ourselves on the basis of constraints of power, the other of attracting each individual to a known and recognized identity, fixed once and for all'.

The individualizing forces may be recognized in neoliberalism's con-struction of the 'free and entrepreneurial' subject, the recognized and fixed identity as your pre-given, 'authentic' subjectivity. The 'struggle for subjectivity', continues Deleuze, 'presents itself, therefore, as the right to difference, variation and metamorphosis'. All vested in potential freedom, in which contemporary organizations allow entrepreneurial creativity to exist in a precarious balance between excessive, bodily gestures and retreated and solemn knowledge work.

NOTE

1. In Foucault's *Archaeology of Knowledge* (1972) he seemingly in passing introduces what he calls 'a *historical a priori*': i.e., something which allegedly is *both* historical *and a priori*. The startling effect consists of something both having a past and being 'prior to' any experience. Yet it is this effect that Foucault aims at: '*juxtaposed*, these two words,' that is, the historical and the a priori, 'produce a rather startling effect' (Foucault, 1972: 126ff).

20 Moving and being moved: ideas, perspectives and 59 theses on entrepreneurial leadership

Daniel Hjorth and William B. Gartner

Leadership, as we will propose and discuss this here, relies on the receptivity to and of the other, as with the relationship between an author and her readers. Leading is in this sense a relational act that relies on my openness to the other, and the other's openness to me, and makes use of this power to be affected so as to increase the other's power to act. This means there is a dynamic of rest and movement, where leadership – of the entrepreneurial kind in particular – moves other bodies from rest (and receptivity) to movement (and spontaneity) for the purpose of increasing social/collective productivity, or again, in the case of entrepreneurial leadership, social/collective *creativity*. However, movement on the part of the led (as with reader) also affect the leader (or author), and a story initiated by an author will thus develop with reception and commentaries to consider. This dynamic between leader and led is crucial for leadership to work as a force that increases a collective's capacity for creativity.

Whereas leadership research in the industrial economic era (nineteenth and twentieth centuries) has emphasised action and determination, conflating it with management or at least downplaying the need to differentiate it from management (Yukl, 1989: 5), we will suggest that for *postindustrial* leadership to be successful, indeed, even meaningful, it would have to shift towards this dynamics between moving people and being moved. Mastering this dynamics will be important for leadership to become entrepreneurial, defined here as mobilising collective creativity in organisational contexts. We will centre on this idea of a dynamics between moving and being moved (cf. Hjorth et al., 2010), using process philosophy as a binding thread. The backdrop to our proposal is outlined in Table 20.1.

We thus emphasise a difference between management and leadership, recognising that the importance of emphasising this has increased with the gradual shift towards the postindustrial economy. Management is no longer to be considered as including all (Grey, 1996), but is more meaningfully limited to a position in a hierarchy with the focused function of securing efficiency and control while attending to existing resources. If

Table 20.1   Transition from industrial to postindustrial economy

	Relative emphasis on management and entrepreneurship	Reflection
Industrial Economy	80 (M) - 20 (E)	Management's preferential right of interpretation (cf. Taylor establishing in 1911; Chandler confirming in 1977)
Postindustrial Economy	50 (M) - 50 (E)	Entrepreneurship's genesis from the confinement to SME- and start-up contexts will be broken
Implications for leadership	The new task for leadership is precisely this balancing of an emphasis on management and entrepreneurship	

organisational entrepreneurship is this collective movement that creates organisation (see introduction to this volume), entrepreneurial leadership is not only mobilisation of collective creativity, but in addition the balancing of the managerial and entrepreneurial forces. This balance is tricky, not the least since 100 years of habit has made rationality almost coincide with management (as indicated by Yukl's lack of interest in differentiating management from leadership).

We have been particularly attracted by two ways of framing this discussion of entrepreneurial leadership. We are perhaps on the brink of inaugurating the study of entrepreneurial leadership (in organisational contexts; see Gupta et al., 2004, for an exception, which, however, does not break with the industrial heritage and approach mentioned above). Given this timing, we have both sought after a framing that allows us to focus on the dynamics between moving people and being moved, and a framing that emphasizes the break with an old system and opens multiple possibilities for a future of entrepreneurial leadership research. The former framing is provided by Odysseus' encounter with the Sirens. The latter is provided by Martin Luther's 95 theses event. As can be seen from the main part of this chapter below, the 95 theses framing guides the bulk of our work. However, the opening is animated by this idea of the Sirens' and Homer's scene of the dynamics of receptivity and spontaneity in the adventures of Odysseus. That scene, to us, carries an important message to scholars as well as practitioners trying to understand and/or practice leadership in the postindustrial era. The Sirens are mastering the dynamics of a power to affect and a power to be affected. The scene displays the power of a call and the power of a calling; the spontaneity and receptivity of bodies.

THE CALL, RECEPTIVITY, SPONTANEITY: MOVING AND BEING MOVED

> They sang these words most musically, and as I longed to hear them further I made by frowning to my men that they should set me free; but they quickened their stroke, and Eurylochus and Perimedes bound me with still stronger bonds till we had got out of hearing of the Sirens' voices. Then my men took the wax from their ears and unbound me. (Odysseus, Book XII)

The 'longing to hear them further' is, from the perspective of this chapter, the key in this quote. The call (in Homer's story it is of course sung) that you long to hear further is one we understand as a call that moves you. This is our definition of entrepreneurial leadership: it produces a call, more often a speech, a story, a vision, an image or metaphor, than a song, that potentialises relationships (often in a team, group, or organisation) and make a collective movement towards creation incipient. The call charges the 'game', which is organisational creativity for innovation. The subject of the game – often more like a play, or like playing together, as in a jazz band – is the movement of the innovation process, towards a market (which may or may not be there in the end), and the 'continual modifications of the field of potential those displacements effect' (Massumi, 2002: 73). The best organisational condition for creativity is the best way to get to an innovation process that generates novelty (what in innovation literature is described as radical innovation; Dewar and Dutton, 1986).

Consider the example of soccer, also a collective achievement. Massumi (2002: 73) writes in an analysis of soccer, drawing on Michel Serres' and Bruno Latour's use of the ball as a way to rethink the relationship between subject and object: 'The ball is the subject of the play. More precisely, the subject of the play is the displacements of the ball and the continual modifications of the field of potential those displacements effect.' The ball is '. . . the catalysis-point of a force-field, a charge-point of potential.' (Ibid.). The question is: can leadership articulate 'the ball', where it is, how it needs to move, and why it should be kicked, so as to make the team play the game (organisational creativity for innovation) better, i.e., more creatively in terms of process and in terms of market impact? Creative movement of the innovation process towards a market, the ball of the innovation-game, has to be described, narrated, nurtured and charged continuously by the entrepreneurial leader. That is what moves the players, the field of potential, and summons a market. This is how they are called and how they are made to desire movement. A skilled narrator creates an articulation of the 'ball' that the players long to hear further (as Odysseus describing the Sirens' song).

'Sweet Music': Collective Creativity and Leadership

Let's play with the theme of music for a while, working our way towards a preliminary description of entrepreneurial leadership, before we turn to the 95 theses declarations, attempting to break with leadership studies by affirming the creative potentials of what it could become.[1]

When jazz legend Miles Davis (Austin and Størmer, 2008) walks amongst the assembled musicians on stage during performance, guiding the focus or centre of gravity of the music that they collectively create, we may observe this as a performance of an engaged leadership-for-creativity. There is not the kind of market-oriented drama we are accustomed to associate with the sweeping gestures of business leadership. Describing Davis' style of leading requires from us to reach for an art criticism concept: it is minimalistic. Being fully present, and attentive to individual musicians, makes Miles' movements energise what we might call the 'field of potential' set up by the group. His movements, and the responding moves by the band members, direct attention to what needs to be done, and affirms what emerges, or, affirms what perishes. He moves the centre of intensity by placing himself, and displacing himself, in the 'field of potential', which includes the relationship to the audience, and invites others to lead. Performing becomes a relational act, between colleagues. Creating happens collectively, within the act of making music. One key element seems to be this ensemble-quality of creation (O'Donnell and Austin, 2007). This, leading creative groups, is the central task for post-industrial entrepreneurial leadership.

Organisations as well as people respond to challenges at hand, and need to form teams with temporary identities. It has become increasingly difficult to say what is 'inside' and 'outside' of organisations (Chesbrough, 2003). Networks and projects span and bridge boundaries (Birley, 1985; Harryson, 2006). The leadership challenge is here not too different from getting a choir sound with one voice. Again, the ensemble-quality of creative, collective performance is important. People can work collectively, they can form a group, they can become a team, but to achieve ensemble-quality (one voice although many) a charge-point of potential (as Massumi put it above) seems needed. This is provided by an entrepreneurial leader.

Becoming entrepreneurial leader is a process itself that can learn and draw inspiration from artistic expressions such as Davis' style: (1) How well you are listening and consider what you hear? (2) What is your organisation's 'sound'? (3) Is your team's actions 'resonant' with the themes and rhythms at play in their innovation networks and in customer tendencies? (4) Is your team/organisation good at articulating ideas/themes in their collective creations?

Following Davis' example, entrepreneurial leadership would centre on attentiveness and careful listening, securing one's presence and openness to those you want to move. This is a condition for directing the focus or centre of gravity, modifying the intensity of the work, and inviting individuals to take the lead. We have called this *receptivity* above.

Furthermore, leaders can open a space for play (Hjorth, 2005). Entrepreneurial leaders know we can become (more than we are) when we practice, that we know by doing. Davis opens space for other musicians to play and exhibit talent. Careful listening seeks to affirm what works, and transform playing by following such leads. Experience is never enough, and sometimes a hindrance, when imagining, sensing the 'nextness' of what needs to be created, or finding the right tune. Making moves, and making other move, belongs to the *spontaneity* of a leader. Timing, rhythm and action are crucial.

When 'ensemble' happens in the creative groups we've studied – such as musical and theatre ensembles (Austin and Devin, 2003), software developers (Austin et al., 2009), and design and product development teams (Austin and Hjorth, 2011) – we've noticed other unusual demonstrations of "leadership." Becoming-leader seems to be expected from every team-member, and answer more to the particular idea or theme at hand. Entrepreneurial leadership would therefore include providing conditions for such dynamic distribution of leadership to happen.

The Guarneri String Quartet, one of America's most honoured and enduring string quartets, is known for its ability to pass leadership deftly and flexibly from person to person, through a more or less unnoticeable process of communication. How is leadership performed and distributed in this group? Four lessons stand out:

- Move and being moved; lead, then follow: First violinist Arnold Steinhardt describes: 'After I give the lead in the Finale of Mozart's K. 589, I'll watch the motion of [second violinist John Dalley's] bow and, if necessary, slightly alter my own motion so that we're perfectly together'[2]. This is not 'simply' about synchronicity, nor even about being fully present and attuned to the other(s), it is crucially also about being receptive and open to become moved.

- Leading "as if": Imagination is central to the dynamic distribution of leadership. Leading is sometimes very demanding when simultaneously engaged in a technically very difficult part. Imagining playing from the other's perspective will then help a substitute leader to step in, and lead 'as if' they were the ones that where called by the idea/theme now being played (cf. Gartner et al., 1992; on 'as if' philosophy, see Vaihinger, 1924 [1952]).

- Least busy person leads: The one who has enough time or capacity at a given moment tend to lead. When team-members are working with exceptionally difficult tasks, and at capacity, leadership needs to be focused on providing the best conditions for members to focus. Distribution of leadership, in musical performance, can happen during an inhale. Speed, flexibility and sense of rhythm characterise styles of leadership that maintain fluency and flow of performance (see Verduyn, 2010, on rhythm).

- Following passionately: As suggested above, entrepreneurial leadership is a dynamic process of receptivity/listening and spontaneity/calling. It requires openness to the responses of the others. Responding passionately will affect leading and transform it by making it desire to move in new directions. What we learn from the string quartet is that homogeneity is rather a problem, while harmony is a key. Sometimes following passionately is the creative response to a lead. A response that will in effect be leading the next lead. This requires strong voices, which can co-create harmony. Weak voices will lead to homogeneity, where 'merely following' is the reactive response. We might describe this as a conversation (Austin and Hjorth, 2011), where we understand what we say when we listen to the responses to it.

Whether we observe Miles Davis' jazz band or a string quartet, heterogeneity is important for an ensemble-quality result. Heterogeneity requires strong voices, distinct skills and passionate followership. On the group level, such conditions enable an integration of new information and adjustment to new conditions. Contextual sensitivity and charged field of potential provide great conditions for innovation[3].

Let's focus on the particularly entrepreneurial qualities or acts that are part of this way of leading – 'ensembling' collective creativity. Ensembling describes a highly interdependent and improvisatory collective process in which team members engage heterogeneous talents and perspectives and respond to dynamic contextual information to rapidly generate variation, push the boundaries, and iterate towards the creation of an emergent, coherent and novel outcome. Teams with ensembling capabilities regularly outperform other kinds of creative groups.

Entrepreneurial leadership, as we have described this here, needs to focus on relations and relational dynamics, rather than on individuals. We have also suggested that leadership that is entrepreneurial is a force that manifests collectively. If we again turn to the example of Miles Davis, we see a distinctly relational constitution and dynamics of leadership: one leads expecting to follow the passionate followers-becoming-leaders; one follows expecting to lead (certain themes, certain ideas) and in effect lead the leader. Leadership moves in order to become-moved. Spontaneity and receptivity in a dynamic becoming-leader.

We have also emphasised entrepreneurial leadership as exercising a visionary or imaginative faculty, performing or playing from the perspective of the other. It is like fabulating, of narrating the future in ways that affects the other; that calls them to move (like Odysseus listening to the Sirens; cf. Hjorth, 2007). Affect functions (in Deluze's philosophy) to produce suspense, a breaking-free from the continuity of reason, creating a pause during which we are powered up in our receptivity so that our capacity to be affected and affect others increases.

Affect-narratives call into being a time of passion: our power to be affected increases and we become changed by the other, and in doing so make the other more receptive to become changed by us in turn, by the impact of our receptivity. Guided by a passionate curiosity for and trust in the capabilities of people, entrepreneurial leaders can embrace heterogeneity, acts of variation, experimentation and play that cannot be planned or anticipated. Here one leads in order to become led – in the sense of being inspired, surprised, moved, and called into action. Impassioned, the leader comes out with increased capacity to affect.

In the post-industrial innovative economy entrepreneurial leadership is not about producing consumers of your ideas, but about creating a collective body of leaders, mobilized to act in ways that multiply opportunities for all involved.

BREAKING BY AFFIRMING THE CREATIVE POTENTIALS: '95 THESES'

What characterises entrepreneurial leadership? What differentiates it from leadership more generally? Playing with Luther's event as an illustration of how entrepreneurial leadership operates, we can learn two things upfront.

Generally, throughout the thesis, one learns that Luther is re-contextualising doctrine and praxis so as to update people's capacity to understand what is meant. From thesis 59,[4] as one example, one can understand this emphasis on contextualisation:

59: St. Laurence said that the poor were the treasures of the church, but he used the term in accordance with the custom of his own time.

Secondly, from several theses (e.g., 25, 36, 37, 79) it is clear that apart from rallying against the Catholic Church's happy translation of repentance into fine, meaning one could purchase indulgence, the theses were much about Luther being against hierarchy.

25: The same power as the pope exercises in general over purgatory is exercised in particular by every single bishop in his bishopric and priest in his parish.

The two are related in Luther's event, for contextualisation requires from readers (or Christians as Luther refers to) that they are endowed with authority to make sense for themselves. Luther in this sense opens for a corporeal transformation: making the word accessible in a more plain language, inviting Christians to become readers and interpreters, rather than merely receivers. In the 95 theses event there is an invitation to become reader, to re-orient oneself into an active relationship to the text (cf. Eco–Rorty debate on competent readers; Eco and Collini, 1992). The 95 theses, as a text, invites its readers to relate 'writerly' rather than 'readerly' to its content (Barthes, 1975), but also to the doctrine it comments. This means that multiple meanings (what is concealed in readerly texts) are made possible and even welcome by the text and, in this way, its reader is placed in an active role as required by the text – the text's meaning has to be constructed, has to *become*. Luther, thus, moves people from passive to active through his intervention. Being against hierarchy becomes meaningful in a plea for contextualisation, and contextualisation becomes meaningful as an act of opposing or rejecting hierarchy.

Two important lessons are provided already by these two: leading for the purpose of enhancing organisations' capacity for entrepreneurship – a form of collective creativity – will require attention to contextual conditions, and stepping away, in practice, from a hierarchical system of organising. This is how the social field is potentialised. The continuity of discursive formations (regularities between statements, themes, choices, objects; Foucault, 1972: 38) is interrupted and postponed, and a space for play is opened (Hjorth, 2005; on space, see also Beyes and Steyaert,

2011). The canvas is extended with clean, white areas and brush and paint is distributed. The existing motif appears as but one of multiple hitherto missing, or indeed as unfinished. And so, people are inclined to, desire to start painting. Here it would be appropriate to use the concept of intensity. For if the social field is potentialised and, as an effect, bodies are bent towards something (the literal meaning of inclinate is to bend towards) intensity is raised. This means the new has become incipient. Massumi describes tendencies as 'pastness opening directly onto a future, but with no present to speak of' (2002: 30), which beautifully resonates with our image of white canvas, of a space for play.

Hierarchy: late Middle English: via Old French and medieval Latin from Greek *hierarkhia*, from *hierarkhēs* from *hieros* 'sacred' + *arkhēs* 'ruler'. The earliest sense was 'system of orders of angels and heavenly beings'; the other senses date from the 17th century (Oxford Online Dictionary)

Leading for the benefit of generous conditions for collective creativity in the postindustrial economy means that hierarchy as an inherited system of order (originally between sacred rulers) represents a problem. The idea of leader has not broken enough with the idea of the ruler, nor with the idea of the proper place for a ruler being that of a system of descending order of power. Foucault said that '[W]e need to cut off the King's head: in political theory that has still to be done.' (1980: 121). The idea of a manager – that has come to dominate organizational life and indeed colonise work-life more generally, disregarding whether there is a for- or non-profit organization to handle – has also inherited too many of the problems belonging to the concept of hierarchy, sovereignty and thus ideas of power as negative/suppressive. The shift from King to manager represents a shift from discipline to control, where the latter becomes immanent to the social field (Deleuze, 1988a; Miller and Rose, 1990; Burchell et al., 1991; Dean and Goodchild, 1996; Dean, 1999; Miller and Rose, 2008). In the firm, the manager is this invention (emerging into its industrial form via F. W. Taylor, Henry Fayol and Elton Mayo in particular) meant to secure control. During the last three decades or so, managing has gradually become a matter of conducting the self while performing efficiently. Managers manage self-managing managers, increasingly performing themselves according to the dominant script for how to be an enterprising employee (what we have called the managerial entrepreneur; Hjorth, 2003).

When we talk about entrepreneurial leadership we thus have to keep this distinction between managerial and entrepreneurial entrepreneurship in mind. We are not interested here in 'enterprising management' in the sense, management for the promotion of the enterprising employee – what we describe as the managerial entrepreneur. This relies too much on an antagonism between the social and the economic, and promotes *individual* strategies for maximising enterprising behaviour. Entrepreneurial leadership (as opposed to management) would be committing a performative contradiction should it operate via hierarchy. It cannot draw on disciplinary or pastoral (sacred) authority, nor rule as exercising ultimate power or authority *over* others (as sovereign). This is management, a role in a hierarchy. Instead, leadership has to *move* others, be *moved* by others and create conditions for creativity wherever such are missing. This is still a question of power. However, it is entrepreneurial leadership (and not management) as it affirms rather than corrects. It is entrepreneurial as what it affirms is desire to create as a social force.

Entrepreneurial leadership affects the social capacity of relationships, increases people's capacity for interaction, which deconstructs hierarchy. It is not focused on individual's enterprising behaviour, but bodies' capacity for belonging and becoming (Massumi, 2002). Entrepreneurial leadership adds a charge point of potential (ibid.) that powers up the force-field of social creativity. The new is thus made incipient and moves closer to the limit where the virtual leaps into the actual. The chance of there being something created increases with such charging of the force field. Foucault opened the way to new understandings of power as force by conceptualizing power as positive-productive, drawing upon the philosophy of Nietzsche. Deleuze continued this work, and we will be exemplifying such a conceptualization when we turn to our '95 theses' framework. This is a framework that seeks to affirm the transmuting potential in what could become (differentiation) and therefore itself practice entrepreneurial leadership.

Somewhat paradoxically, we will see that Luther's protest against the selling of indulgence meant that free reins where given to the becoming-other of the church, resulting in what we now refer to as the Reformation. 'Give free rein to' is the translation of the Latin word *indulgere*.

In a Nietzschean sense, Luther identifies reactive forces as part of the Catholic Church, forces that are negative and serves control. He reacts to this, but in a way characterised by activity. He *acts* his reaction (Deleuze, 2006: 111). Typical for what Nietzsche called ressentiment is that this is where reactive forces prevail over active. Reactions – such as Luther's – become actions when they consciously take as object the intensification of a social field. When we charge the field of potential, when we power up people, when we make them move, we act also when we react. Possibly, Schumpeter was after something similar when he talked about creative response (Schumpeter, 1947 [1991]). When mnemonic imprints, traces, instead take over; when reaction invests in the trace (such as in habit, or institutions), active forces are separated from what they can do, the trace takes the place of intensification and the social field is never potentialised, no movement.

There is a certain economy to such investment in traces. Such traces, in the world of commercial organizations, are often concrete material commitments of resources (the importance of which is confirmed both by resource-based view, Barney, 1991, as well as an effectuation approach to firm creation, Sarasvathy, 2001). Managers are in charge of handling those resources; in charge of maximizing efficiency and control. This also indicates that entrepreneurial leadership needs to balance between two reactive systems – that which prioritises the trace, the investment, and that which prioritises intensification. We could juxtapose this with causation and effectuation processes (Ibid.), and call it 'affectuation'. We may indicate central differences here, to clarify our point (adding merely a fourth column to Sarasvathy's 2001: 251 table; Table 20.2):

This obviously is no more than an opening, a contrast for illustrative reasons. We don't have the purpose to intervene with strategy- or decision-making theory. We seek merely to differentiate by contrast and to relate so as to intensify the dialogic capacity of our proposal. We move now to mobilizing you via this invitational provocation, inspired by Luther's event, that we call 59 (rather than 95) theses for entrepreneurial leadership.

59 Theses for Entrepreneurial Leadership

> an intelligent person fights for lost causes, realizing that others are merely effects (ee cummings, 1953)

We reject the cult of personality that infects the idea of entrepreneur- and leader- ship. Entrepreneurial leadership will not be about the individual. Entrepreneurial leadership will not be about entrepreneurs. Entrepreneurial leadership will not be about leaders.

Whereas entrepreneurship scholars have defined 'entrepreneurial leadership' in more traditional terms, e.g., as 'leadership that creates visionary scenarios that are used to assemble and mobilize a "supporting cast" of participants who become committed by the vision to the discovery and exploitation of strategic value creation' (Gupta et al., 2004: 242), we shall turn our thinking away from vision as static images and away from discovery as the recognition of the concrete, and instead focus on the process of "becoming."

Table 20.2   Causation, effectuation and affectuation processes

Categories of Differentiation	Causation Processes	Effectuation Processes	Affectuation Processes
Givens	Effect is given	Only some means or tools are given	Desire and power to become give us
Decision-making selection criteria	Help choose between means to achieve the given effect	Help choose between possible effects that can be created with given means	Become chosen by potential effects in order to choose which means to affirm
	Selection criteria based on expected return	Selection Criteria based on affordable loss or acceptable risk	Selection criteria based on joy, i.e., increased power to act/produce
	Effect dependent	Actor dependent	Relations dependent
Competencies employed	Excellent at exploiting knowledge	Excellent at exploiting contingencies	Excellent at exploiting or usurping potential for productive becoming
Context of relevance	More ubiquitous in nature	More ubiquitous in human action	More ubiquitous in creative belonging
	More useful in static, linear, and independent environments	Explicit assumption of dynamic, nonlinear, and ecological environments	Virtual in all human sociality (virtually real but lacking actuality)
Nature of unknowns	Focus on the predictable aspects of an uncertain future	Focus on the controllable aspects of an unpredictable future	Focus on the affirmable will to move/create, on directing the tendency (futurity of the present) to become
Underlying logic	To the extent we can predict the future, we can control it	To the extent we can control future, we do not need to predict it	To the extent we can direct the becoming of the present via intensity, control is 'the wrong question'
Outcomes	Market share in existent markets through competitive strategies	New markets created through alliances and other cooperative strategies	New markets, and new ways to create new markets, created through relations of productive desires

1. Entrepreneurial leadership must reside in the dynamic.
2. Entrepreneurial leadership focuses on process.
3. Process evokes the image of movement and transition.
4. Movement involves passion and action – being moved and moving.
5. Entrepreneurial leadership is never about a fixed point in time.
6. Nothing is stationary. Everything moves.
7. Movement = velocity.
8. Being moved = force.
9. Entrepreneurial leadership recognizes that change involves a change in movement.
10. Change is not about the movement of static objects from fixed point to fixed point.
11. Change is about a shift in already occurring movement.
12. Time must never be considered as a fixed point: $T(n)$
13. Time must be recognized as occurring 'over time': between $T(n)$ and $T(n + x)$
14. We believe in the dynamics of passion: the power (force) to be affected and the power (force) to affect.
15. In all cases, entrepreneurial leadership is not about the affecter or the affected. It is the affect itself, affecting, which matters.
16. Therefore, the process of entrepreneurial leadership takes precedence over a focus on either inputs (e.g., the 'entrepreneur', the 'environment', the 'team', etc.) or outputs (e.g., the 'venture', the 'solution', 'success' and 'failure', etc.)
17. The focus of entrepreneurial leadership is on the mechanisms of change: how and why change occurs, rather than on what proceeds or follows the process of change.
18. Entrepreneurial leadership involves the imagination as recognised as images seen through the process of change.
19. Imagination, then, in our view, requires seeing over time, as images become.
20. We believe it is a fallacy to dichotomise 'becoming' as either a process of discovery or creation.
21. Discovery implies the recognition of a possible reality that cannot exist because it has not become. The discovered is realized through resemblance to the possible.
22. Creation imbues the actualized new with a larger sense of intention and omnipresence than becoming or emergence. Creation is differentiation.
23. The imagination (as a process) has its own needs regardless of the imaginator.

24. What the imagination becomes, therefore, cannot be understood by focusing on those that imagine.
25. What the imagination becomes, therefore, cannot be understood by focusing on 'the outcome'.
26. We see the process of imagination as a struggle over time between imaginators and their visions, with visions never being considered as 'fixed' or 'concrete'.
27. A vision is a movie, not a still photo.
28. A vision, then, is inherently in flux.
29. Visions, therefore, are seen in different ways as each person enters the movie at different times and pays attention to different things on the screen.
30. There can never be one 'vision'.
31. The idea of 'vision' is outdated and should be replaced with 'voice' or 'song'.
32. By 'voice/song' we focus on the process of 'saying/singing' what is said and heard.
33. The entrepreneurial leader speaks to intensify and potentialise which requires listeners authorised to become authors. In both cases, 'what to see in what is said' is dynamically negotiated between the speaker-becoming-spoken and the listeners-becoming-authors.
34. The future, then, is called forth, partly anticipated in tendency. The act that makes the future (actualisation) emerges from the pressing crowd of incipiencies and tendencies, from the realm of potential, from the reality of the virtual (adopted from Brian Massumi).
35. The future, then, is negotiable.
36. Indeed, the past and the future are negotiable.
37. The past, then, is called forth.
38. The trace and the intensity are different ways of reacting to the spon-taneity of the world.
39. Negative forces prioritises the trace and this means separating active forces from what they can do. Spinoza called this sadness.
40. Creativity acts its reaction, increases intensity and potentialises the social field. The productivity of the same increases. Spinoza called this joy.
41. 'Art does not come to lie down in the beds that have been made for it; it runs away as soon as anyone utters its name: Its best moments are when it forgets what it's called.' – Jean Dubuffet
42. Substitute 'entrepreneurial leadership' for 'art'.
43. There will never be 'one way' in which entrepreneurial leadership occurs.

44.   Variation in processes of entrepreneurial leadership requires an appreciation of contingency, context, and ones power to be affected.
45.   'We miss more by not seeing than by not knowing' – Sir William Osler
46.   How do we see what we don't know?
47.   'How do I know what I think until I see what I say?' – E. M. Forester
48.   'How can I know what I think until I see what I say?' – Karl Weick
49.   How can I say what I think if I don't know what to see? Thinking participating in its own emergence is imagination.
50.   Contingency recognizes that our language is never final or complete.
51.   To 'say', then, is to never fully understand or be understood.
52.   It is in the incompleteness and inconclusiveness (the openness) of language that variation is possible. Derrida called this the 'play' of language.
53.   Contingency recognizes that we are never final or complete. The actual is thus always also virtual.
54.   To 'be', then, is to 'be-come'. This is Nietzsche's eternal return.
55.   It is in the becoming of being that variation is possible.
56.   Contingency recognizes that community is never final or complete, for in becoming is belonging, and in belonging is potential.
57.   Relationships are 'between', i.e., interactions-in-the-making, rather than 'about'. Affect is a body's potential for interaction (Massumi, 2002).
58.   It is in the between that variation is possible. Differention is creation. Passage is primary to position. Passage is the field of emergence. Positions are what emerged (as Massumi, 2002, phrased this).
59.   In order to arrive at what you do not know you must go by a way which is the way of ignorance. – T. S. Eliot

NOTES

1.   This elaboration on entrepreneurial leadership, using the case of Miles Davis, draws heavily on a previous collaboration with Shannon O'Donnell and Robert Austin, both at Copenhagen Business School. A previous version has been published as a Cutter Advisor (see www.cutter.com)
2.   Blum, D. (1986: 11).
3.   For more about this, see 'Receptivity in crisis: how art helps diagnose the "now" to see the '"what now?"' <http://www.cutter.com/content/innovation/fulltext/advisor/2009/iea090416.html>'," a Cutter Advisor by Shannon O'Donnell, 16 April 2009.
4.   Translation of Luther's 95 theses available at: http://www.spurgeon.org/~phil/history/95theses.htm

References*

Achtenhagen, L. and Welter, F. (2005). (Re-) constructing the entrepreneurial spirit. Paper presented at the Frontiers of Entrepreneurship Research, http://www.babson.edu/entrep/fer/2005FER/chapter_v/paper_v1.html.

Acker, J. (1992). Gendering organizational theory. In A. Mills and P. Tancred (eds.), *Gendering Organizational Analysis*. London: Sage, pp. 248–260.

Acker, J. and Van Houten, D. R. (1974). Differential recruitment and control: the sex structuring of organizations. *Administrative Science Quarterly*, **19**(2), 152–163.

Acs, Z. J. and Karlsson, C. (2002). Introduction to institutions, entrepreneurship and firm growth: From Sweden to the OECD. *Small Business Economics*, **19**(3), 183–187.

Acs, Z.J., Desai, S. and Hessels, J. (2008). Entrepreneurship, economic development and institutions. *Small Business Economics*, **31**(3), 219–234.

Adler, P. S. (2001). Market, hierarchy, and trust: the knowledge economy and the future of capitalism. *Organization Science*, **12**(2), 215–234.

Adorno, T. (1973). *Negative Dialectics*, E. B. Ashton (trans.). London: Routledge.

Agamben, G. (2000). *Means Without Ends*. Minneapolis, MN: University of Minnesota Press.

Ahl, H. (2002). The making of the female entrepreneur: a discourse analysis of research texts on women's entrepreneurship. PhD dissertation. Jönköping: Jönköping International Business School.

Ahl, H. (2004). *The Scientific Reproduction of Gender Inequality: A Discourse Analysis of Research Texts on Women's Entrepreneurship*. Copenhagen: CBS Press.

Ahl, H. (2006a). Motivation in adult education: a problem solver or a euphemism for direction and control? *International Journal of Lifelong Education*, **25**(4), 385–405.

Ahl, H. (2006b). Why research on women entrepreneurs needs new directions. *Entrepreneurship Theory and Practice*, **30**(5), 595–621.

Ahl, H. (2006c). Women and humanities: allies or enemies? In B. Czarniawska and P. Gagliardi (eds.), *Management Education and Humanities*. Cheltenham, UK: Edward Elgar Publishing, pp. 45–66.

Ahl, H. (2007a). Gender stereotypes. In S. Clegg and J. Bailey (eds.), *International Encyclopedia of Organization Studies*. London: Sage.

Ahl, H. (2007b). Sex business in the toy store: a narrative analysis of a teaching case. *Journal of Business Venturing*, **22**(5), 673–693.

Ahl, H. and Berglund, K. (2008). The introduction of entrepreneurship in contemporary Swedish education policy: ugly duckling or beautiful swan? Paper presented at the European Conference on Education Research.

Ahlstrom, D. and Bruton, G. D. (2010). Rapid institutional shifts and the co-evolution of entrepreneurial firms in transition economies. *Entrepreneurship Theory and Practice*, **34**(3), 531–554.

Ahuja, G., and Lampert, C. M. (2001). Entrepreneurship in the large corporation: a longitudinal study of how established firms create breakthrough inventions. *Strategic Management Journal*, **22**, 521–543.

Aidis, R. (2005). 'Institutional barriers to small- and medium-sized enterprise operations in transition countries. *Small Business Economics*, **25**(4), 305–318.

Aidis, R. and van Praag, M. (2007). Illegal entrepreneurship experience: Does it make a difference for business performance and motivation? *Journal of Business Venturing*, **22**(2), 283–310.

Aidis, R., Estrin, S. and Mickiewcz, T. (2008). Institutions and entrepreneurship development in Russia: a comparative perspective. *Journal of Business Venturing*, **23**(6), 656–672.

Albrecht, H.-J. (1997). Ethnic minorities, crime, and criminal justice in Germany. *Crime and Justice*, **21**, 31–99.

Alchian, A. A. and Demsetz, H. (1972). Production, information costs and economic organization. *American Economic Review* **62**(5), 777–795.

Aldrich, H. E. (1999). *Organizations Evolving*. Thousand Oaks, CA: Sage Publications.

Aldrich, H. E. (2009). Lost in space, out of time: why and how we should study organizations comparatively. In B. G. King, T. Felin and D. A. Whetten (eds.), *Studying Differences between Organizations.* Bingley, UK: Emerald Group Publishing Limited, pp. 21–44.

Aldrich, H. E. (2010). Beam me up, Scott(ie)! Institutional theorists' struggles with the emergent nature of entrepreneurship. *Research in the Sociology of Work*, **20**(1), 329–364.

Aldrich, H. E., and Fiol. C. M. (1994). Fools rush in? The institutional context of industry formation. *The Academy of Management Review*, **19**(4), 645–670.

Aldrich, H. E. and Ruef, M. (2006), *Organizations Evolving*. Sage Publications, Thousand Oaks, CA.

Aldrich, H. E. and Staber, U. H. (1988). Organizing business interests:

patterns of trade association foundings, transformations, and deaths. In G. R. Carroll (ed.), *Ecological models of Organizations*. Cambridge, MA: Ballinger, pp. 111–126.

Allen, J. (2006). Ambient power: Berlin's Potsdamer Platz and the seductive logic of public spaces. *Urban Studies*, **43**(2), 441–455.

Almqvist, R. (2006). *Nerw Public Management: om konkurrensutsättning, kontrakt och kontroll.* Malmö, Sweden: Liber.

Alterowitz, R. (1988). *New Corporate Ventures*. New York: Wiley.

Alvarez, S. and Barney, J. (2004). Organizing rent generation and appropriation: toward a theory of the entrepreneurial firm. *Journal of Business Venturing*, **19**(5), 621–635.

Alvarez, S. A. and Barney, J. B. (2005). How do entrepreneurs organize firms under conditions of uncertainty? *Journal of Management*, **31**(5), 776–793.

Alvarez, S. A. and Barney, J. B. (2007a). Discovery and creation: alternative theories of entrepreneurial action. *Strategic Entrepreneurship Journal*, **1**(1–2), 11–26.

Alvarez, S. A. and Barney, J. B. (2007b). The entrepreneurial theory of the firm. *Journal of Management Studies*, **44**(7), 1057–1063.

Alvarez, S. A. and Barney, J. B. (2010). Entrepreneurship and epistemology: the philosophical underpinnings of the study of entrepreneurial opportunities. *The Academy of Management Annals*, **4**(1), 557–558

Alvarez, S. A., Barney, J. B. and Anderson, P. (2012). Forming and exploiting opportunities: The implications of discovery and creation processes for entrepreneurial and organizational research. *Organization Science*, 3 April 2012, doi: 10.1287/orsc.1110.0727.

Alvarez, S. A., Agarwal, R. R. and Sorenson, O. (2005) Introduction. In S. A. Alvarez, R. R. Agarwal and O. Sorenson (eds.), *Handbook of Entrepreneurship Research: Disciplinary Perspectives*. New York: Springer Science.

Alvesson, M. and Willmott, H. (2002). Identity regulation as organizational control: producing the appropriate individual. *Journal of Management Studies*, **39**(5), 619–644.

Alvord, S. H., Brown, D. and Letts, C. W. (2004). Social entrepreneurship and societal transformation: an exploratory study. *Journal of Applied Behavioural Science*, **40**(3), 260–282.

Anderson, C. (2004). The long tail. *Wired*, **12.10**, October. Available at http://www.wired.com/wired/archive/12.10/tail.html.

Anderson, B. S., Covin, J. G. and Slevin, D. P. (2009). Understanding the relationship between entrepreneurial orientation and strategic learning capability: an empirical investigation. *Strategic Management Journal*, **3**(3), 218–240.

Andrade, G., M. Mitchell and E. Stafford (2001). New evidence and perspectives on mergers. *Journal of Economic Perspectives*, **15**, 103–120.

Andrade, G. and Stafford, E. (2004). Investigating the economic role of mergers. *Journal of Corporate Finance*, **10**, 1–36.

Amabile, T. M. (1996). *Creativity in Context: Update To The Social Psychology Of Creativity*. Boulder, CO: Westview Press.

Amabile, T. M. (1997). Entrepreneurial creativity through motivational synergy. *Journal of Creative Behavior*, **31**, 18–26.

Amabile, T. M., Schatzel, E. A., Moneta, G. B. and Kramer, S. J. (2004). Leader behaviors and the work environment for creativity: perceived leader support. *The Leadership Quarterly*, **15**, 5–32.

Amin, A. and Thrift, N. (2002). *Cities: Reimagining the Urban*. Cambridge: Polity Press.

Amin, A. and Thrift, N. (2005). 'What's left? Just the future. *Antipode*, **37**(2), 220–238.

Amin, A. and Thrift, N. (2007). Cultural-economy and cities. *Progress in Human Geography*, **31**(2), 143–161.

Amit, R., Muller, E. and Cockburn, I. (1995). Opportunity costs and entrepreneurial activity. *Journal of Business Venturing*, **10**, 95–106.

Argote, L. (1999). *Organizational Learning: Creating, Retaining and Transferring Knowledge*. New York: Springer.

Armstrong, P. (2005). *Critique of Entrepreneurship*. Basingstoke, UK: Palgrave.

Arrow, K. A. (1974). Limited knowledge and economic analysis. *American Economic Review*, **64**, 1–10.

Artforum (2002). Artforum website. Available at http://artforum.com/.

Ashby, W. R. (1956). *Introduction to Cybernetics*. New York: Methuen.

Aßländer, M. (2011). Corporate social responsibility as subsidiary co-responsibility: a macroeconomic perspective. *Journal of Business Ethics*, **99**(1), 115–128.

Astley, W. G., and Van de Ven, A. H. (1983). Central perspectives and debates in organization theory. *Administrative Science Quarterly*, **28**(2), 245–273.

Atuahene-Gima, K. (2005). Resolving the capability-rigidity paradox in new product innovation. *Journal of Marketing*, **69**(1), 61–83.

Audia, P. G. and Greve, H. R. (2006). Low performance, firm size and factory expansion in the shipbuilding industry. *Management Science*, **52**(1), 83–94.

Audretsch, D. B., Bönte, W. and Tamvada, J. P. (2007). Religion and entrepreneurship. Jena Economic Research Paper, No 2007–075, Friedrich–Schiller-University Jena, Max-Planck-Institute of Economics.

Augier, M. and Teece, D. J. (2009). Dynamic capabilities and the role of managers in business strategy and economic performance. *Organization Science*, **20**(2), 410–421.

Austin, J., Stevenson, H. and Wei-Skillern, J. (2006). Social and commercial entrepreneurship: same, different, or both? *Entrepreneurship Theory and Practice*, January 2006, 1–22.

Austin, R. D. (2000), The People's Light and Theatre Company. Harvard Business School Case No. 600–055, Boston: Harvard Business School Publishing.

Austin, R. D. and Beyersdorfer, D. (2006). Vipp A/S. Harvard Business School Case No. 607–052, Boston: Harvard Business School Publishing.

Austin, R. D. and Devin, L. (2003). *Artful Making: What Managers Need to Know About How Artists Work*. Upper Saddle River, NJ: Financial Times Prentice Hall.

Austin, R. D. and Devin, L. (2010). Not just a pretty face: the economic drivers behind the arts in business movement. *Journal of Business Strategy*, **31**(4), 59–69.

Austin, R. and Hjorth, D. (2012). The unlikely conversation: how the economic 'lives with' the aesthetic in creative companies. In review.

Austin, R. D. and Nolan, R. L. (2007). Bridging the gap between stewards and creators. *MIT Sloan Management Review*, **48**(2), 29–36.

Austin, R. D. and O'Donnell, S. (2007). Paul Robertson and the Medici String Quartet. Harvard Business School Case No. 607–083. Boston, MA: Harvard Business School Publishing.

Austin, R. D. and Størmer, C. (2008). Miles Davis: kind of blue. Harvard Business School Case No. 609–050. Boston, MA: Harvard Business School Publishing.

Austin, R. D., O'Donnell, S. and Friis, S. K. (2006a). e-Types A/S. Harvard Business School Case No. 606–118. Boston, MA: Harvard Business School Publishing.

Austin, R. D., Stevenson, H. and Wei-Skillern, J. (2006b). Social and commercial entrepreneurship: same, different, or both? *Entrepreneurship Theory and Practice*, **30**(1), 1–22.

Austin, R. D., Nolan, R. L. and O'Donnell, S. (2007). The Boeing Company: moonshine shop. Harvard Business School Case No. 607–130. Boston, MA: Harvard Business School Publishing.

Avenier, M. J. (2010). Shaping a constructivist view of organizational design science. *Organization Studies*, **31**, 1229–1255.

Baden-Fuller, C. (1995). Strategic innovation, corporate entrepreneurship and matching outside-in to inside-out approaches to strategy research. *British Journal of Management*, **6** (Special Issue), S3–S16.

Baker, T. and Nelson, R. E. (2005). Creating something from nothing:

resource construction through entrepreneurial bricolage. *Administrative Science Quarterly*, **50**(3), 329–366.

Baker, T. and Pollock, T. G. (2007). Making the marriage work: the benefits of strategy's takeover of entrepreneurship for strategic organization. *Strategic Organization*, **5**, 297–312.

Baker, T., Miner, A. S. and Easley, D. T. (2003). Improvising firms: bricolage, account giving and improvisational competencies in the founding process. *Research Policy*, **32**(2), 255–276.

Baker, T., Gedajlovic, E. and Lubatkin, M. (2005). A framework for comparing entrepreneurship processes across nations. *Journal of International Business Studies*, **36**(5), 492–504.

Banham, G. (2005). *Kant's Transcendental Imagination.* London: Palgrave Macmillan.

Banks, J. A. (1972). *The Sociology of Social Movements.* London: Macmillan Press.

Barinaga, E. (2010). *Powerful Dichotomies: Inclusion and Exclusion in the Information Society.* Stockholm: EFI.

Barinaga, E. (forthcoming). The psychic life of resistance: the ethnic subject in a high-tech region. *Ethnicities.*

Barinaga, E. (in review). The banker, the thief, and the migrant woman: introducing micro-finance in a developed welfare state. *Economic Development Quarterly.*

Barnett, W. P. and Carroll, G. R. (1995). Modeling internal organizational change. *Annual Review of Sociology*, **21**(1), 217–236.

Barnett, W. P. and Hansen, M. T. (1996). The red queen in organizational evolution. *Strategic Management Journal*, **17**, 139–157.

Barnett, W. P., Greve, H. R. and Park, D. Y. (1994), An evolutionary model of organizational performance. *Strategic Management Journal*, **15**(s1), 11–28.

Barney, J. (1991). Firm resources and sustained competitive advantage. *Journal of Management*, **17**(1), 99–120.

Barney, J. B. (2001). Is the resource–based 'view' a useful perspective for strategic management research? Yes. *Academy of Management Review*, **26**(1), 41–56.

Barrett, F. J. (1998). creativity and improvisation in jazz and organizations: implications for organizational learning. *Organization Science*, **9**, 605–622.

Barringer, B. R. and Bluedorn, A. C. (1999). Corporate entrepreneurship and strategic management. *Strategic Management Journal*, **20**, 421–444.

Barthes, R. (1975). *S/Z: An Essay.* New York: Hill and Wang.

Bartlett, D. and Dibben, P. (2002). Public sector innovation and entrepreneurship: case studies from local government. *Local Government Studies*, **28**(4), 107–121.

Barzel, Y. (1987). The entrepreneur's reward for self-policing. *Economic Inquiry*, **25**, 103–116.

Barzel, Y. (1997). *Economic Analysis of Property Rights*. Cambridge: Cambridge University Press.

Basu, A. and Altinay, E. (2002). The interaction between culture and entrepreneurship in London's immigrant businesses. *International Small Business Journal*, **20**(4), 371–393.

Battilana, J., Leca, B. and Boxenbaum, E. (2009). How actors change institutions: towards a theory of institutional entrepreneurship. *Academy of Management Annals*, **3**, 65–107.

Baughn, C. C., Chua, B.-L. and Neupert, K. E. (2006). The normative context for women's participation in entrepreneurship: a multicountry study. *Entrepreneurship Theory and Practice*, **30**(5), 687–708.

Baum, J. R., Locke, E. A., and Smith, K. G. (2001). A multi-dimensional model of venture growth. *The Academy of Management Journal*, **44**(2), 292–303.

Baumol, W. J. (1990). Entrepreneurship: productive, unproductive, and destructive. *Journal of Political Economy*, **98**(5), 893–921.

Baumol, W. J. (1993). *Entrepreneurship, Management, and the Structure of Payoffs*. Cambridge, MA: MIT Press.

Baumol, W. J., (2004). Entrepreneurial cultures and subcultures. *Academy of Management Learning and Education*, 3(3), 316–326.

Baumol, W. (2010). *The Microtheory of Innovative Entrepreneurship*. Princeton, NJ: Princeton University Press.

Becker, G. S. (1964). *Human Capital: A Theoretical and Empirical Analysis, with Special Reference to Education*. Chicago, IL: University of Chicago Press.

Becker, G. S. (1993). *Human Capital: A Theoretical and Empirical Analysis, with Special Reference to Education*, 3rd edn. Chicago, IL: University of Chicago Press.

Becker, H. (1982), *Art Worlds*. Berkeley, CA: University of California Press.

Beckert, J. (1999), Agency, entrepreneurs, and institutional change. The role of strategic choice and institutionalized practices in organizations. *Organization Studies*, **20**(5), 777–799.

Beckert, J. (2010). How do fields change? The interrelations of institutions, networks, and cognition in the dynamics of markets. *Organization Studies*, **31**(5), 605–627.

Beit-Hallahmi, B. and Rabin, A. I. (1977). The kibbutz as a social experiment and as a child-rearing laboratory. *American Psychologist*, **12**, 57–69.

Bejean, M. (2008) Le management des entreprises a prestation artistiques, activites de conception, regimes de signification et potentiel de croissance. PhD thesis, L´ecole des Mines de Paris.

Belak, J. (2009). Business ethics implementation at different stages of enterprise life cycle. Maribor, Slovenia: MER Publishing House.

Bell, D. (1974). *The Coming of Post-Industrial Society*. New York: Harper Colophon Books.

Bell-Rose, S. (2004). Using performance metrics to assess impact. In C. Massarsky, S. Oster and S. Beinhacker (eds.), *Generating and Sustaining Nonprofit Earned Income*. San Francisco, CA: Jossey-Bass, pp. 269–280.

Bellone, C. J. and Goerl, G. F. (1992). Reconciling public entrepreneurship and democracy. *Public Administration Review*, **52**, 130–134.

Belzer, H. and Birnbaum, D. (eds.) (2007) *Kunst Lehren/Teaching Art-Städelschule*. Frankfurt/Main: Verlag der Buchandlung Walther König.

Bem, S. L. (1981). *Bem Sex-role Inventory*. Palo Alto, CA: Mind Garden.

Bem, S. L. (1993). *The Lenses of Gender: Transforming the Debate on Sexual Inequality*. New Haven, CT: Yale University Press.

Benjamin, W. (1982). *Das Passagen-Werk (Gesammelte Schriften, Bd. V)*. Frankfurt, Germany: Suhrkamp.

Benjamin, W. (2003). On the concept of history. In H. Eiland and M. Jennings (eds.), *Selected Writings, Volume 4: 1938–1940*. Cambridge, MA: Bellknap, pp. 389–400.

Benjamin, W. (1936 [1968]) The work of art in the age of mechanical reproduction. In B. Walter and H. Arendt (ed.), *Illuminations*. New York: Harcourt, Brace and World, pp. 219–253.

Ben-Ner, A. and Putterman, L. (1998). Values and institutions in economic analysis. In A. Ben-Ner and L. Putterman (eds.), *Economics, Values and Organization*. Cambridge,: Cambridge University Press, pp. 3–69.

Bennis, W. and Biederman, P. W. (1997). Organizing Genius: The Secrets of Creative Collaboration. New York: Perseus Books.

Berger, P. and Luckmann, T. (1966). The Social Construction of Reality: A Treatise in the Sociology of Knowledge. London: Penguin Books. (1967)

Bergson, H. (2002). *Bergson: Key Writings*. K. W. Pearson and J. Mullarkey (eds.). London: Continuuum.

Bettum, J. and Wigley, M. (2007). Von Raum und Zeit in der Architekturausbildung. In H. Belzer and D. Birnbaum (eds.) *Kunst Lehren/Teaching Art-Städelschule*. Frankfurt, Germany: Verlag der Buchandlung Walther König.

Beuys, J. (1992). *Kunst=Kapital*. Wangen, Germany: FIU-Verlag.

Beyes, T. (2006). City of enterprise, city as prey? On urban entrepreneurial spaces. In C. Steyaert and D. Hjorth (eds.), *Entrepreneurship as Social Change*. Cheltenham, UK: Edward Elgar Publishing, pp. 251–270.

Beyes, T. (2008). Reframing the possible, Rancierian aesthetics and the study of organization. *Asthesis*, **2**, 1.

Beyes, T. (2009). Spaces of intensity: urban entrepreneurship as redistribution of the sensible. In D. Hjorth and C. Steyaert (eds.), *The Politics and Aesthetics of Entrepreneurship*. Cheltenham, UK: Edward Elgar Publishing, pp. 92–112

Beyes, T. (2010). Uncontained: the art and politics of reconfiguring urban space. *Culture and Organization*, **16**(3), 229–245.

Beyes, T. and Michels, C. (2011). The production of educational space: heterotopia and the business university. *Management Learning*, forthcoming.

Beyes, T. and Steyaert, C. (2011). The ontological politics of artistic interventions: implications for performing action research. *Action Research Journal*, **42**(5), 521–536.

Beyes, T. and Steyaert, C. (2012). Spacing organization: non-representational theory and performing organizational space. *Organization*, 19(1), 43–59.

Beyes, T., Krempl, S.-T. and A. Deuflhard (eds.) (2009). *Parcitypate: Art and Urban Space*. Sulgenand and Zurich, Switzerland: Niggli.

Bhide, A. (1992). Bootstrap finance: the art of startups. *Harvard Business Review*, November–December 1992, 109–117.

Biehl, J. and Locke, P. (2010). Deleuze and the anthropology of becoming. *Current Anthropology*, **51**(3), 317–351.

Biggart, N. and Beamish, T. (2003). The economic sociology of conventions: habit, custom, practice, and routine in market order. Annual Review of Sociology, **29**, 443–464.

Bill, F. (2006). *The Apocalypse of Entrepreneurship*. Business administration. Vol. 96. Växjö, Sweden: Växjö University Press.

Bird, B. (1988). Implementing entrepreneurial ideas: the case for intention. *Academy of Management Review*, **13**, 442–453.

Birkinshaw, J. (1997). Entrepreneurship in multinational corporations: the characteristics of subsidiary initiatives. *Strategic Management Journal*, **18**, 207–229.

Birley, S. (1985). The role of networks in the entrepreneurial process. *Journal of Business Venturing*, **1**(1), 107–117.

Birnbaum, D. (1998). *The Hospitality of Presence: Problems of Otherness in Husserl's Phenomenology*. Stockholm, Sweden: Almqvist and Wicksell International.

Birnbaum, D. and Graw, I. (eds.) (2008). *Under Pressure: Pictures, Subjects and the New Spirit of Capitalism*. Berlin: Sternberg Press.

Bishop, J. D. (1991). The moral responsibility of corporate executives for disasters. *Journal of Business Ethics*, **10**(5), 377–384.

Bloom, P. and Sklot, E. (2010). *Scaling Social Impact. New Thinking.* London: Palgrave.

Blum, D. (1986). *The Art of Quartet Playing: The Guarneri Quartet in Conversation with David Blum.* New York, NY: Cornell University Press.

Boltanski, L. and Chiapello, E. (2006). *The New Spirit of Capitalism.* London: Verso.

Bonta, M. and Protevi, J. (2004). *Deleuze and Geophilosopy. A Guide and Glossary.* Edinburgh: Edinburgh University Press.

Boot, A. W.A., Milbourn, T. T. and Thakor, A. V. (1999). Megamergers and expanded scope: theories of bank size and activity diversity. *Journal of Banking and Finance*, **23**, 195–214.

Borch, O.J., Huse, M. and Senneseth, K. (1999), Resource configuration, competitive strategies, and corporate entrepreneurship: an empirical examination of small firms. *Entrepreneurship Theory and Practice*, **24**(1), 49–70.

Borch, O.J., Førde, A., Rønning, L., Vestrum, I. K. and Alsos, G. A. (2008). Resource configuration and creative practices of community entrepreneurship. *Journal of Enterprising Communities: People and Places in the Global Economy*, **2**(2), 100–123.

Borgerson, J. and Rehn, A. (2004). General economy and productive dualisms. *Gender, Work and Organization*, **11**(4), 455–474.

Borins, S. (2001). Innovation, success and failure in public management research: some methodological reflections. *Public Management Review*, **3**(1), 3–17.

Bornstein, D. (2007). *How to Change the World: Social Entrepreneurs and the Power of New Ideas.* London: Penguin Books.

Boudreaux, D. J. and Holcombe, R. G. (1989). The Coasian and Knightian theories of the firm. *Managerial and Decision Economics*, **10**(2), 147–154.

Bourdieu, P. (1977). *Outline of a Theory of Practice.* Cambridge: Polity Press.

Bourdieu, P. (1989). *La Noblesse d'État.* Paris: Les Éditions de Minuit.

Bourdieu, P. (1990). *The Logic of Practice.* Cambridge: Polity Press.

Bourdieu, P. and Haacke, H. (1995). *Free Exchange.* Stanford, CA: Stanford University Press.

Bourgault, J. (2011). Canada's senior public service and the typology of bargains: from the hierarchy of senior civil servants to a community of 'controlled' entrepreneurs. *Public Policy and Administration*, online 7 March 2011.

Bourriaud, N. (2001). *Esthetique Relationelle.* Paris: Les presses du reel.

Bowen, H. P. and De Clercq, D. (2008). Institutional context and the allocation of entrepreneurial effort. *Journal of International Business Studies*, **39**(4), 747–767.

Bowman, E. H. and Hurry, D. (1993). Strategy through the option lens: an integrated view of resource investments and the incremental-choice process. *Academy of Management Review*, **18**, 760–782.

Bradley, L. K., Lowe, K. B. and Gibson, C. B. (2006). A quarter century of culture's consequences: a review of empirical research incorporating Hofstede's cultural values framework. *Journal of International Business Studies*, **37**(3), 285–320.

Braidotti, R. (2002). *Metamorphoses. Towards a Materialist Theory of Becoming*. Cambridge: Polity Press.

Braidotti, R. (2005). Writing. In A. Parr (ed.), *The Deleuze Dictionary*. Edinburgh: Edinburgh University Press, pp. 307–308.

Branson, R. (2008). Creative entrepreneurs can survive the crisis. Insead Knowledge, available at: http://knowledge.insead.edu/Creative EntrepreneursSurviveCrisis081008.cfm?vid=105.

Brenner, N. and Theodore, N. (2002). Cities and geographies of 'actually existing neoliberalism'. *Antipode*, **34**(3), 349–379.

Brent, J. (1993). *Charles Sanders Peirce: A Life*. Bloomington, IN: Indiana University Press.

Brettel, M., Mauer, R., Engelen, A. and Kuepper, D. (2012). Corporate effectuation: entrepreneurial action and its impact on R&D project performance. *Journal of Business Venturing*, **27**(2), 167–184.

Brewis, J. (1994). Signing my life away? Researching sex and organization. *Organization*, **12**(4), 493–510.

Bronson, P. (1999). *The Nudist on the Late Shift and Other Tales of Silicon Valley*. London: Secker and Warburg.

Brown, A. D., Stacey, P. and Nandhakumar, J. (2008). Making sense of sensemaking narratives. *Human Relations*, **61**(8), 1035–1062.

Brown, S. D. (2005). The theatre of measurement: Michel Serres. In C. Jones and R. Munro (eds.), *Contemporary Organization Theory*. Oxford: Blackwell Publishing, pp. 215–227.

Brown, S. D. and Stenner, P. (2009). *Psychology Without Foundations. History, Philosophy and Psychosocial Theory*. London: Sage.

Brown, T. (2008). Design thinking. *Harvard Business Review*, June 2008.

Brundin, E., Patzelt, H. and Shepherd, D.A. (2008). Managers' emotional displays and employees' willingness to act entrepreneurially. *Journal of Business Venturing*, 23(2), 221–243.

Bruner, J. (1986). *Actual Minds, Possible Worlds*. Cambridge, MA: Harvard University Press.

Bruni, A., Gherardi, S. and Poggio, B. (2004). Doing gender, doing entrepreneurship: an ethnographic account of intertwined practices. *Gender, Work and Organization*, **11**(4) 406–429.

Brunsson, N. and Olsen, J. P. (1993). *The Reforming Organization*. London: Routledge.

Bruton, G. D. and Ahlstrom, D. (2003). An institutional view of China's venture capital industry – Explaining the differences between China and the West. *Journal of Business Venturing*, **18**(2), 233–259.

Bruton, G. D., Ahlstrom, D. and Li, H. L. (2010). Institutional theory and entrepreneurship: where are we now and where do we need to move in the future? *Entrepreneurship Theory and Practice*, **34**(3), 421–440.

Bucar, B. and Hisrich, R. D. (2001). Ethics of business managers vs. entrepreneurs. *Journal of Developmental Entrepreneurship*, **6**(1), 59–82.

Bucar, B., Glas, M. and Hisrich, R. D. (2003). Ethics and entrepreneurs: an international comparative study. *Journal of Business Venturing*, **18**, 261–281.

Buchholtz, A. K. and Carroll, A. B. (2009). *Business and Society*. Mason, OH: South-Western.

Bull, I. and Willard, G. E. (1993). Towards a theory of entrepreneurship. *Journal of Business Venturing*, **8**, 183–195.

Buller, P. F. and Kohls, J. J. (1997). A model for addressing cross-cultural conflicts. *Business and Society*, **36**(2), 169–194.

Burchell, D. (1999). The disciplined citizen: Hobbes, neostoicism and the critique of classical citizenship. *Australian Journal of Politics and History*, **45**(4), 506–525.

Burchell, G., Gordon, C. and Miller, P. (eds.) (1991). *The Foucault Effect: Studies in Governmental Rationality*, C. Gordon (trans.). Hemel Hempstead, UK: Harvester Wheatsheaf.

Burgelman, R. A. (1983a). A process model of internal corporate venturing in the major diversified firm. *Administrative Science Quarterly*, **28**(2), 223–244.

Burgelman, R. A. (1983b). Corporate entrepreneurship and strategic management: insights from a process study. *Management Science*, **29**, 1349–1364.

Burgelman, R. A. (1984). Designs for corporate entrepreneurship in established firms. *California Management Review*, **26**(3), 154–166.

Burgelman, R. A. (1996). A process model of strategic business exit: implications for an evolutionary perspective on strategy. *Strategic Management Journal*, **17**, 193–214.

Burgelman, R. A. (2002). *Strategy is Destiny: How Strategy-making Shapes a Company's Future*. Free Press, New York.

Burgelman, R. A. and Sayles, L. R. (1986). *Inside Corporate Innovation: Strategy, Structure, and Managerial Skills*. New York: The Free Press.

Burke, K. (1969). *A Grammar of Motives*. Berkeley, CA: University of California Press.

Burns, P. (2011). *Entrepreneurship and Small Business. Start-up, Growth and Maturity*, 3rd edn. London: Palgrave and Macmillan.

Burns, R. (2008) *Corporate Entrepreneurship. Building the Entrepreneurial Organization*. New York: Palgrave MacMillan.

Burns, T. and Stalker, G. M. (1962) *The Management of Innovation*. Chicago, IL: Quadrangle Books.

Burress, M. J. and Cook, M. L. (2009). A primer on collective entrepreneurship: a preliminary taxonomy. University of Missouri, AEWP 2009-4.

Burress, M. J., Cook, M. L. and Klein, P. G. (2008). The clustering of organizational innovation: developing governance models for vertical integration. *International Food and Agribusiness Management Review*,**11**(4), 49–75.

Busenitz, L. W. (1996). Research on entrepreneurial alertness. *Journal of Small Business Management*, **34**, 35–44.

Busenitz, L. W. and Lau, C.-M. (1996), A cross-cultural cognitive model of new venture creation. *Entrepreneurship Theory and Practice*, **20**(4), 25–39.

Busenitz, L. W., Gómez, C. and Spencer, J. W. (2000). Country institutional profiles: unlocking entrepreneurial phenomena. *The Academy of Management Journal*, **43**(5), 994–1003.

Butler, J. (1990). *Gender Trouble: Feminism and the Subversion of Identity*. London, New York: Routledge.

Butler, J. (1993). Bodies that Matter: On the Discursive Limits of 'Sex'. New York: Routledge.

Bylund, P. L. (2011). Division of labor and the firm: an Austrian attempt at explaining the firm in the market. *Quarterly Journal of Austrian Economics*, forthcoming.

Cadman, L. (2009). Non-representational theory/non-representational geographies. In R. Kitchin and N. Thrift (eds.), *International Encyclopedia of Human Geography*, Vol. 7. London: Elsevier, pp. 456–463.

Calás, M. B., and Smircich, L. (1992). Using the 'F' word: feminist theories and the social consequences of organizational research. In A. Mills and P. Tancred (eds.), *Gendering Organizational Theory*. Newbury Park, CA: Sage.

Calás, M. B., and Smircich, L. (1996). From 'the woman's' point of view: feminist approaches to organization studies. In S. Clegg, C. Hardy and W. Nord (eds.), *Handbook of Organization Studies*. London: Sage, pp. 218–257.

Calás, M. B., Smircich, L. and Bourne, K. (2009). Extending the boundaries: reframing 'entrepreneurship as social change' through feminist perspectives. *Academy of Management Review*, **34**(3), 552–569.

Campbell, D. T. (1969). Variation and selective retention in socio-cultural evolution. *General Systems*, **14**(1), 69–85.

Campbell, J. and Spicer, A. (2009) *Unmasking the Entrepreneur*. Cheltenham, UK: Edward Elgar Publishing.

Cantillon, R. (1755 [2001]). *Essay on the Nature of Commerce*. Piscataway, NJ: Transaction Publishers.

Cantillon, R. (1755 [2010]), *An Essay on Economic Theory*, Auburn, AL: Ludwig von Mises Institute.

Cantwell, J., Dunning, J. H. and Lundan, S. M. (2010). An evolutionary approach to understanding international business activity: the co-evolution of MNEs and the institutional environment. *Journal of International Business Studies*, **41**(4), 567–586.

Carland, J. W., Hoy, F. and Carland, J. A. (1988). Who is an entrepreneur? Is a question worth asking. *American Journal of Small Business*, **12**(4), 33–39.

Carr, P. R., and Lund, D. E. (2007). *The Great White North? Exploring Whiteness, Privilege, and Identity in Education*. Rotterdam, The Netherlands: Sense Publishers.

Carroll, A. B. (1979). A three-dimensional conceptual model of corporate social performance. *Academy of Management Review*, **4**(4), 497–505.

Carroll, A. B. (1998). Social responsibility. In P. H. Werhane and R. E. Freeman (eds.), *Encyclopedic Dictionary of Business Ethics*. Malden, MA: Blackwell Publishing, pp. 593–595.

Carroll, A. B. and Buchholtz, A. K. (2006). *Business and Society: Ethics and Stakeholder Management*, 6th edition. Mason, OH: South-Western Publishing, Thompson.

Carrol, S. J. and Gannon, M. J. (1997). Ethical Dimensions of International Management. Thousand Oaks, CA: Sage Publication.

Carroll, G. R. and Hannan, M. T. (1989). Density dependence in the evolution of populations of newspaper organizations. *American Sociological Review*, **54**(4), 524–541.

Carson, J. B., Tesluk, P. E. and Marrone, J. A. (2007). Shared leadership in teams: an investigation of antecedent conditions and performance. *Academy of Management Journal*, **50**(5), 1217–1234.

Carswell, P. and Rolland, D. (2004). The role of religion in entrepreneurship participation and perception. *International Journal of Entrepreneurship and Small Business*, **1**(3–4), 280–286.

Carter, P. and Jackson, N. (2004). Gilles Deleuze and Felix Guattari.

In S. Linstead (ed.), *Organization Theory and Postmodern Thought*. London: Sage, pp. 105–126.

Casson, M. C. (1982). *The Entrepreneur: An Economic Theory*. Lanham, MD: Rowman and Littlefield Pub Inc.

Casson, M. C. (1997). *Information and Organization: A New Perspective on the Theory of the Firm*. Oxford: Clarendon Press.

Casson, M. C. (2000). An entrepreneurial theory of the firm. In N. J. Foss (ed.), *Competence, Governance and Entrepreneurship: Advances in Economic Strategy Research*. New York: Oxford University Press.

Casson, M. (2004) Entrepreneurship. In A. Kuper and J. Kuper (eds.), *Social Science Encyclopedia*. London: Routledge, pp. 304–305.

Casson, M. C. and Wadeson, N. (2007). The discovery of opportunities: extending the economic theory of the entrepreneur. *Small Business Economics*, **28**, 285–300.

Casson, M. C., Yeung, B., Basu, A. and Wadeson, N. (2006). *The Oxford Handbook of Entrepreneurship*. Oxford: Oxford University Press.

Catmull, E. (2008). How Pixar Fosters Collective Creativity. *Harvard Business Review*, Reprint R0809D, Boston, MA: Harvard Business School Publishing.

Cattani, G. (2008). Reply to Dew's (2007) commentary: 'Pre-adaptation, exaptation and technology speciation: a comment on Cattani (2006)'. *Industrial and Corporate Change*, **17**(3), 585–596.

Caves, R.E. and Porter, M. E. (1977). From entry barriers to mobility barriers: conjectural decisions and contrived deterrence to new competition. *The Quarterly Journal of Economics*, **91**(2), 241–262.

Chandler, A. D. (1962). *Strategy and Structure: Chapters in the History of Industrial Enterprise*. Cambridge MA: MIT Press.

Chandler, A. D. (1977). *The Visible Hand: The Managerial Revolution in American Business*. Cambridge, MA: Belknap Press of Harvard University Press.

Chatterton, P. (2000). Will the real Creative City please stand up? *City*, **4**(3), 390–397.

Chavance, B. (2008). Formal and informal institutional change: the experience of postsocialist transformation. *European Journal of Comparative Economics*, **5**(1), 57–71.

Chell, E. (1985). The entrepreneurial personality. A few ghosts laid to rest. *International Small Business Journal*, **3**(3), 43–54.

Chesbrough, H. (2003). *Open Innovation: The New Imperative for Creating and Profiting from Technology*. Boston, MA: Harvard Business School Press.

Chia, R. (1996). *Organizational Analysis as Deconstructive Practice*. Berlin: Walter de Gruyter.

Chia, R. (ed.) (1998). *Organized Worlds: Explorations in Technology and Organization with Robert Cooper.* London: Routledge.

Chia, R. (1999). A 'rhizomic' model of organizational change and transformation: perspective from a metaphysics of change. *British Journal of Management,* **10**(5), 209–227.

Chia, R. C. H., and Holt, R. (2009) *Strategy Without Design – The silent Efficacy of Indirect Action.* New York: Cambridge University Press.

Chia, R. and Kallinikos, J. (1998). Interview with Robert Cooper. In R. Chia (ed.), *Organized Worlds: Explorations in Technology and Organization with Robert Cooper.* London: Routledge, pp. 121–165.

Child, J. and Tsai, T. (2005). The dynamic between firms' environmental strategies and institutional constraints in emerging economies: evidence from China and Taiwan. *Journal of Management Studies,* **42**(1), 95–125.

Chiles, T. H., Bluedorn, A. C. and Gupta, V. K. (2007). Beyond creative destruction and entrepreneurial discovery: a radical Austrian approach to entrepreneurship. *Organization Studies,* **28**(4), 467–493.

Chiles, T. H., Meyer, A. D. and Hench, T. J. (2004). Organizational emergence: the origin and transformation of Branson, Missouri's musical theaters. *Organization Science,* **15**(5), 499–519.

Chodzinski, A. (2007). *Peter Behrens, Emil Rathenau und der dm-drogerie markt.* Berlin: Kadmos Kulturverlag.

Christensen, C. M., and Bower, J. L. (1996). Customer power, strategic investment, and the failure of leading firms. *Strategic Management Journal,* **17**(3), 197–218.

Christensen, T. and Laegreid, P. (2005). Organisationsteori för offentlig sektor. Malmö, Sweden: Liber.

Christensen, T. and Laegreid, P. (2006). A transformative perspective on administrative reforms. In T. Christensen and P. Laegreid (eds.), *New Public Management. The Transformation of Ideas and Practice.* Farnham, UK: Ashgate, Chapter 2, pp. 13–42

Clegg, S. R. and Kornberger, M. (eds.) (2006) *Space, Organizations and Management Theory.* Copenhagen: Copenhagen Business School Press.

Cloke, P., May, J. and Johnsen, S. (2008). Performativity and affect in the homeless city. *Environment and Planning D: Society and Space,* **26**(2), 241–263.

Coase, R. H. (1937). The nature of the firm. *Economica,* **4**(16), 386–405.

Coase, R. H. (1988a). The nature of the firm: meaning. *Journal of Law, Economics and Organization,* **4**(1), 19–32.

Coase, R. H. (1988b). The nature of the firm: origin. *Journal of Law, Economics and Organization,* **4**(1), 3–17.

Coase, R. H. (1988c). *The Firm, the Market, and the Law.* Chicago, IL: Univerisity of Chicago Press.

Cochrane, A. (2006). Euro-commentary: (Anglo)phoning home from Berlin: a response to Alan Latham. *European Urban and Regional Studies*, **13**(4), 371–376.

Cochrane, A. and Jonas, A. (1999). Reimagining Berlin: world city, national capital or ordinary place? *European Urban and Regional Studies*, **6**(2), 145–164.

Colebrook, C. (2002). *Gilles Deleuze*. London: Routledge.

Colebrook, C. (2005). How can we tell the dancer from the dance? The subject of dance and the subject of philosophy. *Topoi*, **24**(1), 5–14.

Coleman, J. S. (1990). *Foundations of Social Theory*. Cambridge, MA: Harvard University Press.

Collinson, D. L. (2003). Identities and insecurities: selves at work. *Organization*, 10(3), 527–547.

Collis, D. J. (1994). Research note: how valuable are organizational capabilities? *Strategic Management Journal*, **15**, 143.

Colvin, G. (2009). *The Upside of the Downturn: Ten Management Strategies to Prevail in the Recession and Thrive in the Aftermath*. London: Nicholas Bradley.

Cooper, A. C., and Daily, C. M. (1997). Entrepreneurial Teams. In D. Sexton and R. Smilor (eds.), *Entrepreneurship: 2000*. Boston, MA: PWS–Kent Publishing Company, pp. 127–150.

Cooper, R. (2007). Organs of process. Rethinking human organization. *Organization Studies* **28**(10), 1547–1573.

Cooper, R. (1998). Assemblage notes. In R. Chia (ed.) *Organized Worlds*. London: Routledge, pp. 131–180.

Cooper, R. and Law, J. (1995). Organization: distal and proximal views. *Research in the Sociology of Organizations*, **13**, 237–274.

Cornelissen, J. P. and Clarke, J. S. (2010). Imagining and rationalizing opportunities: inductive reasoning and the creation and justification of new ventures. *Academy of Management Review*, **35**(4), 539–557.

Costea, B., Crump, N. and Amiridis, K. (2007). Managerialism and 'infinite human resourcefulness': a commentary on the 'Therapeutic habitus', 'Derecognition of finitude' and the modern sense of self. *Journal for Cultural Research*, **11**(3), 245–264.

Costea, B., Crump, N. and Amiridis, K. (2008). Managerialism, the therapeutic habitus and the self in contemporary organizing. *Human Relations*, **61**(5), 661–685.

Covin, J. G. and Miles, M. P. (2007). Strategic use of corporate venturing. *Entrepreneurship Theory and Practice*, **31**(2), 183–207.

Covin, J. G. and Miles, M. P. (1999). Corporate entrepreneurship and the pursuit of competitive advantage. *Entrepreneurship Theory and Practice*, **23**(3), 47–64.

Covin, J. G. and Slevin, D. P. (1989). Strategic management of small firms in hostile and benign environments. *Strategic Management Journal*, **10**, 75–87.

Covin, J. G. and Slevin, D. P. (1991a). A conceptual model of entrepreneurship as firm behavior. *Entrepreneurship Theory and Practice*, **16**(1), 7–25.

Covin, J. G., and Slevin, D. P. (1991b). Entrepreneurship: critical perspectives on business and management. *Entrepreneurship Theory and Practice*, **16**, 7–25.

Covin, J. G., Ireland, R. D. and Kuratko, D. F. (2003). Exploring and exploitation function of corporate venturing. Paper presented at Academy of Management, Annual Meeting, Seattle, WA.

Covin, J. G., Slevin, D. P. and Heeley, M. B. (2000). Pioneers and followers: competitive tactics, environment, and firm growth. *Journal of Business Venturing*, **15**, 175–210.

Coyne, C. J., Sobel, R. S. and Dove, J. A. (2010). The non-productive entrepreneurial process. *Review of Austrian Economics*, **23**(4), 333–346.

Crandall, W. (2007). Crisis, chaos and creative destruction: getting better from bad. In E. Carayannis and C. Ziemnowicz (eds.), *Rediscovering Schumpeter: Creative Destruction Evolving into 'Mode 3'*. Basingstoke, UK: Palgrave, pp. 432–455.

Critchley, S. (1996). Angel in disguise: Michel Serres' attempt to re-enchant the world. *Times Literary Supplement*, January 19.

Cronin, A. M. and Hetherington, K. (eds.) (2008). *Consuming the Entrepreneurial City: Image, Memory, Spectacle*. London: Routledge.

Crowther-Heyck, H. (2006). Herbert Simon and the GSIA: building an interdisciplinary community. *Journal of the History of the Behavioral Sciences*, **42**(4), 311–334.

Csikszentmihalyi, M. (1997). *Creativity: Flow and the Psychology of Discovery and Invention*. New York: HarperCollins Publishers.

Cummings, E. E. (1953). *i: six nonlectures*. Cambridge, MA: Harvard University Press.

Cunningham, D. (2005). The Concept of Metropolis. *Radical Philosophy*, **133** (September/October 2005), 13–25.

Cupers, K. and Miessen, M. (2002). *Spaces of Uncertainty*. Wuppertal, Germany: Müller + Busmann.

Currie, G., Humpreys, M., Ucsabasaran, D. and McManus, S. (2008). Entrepreneurial leadership in the English public sector: paradoxes or possibility? *Public Administration*, **86**(4), 987–1008.

Cyert, R. M., and March, J. G. (1963). *A Behavioral Theory of the Firm*. Saddle River, NJ: Prentice-Hall.

Czarniawska, B. (1985). The ugly sister: on relationship between the private and the public sector in Sweden. *Scandinavian Journal of Management Studies*, **2**(2), 83–103.

Czarniawska, B. (1997). *Narrating the Organization.* Chicago, IL: University of Chicago Press.

Czarniawska, B. (2000). *A City Reframed: Managing Warsaw in the 1990s.* Amsterdam: Harwood Academic Publishers.

Czarniawska, B. (2003). The styles and the stylists of organization theory. In H. Tsoukas and C. Knudsen (eds.), *The Oxford Handbook of Organization Theory*. Oxford: Oxford University Press, pp. 237–261.

Czarniawska, B. (2008a). *A Theory of Organizing.* Cheltenham, UK: Edward Elgar Publishing.

Czarniawska, B. (2008b). How to misuse institutions and get away with it: some reflections on institutional theory(ies). In R. Greenwood, C. Oliver, R. Suddaby and K. Sahlin (eds.), *The Sage Handbook of Organizational Institutionalism*. Los Angeles, CA: Sage, pp. 769–782.

Czarniawska, B. and Sevón, G. (eds.) (1996). *Translating Organisational Change.* Berlin: Ruyter.

Czarniawska, B. and Sevón, G. (2008). The thin edge of the wedge: foreign women professors as double strangers in academia. *Gender, Work and Organization*, **15**(3), 235–287.

Czarniawska-Joerges, B. and Wolff, R. (1991). Leaders, managers, entrepreneurs on and off the organizational stage. *Organization Studies*, **12**(4), 529–546.

Dacin, M. T., Goodstein, J. and Scott, W. R. (2002). Institutional theory and institutional change: Introduction to the special research forum. *Academy of Management Journal*, **45**(1), 45–56.

Daft, R. and Weick, K. (1984). Toward a model of organizations as interpretation systems, *Academy of Management Review*, **2**(9), 284–295.

Danto, A. (1981). *The Transfiguration of the Commonplace.* Cambridge, MA: Harvard University Press.

Daokui Li, D., Junxin, F. and Hongping, J. (2006). Institutional entrepreneurs. *American Economic Review*, **96**(2), 358–362.

Dart, J. J. and Davies, R. J. (2003). A dialogical story-based evaluation tool: the most significant change technique. *American Journal of Evaluation*, **24**,137–155.

D'Aveni, R. A. (1994). *Hypercompetition.* New York The Free Press.

Davidsson, P. (2003). The domain of entrepreneurship research: some suggestions. In J. A. Katz and D. A. Shepherd (eds.), *Cognitive Approaches to Entrepreneurship Research.* Amsterdam: JAI, pp. 265–314.

Davidsson, P. and Henrekson, M. (2002). Determinants of the prevalence of start-ups and high-growth firms. *Small Business Economics*, **19**(2), 81–104.

Davidsson, P. and Wiklund, J. (1997). Values, beliefs and regional variations in new firm formation rates. *Journal of Economic Psychology*, **18**(2–3), 179–199.

Davidsson, P. and Wiklund, J. (2001). Levels of analysis in entrepreneurship research: current research practice and suggestions for the future. *Entrepreneurship Theory and Practice*, **25**(4), 81.

Davidsson, P., Hunter, E. and Klofsten, M. (2006). Institutional forces: the invisible hand that shapes venture ideas? *International Small Business Journal*, **24**(2), 115–131.

Davis, M. (2002). *Dead Cities and Other Tales*. New York: New Press.

Dean, M. (1999). *Governmentality: Power and Rule in Modern Society*. London: Sage.

de Certeau, M. (1984). *The Practice of Everyday Life*. Berkeley, CA: University of California Press.

De Cock, C. and Sharp, R. J. (2007). Process theory and research: exploring the dialectic tension. *Scandinavian Journal of Management*, **23**(3), 233–250.

de Koning, A. and Dodd, S. D. (2010). Tea and understanding. *Entrepreneurial Narrative Theory Ethnomethodology and Reflexivity*, **1**, 37–53.

Deal, T. and Kennedy, A. A. (1982). *Corporate Cultures: The Rites and Rituals of Corporate Life*. Reading, MA: Addison-Wesley.

Dean, M. (1999). *Governmentality: Power and Rule in Modern Society*. London: Sage.

Debrix, F. (1999). Space quest: surveillance, governance, and the panoptic eye of the United Nations. *Alternatives: Global, Local, Political*, **24**(3), 269.

Dees, J. G. (1998). The meaning of social entrepreneurship. Available at: http://www.caseatduke.org/documents/dees_sedef.pdf.

Dees, J. G. and Anderson, B. (2006). Framing a theory of entrepreneurship: building on two schools of practice and thought. ARNOVA Occasional Paper Series. *Research on Social Entrepreneurship: Understanding and Contributing to an Emerging Field*, **1**(3), 39–66.

Deleuze, G. (1966 [1991]). *Bergsonism*, H. Tomlinson. and B. Habberjam (trans.). New York: Zone Books.

Deleuze, G. (1983). *Nietzsche and Philosophy*. New York: Athlone Press.

Deleuze, G. (1986). *The Movement–Image,* transl. Hugh Tomlinson and Barbara Habberjam. Minneapolis, MN: University of Minnesota Press.

Deleuze, G. (1988a). *Foucault*. Minneapolis, MN: University of Minnesota Press.

Deleuze, G. (1988b). *Spinoza: Practical Philosophy*. San Francisco: City Lights Books.

Deleuze, G. (1990). Mediators. In *Negotiations 1972–1990*. New York: Columbia University Press, pp. 121–143.

Deleuze, G. (1993). *The Fold: Leibniz and the Baroque*. Minneapolis, MN: University of Minnesota Press.

Deleuze, G. (1996) *Difference and Repetition*. New York: Columbia University Press.

Deleuze, G. (1998) *Essays: Critical and Clinical*. London: Verso.

Deleuze, G. (2006). *Nietzsche & Philosophy*, H. Tomlinson (trans.). New York: Columbia University Press.

Deleuze, G. and Guattari, F. (1986). *Kafka: Toward a Minor Literature*. Minneapolis: University of Minnesota Press.

Deleuze, G. and Guattari, F. (1988). *A Thousand Plateaus*. Minneapolis, MN: University of Minnesota Press.

Deleuze, G. and Guattari, F. (1994). *What is Philosophy?* New York: Columbia University Press.

Demsetz, H. (1983). The neglect of the entrepreneur. In J. Ronen (ed.), *Entrepreneurship*. Lexington, MA: Lexington Press.

Demsetz, H. (1988a). Profit as a functional return: reconsidering Knight's views. In H. Demsetz. (ed.), *Ownership, Control and the Firm. The Organization of Economic Activity, Vol. 1*. Oxford: Blackwell.

Demsetz, H. (1988b). The theory of the firm revisited. *Journal of Law, Economics, and Organization*, **4**(1), 141–161.

Den Haan, W. and V. Sterk (2010). The myth of financial innovation and the great moderation. *The Economic Journal*, **121**(June), 707–739.

Denis, J-L., Langley, A. and Rouleau, L. (2007). Rethinking leadership in public organizations. In E. Ferlie, L. E. Lynn Jr, and C. Pollitt (eds.), *The Oxford Handbook of Public Management*. Oxford: Oxford University Press, Chapter 19, pp. 466–467.

Dennett, D. (1995). *Darwin's Dangerous Idea: Evolution and the Meanings of Life*. London: Penguin Books.

Denrell, J. and March, J. G. (2001). Adaptation as information restriction: the hot stove effect. *Organization Science*, **12**(5), 523–538.

Denzau, A.T. and D.C. North (1994), 'Shared mental models – Ideologies and institutions', Kyklos, 47 (1), 3–31.

Dequech, D. (2003). Cognitive and cultural embeddedness: combining institutional economics and economic sociology. *Journal of Economic Issues*, **37**(2), 461–470.

Dess, G. G. and Lumpkin, G. T. (2005). The role of entrepreneurial orientation in stimulating effective corporate entrepreneurship. *Academy of Management Executive*, **19**, 147–156.

Dess, G.G., Lumpkin, G.T. and Covin, J.G. (1997). Entrepreneurial strategy making and firm performance: tests of contingency and configuration models. *Strategic Management Journal*, **18**(9), 677–695.

Dess, G. G., Lumpkin, G. T. and McGee, J. E. (1999). Linking corporate entrepreneurship to strategy, structure, and process: suggested research directions. *Entrepreneurship Theory and Practice*, **23**(3), 85–102.

Dess, G. G., Ireland, R. D., Zahra, S. A., Floyd, S. W., Janney, J. J. and Lane, P. J. (2003). Emerging issues in corporate entrepreneurship. *Journal of Management*, **29**(3), 351–378.

Deutschmann, C. (2001). Capitalism as a religion? An unorthodox analysis of entrepreneurship. European Journal of Social Theory, **4**(4), 387.

Devin, L. and Austin, R. (2004). Planning to get lucky. *Cutter IT Journal*, **17**(11), 21–26.

Dew, N. (2007). Notes and comments. *Industrial and Corporate Change*, **16**(1), 155–160.

Dew, N. (2009). Serendipity in entrepreneurship. *Organization Studies*, **30**(7), 735–753.

Dew, N., Goldfarb, B. and Sarasvathy, S. D. (2006). Optimal inertia: when organizations should fail. *Ecology and Strategy*, **23**, 73–99.

Dew, N., Read, S., Sarasvathy, S. D., and Wiltbank, R. (2008). Outlines of a behavioral theory of the entrepreneurial firm. *Journal of Economic Behavior and Organization*, **66**(1), 37–59.

Dew, N., Read, S., Sarasvathy, S. D. and Wiltbank, R. (2009). Effectual versus predictive logics in entrepreneurial decision-making: differences between experts and novices. *Journal of Business Venturing*, **24**(4), 287–309.

Dew, N., Read, S., Sarasvathy, S. D. and Wiltbank, R. (2011). On the entrepreneurial genesis of new markets: effectual transformations versus causal search and selection. *Journal of Evolutionary Economics*, **21**(2), 231–253.

Dew, N., Sarasvathy, S. D. and Venkataraman, S. (2004). The economic implications of exaptation. *Journal of Evolutionary Economics*, **14**(1), 69–84.

Dewey, J. (1958). *Art as Experience*. New York: Putnam.

Dey, P. and Steyaert, C. (2007). The troubadours of knowledge: passion and invention in management education. *Organization*,**14**(3), 437–461.

Dey, P. and Steyaert, C. (2010). The troubadours of knowledge: passion and invention in management education. *Organization*, **14**(3), 437–461.

Di Stefano, G., Peteraf, M. and Verona, G. (2010). Dynamic capabilities deconstructed: a bibliographic investigation into the origins, development, and future directions of the research domain. *Industrial and Corporate Change*, **19**(4), 1187–1204.

Dieleman, M. and Sachs, W. M. (2008). Coevolution of institutions and corporations in emerging economies: how the Salim group morphed into an institution of Suharto's crony regime. *Journal of Management Studies*, **45**(7), 1274–1300.

DiMaggio, P. J. (1988). Interest and agency in institutional theory. In L. G. Zucker (ed.), *Institutional Patterns and Organizations: Culture and Environment*. Cambridge, MA: Ballinger Publishing Company, pp. 3–22.

DiMaggio, P. J. and Powell, W. W. (1983). The iron cage revisited: institutional isomorphism and collective rationality in organizational fields. *American Sociological Review*, **48**(2), 147–160.

Dimov, D. (2011). Grappling with the unbearable elusiveness of entrepreneurial opportunities. *Entrepreneurship Theory and Practice*, **35**(1), 57–82.

Dixit, A. K. and Pindyck, R. S. (1994). *Investment Under Uncertainty*. Princeton, NJ: Princeton University Press.

Dixon, S. E. A., and Clifford, A. (2007). Ecopreneurship-a new approach to managing the triple bottom line. *Journal of Organizational Change Management*, **20**(3), 326–345.

Djelic, M.-L. and Ainamo, A. (1999). The co evolution of new organizational forms in the fashion industry: a historical and comparative study of France, Italy, and the United States. *Organization Science*, **10**(5), 622–637.

Dobers, P. (2003). Image of Stockholm as an IT city: emerging urban entrepreneurship. In C. Steyaert and D. Hjorth (eds.), *New Movements in Entrepreneurship*. Cheltenham, UK: Edward Elgar Publishing, pp. 200–221.

Dobrev, S. D. (2007). Competing in the looking-glass market: imitation, resources, and crowding. *Strategic Management Journal*, **28**(13), 1267–1289.

Dodd, S. D. and Seaman, P. T. (1998). Religion and enterprise: an introductory exploration. *Entrepreneurship: Theory and Practice*, **23**(1), 71–86.

Donaldson, T. and Preston, L. E. (1995). The stakeholder theory of the corporation: concepts, evidence, and implications. *Academy of Management Review*, **20**(1), 65–91.

Dorado, S. (2005). Institutional entrepreneurship, partaking and convening. *Organization Studies*, 26(3), 385–414.

Donzelot, J. (1988). The promotion of the social. *Economy and Society*, **17**(3), 395–427.

Dorado, S. (2006). Social entrepreneurial ventures: different values so different propositions of creation, no? *Journal of Development Entrepreneurship*, **11**(4), 319–343.

Douhan, R. and Henrekson, M. (2010). Entrepreneurship and second-best institutions: going beyond Baumol's typology. *Journal of Evolutionary Economics*, **20**(4), 629–643.

Doyle, J. A. and Paludi, M. A. (1998). *Sex and Gender: The Human Experience*, 4 edn. San Francisco, CA: McGraw-Hill.

Drucker, P. (1985). *Innovation and Entrepreneurship: Practice and Principles.* London: Heinemann.

Du Gay, P. (2000). *In Praise of Bureaucracy. Weber. Organization. Ethics.* London: SAGE.

Du Gay, P. (2004). Against 'enterprise' (but not against 'enterprise', for that would make no sense). *Organization*, **11**(1), 37–57.

Du Gay, P., ed. (2005). *The Values of Bureaucracy*. Oxford: Oxford University Press.

Duh, M., Belak, J. and Milfelner, B. (2010). Core values, culture and ethical climate as constitutional elements of ethical behavior: exploring differences between family and non-family enterprises. *Journal of Business Ethics*, **97**(3), 473–489.

Dutton, G. (2008). Do the right thing. *Entrepreneur*, 36(5), 92.

Dymski, G. (2009). Racial exclusion and the political economy of the subprime crisis. Historical *Materialism*, **17**(2), 149–179.

Easterby-Smith, M., Lyles, M. A., and Peteraf, M. A. (2009). Dynamic capabilities: current debates and future directions. *British Journal of Management*, **20**, S1–S8.

Eco, U. and Collini, S. (1992). *Interpretation and Overinterpretation.* Cambridge: Cambridge University Press.

Edmondson, A. C. and McManus, S. E. (2007). Methodological fit in management field research. *The Academy of Management Review*, **32**(4), 1155–1179.

Eduards, M. (1995). En allvarsam lek med ord. In E. Witt-Brattström (ed.), *Viljan att veta och viljan att förstå*. Stockholm: Fritzes.

Eisenhardt, K. M. (1989a). Building theories from case study research. *The Academy of Management Review*, **14**(4), 532–550.

Eisenhardt, K. M. (1989b). Making fast strategic decisions in high-velocity environments. *Academy of Management Journal*, **32**, 543–576.

Eisenhardt, K. M. and Martin, J. A. (2000). Dynamic capabilities: what are they? *Strategic Management Journal*, **21**(10/11), 1105.

Elam, A. and Terjesen, S. (2010). Gendered institutions and cross-national patterns of business creation for men and women. *European Journal of Development Research*, **22**, 331–348.

Elango, B., Paul, K., Kundu, S. K. and Paudel, S. K. (2010). Organizational ethics, individual ethics, and ethical intentions in international decision-making. *Journal of Business Ethics*, **97**(4), 543–561.

Eliot, T. S. (1921). *The Sacred Wood: Essays on Poetry and Criticism.* New York: Alfred A. Knopf.

Elliott, J. (1978–1979). Marx's Grundrisse: Vision of capitalism's creative destruction. *Journal of Post Keynesian Economics*, **1**(2), 148–169.

Emerson, J. (2003). The blended value proposition: integrating social and financial returns. *California Management Review*, **45**(4), 35–51.

Emirbayer, M. and Mische, A. (1998). What is agency? *The American Journal of Sociology*, **103**(4), 962–1023.

Erasmus, D. (2005). *Collected Works of Erasmus: Adages III iv 1 to IV ii 100*, D. Drysdall (trans.), John Grant (ed.). Toronto: University of Toronto Press.

Esping-Andersen, G. (1996). *Welfare States in Transition. National Adaptions in Global Economies.* London: SAGE

Esping-Andersen, G. (2009). *The Incomplete Revolution. Adapting to Women's New Roles.* Cambridge, UK: Polity Press.

Ettlie, J. E., Bridges, W. P. and O'Keefe, R. D. (1984). Organization strategy and structural differences for radical versus incremental innovation author. *Management Science*, **30**(6), 682–695.

European Commission (2001), Green Paper Promoting a European Framework for Corporate Social Responsibility COM (2001) 366. Commission of the European Communities, Brussels.

Eurostat 1 (2011). Euroindicators. Available at: http://epp.eurostat.ec.europa.eu/cache/ITY_PUBLIC/3-01082011-AP/EN/3-01082011-AP-EN.PDF.

Evans, G. (2009). Creative cities, creative spaces and urban policy. *Urban Studies*, **46**(5/6): 1003–1040.

Falasca-Zamponi, S. (1997). *Fascist Spectacle: The Aesthetics of Power in Mussolini's Italy.* Davis, CA: University of California Press.

Falkenberg, L. and Herremans, I. (1995). Ethical behaviours in organizations: directed by the formal or informal systems? *Journal of Business Ethics*, 14(2), 133–144.

Faludi, S. (1991). *Backlash the Undeclared War against American Women.* New York: Crown.

Feldman, M., Francis, J. and Bercovitz, J. (2005). Creating a cluster while building a firm: Entrepreneurs and the formation of industrial clusters. *Regional Studies*, **39**(1), 129–141.

Felin, T., and Hesterly, W. S. (2007). The knowledge-based view, nested heterogeneity, and new value creation: Philosophical considerations on the locus of knowledge. *Academy of Management Review*, **32**, 195–218.

Felin, T. and Zenger, T. R. (2009). Entrepreneurs as theorists: on the emergence of collective beliefs and novel strategies. *Strategic Entrepreneurship Journal*, **3**, 127–146.

Ferlie, E., Pettigrew, A., Ashburner, L. and Fitzgerald, L. (1996). *The New Public Management in Action*. Oxford: Oxford University Press.

Ferrell, O. C., Fraedrich, J. and Ferrell, L. (2008). *Business Ethics: Ethical Decision Making and Cases*. Mason, OH: South-Western CENGAGE Learning.

Ferriani, S., Cattani, G., and Baden-Fuller, C. (2009). The relational antecedents of project-entrepreneurship: network centrality, team composition and project performance. *Research Policy*, **38**(10), 1545–1558.

Fincher, D. (Director) (2010). The Social Network. [Film]. Los Angeles: Columbia Pictures

Fiscella, K., Franks, P., Gold, M. R. and Clancy, C. M. (2000). Inequality in quality: addressing socioeconomic, racial, and ethnic disparities in health care. *Journal of the American Medical Association*, **19**, 2579–2584.

Fischer, E. and Reuber, A. R. (2011). Social interaction via new social media: (how) can interactions on Twitter affect effectual thinking and behavior? *Journal of Business Venturing*, **26**(1), 1–18.

Fleming, P. (2007). Sexuality, power and resistance in the workplace. *Organization Studies*, **28**(2), 239–256.

Fleming, P. and Sturdy, A. (2009). Just be yourself! *Employee Relations*, **31**(6), 569–583.

Fligstein, N. (1997). Markets, politics, and globalization. *Acta Universitatis Upsaliensis*, no. 42, Stockholm, Almquist & Wiksell International.

Florida, R. (2002). *The Rise of the Creative Class: And How It's Transforming Work, Leisure, Community, and Everyday Life*. New York: Basic Books.

Floyd, S. W. and Lane, P. J. (2000), Strategizing throughout the organization: managing role conflict in strategic renewal. *Academy of Management Review*, **25**, 154–177.

Floyd, S. W. and Wooldridge, B. (1990). The strategy process, middle management involvement, and organizational performance. *Strategic Management Journal*, **11**, 231–242.

Floyd, S. W. and Wooldridge, B. (1992). Middle management involvement in strategy and its association with strategic type. *Strategic Management Journal*, **13**, 53–168.

Floyd, S. W. and Wooldridge, B. (1994). Dinosaurs or dynamos? Recognizing middle management's strategic role. *Academy of Management Executive*, 8(4), 47–57.

Foerster, H. von (1973 [2003]). On constructing a reality. In H. von Foerster (ed.), *Understanding Understanding*. New York: Springer Verlag, pp. 211–228.

Foss, K. and Foss, N. J. (2002). Economic organization and the trade-offs between productive and destructive entrepreneurship. In N. J. Foss and P. G. Klein (eds.), *Entrepreneurship and the Firm: Austrian Perspectives on Economic Organization.* Cheltenham, UK: Edward Elgar Publishing, pp. 102–127.

Foss, K., Foss, N. J. and Klein, P. G. (2007a). Original and derived judgment: an entrepreneurial theory of economic organization. *Organization Studies*, **28**(12), 1–20.

Foss, K., Foss, N. J., Klein, P. G. and Klein, S. K. (2007b). the entrepreneurial organization of heterogeneous capital. *Journal of Management Studies* **44**(7), 1165–1186.

Foss, N. J. (1993). More on Knight and the theory of the firm. *Managerial and Decision Economics*, **14**(3), 269–276.

Foss, N. J. (1996). Capabilities and the theory of the firm. *Revue D'Économie Industrielle*, **77**, 7–28.

Foss, N. J. (1997). Austrian insights and the theory of the firm. In P. J. Boettke and S. Horwitz (ed.), *Advances in Austrian Economics*, Vol. 4. Greenwich, CT: JAI Press, pp. 175–198.

Foss, N. J. (2003). Herbert Simon's grand theme in the economics of organization: 'much cited and little used'. *Journal of Economic Psychology*, **24**, 245–264.

Foss, N. J. (2011a). *Entrepreneurial Judgment and the Theory of the Firm.* Cambridge: Cambridge University Press.

Foss, N. J. (2011b). Towards a theory of the entrepreneurial established firm. Lund, Sweden: Lund University

Foss, N. J., and Ishikawa, I. (2007). Towards a dynamic resource-based view: insights from austrian capital and entrepreneurship theory. *Organization Studies*, **28**(5), 749–772.

Foss, N. J. and Klein, P. G. (2005). Entrepreneurship and the economic theory of the firm: any gains from trade? In R. Agarwal, S. A. Alvarez and O. Sorenson (eds.), *Handbook of Entrepreneurship: Disciplinary Perspectives*, New York: Springer, pp. 55–80.

Foss, N. J., and Klein, P. G. (2011). *Entrepreneurship and Theory of the Firm.* Cambridge: Cambridge University Press.

Foss, N. J. and Klein, P. G. (2012). *Organizing Entrepreneurial Judgment.* Cambridge: Cambridge University Press.

Foss, N. J. and Lyngsie, J. (2011). Organizational design for firm-level entrepreneurship: understanding the micro-foundations of firm-level entrepreneurial capability. Working Paper.

Foss, K., Foss, N. J., Klein, P. G., and Klein, S. K. (2007). The entrepreneurial organization of heterogeneous capital. *Journal of Management Studies*, **44**(7), 1165–1186.

Foss, N. J., Klein, P. G., Kor, Y. Y. and Mahoney, J. T. (2008). Entrepreneurship, subjectivism, and the resource-based view: towards a new synthesis. *Strategic Entrepreneurship Journal* **2**(1), 73–94.

Foucault, M. (1972). *The Discourse on Language (L'ordre du discourse) The Archaeology of Knowledge and the Discourse on Language.* New York: Pantheon Books, pp. 215–237.

Foucault, M. (1977). Intellectuals and power: a conversation between Michel Foucault and Gilles Deleuze. In D. F. Bouchard (ed.), *Language, Counter-memory, Practice.* Ithaca: Cornell University Press, pp. 205–217.

Foucault, M. (1980). *Power/Knowledge*, C. Gordon (ed.). Hertfordshire, UK: Simon & Schuster.

Foucault, M. (2002). Truth and juridical forms. In J. D. Fabion (ed.), *Michel Foucault. Power: Essential Works of Foucault 1954–1984.* London: Penguin Books, pp. 1–89.

Foucault, M. (2008). *The Birth of Biopolitics: Lectures at the Collège de France, 1978–79*, G. Burchell (trans.). New York: Palgrave Macmillan

Fournier, V. (2002). Keeping the veil of otherness: practising disconnection. In B. Czarniawska and H. Höpfl (eds.), *Casting the Other: The Production and Maintenance of Inequalities in Work Organizations.* London: Routledge, pp. 68–88.

Fowler, A. (2000). NGDOs as a moment in history: beyond aid to social entrepreneurship or civic innovation? *Third World Quarterly*, **21**(4), 637–654.

Friedman, T. L. (2005). *The World is Flat: A Brief History of the 21st Century.* New York: Farrar, Straus and Giroux.

Fuglsang, M. and Sørensen, B. M. (2006). *Deleuze and the Social.* Edinburgh: Edinburgh University Press.

Fulop, G., Hisrich, R.D. and Szegedi, K. (2000), "Business ethics and social responsibility in transition economies," Journal of Management Development, Vol. 19, No. 1, pp. 5–31.

Gagliardi, P. (1996). Exploring the aesthetic side of organizational life. In S. R. Clegg, C. Hardy and W. R. Nord (eds), *Handbook of Organization Studies.* Thousand Oaks, CA, US: Sage Publications, Inc., pp. 565–580.

Gagliardi, P. and Czarniawska, B. (eds.) (2006) *Management Education and Humanities*, Cheltenham: Edward Elgar Publishing.

García-Marzá, D. (2005). Trust and dialogue: theoretical approaches to ethics auditing. *Journal of Business Ethics*, **57**(3), 209–219.

Garrouste, P. and Saussier, S. (2008). The theories of the firm. In É. Brousseau and J.-M. Glachant (eds.), *New Institutional Economics: A Guidebook.* Cambridge: Cambridge University Press, pp. 23–36.

Gartner, W. B. (1985). A framework for describing and classifying the phenomenon of new venture creation. *Academy of Management Review*, **10**(4), 696–706.

Gartner, W. B. (1988). Who is an entrepreneur? Is the wrong question. *American Journal of Small Business*, **12**(4), 11–32.

Gartner, W. B. (1990). What are we talking about when we talk about entrepreneurship? *Journal of Business Venturing*, **5**(1), 15–28.

Gartner, W. B. (1993). Words lead to deeds: towards an organizational emergence vocabulary. *Journal of Business Venturing*, **8**(3), 231–240.

Gartner, W. B. (2001). Is there an elephant in entrepreneurship? Blind assumptions in theory development. *Entrepreneurship, Theory & Practice*, **25**(4), 27–40.

Gartner, W. B. (2004). Achieving 'critical mess' in entrepreneurship scholarship. In J. Katz and D. Shepherd (eds.), *Corporate Entrepreneurship*. Amsterdam: Elsevier, pp. 199–216.

Gartner, W. B. (2007). Entrepreneurial narrative and a science of the imagination. *Journal of Business Venturing*, **22**(5), 613–627.

Gartner, W. B. (2008). Variations in entrepreneurship. *Small Business Economics*, **31**, 351–361.

Gartner, W. B. (in press) Organizing entrepreneurship. In Fayolle, A. (ed.) *Handbook of Research in Entrepreneurship: What Do We Know? What Do We Need to Know?* Cheltenham, UK: Edward Elgar.

Gartner, W. B. and Brush, C. B. (2007). Entrepreneurship as organizing: emergence, newness and transformation. In T. Habbershon and M. Rice (eds.) *Praeger Perspectives on Entrepreneurship*, Vol. 3. Westport, CT: Praeger Publishers, pp. 1–20.

Gartner W. B. and Carter N. M. (2003). Entrepreneurial behavior and firm organizing processes. In Z. J. Acs, and D. B. Audretch (eds.), *Handbook of Entrepreneurship Research*. Boston, MA: Kluwer Academic Publishers, pp. 195–221.

Gartner, W. and Bird, B. J. and Starr, J. A. (1992). Acting as if: differentiating entrepreneurial from organizational behaviour. *Entrepreneurship, Theory and Practice*, **16**(3), 13–32.

Gartner, W. B., Carter, N. M. and Hills, G. E. (2003). The language of opportunity. In C. Steyaert and D. Hjorth, (eds.), *New Movements in Entrepreneurship*. Cheltenham, UK: Edward Elgar Publishing, pp. 103–124.

Gartner, W. B., Shaver, K. G., Carter, N. M. and Reynolds, P. D. (2004). *Handbook of Entrepreneurial Dynamics: The Process of Business Creation*. Thousand Oaks, CA: Sage Publications.

Gawell, M. (2006). Activist entrepreneurship. Attac'ing norms and articulating disclosive stories. PhD thesis, Stockholm University.

Geertz, C. (1964). The transition to humanity. In: S. Tax (ed.), *Horizons of Anthropology*. Chicago, IL: Aldine, pp. 37–48.

George, G. and Zahra, S. A. (2002) Culture and its consequences for entrepreneurship. *Entrepreneurship: Theory and Practice*, **26**(4), 5.

Ghemawat, P. (1991). *Commitment: The Dynamic of Strategy*. New York: The Free Press.

Gherardi, S. (1994). The gender we think, the gender we do in our everyday organizational lives. *Human Relations*, **47**(6), 591–610.

Ghoshal, S. and Moran, P. (1996). Bad for practice: a critique of the transaction cost theory. *Academy of Management Review*, **21**(1), 13–47.

Gibson, C. B. and Birkinshaw, J. (2004). The antecedents, consequences, and mediating role of organizational ambidexterity. *The Academy of Management Journal*, 47(2), 209–226.

Giddens, A. (1984). *The Constitution of Society: Outline of the Theory of Structuration*. Berkeley, CA: University of California Press.

Gillespie, N. and Dietz, G. (2009). Trust repair after an organization-level failure. *Academy of Management Review*, **34**(1), 127–145.

Ginsberg, A. and Buchholtz, A. (1989). Are the entrepreneurs a breed apart? A look at the evidence. *Journal of General Management*, **15**(2), 32–40.

Ginsberg, A. and Hay, M. (1994). Confronting the challenges of corporate entrepreneurship: guidelines for venture managers. *European Management Journal*, **12**, 382–389.

Glaser, B. G. (1978). *Theoretical Sensitivity: Advances in the Methodology of Grounded Theory*. Mill Valley, CA: Sociology Press.

Glaserfeld, E. von (1995). *Radical Constructivism: A Way of Knowing and Learning*. London: The Falmer Press.

Goffmann, E. (1959). *Presentation of Self in Everyday Life*. New York: Doubleday and Company Inc.

Goldsmith, S. (ed.) (1999). *The Entrepreneurial City: A How-To Handbook for Urban Innovators*. New York, Manhattan Institute.

Gordon, R. A., and Howell, J. E. (1959) *Higher Education for Business*. New York: Columbia University Press.

Görling, S. and Rehn, A. (2008). Accidental ventures: a materialist reading of opportunity and entrepreneurial potential. *Scandinavian Journal of Management*, **24**(3), 94–102.

Granovetter, M. (1985). Economic action and social structure: the problem of embeddedness. *American Journal of Sociology*, **91**, 481–510.

Granovetter, M. (2005). The impact of social structure on economic outcomes. *Journal of Economic Perspectives*, **19**(1), 33–50.

Gratton, L. and Erickson, T. J. (2007). Eight ways to build collaborative teams. Harvard Business Review, Reprint R0711F, Boston, MA: Harvard Business School Publishing.

Greenblatt, S. (1980). *Renaissance Self-Fashioning: From More to Shakespeare*. Chicago, IL: University of Chicago Press.

Greenspan, A. (1999). Financial derivatives. Futures Industry Association, Boca Raton, Florida, 19 March. Available at: www.federalreserve.gov/boarddocs/speeches/1999/19990319.htm.

Greenwood, M. and Buren Iii, H. (2010). Trust and stakeholder theory: trustworthiness in the organisation. Stakeholder relationship. *Journal of Business Ethics*, **95**(3), 425–438.

Gregory, R., (2006) Transforming governmental culture: a skeptical view of new public management. In T. Christensen and P. Laegreid (eds.), *New Public Management. The Transformation of Ideas and Practice*. Farnham, UK: Ashgate, Chapter 10, pp. 231–260.

Greenblatt, S. (1980). *Renaissance Self-Fashioning: From More to Shakespeare*. Chicago, IL: University of Chicago Press.

Greif, A. and Laitin, D. D. (2004). A theory of endogenous institutional change. American *Political Science Review*, **98**(4), 633–652.

Greve, H. R. (2008). A behavioral theory of firm growth: sequential attention to size and performance goals. *Academy of Management Journal*, **51**(3), 476–494.

Grey, C. (1996). Towards a critique of managerialism: the contribution of Simone Weil. *Journal of Management Studies*, **33**(5), 591–611.

Gross, N. (2009). A pragmatist theory of social mechanisms. *American Sociological Review*, **74**(3), 358–380.

Grossman, S. J. and Hart, O. D. (1986). The costs and benefits of ownership: a theory of vertical and lateral integration. *The Journal of Political Economy*, **94**(4), 691–719.

Groth, J. and Corijn, E. (2005). Reclaiming urbanity: indeterminate spaces, informal actors and urban agenda setting. *Urban Studies*, **42**(3), 503–526.

Grundy, J. (2003). Staging queer differences in the entrepreneurial city: the politics of pride Toronto. Doctoral Dissertation, Carleton University.

Guillet de Monthoux (2003). Bonk Business Inc. In A. Mir (ed.), *Corporate Mentality: An Archive Documenting the Emergence of Recent Practices within a Cultural Sphere Occupied by Both Business and Art*. New York: Lukas and Sternberg.

Guillet de Monthoux, (2004). *The Art Firm: Aesthetic Management and Metaphysical Marketing* Palo Alto, CA: Stanford UniversityPress.

Guillet de Monthoux, P. (2006). *Masters of Business Art-A Fields of Flow*. Available at: http://www.youtube.com/watch?v=6f698oKcXY0.

Guillet de Monthoux (2007). Hermeneutik des Handelns. In M. Markowski and W. Hergen, (eds.), *Oeconomenta-Wechselspiele zwischen Kunst und Wirtschaft*. Berlin: Kadmos Kulturverlag.

Guillet de Monthoux, P. (2008). Opening the gates to the art firm. In D. Hjorth and C. Steyart (eds.), *The Politics and Aesthetics of Entrepreneurship*. Cheltenham, UK: Edward Elgar Publishing.

Guillet de Monthoux, P. and Sjöstrand, S. (2003). Corporate art or artful corporation. In B. Czarniawska and G. Sévon-Berg (eds.), *Nordic Light: Organization Theory in Scandinavia*, Malmö, Sweden: Liber.

Guillet de Monthoux, P. and Sjöstrand, S. (2007). *Aesthetic Leadership*. Houndsmills, UK: Palgrave Macmillan.

Guldbrandsson, K. and Fossum, B. (2009). An exploration of the theoretical concepts, policy windows and policy entrepreneurs in the Swedish public health care. *Health Promotion International*, **24**(4), 434–444.

Gupta, V., MacMillan, I. C. and Surie, G. (2004). Entrepreneurial leadership: developing and measuring a cross-cultural construct. *Journal of Business Venturing*, **19**, 241–260.

Gustafsson, G. (2011) *The Production of Seriousness*. Houndsmills, UK: Palgrave Macmillan.

Guth, W. D. and Ginsberg A. (1990). Corporate entrepreneurship. *Strategic Management Journal*, **11**(Special Issue), 5–15.

Hackman, J. R. (2002). *Leading Teams: Setting the Stage for Great Performances*. Boston, MA: Harvard Business School Press.

Hagendoorn, L. (1995). Intergroup biases in multiple group systems: the perception of ethnic hierarchies. *European Review of Social Psychology*, **6**, 199–228.

Hales, J. and Williamson, M. G. (2010). Implicit employment contracts: the limits of management reputation for promoting firm productivity. *Journal of Accounting Research*, 48(1), 51–80.

Hall, P. (1999). *Cities in Civilization: Culture, Innovation, and Urban Order*. London: Phoenix Giant.

Halligan, J. (2008) Leadership and the senior service from a comparative perspective. In B. G. Peters and J. Pierre (eds.), *The Handbook of Public Administration*. Thousand Oaks, CA: Sage, Chapter 5, pp. 63–73.

Hamel, G. (2000). *Leading the Revolution*. Boston, MA: Harvard Business School Press.

Hanan, M. (1976). Venturing corporations: think small to stay strong. *Harvard Business Review*, **54**(3), 139–148.

Hancock, P. (2005). Uncovering the semiotic in organizational aesthetics. *Organization*, **12**(1) 29–50.

Hancock, P. and Tyler, M. (2007). Undoing gender and the aesthetics of organizational performance. *Gender, Work and Organization*, **14**(6), 512–533.

Hannan, M. T. and Freeman, J. (1977). *The Population Ecology of Organizations.* Chicago, IL: University of Chicago Press.

Haraway, D. (1991). *Simians, Cyborgs, and Women.* London: Free Association Books.

Harbi, S. E. and A. R. Anderson (2010). Institutions and the shaping of different forms of entrepreneurship. *Journal of Socio-Economics,* **39**(3), 436–444.

Harding, N. (2002). On the manager's body as an aesthetic of control. *TAMARA: Journal of Critical Postmodern Organization Science,* **2**(1), 63–76.

Harding, S. (1986). *The Science Question in Feminism.* Ithaca, NY: Cornell University Press.

Harding, S. (ed.). (1987). *Feminism and Methodology.* Bloomington, IN: Indiana University Press.

Hardt, M. (1993) *Gilles Deleuze: an Apprenticeship in Philosophy,* Minneapolis, MN: University of Minnesota Press.

Hardt, M. and Negri, A. (2009). *Commonwealth.* Cambridge, MA: Bellknap.

Harel, I. and Papert, S. (1991). *Constructionism.* Norwood, NJ: Ablex.

Harper, D. A. (2008). Towards a theory of entrepreneurial teams. *Journal of Business Venturing,* **23**(6), 613–626.

Harryson, S. (2006). *Know-Who Based Entrepreneurship: From Knowledge Creation to Business Implementation.* Cheltenham, UK: Edward Elgar Publishing.

Hart, O. D. (1995). *Firms, Contracts and Financial Structure.* Oxford: Clarendon Press.

Hart, S. and London, T. (2005). Developing native capability: what multinational corporations can learn from the base of the pyramid. *Stanford Social Innovation Review,* **3**(2), 28–33.

Hart, O. D. and Moore, J. (1990). Property rights and the nature of the firm. *Journal of Political Economy,* **98**(6), 1119–1158.

Harvey, D. (1989) From managerialism to entrepreneurialism: the transformation in urban governance in late capitalism. *Geografiska Annaler,* **B71**(1), 3–17.

Harvey, D. (2008). The right to the city. *New Left Review,* **53**, 2340.

Harvey, D. (2010). *The Enigma of Capital and the Crises of Capitalism.* London: Profile.

Hatch, M. J. (1999). Exploring the empty spaces of organizing: how improvisational jazz helps redescribe organizational structure. *Organization Studies,* **20**, 75–100.

Hatch, M. J. and Yanow, D. (2003). Organization theory as an interpretive science. In H. Tsoukas and C. Knudsen (eds.), *The Oxford*

Handbook of Organization Theory. Oxford: Oxford University Press, pp. 63–87.

Haugh, H. (2007). Community-led social venture creation. *Entrepreneurship Theory and Practice*, **31**(2), 161–182.

Haveman, H. A. and Rao, H. (1997). Structuring a theory of moral sentiments: Institutional and organizational co evolution in the early Thrift industry. *The American Journal of Sociology*, **102**(6), 1606–1651.

Hayden, P. (1998) *Multiplicity and Becoming: The Pluralist Empiricism of Gilles Deleuze.* New York: Peter Lang.

Hayek, F. A. von (1945). *Individualism and Economic Order.* Chicago, IL: University of Chicago Press.

Hayek, F. A. von (1978). *New Studies in Philosophy, Politics and Economics.* Chicago, IL: University of Chicago Press.

Hayton, J. C., George, G. and Zahra, S. A. (2002). National culture and entrepreneurship: a review of behavioral research. *Entrepreneurship: Theory and Practice*, **26**(4), 33.

Hazard, T. and Elita, M. (2008). *The Naked Entrepreneur: A Millionaire's Journey from Fear to True Wealth.* El Monte, CA: Wbusiness Books.

He, Z.-L. and Wong, P.-K. (2004). Exploration vs. exploitation: an empirical test of the ambidexterity hypothesis. *Organization Science*, 15(4), 481–494.

Hébert, R. F. and Link, A. N. (1988). *The Entrepreneur.* New York: Praeger.

Hedberg, B., Baumard, P. and Yaklef, A. (2002). *Managing Imaginary Organizations: A New Perspective on Business.* Oxford: Pergamon.

Hederer, C. (2007). Political entrepreneurship and institutional change: evolutionary perspective. Paper presented at the 2007 EAEPE-conference in Porto.

Heidegger, M. (1962). Being and time. J. Macquarrie, and E. Robinson (trans.). New York: Harper and Row.

Helfat, C. E. and Peteraf, M. A. (2009). Understanding dynamic capabilities: progress along a developmental path. *Strategic Organization*, **7**, 91–102.

Helfat, C. E., Finkelstein, S., Mitchell, W., Peteraf, M., Singh, H., Teece, D. and Winter, S. G. (2007). *Dynamic Capabilities: Understanding Strategic Change in Organizations.* Oxford: Blackwell.

Heller, T. (1999). Loosely coupled systems for corporate entrepreneurship: Imagining and managing the innovation project/host organization interface. *Entrepreneurship: Theory and Practice*, **24**(2), 25–31.

Hellman, J. S., Jones, G. and Kaufmann, D. (2003). Seize the state, seize the day: state capture and influence in transition economies. *Journal of Comparative Economics*, **31**(4), 751–773.

Hemingway, C. A. (2005). Personal values as a catalyst for corporate social entrepreneurship. *Journal of Business Ethics*, **60**(3), 233–249.

Henrekson, M. (2007). Entrepreneurship and institutions. *Comparative Labor Law and Policy Journal*, **28**, 717–742.

Henrekson, M. and D. Johansson (1999). Institutional effects on the evolution of the size distribution of firms. *Small Business Economics*, **12**(1), 11–23.

Henrekson, M. and Sanandaji, T. (2010). *The Interaction of Entrepreneurship and Institutions.* Stockholm: Research Institute of Industrial Economics.

Hernes, T. (2008). *Understanding Organization as Process. Theory for a Tangled World.* New York: Routledge.

Hernes, T. and Maithlis, S. (eds.) (2010). *Process, Sensemaking and Organizing.* Oxford: Oxford University Press.

Hetherington, K. and Cronin, A. M. (2008). Introduction. In A. M. Cronin and K. Hetherington (eds.) *Consuming the Entrepreneurial City: Image, Memory, Spectacle.* London: Routledge, pp. 1–18.

Hill, R. M. and Hlavacek, J. D. (1972), The venture team: a new concept in marketing organizations. *Journal of Marketing*, **36**, 44–50.

Hirdman, Y. (2002). *Att lägga livet tillrätta. Studier i svensk forkhemspolitik.* Stockholm, Sweden: Carlsons.

Hisrich, R. D. (2010). International Entrepreneurship. Thousand Oaks, CA: Sage Publications.

Hisrich, R. D., Peters, M. P. and Shepherd, D. A. (2010). *Entrepreneurship*, 8th edn. New York: McGraw-Hill/Irwin.

Hitt, M. A., and Ireland, R. D. (2000). The intersection of entrepreneurship and strategic management research. In D. L. Sexton and H. Landstrom (Eds.), Handbook of entrepreneurship: 45–63. Oxford: Blackwell Publishers.

Hitt, M. A., Ireland, R. D., Camp, S. M. and Sexton, D. L. (2001), Strategic entrepreneurship: entrepreneurial strategies for wealth creation. *Strategic Management Journal*, **22** (Special Issue), 479–491.

Hitt, M. A., Ireland, R. D., Camp, S. M. and Sexton, D. L. (2002). *Strategic Entrepreneurship: Creating a New Mindset.* Oxford: Blackwell.

Hjorth, D. (2003a). In the tribe of Sisyphus: rethinking management education from an entrepreneurial perspective. *Journal of Management Education*, **27**(6), 637–653.

Hjorth, D. (2003b). *Rewriting Entrepreneurship: For a New Perspective on Organisational Creativity.* Copenhagen: Copenhagen Business School Press.

Hjorth, D. (2005). Organizational entrepreneurship. With de Certeau on creating heterotopias (or spaces for play). Journal of management inquiry, 14(4), 386–398.

Hjorth, D. (2007). Narrating the entrepreneurial event: learning from Shakespeare's Iago. *Journal of Business Venturing*, **22**(5), 712–732

Hjorth, D. (2008). Nordic entrepreneurship research. *Entrepreneurship Theory and Practice*, **32**(2), 313–338.

Hjorth, D. (2010). An art of the weak: organisational creativity as transmutive affirmation. Conference Paper, Process Symposium, Rhodes, Greece, June 2010.

Hjorth, D. and Bjerke, B. (2006). Public entrepreneurship: moving from social/consumer to public/citizen. In C. Steyaert and D. Hjorth, D. (eds.) *Entrepreneurship as Social Change.* Cheltenham: Edward Elgar Publishing, Chapter 5, pp. 97–120

Hjorth, D. and Johannisson, B. (2003). Conceptualising the opening phase of regional development as the enactment of a 'collective identity'. *Concepts and Transformation*, **8**(1), 69–82.

Hjorth, D. and Johannisson, B. (2007). Learning as an entrepreneurial process. In A. Fayol (ed.) *Handbook of Research in Entrepreneurship Education*, Vol. 1. Cheltenham, UK: Edward Elgar Publishing, pp. 46–66.

Hjorth, D. and Johannisson, B. (2008). Building new roads for entrepreneurship research to travel by: on the work of William B. Gartner. *Small Business Economics*, **31**, 341–350.

Hjorth, D. and Kostera, M. (eds.) (2007). *Entrepreneurship and the Experience Economy*. Copenhagen, Denmark: Copenhagen Business School Press.

Hjorth, D. and Steyaert, C. (1998). I see death coming. (So) The future is now or never: On forms and concepts that keep us moving", SCANCORE conference, Stanford, USA.

Hjorth, D. and C. Steyaert (2003). Entrepreneurship beyond (a new) economy: creative swarms and pathological zones. In C. Steyaert and D. Hjorth (eds.), *New Movements in Entrepreneurship*. Cheltenham, UK: Edward Elgar Publishing, pp. 286–304.

Hjorth, D. and Steyaert, C. (2004a). Ex(f)iles in Paris. Key Note Performance at the 3rd Art of Management Conference, Paris, France, September.

Hjorth, D. and Steyaert, C. (Eds.) (2004b). *Narrative and Discursive Approaches in Entrepreneurship*. Cheltenham, UK: Edward Elgar Publishing.

Hjorth, D. and Steyaert, C. (2006). American Psycho/European Schizo: stories of managerial elites in a hundred images. In P. Gagliardi and B. Czarniawska (eds.) *Management Education and Humanities*. Cheltenham, UK: Edward Elgar Publishing, pp. 67–97.

Hjorth, D. and Steyaert, C. (eds.) (2009). *The Politics and Aesthetics of Entrepreneurship.* Cheltenham, UK: Edward Elgar Publishing.

Hjorth, D., Johannisson, B. and Steyaert, C. (2003). Entrepreneurship as discourse and life style. In B. Czarniawska and G. Sevón (eds.), *The Northern Lights: Organization Theory in Scandinavia.* Liber, Abstract, Copenhagen Business School, pp. 91–111.

Hjorth, D., Jones, C. and Gartner, W. B. (2008). Introduction: recreating/recontextualising entrepreneurship. *Scandinavian Journal of Management,* **24**(2), 81–84.

Hjorth, D., O'Donnell, S. and Austin, R. (2010). Learning to lead collective creativity from Miles Davis. *Cutter Advisor.* Available at: www.cutter.com.

Hobbes, T. (1968). *Leviathan,* C. B. MacPherson (ed.). Harmondsworth, UK: Penguin.

Hochschild, A. R. (1983) *The Managed Heart. Commercialization of Human Feeling.* London: University of California Press.

Hockerts, K. N. (2006). Chapter 10: Entrepreneurial Opportunity in Social Purpose Business Ventures. In J. Mair, J. Robertson and K. N. Hockerts (eds.), *Social Entrepreneurship,* Vol. 1. London: Palgrave MacMillan.

Hofstede, G. (1980). *Culture's Consequences: International Differences in Work Related Values.* Beverly Hills, CA: Sage.

Hofstede, G. J. (2000). Organizational culture: siren or sea cow? *Strategic Change,* **9**, 135–137.

Holcombe, R. G (2002). Political entrepreneurship and the democratic allocation of economic resources. *Review of Austrian Economics,* **15**(2), 143–159.

Holmström, B. (1982). Moral hazard in teams. *Bell Journal of Economics,* **13**(2), 324–340.

Holmström, B. and Milgrom, P R. (1991). Multitask principal-agent analysis: incentive contracts, asset ownership and job design. *Journal of Law, Economics and Organization,* **7**, 24–54.

Holmström, B. and Milgrom, P R. (1994). The firm as an incentive system. *The American Economic Review,* **84**(4), 972–991.

Honig, B. (2001). Learning strategies and resources for entrepreneurs and intrapreneurs. *Entrepreneurship Theory and Practice,* **26**(1), 21–35.

Honig, B. and Karlsson, T. (2004). Institutional forces and the written business plan. *Journal of Management,* **30**(1), 29–48.

Hood, C. (1991). A public management for all seasons? *Public Administration,* **69**, 3–19.

Hoogendoorn, B. and Pennings, E. (2010). What do we know about social entrepreneurship? An analysis of empirical research. *International Review of Entrepreneurship,* **8**(2), 1–42.

Horkheimer, M. (1972). *Critical Theory: Selected Essays*, Mathew O'Connell (trans.). New York: Continuum.

Hornsby, J. S., Kuratko, D. F. and Montagno, R. V. (1999). Perception of internal factors for corporate entrepreneurship: a comparison of Canadian and U.S. managers. *Entrepreneurship Theory and Practice*, **24**(2), 9–24.

Hornsby, J. S., Kuratko, D. F. and Zahra, S. A. (2002). Middle managers' perception of the internal environment for corporate entrepreneurship: assessing a measurement scale. *Journal of Business Venturing*, **17**, 49–63.

Hornsby, J. S., Kuratko, D. F., Shepherd, D. A. and Bott, J. P. (2009). Managers' corporate entrepreneurial actions: examining perception and position. *Journal of Business Venturing*, **24**(3), 236–247.

Hoskisson, R. E., Eden, L., Lau, C. M. and Wright, M. (2000). Strategy in emerging economies. *Academy of Management Journal*, **43**(3), 249–267.

Howkins, J. (2001), *The Creative Economy: How People Make Money From Ideas*. London: Penguin Books.

Hrebiniak, L. G., and Joyce, W. F. (1985). Organizational adaptation: strategic choice and environmental determinism. *Administrative Science Quarterly*, **30**(3), 336–349.

Hsieh, C., Nickerson, J. and Zenger, T. R. (2007). Opportunity discovery, problem solving, and a theory of the entrepreneurial firm. *Journal of Management Studies*, **44**(7), 1255–1277.

Hsu, G. and Hannan, M. T. (2005). Identities, genres, and organizational forms. *Organization Science*, **16**(5), 474–490.

Hubbard, P. (2006). *City*. London: Routledge.

Hubbard, P. and Hall, T. (1998). The entrepreneurial city and the 'new urban politics'. In T. Hall and P. Hubbard (eds.), *The Entrepreneurial City: Geographies of Politics, Regime and Representation*. West Sussex, UK: John Wiley and Sons, pp. 1–27.

Hulgård, L. and Spear, R. (2007). Social entrepreneurship and the mobilization of social capital in European social enterprises. In M. Nyssens (ed.), *Social enterprise: At the Cross-road of Market, Public Policies and Civil Society*. London: Routledge, pp. 85–107.

Hull, K. P. (2009) Enabling employee driven innovations. Paper presented at the EDI Europe Conference on Bryssels 2.3 09

Hultin, M. (2003). Some take the glass escalator, some hit the glass ceiling? *Work and Occupation*, **30**(1), 30–61.

Humphreys, N., Robin, D. P., Reidenbach, R. E. and Moak, D. L. (1993). The ethical decision making process of small business owner-managers and their customers. *Journal of Small Business Management*, **31**(3), 9–22.

Hunt, S. D. and Vitell, S. (1992). The general theory of marketing ethics:

a retrospective and revision. In J. Quelch and C. Smith (eds.), *Ethics in Marketing*. Chicago, IL: Richard D. Irwin, pp. 775–784.

Huss-Keeler, R. L. (1998). Teacher perception of ethnic and linguistic minority parental involvement and its relationships to children's language and literacy learning: a case study. *Teaching and Teacher Education*, **13**(2), 171–182.

Husted, B. W. (1999). Wealth, culture, and corruption. *Journal of International Business Studies*, **30**(2), 339–360.

Husted, B. W. (2000). The impact of national culture on software piracy. *Journal of Business Ethics*, **26**(3), 197–211.

Husted, B. W. (2005). Culture and ecology: a cross-national study of the determinants of environmental performance. *Management International Review*, **45**(3), 349–371.

Huy, Q. N. (1999). Emotional capability, emotional intelligence, and radical change. *The Academy of Management Review*, **24**(2), 325–345.

Huyssen, A. (1997). The Voids of Berlin. *Critical Inquiry*, **24**(1), 57–81.

Ibarra, H. (1992). Homophily and differential returns: sex differences in network structure and access in an advertising firm. *Administrative Science Quarterly*, **37**(3), 422–447.

Ingold, T. (1995). Building, dwelling, living: how people and animals make themselves at home in the world. In M. Stratgern (ed.), *Shifting Contexts: Transformations in Anthropological Knowledge*. London, Routledge. pp. 57–80.

Ireland, R. D. and Webb, J. W. (2007a). A multi-theoretic perspective on trust and power in strategic supply chains. *Journal of Operations Management*, **25**, 482–497.

Ireland, R. D. and Webb, J. W. (2007b). Strategic entrepreneurship: creating competitive advantage through streams of innovation. *Business Horizons*, **50**, 49–59.

Ireland, R. D., Hitt, M. A., Camp, S. M., and Sexton, D. L. 2001. Integrating Entrepreneurship and Strategic Management Actions to Create Firm Wealth. The Academy of Management Executive, 15: 49–63.

Ireland, R.D., Hitt, M.A., and Vaidyanath, D. (2002), Strategic alliances as a pathway to competitive success. Journal of Management, 28: 413–446.

Ireland, R. D., Hitt, M. A. and Sirmon, D. G. (2003a). A model of strategic entrepreneurship: the construct and its dimensions. *Journal of Management*, **29**(6), 963–989.

Ireland, R. D., Kuratko, D. F., and Covin, J. G. (2003b), Antecedents, elements, and consequences of corporate entrepreneurship strategy. Best Paper Proceedings: Academy of Management, Annual Meeting, Seattle Washington.

Ireland, R. D., Kuratko, D. F. and Morris, M. H. (2006a). A health audit for corporate entrepreneurship: innovation at all levels. Part I. *Journal of Business Strategy*, **27**(1), 10–17.

Ireland, R. D., Kuratko, D. F. and Morris, M. H. (2006b). A health audit for corporate entrepreneurship: innovation at all levels. Part 2. *Journal of Business Strategy*, **27**(2), 21–30.

Ireland, R. D., Covin, J. G. and Kuratko, D. F. (2009), Conceptualizing corporate entrepreneurship strategy. *Entrepreneurship Theory and Practice*, **33**(1), 19–46.

Jackall, R. (1988). *Moral Mazes: The World of Corporate Managers*. New York: Oxford University Press.

Jackson, N. and Carter, P. (1998). Labour as dressage. In A. McKinlay and K. P. Starkey (eds.), *Foucault, Management and Organization Theory*. Thousand Oaks, CA: Sage, pp. 49–64.

James, M. (1992). From welfare state to welfare society. St Leonards, Australia: The Center for Independent Studies.

Jennings, D. F. and Young, D. M. (1990). An empirical comparison between objective and subjective measures of the product innovation domain of corporate entrepreneurship. *Entrepreneurship Theory and Practice*, **15**(1), 53–66.

Jensen, M. and Meckling, W. (1976). Theory of the firm: managerial behavior, agency costs and ownership structure. *Journal of Financial Economics*, **3**(4), 305–360.

Joas, H. (1996). *The Creativity of Action*. Chicago, IL: The University of Chicago Press.

Johannisson, B. (1987). Anarchists and organizers: entrepreneurs in a network perspective. *International Studies of Management and Organization*, **17**(1), 49–64.

Johannisson, B., Ramirez-Pasillas, M. and Karlsson, G. (2002). The institutional embeddedness of local inter-firm networks: a leverage for business creation. *Entrepreneurship and Regional Development*, **14**(4), 297–315.

John, R. (2006). Venture philanthropy: the evolution of high engagement philanthropy in Europe. Skoll Centre for Social Entrepreneurship.

Johnsen, R., Muhr, S. L. and Pedersen, M. (2009). The frantic gesture of interpassivity. *Journal of Organizational Change Management*, **22**(2), 202–213.

Jones, C. (2002). Foucault's Inheritance/Inheriting Foucault. *Culture and Organization*, **8**(3), 225–238.

Jones, C. and Munro, R. (eds.) (2005). *Contemporary Organization Theory* (Sociological Review Monographs). Oxford: Blackwell.

Jones, C. and Spicer, A. (2005). The sublime object of entrepreneurship. *Organization*, **12**(2), 223–246.

Jones, C. and Spicer, A. (2009). *Unmasking the Entrepreneur.* Cheltenham, UK: Edward Elgar Publishing.

Kaish, S. and Gilad, B. (1991). Characteristics of opportunities search of entrepreneurs versus executives: sources, interests and general alertness. *Journal of Business Venturing*, **6**, 45–61.

Kalantaridis, C. (2007). Institutional change in post-socialist regimes: public policy and beyond. *Journal of Economic Issues*, **XLI**(2), 435–442.

Kania, J. and Kramer, M. (2011). Collective impact. *Stanford Social Innovation Review*, Winter, 36–41.

Kant, I. (1991) *The Critique of Judgment.* Oxford: Clarendon Press.

Kant, I. (1998). *Critique of Pure Reason*, Paul Gayer and Allen Wood (trans.). Cambridge: Cambridge University Press.

Kanter, R. (1977). *Men and Women of the Corporation.* New York: Basic Books.

Kanter, R. M. (1985), Supporting innovation and venture development in established companies. *Journal of Business Venturing*, 1, 47–60.

Kantola, J. and Outshoorn, J. (2007). Changing state feminism. In J. Outshoorn and J. Kantola (eds.), *Changing State Feminism.* Hampshire and New York: Palgrave Macmillan, pp. 1–19.

Kaplan, G. and Rogers, L. (1990). The definition of male and female. Biological reductionism and the sanctions of normality. In S. Gunew (ed.), *Feminist Knowledge: Critique and Construct.* London: Routledge.

Kaptein, M. (2002). Guidelines for the development of and ethics safety net. *Journal of Business Ethics*, **41**(3), 217–234.

Kaptein, M. and Avelino, S. (2005). Measuring corporate integrity: a survey-based approach. *Journal of Business Ethics*, **5**(1), 45–54.

Karlsson, C. and Acs, Z. J. (2002). Introduction to institutions, entrepreneurship and firm growth: The case of Sweden. *Small Business Economics*, **19**(2), 63–67.

Kaulingfreks, R. and Warren, S. (2010). SWARM: flash mobs, mobile clubbing and the city. *Culture and Organization*, **16**(3), 211–227.

Kaulingfreks, R. and Bos, R. ten (2005). Are organizations bicycles? On hosophobia and neognosticism in organizational thought. *Culture and Organization*, **11**(2), 83–96.

Kearney, C., Hisrich, R. and Roche, F. (2008). A conceptual model of public sector corporate entrepreneurship. *International Entrepreneurship Management Journal,* **4**, 295–313.

Kelly, P. (2006). The entrepreneurial self and 'youth at-risk': exploring the horizons of identity in the twenty-first century. *Journal of Youth Studies*, **9**(1), 17–32.

Ketchen, D., Ireland, R. D. and Snow, C. (2007). Strategic

entrepreneurship, collaborative innovation, and wealth creation. *Strategic Entrepreneurship Journal*, **1**(1), 371–385.

Kets de Vries, M. (1985). The dark side of entrepreneurship. Harvard Business Review, Nov-Dec, 160–168.

Keuls, E. C. (1993). The reign of the phallus: sexual politics in ancient Athens. California: University of California Press.

Keynes, J. M. (1936 [1967]). *The General Theory of Employment, Interest and Money*. London: Macmillan.

Kim, J. and Mahoney, J. T. (2007). Appropriating economic rents from resources: an integrative property rights and resource-based approach. *International Journal of Learning and Intellectual Capital*, **4**(1/2), 11–28.

Kim, Y. (2010). Stimulating entrepreneurial practices in the public sector: the roles of organizational characteristics. *Administration & Society*, **42**(7), 780–814.

King, A. W., Fowler, S. W. and Zeithaml, C. P. (2001), Managing organizational competencies for competitive advantage: the middle-management edge. *Academy of Management Executive*, **15**(2), 95–106.

King, I. W. (2003). Reassessing organizational structure as a painting of space. *Culture and Organization*, **9**(3), 195–207.

Kingdon, J. W. (1995). *Agendas, Alternatives and Public Policies.* New York: Harper Collins.

Kirzner, I. M. (1973). *Competition and Entrepreneurship*. Chicago, IL: University of Chicago Press.

Kirzner, I. M. (1979). *Perception, Opportunity, and Profit: Studies in the Theory of Entrepreneurship*, Chicago, IL: University of Chicago Press.

Kirzner, I. M. (1982). Competition, regulation and the market process: an 'Austrian' perspective. Cato Institute Policy Analysis No. 18, 30 September 1982.

Kirzner, I. M. (1983). Entrepreneurs and the entrepreneurial function: a commentary. In J. Ronen (ed.), *Entrepreneurship.* Lexington, MA: LexingtonBooks, pp. 281–290.

Kirzner, I. M. (1985). *Discovery and the Capitalist Process*. Chicago, IL: University of Chicago Press.

Kirzner, I. M. (1992). *The Meaning of the Market Process: Essays in the development of Modern Austrian Economics.* London and New York: Routledge.

Kirzner, I. M. (1997a). Entrepreneurial discovery and the competitive market process: an Austrian approach. *Journal of Economic Literature*, 35, 60–85.

Kirzner, I. M. (1997b). Interview with Israel M. Kirzner. *Austrian Economics Newsletter*, 17(1).

Kirzner, I. M. (2009). The alert and creative entrepreneur: a clarification. *Small Business Economics*, **32**(2), 145–152.

Kisor, A. J. and Kendal-Wilson, L. (2002). Older homeless women: reframing the stereotype of the bag lady. *Affilia*, **17**(3), 354–370.

Klein, K. J., Ziegert, J. C., Knight, A. P. and Xiao, Y. (2006). Dynamic delegation: shared, hierarchical, and deindividualized leadership in extreme action teams. *Administrative Science Quarterly*, **51**, 590–621.

Klein, N.(2007). *The Shock Doctrine: The Rise of Disaster Capitalism.* London: Allen Lane.

Klein, P. G. (2008). Opportunity discovery, entrepreneurial action, and economic organization. *Strategic Entrepreneurship Journal*, **2**(3), 175–190.

Klein, P. G. and Klein, S. K. (2001). Do entrepreneurs make predictable mistakes? Evidence from corporate divestitures. *Quarterly Journal of Austrian Economics* **4**, 3–25.

Klein, P. G., Mahoney, J. T., McGahan, A. M. and Pitelis, C. (2010). Toward a theory of public entrepreneurship. *European Management Review*, **7**, 1–15.

Kloosterman, R. C. (2010). Matching opportunities with resources: a framework for analysing (migrant) entrepreneurship from a mixed embeddedness perspective. *Entrepreneurship and Regional Development*, **22**(1), 25–45.

Kloosterman, R. C., Van der Leun, J. and Rath, J. (1999). Mixed embeddedness: (in)formal economic activities and immigrant businesses in the Netherlands. *International Journal of Urban and Regional Research*, **23**(2), 252–277.

Knight, F. H. (1921 [1985]), *Risk, Uncertainty and Profit.* Chicago, IL: University of Chicago Press.

Knight, F. H. (1942). Profit and entrepreneurial functions. *The Journal of Economic History* **2**(2), 126–132.

Knight, J. (1997). Social institutions and human cognition: thinking about old questions in new ways. *Journal of Institutional and Theoretical Economics*, **153**(4), 693–699.

Knights, D. (2002). Writing organizational analysis into Foucault. *Organization*, **9**(4), 575–593.

Knights, D. and Willmott, H. (1989). Power and subjectivity at work. *Sociology*, **23**(4), 535–558.

Knott, A. M., and Posen, H. E. (2005). Is failure good? *Strategic Management Journal*, **26**(7), 617–641.

Knox, H. (2010). Cities and organization: the information city and urban form. *Culture and Organization*, **16**(3), 185–196.

Knudsen, T. and Swedberg, R. (2010). Capitalist entrepreneurship:

making profit through the unmaking of economic orders. *Capitalism and Society*, **4**(2), Art. 3, 1–26.

Kocka, J. (1980). The rise of the modern industrial enterprise in Germany". In Alfred Chandler and Herman Daems (eds.), *Managerial Hierarchies*. Cambridge, MA: Harvard University Press, pp. 77–116

Koene, B. A. S. (2006). Situated human agency, institutional entrepreneurship and institutional change. *Journal of Organizational Change Management*, **19**(3), 365–382.

Kovalainen, A. and Österberg-Högstedt, J. (2011). Changing public sector in Finland: on business, trust and gender in municipalities. *Nordiske Organisasjonsstudier*, **12**(1).

Kozlowski, S. W. J. and Ilgen, D. R. (2006). Enhancing the effectiveness of work groups and teams. *Psychological Science in the Public Interest*, **7**(3), 77–124.

Kramer, R. M. (2010). Collective trust within organizations: conceptual foundations and empirical insights. *Corporate Reputation Review*, **13**(2), 82–97.

Kuratko, D. F. (1993). Intrapreneurship: developing innovation in the corporation. *Advances in Global High Technology Management: High Technology Venturing*, **3**, 3–14.

Kuratko, D. F. (2007). Entrepreneurial leadership for the 21st century. *Journal of Leadership and Organizational Studies*, **14**(1), Summer, 2007.

Kuratko, D. F. (2009). The entrepreneurial imperative of the 21st century. Business Horizons, **52**(5), 421–428.

Kuratko, D. F. and Audretsch, D. B. (2009). Strategic entrepreneurship: exploring different perspectives on an emerging concept. *Entrepreneurship Theory and Practice*, **33**(1), 1–17.

Kuratko, D. F. and Montagno, R. V. (1989). The intrapreneurial spirit. *Training and Development Journal*, **43**(10), 83–87.

Kuratko, D. F., Covin, J. G. and Garrett, R. P. (2009). Corporate venturing: insights from actual performance. *Business Horizons*, **52**(5), 459–467.

Kuratko, D. F., Hornsby, J. S. and Bishop, J. W. (2005a). Managers' corporate entrepreneurial actions and job satisfaction. *International Entrepreneurship and Management Journal*, **1**(3), 275–291.

Kuratko, D. F., Hornsby, J. S. and Goldsby, M. G. (2004). Sustaining corporate entrepreneurship: a proposed model of perceived implementation/outcome comparisons at the organizational and individual levels. *International Journal of Entrepreneurship and Innovation*, **5**(2), 77–89.

Kuratko, D. F, Ireland, R. D. and Hornsby, J. S. (2001). The power of entrepreneurial outcomes: Insights from Acordia, Inc. *Academy of Management Executive*, **15**(4), 60–71.

Kuratko, D. F., Ireland, R. D., and Hornsby, J. (2004). Corporate entrepreneurship behaviour among managers: a review of theory, research and practice. *Advances in Entrepreneurship, Firm Emergence and Growth*, **7**, 7–45.

Kuratko, D. F., Montagno, R. V. and Hornsby, J. S. (1990). Developing an entrepreneurial assessment instrument for an effective corporate entrepreneurial environment. *Strategic Management Journal*, **11** (Special Issue), 49–58.

Kuratko, D. F., Ireland, R. D., Covin, J. G. and Hornsby, J. S. (2005b). A model of middle level managers. *Entrepreneurial Behavior. Entrepreneurship Theory and Practice*, **29**(6), 699–716.

Kwon, M. (2004). *One Place after Another: Site-Specific Art and Locational Identity*. Cambridge, MA: MIT Press.

Lachmann, L. M. (1956 [1978]). *Capital and Its Structure*. Kansas City, MO: Sheed Andrews and McMeel.

Ladkin, D. and Taylor, S. S. (2010). Enacting the 'true self': towards a theory of embodied authentic leadership. *The Leadership Quarterly*, **21**(1), 64–74.

Lake, R. W. (2005). Urban crisis redux. *Urban Geography*, **26**(3), 266–270.

Lakoff, G. and S. Ferguson (2006). *The Framing of Immigration*. Berkeley, CA: The Rockridge Institute.

Lampel, J. and Shamsie, J. (2003). Capabilities in motion: new organizational forms and the reshaping of the Hollywood movie industry. *Journal of Management Studies*, **40**(8), 2189–210.

Landry, C. (2000). *The Creative City: A Toolkit for Urban Innovators*. London: Earthscan.

Lange, B. (2005). Socio-spatial strategies of culturepreneurs. *Zeitschrift für Wirtschaftsgeographie*, **49**(2), 79–96.

Langer, E. J. (1989). *Mindfulness*. Reading, MA: Addison-Wesley/ Addison Wesley Longman.

Langer, E. J. (1997). *The Power of Mindful Learning*. Cambridge, MA: Perseus Publishing.

Langley, A. (1999). Strategies for analyzing from process data. *Academy of Management Review*, **24**(4), 691–711.

Langley, A. (2007). Process thinking in strategic organization. *Strategic Organization*, **5**, 271–282

Langlois, R. N. (1995). Capabilities and coherence in firms and markets. In C. A. Montgomery (ed.), *Resource-based and Evolutionary Theories of the Firm: Towards a Synthesis*. Amsterdam: Dordrecht Kluwer Academic Publishers, pp. 71–100.

Langlois, R. N. (2007). The entrepreneurial theory of the firm and the theory of the entrepreneurial firm. *Journal of Management Studies*, **44**(7), 1107–1124.

Langlois, R. N. and Cosgel, M. M. (1993). Frank Knight on risk, uncertainty, and the firm: a new interpretation. *Economic Inquiry*, **31**(3), 456–465.

Langlois, R. N. and Foss, N. J. (1999). Capabilities and governance: the rebirth of production in the theory of economic organization. *Kyklos*, **52**(2), 201–218.

Lant, T. K., and Mezias, S. J. (1990). Managing discontinuous change: a simulation study of organizational learning and entrepreneurship. *Strategic Management Journal*, **11**(4), 147–179.

Laratta, R. (2010). From welfare state to welfare society: toward a viable system of welfare in Japan and England. *International Journal of Social Welfare*, **19**(2), 131–141.

Latham, A. (1999). Powers of engagement: on being engaged, being indifferent, and urban life. *Area*, **31**(2), 161–168.

Latham, A. (2003). Urbanity, lifestyle and making sense of the new urban cultural economy: notes from Auckland, New Zealand. *European Urban and Regional Studies*, **40**(9), 1699–1724.

Latham, A. (2006a). Euro-Commentary: Anglophone urban studies and the European city: some comments on interpreting Berlin. *European Urban and Regional Studies*, **13**(1), 88–92.

Latham, A. (2006b). Euro-commentary: Berlin and everywhere else: a reply to Allan Cochrane. European Urban and Regional Studies 13(4), 377–379.

Latham, A., McCormack, D. P., McNamara, K. and McNeill, D. (2009). *Key Concepts in Urban Geography*. London: Sage.

Latour, B. (1988). *The Pasteurization of France*. Cambridge, MA: Harvard University Press.

Latour, B. (1993). *We Have Never Been Modern*, transl. by C. Porter. Cambridge, MA: Harvard University Press.

Latour, B. (1997). On actor–network theory: A few clarifications. Centre for Social Theory and Technology (CSTT), Keele University. Available at: www.nettime.org/Lists-Archives/nettime-l-9801/msg00019.html.

Latour, B. and Woolgar, S. (1979). *Laboratory Life: The Construction of Scientific Facts.* Princeton: New Jersey: Princeton University Press.

Law, J. (2004). *After Method: Mess in Social Science Research*. London: Routledge.

Lazzarato, M. (2006). The concepts of life and the living in the societies of control. In M. Fuglsang and B. M. Sørensen (eds.), *Deleuze and the social*. Edinburgh: Edinburgh University Press, pp. 171–190.

Leadbeater, C. (1997). *The Rise of the Social Entrepreneur*. London: Demos.

Leca, B. and Naccache, P. (2006). A critical realist approach to institutional entrepreneurship. *Organization*, **13**(5), 627–651.

Ledeneva, A. V. (2006). *How Russia Really Works: The Informal Practices that Shaped Post-Soviet Politics and Business*. Ithaca, NY: Cornell University Press.

Lee, P. M. (2007). Die Sozialgeschichte der Kunst: in the belly of an architect. In H. Belzer and D. Birnbaum (eds.), *Kunst Lehren/Teaching Art-Städelschule*. Frankfurt/Main: Verlag der Buchandlung Walther König.

Lefebvre, H. (1991). *The Production of Space*, trans. D. Nicholson-Smith. Oxford: Blackwell.

Lefebvre, H. (1996). Right to the City. In E. Kofman and E. Lebas (eds.), *Henri Lefebvre: Writings on Cities*. Oxford: Blackwell, pp. 63–184.

Lefebvre, H. (2003). *The Urban Revolution*, trans. R. Bononno. Minneapolis, MN: University of Minnesota Press.

Leisinger, K. M. (2007). Corporate philanthropy: the top of the pyramid. *Business and Society Review*, **112**(3), 315–342.

Leisinger, K. M. (2009). On corporate responsibility on human rights. In H. Spitzeck, M. Pirson, W. Amann, S. Khan and E. von Kimakowitz (eds.), *Humanism in Business*. Cambridge: Cambridge University Press, pp. 175–203.

Levine, P. (2008). States of undress: nakedness and the colonial imagination. *Victorian Studies*, **50**(2), 189–219.

Levinthal, D. A. (1991). Organizational adaptation and environmental selection-interrelated processes of change. *Organization Science*, 2(1), 140–145.

Levinthal, D. A., and March, J. G. (1993). The myopia of learning. *Strategic Management Journal*, **14**, 95–112.

Levy, D. and Scully, M. (2007). The institutional entrepreneur as modern prince: the strategic face of power in contested fields. *Organization Studies*, **28**(7), 971–991.

Lewis, B. (2009). *The Great Contemporary Art Bubble*. Documentary film on BBC4, 18 May 2009.

Lin, Z., Haibin, Y. and Demirkan, I. (2007). The performance consequences of ambidexterity in strategic alliance formations: empirical investigation and computational theorizing. *Management Science*, **53**(10), 1645–1658.

Lindgreen, A., Swaen, V. and Johnston, W. J. (2008). Corporate social responsibility: an empirical investigation of U.S. organizations. *Journal of Business Ethics*, **85**, 303–324.

Lindenberg, S. M., and Foss, N. (2011). Managing joint production motivation: the role of goal framing and governance mechanisms. *Academy of Management Review*, **36**(3), 500–525.

Lindgren, G. (1996). Broderskapets logik. *Kvinnovetenskaplig tidskrift*, **1**, 4–14.

Lindgren, M. and Packendorff, J. (2008). Woman, teacher, entrepreneur: on identity construction in female entrepreneurs of Swedish independent schools. In I. Aaltio, P. Kyrö and E. Sundin (eds.), *Women Entrepreneurship and Social Capital: A Dialogue and Construction*. Copenhagen: Copenhagen Business School Press, pp. 193–223.

Lindqvist, K. (2003). Exhibition enterprising. PhD dissertation School of Business, Stockholm University, Stockholm.

Ling, Y., Simsek, Z., Lubatkin, M. H. and Veiga, J. F. (2008). Transformational leadership's role in promoting corporate entrepreneurship: examining the CEO–TMT interface. *Academy of Management Journal*, **51**(3), 557–576.

Linstead, A. and Brewis, J. (2004). Editorial. Beyond boundaries: towards fluidity in theorizing and practice. *Gender, Work & Organization*, **11**(4), 355–362.

Linstead, S. A. (2000). Dangerous fluids and the organization-without-organs. In J. Hassard, R. Holliday and H. Willmot (eds.), *Body and Organization*. London: Sage, pp. 31–52.

Linstead, S. A. (2004). *Organization Theory and Postmodern Thought*. London: Sage Publications.

Linstead, S. A. and Mullarkey, J. (2003). Time, creativity and culture: introducing Bergson. *Culture and Organization*, 9(1), 3–13.

Lippman, S. A. and Rumelt, R. P. (1982). Uncertain imitability: an analysis of interfirm differences in efficiency under competition. *The Bell Journal of Economics*, **13**, 418–438.

Lippman, S. A. and Rumelt, R. P. (2003). A bargaining perspective on resource advantage. *Strategic Management Journal*, **24**, 1069–1086.

Lipsky, M. (1980). *Street-level Bureaucrats. Dilemmas of the Individual in Public Services*. New York: Russel Sage Foundation.

Littlechild, S. C. (1986). Three types of market process. In R. N. Langlois (ed.), *Economics as a Process*. Cambridge: Cambridge University Press.

Locke, R. R. and Schöne, K. E. (2004). *The Entrepreneurial Shift*. Cambridge: Cambridge University Press.

Lohmann, P. and Steyaert, C. (2006). In the mean-time: vitalism, affect and metamorphosis in organizational change. In M. Fuglsang and B. Meier Sørensen (eds.), *Deleuze and the Social*. Edinburgh: Edinburgh University Press, pp. 79–95.

Lomi, A., Larsen, E. R. and Wezel, F. C. (2010). Getting there: exploring the role of expectations and preproduction delays in processes of organizational founding. *Organization Science*, **21**(1), 132–149.

Lounsbury, M. and Glynn, M. A. (2001). Cultural entrepreneurship:

stories, legitimacy, and the acquisition of resources. *Strategic Management Journal*, **22**(6–7), 545–564.

Low, M. B. and MacMillan, I. C. (1988). Entrepreneurship: past research and future challenges. *Journal of Management*, **14**, 139–161.

Lubatkin, M. H., Simsek, Z., Ling, Y. and Veiga, J. F. (2006). Ambidexterity and performance in small-to medium-sized firms: the pivotal role of top management team behavioral integration. *Journal of Management*, **32**(5), 646–672.

Luksha, P. (2008). Niche construction: the process of opportunity creation in the environment. *Strategic Entrepreneurship Journal*, 2(4), 269–283.

Lumpkin, G. T. and Dess, G. G. (1996). Clarifying the entrepreneurial orientation construct and linking it to performance. *Academy of Management Review*, **21**, 135–172.

Luna-Garcia, A. (2008). Just another coffee! Milking the Barcelona model, marketing a global image, and the restoration of local identities. In A. M. Cronin and K. Hetherington (eds.), *Consuming the Entrepreneurial City: Image, Memory, Spectacle.* London, Routledge, pp. 143–160.

Lyle, E. (2008). *On the Lower Frequencies: A Secret History of the City.* Berkeley, CA: Soft Skull Press.

Lynn, M. L. (1998). Patterns of micro-enterprise diversification in transitional Eurasian economies. *International Small Business Journal*, **16**(2), 34–49.

Lyotard, J.-F. (1979). *The Postmodern Condition: A Report on Knowledge*, G. Bennington and B. Massumi (trans.). Manchester, UK: Manchester University Press.

Lyotard, J.-F. (1984). *The Postmodern Condition*. Minneapolis, MN: University of Minnesota Press.

Mace, A., Hall, P. and Gallent, N. (2007). New east Manchester: urban renaissance or urban opportunism? *European Planning Studies*, **15**(1), 51–67.

Machiavelli, N. (1513 [1988]) *The Prince*, Q. Skinner and R. Price (eds.). Cambridge: Cambridge University Press.

Mair, V. (2009). 'danger + opportunity ≠ crisis: how a misunderstanding about Chinese characters has led many astray. Available online: www.pinyin.info/chinese/crisis.html.

Mair, J. and Martí, I. (2006). Social entrepreneurship research: a source of explanation, prediction, and delight. *Journal of World Business*, **41**, 36–44.

Manolova, T. S. and Yan, A. (2002). Institutional constraints and entrepreneurial responses in a transforming economy: the case of Bulgaria. *International Small Business Journal*, **20**(2), 163–184.

Manolova, T. S., Eunni, R. V. and Gyoshev, B. S. (2008). Institutional environments for entrepreneurship: evidence from emerging economies in Eastern Europe. *Entrepreneurship Theory and Practice*, **32**(1), 203–218.

Maravelias, C. (2009). Freedom, opportunism and entrepreneurialism in post-bureaucratic organizations. In D. Hjorth and C. Steyaert (eds.), *The Politics and Aesthetics of Entrepreneurship*. Cheltenham, UK: Edward Elgar Publishing, pp. 13–30.

March, J. G. (1982). The technology of foolishness. In J. G. March and J. P. Olsen (eds.), *Ambiguity and Choice in Organizations*. Bergen, Norway: Universitetsforlaget, pp. 69–81.

March, J. G. (1991). Exploration and exploitation in organizational learning. *Organization Science*, **2**(1), 71–87.

March, J. G. and Simon, H. A. (1993), *Organizations*. Oxford: Blackwell Publishers.

March, J. G. (1996). A scholar's quest. *Stanford Graduate School of Business Magazine*.

March, J. G. (2006). Rationality, foolishness, and adaptive intelligence. *Strategic Management Journal*, **27**(3), 201–214.

Marlow, S. and Patton, D. (2005). All credit to men? Entrepreneurship, finance and gender. *Entrepreneurship Theory and Practice*, **29**(6), 717–735.

Marquis, C., and Huang, Z. H. I. (2010). Acquisitions as exaptation: the legacy of founding institutions in the U.S. commercial banking industry. *Academy of Management Journal*, **53**(6), 1441–1473.

Marschak, J. and Radner, R. (1972). *Economic Theory of Teams*. New Haven, CT: Yale University Press.

Marshall, A. (1961 [1920]). *Principles of Economics*, 9th (variorum) edn. 2 vols. London: Macmillan and Company.

Marshall, T. (ed.) (2004). *Transforming Barcelona*. London, Routledge.

Martin, L. H., Gutman, H. and Hutton, P. H. (1988) (eds.) *Technologies of the Self: A Seminar with Michel Foucault*. Amherst, MA: University of Massachusetts Press.

Martin, R. (2010). Roepke lecture in economic geography: rethinking regional path dependence: beyond lock-in to evolution. *Economic Geography*, **86**(1), 1–27.

Martin, R. L. and Osberg, S. (2007). Social entrepreneurship: the case for definition. *Stanford Social Innovation Review*, Spring, 28–39.

Martinez, M. A. and Aldrich, H. E. (2011). Networking strategies for entrepreneurs: balancing cohesion and diversity. *International Journal of Entrepreneurial Behaviour and Research*, **17**(1), 7–38.

Martinez, M. A., Yang, T. and Aldrich, H. E. (2011). Entrepreneurship as an evolutionary process: research progress and challenges. *Entrepreneurship Research Journal*, **1**(1), DOI: 10.2202/2157-5665.1009.

Marx, K. (1972). *The Eighteenth Brumaire of Louis Bonaparte*. New York: International Publishers.

Marx, K. (1973). *Grundrisse: Foundations of the Critique of Political Economy*, trans. M. Nicolas. London: Penguin.

Marx, K. (1976). *Capital: A Critique of Political Economy*, Vol. 1, B. Fawkes (trans.). London: Penguin.

Marx, K. and F. Engels (1998). *The Communist Manifesto*. London: Verso.

Massumi, B. (1987). Realer than real. The simulacrum according to Deleuze and Guattari. *Copyright*, **1**, 90–97.

Massumi, B. (1987). Notes on the translation and acknowledgements. In G. Deleuze and F. Guattari (eds.), *A Thousand Plateaus*. Minneapolis, MN: University of Minnesota Press, pp. xvii–xix.

Massumi, B. (1996). The autonomy of affect. In P. Patton (ed), *Deleuze: A Critical Reader*. Oxford: Blackwell Publishers.

Massumi, B. (2002a). *Parables for the Virtual. Movement, Affect, Sensation*. Durham, NC: Duke University Press.

Massumi, B. (ed.) (2002b). *A Shock to Thought: Expression After Deleuze and Guattari*, London and New York: Routledge.

Mata, J. and Portugal, P. (2000). Closure and divestiture by foreign entrants: the impact of entry and post-entry strategies. *Strategic Management Journal*, **21**(5), 549.

Matsusaka, J. G. (2001). Corporate diversification, value maximization, and organizational capabilities. *Journal of Business* **74**, 409–431.

Matten, D. and Moon, J. (2008). 'Implicit' and 'explicit' CSR: a conceptual framework for a comparative understanding of corporate social responsibility. *Academy of Management Review*, **33**(2), 404–424.

Mayer, M. (2010). *Civic City Cahier 1: Social Movements in the (Post-) Neoliberal City*. London: Bedford Press.

Mayo, E. (1919). *Democracy and Freedom: An Essay in Social Logic*. Melbourne, Australia: A. H. Massina & Co.

Mayo, E. (1923). The irrational factor in human behaviour: the 'night mind' in industry. *Annals of the American Academy of Political and Social Science*, **110**, 117–130.

Mayo, E. (1924). The basis of industrial psychology. *Bulletin of the Taylor Society*, **9**, 249–259.

Mayo, E. (1933). *The Human Problems of an Industrial Civilization*. New York: MacMillan.

Mayo, E. (1945). *The Social Problems of an Industrial Civilization*. Boston, MA: Harvard University Graduate School of Business Administration.

McAfee, A. P. (2006). Enterprise 2.0: the dawn of emergent collaboration. *MIT Sloan Management Review*, **47**(3), 21–28.

McCloskey, D. (1985). *The Rhetoric of Economics*. Madison, WI: The University of Wisconsin Press.

McCraw, T. (2006). Schumpeter's business cycles as business history. *Business History Review*, **80**, 231–261.

McGrath, R. G. and MacMillan, I. C. (1995). Discovery-driven planning. *Harvard Business Review*, **73**(4), 4–12.

McGrath, R. G. and MacMillan, I. C. (2000). *The Entrepreneurial Mindset*. Boston, MA: Harvard Business Press.

McGrath, R. G., Keil, T., and Tukiainen, T. (2006), Extracting value from corporate venturing. *MIT Sloan Management Review*, **48**(1), 50–56.

McGrath, R. G., Venkataraman, S. and MacMillan, I. C. (1994). The advantage chain: antecedents to rents from internal corporate ventures. *Journal of Business Venturing*, **9**, 351–369.

McKelvey, B. (2002). Model-centered organization science epistemology. In J. A. C. Baum (ed.), *Companion to Organizations*. Thousand Oaks, CA: Sage Publications, pp. 752–780.

McKenzie, J. (2001). *Perform or Else: From Discipline to Performance*. London: Taylor and Francis Ltd.

McNeill, D. (2001). Barcelona as imagined community: Pasqual Maragall's spaces of engagement. *Transactions of the Institute of British Geographers*, **26**(3), 340–352.

McNulty, P. (1984). On the nature and theory of economic organization: the role of the firm reconsidered. *History of Political Economy*, **16**, 223–253.

Ménard, C. (2010). Hybrid organisations. In N. J. Foss and P. G. Klein (ed.), *The Elgar Companion to Transaction Cost Economics*. Cheltenham, UK: Edward Elgar Publishing, pp. 176–184.

Merrifield, D. B. (1993). Intrapreneurial corporate renewal. *Journal of Business Venturing*, **8**, 383–389.

Merton, R. (1995). Financial innovation and the management and regulation of financial institutions. *Journal of Banking and Finance*, **19**, 461–481.

Metcalfe, J. S. (2009). Entrepreneurship: an evolutionary perspective. In M. Casson, A. Basu and N. S. Wadeson (eds.), *The Oxford Handbook of Entrepreneurship*. Oxford: Oxford University Press, pp. 59–89

Meydani, A. (2010). Political entrepreneurs and public administration reform: the case of the local authorities' unification reform in Israel. *International Journal of Public Administration*, **33**(4), 200–206.

Meyer, G. D. and Heppard, K. A. (2000). *Entrepreneurship as Strategy*. Thousand Oaks, CA: Sage Publications.

Meyer, J. W. (2008). Reflections on institutional theories of organizations. In R. Greenwood, C. Oliver, R. Suddaby and K. Sahlin (eds.), *The Sage Handbook of Organizational Institutionalism.* Los Angeles, CA: Sage, pp. 790–811.

Meyer, J. W. and Rowan, B. (1977). Institutionalized organizations: formal structure as myth and ceremony. *The American Journal of Sociology*, **83**(2), 340–363.

Meyers, M. K. and Vorsanger, S. (2008). Street-level bureaucrats and the implementation of public policy. In B. G. Peters and J. Pierre (eds.), *The Handbook of Public Administration.* Thousand Oaks, CA: SAGE.

Michaelides, P. and Milios, J. (2009). Joseph Schumpeter and the German historical school. *Cambridge Journal of Economics*, **33**(3), 495–516.

Miles, M. and Huberman, A. M. (1994). *Qualitative Data Analysis.* Thousand Oaks, CA: Sage.

Miles, R. E. and Snow, C. C. (1978). *Organizational Strategy, Structure and Process.* New York: McGraw-Hill.

Miles, M. P. and Covin, J. G. (2002). Exploring the practice of corporate venturing: some common forms and their organizational implications. *Entrepreneurship Theory and Practice*, **26**(3), 21–40.

Miles, S. and Paddison, R. (2005). The rise and rise of culture-led regeneration. *Urban Studies*, **42**(8), 833–839.

Milgrom, P. R. and Roberts, J. (1992). *Economics of Organization and Management*, Englewood Cliffs, NJ: Prentice-Hall.

Miller, D. (1982). Evolution and revolution: a quantum view of structural change in organizations. *Journal of Management Studies*, **19**(2), 131–151.

Miller, D. and Friesen, P. H. (1980). Momentum and revolution in organizational adaptation. *Academy of Management Journal*, **23**, 591–614.

Miller, D. and Friesen, P. H. (1982). Innovation in conservative and entrepreneurial firms: two models of strategic momentum. *Strategic Management Journal*, 3, 1–25.

Miller, P. and Rose, N. (1990). Governing economic life. *Economy and Society*, 19(1), 1–31.

Miller, P. and Rose, N. (2008). *Governing the Present: Administering Economic, Social and Personal Life.* London: Polity Press.

Milliken, F. J. (1987). Three types of perceived uncertainty about the environment: state, effect, and response uncertainty. *The Academy of Management Review*, **12**(1), 133–143.

Mills, P. K. and Lefton, M. (1988). Managing service industries: organizational practices in a postindustrial economy. *Administrative Science Quarterly*, **33**(2), 329–331.

Miner, A. S., Bassoff, P. and Moorman, C. (2001). Organizational improvisation and learning: a field study. *Administrative Science Quarterly*, **46**(2), 304–337.

Minniti, M. (2008). The role of government policy on entrepreneurial activity: productive, unproductive, or destructive? *Entrepreneurship Theory and Practice*, **32**(5), 779.

Minsky, H. (2008). *Stabilizing an Unstable Economy*. New York: McGraw Hill.

Minstrom, M. (1997). Policy entrepreneurs and the diffusion of innovations. *American Journal of Political Science*, **41**(3), 738–770.

Minstrom, M. and Norman, P. (2009). Policy entrepreneurship and policy change. *The Policy Studies Journal*, **37**(4), 649–667.

Mintzberg, H. (1973). *The Nature of Managerial Work*. New York: Harper Row.

Mintzberg, H. (1983). *Structure in Fives. Designing Effective Organizations*. Englewood Cliffs, NJ: Prentice-Hall.

Mir, A.(ed.) (2003) *Corporate Mentality: An Archive Documenting the Emergence of Recent Practices within a Cultural Sphere Occupied by Both Business and Art*. New York: Lukas and Sternberg.

Mises, L. von (1949). *Human Action: A Treatise on Economics*. New Haven, CT: Yale University Press.

Mises, L. von (1978). Planning for freedom. Reprinted in R. Swedberg (ed.), *Entrepreneurship. The Social Science View*. Oxford: Oxford University Press. Oxford, p. 19.

Mitchell, M. and Mulherin, J. H. (1996). The impact of industry shocks on takeover and restructuring activity. *Journal of Financial Economics*, 41, 193–229.

Mitchell, R. K., Smith, B., Seawright K. W. and Morse, E. A. (2000). Cross-cultural cognitions and the venture creation decision. *Academy of Management Journal*, **43**(5), 974–993.

Mokyr, J. (2000). Evolutionary phenomena in technological change. In J. Ziman (ed.), *Technological Innovation as an Evolutionary Process*. Cambridge: Cambridge University Press, pp. 52–65.

Monks, R. A. and Minow, N. (1989). The high cost of ethical retrogression. *Directors and Boards*, **13**(2), 9–10.

Monsen, E., and Boss, R. W. (2009). The impact of strategic entrepreneurship inside the organization: examining job stress and employee retention. *Entrepreneurship: Theory and Practice*, **33**(1), 71–104.

Moor, L. and Littler, J. (2008). Fourth worlds and Neo-Fordism. *Cultural Studies*, **22**(5), 700–723.

Morgan, G. (2006). *Images of Organization*. London: Sage.

Morris, H. H. and Jones, F. F. (1999). Entrepreneurship in established organizations: the case of the public sector. *Entrepreneurship Theory and Practice*, Fall, 71–91.

Morris, M. H., Schindehutte, M. Walton, J. and Allen, J. (2002). The ethical context of entrepreneurship: proposing and testing a developmental framework. *Journal of Business Ethics*, **40**(4), 331–361.

Morris, M. H., Kuratko, D. F. and Covin, J. G. (2011). *Corporate Entrepreneurship and Innovation*, 3rd edn. Mason, OH: South-Western/Thomson Publishers.

Morse, C. W. (1986). The delusion of intrapreneurship. *Long Range Planning*, **19**(6), 92–95.

Mort, G. S., Weerawardena, J. and Carnegie, K. (2003). Social entrepreneurship: towards conceptualization. *International Journal of Nonprofit and Voluntary Sector Marketing*, **8**(1), 76–88.

Mosakowski, E. (1997). Strategy making under causal ambiguity: conceptual issues and empirical evidence. *Organization Science*, **8**, 414–442.

Mosakowski, E. (1998). Entrepreneurial resources, organizational choices, and competitive outcomes. *Organization Science*, **9**, 625–643.

Moschandreas, M. (1997). The role of opportunism in transaction cost economics. *Journal of Economic Issues*, **31**(1), 39.

Mouzelis, N. (2000). The subjectivist–objectivist divide: against transcendence. *Sociology*, **34**(4), 741–762.

Mujtaba, B. G. and Sims, R. L. (2006). Socializing retail employees in ethical values: the effectiveness of the formal versus informal methods. *Journal of Business Ethics*, **21**(2), 261.

Mulholland, K. (1996). Entrepreneurialism, masculinities and the self-made man. In D. L. Collinson and J. Hearn (Eds.), *Men as Managers, Managers as Men.* London: Sage, pp. 123–149.

Mulholland, K. (1998). 'Survivors' versus 'Movers and Shakers': The Reconstitution of management and Careers in the Privatised Utilities. In P. Thompson and C. Warhurst (eds.), *Workplaces of the Future*. Basingstoke, UK: MacMillan Press, pp. 184–203.

Murnighan, K. J. and Conlon, D. E. (1991). The dynamics of intense work groups: a study of British string quartets. *Administrative Science Quarterly*, **36**, 165–186.

Murtola, A.-M. (2008). Redeeming entrepreneurship. *Scandinavian Journal of Management*, **24**(3), 127–129.

Mustard, D. B. (2001). Racial, ethnic, and gender disparities in sentencing: evidence from the US Federal Courts. *The Journal of Law and Economics*, **44**, 285–313.

Myers, S.C, 1977. Determinants of corporate borrowing. Journal of Financial Economics, 5: 147–175.

Nagel, J. (1994). Constructing ethnicity: creating and recreating ethnic identity and culture. *Social Problems*, **41**(1), 152–176.

Nayak, A. (2008). On the way to theory: a processual approach. *Organization Studies*, **29**(2), 173–190.

Najak. A. and Chia, R. (2011). Thinking becoming and emergence: philosophy and organization studies. *Research in the Sociology of Organizations*, **32**, 281–309.

Narayanan, V. K., Yang, Y. and Zahra, S. A. (2009). Corporate venturing and value creation: a review and proposed framework. *Research Policy*, **38**(1), 58–76.

Nathan, M. (2000). The paradoxical nature of crisis. *Review of Business*, Fall, 12–16.

Nationalencyclopedin. Trettonde Bandet. (1994) *Miljonprogrammet*. Bra Böcker: Höganäs.

Nee, V. (1998). Norms and networks in economic and organizational performance. *American Economic Review*, **88**(2), 85–89.

Needham, R. (ed.). (1973). *Right and Left*. Chicago, IL: The University of Chicago Press.

Negri, A. (2003). *Time for Revolution*, Matteo Mandarini (trans.). New York: Continuum.

Nelson, R. R. (2005). *Technology, Institutions and Economic Growth*. Cambridge, MA: Harvard University Press.

Newman, J. (2005). *Bending Bureaucracy: Leadership and Multi-Level Governance*. in P. du Gay (ed.), *The Values of Bureaucracy*. Oxford: Oxford University Press, Chapter 8, pp. 191–210

New York Times Online (2009). Bonus for bad performance. Available at: http://roomfordebate.blogs.nytimes.com/2009/01/29/bonuses-for-bad-performance/.

Nguyen, T. V., Bryant, S. E., Rose, J., Tseng, C.H. and Kapasuwan, S. (2009). Cultural values, market institutions, and entrepreneurship potential: a comparative study of the United States, Taiwan, and Vietnam. *Journal of Developmental Entrepreneurship*, **14**(1), 21–37.

Nicholls, A., Cho, A. H. (2006). Social entrepreneurship: the structuration of a field. In A. Nicholls (ed.), *Social Entrepreneurship. New Models of Sustainable Social Change*. Oxford: Oxford University Press, pp. 99–143.

Nietzsche, F. W. (1967). *On the Genealogy of Morals*, W. Kaufmanna and R. J. Hollingdale (trans.). New York: Vintage.

Nietzsche, F. W. (1969). *Thus Spoke Zarathustra*, R. J. Hollingdale (trans.). Harmondsworth, UK: Penguin Books.

NION (2010). Not in our name! Jamming the gentrification machine: a manifesto. *City*, **14**(3), 323–325.

Nisbett, R. E. and Wilson, T. D. (1977). Telling more than we can know: verbal reports on mental processes. *Psychological Review*, **84**(3), 231–259.

Nooteboom, B. (2002). Trust. Forms, Foundations, Functions, Failures and Figures. Cheltenham, UK: Edward Elgar Publishing.

Nordström, L. (1938). *Lort-Sverige*. Stockholm: Sveriges Radios Förlag.

North, D. C. (1981). *Structure and Change in Economic History*. New York and London: Norton.

North, D. C. (1990). *Institutions, Institutional Change, and Economic Performance*. Cambridge: Cambridge University Press.

North, D. C. (1994). Economic performance through time. *American Economic Review*, **84**(3), 359–368.

North, D. C. (2005). *Understanding the Process of Economic Change*. Princeton, NJ: Princeton University Press.

Nussbaum, B. (2004). The power of design. *BusinessWeek*, May 17, 2004.

Nyssens, M. (ed.). (2006). *Social Enterprise: At the Crossroads of Markets, Public Policies and Civil Society*. London: Routledge.

Nählinder, J. (2010). Where are all the female innovators? Nurses as innovators in a public sector innovation project. *Journal of Technology Management and Innovation*, **5**(1), 13–29.

O'Brien, D. P. (1984). The evolution of the theory of the firm. In F. H. Stephen (ed.), *Firms, Organization and Labour: Approaches to the Economics of Work Organization*. London: MacMillan, pp. 25–62.

O'Connor, E. S. (1999a). Minding the workers: the meaning of 'human' and 'human relations' in Elton Mayo. *Organization*, **6**(2), 223–246.

O'Connor, E. S. (1999b). The politics of management thought: a case study of the Harvard Business School and the Human Relations School. *The Academy of Management Review*, **24**(1), 117–131.

O'Connor, E. S. (2007). Reader beware: doing business with a store(y) of knowledge. *Journal of Business Venturing*, **22**, 637–648.

O'Donnell, S. (2010). *Organizing the Creative Crowd for Innovation*. Boston: Cutter Consortium.

O'Donnell, S. and Austin, R. D. (2008). Extreme collaboration; group work at the frontier of human experience. Presented at the Fourth Annual Art of Management Conference, BANFF.

Ogbor, J. (2000). Mythicizing and reification in entrepreneurial discourse: ideology-critique of entrepreneurial studies. *Journal of Management Studies*, **37**(5), 605–635.

Ohmae, K. (1999). *The Borderless World*, revised edn. New York: Harper.

Oliver, C. (1991). Strategic responses to institutional processes. *Academy of Management Review*, **16**(1), 145–179.

Orlikowski, W. (2002). Knowing in practice: enacting a collective capability in distributed organizing. *Organization Science*, **13**(3), 249–273.

Osborn, D. and Gaebler, T. (1993). *Reinventing Government: How the Entrepreneurial Spirit is Transforming the Public Sector*. New York: Plume.

Oswald, P. (2000). *Berlin: Stadt ohne Form*. Munich: Prestel Verlag.

Oudenampsen, M. (2007). AmsterdamTM, the city as a business. In BAVO (ed.) *Urban Politics Now: Re-Imagining Democracy in the Neoliberal City*. Rotterdam: NAi Publishers, pp. 110–127

Pacheco-de-Almeida, G. (2010). Erosion, time compression, and self-displacement of leaders in hypercompetitive environments. *Strategic Management Journal*, **31**(13), 1498–1526. Special Issue: The Age of Temporary Advantage?

Pacheco, D. F., York, J. G., Dean T. J. and Sarasvathy, S. D. (2010). The coevolution of institutional entrepreneurship: a tale of two theories. *Journal of Management*, **36**(4), 974–1010.

Painter, J. (1998). Entrepreneurs are made, not born: learning and urban regimes in the production of entrepreneurial cities. In T. Hall and P. Hubbard (eds.), *The Entrepreneurial City: Geographies of Politics, Regime and Representation*. West Sussex, UK: John Wiley and Sons, pp. 259–275.

Parr, A. (2005). The art of privacy: assaulting the phallocentric organization of capital. *Women*, **16**(3), 321–339.

Pasquinelli, M. (2008). *Animal Spirits: A Bestiary of the Commons*. Rotterdam: NAi Publishers.

Patton, P. (ed.) (1996). *Deleuze: A Critical Reader*. Oxford: Blackwell.

Patton, P. (2000). *Deleuze and the Political*. London: Routledge.

Pearce, J. A., Kramer, T. R. and Robbins, D. K. (1997). Effects of managers' entrepreneurial behavior on subordinates. *Journal of Business Venturing*, **12**, 147–160.

Peck, J. (2005). Struggling with the creative class. *International Journal of Urban and Regional Research*, **29**(4), 740–770.

Peirce, C. S. (1901). The proper treatment of hypotheses. MS 692, Houghton Library, Harvard University.

Peirce, C. S. (1992–1998). *The Essential Peirce*, 2 vols. Bloomington, IN: Indiana University Press.

Peng, M. W. (2001). How entrepreneurs create wealth in transition economies. *Academy of Management Executive*, **15**(1), 95–108.

Peng, M. W. (2003). Institutional transitions and strategic choices. *Academy of Management Review*, **28**(2), 275–286.

Peng, M. W. and Heath, P. S. (1996). The growth of the firm in planned economies in transition: institutions, organizations, and strategic choice. *Academy of Management Journal*, **21**(2), 492–528.

Penrose, E. T. (1959). *The Theory of the Growth of the Firm*. Oxford: Oxford University Press.

Peteraf, M. A. (1993). The cornerstones of competitive advantage: a resource-based view. *Strategic Management Journal*, **14**, 179–191.

Peteraf, M. A. and Barney, J. B. (2003). Unraveling the resource-based tangle. *Managerial and Decision Economics*, **24**, 309–323.

Peters, B. G. and Pierre, J. (eds.) (2008). *The Handbook of Public Administration*. Thousand Oaks, CA: SAGE.

Peters, T. and Waterman, R. (1982). *In Search of Excellence*. New York: Warner Books/Harper & Row.

Peterson, R. and Berger D. (1972). Entrepreneurship in organizations. *Administrative Science Quarterly*, **16**, 97–106.

Pettigrew, A. and Longshore, J. M. (1990). The management of strategic change. *Academy of Management Review*, **15**(1), 168–171.

Pfeffer, J. and Salancik, G. R. (1978). *The External Control of Organizations: A Resource Dependence Perspective*. New York: Harper and Row.

Phelan, J., Link, B G., Moore, R. E. and Stueve, A. (1997). The stigma of homelessness: the impact of the label 'homeless' on attitudes toward poor persons. *Social Psychology Quarterly*, **60**(4), 323–337.

Phillips, D. J. and Zuckerman, E. W. (2001). Middle-status conformity: theoretical restatement and empirical demonstration in two markets. *The American Journal of Sociology*, **107**(2), 379–429.

Pierson, F. C. (1959). *The Education of American Businessmen: A Study of University-College Programs in Business Administration*. New York: McGraw-Hill.

Pierson, P. (2001). Investigating the welfare state futures: an introduction. In S. Leibfried (ed.), *Welfare State Futures*. Cambridge: Cambridge University Press.

Pinchott, G. (1985). Intrapreneurship. New York: Harper and Row.

Pine, B. J. and Gilmore, J. H. (1999). The experience economy: work is theatre and every business a stage. Boston, MA: Harvard Business School Press.

Pipan, T. and Porsander, L. (2000). Imitating uniqueness: how big cities organize big events. *Organization Studies*, **21**, 1–27.

Piras (2005). La routinizzazione della passione et la passione nelle practice organizzative. Etnografie di una fondazione d'arte contemporanea. Doctoral dissertation, Trento.

Pitti, S. J. (2004). *The Devil in Silicon Valley: Northern California, Race and Mexican Americans*. Princeton, NJ: Princeton University Press.

Poklinghorne, D. E. (1988). *Narrative Knowing and the Human Sciences.* Albany, NY: State University of New York Press.

Polishchuk, L. (2001). *Small Businesses in Russia: Institutional Environment.* College Park, MD: University of Maryland.

Pólos, L., Hannan, M. T. and Carroll, G. R. (2002). *Foundations of a Theory of Social Forms. Industrial and Corporate Change.* Oxford: Oxford University Press.

Porter, M. E. (1980). *Competitive Strategy.* New York: Free Press.

Porter, M. E. (1985). *Competitive Advantage.* New York: Free Press.

Powell, T. C., Lovallo, D. and Caringal, C. (2006). Causal ambiguity, management perception, and firm performance. *Academy of Management Review,* **31**(1), 175–196.

Powell, W. and DiMaggio, P. (eds.) (1991). *The New Institutionalism in Organizational Analysis.* Chicago, IL: University of Chicago Press.

Prahalad, C. K. (2005). *The Fortune at the Bottom of the Pyramid.* Upper Saddle River, NJ: Wharton Publishing.

Pratt, A. C. (2008). Creative cities: the cultural industries and the creative class. *Geografiska Annaler: Series B, Human Geography,* **90**(2), 107–117.

Priem, R. L. and Butler, J. E. (2001). Tautology in the resource-based view and the implications of externally determined resource value: further comments. *Academy of Management Review,* **26**(1), 57–66.

Puffer, S. M., McCarthy, D. J. and Boisot, M. (2010). Entrepreneurship in Russia and China: the impact of formal institutional voids. *Entrepreneurship Theory and Practice,* **34**(3), 441–467.

Putnam, L. I. and Mumby, D. K. (1993). Organizations, emotion and the myth of rationality. In S. Fineman (ed.), *Emotions in Organizations.* London: Sage, pp. 36–57.

Putterman, L. (ed.) (1996). *The Economic Nature of the Firm: A Reader.* Cambridge: Cambridge University Press.

Quilley, S. (2000). Manchester first: from municipal socialism to the entrepreneurial city. *International Journal of Urban and Regional Research,* **24**(3), 601–615.

Quinn, R. E., Cameron, K. S., Berlinger, L. R. and Sitkin, S. B. (1990). Paradox and transformation: toward a theory of change in organization and management. *Administrative Science Quarterly,* **35**(4), 740–744.

Radaev, V. (2004). How trust is established in economic relationships when institutions and individuals are not trustworthy: the case of Russia. In J. Kornai, B. Rothstein and S. Rose-Ackerman (eds.), *Creating Social trust in Post-socialist Transition.* New York: Palgrave Macmillan, pp. 91–110.

Raisch, S. and Birkinshaw, J. (2008). Organizational ambidexterity:

antecedents, outcomes and moderators. *Journal of Management*, **34**(3), 375–409.

Raiser, M. (1997). Informal institutions, social capital and economic transition: reflections on a neglected dimension. Working paper // European Bank for Reconstruction and Development, Retrieved from http://www.ebrd.co.uk/pubs/econo/wp0025.htm.

Raiser, M. (1999). *Trust in Transition*, Vol. 39. London: European Bank for Reconstruction and Development.

Rajan, R., Servaes, H. and Zingales, L. (2000). The cost of diversity: the diversification discount and inefficient investment. *The Journal of Finance* **55**(1), 35–80.

Rajchman, J. (2000). *The Deleuze Connections*. Cambridge, MA: The MIT Press.

Ramirez, R. (1991). *The Beauty of Social Organization*. Munich, Germany: Accedo.

Rancière, J. (2004a). *The Philosopher and his Poor*, A. Parker (trans.). Durham, NC: Duke University Press.

Ranciére, J. (2004b). *The Politics of Aesthetics*. London: Continuum.

Rauch, A., Wiklund, J., Lumpkin, G. T. and Frese, M. (2009). Entrepreneurial orientation and business performance: an assessment of past research and suggestions for the future. *Entrepreneurship Theory and Practice*, **33**, 761–787.

Read, S., Dew, N., Sarasvathy, S. D., Song, M. and Wiltbank, R. (2009). Marketing under uncertainty: the logic of an effectual approach. *Journal of Marketing*, **73**(3), 1–18.

Read, S., Sarasvathy, S. D., Dew, N., Wiltbank, R. and Ohlsson, A. V. (2011). *Effectual Entrepreneurship*. New York: Routledge.

Rehn, A. and Taalas, S. (2004a). Of crime and assumptions in entrepreneurship. In D. Hjorth and C. Steyaert (eds), *Narrative and Discursive Approaches in Entrepreneurship: A Second Movements in Entrepreneurship Book*. Cheltenham, UK: Edward Elgar Publishing, pp. 144–159.

Rehn, A. and Taalas, S. (2004b). 'Znakomstva i svyazi' (acquaintances and connections): Blat, the Soviet Union, and mundane entrepreneurship. *Entrepreneurship and Regional Development*, **16** (May), 235–250.

Rehnberg, H. and Ruin, H. (1997). *Herakleitos – Fragment*. Lund, Sweden: Propexus.

Reich, R. B. (1987). Entrepreneurship reconsidered: the team as hero. *Harvard Business Review*, May–June, 77–83.

Reimers, C. W. (1983). Labor market discrimination against hispanic and black men. *The Review of Economics and Statistics*, **65**(4), 570–579.

Reinert, H. and Reinert, E. (2006). Creative destruction in economics:

Nietzsche, Sombart, Schumpeter. In J. Backhaus and W. Drechsler (eds.), *Friedrich Nietzsche 1844–2000: Economy and Society*. Boston, MA: Kluwer.

Reynolds, P. (1987), New firms: societal contribution versus survival potential. *Journal of Business Venturing*, **2**, 231–246.

Reynolds, P. D. (2007). New firm creation in the United States: a PSED I overview. *Foundations and Trends in Entrepreneurship*, **3**(1), 1–107.

Reynolds, P. D. and Curtin, R. (2007). Panel study of entrepreneurial dynamics II: data overview. SSRN eLibrary.

Reynolds, P. D., Bosma, N., Autio, E., Hunt, S., De Bono, N., Servais, I., Lopez-Garcia, P. and Chin, N. (2005). Global entrepreneurship monitor: data collection design and implementation 1998–2003. *Small Business Economics*, **24**(3), 205–231.

Rindova, V., Barry, D. and Ketchen, D. J., Jr. (2009). Entrepreneuring as emancipation. *Academy of Management Review*, **34**(3), 477–491.

Rizzolatti, G. and Craighero, L. (2004). The mirror-neuron system. *Annual Review of Neuroscience*, **27**, 169–192.

Robertson, D. (2009). Don't be gloomy; the time is just right to be like me. *The Times*, 9 March. Available online at: http://business.timesonline. co.uk/tol/business/movers_and_shakers/article5870683.ece.

Rodger, J. J. (2000). *From a Welfare State to a Welfare Society: The Changing Context of Social Policy in a Postmodern Era*. New York: St. Martin's Press.

Rodrigues, S. and Child, J. (2003). Co-evolution in an institutionalized environment. *Journal of Management Studies*, **40**(8), 2137–2162.

Ronneberger, K., Lanz, S. and Jahn, W. (1999). *Die Stadt als Beute*. Bonn, Germany: Dietz.

Rorty, R. (1980). *Philosophy and the Mirror of Nature*. Princeton, NJ: Princeton University Press.

Rorty, R. (1989). *Contingency, Irony and Solidarity*. Cambridge: Cambridge University Press.

Rose, N. (1998). *Inventing Our Selves. Psychology, Power and Personhood*. Cambridge: Cambridge University Press.

Rosenheck, R., Morrissey, J., Lam, J., Calloway, M., Stolar, M. S., Johnsen, M., Randolph, F., Blasinsky, M. and Goldman, H. (2001). Service delivery and community: social capital, service systems integration, and outcomes among homeless persons with severe mental illness. *Health Services Research*, **36**(4), 691–710.

Rossbach, S. (1996). Gnosis, science, and mysticism: a history of self-referential theory designs. *Social Science Information*, **35**(2), 233–255.

Rothbard, M. N. (1985 [1997]). Professor Hébert on Entrepreneurship. In M. N. Rothbard (ed.), *The Logic of Action Two: Applications and*

Criticism from the Austrian School. Aldershott, UK: Edward Elgar Publishing, pp. 245–253.

Ruef, M., Aldrich, H. E. and Carter, N. M. (2003). The structure of founding teams: homophily, strong ties, and isolation among US entrepreneurs. *American Sociological Review*, **68**(2), 195–222.

Rumbaut, R. G. (1994). The crucible within: ethnic identity, self-esteem, and segmented assimilation among children of immigrants. *International Migration Review*, **20**(4), 748–794.

Rumelt, R. P. (1987). Theory, strategy, and entrepreneurship. In D. Teece (ed.), *The Competitive Challenge*. Cambridge, MA: Ballinger, pp. 11–32.

Russell, R. D. (1999). Developing a process model of intrapreneurial systems: a cognitive mapping approach. *Entrepreneurship: Theory and Practice*, **23**(3), 65–84.

Rycroft, S. (2005). The nature of Op Art: Bridget Riley and the art of non-representation. *Environment and Planning D: Society and Space*, **23**(3), 351–371.

Saario, S. and Raitakari, S. (2010). Contractual audit and mental health rehabilitation: a study of formulating effectiveness in a Finnish supported housing unit. *International Journal of Social Welfare*, **19**, 321–329.

Sadler, R. J. (2000). Corporate entrepreneurship in the public sector: the dance of the chameleon. *Australian Journal of Public Administration*, **59**(2), 25–43.

Sahlin-Andersson, K. (2006). National, international and transnational construction of new public management. In T. Christensen and P. Laegreid (eds.), *New Public Management. The Transformation of Ideas and Practice*. Aldershot, UK: Ashgate, Chapter 3, pp. 43–72.

Salaman, G. (2005). Bureaucracy and beyond: managers and leaders in the 'post-bureaucratic' organization. In P. du Gay (ed.), *The Values of Bureaucracy*. Oxford: Oxford University Press, pp. 141–164.

Salerno, J. T. (1993). Mises and Hayek dehomogenized. *Review of Austrian Economics*, **6**(2), 113–146.

Salimath, M. S. and Cullen, J. B. (2010). Formal and informal institutional effects on entrepreneurship: a synthesis of nation-level research. *International Journal of Organizational Analysis*, **18**(3), 358–385.

Samuelson, P. (1970). *Economics*, 8th edn. New York: McGraw-Hill.

Santos, F. M. and Eisenhardt, K. M. (2009). Constructing markets and shaping boundaries: entrepreneurial power in nascent fields. *Academy of Management Journal*, **52**(4), 643–671.

Sarasvathy, S. D. (2001). Causation and effectuation: toward a theoretical shift from economic inevitability to entrepreneurial contingency. *Academy of Management Review*, **26**(2), 243–263.

Sarasvathy, S. D. (2003). Entrepreneurship as a science of the artificial. *Journal of Economic Psychology*, **24**(2), 203–220.

Sarasvathy, S. D. (2008). Effectuation: elements of entrepreneurial expertise. *New Horizons in Entrepreneurship*, xxii.

Sarasvathy, S. D. and Dew, N. (2005a). Entrepreneurial logics for a technology of foolishness. *Scandinavian Journal of Management*, **21**(4), 385–406.

Sarasvathy, S. D. and Dew, N. (2005b). New market creation through transformation. *Journal of Evolutionary Economics*, **15**(5), 533–565.

Sarasvathy, S. D. and Venkataraman, S. (2011). Entrepreneurship as method: open questions for an entrepreneurial future. *Entrepreneurship Theory and Practice*, **35**(1), 113.

Sarasvathy, S. D., Menon, A. R. and Kuechle, G. (2012). Failing firms and successful entrepreneurs: Serial entrepreneurship as a temporal portfolio. *Small Business Economics*, forthcoming.

Sathe, V. (1984). Implications of corporate culture: a manager's guide to action. *Organizational Dynamics*, **12**(2), 5–23.

Sathe, V. (1989). Fostering entrepreneurship in large diversified firm. *Organizational Dynamics*, **18**(1), 20–32.

Savage, M. (1995). Walter Benjamin's urban thought: a critical analysis. *Environment and Planning D: Society and Space*, **13**, 201–216.

Sawyer, K. (2007). *Group Genius: The Creative Power of Collaboration.* Cambridge, MA: Basic Books.

Saxenian, A. (2002). Silicon Valley's new immigrant high-growth entrepreneurs. *Economic Development Quarterly*, **16**(1), 20–31.

Say, J-B. (1800 [2010]). *A Treatise on Political Economy.* Memphis, TN: General Books LLC.

Scharfstein, D. S., and Stein, J. C. (2000). The dark side of internal capital markets: divisional rent-seeking and inefficient investment. *Journal of Finance*, **55**, 2537–2564.

Scharder, H. (2010). Meanwhile Wham, comic and its communication value in organizational context. Doctoral thesis University of Essex, Essex.

Schein, E. H. (1992). Organizational Culture and Leadership. San Francisco, CA: Jossey-Bass.

Scherdin, M. (2007). The invisible foot: survival of new art ideas on the Swedish art arena. Doctoral thesis in business administration no. 127, Uppsala.

Scherdin, M. and Zander, I. (eds.) (2001). *Art Entrepreneurship.* Cheltenham, UK: Edward Elgar Publishing.

Schindehutte, M. and Morris, M. H. (2009). Advancing strategic entrepreneurship research: the role of complexity science in shifting the paradigm. *Entrepreneurship Theory and Practice*, 33(1), 241–276.

Schiuma, G. (2001). *The Value of Art for Business.* Cambridge, UK: Cambridge University Press.

Schneiberg, M. (2005). Combining new institutionalisms: explaining institutional change in American property insurance. *Sociological Forum*, 21(1), 93–137.

Schollhammer, H. (1982). Internal corporate entrepreneurship. In C. Kent, D. Sexton and K. Vesper (eds.), *Encyclopedia of Entrepreneurship*. Englewood Cliffs, NJ: Prentice-Hall.

Schoonhoven, C. B. and Romanelli, E. (2001). *The Entrepreneurship Dynamic: Origins of Entrepreneurship and the Evolution of Industries.* Stanford, CA: Stanford Business Books.

Schultz, M., Hatch, M. J. and Larsen, M. H. (2000). *The Expressive Organization.* Oxford: Oxford University Press.

Schumpeter, J. (1911). *The Theory of Economic Development: An Inquiry into Profits, Capital, Credit, Interest, and the Business Cycle*, R. Opie, trans. Cambridge, MA: Harvard University Press.

Schumpeter, J. A. (1928 [1991]). The instability of capitalism. In R. V. Clemence (ed.), *Essays on Entrepreneurs, Innovations, business Cycles, and the Evolution of Capitalism. Joseph A. Schumpeter.* New Brunswick and London: Transaction Publishers, pp. 361–386.

Schumpeter, J. A. (1934 [1983]). *The Theory of Economic Development*, trans. Redvers Opine. (Reprint 1971 edn.). New Brunswick: Transaction Publishers.

Schumpeter, J. A. (1939). *Business Cycles: A Theoretical, Historical and Statistical Analysis of the Capitalist Process*, 2 vols. New York: McGraw-Hill Company.

Schumpeter, J. (1942 [1962]). *Capitalism. Socialism and Democracy*. New York: Harper and Row.

Schumpeter, J. A. (1947 [1991]). The creative response in economic history. In R. V. Clemence (ed.) *Joseph A. Schumpeter: Essays.* London: Transaction Publishers, pp. 221–231.

Schumpeter, J. A. (1949). *Economic Theory and Entrepreneurial History: Change and the Entrepreneur; Postulates and Patterns for Entrepreneurial History.* Cambridge, MA: Harvard University Press (Swedish Translation, p. 255)

Schumpeter, J. A. (1950). *Capitalism, Socialism and Democracy*, 3rd edn. New York: Harper and Row.

Schumpeter, J. A. (1951). Economic theory and entrepreneurial history. In R. Clemency (ed.), *Essays of J. A. Schumpeter*. Cambridge, MA: Addison-Wesley.

Schwartz, H. and Davis, S. (1981), "Matching corporate culture and business strategy," Organizational Dynamics, Vol. 10, No. 1, pp. 30–49.

Scott, W. R. (1995). *Institutions and Organizations.* Thousand Oaks, CA: Sage.

Scott, W.R. (1999). The new institutionalism in sociology. *Contemporary Sociology: A Journal of Reviews*, **28**(4), 425–426.

Scott, W. R. (2008). Approaching adulthood: the maturing of institutional theory. *Theory and Society*, **37**(5), 427–442.

Scott, W. R. (2008a). Approaching adulthood: the maturing of institutional theory. *Theory and Society*, **37**(5), 427–442.

Scott, W. R. (2008b). *Institutions and Organizations: Ideas and Interests.* London: Sage.

Sea Jin, C. and Singh, H. (1999). The impact of modes of entry and resource fit on modes of exit by multibusiness firms. *Strategic Management Journal*, **20**(11), 1019–1035.

Secchi, L. (2010). Entrepreneruship and participation in public management reforms at the local level. *Local Government Studies,* **36**(4), 511–527.

Seelos, C., Mair, J., Battilana, J. and Dacin, M. T. (2011). The embeddedness of social entrepreneurship: understanding variation across local communities. Research in the sociology of organizations, **33**, 333–363.

Sehested, K. (2002). How new public management reforms challenge the roles of professionals. *International Journal of Public Administration*, **25**(12), 1513–1537.

Semetsky, I. (2004). The complexity of individuation. *International Journal of Applied Psychoanalytic Studies*, 1(4), 324–346.

Sent, E.-M. (2000). Herbert A. Simon as a cyborg scientist. *Perspectives on Science*, **8**(4), 380–406.

Seo, M.-G. and Creed, W. E. D. (2002). Institutional contradictions, praxis, and institutional change: a dialectical perspective. *The Academy of Management Review*, 27(2), 222–247.

Serres, M. (1995a). *Angels, A Modern Myth.* Paris: Flammarion.

Serres, M. (1995b). *Genesis.* Ann Arbor, MI: The University of Michigan Press.

Shah, S. K. and Tripsas, M. (2007). The accidental entrepreneur: the emergent and collective process of user entrepreneurship. *Strategic Entrepreneurship Journal*, **1**(1–2), 123–140.

Shane, S. (2000). Prior knowledge and the discovery of entrepreneurial opportunities. *Organization Science*, 11(4), 448–469.

Shane, S. (2004). *A General Theory of Entrepreneurship: The Individual–Opportunity Nexus.* Cheltenham, UK: Edward Elgar Publishing.

Shane, S. and Venkataraman, S. (2000). The promise of entrepreneurship as a field of research. *Academy of Management Review*, **25**(1), 217–226.

Sharir, M. and Lerner, M. (2006). Gauging the success of social ventures initiated by individual social entrepreneurs. *Journal of World Business*, **41**(1), 6–20.

Sharma, P. and Chrisman, J. J. (1999). Toward a reconciliation of the definitional issues in the field of corporate entrepreneurship. *Entrepreneurship Theory and Practice*, **23**(3), 11–28.

Shepherd, D. A.. and Kuratko, D. F. (2009). The death of an innovative project: how grief recovery enhances learning. *Business Horizons*, **52**(5), 451–458.

Shepherd, D. A., Covin, J. G. and Kuratko, D. F. (2009), Project failure from corporate entrepreneurship: managing the grief process. *Journal of Business Venturing*, **24**(6), 588–600.

Shockley, G. E., Frank, P. M. and Stough, R. R. (2002). Toward a theory of public sector entrepreneurship. Paper presented at the NCIIA 7th Annual Meeting: Big Ideas in a Small World.

Shin, H.-H. and Stulz, R. M. (1998). Are internal capital markets efficient? *The Quarterly Journal of Economics*, **113**(2), 531–552.

Short, J. C., Moss, T. W. and Lumpkin, G. T. (2009). Research in social entrepreneurship: past contributions and future opportunities. *Strategic Entrepreneurship Journal*, **3**(2), 161–194.

Short, J., Ketchen Jr., D., Shook, C. and Ireland, D. (2010). The concept of 'opportunity' in entrepreneurship research: past accomplishments and future challenges. *Journal of Management*, **36**(1), 40–65.

Shotter, J. (1995). *The Cultural Politics of Everyday Life*. Milton Keynes, UK: Open University Press.

Simmel, G. (2002). The metropolis and mental life. In G. Bridge and S. Watson (eds.), *The Blackwell City Reader*. Oxford: Blackwell, pp. 11–20.

Simon, H. A. (1945) *Administrative Behaviour*. New York: The Free Press.

Simon, H. A. (1991). Organizations and markets. *Journal of Economic Perspectives*, **5**(2), 25–44.

Simon, H. A. (1993a). Altruism and economics. *American Economic Review*, **83**(2), 156–161.

Simon, H. A. (1993b). A mechanism for social selection and successful altruism. *Science*, **250**(4988), 1665–1668.

Simon, H. A. (1996). The Sciences of the Artificial, 3rd edn. Cambridge and London: MIT Press.

Simsek, Z. (2009). Organizational ambidexterity: towards a multilevel understanding. *Journal of Management Studies*, **46**(4), 597–624.

Sine, W. D. and Lee, B. (2009). Tilting at windmills? The

environmental movement and the emergence of the U.S. wind energy sector. *Administrative Science Quarterly*, 54(1), 123–155.

Sine, W. D., Haveman, H. A. and Tolbert, P. S. (2005). Risky business? Entrepreneurship in the new independent-power sector. *Administrative Science Quarterly*, **50**(2), 200–232.

Small, M. (2009). *Unanticipated Gains: Origins of Network Inequality in Everyday Life.* Oxford New York: University Press.

Smallbone, D. and Welter, F. (2001). The distinctiveness of entrepreneurship in transition economies. *Small Business Economics*, **16**(4), 249–262.

Smallbone, D. and Welter, F. (2009a). Entrepreneurial behaviour in transition environments. In M.-À. Galindo, J. Guzman and D. Ribeiro (eds.), *Entrepreneurship and Business in Regional Economics.* New York: Springer, pp. 211–228.

Smallbone, D. and Welter, F. (2009b). *Entrepreneurship and Small Business Development in Post-socialist Economies.* London: Routledge.

Smallbone, D. and Welter, F. (2010a). Entrepreneurship and government policy in former Soviet republics: Belarus and Estonia compared. *Environment and Planning C. Government and Policy*, **28**, 195–210.

Smallbone, D. and Welter, F. (2010b). Entrepreneurship and the role of government in post-socialist economies: some institutional challenges. *Historical Social Research-Historische Sozialforschung*, **35**(2), 320–333.

Smallbone, D. and Welter, F. (2012). Entrepreneurship and institutional change in transition economies: the Commonwealth of Independent States, Central and Eastern Europe and China compared. *Entrepreneurship and Regional Development*, **24**(3–4), 215–233.

Smallbone, D., Welter, F., Voytovich, A., and Egorov, I. (2010). Government and entrepreneurship in transition economies: the case of small firms in business services in Ukraine. *Service Industries Journal*, **30**(5), 655–670.

Smircich, L. and Stubbart, C. (1985). Strategic management in an enacted world. *The Academy of Management Review*, 10(4), 724–736.

Smith, A. (1976 [1776]). *An Inquiry into the Nature and Causes of the Wealth of Nations*, 2 vols. Oxford: Oxford University Press.

Smith, D. W. (2007a). The Conditions of the New. *Deleuze Studies*, **1**(1), 1–21.

Smith, D. W. (2007b). Deleuze and the question of desire: towards an immanent theory of ethics. *Parrhesia*, **2**, 66–78.

Smith, N. (1996). *The New Urban Frontier: Gentrification and the Revanchist City.* London: Routledge.

Smith, R. (2003). Constructing the heroic/fabled entrepreneur: a biographical analysis. Paper presented at the Babson Kauffman Entrepreneurship Research Conference 2003, Boston.

Smith, R. and Anderson, A. R. (2004). The devil is in the e-tail: forms and structures in the entrepreneurial narratives. In D. Hjorth and C. Steyaert (eds.), *Narrative and Discursive Approaches in Entrepreneurship.* Cheltenham, UK: Edward Elgar Publishing, pp. 125–143.

Smith, W. K. and Tushman, M. L. (2005). Managing strategic contradictions: a top management model for managing innovation streams. *Organization Science,* **16**(5), 522–536.

Snow, D. A. and Anderson, L. (1987). Identity work among the homeless: the verbal construction and avowal of personal identities. *American Journal of Sociology,* **92**(6), 1336–1371.

Soja, E. W. (1996). *Thirdspace: Journeys to Los Angeles and Other Real-and-Imagined Places.* Oxford: Blackwell.

Soja, E. W. (2003). Writing the city spatially. *City,* **7**(3), 269–281.

Sombart, W. (1913). *Krieg und Kapitalismus.* Leipzig, Germany: Duncker and Humblot.

Sombart, W. (1927). *Der moderne Kapitalismus.* Leipzig, Germany: Duncker and Humblot.

Spear, R. (2006). Social entrepreneurship: A different model? *International Journal of Social Economics,* **33**(5), 399–410.

Spencer, J. W. and Gómez, C. (2004). The relationship among national institutional structures, economic factors, and domestic entrepreneurial activity: a multicountry study. *Journal of Business Research,* **57**(10), 1098–1107.

Spiegel Online (2000). Hamburg als Modell: US-Ökonom Florida will Künstler an öffentlichem Eigentum beteiligen. Available at: http://www.spiegel.de/kultur/gesellschaft/0,1518,659833,00.html (accessed 22 February, 2011).

Spindler, F. (2009). *Spinoza: multitud, affect, kraft [multitute, affect, force],* Munkedal, Sweden: Glönta Produktion.

Spinosa, C., Flores, F. and Dreyfus, H. L. (1997). *Disclosing New Worlds: Entrepreneurship, Democratic Action and the Cultivation of Solidarity.* Cambridge, MA: MIT Press.

Starbuck, W. (1976). Organizations and their environments. In M. Dunnette (ed.), *Handbook of Industrial and Organizational Psychology.* Chicago, IL: Rand McNally, pp. 1069–123.

Stark, D. (1996). Recombinant property in East European capitalism. *American Journal of Sociology,* **101**(4), 993–1027.

Stark, D. and Bruszt, L. (2001). One way or multiple paths: for a comparative sociology of East European capitalism. *American Journal of Sociology,* **106**(4), 1129–1137.

Statistics Sweden (2010). Women and men in Sweden. Available at:

http://www.scb.se/statistik/_publikationer/LE0201_2010A01_BR_X10B
R1001ENG.pdf.

Statistics Sweden (1969). Historisk statistic för Sverige. Del 1. Befolkning.
Available at:http://www.scb.se/Grupp/Hitta_statistik/Historisk_statist
ik/_Dokument/Historisk%20statistik%20för%20Sverige_%20Del%201.
pdf.

Steier, L. and Greenwood, R. (1995). Venture capitalist relationships in
the deal structuring and post-investment stages of new firm creation.
Journal of Management Studies, **32**(3), 337–357.

Stepanova, E. (2011). The role of information communication technologies in the 'Arab Spring': implications beyond the region. *PONARS
Eurasia Policy*, Memo No. 159, –6.

Stevenson, H. (1984). A perspective on entrepreneurship. In H. Stevenson,
M. Roberts and H. Grousebeck (eds.), *New Business Venture and the
Entrepreneur*. Boston, MA: Harvard Business School, pp. 3–14

Stewart, A. (1989). *Team Entrepreneurship*. Newbury Park, CA: Sage.

Steyaert, C. (2006). Cities as heterotopias and third spaces: the example
of ImagiNation, the Swiss Expo02. In S. R. Clegg and M. Kornberger
(eds.), *Space, Organizations and Management Theory*. Copenhagen,
Denmark: Copenhagen Business School Press, pp. 248–265.

Steyaert, C. (2007). 'Entrepreneuring' as a conceptual attractor? A
review of process theories in 20 years of entrepreneurship studies.
Entrepreneurship and Regional Development, **19**(6), 453–477.

Steyaert, C. (2009). Enacting urban ethnographies of artistic interventions
in the entrepreneurial city. In T. Beyes, S.-T. Krempl and A. Deuflhard
(eds.), *Parcitypate: Art and Urban Space*. Zurich: Niggli, pp. 383–465.

Steyaert, C. and Hjorth, D. (1997). In the museum of last things: performing organizing. Performance at the SCOS conference, July, Warsaw,
Poland.

Steyaert, C. and Hjorth, D. (2006). *Entrepreneurship as Social Change*.
Cheltenham, UK: Edward Elgar Publishing.

Steyaert, C. (2011). Entrepreneurship as in(ter)vention: reconsidering the conceptual politics of method in entrepreneurship studies.
Entrepreneurship and Regional Development, **23**(1/2), 77–88.

Steyaert, C. and Beyes, T. (2009). Narrating urban entrepreneurship:
a matter of imagineering? In B. Lange et al. (eds.), *Governance der
Creative Industries*. Bielefeld, Germany: Verlag, pp. 207–221.

Steyaert, C. and Dey, P. (2007). Post-Weickian organization theory: notes
on the aesthetics and politics of theorizing. In Th. S. Eberle, S. Hoidn
and K. Sikavica (eds.), *Fokus Organisation, Sozialwissenschaftliche
Perspektiven und Analysen*. Konstanz, Germany: UVK
Verlagsgesellschaft mbH, pp. 41–62.

Steyaert, C. and Hjorth, D. (2002). Thou art a scholar, speak to it: on spaces of speech. A script. *Human Relations*, **55**(7), 767–797.

Steyaert, C. and Hjorth, D. (eds.) (2003). *New Movements in Entrepreneurship*. Cheltenham, UK: Edward Elgar Publishing.

Steyaert, C. and Hjorth, D. (eds.) (2006). Entrepreneurship as Social Change. Cheltenham, UK: Edward Elgar Publishing.

Steyaert, C. and Katz, J. (2004). Reclaiming the space of entrepreneurship: geographical, discursive and social dimensions. *Entrepreneurship and Regional Development*, **16**(3), 179–196.

Steyaert, C., Marti, L. and Michels, C. (2012). Multiplicity and reflexivity in organizational research: towards a performative approach to the visual. *Qualitative Research in Organizations and Management*, **7**(1), 34–53.

Stopford, J. M. and Baden-Fuller, C. W. F. (1994). Creating corporate entrepreneurship. *Strategic Management Journal*, **15**(7), 521–536.

Storper, M. and Walker, R. (1989). *The Capitalist Imperative: Territory, Technology, and Industrial Growth*. New York: Blackwell.

Strati, A. (1999). *Aesthetics and Organization.* London: Sage.

Strauss, A. and Corbin, J. (1998). *Basics of Qualitative Research: Techniques and Procedures for Developing Grounded Theory*, 2nd edn. Thousand Oaks, CA: Sage.

Styhre, A. (2002). How process philosophy can contribute to strategic management. *Systems Research and Behavioral Science*, **19**(6), 577–587.

Styhre, A. (2005). Deleuze, desire and motivation theory. In J. Brewis, S. Linstead, A. O'Shea and D. M. Boje (eds.), *The Passion of Organizing*. Oslo, Norway: Abstrakt.

Suhomlinova, O. (2006). Toward a model of organizational co-evolution in transition economies. *Journal of Management Studies*, **43**(7), 1537–1558.

Sullivan, G. (2005). *Art Practice as Research*. Thousand Oaks, CA: Sage.

Sundaramurthy, C. (2008). Sustaining trust within family businesses. *Family Business Review*, **21**(1), 89–102.

Sundin, E. (2004). *Den offentliga sektorns entreprenörer*. Stockholm: Kommentus.

Sundin, E. (2010). Street-level bureaucrats in the era of New Public Management. Example: the production of meals for elderly and children in a Swedish municipality. Paper presented at the conference Dilemmas for Human Services 2010, Luleå.

Sundin, E. and Holmquist, C. (1991). The growth of women entrepreneurship: push or pull factors? In L. G. Davies and A. A. Gibbs (eds.), *Recent Research in Entrepreneurship*. Aldershot, UK: Avebury, pp. 106–114.

Sundin, E. and Tillmar, M (2008). A nurse and a civil servant changing institutions. entrepreneurial processes in different public sector organizations. *Scandinavian Journal of Management*, 24, 113–124.

Sundquist, J. (1993). Ethnicity as a risk factor for consultations in primary health care and out-patient care. *Scandinavian Journal of Primary Health Care*, **11**(3), 169–173.

Sutton, R. (2001). The weird rules of creativity. *Harvard Business Review*, **79**, 94–103.

Swedberg, R. (2000). *Entrepreneurship. The Social Science View*. Oxford: Oxford University Press.

Swedberg, R. (2009a). Rebuilding Schumpeter's theory of entrepreneurship. In Y. Shionoya and T. Nishizawa (eds.), *Marshall and Schumpeter on Evolution: Economic Sociology of Capitalist Development*. Cheltenham, UK: Edward Elgar Publishing, pp. 188–203.

Swedberg, R. (2009b). Tocqueville as a pioneer in organization theory. In P. Adler (ed.), *The Oxford Handbook of Sociology and Organizational Studies: Classical Foundations*. New York: Oxford University Press, pp. 39–61

Sydow, J., Schreyogg, G. and Koch, J. (2009). Organizational path dependence: opening the black box. *Academy of Management Review*, **34**(4), 689–709.

Sykes, H. B. and Block, Z. (1989). Corporate venturing obstacles: sources and solutions. *Journal of Business Venturing*, **4**, 159–167.

Sørensen, B. M. (2006). Identity sniping: innovation, imagination and the body. *Creativity and Innovation Management*, **15**(2), 135–142.

Sørensen, B. M. (2008). 'Behold, I am making all things new': the entrepreneur as savior in the age of creativity. *Scandinavian Journal of Management*, **24**(3), 85–93.

Sørensen, B. M. (2009a). The entrepreneurial utopia: Miss Black Rose and the holy communion. In D. Hjorth and C. Steyaert (eds.), *The Politics and Aesthetics of Entrepreneurship*. Cheltenham, UK: Edward Elgar Publishing, pp. 202–220.

Sørensen, B. M. (2009b). How to surf: technologies at work in the societies of control. In M. Poster and D. Savat (eds.), *Deleuze and New Technology*. Edinburgh: Edinburgh University Press, pp. 63–81.

Sørensen, B. M. (2010). St Paul's conversion: The aesthetic organization of labour. *Organization Studies,* **31**(3), 307–326.

Sørensen, J. B. (2007) Bureaucracy and entrepreneurship. Workplace effects on entrepreneurial entry. *Administrative Science Quarterly*, **52**, 387–412.

Sørensen, J. B. and M. A. Fassiotto (2011). Organizations as fonts of entrepreneurship. *Organization Science*, **22**(5), 1322–1331.

Tan, J. (2002). Culture, nation, and entrepreneurial strategic orientations: implications for an emerging economy. *Entrepreneurship: Theory and Practice*, **26**(4), 95.

Tan, J. and Tan, D. (2004). Entry, growth, and exit strategies of Chinese technology start-ups: choosing between short-term gain or long-term potential. *Journal of Management Inquiry*, **13**(1), 49–54.

Taylor, C. (2004). *Modern Social Imaginaries.* Durham, NC: Duke University Press.

Taylor, F. W. (1911). *Principles of Scientific Management.* New York: Harper & Brothers.

Teece, D. J. (1986). Profiting from technological innovation: implications for integration, collaboration, licensing and public policy. *Research Policy*, **15**, 285–305.

Teece, D. J. (2007a). Explicating dynamic capabilities: the nature and microfoundations of (sustainable) enterprise performance. *Strategic Management Journal*, **28**(13), 1319–1350.

Teece, D. J. (2007b). The role of managers, entrepreneurs and the literati in enterprise performance and economic growth. *International Journal of Technological Learning, Innovation and Development*, **1**(1), 43–64.

Teece, D. J., Pisano, G. and Shuen, A. (1997). Dynamic capabilities and strategic management. *Strategic Management Journal*, **18**(7), 509–533.

Tett, G. (2009). *Fool's Gold: How Unrestrained Greed Corrupted a Dream, Shattered Global Markets and Unleashed a Catastrophe.* London: Little Brown.

Thake, S. and Zadek, S. (1997). *Practical People, Noble Causes: How to Support Community-based Social Entrepreneurs.* London: New Economic Foundation.

Thatcher, M. (1987). Interview. *Woman's Own*, 31 October.

Thommen, J.-P. (2002). *Management and Organization.* Zurich, Germany: Versus Verlag.

Thompson, J., Alvy, G. and Lees, A. (2000). Social entrepreneurship: a new look at the people and the potential. *Management Decision*, **38**(5), 328–338.

Thompson, M. (2011). Ontological shift or ontological drift? Reality claims, epistemological frameworks, and theory generation in organization studies. *Academy of Management Review*, **36**(4), 754–773.

Thompson, P. and McHugh, D. (2002). *Work Organizations.* London: Palgrave.

Thrift, N. (1999). Steps to an ecology of place. In D. Massey, J. Allenand and P. Sarre (eds.) *Human Geography Today*. Polity Press: Cambridge, pp. 295–323.

Thrift, N. (2000). Afterwords. *Environment and Planning D: Society and Space*, **18**(2), 213–255.

Thrift, N. (2005). But malice aforethought: cities and the natural history of hatred. *Transactions of the Institute of British Geographers*, **30**(2), 133–150.

Thrift, N. (2007). *Non-Representational Theory: Space, Politics, Affect*. London: Routledge.

Thrift, N. (2009). Cityescapes. In T. Beyes, S.-T. Krempl and A. Deuflhard (eds.), *Parcitypate: Art and Urban Space*. Zurich, Germany: Niggli.

Thrift, N. and Dewsbury, J.-D. (2000). Dead geographies: and how to make them live. *Environment and Planning D: Society and Space*, **18**(4), 411–432.

Thyrstrup, M. (1993). *Företagsledares arbete* [*The Work of Leaders in Business*]. Stockholm: Handelshögskolan.

Tidd, J. and Taurins, S. (1999). Learn or leverage? Strategic diversification and organizational learning through corporate ventures. *Creativity and Innovation Management*, **8**(2), 122–129.

Tocqueville, A. de (1945 [1835–40]). *Democracy in America*, 2 vols., H. Reeve (trans.). New York: Vintage Books.

Todd, P. M., and Gigerenzer, G. (2003). Bounding rationality to the world. *Journal of Economic Psychology*, **24**(2), 143–165.

Toffler, A. (1980). *The Third Wave*. New York: Bentham Books.

Toffler, B. L. and Reingold, J. (2004). *Final Accounting: Ambition, Greed and the Fall of Arthur Andersen*. New York: Doubleday.

Thornqvist C. (2010). *Artistic Direction: The Ways of Robert Wilson*. Borås, Sweden: Textile Research Centre, The Swedish School of Textiles.

Townley, B. (1993). Foucault, power/knowledge, and its relevance for human resource management. *Academy of Management Review*, **18**(3), 518–545.

Townley, B. (1999). Nietzsche, competencies and übermensch: reflections on human and inhuman resource management. *Organization*, 6(2), 285–305.

Townley, B. (2002). The role of competing rationalities in organizational change. *Academy of Management Journal,* **45**(1), 163–179.

Tracey, P., Phillips, N. and Haugh, H. (2005). Beyond philanthropy: community enterprise as a basis for corporate citizenship. *Journal of Business Ethics*, **58**(4), 327–344.

Tréhin-Marçot, P. (2004). *One Day with Peter*. Poland: Zentropa Production.

Trivedi, C. and Stokols, D. (2011). Social enterprises and commercial enterprises: fundamental differences and defining features. *The Journal of Entrepreneurship*, **20**(1), 1–32.

Tsoukas, H. and Chia, R. (2002). On organizational becoming: rethinking organization change. *Organization Science*, **13**(5), 567–582.

Tsoukas, H. and Chia, R. (2011). Introduction: why philosophy matters to organization theory. *Research in the Sociology of Organizations*, **32**, 1–21.

Tullberg, M, (2002). Orden som förnyar. *Nordiske Organisasjons Studier*, **3**(4), 2002

Tushman, M. L. and O'Reilly III, C. A. (1996). Ambidextrous organizations: managing evolutionary and revolutionary change. *California Management Review*, **38**(4), 8–30.

Uhlaner, L. and Thurik, R. (2007). Postmaterialism influencing total entrepreneurial activity across nations. *Journal of Evolutionary Economics*, **17**(2), 161–185.

Ullrich, W. (2000). *Mit dem Rücken zur Kunst*. Berlin: Verlag Klaus Wagenbach.

Vaihinger, H. (1924 [1952]). *The Philosophy of 'as if'*, C.K. Ogden (trans.). London: Routledge.

van der Haar, D.and Hosking, D. M. (2004). Evaluating appreciative inquiry: a relational constructionist perspective. *Human Relations*, **57**, 1017–1036.

Van de Ven, A. H. and Poole, M. S. (2005). Alternative approaches for studying organizational change. *Organization Studies*, **26**(9), 1377–1404.

Van Parijs, P. (1995). *Real Freedom for All, What (If Anything) Can Justify Capitalism?* Oxford: Clarendon Press.

Varadarajan, P. R. (1985). A two-factor classification of competitive strategy variables. *Strategic Management Journal*, **6**(4), 357–375.

Venkataraman, S. (1997). The distinctive domain of entrepreneurship research. In J. A. Katz (ed.), *Advances in Entrepreneurship, Firm Emergence and Growth*. Bradford, UK: JAI Press Inc., pp. 119–138.

Venkataraman, S., Sarasvathy, S. D., Dew, N. and Forster, W. (2012). Reflections on the 2010 AMR decade award: Whither the promise? Moving forward with entrepreneurship as a science of the artificial. *Academy of Management Review*, **37**(1), 21–33.

Verduyn, J. K. (2010). Rhythmanalyzing the emergence of 'the republic of tea'. In W. B. Gartner (ed.), *ENTER (Entrepreneurial Narrative Theory Ethnomethodology and Reflexivity)*. Clemson, SC: Clemson University Digital Press.

Verheul, I., Van Stel, A. and Thurik, R. (2006). Explaining female and male entrepreneurship at the country level. *Entrepreneurship and Regional Development*, **18**(2), 151–183.

Verwoert, J. (2007). Frei sind wir schon. Was wir jetzt brauchen, ist ein besseres Leben. In H. Belzer and D. Birnbaum (eds.), *Kunst Lehren/*

Teaching Art-Städelschule. Frankfurt/Main, Germany: Verlag der Buchandlung Walther König.

Vestrum, I. K. and Borch, O. J. (2006). Community entrepreneurship within the cultural sector. Paper presented at the Nordic Conference on Small Business Research, Stockholm, 11–13 May.

Virilio, P. (2005). *City of Panic.* Oxford: Berg.

Virno, P. (2002). *A Grammar of Multitude.* New York: Semiotext(e).

Vitell, S. J., Nwachukwu, S. L. and Barnes, J. H. (1993). The effects of culture on ethical decision-making: an application of Hofstede's typology. *Journal of Business Ethics*, **12**, 753–760.

Viteritti, A. (2004). Gianni Vattimo, Umberto Eco and Franco Rella. In S. Linstead (ed.), *Organization Theory and Postmodern Thought.* London: Sage, pp. 149–172.

Volberda, H. W., and Lewin, A. Y. (2003). Co-evolutionary dynamics within and between firms: from evolution to co- evolution. *Journal of Management Studies,* **40**, 2111–2136.

Volkov, V. (2002). *Violent Entrepreneurs: The Use of Force in the Making of Russian Capitalism.* Ithaca, NY: Cornell University Press.

von Mises, L.(1996). *Human Action: A Treatise on Economics.* San Francisco, CA: Fox and Wilkes.

Vozikis, G. S., Bruton, G. D., Prasad, D. and Merikas, A. A. (1999). Linking corporate entrepreneurship to financial theory through additional value creation. *Entrepreneurship Theory and Practice*, **24**(2), 33–43.

Wageman, R. (1995). Interdependence and group effectiveness. *Administrative Science Quarterly*, **40**(1), 145–180.

Waldinger, R., Aldrich, H. E. and Ward, R. (1990). Opportunities, group characteristics and strategies. In R. Waldinger, H. E. Aldrich and R. Ward (eds.), *Ethnic Entrepreneurs: Immigrant Businesses in Industrial Societies.* Newbury Park, CA: Sage Publications, pp. 13–48.

Wall Street Journal (2008). Rahm Emanuel on the opportunities of crisis. Available at www.youtube.com/watch?v=_mzcbXi1Tkk.

Walter, A., Auer, M. and Ritter, T. (2006). The impact of network capabilities and entrepreneurial orientation on university spin-off performance. *Journal of Business Venturing*, **21**(4), 541–567.

Ward, K. (2003). The limits to contemporary urban development: 'doing' entrepreneurial urbanism in Birmingham, Leeds and Manchester. *City*, **7**(2), 199–211.

Waris, H. (1961). *Suomalaisen yhteiskunnan sosiaalipolitiikka.* Porvoo, Finland: WSOY.

Wastell, D., White, S., Broadhurst, K., Peckover, S. and Pithouse, A. (2010). Children's services in the iron cage of performance management: street-level bureaucracy and the spectre of Svejkism. *International Journal of Social Welfare*, **19**, 321–329.

Weatherston, M. (2002). *Heidegger's Interpretation of Kant: Categories, Imagination, and Temporality*. London: Palgrave Macmillan.

Weaver, G. R., Trevino, L. K. and Cochran, P. L. (1999). Corporate ethics programs as control systems: influences on executive commitment and environmental factors. *Academy of Management Journal*, **42**, 539–552.

Weber, M. (1947). *The Theory of Social and Economic Organization*, A. M. Henderson and T. Parsons (eds.). London: The Free Press.

Weber, M. (1904–05 [1958]). *The Protestant Ethic and the Spirit of Capitalism*. New York: Charles Scribner's Sons.

Weber, M. (1978). *Economy and Society: An Outline of Interpretive Sociology*, E. Fischoff et al. (eds.), 2 vols. Berkeley, CA: University of California Press.

Weber, M. (1980). Die Stadt. In *Wirtschaft und Gesellschaft: Grundriß der verstehenden Soziologie*. Tübingen, Germany: Mohr Siebeck, pp. 727–814.

Weber, M. (1985). *The Protestant Ethic and the Spirit of Capitalism*. London: Unwin Paperbacks.

Weedon, C. (1999). *Feminism, Theory and the Politics of Difference*. Oxford: Blackwell.

Weerawardena, J. and Mort, G. S. (2005). Investigating social entrepreneurship: a multidimensional model. *Journal of World Business*, **41**(1), 21–35.

Weick, K. E. (1979). *The Social Psychology of Organizing*, 2nd edn. Reading, MA: Addison-Wesley.

Weick, K. E. (1989). Theory construction as disciplined imagination. *Academy of Management Review*, **14**(4), 516–531.

Weick, K. E. (1992). Agenda setting in organizational behavior: a theory-focused approach. *Journal of Management Inquiry*, **1**(3), 171–182.

Weick, K. E. (1993). Organizational redesign as improvisation. In G. Huber and W. Glick (eds.), *Mastering Organizational Change*. New York: Oxford University Press, pp. 346–379.

Weick, K. E. (1995). What theory is not, theorizing is. *Administrative Science Quarterly*, **40**(3), 385–390.

Weick, K. E. (1996). Drop your tools: an allegory for organizational studies. *Administrative Science Quarterly*, **41**, 301–313

Weick, K. E. (1999a). Theory construction as disciplined reflexivity: trade-offs in the 90s. *Academy of Management Review*, **24**(4), 797–806.

Weick, K. E. (1999b). That's moving. Theories that matter. *Journal of Management Inquiry*, **8**(2), 134–142.

Weick, K. E. (2001). *Making Sense of the Organization*. Oxford: Blackwell.

Weick, K. E. 2004. Mundane poetics: Searching for wisdom in organization studies. Organization Studies, 25(4), 653–668.

Weick, K. E. and Westley, F. (1996). Organizational learning: affirming an oxymoron. In S. R. Clegg, C. Hardy and W. Nord (eds.), *Handbook of Organization Studies*. London: Sage Publications, pp. 440–458.

Weik, E. (2011). In deep waters: process theory between Scylla and Charybdis. *Organization*, 11(5), 655–672.

Weinberg, T. (2009). *The New Community Rules: Marketing on the Social Web.* Sebastopol, CA: O'Reilly Media Inc.

Weinick, R. M., Zuvekas, S. H. and Cohen, J. W. (2000). Racial and ethnic differences in access to and use of health care services, 1977 to 1996. *Medical Care Research and Review*, 57(4), 36–54.

Weiskopf, R. and Loacker, B. (2006). A snake's coils are even more intricate than a mole's burrow: individualization and subjectification in post-disciplinary regimes of work. *Management Revue*, 17, 395–419.

Weiskopf, R. and Steyaert, C. (2009). Metamorphoses in entrepreneurship studies: towards an affirmative politics of entrepreneuring. In D. Hjorth and C. Steyaert (eds.), *The Politics and Aesthetics of Entrepreneurship*. Cheltenham, UK: Edward Elgar Publishing, pp. 183–201.

Weldon, T. D. (1953). *The Vocabulary of Politics: An Enquiry into the Use and Abuse of Language in the Making of Political Theories.* Baltimore, MD: Penguin Books.

Welter, F. (2011), 'Contextualising Entrepreneurship – Challenges and Ways Forward', Entrepreneurship Theory and Practice, 35 (1), 165–184.

Welter, F. and Smallbone, D. (2003). Entrepreneurship and enterprise strategies in transition economies: an institutional perspective. In D. Kirby and A. Watson (eds.), *Small Firms and Economic Development in Developed and Transition Economies: A Reader*. Aldershot, UK: Ashgate, pp. 95–114.

Welter, F. and Smallbone, D. (2008). Women's entrepreneurship from an institutional perspective: the case of Uzbekistan. *International Entrepreneurship and Management Journal*, 4, 505–520.

Welter, F. and Smallbone, D. (2009). The emergence of entrepreneurial potential in transition environments: a challenge for entrepreneurship theory or a developmental perspective? In D. Smallbone, H. Landström and D. Jones-Evans (eds.), *Entrepreneurship and Growth in Local, Regional and National Economies: Frontiers in European Entrepreneurship Research.* Cheltenham, UK: Edward Elgar Publishing, pp. 339–353.

Welter, F. and Smallbone, D. (2010). The embeddedness of women's entrepreneurship in a transition context. In C. G. Brush, A. De Bruin,

E. Gatewood and C. Henry (eds.), *Women Entrepreneurs and the Global Environment for Growth: A Research Perspective*, Cheltenham, UK: Edward Elgar Publishing, pp. 96–117.

Welter, F. and Smallbone, D. (2011). Institutional perspectives on entrepreneurial behaviour in challenging environments. *Journal of Small Business Management*, **49**(1), 107–125.

Wennekers, A. R. M. and Thurik, A. R. (1999). Linking entrepreneurship and economic growth. *Small Business Economics*, **13**(1), 27–55.

Wensley, R. (1996). Isabella Beeton: management as 'everything in its place'. *Business Strategy Review*, **7**(1), 37–46.

Wernerfelt, B. (1984). A resource-based view of the firm. *Strategic Management Journal*, **5**(2), 171–180.

West, G. Page III. (2007). Collective cognition: when entrepreneurial teams, not individuals, make decisions. *Entrepreneurship Theory and Practice*, **31**(1), 77–102.

West, C., and Zimmerman, D. (1987). Doing gender. *Gender and Society*, **1**(2), 125–151.

White, M. and Hunt, A. (2000). Citizenship: care of the self, character and personality. *Citizenship Studies*, **4**(2), 93–116.

Whitener, E. M., Brodt, S. E. Korsgaard, M. A. and Werner, J. M. (1998). Managers as initiators of trust: an exchange relationship framework for understanding managerial trustworthy behavior. *Academy of Management Review*, **23**(3), 513–530.

WHO (2010). World health statistics. Available at: http://www.who.int/whosis/whostat/EN_WHS10_Full.pdf.

Whybrow, N. (2010) Introduction. In N. Whybrow (ed.) *Performance and the Contemporary City: An Interdisciplinary Reader*. Basingstoke, UK: Palgrave Macmillan.

Whyte, G., Saks, A. M. and Hook, S. (1997). When success breeds failure: the role of self-efficacy in escalating commitment to a losing course of action. *Journal of Organizational Behavior*, **18**(5), 415–432.

Wickham, P. (2008). *Strategic Entrepreneurship*. Upper Saddle River, NJ: Prentice Hall.

Wicks, A. C., Berman, S. L., and Jones, T. M. (1999). The structure of optimal trust: moral and strategic implications. *Academy of Management Review*, **24**(1), 99–116.

Wiggins, R. R. and Rueffli, T. W. (2002). Sustained competitive advantage: temporal dynamics and the incidence and persistence of superior economic performance. *Organization Science*, **13**, 82–105.

Wigren, C. (2003). The spirit of Gnosjö: the grand narrative and beyond. Doctoral dissertation. Jönköping: Jönköping International Business School.

Wiklund, J. and Shepherd, D. (2003). Aspiring for and achieving growth: the moderating role of resources and opportunities. *Journal of Management Studies*, **40**(8), 1911–1941.

Williams, G. (2003). *The Enterprising City Centre: Manchester's Development Challenge*. London: Routledge.

Williamson, O. E. (1973). Markets and hierarchies: some elementary considerations. *The American Economic Review*, **63**(2), 316–325.

Williamson, O. E. (1975). *Markets and Hierarchies, Analysis and Antitrust Implications: A Study in the Economics of Internal Organization*. New York: Free Press.

Williamson, O. E. (1985). *The Economic Insitutions of Capitalism*. New York: Free Press.

Williamson, O. E. (1991). Comparative economic organization: the analysis of discrete structural alternatives. *Administrative Science Quarterly*, **36**(2), 269–296.

Williamson, O. E. (1993a). Calculativeness, trust, and economic organization. *Journal of Law and Economics*, **36**(1), 453–486.

Williamson, O. E. (1993b). Opportunism and its critics. *Managerial and Decision Economics*, **14**(2), 97–107.

Williamson, O. E. (1996). *The Mechanisms of Governance*. Oxford: Oxford University Press.

Williamson, O. E. (2000). The new institutional economics: taking stock, looking ahead. *Journal of Economic Literature*, **38**(3), 595–613.

Williamson, O. E., Wachter, M. L. and Harris, J. E. (1975). Understanding the employment relation: the analysis of idiosyncratic exchange. *The Bell Journal of Economics*, **6**(1), 250–278.

Wilson, K. L., and Portes, A. (1980). Immigrant enclaves: an analysis of the labor market experiences of Cubans in Miami. *The American Journal of Sociology*, **86**(2), 295–319.

Wilson, T. D. and Dunn, E. W. (2004). Self-knowledge: its limits, value, and potential for improvement. *Annual Review of Psychology*, **55**, 17.1–17.26.

Wilson, T. D. and Schooler, J. W. (1991). Thinking too much: introspection can reduce the quality of preferences and decisions. *Journal of Personality and Social Psychology*, **60**(2), 181–192.

Wimmer, A. (2008). The making and unmaking of ethnic boundaries: a multilevel process theory. *American Journal of Sociology*, **113**(4), 970–1022.

Winter, S. G. (2000). The satisficing principle in capability learning. *Strategic Management Journal*, **21**(10/11), 981–996.

Winter, S. G. (2003). Understanding dynamic capabilities. *Strategic Management Journal*, **24**(10), 991.

Witt, U. (1998). Imagination and leadership: the neglected dimension of an evolutionary theory of the firm. *Journal of Economic Behavior and Organization*, **35**, 161–177.

Witt, U. (1999). Do entrepreneurs need firm? A contribution to a missing chapter in Austrian economics. *Review of Austrian Economics*, **11**, 99–109.

Woessner, M. (2009). Rescuing the 'Right to the City'. *City*, **13**(4), 474–475.

Wood, A. (1998). Making sense of urban entrepreneurialism. *Scottish Geographical Journal*, **114**(2), 120–123.

Wood, M. (2002). Mind the gap. A processual reconsideration of organizational knowledge. *Organization*, **9**(1), 151–171.

World Bank (2011). *Entrepreneurial Snapshots 2010: Measuring the Impact of the Financial Crisis on New Business Registration*. Washington DC: World Bank.

Wulf, J. (2002). Internal capital markets and firm-level compensation incentives for division managers. *Journal of Labor Economics*, **20**(2), S219–S262.

Yan, A. and T. S. Manolova (1998). New and small players on shaky ground: a multicase study of emerging entrepreneurial firms in a transforming economy. *Journal of Applied Management Studies*, **7**(1), 139–143.

Yang, K. (2007). *Entrepreneurship in China*. Aldershot, UK: Ashgate.

Yin, R. (1984). *Case Study Research*. Beverly Hills, CA: Sage Publications.

Young, I. (1995). Gender as seriality. In L. Nicholson and S. Seidman (eds.), *Social Postmodernism*. Cambridge: Cambridge University Press, pp. 187–215.

Yukl, G. A. (1989). *Leadership in Organizations*. Englewood Cliffs, NJ: Prentice Hall.

Zafirovski, M. (1999). Probing into the social layers of entrepreneurship: outlines of the sociology of enterprise. *Entrepreneurship and Regional Development*, **11**(4), 351–371.

Zahra, S. A. (1991), Predictors and financial outcomes of corporate entrepreneurship: an exploratory study. *Journal of Business Venturing*, **6**, 259–286.

Zahra, S. A. (1993). Environment, corporate entrepreneurship and financial performance: a taxonomic approach. *Journal of Business Venturing*, **8**, 319–340.

Zahra, S. A. (1996). Governance, ownership, and corporate entrepreneurship: the moderating impact of industry technological. *Academy of Management Journal*, **39**, 1713–1735.

Zahra, S. A., Jennings, D. F. and Kuratko, D. (1999). The antecedents and consequences of firm-level entrepreneurship: the state of the field. *Entrepreneurship Theory and Practice*, **24**, 45–65.

Zahra, S. A., Neilsen, A. P. and Bogner, W. C. (1999), Corporate entrepreneurship, knowledge, and competence development. *Entrepreneurship Theory and Practice*, **23**(3), 169–189.

Zahra, S. A., Kuratko, D. F. and Jennings, D. F. (1999). Entrepreneurship and the acquisition of dynamic organizational capabilities. *Entrepreneurship Theory and Practice*, **23**(3), 5–10.

Zahra, S. A., Gedajlovic, E., Neubaum, D. O. and Shulman, J. M. (2009). A typology of social entrepreneurs: motives, search processes and ethical challenges. *Journal of Business Venturing*, **24**(5), 519–532.

Zald, M. N. (1993). Organization Studies as a scientific and humanistic enterprise: toward a reconceptualization of the foundations of the field. *Organization Science*, **4**(4), 513–528

Zampetakis, L. and Moustakis, V. (2007). Fostering corporate entrepreneurship through internal marketing. *European Journal of Innovation Management*, **10**(4), 413–433.

Zerbinati, S. and Souitaris, V. (2005). Entrepreneurship in the public sector: a framework of analysis in European local governments. *Entrepreneurship & Regional Development*, **17**(1), 43–64.

Zhang, J. J., Baden-Fuller, C. and Pool, J. K. (2011). Resolving the tensions between monitoring, resourcing and strategizing: structures and processes in high technology venture boards. *Long Range Planning*, **44**(2), 95–117.

Zietlow, J. T. (2001). Social entrepreneurship: managerial, finance and marketing aspects. *Journal of Nonprofit and Public Sector Marketing*, **9**(1), 19–43.

Zizek, S. (2001). *Enjoy Your Symptom!* New York: Routledge.

Zizek, S. (2008). *In Defense of Lost Causes*. London: Verso.

Zlolniski, C. (2006). *Janitors, Street Vendors and Activists: The Lives of Mexican Immigrants in Silicon Valley*. Berkeley, CA: University of California Press.

Zollo, M. and Winter, S. G. (2002). Deliberate learning and the evolution of dynamic capabilities. *Organization Science*, **13**(3), 339–351.

Zott, C. (2002). Dynamic capabilities and the emergence of intraindustry differential firm performance: insights from a simulation study. *Strategic Management Journal*, **24**(2), 97–125.

Zucker, L. G. (1977). The role of institutionalization in cultural persistence. *American Sociological Review*, 42(5), 726–743.

Zuckerman, E. W., Kim, T.-Y., Ukanwa, K. and James von, R. (2003). Robust identities or nonentities? Typecasting in the feature-film labor market. *The American Journal of Sociology*, **108**(5), 1018–1074.

Zukin, S. (1989). *Loft Living: Culture and Capital in Urban Change*. New York: Rutgers University Press.

Zukin, S. (1995). *The Culture of Cities*. Oxford: Blackwell.

Zukin, S. (2008). Foreword. In A. M. Cronin and K. Hetherington (eds.), *Consuming the Entrepreneurial City: Image, Memory, Spectacle*. London: Routledge, pp. xi–xiii

Zukin, S. and DiMaggio, P. (1990). Introduction. In S. Zukin and P. DiMaggio (eds.), *Structures of Capital: The Social Organization of the Economy*. Cambridge: Cambridge University Press, pp. 1–36.

Zuzul, T. and Edmondson, A. C. (2001). Strategy as innovation: emergent goal formation in a nascent industry. Harvard Business School Working Paper, No. 11–099.

NOTE

*. All websites last accessed August 2012.

Index

Aacorn 302
Aalbaek, P. 338, 343, 344, 346, 347–8, 351, 355, 357, 358, 359
abduction 44–6
abiding 74–5
academic entrepreneurs 128
academic praxis 167
Academy of Management Review 22
accountability 100, 103, 109, 110, 113, 244
Acker, J. 138
acquiescence 74
acquisitions 60
actants 162, 172
action(s) 65, 67, 170, 173, 188, 189, 282, 303
    see also collective action;
        entrepreneurial actions
action approaches, to entrepreneurship 51
active force(s) 185, 186, 187, 372
active responses 7, 8, 10, 11
actor network/theory 156, 172
actor(s) 172–3, 174–5, 184, 186
actorship 173, 183, 184, 187
actualization 172, 176, 182–3
actualized newness 184
ad-hoc problem solving 202
adaptation 81–4, 96, 205–6
    barriers to organizational 84–7
    firms 59–61
    strategic 231, 232
    variation and 87–90
'add women and stir' approach 139
adjusting roles 238
adjustment 6, 52
adjustment costs 59
Adorno, T. 129, 132
advantage seeking 208, 214, 220, 225, 230
aesthetic analysis 339–43, 344, 350–55
aesthetic enlightenment 300–18
aesthetic landscaping 340, 350

aesthetic performance 339
aestheticized body 347
affect(s) 165, 182, 185, 343–4, 368
    see also cartography of affects;
        power to affect; power to be
        affected; production of affects
affect-narratives 368
affections 187
affectivity 165, 187
affectuation 372, 373
affirmation 170, 172, 173, 176, 177–9, 180, 186–8
affirmative creativity 167
'affordable loss' principle 196
affordable risks 232
Agamben, G. 315, 316
agency 6, 73–4, 77, 82, 92, 169, 170, 171, 172, 173, 175, 183, 184, 187, 249, 250, 253, 256, 328
agent(s) 170, 172, 183
agreement, culture evaluation 102
Ahuja, G. 218
Aidis, R. 72
Aldrich, H.E. 87
alertness 51, 52, 144, 179
altering 74
altruists, intelligent 205
Aluma 251
Alvarez, S. 57
Alvesson, M. 340, 350
ambidexterity 89–90, 208
American International Group (AIG) 103
Amin, A. 334
analysability, environments 90
analysis 163
anchoring, culture evaluation 102
Anderson, B.S. 218
Angel of History 130
Angelus Novus 130
Anglophone urban literature 333
anti-interpretive movement 163
antitrust law 110–11

appropriate individual 340, 350
Arab Spring 1–2, 8
archives, aesthetic analysis of 339–43, 350–55
Aristotle 99, 112
Arrow, K.A. 193
art 2, 165, 326
Art=Capital 302, 318
'art and enterprise' 314
art firms 304–6, 314
'art of the weak' 170, 174, 177, 179, 187, 188–90
Art-Capital 318
artepreneurs 304, 305, 306–16, 317, 318
artepreneurship 301–6
Arthur Anderson 103
artistic criticism 315
'artistic mode of production' 321, 322, 326, 330
artists 300–301, 303–4, 312, 317, 320–21, 327
'as if' 29–30, 367
Asia 73, 115
aspirations 91
ass (Nietzschean) 188, 189
asset ownership 50, 52–3, 55, 57, 62
asset specificity 55, 59
assumptions 153, 204–5
Astley, W.G. 205
attitudes 88
attributes 56–7, 58, 61
Audretsch, D.B. 217, 221
Austin, R.D. 282, 309
authentic self 301, 341, 358
authority 5, 6, 54
autonomous strategic behaviour 233
autonomy 220, 345
avant-garde art 301, 303, 304, 317, 318
avoidance 74

Baldessari, J. 309
'ball' analogy 364–5
Banks, J.A. 246
bargaining 198
Barnett, W.P. 203
Barney, J. 57, 199
Barringer, B.R. 215, 226
Barzel, Y. 57
Battilana, J. 76
Baumol, W.J. 125, 208

Bayerle, T. 313
Becker, G. 188, 189
becoming(s) 2, 10, 12, 156, 157, 171, 172, 174, 182, 185, 189, 341
becoming ontology 155
becoming-active 11, 12, 170, 173, 178, 183, 186, 187
becoming-entrepreneur 170
becoming-entrepreneurial leader 366, 372, 374–6
becoming-organizational 166
becoming-other 8, 180–81, 189, 371
becoming-post-industrial 1–2, 4, 10
becoming-reactive 187, 190
becoming-urbanist 335–6
behaviour 67, 68, 71
    see also entrepreneurial behaviour; ethics
behavioural assumptions 204–5
behavioural responses, to institutions 74–5
The Behavioural Theory of the Firm 198
Being 171, 172
Benjamin, W. 130, 132, 322
Berger, P. 134
Bergson, H. 24, 155, 156, 166, 172, 175, 178, 181, 182, 188
Berlin 332, 333
Bern, S. 145, 146
Beuys, J. 302, 304, 310, 314, 318
Bible 175
Biella 306
bilateral dependence 59
'bird-in-hand' principle 196
Birnbaum, D. 309, 310, 311
Bjerke, B. 276
Black Rose, Miss 347
blind variation 82
Block, Z. 232
Bluedorn, A.C. 215, 226
body
    and affects 343–4
    creative work 289–90
    language and the understanding of 137
    openness of 172, 183
    physical body/thought body 340
    power to affect/be affected 173, 185, 186–7

subjectivity, entrepreneurship and
344–7
body-mind capacity 186–7
bohèmes 312
Boltanski, L. 315
Bonk Business, Inc. 303
Bonta, M. 164, 165
Borch, O.J. 266
Borins, S. 271
Bornstein, D. 246
Boss, R.W. 217, 221
boundaries, firm/organizational 55, 60,
83, 234, 235
boundary changes 60
bounded environments 27
bounded rationality 59, 68
Bourdieu, P. 250, 253, 254
Bourriaud, N. 310, 316
Bowen, H.P. 71
Bower, J.L. 203
bracketing 25, 27, 28
Braidotti, R. 155, 157, 166, 167, 168
Branson, R. 120
breakthrough inventions 218
Brewis, J. 141
bribery 111, 113
Bronson, P. 353
Brundin, E. 238
Bruner, J. 29
Bruton, G.D. 73
Buchholtz, A.K. 104, 107
budgets, public sector 267
'building' metaphor, rejection of 156
bureaucracy 32, 257, 261–2, 269, 300,
359
bureaucratic man 359
bureaucratic subjectivity 345
bureaucrats 264, 273, 277, 359
Burgelman, R.A. 221, 225, 233, 235,
236
Burke, K. 172
Burns, R. 259
Burns, T. 2, 3
business art 302, 305
Business Cycles 31, 35–7, 40, 41, 47,
124
business entrepreneurs 76
business ethics 97, 98–9, 109–14
business methods 247
business registration 118

Butler, J. 137, 166, 172, 348
Butler, J.E. 199
Bylund, P.L. 58

calculative rationality 11
the call 364
Canada 234, 235
Cantillon, R. 50, 143
capital 59, 107, 124
capital theory 59, 60, 199
capitalism 46, 120, 123–4, 126, 127–9,
315
Capitalism, Socialism and Democracy
31, 37–9
Carnegie Foundation 6
Carnegie School of Decision-making 6
Carrol, S.J. 102
Carroll, A.B. 104
Carter, N.M. 209
Cartesian subject 158, 174, 183, 186
cartography(er) of affects 161, 167
case studies, collective creativity
282–3
Casson, M.C. 57
Catholic Church 5, 371
causal ambiguity 90
causal logics 195
causality 93, 328
causation 372, 373
Central and Eastern Europe 66, 72, 76
champions 219, 265
Chandler, A.D. 38, 107
change agents 76–7, 236, 244
charismatic leadership 51
Charney, D. 354
Chia, R. 151, 166
Chiapello, E. 315
Chihuly, D. 296
China 71, 72, 76, 87, 113, 114
Chinese vocabulary 120, 132
Chrisman, J.J. 228
Christensen, C.M. 203
Christianity 126, 186
Christianity, Communism and
Capitalism 354
'circular flow of economic life' 33, 34
cities 322, 323
see also entrepreneurial city; urban
problematic
Cities in Civilization 323, 328

Cittadellarte Pistoletto Foundation 305, 306
civic-regarding entrepreneurship 259
civilisation 6
classical economics 193
classical entrepreneurship theory 142
classics, use of 31, 47
Claude, J. 302
clothed body 354
co-evolution 78, 83–4
Coase, R.H. 53–4, 193, 201
codes of conduct 66, 67, 113
codes of ethics 100–101, 105, 106, 108
codified institutions 67–8
coercion 68
cogito ergo sum 158, 186
cognition 90–91, 96, 132
cognitive basis, entrepreneurial firms 194–7
cognitive embeddedness 78
cognitive filters 95
cognitive institutions 71
cognitive leadership 51
cognitive psychology 90, 91
Coleman, J. 205
collaboration 283–5, 297
collaborative attitude 202–3
collateralised debt obligations (CDOs) 121, 122
collective action 82, 84, 90, 96, 149, 213
collective creativity 4, 7, 8, 281–3, 363, 365–8, 370
collective entrepreneurship 61
collective impact 255, 256
Collis, D.J. 200
colonial gaze 353, 354
combinations 33, 206
commercial spaces 331
Commonwealth of Independent States (CIS) 72, 76
comparative research 78, 115
comparative studies 328
'competing down/up' 43
competition 43, 45, 51, 81, 217
competitive advantage(s) 84, 199, 200, 208, 211, 212, 214, 225, 226, 239
competitive aggressiveness 220
competitive imperfection 211
competitive pressures 108

competitive struggles 80
complementarity 59, 60
complex environments 87
complexity 59, 60, 85, 95
compromise 74
conatus 185, 186
concepts 166
concrete newness 183
confidence 238
conforming roles 238
conformity 74, 87
Confucius 112
consciousness 132, 133, 165, 185, 186
consciousness raising 148–9
constraint(s) 51, 62, 81, 85–6, 92, 95, 249, 290, 297, 323, 361
constructionist view, of gender 137, 139
contextualization 369
contingency 172
contingency theorists 205
contractual incompleteness 55, 58, 62
control 108, 240, 277, 330–31, 370, 371, 372
    of destructive entrepreneurship 61–2
    formal structures and 11
    moved from manager to machine 5–6
    moved to the worker 6–7
    technologies 6, 342
    see also managerial control; non-predictive control; perfect control; self-control
control-driven opposition 177
control-oriented management 5
controlled change 184, 188
controlled experiments, firms as 58–9
conventions 66
convergence 294–5
conversion 75
Cooper, R. 151
cooperation 80, 81, 97
cooperative corporate venturing 229
coordinating entrepreneurs 51
core competencies 103, 237, 238, 239
core values 101–2, 104, 106
corporate accountability 105
corporate citizenship 105

corporate entrepreneurship 208, 215,
221, 226–41, 259
encouragement of entrepreneurial
behaviour 267
evolution of academic field 227–31
leadership 239–40
managerial roles 235–9
organizational architecture 234–5
strategy 231–4
Corporate Entrepreneurship
Assessment Instrument (CEAI)
234–5, 238, 239
corporate mentalities 303, 304
corporate philanthropy 105
corporate policies 105
corporate production 346
corporate responsibility 105
corporate responsiveness 105
corporate social responsibility 104–9
corporate sustainability 105
corporate venturing 219, 221, 228–30,
236
corruption 111
Corruption Perceptions Index 111,
112
Costea, B. 345
counselling interview 6
Covin, J.G. 215, 227, 230
Crandall, W. 124
'crazy quilt' principle 196
creation
of multiplicity *see* multiplicity
in non-processual thinking 172
representing 175–6
space for 11
theorizing as 157
see also organization-creation;
self-creation; venture creation;
wealth creation
creative capitals 328
creative class 300, 301, 315, 327, 328–9,
346
creative destruction 122–6, 143, 144,
176, 330
creative economy(ies) 280, 286, 302,
320
creative industries 301, 303
entrepreneurial subjectivity 338–61
creative living 159
creative response 3, 367, 371

creativity 52, 145, 166
in process thinking 180–83
urban 326, 327, 328, 331
see also collective creativity;
organizational creativity
credibility 103
credit derivatives 121, 122
crisis
creative destruction and 124–5
entrepreneurial opportunity 119–20
entrepreneurship as a solution to
118–19
role of entrepreneurship in creating
121–2
and system-level changes 84
see also financial crises
critical thinking 29
critique 116, 126–32, 133
Critique is not enough 304
cross-border entrepreneurship 71
cross-cultural conflicts 99
cross-cultural studies 110
Cubism 303
Cullen, J.B. 73
cultural codes 91
cultural consumption 322, 326
cultural embeddedness 70, 71, 78
cultural industry(ies) 326–7
cultural institutions 70
cultural norms 70
cultural performance 326
cultural resources 88
cultural values 101, 343
cultural-cognitive institutions 66
culture 67, 71, 85, 86, 101–2, 219, 325
curating 310–11
Currie, G. 271, 273, 277
Curzon, C. 288, 292
Cyert, R.M. 198
Czarniawska, B. 149, 151, 257
Czarniawska-Joerges, B. 142

Dada 303
Dali, S. 316, 318
Daly, M. 137
dance 12, 177, 180, 181, 182, 188, 190
Danto, A. 314
Daokui Li, D. 76
Davidsson, P. 70, 77
Davis, M. 296, 365, 366, 368

Davis, S. 102
de Certeau, M. 177, 178, 179, 184
De Clercq, D. 71
De Cock, C. 163
Deal, T. 102
decentralization 61, 223, 266, 268
decision-making 10, 91, 102, 195, 202,
    235, 266
    see also judgement
deep listening 289, 291, 292, 295
Dees, J.G. 244, 245
defiance 74
delegation 61, 223, 235
Deleuze, G. 151, 152, 155, 157–8, 164,
    165, 166, 167, 170–71, 172, 173,
    175, 177–8, 179, 181, 182, 184,
    185, 186, 187, 338–9, 341, 342,
    359, 361, 371
democracy 6, 264, 268, 269
Democracy in America 47
Democracy and Freedom 6
Denis, J-L. 271
Denrell, J. 203
deployment of resources 237
deregulation 87, 161
derived entrepreneurship 61
Derrida, J. 314
Descartes, R. 158, 172
descriptive evidence 77
desire 173
Dess, G.G. 215, 219, 226, 232
destructive entrepreneurship 61–2,
    122
determinism 249, 250
Deutsche Edelstahlwerke 37
deviations, unplanned 82
Dew, N. 195, 204, 206
Dewey, J. 318
difference(s) 28, 170, 171, 172, 178,
    179, 181, 182, 186, 188, 311
differentiation 2, 184, 371
difficulties 285
DiMaggio, P.J. 75, 78
Dimov, D. 22
directing role 236
disaster capitalism 120
disciplinary oriented management 5
disconfirmed assumptions 153
discontinuous change 89
discourses 134

discovery 22–3, 25, 27, 29, 51, 210, 220,
    221, 222, 223, 224, 225
discretion 276
disequilibrium 124, 143
divergence 294–5
diversification 74, 83
divestitures 60, 61
division of labor 54, 58, 59, 222, 328
docility 205
dogmatism 117
Doing Business 69
doing gender 137
double entrepreneurship 72
doubt 117
Douhan, R. 67, 76
downsizing 241, 268, 269
drama 172
dreams 133, 179, 304, 329
Drucker, P. 10, 257
Du Gay, P. 269–70, 271
Duchamp, M. 303, 316, 318
duration 182–3
Dürer, A. 357
dynamic capabilities 199, 200, 208,
    213–14

E-teams 280–81, 286–98
economic development 33, 36, 143
economic efficiency 6, 10, 11, 121
economic life 33, 46, 190
economic rationality 10
economic theory of the firm 49–63
education, and artepreneurs 308–9
educational institutions 86
effective institutions 68
effectual logic 195–7, 201–2
effectuation 197, 372, 373
efficiency 83, 268, 269, 277, 285, 297,
    372
Elam, A. 72
élan vital 44, 188
Eliasson, O. 316
Elliot, T.S. 47
Emanuel, R. 120
embeddedness 64, 65, 66, 69, 70, 71,
    77–8, 243
embodiment 343, 347
emergence 26, 59–61, 80–81
emerging economies 71, 84
emotions 154, 238, 240

employee-driven innovations 273
employees, public sector 276
empowered champion 265
enables, institutions as 64
'enabling entrepreneurial activities' 271
enactment 22, 26, 27, 90
endogenous changes 87
endorsement of opportunities 236
enforcement mechanisms, institutional
    66, 67–8
Enron 103
ensemble 280, 285–6, 297, 366
ensembling 367–8
enterprise 33
entrepreneur words 146
entrepreneurial actions 224–5, 241
entrepreneurial behaviour 222, 226–7,
    232, 233, 234, 235, 236–7, 238, 267
entrepreneurial city 321, 324–6
entrepreneurial creativity 56
entrepreneurial culture 219
entrepreneurial ethics 97, 106–9
entrepreneurial feats 34
entrepreneurial firm 193–207
    cognitive elements in the organizing
        of 194–7
    social, behavioural and evolutionary
        elements 197–207
entrepreneurial function(s) 57, 61, 122,
    123, 124, 205
entrepreneurial government/
    governance 270
entrepreneurial leadership 46, 362–76
    the call, receptivity, spontaneity
        364–8
    characteristics 368–76
    collective creativity 281, 283–4,
        296–7
    corporate 239–40
    public sector 271
entrepreneurial management 246–8
entrepreneurial mindset 219, 239
entrepreneurial orientation 220, 225
entrepreneurial ownership 56–7, 108
entrepreneurial profit 43
entrepreneurial self 344, 345, 355
entrepreneurial society 207
entrepreneurial spirit 47, 98, 241, 359
entrepreneurial subjectivity, creative
    industries 338–61

entrepreneurial theory of the firm 201
entrepreneurs 12, 33–5, 142, 143
    aggressive 86–7
    body-mind capacity 186
    economic function 51
    ethics and CSR 106–9
    fetishisation of 123
    firm's need for 53–6
    gendering of 145–7
    'helplessness before deepening crises'
        116, 118
    motivation 143–4
    mythological status 346
    profit-seeking 52, 57, 60
    prospects of adaptive change 88–9
    small-scale 71
    as speculators 52
    successful 56–7
    see also academic entrepreneurs;
        artepreneurs; nascent
        entrepreneurs; policy
        entrepreneurs; proxy
        entrepreneurs; social
        entrepreneurs
entrepreneurship 2
    biases in research 209–11
    and crisis *see* crisis
    critique of 116–17, 126–32, 133
    depoliticisation of 128, 129
    economic theory of the firm 49–63
    functional concepts 51
    as gendered 142–50
    institutional theory 64–78
    key ideas of 259–60
    moral vacuum in the thinking of 133
    as organization-creation 2, 3, 4, 7,
        10, 21–30, 170, 176
    theorizing processes 151–68
    see also artepreneurship;
        managerial entrepreneurship;
        organizational
        entrepreneurship; public sector
        entrepreneurship; strategic
        entrepreneurship
*Entrepreneurship Snapshots 2010:
    Measuring the Impact of the
    Financial Crisis on New Business
    Registration* 118
entrepreneurship-organization
    relationship 3–5, 7

environmental signals 93
environmental triggers 232
environments 25–6, 27, 42, 61, 71, 84,
    85, 87, 90, 93, 94, 96, 104, 123, 255
equilibrium 143
equilibrium capitalism 124
Erasmus, D. 133
Esping-Andersen, G. 260–61
essentialism 135
eternal return 179
ethical joy 187
ethical responsibility 105
ethical standards 98, 100, 101, 104,
    105, 107, 110
ethics 98–100
    codes, core values and corporate
        culture 100–104
    corporate social responsibility 104–9
    global perspective of business ethics
        109–14
ethnic enclaves 88–9
ethnic entrepreneurs 77
ethnic inertia 251–3
ethnicity 252–3
ethnomethodology 249
êthos 99
Europe 104–5, 115, 140, 320, 330
European Commission 105
European School of Entrepreneurship
    Research 9
European Union 72, 266
evasion 75
event, multiplicity and 182–3
evolution 36, 78, 171
evolutionary change 90–93
evolutionary models 93
evolutionary theory 79–96
    barriers to organizational
        adaptation 84–7
    cognition, identity and evolutionary
        change 90–93
    evolutionary processes 79, 80–81
    firm emergence 59–61
    as a meta-theory 79
    research methodology 93–5
    selection and adaptation 81–4
    variation and adaption in 87–9
exaptation 206
exit 204
exogenous changes 87

expectations, ethical 100, 104, 107,
    110, 113, 114
experience(s) 26, 27, 195, 311, 318
experience economy 300, 301, 303, 325,
    332
experimentation 43, 45, 50, 52, 61, 62,
    152, 161, 162–5
experimenting roles 237, 238
exploitation 89, 203, 210, 211, 222,
    223, 230
expressive organization 346
expressivity 346–7
extensive multiplicities 182
external corporate venturing 229–30
external environment 71

Facebook 1, 2, 29
failure 203, 204, 219, 240
Faludi, S. 148
Fassiotto, M.A. 223
Fayol, H. 370
feeling of power 183–4, 187
female subordination 134, 135, 141
feminine traits 135
femininity 134, 136, 137, 145
femininity words 146–7
feminist activism 135, 148
feminist empiricism 138–9
feminist process thinkers 166
feminist research 134, 135–8, 138–9
Ferlie, E. 268, 272
fetishisation, of the entrepreneur 123
figurations 157, 168
financial crises 97, 108, 113, 116, 118,
    122, 124, 129, 330
financial innovation 121–2
financial institutions 113, 122
financial risks 107
Finland 262, 263
firm(s)
    co-evolution between institutions
        and 83–4
    Schumpeterian theories 34, 36, 38–9
    see also economic theory of the firm;
        entrepreneurial firm
firm performance 215, 220
firm-level entrepreneurship 209, 210,
    212, 221, 224, 225
firm-level wealth creation 214
first-level managers 237–8, 239

fit, organizational-environmental 79
flexibility 233, 269
Fligstein, N. 75
Florida, R. 320, 321, 327–8
flow(s) 152, 172, 174, 186
Floyd, S.W. 237
Foerster, H. von 30
fold/folding 338–9, 339–43, 347–55, 359
foolishness, technology of 197, 202, 203
for profit institutions 91–2
Ford Foundation 6
Fordism 46
forecasting 10, 56, 212
Foreign Corrupt Practices Act (1977) 111
form/forming 4, 91, 92
formal institutions 66, 67–9, 69–70, 71
Foucault, M. 5, 134, 172, 339, 341, 369, 370, 371
Fournier, V. 149
frames/framing 172
Freud, S. 6, 317
From managerialism to entrepreneurialism 324–5
Fuglsang, M. 164
Fuld, R. 8

Gagliardi, P. 344
Gängeviertel 320–21
Gannon, M.J. 102
Garciá-Marzá, D. 97
Gartner, W.B. 77, 144, 209
Geertz, C. 156, 172
gender 134–50
    entrepreneurship and 72–3, 142–50
    women and organizations 138–42
gender blindness 138
gender equality 148
gender identity 141
gender segregation 139
gendered norms 139, 141–2, 148, 149
general equilibrium theory 143
general strike, first US 6
General Theory 35
Genèse (Genesis) 158, 166, 175
gentrification 320, 321, 330
gestures 315–16
Gherardi, S. 141

giant corporation 38–9
Giddens, A. 75, 250
Ginsberg, A. 107, 228
given circumstances, discovering and creating 291–2
glass ceiling 139
glass escalator 141
global economy 8, 85, 97, 118, 119, 226, 241
Global Entrepreneurship Monitor (GEM) 69, 71, 72, 94–5
global financial crises 97, 113, 116, 118, 122, 124, 129
globalization 85, 92, 103, 109–14, 276
gnosis 355, 357
goals 51, 91, 198, 237
Goffmann, E. 172, 173
Goméz, C. 70
Google 1, 47, 100
governance 55, 213–14, 219, 260, 262, 263, 269–70, 324–5
government/policy 70, 86, 87–8, 108
governmentality 5
Graham, M. 288
gravity 239–40
greed 108
green energy industry 88
Greenblatt, S. 172
Greenspan, A. 122
Gregory, R. 276, 277
grief 240
grounded theory studies 282
group work 285
Guarneri String Quartet 366–7
Guattari, F. 152, 158, 164, 165, 339, 359, 360
Guth, W.D. 228

habit(s) 33, 99
Hall, P. 323, 328
Hamburg manifesto 321, 334
Hamel, G. 226
Hancock, P. 343
hands-on-professional management 271
Hansen, M.T. 203
Haraway, D. 137
Harding, N. 340, 358
Harvard Business School 5, 283, 298, 309

Harvey, D. 124, 321, 324, 325, 329, 330
Hawthorne Experiments 138
Hayek, F.A. von 51
Hébert, R.F. 143
Heidegger, M. 154, 359
Helfat, C.E. 213
'helplessness before deepening crises' 116, 118
Henrekson, M. 67, 74, 76
Heraclitus 175, 177
Hernes, T. 163, 165
hero-entrepreneurs 302
heterogeneity 56, 64, 221, 367, 368
heterogeneous assets 56–7, 58
heterogenesis 174
heterosexual matrix 141, 348
hierarchy(ies) 166, 184, 223, 272–3, 276, 369, 370
'higher men' 12, 180
Hinduism 99, 126
Hirst, D. 302, 305
historical events 353
Historische Schule 65
history 36, 130
Hitt, M.A. 217, 219, 221
Hjorth, D. 24, 145, 160, 161, 162, 259, 276
Hofstede, G. 101, 102
homo economicus 73, 188, 189
homogeneity 183, 367
homosexuals 327–8
homosocial reproduction 140
Hood, C. 271
horizontal gender segregation 139
Horkheimer, M. 116, 118
Hornsby, J.S. 234, 238, 239
Hrebiniak, L.G. 206
Huang, Z.H.I. 206
human capital/theory 11, 57
Human Relations School 138
human resource departments 86
humanities 2
Hunt, S.D. 102
Huyghe, P. 310
hyper-aestheticization 332
hyper-competition 208, 211–12

IBM 86
ICT 8

idea(s)
    entrepreneurial 271
    entrepreneurship as an 130–32
ideal worker 339, 344
identification of resources 237
identity 91–3, 101, 141, 172, 181, 184, 186, 241, 342
ignorance 55–6
Ilgen, D.R. 281
illegal entrepreneurial activities 71, 72
image(s)
    entrepreneurial city 325, 326
    see also aesthetic analysis
image-based performance 160–61
imaginary constructions 124
imagination 12, 29, 52, 153, 154, 179, 293, 367
imitators 42–3, 54
implicit theories 154
impulse 293–4
In Praise of Bureaucracy 270
inauguration-story 175
incomplete markets 57, 58
incremental change 89
incremental innovation 2–3
individual-level, social change matrix 251, 252, 253
individual-level research 107–8, 210, 224, 246–7
individuation 181, 183, 184, 187
'induced innovation of a technical type' 37
induced strategic behaviour 233
industrial district 39
industrial economy 1, 8, 169, 177, 362, 363
industry leaders 91
inertial informality 75
informal institutions 66–9, 70, 71
information 23, 223, 297
ingenuity 129, 144, 339
Ingold Airlines 303
inner structure, of the firm 36
innovation
    E-Team 295–6
    entrepreneurial orientation 220
    financial 121–2
    institutional entrepreneurs 76
    risk calculations 91

Schumpeter on 34, 35, 36, 37, 38–9, 39–43, 45, 51
social entrepreneurship 244, 245
strategic entrepreneurship 228, 230–31
see also incremental innovation; radical innovation
innovation clouds 7
innovation processes 7
innovators 143, 177, 273
inquiry/learning 24
insight 24, 28, 29
institutional change 68–9, 71–2, 72–3, 74–5, 76–7
institutional constraints 85–6
institutional deficiencies 64, 71, 72
institutional entrepreneurship 75–6
institutional instability 84
institutional legacies 72
institutional theory, entrepreneurship 64–78
  empirical insights 69–73
  further research directions 73–6
  rationality 10
  theoretical overview 65–9
institutionalists, American 65
institutions 184
  co-evolution between firms and 83–4
  dimensions and functions of 65–7
  enabling and constraining forces 64, 65–6
  need for high quality 115
instrumental view of the firm 203
integrity 101, 104, 106, 110
intellectualisation 314, 315
intelligent altruists 205
intensified entrepreneurialism 332
intensity(ies) 10, 12, 165, 172, 178, 182, 183, 189
intensive images 11
intensive multiplicities 182
intentionality 74, 75, 82, 84, 86
interactions, organizational-environmental 80
interactive learning, institutional change as 74
intermediaries 143, 205
internal corporate venturing 229, 230
internal gender segregation 139
internal organization 61

internet 83
interorganizational analysis, social enterprises 247
interpretation
  objective environments 90
  of opportunities 238
interpretive logic, in theorizing 152, 153–5
interpretive paradigm 250
introspections 23, 24, 28
intuition 12
'invention x entrepreneurship = innovation' 2
inventiveness 179
investment banks 122
Ireland, R.D. 216, 217, 219, 226, 233
irony art 303–4, 314
irrationalism 125, 300
iteration 286, 291–2, 293, 295

Javacheff, C. 301, 302, 303, 304, 305, 309, 314
Johannisson, B. 24
joint surplus 61
joint ventures 97, 111
Jones, F.F. 265
Jones, R. 309
Journal of European Urban and Regional Studies 332
joy 170, 185, 186, 187, 189, 190
Joyce, W.F. 206
J.P. Morgan 122
Judaism 99
Judeo-Christian heritage 99
judgement 50, 51–3, 58, 133
juxtaposition method 338, 339–43, 350–55, 358, 359

Kania, J. 255
Kant, I. 24, 117, 316
Kaplan, G. 136–7
Katz, J. 324
Kennedy, A.A. 102
Ketchen, D. 216
Keynes, J.M. 35, 130–31
Kierkegaard, S.A. 154
King, I.W. 339
Kippenberger, M. 312
Kirzner, I.M. 23–4, 51, 57, 124, 179, 210, 222

Klee, P. 130
Klein, N. 120
Klein, P.G. 51, 210, 264, 265–6, 269, 270
Klein, Y. 318
Knight, F. 50, 51, 52, 55, 56, 62, 66, 143, 194–5
Knightian uncertainty 52, 56, 58, 59, 194, 195, 201, 203, 206
Knott, A.M. 203
knowledge(s) 5, 7, 33, 169, 223, 237
    see also prior knowledge; scientific knowledge; social knowledge
knowledge worker/work 350–51, 355–8, 358–9, 360
Koons, J. 302
Koslowski, S.W.J. 281
Kovalainen, A. 275
Kramer, M. 255
Kuratko, D.F. 217, 221, 234, 236

Lacan, J. 133
Lachmann, L.M. 59, 60
Ladkin, D. 358
Lampert, C.M. 218
Lane, P.J. 237
Langley, A. 163
Langlois, R.N. 193, 201
language 137, 281
Lant, T.K. 203
Latham, A. 326, 329, 332, 333
Latour, B. 156, 166, 172, 314, 364
laughter 12, 176, 177, 180, 188, 190
laws 66, 110–11
leadership 52, 140–41
    see also charismatic leadership; cognitive leadership; entrepreneurial leadership
learned behaviour 68, 71
Lee, P.M. 88, 310
Lefebvre, H. 322–3, 323, 332, 334
legitimacy 87
Lehman Brothers 1, 8
'lemonade' principle 197, 202
leveraging 214, 220, 227, 230
Levinthal, D.A. 203
liability 107
liberal feminism 135, 148
Lilja, T. 301, 302, 305
Lindgren, M. 275

Ling, Y. 236
linguistic turn 137, 167
Link, A.N. 143
Linstead, S.A. 162
Lipsky, M. 273, 276
listening 367
literature 165
Loacker, B. 344
lobbying 81
Logos 175
Lohmann, P. 161, 162
long tails 8
long-term decision framework 104
longitudinal studies, need for 78
Love Difference 313
Luckmann, T. 134
Lumpkin, G.T. 219, 232
Luthers' 95 theses 368–76
Lyotard, F. 314

McCraw, T. 35
Machiavelli, N. 176, 177, 179, 184, 187–8
machine-worker relationship 5–7
McKenzie, J. 346
macroeconomics 88, 118, 121
Mair, V. 120
maladaptation 59
male superiority 134
management 11, 105, 139, 140, 362
    see also new public management; self-management; strategic management
management knowledge 7
management science 89
management support 234, 235, 238–9
management-organization relationship 4, 5, 7
manager-worker relationship 5
managerial control 7, 10, 107, 177, 277
managerial entrepreneurship 11, 12, 170, 267, 371
managerialism 145, 267, 278, 324
managers 9, 34–5, 89, 106–9, 169, 189, 235–9, 270, 271, 274–5, 370
manipulation 74, 84, 85, 330–32
Maravelias, C. 340, 345, 350
March, J.G. 198, 202, 203
market institutions 71
markets 193, 245

Marquis, C. 206
Marshall, A. 39
Marx, K. 124, 126, 353
Marxism 249, 332
masculinity 134, 136, 137, 145
masculinity words 146
Massumi, B. 162, 166, 182, 183, 340, 343, 364, 370
material level, social change matrix 251, 252, 253
materialistic mappings 157
mathematical modeling 53
Matta-Clark, G. 310
Mayo, E. 5, 6–7, 138, 370
mechanic-organic metaphorisation 2–3
mediators 164
Medici String Quartet 288, 290, 292
mental models 51
mere managers 34–5
mergers 36, 60, 61
Merleau-Ponty, M. 156
Merton, R.C. 121
meta-theory 79
metamorphic research 157
Metcalfe, J.S. 271
Meyer, J.W. 92
Meyers, M.K. 273
Mezias, S.J. 203
micro-level studies 94, 221, 224, 250, 282
microeconomics 49, 207
middle-level managers 235, 236–7, 238, 239, 271
Miles, M.P. 227, 230
A Millionaire's Journey From Fear to True Wealth 347
mimetic enforcement mechanisms 68
mind 186–7, 289
Minniti, M. 70
Minsky, H. 124
Minstrom, M. 278
Mintzberg, H. 339
Mir, A. 303
Mises, L. von 50, 52, 56, 124
mistakes 82
mixed embeddedness 77
modern theories of the firm 49, 50, 54, 55
Mokyr, J. 206
monitoring 240

Monsen, E. 217, 221
Moonshine Shop 294
moral entrepreneurship 128
moral hazard 55, 57, 61
moral norms 66
morality 98, 99
Morris, H.H. 233, 265
Moustakis, V. 257, 277
moved and being moved, in leadership 368, 371
movement 159, 160, 172, 174, 184, 189, 362
movements 152
moving 154
Mulholland, K. 274
multi-national organizations 100, 106
multilevel research 77
multiple becomings 2, 10, 174
multiple goals 91
multiple innovations 43
multiplicity 172, 174, 177, 181
    creation of 152, 157–60
    and event 182–3
    performing series 160–62
    stepping aside 157–60
    through experimentation 162–5
Myers, S.C. 212

nakedness 343, 347
'nakedness' image, juxtaposition/ folding of 351–5, 360
The Naked Entrepreneur 347
narrative(s) 11, 29, 326–34
narrative knowing 29
narrative rationality 12
narrativization 10, 173, 174
nascent entrepreneurs 68, 80, 82, 88, 91, 94
national culture(s) 73, 102, 114, 234
National Expert Surveys 95
national institutions 84
The nature of the firm 54
Nayak, A. 167
negative externalities 125
negative forces 188
negative-reactive 170, 178, 180
negativity 178, 179, 186, 190
negligence 108, 113
Negri, A. 360

neoclassical economics 49, 53, 54, 55,
    193
neoliberalism 124–5, 128, 269, 276,
    324, 332, 334, 361
nerds 327
networks 243, 247
'new' 176–7, 179, 181
new combinations 33, 34, 40, 42, 44,
    206, 223, 266
new firms 36, 88
new institutionalism 10, 65, 79
new organizations 34, 36, 81, 87, 91,
    228
new public management (NPM) 258,
    268–75, 276, 277
newness 4, 183, 184, 188
Nguyen, T.V. 71
Nicholas de Cusa 355
Nietzsche, F.W. 12, 126, 155, 170, 175,
    176, 177, 178, 179, 180, 183, 186,
    187, 188, 371
nihilism 180, 186, 188
Nike 113
noise 158
nomadology 159
non-consequential decision-making
    202
non-contractability 57
non-entrepreneurial firms 34, 43
non-predictive control 195–6
non-predictive logic 201, 202–3
non-profit organizations 143, 247, 267
non-representational theory 155–7
non-Western body 354
normalization 5, 7
Norman, P. 278
normative enforcement mechanisms
    68
normative institutions 66, 70
norms
    influence on entrepreneurs 88
    innovation as the creation of new
        41–3, 44, 45
    see also cultural norms; gendered
        norms; social norms
North, D.C. 65, 73–4
'Not in our name' (Hamburg)
    manifesto 321, 334
*The Nudist on the Late Shift, and other
    Tales of Silicon Valley* 353

objective environments 90, 95
objectivism 249, 250
obligation 104
Odysseus 363, 364
Ohmae, K. 102–3
old firms 36
Oliver, C. 74
On the Concept of History 130
One Day with Peter 338, 339, 344, 347
ontogenesis 171
openness 172, 183, 189, 292, 362, 367
opportunism 204, 205
opportunists 345
opportunity 144, 187, 199
    crisis and entrepreneurial 119–20
    discovery 22–3, 25, 29, 210, 220, 221,
        222, 223, 224, 225
    evaluation 210, 211, 222, 225
    exploitation 210, 211, 222, 223
    interpretation of 238
    middle-level managerial role 236–7
    research focus on 22
opportunity costs 232–3
opportunity-seeking 208, 214, 220,
    225, 230
opposition, control-driven 177
order 179, 184, 185, 188
'organism' metaphor 47
organization 3–5, 158, 166, 323
organization-creation 2, 3, 4, 7, 10,
    21–30, 170, 176, 184
organization-environment relations 27
organizational art 309
organizational bodies 344
organizational boundaries 55, 60, 83,
    234, 235
organizational capabilities 200, 206
organizational capacity 8
organizational change 80–81, 86,
    161–2, 166, 184, 272, 278
organizational creativity 7, 9, 11, 364
    as affirmation 177–9, 180
    dilemma of 176–7, 179, 184, 187–8
organizational culture 101, 102–3, 234
organizational design 61–2, 223–5
organizational entrepreneurship 145
    an art of the weak 169–90
    history of incubation 11
    and innovation 7
    opening a research agenda 8–12

processual approaches 167
reasons for focusing on 1–7
Schumpeter's theories 31–48
significance of 2011 1–2
organizational forms 91, 92
organizational innovations 37, 41
organizational knowledge 237
organizational learning 82, 203, 208,
    230, 240
organizational performance 343
organizational rationalization 37
organizational size 267
organizational structure(s) 10–11, 36,
    176, 198, 205, 213–14, 222, 234,
    240
organizational theory 84, 138, 166,
    322–4
organizational-level analysis, social
    entrepreneurship 247
organizations, and women 138–42
organizing 2–3, 21, 22, 23, 25, 26, 28,
    29, 153, 301–3, 346
Organizing reality machines 316–18
Osborne, W. 113
Österberg-Högstedt, J. 275
Ostrom, E. 266
outcome approaches, to
    entrepreneurship 50–51
the outside 341
ownership 56–7, 108

Pacheco-de-Almeida, G. 212
Packendorff, J. 275
Panel Study of Entrepreneurial
    Dynamics (PSED) 94
passage 152, 182, 187
passion(s) 170, 173, 183, 185, 187, 368
path dependency 59, 75, 86, 89
pathos 339, 343, 344, 355
peer pressure 108
Peirce, C. 43–6
Penrose, E.T. 199, 208
People's Light 283, 293
perceiver-world separation 156
perception of gender 137
perception of reality 343
perception of the situation 57
'perennial gale of creative destruction'
    123, 130
perfect control 91

performance 160–61, 172, 215, 220,
    326, 333–4, 339, 343
performative mode, of theorizing 152,
    155–7
performative view, of gender 137
performativity 346
performing series 160–62
personal networking 185
personality 38, 107, 342
Peters, B.G. 264
Peters, T. 267
petty traders 71
phenomenology 249
philosophy 2, 166, 314
Phoenix 126
Picasso, P. 316, 318
Pierre, J. 264
Pierson, P. 276
'pilot-in-the-plane' principle 197
Pink, D. 309
Pioppi, M. 305
pipeline problem 139
Pistoletto, M. 304, 305–6, 313
place marketing/promotion 325, 326,
    333
planning (E-Team) 286–7
Plato 99, 112, 355
plausibility 154
play 12, 177, 180, 181, 188, 190
policy entrepreneurs 262–4
political conception, organizational
    goals 198
political context, CSR in 105
political economy perspective 76
political embeddedness 78
political turbulence 87
Polkinghorne 29
Poole, M.S. 163
population ecology 36, 79, 81, 92, 205
Porticus 310
Posen, H.E. 203
positive path-dependent informality 75
post-bureaucratic organization 345
post-disciplinary mode, of organizing
    346
post-facto rationalizations 91
post-industrial becoming 1–2, 4, 10
post-industrial cities 325
post-industrial economy 4, 8, 9, 177,
    363, 368, 370

post-industrial leadership 362
post-industrial organization 7
post-industrialism 169
post-materialism 70
post-socialist countries 66, 71, 75
post-Soviet states 73, 74
post-structuralism 172, 175
postmodern boss 358
potentiality 10, 11, 172, 173, 174, 176,
    180, 189
Potsdamer Platz 333
Powell, W.W. 78
power 5, 107, 132, 134, 138, 268, 269,
    275, 371
  to act 185, 187, 362
  to affect 170, 173, 179, 185
  to be affected 170, 173, 179, 183,
      185, 189, 362
  to become 182
  see also feeling of power; will power;
      will to power
Praag, M. van 72
practice, theory of 250
preparation, E-Teams 286–91
price theory, neoclassical 49, 54
Priem, R.L. 199
principal-agent theory 54, 55
Principles of Scientific Management 1
prior knowledge 26, 225
Prior Knowledge and the discovery of
    entrepreneurial opportunities 22,
    23, 25, 28, 29, 30
prior selection 86
'the private is public' 140
privatizations 84, 161, 268, 269, 274
proactive conception 199
proactiveness 106, 217, 220, 226, 236
problems 285
process
  as emergence 26
  innovation as 39–41, 42
  social entrepreneurial 248
process data 163
process philosophy 12, 163, 166, 167,
    175, 176, 362
process theory 151–68
process thinking 169–90
process-oriented approach, collective
    creativity 282
production of affects 343, 355

production function 35–6, 53
production plans 59
productive entrepreneurship 61, 62, 64,
    66, 70
productivity 6, 59, 138, 272, 346
professions, public sector 272, 276, 277
profit, entrepreneurial 43
profit-seeking entrepreneurs 52, 57, 60
property rights 54, 55, 57, 65, 66, 73
*The Protestant Ethic and the Spirit of
    Capitalism* 35, 46
Protevi, J. 164, 165
proxy-entrepreneurs 58
Prudential 113
psychological traits 144
psychology 195
public champion 265
public choice 65
public sector
  corruption perceptions index 112
  key ideas 260–61
  organizations 100
public sector entrepreneurship 257–78
  bureaucracy mingling 266–7
  comparison with private sector
      264–6
  key ideas about 261–4
  and new public management 270–75
Puffer, S.M. 71
pure entrepreneur 210

qualitative transformation 171, 174,
    177, 189
quantitative change 170, 171, 177, 179,
    182
quantitative homogeneity 183
queer difference 328
Quixote 202
quotas (gender) 148

radical feminism 135
radical innovation 2, 3, 364
Raiser 66
Rajchman, J. 164
Rancière, J. 315, 316
ratification work 141
rational capitalism 46
rationality(ies) 5, 10, 11, 12, 59, 68, 316
rationalization(s) 37, 91, 235–6
re-acting 173

reactions 371
reactive forces 184, 185, 186, 187, 371
reactive responses 7, 10, 11, 188
reactive-negative 170, 178, 180
Read, S. 195
'Real', of entrepreneurship 133
real options theory 212–13
realism 314
realists, artists as 303–4
reality 26, 45, 46, 51, 156, 314
realizations 24
realized change 184
reason 10, 133, 317
receptivity 171, 179, 183, 185, 189, 362, 363, 366, 367, 368
recombination 75
reconceiving 292–4
recovery, out of crisis 119
Red Queen phenomenon 203
refinement of opportunities 236–7
reflexivity 152, 153
Reformation (Protestant) 46, 371
regrouping/reshuffling 59, 60
regulation 87, 88, 108, 110, 113–14
regulative institutions 66, 71
Rehberger, T. 312
Rehn, A. 72
Reichert, D. 304
Reinart, H. and E. 126
relatedness 12
relation(s) 159, 182–3
relational aesthetics 310, 316
relational capacity 8
relational materialism 155
relational theorizing 156
relationality 172, 183, 184
relationships 4, 51, 81, 93, 97, 113, 159, 203, 282, 292, 327, 371
religion 70, 99, 102, 117
Research Triangle Park Area (North Carolina) 82
resentment 180, 371
resistance 42, 43, 86, 140, 142, 264, 361
resource acquisition 59, 83, 237
resource allocation 52, 84, 107, 212, 287
resource availability 70, 81, 84, 234
resource base 213
resource combinations 59, 60
resource dependence 79, 96

resource distribution 81
resource identification 237
resource-based view (RBV) 198–201, 372
resources 50, 56–7, 81, 87, 88, 211
responsible microeconomics 207
rest/movement 186, 362
retention 80
retroactive rationalization 235–6
revanchism 330
reward 234, 235
rhizomatic becomings 156
rhizomatic subjectivity 158
rhizomatic theorizing 166
'right to the city' 334
The Rise of the Creative Class 321, 327
risk(s) 107, 122, 143, 232
risk calculations 91
risk-taking 107, 143, 144, 217, 219, 220, 234, 266
Robertson, P. 288, 290, 292
Rockefeller Foundation 6
Rogers, L. 136–7
Ruef, M. 87
rules of the game, institutions as 65–6
Rumelt, R.P. 208
Rumsfeld, D. 120
Russia 71

sadness 170, 187, 189
St Jerome in His Study 357, 359
Saint-Simon 143
Salaman, G. 270
Salimath, M.S. 73
sameness, of entrepreneurial cities 329–30
Samuelson, P. 35
Sanandaji, T. 74
Sarasvathy, S.D. 195
Sathe, V. 102
satisfaction 238
Sayles, L.R. 233
scandals 103
Scandinavia 148
Scandinavian Journal of Management 274
scarcity 89, 96, 203
Schmoller, G. 65
'scholar-saint at work' 357

Schumpeter, J. 1, 5, 31–48, 51, 122–6, 127, 143–4, 176, 190, 209, 259, 371
Schwartz, H. 102
science 182
scientific knowledge 12, 159
scientific management 6, 10
Scott, W.R. 66, 68, 87
Secchi, L. 264
second wave feminism 135, 148
Sehested, K. 270
selecting role 236
selection 79, 80, 81–4, 96
self 5, 184
   see also authentic self; entrepreneurial self
self-control 6
self-creation 345, 346
self-employment 50, 58, 70
self-expression 338, 346
self-grounded subject 172, 181, 182, 183
self-management 346, 370
Semenya, C. 136
Semetsky, I. 185
semiotic approach 43–7
senior-level managers 235–6, 238, 239
sensation(s) 12, 165, 171, 174, 178, 182
sensemaking 151, 153, 154
senses 316
sensing ability 213
separatist imagery 27
separatist strategy 135
serial entrepreneurs 203
seriality, gender as 137
Serres, M. 152, 157–60, 166, 357, 364
services, public sector 260, 261, 267, 274
Sevón, G. 149
sex differences, studies 135–6
sex role stereotyping 140
sex/gender distinction 136–7
sexual identity 141
sexuality 135, 354, 359, 360
Shane, S. 22, 23, 24, 25, 199, 222
shared vision 51
Sharma, P. 228
Sharp, R.J. 163
shepherding, of opportunities 237
shock doctrine 120
Shotter, J. 156

Simmel, G. 322
Simon, H. 6, 205
sine ire et studio 345
Sine, W.D. 88
singularity 312–13, 318
Sirens 363, 364
sites of organization, cities as 323, 332
skills 222, 223, 224, 240, 283, 288, 289
skinny-dipping 354
Slevin, D.P. 215
small and medium-sized enterprises (SMEs) 100, 273
small-scale entrepreneurs 71
Smallbone, D. 70, 71, 72, 76
Smith, A. 47, 143
Smith, N. 330
'social atmosphere' of firms 47
social capital 223, 243, 247, 250, 311
social change 8–9, 88, 145, 243, 245, 248
social change matrix 248–51, 252–3, 254–6
social comparisons 91
social construction(s) 35, 80, 134, 137, 145
social costs, urban entrepreneurialism 330
social destruction 80
social embeddedness 64, 65, 66, 69, 78, 243
social engineers 246
Social Enterprise School 247
social entrepreneurs 244, 246–7
social entrepreneurship 128, 143, 242–56, 259
   further research, overcoming inertia 253–6
   research field 243–53
social environments 42, 61, 96, 104, 123, 255
social field 11, 173, 369, 370, 372
social forces, access to resources 81
social imaginaries 339
Social Innovation School 245
social interaction(s) 249, 250, 282, 312
social knowledge 311–12
social mechanisms 88
social mission 243, 244, 245, 248
The Social Network 29
social norms 66, 67, 70, 108, 138

social polarization 330
social reality(ies) 116, 134, 141, 250, 253, 318, 331
social reproduction 80, 87
social responsibility 97, 104
   see also corporate social responsibility
social structures 249, 250
societies, becoming of 2
sociology 166, 195, 249–50, 253, 314
Socrates 24, 99
Sombart, W. 65, 126
Sørensen, B.M. 131, 164, 339
Sørensen, J.B. 223
Souitaris, V. 266
sound-noise 159
Soviet Union 72
space-related contexts, investigation of 94
space-time complexity 156
speculative affirmation 186–8
speculators 52
speech, performance based on 161
Spencer, J.W. 70
Spinoza, C. 155, 166, 170, 176, 185, 186, 189
'spirit' of the firm 35, 36, 46, 47
Splintermind 307, 308, 316
spontaneity 173, 183, 184, 185, 362, 363, 366, 367, 368
spontaneous initiatives 225
Städel Schule 309, 310, 313, 314, 315
stakeholder self-selection 197, 198
Stalker, G.M. 2, 3
standpoint 137–8
state capture 74
state intervention 330
stepping aside 157–60
stereotypes/stereotyping (gendered) 140, 141, 148
stewardship model 271
Steyaert, C. 160, 161, 162, 259, 324
strata 341, 342, 350
strategic alliances 203
strategic behaviour 233
strategic change 184
strategic entrepreneurship 208–25
   emergence of specialized research literature 209–14
   innovation 228, 230–31

literature 214–20
micro-foundations and division of labour 221–2
organizational design 223–5
Strategic Entrepreneurship Journal 208
strategic focus 203–4
strategic intent 214, 221, 225, 227, 237
strategic learning 218
strategic management 96, 200, 203, 206, 208
Strategic Management Journal 206, 214
strategic renewal 228, 231, 236
strategy 9–10, 90, 174, 178, 188, 231–4
strategy making 201–3, 298
street-level bureaucrats 264, 273, 277
striving 185
structural change(s) 120, 148
structural constraint 92
structural discrimination 135
structural functionalism 249
structural violence 130
structural-level, social change matrix 251, 252, 253
structuration theory 74, 250
structure(s) 35, 75, 85, 86, 174, 184, 253, 262
   see also organizational structure(s); social structures
subject 174, 181, 189, 341, 342
subjectification 7, 170, 171, 172, 173, 181, 183, 184, 186–8, 187, 189, 346
subjective opportunity set 208
subjectivism 249–50
subjectivity(ies) 12, 172, 173, 181, 184, 185, 186, 187, 313
   see also entrepreneurial subjectivity
success 203, 204, 232, 285
suffering 117, 129–30
Sundin, S. 274
surprise 23–5, 28, 55–6, 82
Surrealism 303
sustainable competitive advantage 199, 200, 211, 225, 239
Sweden 139, 140, 251, 262–3, 274
swëdêthos 99
Sykes, H.B. 232
symbolic classifications 250
symbolic economy 325

symbolic level, social change matrix 251, 252, 253
symbolic violence 117
system compatibility, culture evaluation 102
system expansion 255
system maintenance 254, 255
system transformation 255
system-level changes 84

Taalas, S. 72
tactics 174, 177, 178, 179, 189, 240
task-level judgement 58
taxation 257, 267
Taylor, C. 339
Taylor, F.W. 1, 5, 6, 10, 169, 370
Taylor, S.S. 358
'Taylorization of work' 36
technology(ies) 85, 125
    of control 6, 342
    of extension 353
    of foolishness 197, 202, 203
    green 88
    of self 5
Teece, D.J. 199, 213
Terjesen, S. 72
tertiary gaudens 204–5
text 174–5
Thatcher, M. 346
That's moving 154
theatre of everyday life 173
Theorie der Wirtschaftlichen Entwicklung 1
theorizing processes 151–68
theory construction 154
The Theory of Economic Development 31, 32–5, 40, 41
thickness 172
third sector organizations 266
third wave feminism 136
Thommen, J.-P. 102
Thompson, J. 277
thought 174, 189
thought body 340, 341
3 Ts formula 327
Thrift, N. 155–6, 331, 334
Thurik, R. 70
time 287
time availability 234, 235
time series data 93

time-economy link 5, 10
time-related contexts 94
time-space 156, 178
Tiravanija, R. 310
Tocqueville, A. de 47
tokenism 139–40
top managers/management 235, 270, 271
Toys 'R' Us 106
trace-oriented management 10, 11
traces/investments 184, 185, 188, 372
traditional firm 46
traditional management 109
traditional theory of the firm 53–4
traits 135, 144, 246–7
transaction costs/theory 54, 55, 58, 64, 65, 79, 193, 204
transcendental enlightenment 317, 318
transformation(s) 123, 152, 206, 207, 241
transformation model 271
transformational CEOs 236
transformative affirmation 177
transmutation 170, 171, 177, 180, 188, 189, 371
transparency 110, 114, 267
Transparency International 111, 112
Tréhin-Marçot, P. 347
Trier, Lars von 338, 347
trust 68, 97, 103, 115, 204, 205, 262, 368
truth-making 159
trystorming 294
Tsoukas, H. 151, 166
Twitter 1, 2
Tyler, M. 343

Übermensch 126
Uhlaner, L. 70
Ukraine 71
'unattended to' 28
uncertainty 52, 55–6, 58, 59, 64, 89, 194, 195, 201, 203, 206, 239
unethical behaviour 99, 103, 108, 113, 115
Unfolding 351, 352, 356, 357
United States 6, 8, 71, 81, 88, 92, 93, 99, 105, 111, 114, 115, 139, 140, 234, 235, 328

universities 92, 128
urban entrepreneurialism 321, 325
  celebratory narrative 326–9
  counter-narrative 329–31, 332–3
  towards prosaic narratives 331–4
urban problematic 321, 322–4
urban (re)generation, culture-driven
  325
urban sensibility 336

valuable, rare, inimitable and non-
  substitutable (VRIN) resources
  199
value spheres 11
value statements 101, 103, 104, 105,
  106, 114
value systems 108
values 66, 67, 70, 88, 99, 101, 104, 141,
  223, 343
Van de Ven, A.H. 163, 205
Van Houten, D.R. 138
variation(s) 28, 30, 80, 81, 82, 86,
  87–90
Venkataraman, S. 22, 199, 222
venture creation 70, 71, 88, 228
Vereinigte Stahlwerke 37
vertical sex segregation 139
Verwoert, J. 311, 312
Vestrum, I.K. 266
Vietnam 71, 114
vigilance 113
violent entrepreneurs 130
Virno, P. 315
virtual value 8
virtuality(ies) 173, 174, 176
The Visible Hand 38
vision 51, 198, 236, 283
Vitell, S. 102
Vorsanger, S 273
vulgar economists 124

Walras, M.E.L. 143
Warhol, A. 302, 304, 305, 314
Waterman, R. 267

wealth creation 119, 200, 214, 216, 219,
  220, 221, 222, 224
The Wealth of Nations 47
Weber, M. 11, 32, 35, 38, 46, 322
Weick, K. 21, 22, 25, 26, 27, 151, 152,
  153–5, 163, 166
Weiskopf, R. 344
Weldon, T.D. 285
welfare regimes 261, 263–4
Welter, F. 70, 71, 72, 76
West, C. 137
Western body 354, 360
What is Philosophy? 158
What theory is not, theorizing is 153–5
Wickham, P. 257
Wiklund, J. 70, 77
will power 38
will to power 12, 170, 173, 180, 183,
  185, 186, 187, 188
Williamson, O.E. 65, 67, 68
willingness to act entrepreneurially
  209, 238
Willmott, H. 340, 350
Winter, S.G. 202
Wissenschaftstheorie 164
Wolff, R. 142
women *see* gender
work discretion/autonomy 235
work intensification 274, 345
work orientation 272
World Bank 69, 95, 118, 119, 121, 122,
  125, 129, 130
writing 165, 167
'writing is organizing' 153

Young, I. 137

Zahra, S.A. 228, 241
Zampetakis, L. 257, 277
Zentropa 338, 340, 343, 344, 347–55
Zerbinati, S. 266
Zimmerman, D. 137
Zizek, S. 358
Zukin, S. 326, 329–30